Data Structures
And
Algorithms
Made Easy In JAVA

By
Narasimha Karumanchi

☀ **Concepts**   ☀ **Problems**   ☀ **Interview Questions**

Acknowledgements

Mother and *father*, it is impossible to thank you adequately for everything you have done, from loving me unconditionally to raising me in a stable household, where you persistent efforts traditional values and taught your children to celebrate and embrace life. I could not have asked for better parents or role-models. You showed me that anything is possible with faith, hard work and determination.

This book would not have been possible without the help of many people. I would like to thank them for their efforts in improving the end result. Before we do so, however, I should mention that I have done my best to correct the mistakes that the reviewers have pointed out and to accurately describe the protocols and mechanisms. I alone am responsible for any remaining errors.

First and foremost, I would like to express my gratitude to many people who saw me through this book, to all those who provided support, talked things over, read, wrote, offered comments, allowed me to quote their remarks and assisted in the editing, proofreading and design. In particular, I would like to thank the following individuals.

- *Mohan Mullapudi*, IIT Bombay, Architect, dataRPM Pvt. Ltd.
- *Navin Kumar Jaiswal*, Senior Consultant, Juniper Networks Inc.
- *Kishore Kumar Jinka*, IIT Bombay
- *A.Vamshi Krishna*, IIT Kanpur, Mentor Graphics Inc.
- *Hirak Chatterjee*, Yahoo Inc.
- *Kondrakunta Murali Krishna*, B-Tech., Technical Lead, HCL
- *Chaganti Siva Rama Krishna Prasad*, Founder, StockMonks Pvt. Ltd.
- *Naveen Valsakumar*, Co-Founder, NotionPress Pvt. Ltd.
- *Ramanaiah*, Lecturer, Nagarjuna Institute of Technology and Sciences, MLG

Last but not least, I would like to thank *Directors* of *Guntur Vikas College*, *Prof.Y.V.Gopala Krishna Murthy & Prof.Ayub Khan [ACE Engineering Academy]*, *T.R.C.Bose [Ex. Director of APTransco]*, *Ch.Venkateswara Rao VNR Vignanajyothi [Engineering College, Hyderabad]*, *Ch.Venkata Narasaiah [IPS]*, *Yarapathineni Lakshmaiah [Manchikallu, Gurazala]* and *all our well – wishers* for helping me and my family during our studies.

-*Narasimha Karumanchi*
M-Tech, *IIT Bombay*
Founder, *CareerMonk.com*

Motivational and Inspirational Quotes

A stone is broken by the last stroke. This does not mean that first stroke was useless. Success is a result of continuous daily effort.   *--Unknown*

Stand up, be bold, be strong. Take the whole responsibility on your own shoulders, and know that you are the creator of your own destiny.   *--Swami Vivekananda*

Preface

Dear Reader,

Please Hold on! I know many people do not read the preface. But I would strongly recommend that you go through the preface of this book at least. The reason for this is that this preface has *something different* to offer.

The main objective of the book is not to give you the theorems and proofs about *Data Structures* and *Algorithms*. I have followed a pattern of improving the problem solutions with different complexities (for each problem, you will find multiple solutions with different, and reduced complexities). Basically, it's an enumeration of possible solutions. With this approach, even if you get a new question it will show you a way to think about all possible solutions. This book is very useful for interview preparation, competitive exams preparation, and campus interview preparations.

As a *job seeker* if you read the complete book with good understanding, I am sure you will challenge the interviewers and that is the objective of this book. If you read it as an *instructor*, you will deliver better lectures with an easy approach and as a result your students will appreciate the fact that they have opted for Computer Science / Information Technology as their degree.

This book is very useful for the *students* of *Engineering Degree* and *Masters* during their academic preparations. In all the chapters you will see that more importance has been given to problems and their analysis instead of theory. For each chapter, first you will read about the basic required theory and this will be followed by a section on problem sets. There are approximately 700 algorithmic problems and all of them are with solutions.

If you read as a *student* preparing for competitive exams for Computer Science/Information Technology, the content of this book covers *all* the *required* topics in full detail. While writing this book, my focus has been to help students who are preparing for these exams.

In all the chapters you will see more importance given to problems and analyzing them instead of concentrating more on theory. For each chapter, first you will see the basic required theory and then followed by problems.

For many problems, *multiple* solutions are provided with different levels of complexities. We start with *brute force* solution and slowly move towards the *best solution* possible for that problem. For each problem we will try to understand how much time the algorithm is taking and how much memory the algorithm is taking.

It is *recommended* that the reader does at least one complete reading of this book to get full understanding of all the topics. In the subsequent readings, you can go directly to any chapter and refer. Even though, enough readings were given for correcting the errors, there could be some minor typos in the book. If any such typos are found, they will be updated at *www.CareerMonk.com*. I request you to constantly monitor this site for any corrections, new problems and solutions. Also, please provide your valuable suggestions at: *Info@CareerMonk.com*.

Wish you all the best. I am sure that you will find this book useful.

-Narasimha Karumanchi
M-Tech, *IIT Bombay*
Founder of *CareerMonk.com*

Other Titles by Narasimha Karumanchi

- ◭ IT Interview Questions
- ◭ Elements of Computer Networking
- ◭ Data Structures and Algorithms Made Easy (C/C++)
- ◭ Coding Interview Questions
- ◭ Data Structures and Algorithms for GATE
- ◭ Peeling Design Patterns

Table of Contents

1. Introduction --- 15
   1.1 Variables-- 15
   1.2 Data types -- 15
   1.3 Data Structure -- 16
   1.4 Abstract Data Types (ADTs) --- 16
   1.5 What is an Algorithm?--- 16
   1.6 Why Analysis of Algorithms? -- 17
   1.7 Goal of Analysis of Algorithms -- 17
   1.8 What is Running Time Analysis? --- 17
   1.9 How to Compare Algorithms? -- 17
   1.10 What is Rate of Growth?-- 17
   1.11 Commonly used Rate of Growths --- 17
   1.12 Types of Analysis --- 18
   1.13 Asymptotic Notation--- 19
   1.14 Big-O Notation -- 19
   1.15 Omega-Ω Notation -- 20
   1.16 Theta-Θ Notation --- 21
   1.17 Important Notes--- 22
   1.18 Why is it called Asymptotic Analysis? --- 22
   1.19 Guidelines for Asymptotic Analysis -- 22
   1.20 Properties of Notations--- 23
   1.21 Commonly used Logarithms and Summations -- 23
   1.22 Master Theorem for Divide and Conquer --- 24
   1.23 Problems on Divide and Conquer Master Theorem-- 24
   1.24 Master Theorem for Subtract and Conquer Recurrences --- 25
   1.25 Variant of Subtraction and Conquer master theorem -- 26
   1.26 Method of Guessing and Confirm --- 26
   1.27 Amortized Analysis --- 27
   1.28 Problems on Algorithms Analysis --- 27

2. Recursion and Backtracking--- 38
   2.1 Introduction-- 38
   2.2 What is Recursion? --- 38
   2.3 Why Recursion? -- 38
   2.4 Format of a Recursive Function -- 38
   2.5 Recursion and Memory (Visualization)--- 39
   2.6 Recursion versus Iteration--- 39
   2.7 Notes on Recursion -- 40

o

2.8 Example Algorithms of Recursion -- 40

2.9 Problems on Recursion -- 40

2.10 What is Backtracking? --- 41

2.11 Example Algorithms of Backtracking -- 41

2.12 Problems on Backtracking --- 41

3. Linked Lists -- 42

3.1 What is a Linked List? -- 42

3.2 Linked Lists ADT -- 42

3.3 Why Linked Lists? -- 42

3.4 Arrays Overview -- 42

3.5 Comparison of Linked Lists with Arrays & Dynamic Arrays -- 43

3.6 Singly Linked Lists --- 44

3.7 Doubly Linked Lists -- 49

3.8 Circular Linked Lists --- 53

3.9 A Memory-Efficient Doubly Linked List --- 59

3.10 Unrolled Linked Lists --- 60

3.11 Problems on Linked Lists --- 62

4. Stacks --- 77

4.1 What is a Stack? -- 77

4.2 How Stacks are used? -- 77

4.3 Stack ADT --- 77

4.4 Exceptions -- 78

4.5 Applications -- 78

4.6 Implementation -- 78

4.7 Comparison of Implementations -- 82

4.8 Problems on Stacks --- 82

5. Queues -- 99

5.1 What is a Queue? --- 99

5.2 How are Queues Used? --- 99

5.3 Queue ADT -- 99

5.4 Exceptions -- 99

5.5 Applications --- 100

5.6 Implementation --- 100

5.7 Problems on Queues --- 104

6. Trees --- 109

6.1 What is a Tree? -- 109

6.2 Glossary -- 109

6.3 Binary Trees --- 110

6.4 Binary Tree Traversals --112

6.5 Generic Trees (N-ary Trees) --130

6.6 Threaded [Stack or Queue less] Binary Tree Traversals ----------------------------------136

6.7 Expression Trees ---141

6.8 XOR Trees --143

6.9 Binary Search Trees (BSTs)--144

6.10 Balanced Binary Search Trees---156

6.11 AVL (Adelson-Velskii and Landis) Trees--156

6.12 Other Variations in Trees--169

7.   Priority Queue and Heaps --- 172

7.1 What is a Priority Queue?--172

7.2 Priority Queue ADT --172

7.3 Priority Queue Applications ---172

7.4 Priority Queue Implementations --172

7.5 Heaps and Binary Heap ---173

7.6 Binary Heaps --174

7.7 Problems on Priority Queues [Heaps] --180

8.   Disjoint Sets ADT--- 189

8.1 Introduction--189

8.2 Equivalence Relations and Equivalence Classes --189

8.3 Disjoint Sets ADT ---189

8.4 Applications ---189

8.5 Tradeoffs in Implementing Disjoint Sets ADT---190

8.6 Fast UNION implementation (Slow FIND) --190

8.7 Fast UNION implementations (Quick FIND)---193

8.8 Path Compression--195

8.9 Summary --196

8.10 Problems on Disjoint Sets ---196

9.   Graph Algorithms--- 197

9.1 Introduction--197

9.2 Glossary ---197

9.3 Applications of Graphs --199

9.4 Graph Representation --200

9.5 Graph Traversals---202

9.6 Topological Sort --209

9.7 Shortest Path Algorithms ---211

9.8 Minimal Spanning Tree ---215

9.9 Problems on Graph Algorithms ---219

10. Sorting -- 237

10.1 What is Sorting? --237

10.2 Why is Sorting Necessary? --237

10.3 Classification --237

10.4 Other Classifications --238

10.5 Bubble sort ---238

10.6 Selection Sort---239

10.7 Insertion sort --239

10.8 Shell sort ---241

10.9 Merge sort--242

10.10 Heapsort --243

10.11 Quicksort --243

10.12 Tree Sort ---246

10.13 Comparison of Sorting Algorithms --246

10.14 Linear Sorting Algorithms --246

10.15 Counting Sort--246

10.16 Bucket sort [or Bin Sort] ---247

10.17 Radix sort ---247

10.18 Topological Sort ---248

10.19 External Sorting---248

10.20 Problems on Sorting ---249

11. Searching --- 257

11.1 What is Searching?--257

11.2 Why do we need Searching? ---257

11.3 Types of Searching---257

11.4 Symbol Tables and Hashing --258

11.5 String Searching Algorithms ---258

11.6 Problems on Searching ---259

12. Selection Algorithms [Medians]-- 278

12.1 What are Selection Algorithms? ---278

12.2 Selection by Sorting --278

12.3 Partition-based Selection Algorithm --278

12.4 Linear Selection algorithm - Median of Medians algorithm ------------------------------------278

12.5 Finding the K Smallest Elements in Sorted Order--278

12.6 Problems on Selection Algorithms --278

13. Symbol Tables -- 286

13.1 Introduction --286

13.2 What are Symbol Tables? ---286

13.3 Symbol Table Implementations --- 286

13.4 Comparison of Symbol Table Implementations --- 287

Imp 14. Hashing -- 288

14.1 What is Hashing? -- 288

14.2 Why Hashing? -- 288

14.3 HashTable ADT --- 288

14.4 Understanding Hashing --- 288

14.5 Components of Hashing --- 289

14.6 Hash Table -- 289

14.7 Hash Function -- 290

14.8 Load Factor -- 290

14.9 Collisions --- 290

14.10 Collision Resolution Techniques -- 290

14.11 Separate Chaining -- 290

14.12 Open Addressing --- 291

14.13 Comparison of Collision Resolution Techniques -- 292

14.14 How Hashing Gets O(1) Complexity? -- 293

14.15 Hashing Techniques --- 293

14.16 Problems for which Hash Tables are not Suitable -- 293

14.17 Bloom Filters --- 293

14.18 Problems on Hashing -- 295

Imp 15. String Algorithms -- 303

15.1 Introduction -- 303

15.2 String Matching Algorithms -- 303

15.3 Brute Force Method -- 303

15.4 Robin-Karp String Matching Algorithm --- 304

15.5 String Matching with Finite Automata --- 304

15.6 KMP Algorithm -- 305

15.7 Boyce-Moore Algorithm -- 308

15.8 Data Structures for Storing Strings --- 308

15.9 Hash Tables for Strings --- 308

15.10 Binary Search Trees for Strings -- 308

15.11 Tries -- 309

15.12 Ternary Search Trees --- 311

15.13 Comparing BSTs, Tries and TSTs --- 314

15.14 Suffix Trees --- 315

15.15 Problems on Strings --- 317

16. Algorithms Design Techniques -- 324

16.1 Introduction -- 324

16.2 Classification --324

16.3 Classification by Implementation Method ---324

16.4 Classification by Design Method --324

16.5 Other Classifications ---325

17. Greedy Algorithms -- 326

17.1 Introduction --326

17.2 Greedy strategy --326

17.3 Elements of Greedy Algorithms---326

17.4 Does Greedy Always Work? --326

17.5 Advantages and Disadvantages of Greedy Method -----------------------------326

17.6 Greedy Applications --326

17.7 Understanding Greedy Technique ---327

17.8 Problems on Greedy Algorithms ---329

18. Divide and Conquer Algorithms --- 335

18.1 Introduction --335

18.2 What is Divide and Conquer Strategy?---335

18.3 Does Divide and Conquer Always Work? --335

18.4 Divide and Conquer Visualization ---335

18.5 Understanding Divide and Conquer --336

18.6 Master Theorem---337

18.7 Divide and Conquer Applications --337

18.8 Problems on Divide and Conquer ---337

19. Dynamic Programming -- 348

19.1 Introduction --348

19.2 What is Dynamic Programming Strategy? ---348

19.3 Properties of Dynamic Programming Strategy -----------------------------------348

19.4 Can Dynamic Programming Solve All Problems? --------------------------------348

19.5 Dynamic Programming Approaches --348

19.6 Examples of Dynamic Programming Algorithms---------------------------------349

19.7 Understanding Dynamic Programming ---349

19.8 Problems on Dynamic Programming ---353

20. Complexity Classes -- 378

20.1 Introduction --378

20.2 Polynomial/Exponential time --378

20.3 What is Decision Problem?---378

20.4 Decision Procedure ---378

20.5 What is a Complexity Class?---378

20.6 Types of Complexity Classes --379

20.7 Reductions --381

20.8 Problems on Complexity Classes --383

21. Miscellaneous Concepts --- 385

21.1 Introduction ---385

21.2 Hacks on Bitwise Programming --385

21.3 Other Programming Questions ---388

Design patterns

Chapter-1

INTRODUCTION

The objective of this chapter is to explain the importance of analysis of algorithms, their notations, relationships and solving as many problems as possible. Let us first focus on understanding the basic elements of algorithms, importance of analysis and then slowly move towards the other topics as mentioned above. After completing this chapter you should be able to find the complexity of any given algorithm (especially recursive functions).

1.1 Variables

Before getting in to the definition of variables, let us relate them to an old mathematical equation. Many of us would have solved many mathematical equations since childhood. As an example, consider the equation below:

$$x^2 + 2y - 2 = 1$$

We don't have to worry about the use of this equation. The important thing that we need to understand is, the equation has some names (x and y), which hold values (data). That means, the *names* (x and y) are placeholders for representing data. Similarly, in computer science we need something for holding data, and *variables* is the way to do that.

1.2 Data types

In the above-mentioned equation, the variables x and y can take any values such as integral numbers (10, 20.), real numbers (0.23, 5.5) or just 0 and 1. To solve the equation, we need to relate them to kind of values they can take and *data type* is the name used in computer science for this purpose.

→ A *data type* in a programming language is a set of data with predefined values. Examples of data types are: integer, floating point unit number, character, string, etc.

Computer memory is all filled with zeros and ones. If we have a problem and wanted to code it, it's very difficult to provide the solution in terms of zeros and ones. To help users, programming languages and compilers provide us with data types.

For example, *integer* takes 2 bytes (actual value depends on compiler), *float* takes 4 bytes, etc. This says that, in memory we are combining 2 bytes (16 bits) and calling it as *integer*. Similarly, combining 4 bytes (32 bits) and calling it as *float*. A data type reduces the coding effort. At the top level, there are two types of data types:

- System-defined data types (also called *Primitive* data types)
- User-defined data types

System-defined data types (Primitive data types)

Data types that are defined by system are called *primitive* data types. The primitive data types provided by many programming languages are: int, float, char, double, bool, etc.The number of bits allocated for each primitive data type depends on the programming language, compiler and operating system. For the same primitive data type, different languages may use different sizes. Depending on the size of the data types the total available values (domain) will also change.

For example, "*int*" may take 2 bytes or 4 bytes. If it takes 2 bytes (16 bits) then the total possible values are -32,768 to +32,767 ($-2^{15}\ to\ 2^{15}$-1). If it takes, 4 bytes (32 bits), then the possible values are between $-2,147,483,648$ and $+2,147,483,648$ ($-2^{31}\ to\ 2^{31}$-1). Same is the case with remaining data types too.

User-defined data types

If the system-defined data types are not enough, then most programming languages allow the users to define their own data types called as user-defined data types. Good example of user-defined data types are: structures in $C/C++$ and classes in *Java*.

For example, in the snippet below, we are combining many system-defined data types and call it as user-defined data type with name "*newType*". This gives more flexibility and comfort in dealing with computer memory.

```
public class newType {
    public int data1;
    public int data 2;
    private float data3;
    ...
    private char data;
    //Operations
}
```

1.3 Data Structure

Based on the discussion above, once we have data in variables, we need some mechanism for manipulating that data to solve problems. [Data structure is a particular way of storing and organizing data in a computer so that it can be used efficiently. A *data structure* is a special format for organizing and storing data.] General data structure types include arrays, files, linked lists, stacks, queues, trees, graphs and so on.

Depending on the organization of the elements, data structures are classified into two types:

1) *Linear data structures*: Elements are accessed in a sequential order but it is not compulsory to store all elements sequentially (say, Linked Lists). *Examples*: Linked Lists, Stacks and Queues.

2) *Non − linear data structures*: Elements of this data structure are stored/accessed in a non-linear order. *Examples*: Trees and graphs.

1.4 Abstract Data Types (ADTs)

Before defining abstract data types, let us consider the different view of system-defined data types. We all know that, by default, all primitive data types (int, float, etc.) support basic operations such as addition and subtraction. The system provides the implementations for the primitive data types. For user-defined data types also we need to define operations. The implementation for these operations can be done when we want to actually use them. That means, in general user defined data types are defined along with their operations.

To simplify the process of solving the problems, we combine the data structures along with their operations and call it as *Abstract Data Types* (ADTs). An ADT consists of *two* parts:

1. Declaration of data
2. Declaration of operations

Commonly used ADTs *include*: Linked Lists, Stacks, Queues, Priority Queues, Binary Trees, Dictionaries, Disjoint Sets (Union and Find), Hash Tables, Graphs, and many other. For example, stack uses LIFO (Last-In-First-Out) mechanism while storing the data in data structures. The last element inserted into the stack is the first element that gets deleted. Common operations of it are: creating the stack, pushing an element onto the stack, popping an element from stack, finding the current top of the stack, finding number of elements in the stack, etc.

While defining the ADTs do not worry about the implementation details. They come into picture only when we want to use them. Different kinds of ADTs are suited to different kinds of applications, and some are highly specialized to specific tasks. By the end of this book, we will go through many of them and you will be in a position to relate the data structures to the kind of problems they solve.

1.5 What is an Algorithm?

Let us consider the problem of preparing an omelet. For preparing omelet, general steps we follow are:

1) Get the frying pan.
2) Get the oil.
    a. Do we have oil?
        i. If yes, put it in the pan.
        ii. If no, do we want to buy oil?
            1. If yes, then go out and buy.
            2. If no, we can terminate.
3) Turn on the stove, etc...

What we are doing is, for a given problem (preparing an omelet), giving step-by-step procedure for solving it. Formal definition of an algorithm can be given as:

An algorithm is the step-by-step instructions to solve a given problem.

Note: we do not have to prove each step of the algorithm.

1.6 Why Analysis of Algorithms?

To go from city "*A*" to city "*B*", there can be many ways of accomplishing this: by flight, by bus, by train and also by bicycle. Depending on the availability and convenience we choose the one that suits us. Similarly, in computer science t multiple algorithms are available for solving the same problem (for example, sorting problem has many algorithms like insertion sort, selection sort, quick sort and many more). Algorithm analysis helps us determining which of them is efficient in terms of time and space consumed.

1.7 Goal of Analysis of Algorithms

The goal of *analysis of algorithms* is to compare algorithms (or solutions) mainly in terms of running time but also in terms of other factors (e.g., memory, developers effort, etc.)

1.8 What is Running Time Analysis?

It is the process of determining how processing time increases as the size of the problem (input size) increases. Input size is the number of elements in the input and depending on the problem type the input may be of different types. The following are the common types of inputs.

- Size of an array
- Polynomial degree
- Number of elements in a matrix
- Number of bits in binary representation of the input
- Vertices and edges in a graph

1.9 How to Compare Algorithms?

To compare algorithms, let us define few *objective measures*.

Execution times? *Not a good measure* as execution times are specific to a particular computer.

Number of statements executed? *Not a good measure*, since the number of statements varies with the programming language as well as the style of the individual programmer.

Ideal Solution? Let us assume that we expressed running time of given algorithm as a function of the input size n (i.e., $f(n)$) and compare these different functions corresponding to running times. This kind of comparison is independent of machine time, programming style, etc.

1.10 What is Rate of Growth?

The rate at which the running time increases as a function of input is called *rate of growth*. Let us assume that you went to a shop to buy a car and a cycle. If your friend sees you there and asks what you are buying then in general you say *buying a car*. This is because, cost of car is too big compared to cost of cycle (approximating the cost of cycle to cost of car).

$$Total\ Cost = cost\_of\_car + cost\_of\_cycle$$
$$Total\ Cost \approx cost\_of\_car\ (approximation)$$

For the above-mentioned example, we can represent the cost of car and cost of cycle in terms of function and for a given function ignore the low order terms that are relatively insignificant (for large value of input size, n). As an example in the case below, $n^4, 2n^2, 100n$ and 500 are the individual costs of some function and approximate it to n^4. Since, n^4 is the highest rate of growth.

$$n^4 + 2n^2 + 100n + 500 \approx n^4$$

1.11 Commonly used Rate of Growths

Given below is the list of rate of growths which come across in remaining chapters.

Time complexity	Name	Example
1	Constant	Adding an element to the front of a linked list
$logn$	Logarithmic	Finding an element in a sorted array
n	Linear	Finding an element in an unsorted array
$nlogn$	Linear Logarithmic	Sorting n items by 'divide-and-conquer'-Mergesort
n^2	Quadratic	Shortest path between two nodes in a graph
n^3	Cubic	Matrix Multiplication

| 2^n | Exponential | The Towers of Hanoi problem |

Below diagram shows the relationship between different rates of growth.

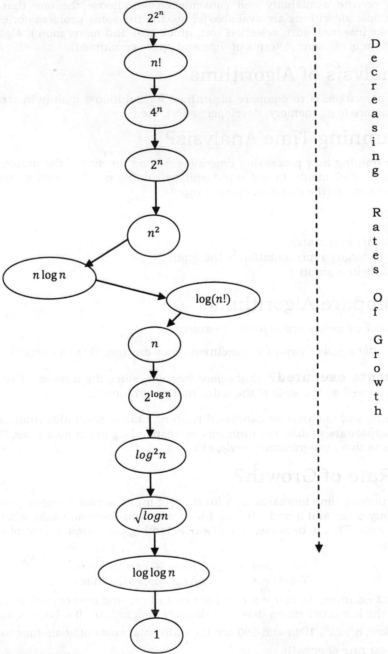

1.12 Types of Analysis

To analyze the given algorithm we need to know on what inputs the algorithm takes less time (performing well) and on what inputs the algorithm takes long time. We have already seen that an algorithm can be represented in the form of an expression. That means we represent the algorithm with multiple expressions: one for the case where it takes less time and other for the case where it takes the more time. In general the first case is called the *best case* and second case is called the *worst case* of the algorithm. To analyze an algorithm we need some kind of syntax and that forms the base for asymptotic analysis/notation.

There are three types of analysis:

- **Worst case**
  - Defines the input for which the algorithm takes long time.
  - Input is the one for which the algorithm runs the slower.

- **Best case**
  - o Defines the input for which the algorithm takes lowest time.
  - o Input is the one for which the algorithm runs the fastest.
- **Average case**
  - o Provides a prediction about the running time of the algorithm
  - o Assumes that the input is random

Lower Bound <= Average Time <= Upper Bound

For a given algorithm, we can represent the best, worst and average cases in the form of expressions. As an example, let $f(n)$ be the function, which represents the given algorithm.

$f(n) = n^2 + 500$, for worst case
$f(n) = n + 100n + 500$, for best case

Similarly, for average case too. The expression defines the inputs with which the algorithm takes the average running time (or memory).

1.13 Asymptotic Notation

Having the expressions for the best, average case and worst cases, for all the three cases we need to identify the upper and lower bounds. To represent these upper and lower bounds we need some kind of syntax and that is the subject of the following discussion. Let us assume that the given algorithm is represented in the form of function $f(n)$.

1.14 Big-O Notation

This notation gives the *tight* upper bound of the given function. Generally, it is represented as $f(n) = O(g(n))$. That means, at larger values of n, the upper bound of $f(n)$ is $g(n)$.

For example, if $f(n) = n^4 + 100n^2 + 10n + 50$ is the given algorithm, then n^4 is $g(n)$. That means, $g(n)$ gives the maximum rate of growth for $f(n)$ at larger values of n.

Let us see the O−notation with little more detail. O−notation defined as $O(g(n)) = \{f(n)$: there exist positive constants c and n_0 such that $0 \le f(n) \le cg(n)$ for all $n \ge n_0\}$. $g(n)$ is an asymptotic tight upper bound for $f(n)$. Our objective is to give smallest rate of growth $g(n)$ which is greater than or equal to given algorithms rate of growth $f(n)$.

Generally we discard lower values of n. That means the rate of growth at lower values of n is not important. In the figure below, n_0 is the point from which we need to consider the rate of growths for a given algorithm. Below n_0 the rate of growths could be different.

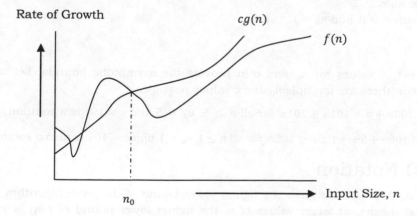

Big-O Visualization

$O(g(n))$ is the set of functions with smaller or same order of growth as $g(n)$. For example, $O(n^2)$ includes $O(1), O(n), O(nlogn)$ etc..

Note: Analyze the algorithms at larger values of n only. What this means is, below n_0 we do not care for rate of growth.

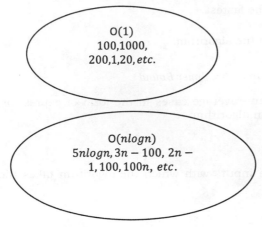

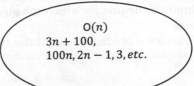

Big-O Examples

Example-1 Find upper bound for $f(n) = 3n + 8$
Solution: $3n + 8 \leq 4n$, for all $n \geq 8$
$\therefore 3n + 8 = O(n)$ with c = 4 and $n_0 = 8$

Example-2 Find upper bound for $f(n) = n^2 + 1$
Solution: $n^2 + 1 \leq 2n^2$, for all $n \geq 1$
$\therefore n^2 + 1 = O(n^2)$ with $c = 2$ and $n_0 = 1$

Example-3 Find upper bound for $f(n) = n^4 + 100n^2 + 50$
Solution: $n^4 + 100n^2 + 50 \leq 2n^4$, for all $n \geq 11$
$\therefore n^4 + 100n^2 + 50 = O(n^4)$ with $c = 2$ and $n_0 = 11$

Example-4 Find upper bound for $f(n) = 2n^3 - 2n^2$
Solution: $2n^3 - 2n^2 \leq 2n^3$, for all $n \geq 1$
$\therefore 2n^3 - 2n^2 = O(2n^3)$ with $c = 2$ and $n_0 = 1$

Example-5 Find upper bound for $f(n) = n$
Solution: $n \leq n$, for all $n \geq 1$
$\therefore n = O(n)$ with $c = 1$ and $n_0 = 1$

Example-6 Find upper bound for $f(n) = 410$
Solution: $410 \leq 410$, for all $n \geq 1$
$\therefore 410 = O(1)$ with $c = 1$ and $n_0 = 1$

No Uniqueness?

There are no unique set of values for n_0 and c in proving the asymptotic bounds. Let us consider, $100n + 5 = O(n)$. For this function there are multiple n_0 and c values possible.

Solution1: $100n + 5 \leq 100n + n = 101n \leq 101n$, for all $n \geq 5$, $n_0 = 5$ and $c = 101$ is a solution.

Solution2: $100n + 5 \leq 100n + 5n = 105n \leq 105n$, *for all* $n \geq 1$, $n_0 = 1$ *and* $c = 105$ *is also a solution.*

1.15 Omega-Ω Notation

Similar to O discussion, this notation gives the tighter lower bound of the given algorithm and we represent it as $f(n) = \Omega(g(n))$. That means, at larger values of n, the tighter lower bound of $f(n)$ is $g(n)$. For example, if $f(n) = 100n^2 + 10n + 50$, $g(n)$ is $\Omega(n^2)$.

The Ω notation can be defined as $\Omega(g(n)) = \{f(n):$ there exist positive constants c and n_0 such that $0 \leq cg(n) \leq f(n)$ for all $n \geq n_0\}$. $g(n)$ is an asymptotic tight lower bound for $f(n)$. Our objective is to give largest rate of growth $g(n)$ which is less than or equal to given algorithms rate of growth $f(n)$.

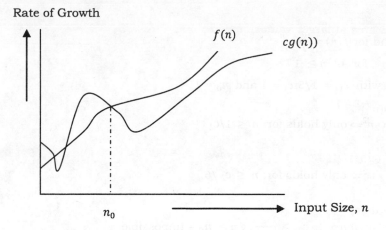

Ω Examples

Example-1 Find lower bound for $f(n) = 5n^2$

Solution: $\exists\, c, n_0$ Such that: $0 \leq cn^2 \leq 5n^2 \Rightarrow cn^2 \leq 5n^2 \Rightarrow c = 1$ and $n_0 = 1$

$\therefore 5n^2 = \Omega(n^2)$ with $c = 1$ and $n_0 = 1$

Example-2 Prove $f(n) = 100n + 5 \neq \Omega(n^2)$

Solution: $\exists\, c, n_0$ Such that: $0 \leq cn^2 \leq 100n + 5$

$100n + 5 \leq 100n + 5n\,(\forall n \geq 1) = 105n$

$cn^2 \leq 105n \Rightarrow n(cn - 105) \leq 0$

Since n is positive $\Rightarrow cn - 105 \leq 0 \Rightarrow n \leq 105/c$

$\Rightarrow$ Contradiction: n cannot be smaller than a constant

Example-3 $2n = \Omega(n)$, $n^3 = \Omega(n^3)$, $logn = \Omega(logn)$

1.16 Theta-Θ Notation

This notation decides whether the upper and lower bounds of a given function (algorithm) are same. The average running time of algorithm is always between lower bound and upper bound. If the upper bound (O) and lower bound (Ω) give the same result then Θ notation will also have the same rate of growth. As an example, let us assume that $f(n) = 10n + n$ is the expression. Then, its tight upper bound $g(n)$ is O(n). The rate of growth in best case is $g(n) = O(n)$.

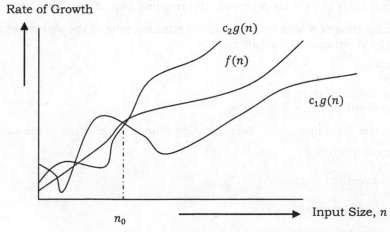

In this case, rate of growths in the best case and worst are same. As a result, the average case will also be same. For a given function (algorithm), if the rate of growths (bounds) for O and Ω are not same then the rate of growth Θ case may not be same. In this case, we need to consider all possible time complexities and take average of those (for example, quick sort average case, refer *Sorting* chapter).

Now consider the definition of Θ notation. It is defined as $\Theta(g(n)) = \{f(n)$: there exist positive constants c_1, c_2 and n_0 such that $0 \leq c_1 g(n) \leq f(n) \leq c_2 g(n)$ for all $n \geq n_0\}$. $g(n)$ is an asymptotic tight bound for $f(n)$. $\Theta(g(n))$ is the set of functions with the same order of growth as $g(n)$.

Θ Examples

Example-1 Find Θ bound for $f(n) = \frac{n^2}{2} - \frac{n}{2}$

Solution: $\frac{n^2}{5} \leq \frac{n^2}{2} - \frac{n}{2} \leq n^2$, for all, $n \geq 1$

$\therefore \frac{n^2}{2} - \frac{n}{2} = \Theta(n^2)$ with $c_1 = 1/5, c_1 = 1$ and $n_0 = 1$

Example-2 Prove $n \neq \Theta(n^2)$

Solution: $c_1 n^2 \leq n \leq c_2 n^2 \Rightarrow$ only holds for: $n \leq 1/c_1$

$\therefore n \neq \Theta(n^2)$

Example-3 Prove $6n^3 \neq \Theta(n^2)$

Solution: $c_1 n^2 \leq 6n^3 \leq c_2 n^2 \Rightarrow$ only holds for: $n \leq c_2/6$

$\therefore 6n^3 \neq \Theta(n^2)$

Example-4 Prove $n \neq \Theta(log n)$

Solution: $c_1 log n \leq n \leq c_2 log n \Rightarrow c_2 \geq \frac{n}{\log n}, \forall n \geq n_0$ – Impossible

1.17 Important Notes

For analysis (best case, worst case and average) we try to give upper bound (O) and lower bound (Ω) and average running time (Θ). From the above examples, it should also be clear that, for a given function (algorithm) getting upper bound (O) and lower bound (Ω) and average running time (Θ) may not be possible always. For example, if we are discussing the best case of an algorithm, then we try to give upper bound (O) and lower bound (Ω) and average running time (Θ).

In the remaining chapters we generally focus on upper bound (O) because knowing lower bound (Ω) of an algorithm is of no practical importance and we use θ notation if upper bound (O) and lower bound (Ω) are same.

1.18 Why is it called Asymptotic Analysis?

From the discussion above (for all the three notations: worst case, best case and average case), we can easily understand that, in every case for a given function $f(n)$ we are trying to find other function $g(n)$ which approximates $f(n)$ at higher values of n. That means, $g(n)$ is also a curve which approximates $f(n)$ at higher values of n. In mathematics we call such curve as *asymptotic curve*. In other terms, $g(n)$ is the asymptotic curve for $f(n)$. For this reason, we call algorithm analysis as *asymptotic analysis*.

1.19 Guidelines for Asymptotic Analysis

There are some general rules to help us determine the running time of an algorithm.

1) Loops: The running time of a loop is, at most, the running time of the statements inside the loop (including tests) multiplied by the number of iterations.

```
// executes n times
for (i=1; i<=n; i++)
    m = m + 2; // constant time, c
Total time = a constant c × n = c n = O(n).
```

2) Nested loops: Analyze from inside out. Total running time is the product of the sizes of all the loops.

```
//outer loop executed n times
for (i=1; i<=n; i++) {
    // inner loop executed n times
    for (j=1; j<=n; j++)
            k = k+1; //constant time
}
Total time = c × n × n = cn² = O(n²).
```

3) Consecutive statements: Add the time complexities of each statement.

```
x = x +1; //constant time
// executed n times
for (i=1; i<=n; i++)
    m = m + 2; //constant time
//outer loop executed n times
for (i=1; i<=n; i++) {
```

```
          //inner loop executed n times
        for (j=1; j<=n; j++)
                k = k+1; //constant time
    }
```
Total time $= c_0 + c_1 n + c_2 n^2 = O(n^2)$.

4) **If-then-else statements:** Worst-case running time: the test, plus *either* the *then* part *or* the *else* part (whichever is the larger).

```
    //test: constant
    if(length( ) == 0 ) {
        return false; //then part: constant
    }
    else { // else part: (constant + constant) * n
        for (int n = 0; n < length( ); n++) {
                // another if : constant + constant (no else part)
                if(!list[n].equals(otherList.list[n]))
                        //constant
                        return false;
        }
    }
```
Total time $= c_0 + c_1 + (c_2 + c_3) * n = O(n)$.

5) **Logarithmic complexity:** An algorithm is $O(logn)$ if it takes a constant time to cut the problem size by a fraction (usually by ½). As an example let us consider the following program:

```
    for (i=1; i<=n;)
        i = i*2;
```

If we observe carefully, the value of i is doubling every time. Initially $i = 1$, in next step $i = 2$, and in subsequent steps $i = 4, 8$ and so on. Let us assume that the loop is executing some k times. At k^{th} step $2^k = n$ and we come out of loop. Taking logarithm on both sides, gives

$$log(2^k) = logn$$
$$klog2 = logn$$
$$k = logn \qquad //\text{if we assume base-2}$$
Total time $= O(logn)$.

Note: Similarly, for the case below also, worst case rate of growth is $O(logn)$. The same discussion holds good for decreasing sequence as well.

```
    for (i=n; i>=1;)
        i = i/2;
```

Another example: binary search (finding a word in a dictionary of n pages)
- Look at the center point in the dictionary
- Is word towards left or right of center?
- Repeat process with left or right part of dictionary until the word is found

1.20 Properties of Notations

- Transitivity: $f(n) = \Theta(g(n))$ and $g(n) = \Theta(h(n)) \Rightarrow f(n) = \Theta(h(n))$.
- Reflexivity: $f(n) = \Theta(f(n))$. Valid for O and Ω also.
- Symmetry: $f(n) = \Theta(g(n))$ if and only if $g(n) = \Theta(f(n))$.
- Transpose symmetry: $f(n) = O(g(n))$ if and only if $g(n) = \Omega(f(n))$.

1.21 Commonly used Logarithms and Summations

Logarithms

$$log\, x^y = y\, log\, x \qquad\qquad logn = log_{10}^n$$
$$log\, xy = logx + logy \qquad\qquad log^k n = (logn)^k$$
$$log\, logn = log(logn) \qquad\qquad log\frac{x}{y} = logx - logy$$
$$a^{log_b^x} = x^{log_b^a} \qquad\qquad\qquad log_b^x = \frac{log_a^x}{log_a^b}$$

Arithmetic series

$$\sum_{K=1}^{n} k = 1 + 2 + \cdots + n = \frac{n(n+1)}{2}$$

Geometric series

$$\sum_{k=0}^{n} x^k = 1 + x + x^2 \ldots + x^n = \frac{x^{n+1} - 1}{x - 1} (x \neq 1)$$

Harmonic series

$$\sum_{k=1}^{n} \frac{1}{k} = 1 + \frac{1}{2} + \ldots + \frac{1}{n} \approx \log n$$

Other important formulae

$$\sum_{k=1}^{n} \log k \approx n \log n$$

$$\sum_{k=1}^{n} k^p = 1^p + 2^p + \cdots + n^p \approx \frac{1}{p+1} n^{p+1}$$

1.22 Master Theorem for Divide and Conquer

All divide and conquer algorithms (Also discussed in detail in the *Divide and Conquer* chapter) divide the problem into sub-problems, each of which is part of the original problem, and then perform some additional work to compute the final answer. As an example, merge sort algorithm [for details, refer *Sorting* chapter] operates on two sub-problems, each of which is half the size of the original and then performs $O(n)$ additional work for merging. This gives the running time equation:

$$T(n) = 2T\left(\frac{n}{2}\right) + O(n)$$

The following theorem can be used to determine the running time of divide and conquer algorithms. For a given program (algorithm), first we try to find the recurrence relation for the problem. If the recurrence is of the below form then we can directly give the answer without fully solving it. If the recurrence is of the form $T(n) = aT\left(\frac{n}{b}\right) + \Theta(n^k \log^p n)$, where $a \geq 1, b > 1, k \geq 0$ and p is a real number, then:

1) If $a > b^k$, then $T(n) = \Theta\left(n^{\log_b^a}\right)$
2) If $a = b^k$
   a. If $p > -1$, then $T(n) = \Theta\left(n^{\log_b^a} \log^{p+1} n\right)$
   b. If $p = -1$, then $T(n) = \Theta\left(n^{\log_b^a} \log\log n\right)$
   c. If $p < -1$, then $T(n) = \Theta\left(n^{\log_b^a}\right)$
3) If $a < b^k$
   a. If $p \geq 0$, then $T(n) = \Theta(n^k \log^p n)$
   b. If $p < 0$, then $T(n) = O(n^k)$

1.23 Problems on Divide and Conquer Master Theorem

For each of the following recurrences, give an expression for the runtime $T(n)$ if the recurrence can be solved with the Master Theorem. Otherwise, indicate that the Master Theorem does not apply.

Problem-1 $T(n) = 3T(n/2) + n^2$

Solution: $T(n) = 3T\left(\frac{n}{2}\right) + n^2 \Rightarrow T(n) = \Theta(n^2)$ (Master Theorem Case 3.a)

Problem-2 $T(n) = 4T(n/2) + n^2$

Solution: $T(n) = 4T(n/2) + n^2 \Rightarrow T(n) = \Theta(n^2 \log n)$ (Master Theorem Case 2.a)

Problem-3 $T(n) = T(n/2) + n^2$

Solution: $T(n) = T(n/2) + n^2 \Rightarrow \Theta(n^2)$ (Master Theorem Case 3.a)

Problem-4 $T(n) = 2^n T(n/2) + n^n$

Solution: $T(n) = 2^n T(n/2) + n^n \Rightarrow$ Does not apply (a is not constant)

Problem-5 $T(n) = 16T(n/4) + n$

Solution: $T(n) = 16T(n/4) + n \implies T(n) = \Theta(n^2)$ (Master Theorem Case 1)

Problem-6 $T(n) = 2T(n/2) + nlogn$

Solution: $T(n) = 2T(n/2) + n\,logn \implies T(n) = \Theta(nlog^2 n)$ (Master Theorem Case 2.a)

Problem-7 $T(n) = 2T(n/2) + n/logn$

Solution: $T(n) = 2T(n/2) + n/logn \implies T(n) = \Theta(nloglogn)$ (Master Theorem Case 2.b)

Problem-8 $T(n) = 2T(n/4) + n^{0.51}$

Solution: $T(n) = 2T(n/4) + n^{0.51} \implies T(n) = \Theta(n^{0.51})$ (Master Theorem Case 3.b)

Problem-9 $T(n) = 0.5T(n/2) + 1/n$

Solution: $T(n) = 0.5T(n/2) + 1/n \implies$ Does not apply $(a < 1)$

Problem-10 $T(n) = 6T(n/3) + n^2 logn$

Solution: $T(n) = 6T(n/3) + n^2 logn \implies T(n) = \Theta(n^2 logn)$ (Master Theorem Case 3.a)

Problem-11 $T(n) = 64T(n/8) - n^2 logn$

Solution: $T(n) = 64T(n/8) - n^2 logn \implies$ Does not apply (function is not positive)

Problem-12 $T(n) = 7T(n/3) + n^2$

Solution: $T(n) = 7T(n/3) + n^2 \implies T(n) = \Theta(n^2)$ (Master Theorem Case 3.as)

Problem-13 $T(n) = 4T(n/2) + logn$

Solution: $T(n) = 4T(n/2) + logn \implies T(n) = \Theta(n^2)$ (Master Theorem Case 1)

Problem-14 $T(n) = 16T(n/4) + n!$

Solution: $T(n) = 16T(n/4) + n! \implies T(n) = \Theta(n!)$ (Master Theorem Case 3.a)

Problem-15 $T(n) = \sqrt{2}T(n/2) + logn$

Solution: $T(n) = \sqrt{2}T(n/2) + logn \implies T(n) = \Theta(\sqrt{n})$ (Master Theorem Case 1)

Problem-16 $T(n) = 3T(n/2) + n$

Solution: $T(n) = 3T(n/2) + n \implies T(n) = \Theta(n^{log3})$ (Master Theorem Case 1)

Problem-17 $T(n) = 3T(n/3) + \sqrt{n}$

Solution: $T(n) = 3T(n/3) + \sqrt{n} \implies T(n) = \Theta(n)$ (Master Theorem Case 1)

Problem-18 $T(n) = 4T(n/2) + cn$

Solution: $T(n) = 4T(n/2) + cn \implies T(n) = \Theta(n^2)$ (Master Theorem Case 1)

Problem-19 $T(n) = 3T(n/4) + nlogn$

Solution: $T(n) = 3T(n/4) + nlogn \implies T(n) = \Theta(nlogn)$ (Master Theorem Case 3.a)

Problem-20 $T(n) = 3T(n/3) + n/2$

Solution: $T(n) = 3T(n/3) + n/2 \implies T(n) = \Theta(nlogn)$ (Master Theorem Case 2.a)

1.24 Master Theorem for Subtract and Conquer Recurrences

Let $T(n)$ be a function defined on positive n, and having the property

$$T(n) = \begin{cases} c, & \text{if } n \leq 1 \\ aT(n-b) + f(n), & \text{if } n > 1 \end{cases}$$

for some constants $c, a > 0, b > 0, k \geq 0$, and function $f(n)$. If $f(n)$ is in $O(n^k)$, then

$$T(n) = \begin{cases} O(n^k), & \text{if } a < 1 \\ O(n^{k+1}), & \text{if } a = 1 \\ O\left(n^k a^{\frac{n}{b}}\right), & \text{if } a > 1 \end{cases}$$

1.25 Variant of Subtraction and Conquer master theorem

The solution to the equation $T(n) = T(\alpha n) + T((1 - \alpha)n) + \beta n$, where $0 < \alpha < 1$ and $\beta > 0$ are constants, is $O(nlogn)$.

1.26 Method of Guessing and Confirm

Now, let us discuss about a method which can be used to solve any recurrence. The basic idea behind this method is,

guess the answer; and then *prove* it correct by induction.

In other words, it addresses the question: What if the given recurrence doesn't seem to match with any of these (master theorems) methods? If we guess a solution and then try to verify our guess inductively, usually either the proof will succeed (in which case we are done), or the proof will fail (in which case the failure will help us refine our guess).

As an example, consider the divide-and-conquer recurrence $T(n) = \sqrt{n}\ T(\sqrt{n}) + n$. This doesn't fit into the form required by the Master Theorems. Carefully observing the recurrence gives us the impression that it is similar to divide and conquer method (diving the problem into $\sqrt{n}$ subproblems each with size $\sqrt{n}$). As we can see, the size of the subproblems at the first level of recursion is n. So, let us guess that $T(n) = O(nlogn)$, and then try to prove that our guess is correct.

Let's start by trying to prove an *upper* bound $T(n) \le cnlogn$:

$$\begin{aligned} T(n) &= \sqrt{n}\ T(\sqrt{n}) + n \\ &\le \sqrt{n}.\ c\sqrt{n}\ log\sqrt{n} + n \\ &= n.\ c\ log\sqrt{n} + n \\ &= n.c.\frac{1}{2}.\ logn + n \\ &\le cnlogn \end{aligned}$$

The last inequality assumes only that $1 \le c.\frac{1}{2}.\ logn$. This is correct if n is sufficiently large and for any constant c, no matter how small. From the above proof, we can see that our guess is correct for upper bound. Now, let us prove the lower bound for this recurrence.

$$\begin{aligned} T(n) &= \sqrt{n}\ T(\sqrt{n}) + n \\ &\ge \sqrt{n}.\ k\ \sqrt{n}\ log\sqrt{n} + n \\ &= n.\ k\ log\sqrt{n} + n \\ &= n.k.\frac{1}{2}.\ logn + n \\ &\ge knlogn \end{aligned}$$

The last inequality assumes only that $1 \ge k.\frac{1}{2}.\ logn$. This is incorrect if n is sufficiently large and for any constant k. From the above proof, we can see that our guess is incorrect for lower bound.

From the above discussion, we understood that $\Theta(nlogn)$ is too big. How about $\Theta(n)$? The lower bound is easy to prove directly:

$$T(n) = \sqrt{n}\ T(\sqrt{n}) + n\ \ge n$$

Now, let us prove the upper bound for this $\Theta(n)$.

$$\begin{aligned} T(n) &= \sqrt{n}\ T(\sqrt{n}) + n \\ &\le \sqrt{n}.c.\ \sqrt{n} + n \\ &= n.\ c + n \\ &= n\ (c + 1) \\ &\nleq cn \end{aligned}$$

From the above induction, we understood that $\Theta(n)$ is too small and $\Theta(nlogn)$ is too big. So, we need something bigger than n and smaller than $nlogn$? How about $n\sqrt{logn}$?

Proving upper bound for $n\sqrt{logn}$:

$$\begin{aligned} T(n) &= \sqrt{n}\ T(\sqrt{n}) + n \\ &\le \sqrt{n}.c.\ \sqrt{n}\ \sqrt{log\sqrt{n}} + n \end{aligned}$$

$$= n. c.\frac{1}{\sqrt{2}} \, log\sqrt{n} + n$$
$$\leq cnlog\sqrt{n}$$

Proving lower bound for $n\sqrt{logn}$:

$$T(n) = \sqrt{n} \, T(\sqrt{n}) + n$$
$$\geq \sqrt{n}.k.\sqrt{n}\sqrt{log\sqrt{n}} + n$$
$$= n. k.\frac{1}{\sqrt{2}} \, log\sqrt{n} + n$$
$$\ngeq knlog\sqrt{n}$$

The last step doesn't work. So, $\Theta(n\sqrt{logn})$ doesn't work. What else is between n and $nlogn$? How about $nloglogn$?

Proving upper bound for $nloglogn$:

$$T(n) = \sqrt{n} \, T(\sqrt{n}) + n$$
$$\leq \sqrt{n}.c.\sqrt{nloglog\sqrt{n}} + n$$
$$= n. c. loglogn - c.n + n$$
$$\leq cnloglogn, \text{ if } c \geq 1$$

Proving lower bound for $nloglogn$:

$$T(n) = \sqrt{n} \, T(\sqrt{n}) + n$$
$$\geq \sqrt{n}.k.\sqrt{nloglog\sqrt{n}} + n$$
$$= n. k. loglogn - k.n + n$$
$$\geq knloglogn, \text{ if } k \leq 1$$

From the above proofs, we can see that $T(n) \leq cnloglogn$, if $c \geq 1$ and $T(n) \geq knloglogn$, if $k \leq 1$. Technically, we're still missing the base cases in both proofs, but we can be fairly confident at this point that $T(n) = \Theta(nloglogn)$.

1.27 Amortized Analysis

Amortized analysis refers to determining the time-averaged running time for a sequence of operations. It is different from average case analysis, because amortized analysis does not make any assumption about the distribution of the data values, whereas average case analysis assumes the data are not "bad" (e.g., some sorting algorithms do well on "average" over all input orderings but very badly on certain input orderings). That is, amortized analysis is a worst-case analysis, but for a sequence of operations, rather than for individual operations.

The motivation for amortized analysis is to better understand the running time of certain techniques, where standard worst case analysis provides an overly pessimistic bound. Amortized analysis generally applies to a method that consists of a sequence of operations, where the vast majority of the operations are cheap, but some of the operations are expensive. If we can show that the expensive operations are particularly rare we can "charge them" to the cheap operations, and only bound the cheap operations.

The general approach is to assign an artificial cost to each operation in the sequence, such that the total of the artificial costs for the sequence of operations bounds total of the real costs for the sequence. This artificial cost is called the amortized cost of an operation. To analyze the running time, the amortized cost thus is a correct way of understanding the overall running time — but note that particular operations can still take longer so it is not a way of bounding the running time of any individual operation in the sequence.

When one event in a sequence affects the cost of later events:

- One particular task may be expensive.
- But it may leave data structure in a state that next few operations becomes easier.

Example: Let us consider an array of elements from which we want to find k^{th} smallest element. We can solve this problem using sorting. After sorting the given array, we just need to return the kth element from it. Cost of performing sort (assuming comparison based sorting algorithm) is $O(nlogn)$. If we perform n such selections then the average cost of each selection is $O(nlogn/n) = O(logn)$. This clearly indicates that sorting once is reducing the complexity of subsequent operations.

1.28 Problems on Algorithms Analysis

Note: From the following problems, try to understand the cases which give different complexities ($O(n), O(logn)$, $O(loglogn)$ etc...).

Problem-21   Find the complexity of the below recurrence:

$$T(n) = \begin{cases} 3T(n-1), if\ n > 0, \\ 1, \qquad otherwise \end{cases}$$

Solution: Let us try solving this function with substitution.

$T(n) = 3T(n-1)$

$T(n) = 3(3T(n-2)) = 3^2 T(n-2)$

$T(n) = 3^2(3T(n-3))$

.

.

.

$T(n) = 3^n T(n-n) = 3^n T(0) = 3^n$

This clearly shows that the complexity of this function is $O(3^n)$.

Note: We can use the *Subtraction and Conquer* master theorem for this problem.

Problem-22 Find the complexity of the below recurrence:

$$T(n) = \begin{cases} 2T(n-1) - 1, if\ n > 0, \\ 1, \qquad otherwise \end{cases}$$

Solution: Let us try solving this function with substitution.

$T(n) = 2T(n-1) - 1$

$T(n) = 2(2T(n-2) - 1) - 1 = 2^2 T(n-2) - 2 - 1$

$T(n) = 2^2(2T(n-3) - 2 - 1) - 1 = 2^3 T(n-4) - 2^2 - 2^1 - 2^0$

$T(n) = 2^n T(n-n) - 2^{n-1} - 2^{n-2} - 2^{n-3} \dots 2^2 - 2^1 - 2^0$

$T(n) = 2^n - 2^{n-1} - 2^{n-2} - 2^{n-3} \dots 2^2 - 2^1 - 2^0$

$T(n) = 2^n - (2^n - 1)\ [note: 2^{n-1} + 2^{n-2} + \dots + 2^0 = 2^n]$

$T(n) = 1$

∴Complexity is $O(1)$. Note that while the recurrence relation looks exponential the solution to the recurrence relation here gives a different result.

Problem-23 What is the running time of the following function?

```java
void Function(int n) {
        int i=1, s=1;
        while( s <= n) {
                i++;
                s= s+i;
                System.out.println("*");
        }
}
```

Solution: Consider the comments in below function:

```java
void Function (int n) {
        int i=1, s=1;
        // s is increasing not at rate 1 but i
        while( s <= n) {
                i++;
                s= s+i;
                System.out.println("*");
        }
}
```

We can define the terms 's' according to the relation $s_i = s_{i-1} + i$. The value of 'i' increases by 1 for each iteration. The value contained in 's' at the ith iteration is the sum of the first 'i' positive integers. If k is the total number of iterations taken by the program, then *while* loop terminates if:

$$1 + 2 + \dots + k = \frac{k(k+1)}{2} > n \implies k = O(\sqrt{n}).$$

Problem-24 Find the complexity of the function given below.

```java
void Function(int n) {
        int i, count =0;
        for(i=1; i*i<=n; i++)
                count++;
}
```

Solution:

```
void Function(int n) {
        int i, count =0;
        for(i=1; i*i<=n; i++)
                count++;
}
```

In the above-mentioned function the loop will end, if $i^2 \leq n \Rightarrow T(n) = O(\sqrt{n})$. The reasoning is same as that of Problem-23.

Problem-25   What is the complexity of the program given below?

```
void function(int n) {
        int i, j, k , count =0;
        for(i=n/2; i<=n; i++)
                for(j=1; j + n/2<=n; j= j++)
                        for(k=1; k<=n; k= k * 2)
                                count++;
}
```

Solution: Consider the comments in the following function.

```
void function(int n) {
        int i, j, k , count =0;
        //outer loop execute n/2 times
        for(i=n/2; i<=n; i++)
                //Middle loop executes n/2 times
                for(j=1; j + n/2<=n; j= j++)
                        //outer loop execute logn times
                        for(k=1; k<=n; k= k * 2)
                                count++;
}
```

The complexity of the above function is $O(n^2 logn)$.

Problem-26   What is the complexity of the program given below?

```
void function(int n) {
        int i, j, k , count =0;
        for(i=n/2; i<=n; i++)
                for(j=1; j<=n; j= 2 * j)
                        for(k=1; k<=n; k= k * 2)
                                count++;
}
```

Solution: Consider the comments in the following function.

```
void function(int n) {
        int i, j, k , count =0;
        //outer loop execute n/2 times
        for(i=n/2; i<=n; i++)
                //Middle loop executes logn times
                for(j=1; j<=n; j= 2 * j)
                        //outer loop execute logn times
                        for(k=1; k<=n; k= k*2)
                                count++;
}
```

The complexity of the above function is $O(nlog^2 n)$.

Problem-27   Find the complexity of the program given below.

```
function( int n ) {
        if(n == 1) return;
        for(int i = 1 ; i <= n ; i + + ) {
                for(int j= 1 ; j <= n ; j + + ) {
                        System.out.println("*" );
                        break;
                }
        }
}
```

Solution: Consider the comments in the following function.

```
function( int n ) {
        //constant time
        if( n == 1 ) return;
```

```
//outer loop execute n times
for(int i = 1 ; i <= n ; i + + ) {
        // inner loop executes only time due to break statement.
        for(int j= 1 ; j <= n ; j + + )        {
                System.out.println("*" );
                break;
        }
}
```

The complexity of the above function is O(n). Even though the inner loop is bounded by n, but due to the break statement it is executing only once.

Problem-28   Write a recursive function for the running time $T(n)$ of the function given below. Prove using the iterative method that $T(n) = \Theta(n^3)$.

```
function( int n ) {
        if( n == 1 ) return;
        for(int i = 1 ; i <= n ; i + + )
                for(int j = 1 ; j <= n ; j + + )
                        System.out.println("*" ) ;
        function( n-3 );
}
```

Solution: Consider the comments in the function below:

```
function (int n) {
        //constant time
        if( n == 1 ) return;
        //outer loop execute n times
        for(int i = 1 ; i <= n ; i + + )
                //inner loop executes n times
                for(int j = 1 ; j <= n ; j + + )
                        //constant time
                        System.out.println("*" ) ;
        function( n-3 );
}
```

The recurrence for this code is clearly $T(n) = T(n - 3) + cn^2$ for some constant $c > 0$ since each call prints out n^2 asterisks and calls itself recursively on n - 3. Using the iterative method we get: $T(n) = T(n - 3) + cn^2$. Using the *Subtraction and Conquer* master theorem, we get $T(n) = \Theta(n^3)$.

Problem-29   Determine Θ bounds for the recurrence relation: $T(n) = 2T\left(\frac{n}{2}\right) + nlogn$.

Solution: Using Divide and Conquer master theorem, we get O($nlog^2n$).

Problem-30   Determine Θ bounds for the recurrence: $T(n) = T\left(\frac{n}{2}\right) + T\left(\frac{n}{4}\right) + T\left(\frac{n}{8}\right) + n$.

Solution: Substituting in the recurrence equation, we get:
$$T(n) \le c1 * \frac{n}{2} + c2 * \frac{n}{4} + c3 * \frac{n}{8} + cn \le k * n \text{ , where } k \text{ is a constant.}$$

Problem-31   Determine Θ bounds for the recurrence relation: $T(n) = T(\lceil n/2 \rceil) + 7$.

Solution: Using Master Theorem we get $\Theta(logn)$.

Problem-32   Prove that the running time of the code below is $\Omega(logn)$.

```
Read(int n) {
        int k = 1;
        while( k < n )
                k = 3k;
}
```

Solution: The *while* loop will terminate once the value of 'k' is greater than or equal to the value of 'n'. In each iteration the value of 'k' is multiplied by 3. If i is the number of iterations, then 'k' has the value of $3i$ after i iterations. The loop is terminated upon reaching i iterations when $3^i \ge n \leftrightarrow i \ge \log_3 n$, which shows that $i = \Omega(logn)$.

Problem-33   Solve the following recurrence.
$$T(n) = \begin{cases} 1, & if\ n = 1 \\ T(n - 1) + n(n - 1), & if\ n \ge 2 \end{cases}$$

Solution: By iteration:
$$T(n) = T(n - 2) + (n - 1)(n - 2) + n(n - 1)$$

...

$$T(n) = T(1) + \sum_{i=1}^{n} i(i-1)$$

$$T(n) = T(1) + \sum_{i=1}^{n} i^2 - \sum_{i=1}^{n} i$$

$$T(n) = 1 + \frac{n((n+1)(2n+1)}{6} - \frac{n(n+1)}{2}$$

$$T(n) = \Theta(n^3)$$

Note: We can use the *Subtraction and Conquer* master theorem for this problem.

Problem-34   Consider the following program:
```
Fib[n]
if(n==0) then return 0
else if(n==1) then return 1
else return Fib[n-1]+Fib[n-2]
```

Solution: The recurrence relation for running time of this program is
$$T(n) = T(n-1) + T(n-2) + c.$$

Note T(n) has two recurrence calls indicating a binary tree. Each step recursively calls the program for n reduced by 1 and 2, so the depth of the recurrence tree is O(n). The number of leaves at depth n is 2^n since this is a full binary tree, and each leaf takes at least O(1) computation for the constant factor. Running time is clearly exponential in n.

Problem-35   Running time of following program?
```
function(n) {
        for(int i = 1 ; i <= n ; i++ )
                for(int j = 1 ; j <= n ; j+ = i )
                        System.out.println("*") ;
}
```

Solution: Consider the comments in the function below:
```
function (n) {
        //this loop executes n times
        for(int i = 1 ; i <= n ; i++ )
                //this loop executes j times with j increase by the rate of i
                for(int j = 1 ; j <= n ; j+ = i )
                        System.out.println("*") ;
}
```

In the above program, the inner loop executes n/i times for each value of i. Its running time is $n \times (\sum_{i=1}^{n} n/i) = O(n \log n)$.

Problem-36   What is the complexity of $\sum_{i=1}^{n} \log i$?

Solution: Using the logarithmic property, $\log xy = \log x + \log y$, we can see that this problem is equivalent to

$$\sum_{i=1}^{n} \log i = \log 1 + \log 2 + \cdots + \log n = \log(1 \times 2 \times \ldots \times n) = \log(n!) \le \log(n^n) \le n \log n$$

This shows that that the time complexity = O($n \log n$).

Problem-37   What is the running time of the following recursive function (specified as a function of the input value n)? First write the recurrence formula and then find its complexity.
```
function(int n) {
        if(n <= 1) return ;
        for (int i=1 ; i <= 3; i++ )
                f(⌈n/3⌉);
}
```

Solution: Consider the comments in the function below:
```
function (int n) {
        //constant time
        if(n <= 1) return;
        //this loop executes with recursive loop of n/3 value
        for (int i=1 ; i <= 3; i++ )
                f(⌈n/3⌉);
}
```

We can assume that for asymptotical analysis $k = \lceil k \rceil$ for every integer $k \geq 1$. The recurrence for this code is $T(n) = 3T(\frac{n}{3}) + \Theta(1)$. Using master theorem, we get $T(n) = \Theta(n)$.

Problem-38   What is the running time of the following recursive function (specified as a function of the input value n)? First write a recurrence formula, and show its solution using induction.

```
function(int n) {
        if(n <= 1) return;
        for (int i=1 ; i <= 3 ; i++ )
                function (n − 1).
}
```

Solution: Consider the comments in below function:

```
function (int n) {
        //constant time
        if(n <= 1) return;
        //this loop executes 3 times with recursive call of n-1 value
        for (int i=1 ; i <= 3 ; i++ )
                function (n − 1).
}
```

The *if* statement requires constant time (O(1)). With the *for* loop, we neglect the loop overhead and only count three times that the function is called recursively. This implies a time complexity recurrence:

$$T(n) = c, if\ n \leq 1;$$
$$= c + 3T(n - 1), if\ n > 1.$$

Using the *Subtraction and Conquer* master theorem, we get $T(n) = \Theta(3^n)$.

Problem-39   Write a recursion formula for the running time $T(n)$ of the function f, whose code is given below. What is the running time of *function*, as a function of n?

```
function (int n) {
        if(n <= 1)  return;
        for(int i = 1; i < n; i + +)
                System.out.println("*");
        function ( 0.8n ) ;
}
```

Solution: Consider the comments in below function:

```
function (int n) {
        //constant time
        if(n <= 1)  return;
        // this loop executes n times with constant time loop
        for(int i = 1; i < n; i + +)
                System.out.println("*");
        //recursive call with 0.8n
        function ( 0.8n ) ;
}
```

The recurrence for this piece of code is $T(n) = T(.8n) + O(n) = T\left(\frac{4}{5n}\right) + O(n) = \frac{4}{5}T(n) + O(n)$. Applying master theorem, we get $T(n) = O(n)$.

Problem-40   Find the complexity of the recurrence: $T(n) = 2T(\sqrt{n}) + logn$

Solution: The given recurrence is not in the master theorem form. Let us try to convert this to master theorem format by assuming $n = 2^m$. Applying logarithm on both sides gives, $logn = mlog2 \Rightarrow m = logn$. Now, the given function becomes,

$$T(n) = T(2^m) = 2T\left(\sqrt{2^m}\right) + m = 2T\left(2^{\frac{m}{2}}\right) + m.$$

To make it simple we assume $S(m) = T(2^m) \Rightarrow S(\frac{m}{2}) = T(2^{\frac{m}{2}}) \Rightarrow S(m) = 2S\left(\frac{m}{2}\right) + m$. Applying the master theorem would result $S(m) = O(mlogm)$. If we substitute $m = logn$ back, $T(n) = S(logn) = O((logn)\ loglogn)$.

Problem-41   Find the complexity of the recurrence: $T(n) = T(\sqrt{n}) + 1$

Solution: Applying the logic of Problem-40, gives $S(m) = S\left(\frac{m}{2}\right) + 1$. Applying the master theorem would result $S(m) = O(logm)$. Substituting $m = logn$, gives $T(n) = S(logn) = O(loglogn)$.

Problem-42   Find the complexity of the recurrence: $T(n) = 2T(\sqrt{n}) + 1$

Solution: Applying the logic of Problem-40, gives: $S(m) = 2S\left(\frac{m}{2}\right) + 1$. Using the master theorem results $S(m) = O(m^{log_2^2}) = O(m)$. Substituting $m = logn$ gives $T(n) = O(logn)$.

Problem-43   Find the complexity of the function given below.
```
int Function (int n) {
        if(n <= 2) return 1;
        else
                return (Function (floor(sqrt(n))) + 1);
}
```
Solution: Consider the comments in below function:
```
int Function (int n) {
        if(n <= 2) return 1;          //constant time
        else
                // executes √n + 1 times
                return (Function (floor(sqrt(n))) + 1);
}
```
For the above function, recurrence function can be given as: $T(n) = T(\sqrt{n}) + 1$. This is same as that of Problem-41.

Problem-44   Analyze the running time of the following recursive psuedocode as a function of n.
```
void function(int n) {
        if( n < 2 ) return;
        else    counter = 0;
        for i = 1 to 8 do
                function (n/2);
        for i =1 to n³ do
                counter = counter + 1;
}
```
Solution: Consider the comments in below psuedocode and call running time of function(n) as $T(n)$.
```
void function(int n) {
        if( n < 2 ) return;          //constant time
        else    counter = 0;
        // this loop executes 8 times with n value half in every call
        for i = 1 to 8 do
                function (n/2);
        // this loop executes n³ times with constant time loop
        for i =1 to n³ do
                counter = counter + 1;
}
```
$T(n)$ can be defined as follows:
$$T(n) = 1 \; if \; n < 2,$$
$$= 8T(\frac{n}{2}) + n^3 + 1 \; otherwise.$$
Using the master theorem gives, $T(n) = \Theta(n^{\log_2 8} \log n) = \Theta(n^3 \log n)$.

Problem-45   Find the complexity of the psuedocode given below.
```
temp = 1
repeat
        for i = 1 to n
                temp = temp + 1;
        n = n/2;
until n <= 1
```
Solution: Consider the comments in the psuedocode given below:
```
temp = 1          //const time
repeat
        // this loops executes n times
        for i = 1 to n
                temp = temp + 1;
        //recursive call with n/2 value
        n = n/2;
until n <= 1
```
The recurrence for this function is $T(n) = T(n/2) + n$. Using master theorem we get, $T(n) = O(n)$.

Problem-46   Running time of following program?
```
function(int n) {
```

```
for(int i = 1 ; i <= n ; i + + )
        for(int j = 1 ; j <= n ; j * = 2 )
                System.out.println("*");
}
```

Solution: Consider the comments in the function given below:

```
function(int n) {
        // this loops executes n times
        for(int i = 1 ; i <= n ; i + + )
                // this loops executes logn times from our logarithms
                //guideline
                for(int j = 1 ; j <= n ; j * = 2 )
                        System.out.println("*");
}
```

Complexity of above program is : $O(nlogn)$.

Problem-47   Running time of following program?

```
function(int n) {
        for(int i = 1 ; i <= n/3 ; i + + )
                for(int j = 1 ; j <= n ; j += 4 )
                        System.out.println(" * ");
}
```

Solution: Consider the comments in the function given below:

```
function(int n) {
        // this loops executes n/3 times
        for(int i = 1 ; i <= n/3 ; i + + )
                // this loops executes n/4 times
                for(int j = 1 ; j <= n ; j += 4)
                        System.out.println(" * ");
}
```

The time complexity of this program is: $O(n^2)$.

Problem-48   Find the complexity of the below function.

```
void function(int n) {
        if(n <= 1) return;
        if(n > 1) {
                System.out.println(" * ");
                function( n/2 );
                function( n/2 );
        }
}
```

Solution: Consider the comments in the function given below:

```
void function(int n) {
        if(n <= 1) return;                        //constant time
        if(n > 1) {
                System.out.println(" * ");        //constant time
                //recursion with n/2 value
                function( n/2 );
                //recursion with n/2 value
                function( n/2 );
        }
}
```

The recurrence for this function is: $T(n) = 2T\left(\frac{n}{2}\right) + 1$. Using master theorem, we get $T(n) = O(n)$.

Problem-49   Find the complexity of the below function.

```
function(int n) {
        int i=1;
        while (i < n) {
                int j=n;
                while(j > 0)
                        j = j/2;
                i=2*i;
        } // i
}
```

Solution:
```
function(int n) {
        int i=1;
        while (i < n) {
                int j=n;
                while(j > 0)
                        j = j/2;   //logn code
                i=2*i; //logn times
        } // i
}
```
Time Complexity: $O(logn * logn) = O(log^2 n)$.

Problem-50 $\sum_{1 \le k \le n} O(n)$, where $O(n)$ stands for order n is:
    (a) $O(n)$ (b) $O(n^2)$ (c) $O(n^3)$ (d) $O(3n^2)$ (e) $O(1.5n^2)$

Solution: (b). $\sum_{1 \le k \le n} O(n) = O(n) \sum_{1 \le k \le n} 1 = O(n^2)$.

Problem-51 Which of the following three claims are correct
    I $(n + k)^m = \Theta(n^m)$, where k and m are constants   II $2^{n+1} = O(2^n)$ III $2^{2n+1} = O(2^n)$
    (a) I and II   (b) I and III   (c) II and III   (d) I, II and III

Solution: (a).   (I) $(n + k)^m = n^k + c1 * n^{k-1} + \dots k^m = \Theta(n^k)$ and (II) $2^{n+1} = 2 * 2^n = O(2^n)$

Problem-52 Consider the following functions:
    $f(n) = 2^n$ $g(n) = n!$ $h(n) = n^{logn}$
    Which of the following statements about the asymptotic behavior of $f(n)$, $g(n)$, and $h(n)$ is true?
    (A) $f(n) = O(g(n))$; $g(n) = O(h(n))$ (B) $f(n) = \Omega(g(n))$; $g(n) = O(h(n))$
    (C) $g(n) = O(f(n))$; $h(n) = O(f(n))$ (D) $h(n) = O(f(n))$; $g(n) = \Omega(f(n))$

Solution: (D). According to rate of growths: $h(n) < f(n) < g(n)$ ($g(n)$ is asymptotically greater than $f(n)$ and $f(n)$ is asymptotically greater than $h(n)$). We can easily see the order above taking logarithms of the given 3 functions: $lognlogn < n < log(n!)$. Note that, $log(n!) = O(nlogn)$.

Problem-53 Consider the following segment of C-code:
```
int j=1, n;
while (j <=n)
        j = j*2;
```
    The number of comparisons made in the execution of the loop for any $n > 0$ is:
    (A) $ceil(log_2^n) + 1$ (B) n (C) $ceil(log_2^n)$ (D) $floor(log_2^n) + 1$

Solution: (a). Let us assume that the loop executes k times. After k^{th} step the value of j is 2^k. Taking logarithms on both sides gives $k = log_2^n$. Since we are doing one more comparison for exiting from loop, the answer is $ceil(log_2^n) + 1$.

Problem-54 Consider the following C code segment. Let $T(n)$ denotes the number of times the for loop is executed by the program on input n. Which of the following is TRUE?
```
int IsPrime(int n){
   for(int i=2;i<=sqrt(n);i++)
   if(n%i == 0)
     {printf("Not Prime\n"); return 0;}
   return 1;
}
```
    (A) $T(n) = O(\sqrt{n})$ and $T(n) = \Omega(\sqrt{n})$ (B) $T(n) = O(\sqrt{n})$ and $T(n) = \Omega(1)$
    (C) $T(n) = O(n)$ and $T(n) = \Omega(\sqrt{n})$ (D) None of the above

Solution: (B). Big O notation describes the tight upper bound and Big Omega notation describes the tight lower bound for an algorithm. The *for* loop in the question is run maximum $\sqrt{n}$ times and minimum 1 time. Therefore, $T(n) = O(\sqrt{n})$ and $T(n) = \Omega(1)$.

Problem-55 In the following C function, let n ≥ m. How many recursive calls are made by this function?
```
int gcd(n,m){
        if (n%m ==0) return m;
        n = n%m;
        return gcd(m,n);
}
```
    (A) $\Theta(log_2^n)$ (B) $\Omega(n)$ (C) $\Theta(log_2 log_2^n)$ (D)
    $\Theta(n)$

Solution: No option is correct. Big O notation describes the tight upper bound and Big Omega notation describes the tight lower bound for an algorithm. For $m = 2$ and for all $n = 2^i$, running time is $O(1)$ which contradicts every option.

Problem-56   Suppose $T(n) = 2T(n/2) + n$, $T(0)=T(1)=1$. Which one of the following is FALSE?

(A) $T(n) = O(n^2)$ (B) $T(n) = \Theta(nlogn)$ (C) $T(n) = \Omega(n^2)$ (D) $T(n) = O(nlogn)$

Solution: (C). Big O notation describes the tight upper bound and Big Omega notation describes the tight lower bound for an algorithm. Based on master theorem, we get $T(n) = \Theta(nlogn)$. This indicates that tight lower bound and tight upper bound are same. That means, $O(nlogn)$ and $\Omega(nlogn)$ are correct for given recurrence. So option (C) is wrong.

Problem-57   Find the complexity of the below function.

```
function(int n) {
    for (int i = 0; i<n; i++)
        for(int j=i; j<i*i; j++)
            if (j %i == 0){
                for (int k = 0; k < j; k++)
                    printf(" * ");
            }
}
```

Solution:

```
function(int n) {
    for (int i = 0; i<n; i++)           // Executes n times
        for(int j=i; j<i*i; j++)        // Executes n*n times
            if (j %i == 0){
                for (int k = 0; k < j; k++)   // Executes j times = (n*n) times
                    printf(" * ");
            }
}
```

Time Complexity: $O(n^5)$.

Problem-58   To calculate 9^n, give algorithm and discuss its complexity.

Solution: Start with 1 and multiply by 9 until reaching 9^n.

Time Complexity: There are $n - 1$ multiplications and each takes constant time giving a $\Theta(n)$ algorithm.

Problem-59   For Problem-58, can we improve the time complexity?

Solution: Refer *Divide and Conquer* chapter.

Problem-60   Find the complexity of the below function.

```
function(int n) {
    int sum = 0;
    for (int i = 0; i<n; i++)
        if (i>j)
            sum = sum +1;
        else {
            for (int k = 0; k < n; k++)
                sum = sum -1;
        }
}
```

Solution: Consider the worst-case.

```
function(int n) {
    int sum = 0;
    for (int i = 0; i<n; i++)             // Executes n times
        if (i>j)
            sum = sum +1;                 // Executes n times
        else {
            for (int k = 0; k < n; k++)   // Executes n times
                sum = sum -1;
```

```
        }
    }
}
```

Time Complexity: $O(n^2)$.

Chapter-2

RECURSION AND BACKTRACKING

2.1 Introduction

In this chapter, we will look at one of the important topics *"recursion"*, which will be used in almost every chapter and also its relative *"backtracking"*.

2.2 What is Recursion?

Any function which calls itself is called *recursive*. A recursive method solves a problem by calling a copy of itself to work on a smaller problem. This is called the recursion step. The recursion step can result in many more such recursive calls. It is important to ensure that the recursion terminates. Each time the function calls itself with a slightly simpler version of the original problem. The sequence of smaller problems must eventually converge on the base case.

2.3 Why Recursion?

Recursion is a useful technique borrowed from mathematics. Recursive code is generally shorter and easier to write than iterative code. Generally, loops are turned into recursive functions when they are compiled or interpreted. Recursion is most useful for tasks that can be defined in terms of similar subtasks. For example, sort, search, and traversal problems often have simple recursive solutions.

2.4 Format of a Recursive Function

A recursive function performs a task in part by calling itself to perform the subtasks. At some point, the function encounters a subtask that it can perform without calling itself. This case, where the function does not recur, is called the *base case*, the former, where the function calls itself to perform a subtask, is referred to as the *recursive case*. We can write all recursive functions using the format:

```
if(test for the base case)
        return some base case value
else if(test for another base case)
        return some other base case value
// the recursive case
else     return (some work and then a recursive call)
```

As an example consider the factorial function: $n!$ is the product of all integers between n and 1. Definition of recursive factorial looks like:

$$n! = 1, \qquad\qquad \text{if } n = 0$$
$$n! = n * (n-1)! \qquad \text{if } n > 0$$

This definition can easily be converted to recursive implementation. Here the problem is determining the value of $n!$, and the subproblem is determining the value of $(n-l)!$. In the recursive case, when n is greater than 1, the function calls itself to determine the value of $(n-l)!$ and multiplies that with n. In the base case, when n is 0 or 1, the function simply returns 1. This looks like the following:

```
// calculates factorial of a positive integer
int Fact(int n) {
        // base cases: fact of 0 or 1 is 1
        if(n == 1)
                return 1;
        else if(n == 0)
                return 1;
        // recursive case: multiply n by (n - 1) factorial
        else
                return n*Fact(n-1);
}
```

2.5 Recursion and Memory (Visualization)

Each recursive call makes a new copy of that method (actually only the variables) in memory. Once a method ends (that is, returns some data), the copy of that returning method is removed from memory. The recursive solutions look simple but visualization and tracing takes times. For better understanding, let us consider the following example.

```java
int Print(int n) {
        if( n = = 0) // this is the terminating base case
                return 0;
        else {   System.out.println(n);
                return Print(n-1); // recursive call to itself again
        }
}
```

For this example, if we call the print function with n=4, visually our memory assignments may look like:

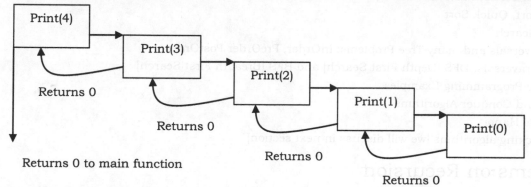

Now, let us consider our factorial function. The visualization of factorial function with n=4 will look like:

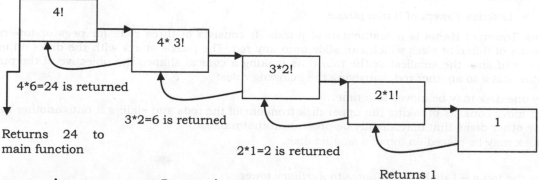

2.6 Recursion versus Iteration

While discussing recursion the basic question that comes to mind is, which way is better? – Iteration or recursion? Answer to this question depends on what we are trying to do. A recursive approach mirrors the problem that we are trying to solve. A recursive approach makes it simpler to solve a problem, which may not have the most obvious of answers. But, recursion adds overhead for each recursive call (needs space on the stack frame).

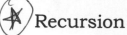

Recursion

- Terminates when a base case is reached.
- Each recursive call requires extra space on the stack frame (memory).
- If we get infinite recursion, the program may run out of memory and gives stack overflow.
- Solutions to some problems are easier to formulate recursively.

Iteration

- Terminates when a condition is proven to be false.
- Each iteration does not require any extra space.
- An infinite loop could loop forever since there is no extra memory being created.
- Iterative solutions to a problem may not always be as obvious as a recursive solution.

2.7 Notes on Recursion

- Recursive algorithms have two types of cases, recursive cases and base cases.
- Every recursive function case must terminate at base case.
- Generally iterative solutions are more efficient than recursive solutions [due to the overhead of function calls].
- A recursive algorithm can be implemented without recursive function calls using a stack, but it's usually more trouble than its worth. That means any problem that can be solved recursively can also be solved iteratively.
- For some problems, there are no obvious iterative algorithms.
- Some problems are best suited for recursive solutions while others are not.

2.8 Example Algorithms of Recursion

- Fibonacci Series, Factorial Finding
- Merge Sort, Quick Sort
- Binary Search
- Tree Traversals and many Tree Problems: InOrder, PreOrder PostOrder
- Graph Traversals: DFS [Depth First Search] and BFS [Breadth First Search]
- Dynamic Programming Examples
- Divide and Conquer Algorithms
- Towers of Hanoi
- Backtracking algorithms [we will discuss in next section]

2.9 Problems on Recursion

In this chapter we cover few problems on recursion and will discuss the rest in other chapters. By the time you complete the reading of entire book you will encounter many problems on recursion.

Problem-1   Discuss Towers of Hanoi puzzle.

Solution: The Tower of Hanoi is a mathematical puzzle. It consists of three rods (or pegs or towers), and a number of disks of different sizes which can slide onto any rod. The puzzle starts with the disks on one rod in ascending order of size, the smallest at the top, thus making a conical shape. The objective of the puzzle is to move the entire stack to another rod, satisfying the following rules:

- Only one disk may be moved at a time.
- Each move consists of taking the upper disk from one of the rods and sliding it onto another rod, on top of the other disks that may already be present on that rod.
- No disk may be placed on top of a smaller disk.

Algorithm

- Move the top $n - 1$ disks from *Source* to *Auxiliary* tower,
- Move the nth disk from *Source* to *Destination* tower,
- Move the $n - 1$ disks from Auxiliary tower to *Destination* tower.
- Transferring the top $n - 1$ disks from *Source* to *Auxiliary* tower can again be thought as a fresh problem and can be solved in the same manner. Once we solve *Tower of Hanoi* with three disks, we can solve it with any number of disks with the above algorithm.

```java
void TowersOfHanoi(int n, char frompeg, char topeg, char auxpeg) {
    /* If only 1 disk, make the move and return */
    if(n==1) {
        System.out.println("Move disk 1 from peg " + frompeg + " to peg " + topeg);
        return;
    }
    /* Move top n-1 disks from A to B, using C as auxiliary */
    TowersOfHanoi(n-1,frompeg,auxpeg,topeg);
    /* Move remaining disks from A to C */
    System.out.println("Move disk from peg" + frompeg + " to peg " + topeg);
    /* Move n-1 disks from B to C using A as auxiliary */
    TowersOfHanoi(n-1,auxpeg,topeg,frompeg);
}
```

Problem-2   Given an array, check whether the array is in sorted order with recursion.

Solution:
```
int isArrayInSortedOrder(int[] A, int index){
        if(A.length() == 1) return 1;
        return (A[index -1] <= A[index -2])?0:isArrayInSortedOrder(A, index -1);
}
```

Time Complexity: $O(n)$. Space Complexity: $O(n)$ for stack space.

2.10 What is Backtracking?

Backtracking is a method of exhaustive search using divide and conquer.
- Sometimes the best algorithm for a problem is to try all possibilities.
- This is always slow, but there are standard tools that can be used to help.
- Tools: algorithms for generating basic objects, such as binary strings [2^n possibilities for n-bit string], permutations [$n!$], combinations [$n!/r!(n-r)!$], general strings [$k-$ary strings of length n has k^n possibilities], etc...
- Backtracking speeds the exhaustive search by pruning.

2.11 Example Algorithms of Backtracking

- Binary Strings: generating all binary strings
- Generating k-ary Strings
- The Knapsack Problem
- Generalized Strings
- Hamiltonian Cycles [refer *Graphs* chapter]
- Graph Coloring Problem

2.12 Problems on Backtracking

Problem-3   Generate all the strings of n bits. Assume $A[0..n-1]$ is an array of size n.

Solution:
```
void Binary(int n) {
        if(n < 1 )
                System.out.println(A);              //Assume array A is a global variable
        else {   A[n-1] = 0;
                Binary (n - 1);
                A[n-1] = 1;
                Binary(n - 1);
        }
}
```

Let $T(n)$ be the running time of $binary(n)$. Assume function $System.out.println$ takes time $O(1)$.
$$T(n) = \begin{cases} c, & \text{if } n < 0 \\ 2T(n-1) + d, & \text{otherwise} \end{cases}$$
Using Subtraction and Conquer Master theorem we get, $T(n) = O(2^n)$. This means the algorithm for generating bit-strings is optimal.

Problem-4   Generate all the strings of length n drawn from $0...k-1$.

Solution: Let us assume we keep current k-ary string in an array $A[0..n-1]$. Call function $k-string$(n, k):
```
void k-string(int n, int k) {
        //process all k-ary strings of length m
        if(n < 1 )
                System.out.println(A);              //Assume array A is a global variable
        else {   for (int j = 0 ; j < k ; j++) {
                        A[n-1] = j;
                        k-string(n- 1, k);
                }
        }
}
```

Let $T(n)$ be the running time of $k-string(n)$. Then,
$$T(n) = \begin{cases} c, & \text{if } n < 0 \\ kT(n-1) + d, & \text{otherwise} \end{cases}$$
Using Subtraction and Conquer Master theorem we get, $T(n) = O(k^n)$.

Note: For more problems, refer *String Algorithms* chapter.

Chapter-3

LINKED LISTS

3.1 What is a Linked List?

Linked list is a data structure used for storing collections of data. Linked list has the following properties.

- Successive elements are connected by pointers
- Last element points to NULL
- Can grow or shrink in size during execution of a program
- Can be made just as long as required (until systems memory exhausts)
- It does not waste memory space (but takes some extra memory for pointers)

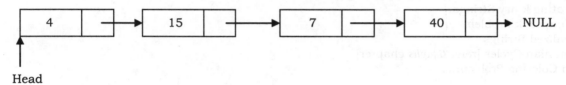

Head

3.2 Linked Lists ADT

The following operations make linked lists an ADT:

Main Linked Lists Operations

- Insert: inserts an element into the list
- Delete: removes and returns the specified position element from the list

Auxiliary Linked Lists Operations

- Delete List: removes all elements of the list (disposes the list)
- Count: returns the number of elements in the list
- Find n^{th} node from the end of the list

3.3 Why Linked Lists?

There are many other data structures that do the same thing as that of linked lists. Before discussing linked lists it is important to understand the difference between linked lists and arrays. Both linked lists and arrays are used to store collections of data. Since both are used for the same purpose, we need to differentiate their usage. That means in which cases *arrays* are suitable and in which cases *linked lists* are suitable.

3.4 Arrays Overview

One memory block is allocated for the entire array to hold the elements of the array. The array elements can be accessed in a constant time by using the index of the particular element as the subscript.

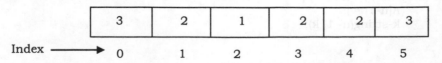

Index

Why Constant Time for Accessing Array Elements?

To access an array element, address of an element is computed as an offset from the base address of the array and one multiplication is needed to compute what is supposed to be added to the base address to get the memory address of the element. First the size of an element of that data type is calculated and then it is multiplied with the index of the element to get the value to be added to the base address. This process takes one multiplication and one addition. Since these two operations take constant time, we can say the array access can be performed in constant time.

Advantages of Arrays

- Simple and easy to use
- Faster access to the elements (constant access)

Disadvantages of Arrays

- **Fixed size:** The size of the array is static (specify the array size before using it).
- **One block allocation**: To allocate the array at the beginning itself, sometimes it may not be possible to get the memory for the complete array (if the array size is big).
- **Complex position-based insertion**: To insert an element at a given position we may need to shift the existing elements. This will create a position for us to insert the new element at the desired position. If the position at which we want to add an element is at the beginning then the shifting operation is more expensive.

Dynamic Arrays

Dynamic array (also called as *growable array, resizable array, dynamic table,* or *array list*) is a random access, variable-size list data structure that allows elements to be added or removed.

One simple way of implementing dynamic arrays is, initially start with some fixed size array. As soon as that array becomes full, create the new array of size double than the original array. Similarly, reduce the array size to half if the elements in the array are less than half.

Note: We will see the implementation for *dynamic arrays* in the *Stacks, Queues* and *Hashing* chapters.

Advantages of Linked Lists

Linked lists have both advantages and disadvantages. The advantage of linked lists is that they can be *expanded* in constant time. To create an array we must allocate memory for a certain number of elements. To add more elements to the array then we must create a new array and copy the old array into the new array. This can take lot of time.

We can prevent this by allocating lots of space initially but then you might allocate more than you need and wasting memory. With a linked list we can start with space for just one element allocated and *add* on new elements easily without the need to do any copying and reallocating.

Issues with Linked Lists (Disadvantages)

There are a number of issues in linked lists. The main disadvantage of linked lists is *access time* to individual elements. Array is random-access, which means it takes O(1) to access any element in the array. Linked lists takes O(n) for access to an element in the list in the worst case. Another advantage of arrays in access time is *spacial locality* in memory. Arrays are defined as contiguous blocks of memory, and so any array element will be physically near its neighbors. This greatly benefits from modern CPU caching methods.

Although the dynamic allocation of storage is a great advantage, the *overhead* with storing and retrieving data can make a big difference. Sometimes linked lists are *hard* to *manipulate*. If the last item is deleted, the last but one must now have its pointer changed to hold a NULL reference. This requires that the list is traversed to find the last but one link, and its pointer set to a NULL reference.

Finally, linked lists wastes memory in terms of extra reference points.

3.5 Comparison of Linked Lists with Arrays & Dynamic Arrays

Parameter	Linked list	Array	Dynamic array
Indexing	O(n)	O(1)	O(1)
Insertion/deletion at beginning	O(1)	O(n), if array is not full (for shifting the elements)	O(n)
Insertion at ending	O(n)	O(1), if array is not full	O(1), if array is not full O(n), if array is full
Deletion at ending	O(n)	O(1)	O(n)
Insertion in middle	O(n)	O(n), if array is not full (for shifting the	O(n)

		elements)	
Deletion in middle	O(n)	O(n), if array is not full (for shifting the elements)	O(n)
Wasted space	O(n)	0	O(n)

3.6 Singly Linked Lists

Generally "linked list" means a singly linked list. This list consists of a number of nodes in which each node has a *next* pointer to the following element. The link of the last node in the list is NULL, which indicates end of the list.

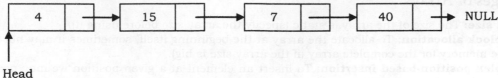

Head

Following is a type declaration for a linked list:

```java
public class ListNode {
        private int data;
        private ListNode next;
        public ListNode(int data){
                this.data = data;
        }
        public void setData(int data){
                this.data = data;
        }
        public int getData(){
                return data;
        }
        public void setNext(ListNode next){
                this.next = next;
        }
        public ListNode getNext(){
                return this.next;
        }
}
```

Basic Operations on a List

- Traversing the list
- Inserting an item in the list
- Deleting an item from the list

Traversing the Linked List

Let us assume that the *head* points to the first node of the list. To traverse the list we do the following.

- Follow the pointers.
- Display the contents of the nodes (or count) as they are traversed.
- Stop when the next pointer points to NULL.

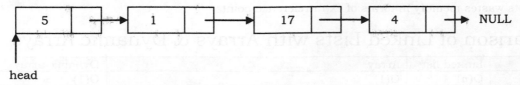

head

The ListLength() function takes a linked list as input and counts the number of nodes in the list. The function given below can be used for printing the list data with extra print function.

```java
int ListLength(ListNode headNode) {
        int length = 0;
        ListNode currentNode = headNode;
```

```
        while(currentNode != null){
                length++;
                currentNode = currentNode.getNext();
        }
        return length;
}
```

Time Complexity: O(*n*), for scanning the list of size *n*. Space Complexity: O(1), for creating temporary variable.

Singly Linked List Insertion

Insertion into a singly-linked list has three cases:
- Inserting a new node before the head (at the beginning)
- Inserting a new node after the tail (at the end of the list)
- Inserting a new node at the middle of the list (random location)

Note: To insert an element in the linked list at some position *p*, assume that after inserting the element the position of this new node is *p*.

Inserting a Node in Singly Linked List at the Beginning

In this case, a new node is inserted before the current head node. *Only one next pointer* needs to be modified (new node's next pointer) and it can be done in two steps:

- Update the next pointer of new node, to point to the current head.

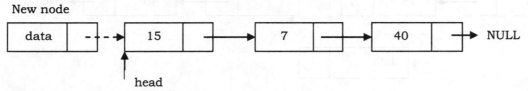

- Update head pointer to point to the new node.

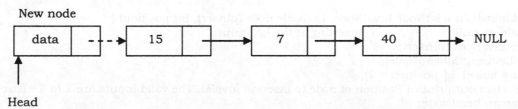

Inserting a Node in Singly Linked List at the Ending

In this case, we need to modify *two next pointers* (last nodes next pointer and new nodes next pointer).

- New nodes next pointer points to NULL.

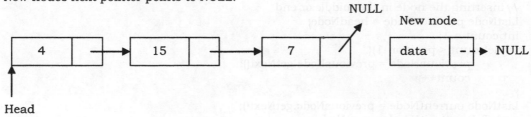

- Last nodes next pointer points to the new node.

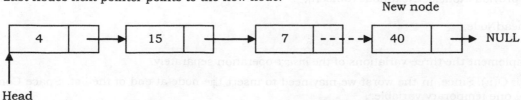

Inserting a Node in Singly Linked List at the Middle

Let us assume that we are given a position where we want to insert the new node. In this case also, we need to modify two next pointers.

- If we want to add an element at position 3 then we stop at position 2. That means we traverse 2 nodes and insert the new node. For simplicity let us assume that second node is called *position* node. New node points to the next node of the position where we want to add this node.

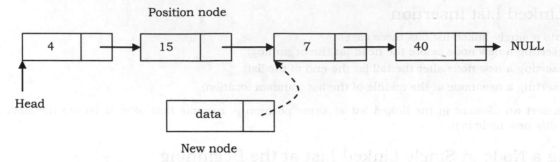

- Position nodes next pointer now points to the new node.

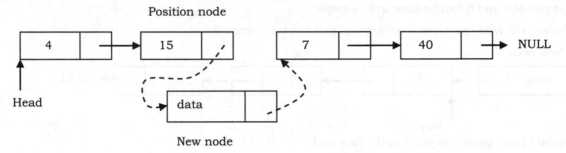

```
ListNode InsertInLinkedList (ListNode headNode, ListNode nodeToInsert, int position) {
        if(headNode == null)              //inserting at the beginning
                return nodeToInsert;
        int size = ListLength(headNode);
        if(position > size+1 || position < 1){
                System.out.println("Position of node to insert is invalid. The valid inputs are 1 to " + (size+1));
                return headNode;
        }
        if(position == 1){                //inserting the node in the beginning
                nodeToInsert.setNext(headNode);
                return nodeToInsert;
        }else{
                //inserting the node in the middle or end
                ListNode previousNode = headNode;
                int count = 1;
                while(count < position-1){
                        previousNode = previousNode.getNext();
                        count++;
                }
                ListNode currentNode = previousNode.getNext();
                nodeToInsert.setNext(currentNode);
                previousNode.setNext(nodeToInsert);
        }
        return headNode;
}
```

Note: We can implement the three variations of the *insert* operation separately.

Time Complexity: O(n). Since, in the worst we may need to insert the node at end of the list. Space Complexity: O(1), for creating one temporary variable.

Singly Linked List Deletion

As similar to insertion here also we have three cases.

- Deleting the first node
- Deleting the last node
- Deleting an intermediate node

Deleting the First Node in Singly Linked List

First node (current head node) is removed from the list. It can be done in two steps:

- Create a temporary node which will point to same node as that of head.

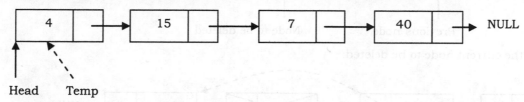

- Now, move the head nodes pointer to the next node and dispose the temporary node.

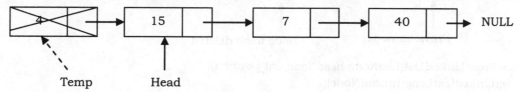

Deleting the Last node in Singly Linked List

In this case, last node is removed from the list. This operation is a bit trickier than removing the first node, because algorithm should find a node, which is previous to the tail first. It can be done in three steps:

- Traverse the list and while traversing maintain the previous node address also. By the time we reach the end of list, we will have two pointers one pointing to the *tail* node and other pointing to the node *before* tail node.

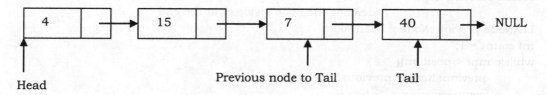

- Update previous nodes next pointer with NULL.

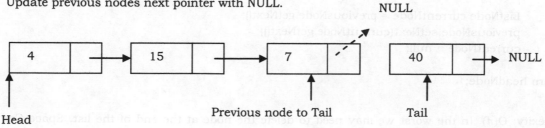

- Dispose the tail node.

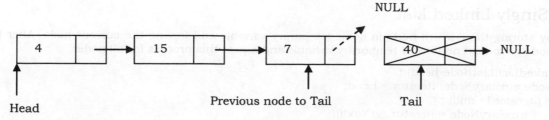

Deleting an Intermediate Node in Singly Linked List

In this case, node to be removed is *always located between* two nodes. Head and tail links are not updated in this case. Such a removal can be done in two steps:

- As similar to previous case, maintain previous node while traversing the list. Once we found the node to be deleted, change the previous nodes next pointer to next pointer of the node to be deleted.

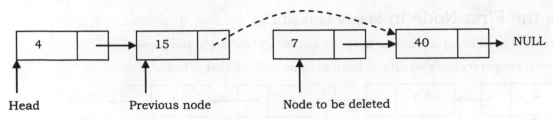

Head   Previous node   Node to be deleted

- Dispose the current node to be deleted.

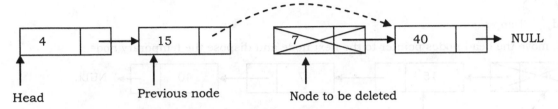

Head   Previous node   Node to be deleted

```java
ListNode DeleteNodeFromLinkedList(ListNode headNode, int position){
        int size = getLinkedListLength(headNode);
        if(position > size || position < 1){
                System.out.println("Position of node to delete is invalid. The valid inputs are 1 to " + size);
                return headNode;
        }
        if(position == 1){                      //deleting the node in the beginning
                ListNode currentNode = headNode.getNext();
                headNode = null;
                return currentNode;
        }else{                                  //deleting the node inside or at the end
                ListNode previousNode = headNode;
                int count = 1;
                while(count < position){
                        previousNode = previousNode.getNext();
                        count++;
                }
                ListNode currentNode = previousNode.getNext();
                previousNode.setNext(currentNode.getNext());
                currentNode = null;
        }
        return headNode;
}
```

Time Complexity: O(n). In the worst we may need to delete the node at the end of the list. Space Complexity: O(1). Since, we are creating only one temporary variable.

Deleting Singly Linked List

This works by storing the current node in some temporary variable and freeing the current node. After freeing the current node go to next node with temporary variable and repeat this process for all nodes.

```java
void DeleteLinkedList(ListNode head) {
        ListNode auxilaryNode, iterator = head;
        while (iterator != null) {
                auxilaryNode = iterator.getNext();
```

```
            iterator = null;            //In Java, it will be taken care by garbage collector
            iterator = auxilaryNode;  //In reality we need not implement this.
       }
}
```

Time Complexity: O(n), for scanning the complete list of size n.
Space Complexity: O(1), for temporary variable.

3.7 Doubly Linked Lists

The *advantage* of a doubly linked list (also called *two − way linked list*) is that given a node in the list, we can navigate in both directions. A node in a singly linked list cannot be removed unless we have the pointer to its predecessor. But in doubly linked list we can delete a node even if we don't have previous nodes address (since, each node has left pointer pointing to previous node and we can move backward).

The primary *disadvantages* of doubly linked lists are:

*   Each node requires an extra pointer, requiring more space.
*   The insertion or deletion of a node takes a bit longer (more pointer operations).

As similar to singly linked list, let us implement the operations of doubly linked lists. Following is a type declaration for a doubly linked list:

```
public class DLLNode {
        private int data;
        private DLLNode next;
        private DLLNode previous;
        public DLLNode(int data){
                this.data = data;
        }
        public void setData(int data){
                this.data = data;
        }
        public int getData(){
                return data;
        }
        public void setNext(DLLNode next){
                this.next = next;
        }
        public DLLNode getNext(){
                return this.next;
        }
        public void setPrevious(DLLNode previous){
                this.previous = previous;
        }
        public DLLNode getPrevious(){
                return this.previous;
        }
}
```

Doubly Linked List Insertion

Insertion into a doubly-linked list has three cases (same as singly linked list).
*   Inserting a new node before the head.
*   Inserting a new node after the tail (at the end of the list).
*   Inserting a new node at the middle of the list.

Inserting a Node in Doubly Linked List at the Beginning

In this case, new node is inserted before the head node. Previous and next pointers need to be modified and it can be done in two steps:

- Update the right pointer of new node to point to the current head node (dotted link in below figure) and also make left pointer of new node as NULL.

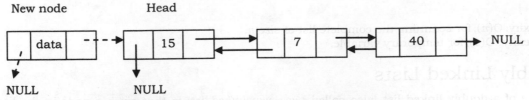

- Update head nodes left pointer to point to the new node and make new node as head.

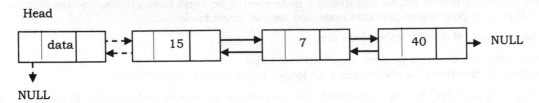

Inserting a Node in Doubly Linked List at the Ending

In this case, traverse the list till the end and insert the new node.

- New node right pointer points to NULL and left pointer points to the end of the list.

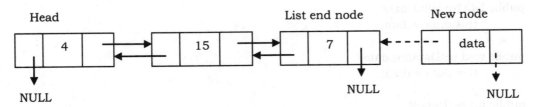

- Update right of pointer of last node to point to new node.

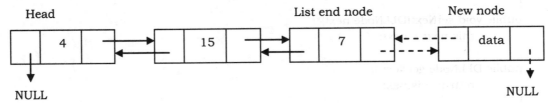

Inserting a Node in Doubly Linked List in the Middle

As discussed in singly linked lists, traverse the list till the position node and insert the new node.

- *New node* right pointer points to the next node of the *position node* where we want to insert the new node. Also, *new node* left pointer points to the *position node*.

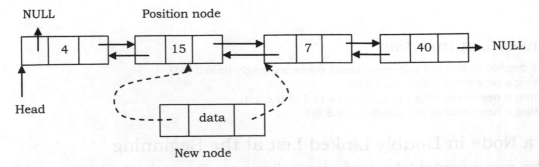

- Position node right pointer points to the new node and the *next node* of position nodes left pointer points to new node.

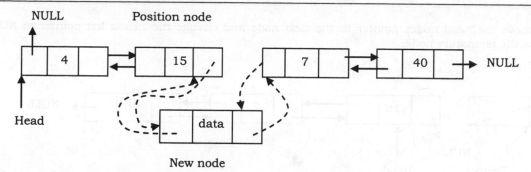

New node

```
DLLNode DLLInsert(DLLNode headNode, DLLNode nodeToInsert, int position){
        if(headNode == null)                    //inserting at the beginning
                return nodeToInsert;
        int size = getDLLLength(headNode);
        if(position > size+1 || position < 1){
                System.out.println("Position of nodeToInsert is invalid. " + "The valid inputs are 1 to " + (size+1));
                return headNode;
        }
        if(position == 1){//inserting the node in the beginning
                nodeToInsert.setNext(headNode);
                headNode.setPrevious(nodeToInsert);
                return nodeToInsert;
        }else{   //inserting the node in the middle or end
                DLLNode previousNode = headNode;
                int count = 1;
                while(count < position-1){
                        previousNode = previousNode.getNext();
                        count++;
                }
                DLLNode currentNode = previousNode.getNext();
                nodeToInsert.setNext(currentNode);
                if(currentNode != null)
                        currentNode.setPrevious(nodeToInsert);
                previousNode.setNext(nodeToInsert);
                nodeToInsert.setPrevious(previousNode);
        }
        return headNode;
}
```

Time Complexity: O(n). In the worst we may need to insert the node at the end of the list.
Space Complexity: O(1), for creating one temporary variable.

Doubly Linked List Deletion

As similar to singly linked list deletion, here also we have three cases:
- Deleting the first node
- Deleting the last node
- Deleting an intermediate node

Deleting the First Node in Doubly Linked List

In this case, first node (current head node) is removed from the list. It can be done in two steps:
- Create a temporary node which will point to same node as that of head.

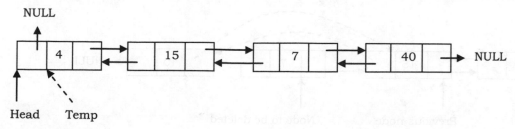

- Now, move the head nodes pointer to the next node and change the heads left pointer to NULL and dispose the temporary node.

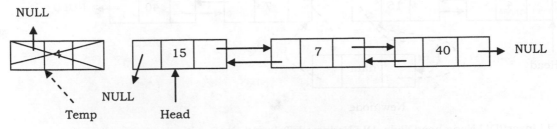

Deleting the Last Node in Doubly Linked List

This operation is a bit trickier, than removing the first node, because algorithm should find a node, which is previous to the tail first. This can be done in three steps:

- Traverse the list and while traversing maintain the previous node address. By the time we reach the end of list, we will have two pointers one pointing to the tail and other pointing to the node before tail node.

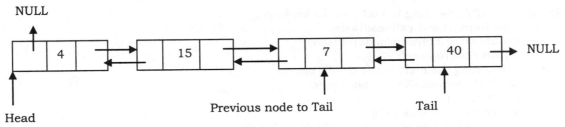

- Update tail nodes previous nodes next pointer with NULL.

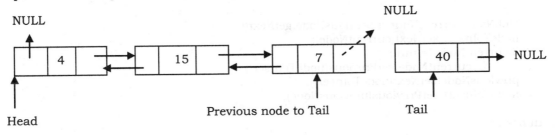

- Dispose the tail node.

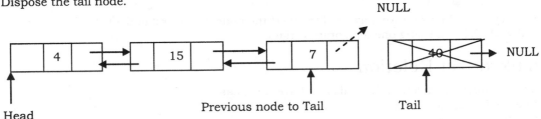

Deleting an Intermediate Node in Doubly Linked List

In this case, node to be removed is *always located between* two nodes. Head and tail links are not updated in this case. Such a removal can be done in two steps:

- Similar to previous case, maintain previous node also while traversing the list. Once we found the node to be deleted, change the previous nodes next pointer to the next node of the node to be deleted.

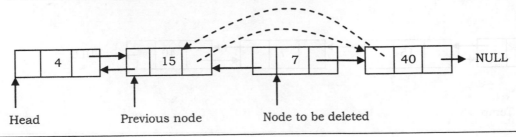

- Dispose the current node to be deleted.

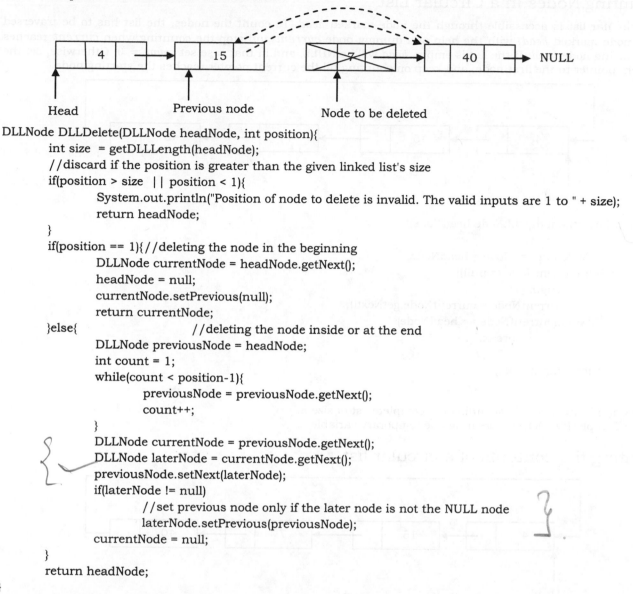

```
DLLNode DLLDelete(DLLNode headNode, int position){
        int size  = getDLLLength(headNode);
        //discard if the position is greater than the given linked list's size
        if(position > size  || position < 1){
                System.out.println("Position of node to delete is invalid. The valid inputs are 1 to " + size);
                return headNode;
        }
        if(position == 1){//deleting the node in the beginning
                DLLNode currentNode = headNode.getNext();
                headNode = null;
                currentNode.setPrevious(null);
                return currentNode;
        }else{                          //deleting the node inside or at the end
                DLLNode previousNode = headNode;
                int count = 1;
                while(count < position-1){
                        previousNode = previousNode.getNext();
                        count++;
                }
                DLLNode currentNode = previousNode.getNext();
                DLLNode laterNode = currentNode.getNext();
                previousNode.setNext(laterNode);
                if(laterNode != null)
                        //set previous node only if the later node is not the NULL node
                        laterNode.setPrevious(previousNode);
                currentNode = null;
        }
        return headNode;
}
```

Time Complexity: O(n), for scanning the complete list of size n.
Space Complexity: O(1), for creating one temporary variable.

3.8 Circular Linked Lists

In singly linked lists and doubly linked lists the end of lists are indicated with NULL value. But circular linked lists do not have ends. While traversing the circular linked lists we should be careful otherwise we will be traversing the list infinitely. In circular linked lists each node has a successor.

Note that unlike singly linked lists, there is no node with NULL pointer in a circularly linked list. In some situations, circular linked lists are useful. For example, when several processes are using the same computer resource (CPU) for the same amount of time, we have to assure that no process accesses the resource before all other processes did (round robin algorithm).

In circular linked list we access the elements using the *head* node (similar to *head* node in singly linked list and doubly linked lists). For readability let us assume that the class name of circular linked list is CLLNode.

Counting Nodes in a Circular List

The circular list is accessible through the node marked *head*. To count the nodes, the list has to be traversed from node marked *head*, with the help of a dummy node *current* and stop the counting when *current* reaches the starting node *head*. If the list is empty, *head* will be NULL, and in that case set *count* = 0. Otherwise, set the current pointer to the first node, and keep on counting till the current pointer reaches the starting node.

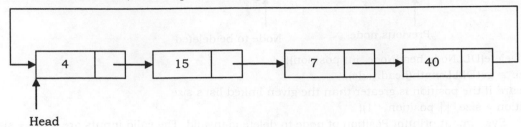

Head

```java
int CircularListLength(CLLNode headNode){
        int length = 0;
        CLLNode currentNode = headNode;
        while(currentNode != null){
                length++;
                currentNode = currentNode.getNext();
                if(currentNode == headNode)
                        break;
        }
        return length;
}
```

Time Complexity: O(n), for scanning the complete list of size n.
Space Complexity: O(1), for creating one temporary variable.

Printing the contents of a circular list

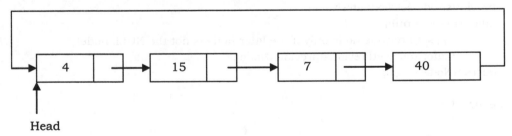

Head

We assume here that the list is being accessed by its *head* node. Since all the nodes are arranged in a circular fashion, the *tail* node of the list will be the node previous to the *head* node. Let us assume we want to print the contents of the nodes starting with the *head* node. Print its contents, move to the next node and continue printing till we reach the *head* node again.

```java
void PrintCircularListData(CLLNode headNode){
        CLLNode CLLNode = headNode;
        while(CLLNode != null){
                System.out.print(CLLNode.getData()+"->");
                CLLNode = CLLNode.getNext();
                if(CLLNode == headNode) break;
        }
        System.out.println("(" + CLLNode.getData() + ")headNode");
}
```

Time Complexity: O(n), for scanning the complete list of size n.
Space Complexity: O(1), for creating ne temporary variable.

Inserting a Node at the End of a Circular Linked List

Let us add a node containing *data*, at the end of a list (circular list) headed by ***head***. The new node will be placed just after the tail node (which is the last node of the list), which means it will have to be inserted in between the tail node and the first node.

- Create a new node and initially keep its next pointer points to itself.

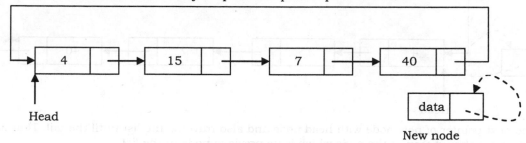

Head

New node

- Update the next pointer of new node with head node and also traverse the list until the tail. That means in circular list we should stop at a node whose next node is head.

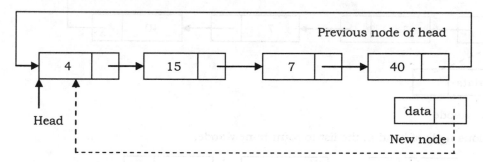

Previous node of head

Head

New node

- Update the next pointer of previous node to point to new node and we get the list as shown below.

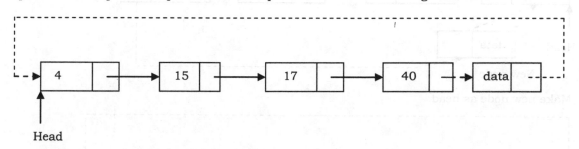

Head

```
void InsertAtEndInCLL (LLNode headNode, LLNode nodeToInsert) {
        CLLNode currentNode = headNode;

        while (currentNode.getNext() != headNode) {
                currentNode.setNext(currentNode.getNext());
        }
        nodeToInsert.setNext(nodeToInsert);
        if(headNode == null)
                headNode = nodeToInsert;
        else {
                nodeToInsert.setNext(headNode);
                currentNode.setNext(nodeToInsert);
        }
}
```

Time Complexity: O(*n*), for scanning the complete list of size *n*.
Space Complexity: O(1), for creating one temporary variable.

Inserting a Node at Front of a Circular Linked List

The only difference between inserting a node at the beginning and at the ending is that, after inserting the new node we just need to update the pointer. The steps for doing this is given below:

- Create a new node and initially keep its next pointer points to itself.

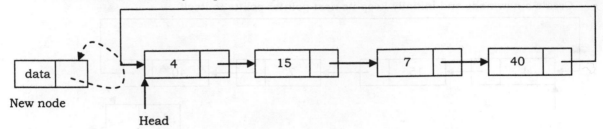

- Update the next pointer of new node with head node and also traverse the list until the tail. That means in circular list we should stop at the node which is its previous node in the list.

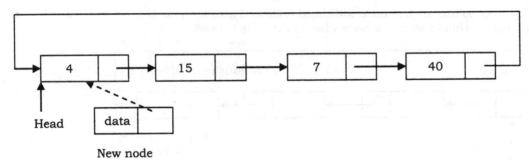

- Update the previous node of head in the list to point to new node.

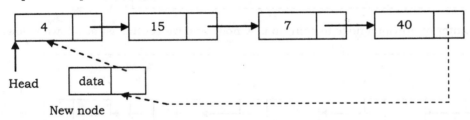

- Make new node as head.

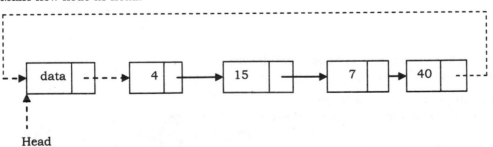

```
void InsertAtBeginInCLL (LLNode headNode, LLNode nodeToInsert) {
        CLLNode currentNode = headNode;

        while (currentNode.getNext() != headNode) {
                currentNode.setNext(currentNode.getNext());
        }
        nodeToInsert.setNext(nodeToInsert);
        if(headNode == null)
                headNode = nodeToInsert;
        else {
                nodeToInsert.setNext(headNode);
                currentNode.setNext(nodeToInsert);
                headNode = nodeToInsert;
```

}

}

Time Complexity: O(n), for scanning the complete list of size n.

Space Complexity: O(1), for creating only one temporary variable.

Deleting the Last Node in a Circular List

The list has to be traversed to reach the last but one node. This has to be named as the tail node, and its next field has to point to the first node. Consider the following list. To delete the last node 40, the list has to be traversed till you reach 7. The next field of 7 has to be changed to point to 60, and this node must be renamed *pTail*.

• Traverse the list and find the tail node and its previous node.

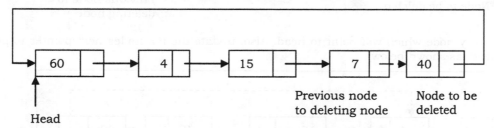

• Update the tail nodes previous node next pointer to point to head.

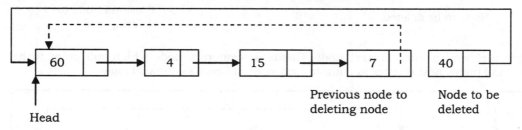

• Dispose the tail node.

```
void DeleteLastNodeFromCLL (CLLNode head) {
        CLLNode temp = head;
        CLLNode currentNode = head;
        if(head == null) {
                System.out.println("List Empty");
                return;
        }
        while (currentNode.getNext() != headNode) {
                temp = currentNode;
                currentNode = currentNode.getNext();
        }
        currentNode = null;
        return;
}
```

Time Complexity: O(n), for scanning the complete list of size n.

Space Complexity: O(1), for creating one temporary variable.

Deleting the First Node in a Circular List

The first node can be deleted by simply replacing the next field of tail node with the next field of the first node.

- Find the tail node of the linked list by traversing the list. Tail node is the previous node to the head node which we want to delete.

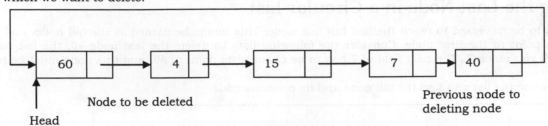

- Create a temporary node which will point to head. Also, update the tail nodes next pointer to point to next node of head (as shown below).

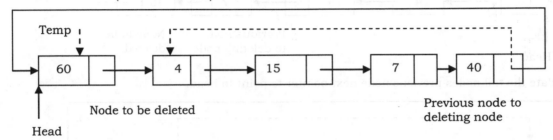

- Now, move the head pointer to next node. Create a temporary node which will point to head. Also, update the tail nodes next pointer to point to next node of head (as shown below).

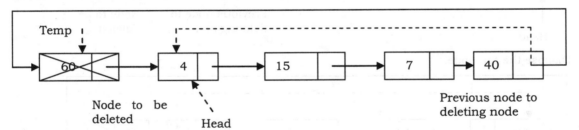

```
void DeleteFrontNodeFromCLL(CLLNode head) {
        CLLNode temp = head;
        CLLNode current = head;

        if(head == null) {
                System.out.println("List Empty");
                return;
        }
        while (current.getNext() != head)
                current.setNext(current.getNext());
        current.setNext(head.getNext());
        head = head.getNext();
        temp = null;
        return;
}
```

Time Complexity: O(n), for scanning complete list of size n.
Space Complexity: O(1), for creating temporary variable.

Applications of Circular List

Circular linked lists are used in managing the computing resources of a computer. We can use circular lists for implementing stacks and queues.

3.9 A Memory-Efficient Doubly Linked List

In conventional implementation, we need to keep a forward pointer to the next item on the list and a backward pointer to the previous item. That means, elements in doubly linked list implementations consist of data, a pointer to the next node and a pointer to the previous node in the list as shown below.

Conventional Node Definition

```
class DLLNode {
    private int data;
    private DLLNode next;
    private DLLNode previous;
    ........
}
```

Recently a journal (Sinha) presented an alternative implementation of the doubly linked list ADT, with insertion, traversal and deletion operations. This implementation is based on pointer difference. Each node uses only one pointer field to traverse the list back and forth.

New Node Definition

```
public class ListNode {
    private int data;
    private ListNode ptrdiff;
    ........
}
```

The *ptrdiff* pointer field contains the difference between the pointer to the next node and the pointer to the previous node. The pointer difference is calculated by using exclusive-or (⊕) operation.

$$ptrdiff = pointer\ to\ previous\ node \oplus pointer\ to\ next\ node.$$

The *ptrdiff* of the start node (head node) is the ⊕ of NULL and *next* node (next node to head). Similarly, the *ptrdiff* of end node is the ⊕ of *previous* node (previous to end node) and NULL. As an example, consider the following linked list.

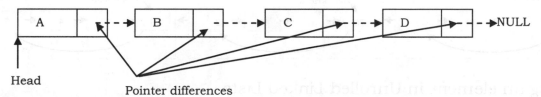

Head

Pointer differences

In the example above,

- The next pointer of A is: NULL ⊕ B
- The next pointer of B is: A ⊕ C
- The next pointer of C is: B ⊕ D
- The next pointer of D is: C ⊕ NULL

Why does it work? To have answer for this question let us consider the properties of ⊕:

$$X \oplus X = 0$$
$$X \oplus 0 = X$$
$$X \oplus Y = Y \oplus X \text{ (symmetric)}$$
$$(X \oplus Y) \oplus Z = X \oplus (Y \oplus Z) \text{ (transitive)}$$

For the example above, let us assume that we are at C node and want to move to B. We know that Cs *ptrdiff* is defined as B ⊕ D. If we want to move to B, performing ⊕ on Cs *ptrdiff* with D would give B. This is due to fact that,

$$(B \oplus D) \oplus D = B \text{ (since, } D \oplus D=0)$$

Similarly, if we want to move to D, then we have to apply ⊕ to Cs *ptrdiff* with B would give D.

$$(B \oplus D) \oplus B = D \text{ (since, } B \oplus B=0)$$

From the above discussion we can see that just by using single pointer, we can move back and forth. A memory-efficient implementation of a doubly linked list is possible without compromising much timing efficiency.

3.10 Unrolled Linked Lists

One of the biggest advantages of linked lists over arrays is that inserting an element at any location takes only O(1) time. However, it takes O(n) to search for an element in a linked list. There is a simple variation of the singly linked list called *unrolled linked lists*.

An unrolled linked list stores multiple elements in each node (let us call it a block for our convenience). In each block, a circular linked list is used to connect all nodes.

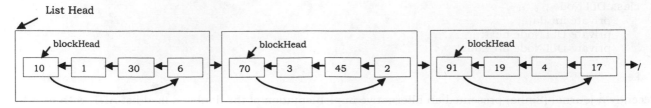

Assume that there will be no more than n elements in the unrolled linked list at any time. To simplify this problem, all blocks, except the last one, should contain exactly $\lceil\sqrt{n}\rceil$ elements. Thus, there will be no more than $\lceil\sqrt{n}\rceil$ blocks at any time.

Searching for an element in Unrolled Linked Lists

In unrolled linked lists, we can find the kth element in $O(\sqrt{n})$:

1. Traverse on the *list of blocks* to the one that contains the kth node, i.e., the $\left\lceil\frac{k}{\lceil\sqrt{n}\rceil}\right\rceil$th block. It takes $O(\sqrt{n})$ since we may find it by going through no more than $\sqrt{n}$ blocks.
2. Find the $(k \bmod \lceil\sqrt{n}\rceil)^{th}$ node in the circular linked list of this block. It also takes $O(\sqrt{n})$ since there are no more than $\lceil\sqrt{n}\rceil$ nodes in a single block.

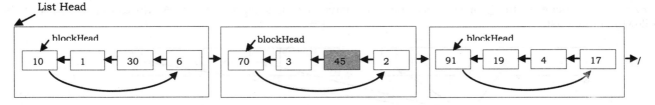

Inserting an element in Unrolled Linked Lists

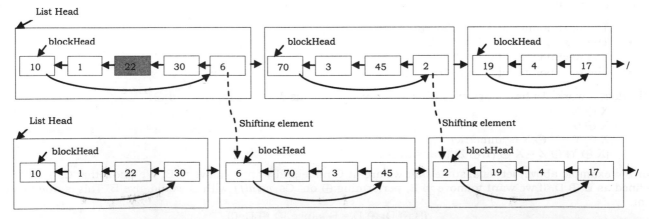

When inserting a node, we have to re-arrange the nodes in the unrolled linked list to maintain the properties previously mentioned, that each block contains $\lceil\sqrt{n}\rceil$ nodes. Suppose that we insert a node x after the ith node, and x should be placed in the jth block.

Nodes in the jth block and in the blocks after the jth block have to be shifted toward the tail of the list so that each of them still have $\lceil\sqrt{n}\rceil$ nodes. In addition, a new block needs to be added to the tail if the last block of the list is out of space, i.e., it has more than $\lceil\sqrt{n}\rceil$ nodes.

Performing Shift Operation

Note that each *shift* operation, which includes removing a node from the tail of the circular linked list in a block and inserting a node to the head of the circular linked list in the block after, takes only O(1). The total time complexity of an insertion operation for unrolled linked lists is therefore $O(\sqrt{n})$; there are at most $O(\sqrt{n})$ blocks and therefore at most $O(\sqrt{n})$ shift operations.

1. A temporary pointer is needed to store the tail of *A*.

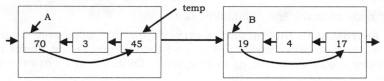

2. In block *A*, move the next pointer of the head node to point to the second to-the-last node, so that the tail node of *A* can be removed.

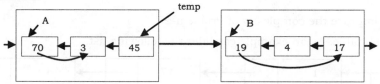

3. Let the next pointer of the node which will be shifted (the tail node of *A*) point to the tail node of *B*.

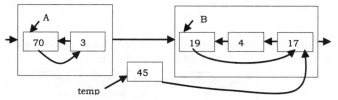

4. Let the next pointer of the head node of *B* point to the node temp points to.

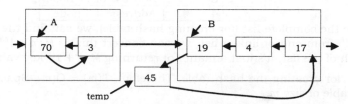

5. Finally, set the head pointer of *B* to point to the node temp points to. Now the node temp points to become the new head node of *B*.

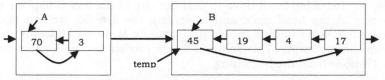

6. *temp* pointer can be thrown away. We have completed the shift operation to move the original tail node of *A* to become the new head node of *B*.

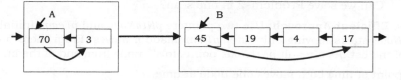

Performance

With unrolled linked lists, there are a couple of advantages, one in speed and one in space.

First, if the number of elements in each block is appropriately sized (e.g., at most the size of one cache line), we get noticeably better cache performance from the improved memory locality.

Second, since we have O(n/m) links, where n is the number of elements in the unrolled linked list and m is the number of elements we can store in any block, we can also save an appreciable amount of space, which is particularly noticeable if each element is small.

3.11 Problems on Linked Lists

Problem-1   Implement Stack using Linked List

Solution: Refer *Stacks* chapter.

Problem-2   Find n^{th} node from the end of a Linked List.

Solution: Brute-Force Approach: In this method, start with the first node and count the number of nodes present after that node. If the number of nodes are $< n - 1$ then return saying "fewer number of nodes in the list". If the number of nodes are $> n - 1$ then go to next node. Continue this until the numbers of nodes after current node are $n - 1$.

Time Complexity: O(n^2), for scanning the remaining list (from current node) for each node.
Space Complexity: O(1).

Problem-3   Can we improve the complexity of Problem-2?

Solution: Yes, using hash table. As an example consider the following list.

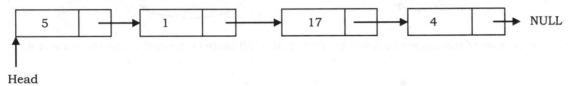

Head

In this approach, create a hash table whose entries are $< position\ of\ node,\ node\ address >$. That means, key is the position of the node in the list and value is the address of that node.

Position in List	Address of Node
1	Address of 5 node
2	Address of 1 node
3	Address of 17 node
4	Address of 4 node

By the time we traverse the complete list (for creating hash table), we can find the list length. Let us say, the list length is M. To find n^{th} from end of linked list, we can convert this to $M\text{-}n + 1^{th}$ from the beginning. Since we already know the length of the list, it's just a matter of returning $M\text{-}n + 1^{th}$ key value from the hash table.

Time Complexity: Time for creating the hash table. Therefore, $T(m) = $ O(m). Space Complexity: O(m). Since, we need to create a hash table of size m.

Problem-4   Can we use Problem-3 approach for solving Problem-2 without creating the hash table?

Solution: Yes. If we observe the Problem-3 solution, what actually we are doing is finding the size of the linked list. That means, we are using hash table to find the size of the linked list. We can find the length of the linked list just by starting at the head node and traversing the list. So, we can find the length of the list without creating the hash table. After finding the length, compute $M - n + 1$ and with one more scan we can get the $M - n + 1^{th}$ node from the beginning. This solution needs two scans: one for finding the length of list and other for finding $M - n + 1^{th}$ node from the beginning.

Time Complexity: Time for finding the length + Time for finding the $M - n + 1^{th}$ node from the beginning. Therefore, $T(n) = $ O(n) +O(n) $\approx$O(n). Space Complexity: O(1). Since, no need of creating the hash table.

Problem-5   Can we solve Problem-2 in one scan?

Solution: Yes. Efficient Approach: Use two pointers *pNthNode* and *pTemp*. Initially, both points to head node of the list. *pNthNode* starts moving only after *pTemp* made n moves. From there both moves forward until *pTemp* reaches end of the list. As a result *pNthNode* points to n^{th} node from end of the linked list.

Note: at any point of time both moves one node at time.

```
ListNode  NthNodeFromEnd(ListNode head , int NthNode) {
    ListNode pTemp = head, pNthNode = null;
    for(int count =1; count< NthNode;count++) {
        if(pTemp != null)
            pTemp = pTemp.getNext();
    }
```

```
            while(pTemp!= null){
                if(pNthNode == null)
                    pNthNode = head;
                else
                    pNthNode = pNthNode.getNext();
                pTemp = pTemp.getNext();
            }
            if(pNthNode != null)
                return pNthNode;
            return null;
        }
```

Time Complexity: O(n). Space Complexity: O(1).

Problem-6   Check whether the given linked list is either NULL-terminated or ends in a cycle (cyclic)

Solution: Brute-Force Approach. As an example consider the following linked list which has a loop in it. The difference between this list and the regular list is that, in this list there are two nodes whose next pointers are same. In regular singly linked lists (without loop) each nodes next pointer is unique. That means, the repetition of next pointers indicates the existence of loop.

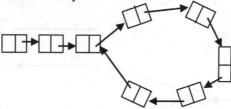

One simple and brute force way of solving this is, start with the first node and see whether there is any node whose next pointer is current node's address. If there is a node with same address then that indicates that some other node is pointing to the current node and we can say loops exists. Continue this process for all the nodes of the linked list.

Does this method works? As per the algorithm we are checking for the next pointer addresses, but how do we find the end of the linked list (otherwise we will end up in infinite loop)?

Note: If we start with a node in loop, this method may work depending on the size of the loop.

Problem-7   Can we use hashing technique for solving Problem-6?

Solution: Yes. Using Hash Tables we can solve this problem.
Algorithm
 - Traverse the linked list nodes one by one.
 - Check if the address of the node is available in the hash table or not.
 - If it is already available in the hash table then that indicates that we are visiting the node that was already visited. This is possible only if the given linked list has a loop in it.
 - If the address of the node is not available in the hash table then insert that nodes address into the hash table.
 - Continue this process until we reach end of the linked list *or* we find loop.

Time Complexity: O(n) for scanning the linked list. Note that we are doing only scan of the input. Space Complexity: O(n) for hash table.

Problem-8   Can we solve the Problem-6 using sorting technique?

Solution: No. Consider the following algorithm which is based on sorting. And then, we see why this algorithm fails.

Algorithm
 - Traverse the linked list nodes one by one and take all the next pointer values into some array.
 - Sort the array that has next node pointers.
 - If there is a loop in the linked list, definitely two nodes next pointers will pointing to the same node.
 - After sorting if there is a loop in the list, the nodes whose next pointers are same will come adjacent in the sorted list.
 - If any such pair exists in the sorted list then we say the linked list has loop in it.

Time Complexity: O($nlogn$) for sorting the next pointers array. Space Complexity: O(n) for the next pointers array.

Problem with above algorithm? The above algorithm works only if we can find the length of the list. But if the list is having loop then we may end up in infinite loop. Due to this reason the algorithm fails.

Problem-9   Can we solve the Problem-6 in O(*n*)?

Solution: Yes. Efficient Approach (Memory less Approach): This problem was solved by *Floyd*. The solution is named as Floyd cycle finding algorithm. It uses 2 pointers moving at different speeds to walk the linked list. Once they enter the loop they are expected to meet, which denotes that there is a loop. This works because the only way a faster moving pointer would point to the same location as a slower moving pointer is, if somehow the entire list or a part of it is circular.

Think of a tortoise and a hare running on a track. The faster running hare will catch up with the tortoise if they are running in a loop. As an example, consider the following example and trace out the Floyd algorithm. From the diagrams below we can see that after the final step they are meeting at some point in the loop which may not be the starting of the loop.

Note: *slowPtr* (*tortoise*) moves one pointer at a time and *fastPtr* (*hare*) moves two pointers at a time

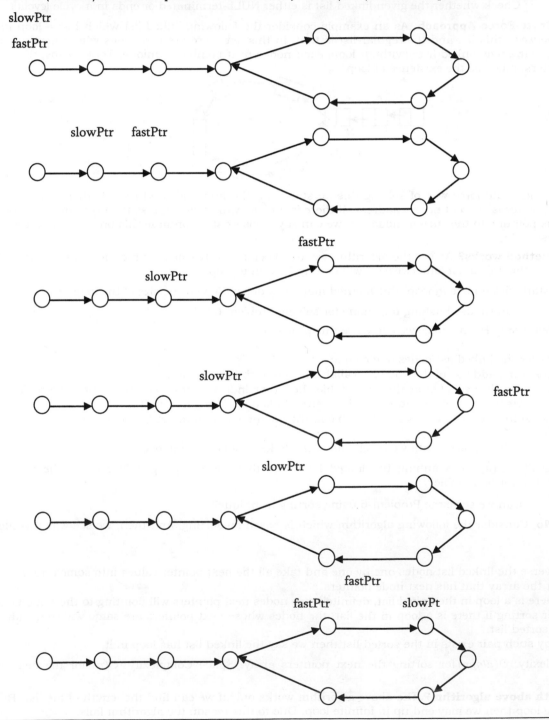

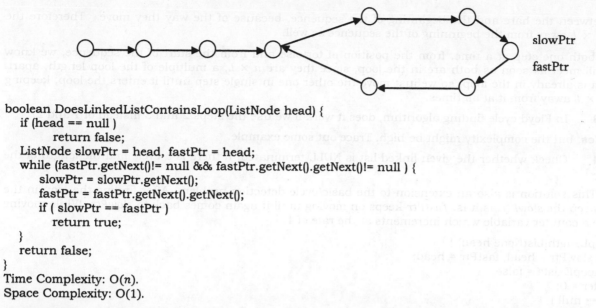

```
boolean DoesLinkedListContainsLoop(ListNode head) {
    if (head == null )
        return false;
    ListNode slowPtr = head, fastPtr = head;
    while (fastPtr.getNext()!= null && fastPtr.getNext().getNext()!= null ) {
        slowPtr = slowPtr.getNext();
        fastPtr = fastPtr.getNext().getNext();
        if ( slowPtr == fastPtr )
            return true;
    }
    return false;
}
```

Time Complexity: O(*n*).
Space Complexity: O(1).

Problem-10   You are given a pointer to the first element of a linked list *L*. There are two possibilities for *L*, it either ends (snake) or its last element points back to one of the earlier elements in the list (snail). Task is to devise an algorithm that tests whether a given list *L* is a snake or a snail.

Solution: It is same as Problem-6.

Problem-11   Check whether the given linked list is either NULL-terminated or not. If there is a cycle find the start node of the loop.

Solution: The solution is an extension to the previous solution (Problem-9). After finding the loop in the linked list, we initialize the *slowPtr* to head of the linked list. From that point onwards both *slowPtr* and *fastPtr* moves only one node at a time. The point at which they meet is the start of the loop. Generally we use this method for removing the loops.

```
int FindBeginofLoop (ListNode head) {
    ListNode slowPtr = head, fastPtr = head;
    boolean loopExists = false;
    if (head == null )
        return false;
    while(fastPtr.getNext()!= null && fastPtr.getNext().getNext() != null) {
        slowPtr = slowPtr.next;
        fastPtr = fastPtr.getNext().getNext();
        if ( slowPtr == fastPtr ) {
            loopExists = true;
            break;
        }
    }
    if(loopExists) {
        slowPtr = head;
        while(slowPtr != fastPtr) {
            fastPtr = fastPtr.getNext();
            slowPtr = slowPtr.getNext();
        }
        return slowPtr;
    }
    return null;
}
```

Time Complexity: O(*n*). Space Complexity: O(1).

Problem-12   From the previous problems we understand that the meeting of tortoise and hare meeting concludes the existence of loop, but how does moving tortoise to beginning of linked list while keeping the hare at meeting place, followed by moving both one step at a time make them meet at starting point of cycle?

Solution: This problem is the heart of number theory. In Floyd cycle finding algorithm, notice that the tortoise and the hare will meet when they are *n* × *L*, where *L* is the loop length. Furthermore, the tortoise is at the midpoint between the hare and the beginning of the sequence, because of the way they move. Therefore the tortoise is $n \times L$ away from the beginning of the sequence as well.

If we move both one step at a time, from the position of tortoise and from the start of the sequence, we know that they will meet as soon as both are in the loop, since they are $n \times L$, a multiple of the loop length, apart. One of them is already in the loop, so we just move the other one in single step until it enters the loop, keeping the other $n \times L$ away from it at all times.

Problem-13   In Floyd cycle finding algorithm, does it work if we use the steps 2 and 3 instead of 1 and 2?

Solution: Yes, but the complexity might be high. Trace out some example.

Problem-14   Check whether the given linked list is NULL-terminated. If there is a cycle find the length of the loop.

Solution: This solution is also an extension to the basic cycle detection problem. After finding the loop in the linked list, keep the *slowPtr* as it is. *fastPtr* keeps on moving until it again comes back to *slowPtr*. While moving *fastPtr*, use a counter variable which increments at the rate of 1.

```
int FindLoopLength(ListNode head) {
    ListNode slowPtr = head, fastPtr = head;
    boolean loopExists = false;
    int counter = 0;
    if (head == null )
        return 0;
    while (fastPtr.getNext()!= null && fastPtr.getNext().getNext() != null ) {
        slowPtr = slowPtr.next;
        fastPtr = fastPtr.getNext().getNext();
        if ( slowPtr == fastPtr ) {
            loopExists = true;
            break;
        }
    }
    if(loopExists) {
        fastPtr = fastPtr.getNext();
        while(slowPtr  != fastPtr) {
            fastPtr = fastPtr.getNext();
            counter++;
        }
        return counter;
    }
    return 0;                          //If no loops exists
}
```

Time Complexity: O(n). Space Complexity: O(1).

Problem-15   Insert a node in a sorted linked list

Solution: Traverse the list and find a position for the element and insert it.
```
ListNode InsertInSortedList(ListNode head, ListNode newNode) {
        ListNode current = head;
        if(head == null) return newNode;
        // traverse the list until you find item bigger the new node value
        while (current != null && current.getData() <  newNode.getData()){
                temp = current;
                current = current.getNext();
        }
        // insert the new node before the big item
        newNode.setNext(current);
        temp.setNext(newNode);
        return head;
}
```
Time Complexity: O(n). Space Complexity: O(1).

Problem-16   Reverse a singly linked list

Solution:
```
// iterative version
ListNode ReverseList(ListNode head ){
        ListNode temp = null, nextNode = null;
        while ( head != null ) {
```

```
                    nextNode = head.getNext();
                    head.setNext(temp);
                    temp = head;
                    head = nextNode;
          }
          return temp;
}
```

Time Complexity: O(n). Space Complexity: O(1).

Problem-17 Suppose there are two singly linked lists both of which intersect at some point and become a single linked list. The head or start pointers of both the lists are known, but the intersecting node is not known. Also, the number of nodes in each of the list before they intersect are unknown and both list may have it different. *List*1 may have n nodes before it reaches intersection point and *List*2 might have m nodes before it reaches intersection point where m and n may be $m = n, m < n$ or $m > n$. Give an algorithm for finding the merging point.

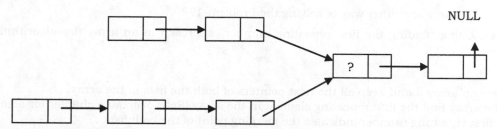

Solution: Brute-Force Approach: One easy solution is to compare every node pointer in the first list with every other node pointer in the second list by which the matching node pointers will lead us to the intersecting node. But, the time complexity in this case will O(mn) which will be high.

Time Complexity: O(mn). Space Complexity: O(1).

Problem-18 Can we solve Problem-17 using sorting technique?

Solution: No. Consider the following algorithm which is based on sorting and see why this algorithm fails.

Algorithm
- Take first list node pointers and keep in some array and sort them.
- Take second list node pointers and keep in some array and sort them.
- After sorting, use two indexes: one for first sorted array and other for second sorted array.
- Start comparing values at the indexes and increment the index whichever has lower value (increment only if the values are not equal).
- At any point, if we were able to find two indexes whose values are same then that indicates that those two nodes are pointing to the same node and we return that node.

Time Complexity: Time for sorting lists + Time for scanning (for comparing) $=O(mlogm) + O(nlogn) + O(m + n)$. We need to consider the one that gives the maximum value. Space Complexity: O(1).

Problem with the above algorithm? Yes. In the algorithm, we are storing all the node pointers of both the lists and sorting. But we are forgetting the fact that, there can be many repeated elements. This is because after the merging point all node pointers are same for both the lists. The algorithm works fine only in one case and it is when both lists have ending node at their merge point.

Problem-19 Can we solve Problem-17 using hash tables?

Solution: Yes.

Algorithm:
- Select a list which has less number of nodes (If we do not know the lengths beforehand then select one list randomly).
- Now, traverse the other list and for each node pointer of this list check whether the same node pointer exists in the hash table.
- If there is a merge point for the given lists then we will definitely encounter the node pointer in the hash table.

Time Complexity: Time for creating the hash table + Time for scanning the second list = O(m) + O(n) (or O(n) + O(m), depends on which list we select for creating the hash table). But in both cases the time complexity is same. Space Complexity: O(n) or O(m).

Problem-20 Can we use stacks for solving the Problem-17?

Solution: Yes.

Algorithm:
- Create two stacks: one for the first list and one for the second list.
- Traverse the first list and push all the node address on to the first stack.
- Traverse the second list and push all the node address on to the second stack.
- Now both stacks contain the node address of the corresponding lists.
- Now, compare the top node address of both stacks.
- If they are same, then pop the top elements from both the stacks and keep in some temporary variable (since both node addresses are node, it is enough if we use one temporary variable).
- Continue this process until top node addresses of the stacks are not same.
- This point is the one where the lists merge into single list.
- Return the value of the temporary variable.

Time Complexity: $O(m + n)$, for scanning both the lists. Space Complexity: $O(m + n)$, for creating two stacks for both the lists.

Problem-21   Is there any other way of solving the Problem-17?

Solution: **Yes**. Using "finding the first repeating number" approach in an array (for algorithm refer *Searching* chapter).

Algorithm:
- Create an array A and keep all the next pointers of both the lists in the array.
- In the array find the first repeating element in the array [Refer *Searching* chapter for algorithm].
- The first repeating number indicates the merging point of the both lists.

Time Complexity: $O(m + n)$. Space Complexity: $O(m + n)$.

Problem-22   Can we still think of finding an alternative solution for the Problem-17?

Solution: Yes. By combining sorting and search techniques we can reduce the complexity.

Algorithm:
- Create an array A and keep all the next pointers of the first list in the array.
- Sort these array elements.
- Then, for each of the second list element, search in the sorted array (let us assume that we are using binary search which gives $O(logn)$).
- Since we are scanning the second list one by one, the first repeating element that appears in the array is nothing but the merging point.

Time Complexity: Time for sorting + Time for searching = $O(Max(mlogm, nlogn))$. Space Complexity: $O(Max(m, n))$.

Problem-23   Can we improve the complexity for the Problem-17?

Solution: Yes.

Efficient Approach:
- Find lengths (L1 and L2) of both list -- $O(n) + O(m) = O(max(m, n))$.
- Take the difference d of the lengths -- $O(1)$.
- Make d steps in longer list -- $O(d)$.
- Step in both lists in parallel until links to next node match -- $O(min(m, n))$.
- Total time complexity = $O(max(m, n))$.
- Space Complexity = $O(1)$.

```
ListNode FindIntersectingNode(ListNode list1, ListNode list2) {
    int L1=0, L2=0, diff=0;
    ListNode head1 = list1, head2 = list2;
    while(head1 != null) {
        L1++;
        head1 = head1.getNext();
    }
    while(head2 != null) {
        L2++;
        head2 = head2.getNext();
    }
    if(L1 < L2) {
        head1 = list2;
        head2 = list1;
```

```
                    diff = L2 - L1;
        } else{
                    head1 = list1;
                    head2 = list2;
                    diff = L1 – L2;
        }
        for(int i = 0; i < diff; i++)
                    head1 = head1.getNext();
        while(head1 != null && head2 != null) {
                    if(head1 == head2)
                              return head1.getData();
                    head1= head1.getNext();
                    head2= head2.getNext();
        }
        return null;
    }
```

Problem-24   How will you find the middle of the linked list?

Solution: Brute-Force Approach: For each of the node count how many nodes are there in the list and see whether it is the middle.

Time Complexity: $O(n^2)$. Space Complexity: O(1).

Problem-25   Can we improve the complexity of Problem-24?

Solution: Yes.
Algorithm:
   • Traverse the list and find the length of the list.
   • After finding the length, again scan the list and locate $n/2$ node from the beginning.

Time Complexity: Time for finding the length of the list + Time for locating middle node = $O(n) + O(n) \approx O(n)$. Space Complexity: O(1).

Problem-26   Can we use hash table for solving Problem-24?

Solution: Yes. The reasoning is same as that of Problem-3.

Time Complexity: Time for creating the hash table. Therefore, $T(n) = O(n)$. Space Complexity: O(n). Since, we need to create a hash table of size n.

Problem-27   Can we solve Problem-24 just in one scan?

Solution: Efficient Approach: Use two pointers. Move one pointer at twice the speed of the second. When the first pointer reaches end of the list, the second pointer will be pointing to the middle node.

Note: If the list has even number of nodes, the middle node will be of $\lfloor n/2 \rfloor$.

```
ListNode FindMiddle(ListNode head) {
        ListNode ptr1x, ptr2x;
        ptr1x = ptr2x = head;
        int i=0;
        // keep looping until we reach the tail (next will be NULL for the last node)
        while(ptr1x.getNext() != null) {
                    if(i == 0) {
                              ptr1x = ptr1x.getNext(); //increment only the 1st pointer
                              i=1;
                    }
                    else if( i == 1) {
                              ptr1x = ptr1x.getNext(); //increment both pointers
                              ptr2x = ptr2x.getNext();
                              i = 0;
                    }
        }
        return ptr2x;        //now return the ptr2 which points to the middle node
}
```

Time Complexity: $O(n)$. Space Complexity: O(1).

Problem-28   How will you display a linked list from the end?

Solution: Traverse recursively till end of the linked list. While coming back, start printing the elements.

```java
//This Function will print the linked list from end
void PrintListFromEnd(ListNode head) {
        if(head == null)
            return;
        PrintListFromEnd(head.getNext());
        System.out.println(head.getData());
}
```
Time Complexity: O(*n*). Space Complexity: O(*n*)→ for Stack.

Problem-29   Check whether the given Linked List length is even or odd?

Solution: Use $2x$ pointer. Take a pointer that moves at $2x$ [two nodes at a time]. At the end, if the length is even then pointer will be NULL otherwise it will point to last node.

```java
int IsLinkedListLengthEven(ListNode listHead) {
    while(listHead != null && listHead.getNext() != null)
        listHead = listHead.getNext().getNext();
    if(listHead == null) return 0;
    return 1;
}
```
Time Complexity: O($\lfloor n/2 \rfloor$) ≈O(*n*). Space Complexity: O(1).

Problem-30   If the head of a linked list is pointing to *kth* element, then how will you get the elements before *kth* element?

Solution: Use Memory Efficient Linked Lists [XOR Linked Lists].

Problem-31   Given two sorted Linked Lists, we need to merge them into the third list in sorted order.

Solution:
```java
ListNode MergeList(ListNode a, ListNode b) {
    ListNode result = null;
    if(a==null) return b;
    if(b==null) return a;
    if(a.getData() <= b.getData()) {
        result =a;
        result.setNext(MergeList(a.getNext(), b));
    }
    else {
        result =b;
        result.setNext(MergeList(b.getNext(),a));
    } .
    return result;
}
```
Time Complexity – O(*n*).

Problem-32   Reverse the linked list in pairs. If you have a linked list that holds 1→2→3→4→X, then after the function has been called the linked list would hold 2→1→4→3→X.

Solution:
```java
//Recursive Version
ListNode ReversePairRecursive(ListNode head) {
        ListNode temp;
        if(head ==NULL || head.next ==NULL)
                return;   //base case for empty or 1 element list
        else {
                //Reverse first pair
                temp = head.next;
                head.next = temp.next;
                temp.next = head;
                head = temp;

                //Call the method recursively for the rest of the list
                head.next.next = ReversePairRecursive(head.next.next);
                return head;
        }
}
```

```
/*Iterative version*/
ListNode ReversePairIterative(ListNode head) {
    ListNode temp1 = null;
    ListNode temp2 = null;
    while (head != null && head.next != null) {
        if (temp1 != null) {
            temp1.next.next = head.next;
        }
        temp1 = head.next;
        head.next = head.next.next;
        temp1.next = head;
        if (temp2 == null)
            temp2 = temp1;
        head = head.next;
    }
    return temp2;
}
```

Time Complexity – O(n). Space Complexity - O(1).

Problem-33   Given a binary tree convert it to doubly linked list.

Solution: Refer *Trees* chapter.

Problem-34   How do we sort the Linked Lists?

Solution: Refer *Sorting* chapter.

Problem-35   If we want to concatenate two linked lists which of the following gives O(1) complexity?
    1)   Singly linked lists   2) Doubly linked lists   3) Circular doubly linked lists

Solution: Circular Doubly Linked Lists. This is because for singly and doubly linked lists, we need to traverse the first list till the end and append the second list. But in case of circular doubly linked lists we don't have to traverse the lists.

Problem-36   Split a Circular Linked List into two equal parts. If the number of nodes in the list are odd then make first list one node extra than second list.

Solution:
Algorithm
- Store the mid and last pointers of the circular linked list using Floyd cycle finding algorithm.
- Make the second half circular.
- Make the first half circular.
- Set head pointers of the two linked lists.

As an example, consider the following circular list.

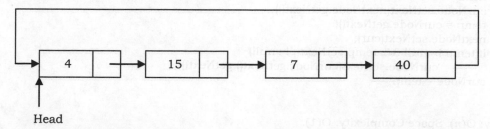

Head

After the split, the above list will look like:

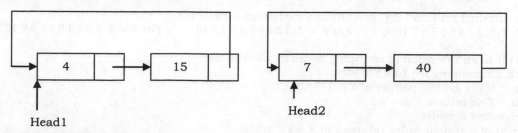

Head1   Head2

```
void SplitList(ListNode head, ListNode head1, ListNode head2) {
    ListNode slowPtr = head, fastPtr = head;
```

```
if(head == nlu) return;
/* If there are odd nodes in the circular list then fastPtr.getNext() becomes
    head and for even nodes fastPtr.getNext().getNext() becomes head */
while(fastPtr.getNext() != head && fastPtr.getNext().getNext() != head)        {
        fastPtr = fastPtr.getNext().getNext();
        slowPtr = slowPtr.getNext();
}
/* If there are even elements in list then move fastPtr */
if(fastPtr.getNext().getNext() == head)
        fastPtr = fastPtr.getNext();
/* Set the head pointer of first half */
head1 = head;
/* Set the head pointer of second half */
if(head.getNext() != head)
        head2 = slowPtr.getNext();
/* Make second half circular */
fastPtr.setNext(slowPtr.getNext());
/* Make first half circular */
slowPtr.setNext(head);
}
```

Time Complexity: O(n). Space Complexity: O(1).

Problem-37   How will you check if the linked list is palindrome or not?

Solution:
Algorithm
1. Get the middle of the linked list.
2. Reverse the second half of the linked list.
3. Compare the first half and second half.
4. Construct the original linked list by reversing the second half again and attaching it back to the first half.

Time Complexity: O(n). Space Complexity: O(1).

Problem-38   Exchange the adjacent elements in a link list.
Solution:
```
void ExchangeAdjacentNodes(ListNode head) {
        ListNode curNode, temp, nextNode;
        curNode = head;
        if(curNode ==null || curNode.getNext() == null) return;
        head = curNode.getNext();
        while(curNode != null && curNode.getNext() != null) {
                nextNode = curNode.getNext();
                curNode.setNext(nextNode.getNext());
                temp = curNode.getNext();
                nextNode.setNext(cur);
                if(temp != null && temp.getNext() != null)
                        curNode.setNext(curNode.getNext().getNext());
                curNode = temp;
        }
}
```
Time Complexity: O(n). Space Complexity: O(1).

Problem-39   For a given K value ($K > 0$) reverse blocks of K nodes in a list.

   Example: Input: 1 2 3 4 5 6 7 8 9 10, Output for different K values:
       For $K = 2$: 2 1 4 3 6 5 8 7 10 9,   For $K = 3$: 3 2 1 6 5 4 9 8 7 10,   For $K = 4$: 4 3 2 1 8 7 6 5 9 10
Solution:
Algorithm: This is an extension of swapping nodes in a linked list.
   1) Check if remaining list has K nodes.
        a.   If yes get the pointer of $K + 1^{th}$ node.
        b.   Else return.
   2) Reverse first K nodes.
   3) Set next of last node (after reversal) to $K + 1^{th}$ node.
   4) Move to $K + 1^{th}$ node.
   5) Go to step 1.

6) $K - 1^{th}$ node of first K nodes becomes the new head if available. Otherwise, we can return the head.

```
ListNode GetKPlusOneThNode(int K, ListNode head) {
    ListNode Kth;
    int i;
    if(head != null) return head;
    for (int i=0, Kth=head; Kth != null && (i < K); i++, Kth=Kth.getNext());
    if(i==K && Kth!=null)
        return Kth;
    return head.getNext();
}
int HasKnodes(ListNode head, int K) {
    int i;
    for(i=0; head != null && (i < K); i++, head=head.getNext());
    if(i == K)
        return 1;
    return 0;
}
ListNode ReverseBlockOfK-nodesInLinkedList(ListNode head, int K) {
    ListNode temp, next, cur = head, newHead;
    if(K==0 || K==1)
        return head;
    if(HasKnodes(cur, K-1))
        newHead = GetKPlusOneThNode(K-1, cur);
    else newHead = head;
    while(cur != null && HasKnodes(cur, K)) {
        //Take care of below step
        temp = GetKPlusOneThNode(K, cur);
        int i=0;
        while(i<K) {
            next = cur.getNext();
            cur.setNext(temp);
            temp = cur;
            cur = next;
            i++;
        }
    }
    return newHead;
}
```

Problem-40   Is it possible to get O(1) access time for Linked Lists?

Solution: Yes. Create a linked list at the same time keep it in a hash table. For n elements we have to keep all the elements into hash table which gives preprocessing time of O(n). To read any element we require only constant time O(1) and to read n elements we require $n * 1$ unit of time = n units. Hence by using amortized analysis we can say that element access can be performed within O(1) time.

Time Complexity – O(1) [Amortized]. Space Complexity - O(n) for Hash.

Problem-41   JosephusCircle: N people have decided to elect a leader by arranging themselves in a circle and eliminating every M^{th} person around the circle, closing ranks as each person drops out. Find which person will be the last one remaining (with rank 1).

Solution: Assume the input is a circular linked list with N nodes and each node has a number (range 1 to N) associated with it. The head node has number 1 as data.

```
ListNode  GetJosephusPosition(int N, int M) {
    ListNode p, q;
    // Create circular linked list containing all the players:
    p.setData(1);
    q = p;
    for (int i = 2; i <= N; ++i) {
        p = p.getNext();
        p.setData(i);
    }
    p.setNext(q);  // Close the circular linked list by having the last node point to the first.
    // Eliminate every M-th player as long as more than one player remains:
```

```
        for (int count = N; count > 1; --count) {
                for (int i = 0; i < M - 1; ++i)
                        p = p.getNext();
                p.setNext(p.getNext().getNext());  // Remove the eiminated player from the list.
        }
        System.out.println("Last player left standing (Josephus Position) is " + p.getData());
}
```

Problem-42   Given a linked list consists of data, next pointer and also a random pointer which points to a random node of the list. Give an algorithm for cloning the list.

Solution: We can use the hash table to associate newly created nodes with the instances of node in the given list.

Algorithm:
* Scan the original list and for each node X create a new node Y with data of X, then store the pair (X, Y) in hash table using X as a key. Note that during this scan we set $Y.next$ and $Y.random$ to *NULL* and we will fix them in the next scan
* Now for each node X in the original list we have a copy Y stored in our hash table. We scan again the original list and set the pointers buildings the new list

```
ListNode Clone(ListNode head){
        ListNode X = head, Y;
        Map<ListNode, ListNode> HT = new HashMap<ListNode, ListNode>();
        while (X != null) {
                Y = new ListNode();
                Y.setData(X.getData());
                Y.setNext(null);
                Y.setRandom(null);
                HT.put(X, Y);
                X = X.getNext();
        }
        X = head;
        while (X != null) {
                // Get the node Y corresponding to Y from the hash table
                Y = HT.get(X);
                Y.setNext(HT.get(X.getNext()));
                Y.setRandom(HT.get(X.getRandom()));
                X = X.getNext();
        }
        // Return the head of the new list, that is the node Y
        return HT.get(head);
}
```

Time Complexity: O(n). Space Complexity: O(n).

Problem-43   In a linked list with n nodes, the time taken to insert an element after an element pointed by some pointer is

(A) O(1)   (B) O($logn$)   (C) O(n)   (D) O($n logn$)

Solution: A.

Problem-44   **Find modular node:** Given a singly linked list, write a function to find the last element from the beginning whose $n\%k == 0$, where n is the number of elements in the list and k is an integer constant. For example, if $n = 19$ and $k = 3$ then we should return 18th node.

Solution: For this problem the value of n is not known in advance.

```
ListNode modularNodes(ListNode head, int k){
        ListNode modularNode;
        int i=0;
        if(k<=0)
                return null;
        for (;head!= null; head = head.getNext()){
                if(i%k == 0){
                        modularNode = head;
                }
                i++;
        }
}
```

```
        return modularNode;
}
```

Time Complexity: O(n). Space Complexity: O(1).

Problem-45   Find modular node from end: Given a singly linked list, write a function to find the first element from the end whose $n\%k == 0$, where n is the number of elements in the list and k is an integer constant. For example, if $n = 19$ and $k = 3$ then we should return 16^{th}node.

Solution: For this problem the value of n is not known in advance and it is same as finding the k^{th}element from end of the linked list.

```java
ListNode modularNodes(ListNode *head, int k){
    ListNode modularNode=null;
    int i=0;
    if(k<=0)
        return null;
    for (i=0; i < k; i++){
        if(head!=null)
            head = head.getNext();
        else
            return null;
    }
    while(head!= null)
        modularNode = modularNode.getNext();
        head = head.getNext();
    }
    return modularNode;
}
```

Time Complexity: O(n). Space Complexity: O(1).

Problem-46   Find fractional node: Given a singly linked list, write a function to find the $\frac{n}{k}th$ element, where n is the number of elements in the list.

Solution: For this problem the value of n is not known in advance.

```java
ListNode fractionalNodes(ListNode head, int k){
    ListNode fractionalNode;
    int i=0;
    if(k<=0)
        return null;
    for (;head!= null; head = head.getNext()){
        if(i%k == 0){
            if(fractionalNode!=null)
                fractionalNode = head;
            else fractionalNode = fractionalNode.getNext();
        }
        i++;
    }
    return fractionalNode;
}
```

Time Complexity: O(n). Space Complexity: O(1).

Problem-47   Median in an infinite series of integers

Solution: Median is the middle number in a sorted list of numbers (if we have odd number of elements). If we have even number of elements, median is the average of two middle numbers in a sorted list of numbers.

We can solve this problem with linked lists (with both sorted and unsorted linked lists).

First, let us try with *unsorted* linked list. In an unsorted linked list, we can insert the element either at the head or at the tail. The disadvantage with this approach is that, finding the median takes O(n). Also, the insertion operation takes O(1).

Now, let us with *sorted* linked list. We can find the median in O(1) time if we keep track of the middle elements. Insertion to a particular location is also O(1) in any linked list. But, finding the right location to insert is not O($logn$) as in sorted array, it is instead O(n) because we can't perform binary search in a linked list even if it is sorted.

So, using a sorted linked list doesn't worth the effort, insertion is O(n) and finding median is O(1), same as the sorted array. In sorted array insertion is linear due to shifting, here it's linear because we can't do binary search in a linked list.

Note: For efficient algorithm refer *Priority Queues and Heaps* chapter.

Chapter-4
STACKS

4.1 What is a Stack?

A stack is a simple data structure used for storing data (similar to Linked Lists). In stack, the order in which the data arrives is important. The pile of plates of a cafeteria is a good example of stack. The plates are added to the stack as they are cleaned. They are placed on the top. When a plate is required it is taken from the top of the stack. The first plate placed on the stack is the last one to be used.

Definition: A *stack* is an ordered list in which insertion and deletion are done at one end, called as *top*. The last element inserted is the first one to be deleted. Hence, it is called Last in First out (LIFO) or First in Last out (FILO) list.

Special names are given to the two changes that can be made to a stack. When an element is inserted in a stack, the concept is called as *push*, and when an element is removed from the stack, the concept is called as *pop*. Trying to pop out an empty stack is called *underflow* and trying to push an element in a full stack is called *overflow*. Generally, we treat them as exceptions. As an example, consider the snapshots of the stack.

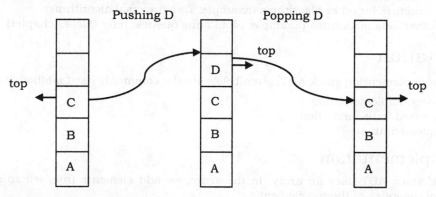

4.2 How Stacks are used?

Consider a working day in the office. Let us assume a developer is working on a long-term project. The manager then gives the developer a new task, which is more important. The developer places the long-term project aside and begins work on the new task. The phone rings, this is the highest priority, as it must be answered immediately. The developer pushes the present task into the pending tray and answers the phone. When the call is complete the task abandoned to answer the phone is retrieved from the pending tray and work progresses. To take another call, it may have to be handled in the same manner, but eventually the new task will be finished, and the developer can draw the long-term project from the pending tray and continue with that.

4.3 Stack ADT

The following operations make a stack an ADT. For simplicity, assume the data is of integer type.

Main stack operations

- void push(int data): Inserts *data* onto stack.
- int pop(): Removes and returns the last inserted element from the stack.

Auxiliary stack operations

- int top(): Returns the last inserted element without removing it.
- int size(): Returns the number of elements stored in stack.
- int isEmpty(): Indicates whether any elements are stored in stack or not.
- int isStackFull(): Indicates whether the stack is full or not.

4.4 Exceptions

Attempting the execution of an operation may sometimes cause an error condition, called an exception. Exceptions are said to be "thrown" by an operation that cannot be executed. In the Stack ADT, operations pop and top cannot be performed if the stack is empty. Attempting the execution of pop (top) on an empty stack throws an exception. Trying to push an element in a full stack throws an exception.

4.5 Applications

Following are some of the applications in which stacks plays an important role.

Direct applications

- Balancing of symbols
- Infix-to-postfix conversion
- Evaluation of postfix expression
- Implementing function calls (including recursion)
- Finding of spans (finding spans in stock markets, refer *Problems* section)
- Page-visited history in a Web browser [Back Buttons]
- Undo sequence in a text editor
- Matching Tags in HTML and XML

Indirect applications

- Auxiliary data structure for other algorithms (Example: Tree traversal algorithms)
- Component of other data structures (Example: Simulating queues, refer *Queues* chapter)

4.6 Implementation

There are many ways of implementing stack ADT, given below are the commonly used methods.

- Simple array based implementation
- Dynamic array based implementation
- Linked lists implementation

Simple Array Implementation

This implementation of stack ADT uses an array. In the array, we add elements from left to right and use a variable to keep track of the index of the top element.

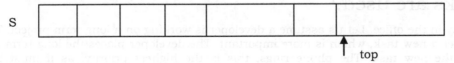

The array storing the stack elements may become full. A push operation will then throw a *full stack exception*. Similarly, if we try deleting an element from empty stack then it will throw *stack empty exception*.

```java
public class  ArrayStack{
        private int top;
        private int capacity;
        private int[] array;
        public ArrayStack(){
                capacity = 1;
                array= new int[capacity];
                top = -1;
        }
        public boolean isEmpty (){
                // if the condition is true then 1 is returned else 0 is returned
                return (top == -1);
        }
        public int isStackFull(){
                //if the condition is true then 1 is returned else 0 is returned
                return (top == capacity - 1);  //or return (top == array.length);
        }
```

```java
        public void push(int data){
                if(isStackFull(S)) System.out.println( "Stack Overflow");
                else /*Increasing the 'top' by 1 and storing the value at 'top' position*/
                        array[++top]= data;
        }
        public int pop(){
                if(isEmpty(S)){                          /* top == - 1 indicates empty stack*/
                        System.out.println("Stack is Empty");
                        return 0;
                }
                else      return ( array[top--]);
        }
        public void deleteStack(){
                top = -1;
        }
}
```

Performance & Limitations

Performance: Let n be the number of elements in the stack. The complexities of stack operations with this representation can be given as:

Space Complexity (for n push operations)	$O(n)$
Time Complexity of push()	$O(1)$
Time Complexity of pop()	$O(1)$
Time Complexity of size()	$O(1)$
Time Complexity of isEmpty()	$O(1)$
Time Complexity of isFullStack()	$O(1)$
Time Complexity of deleteStack()	$O(1)$

Limitations: The maximum size of the stack must be defined in prior and cannot be changed. Trying to push a new element into a full stack causes an implementation-specific exception.

Dynamic Array Implementation

First, let's consider how we implemented a simple array based stack. We took one index variable *top* which points to the index of the most recently inserted element in the stack. To insert (or push) an element, we increment *top* index and then place the new element at that index. Similarly, to delete (or pop) an element we take the element at *top* index and then decrement the *top* index. We represent empty queue with *top* value equal to −1. The issue still need to be resolved is that what we do when all the slots in fixed size array stack are occupied?

First try: What if we increment the size of the array by 1 every time the stack is full?
- Push(): increase size of S[] by 1
- Pop(): decrease size of S[] by 1

Problems with this approach?

This way of incrementing the array size is too expensive. Let us a see the reason for this. For example, at $n = 1$, to push an element create a new array of size 2 and copy all the old array elements to new array and at the end add the new element. At $n = 2$, to push an element create a new array of size 3 and copy all the old array elements to new array and at the end add the new element.

Similarly, at $n = n - 1$, if we want to push an element create a new array of size n and copy all the old array elements to new array and at the end add the new element. After n push operations the total time $T(n)$ (number of copy operations) is proportional to $1 + 2 + ... + n \approx O(n^2)$.

Alternative Approach: Repeated Doubling

Let us improve the complexity by using array *doubling* technique. If the array is full, create a new array of twice the size, and copy items. With this approach, pushing n items takes time proportional to n (not n^2).

For simplicity, let us assume that initially we started with $n = 1$ and moved till $n = 32$. That means, we do the doubling at $1, 2, 4, 8, 16$. The other way of analyzing the same is, at $n = 1$, if we want to add (push) an element then double the current size of array and copy all the elements of old array to new array.

At, $n = 1$, we do 1 copy operation, at $n = 2$, we do 2 copy operations, and n = 4, we do 4 copy operations and so on. By the time we reach $n = 32$, the total number of copy operations is $1 + 2 + 4 + 8 + 16 = 31$ which is approximately equal to $2n$ value (32). If we observe carefully, we are doing the doubling operation $logn$ times.

Now, let us generalize the discussion. For n push operations we double the array size $logn$ times. That means, we will have $logn$ terms in the expression below. The total time $T(n)$ of a series of n push operations is proportional to

$$1 + 2 + 4 + 8 \dots + \frac{n}{4} + \frac{n}{2} + n = n + \frac{n}{2} + \frac{n}{4} + \frac{n}{8} \dots + 4 + 2 + 1$$
$$= n\left(1 + \frac{1}{2} + \frac{1}{4} + \frac{1}{8} \dots + \frac{4}{n} + \frac{2}{n} + \frac{1}{n}\right)$$
$$= n(2) \approx 2n = O(n)$$

$T(n)$ is O(n) and the amortized time of a push operation is O(1).

```java
public class DynArrayStack{
        private int top;
        private int capacity;
        private int[] array;
        public DynArrayStack(){
                capacity = 1;
                array= new int[capacity];
                top = -1;
        }
        public boolean isEmpty(){
                // if the condition is true then 1 is returned else 0 is returned
                return (top == -1);
        }
        public int isStackFull(){
                //if the condition is true then 1 is returned else 0 is returned
                return (top == capacity - 1);  //or return (top == array.length);
        }
        public void push(int data){
                if(isStackFull(S))
                            doubleStack(S);
                 array[++top]= data;
        }
        private void doubleStack(){
                int newArray[] = new int[capacity*2];
                System.arraycopy(array, 0, newArray, 0, capacity);
                capacity = capacity*2;
                array = newArray;
        }
        public int pop() {
                if(isEmpty(S))   System.out.println( "Stack Overflow");
                else     return ( array[top--]);
        }
        public void deleteStack(){
                top = -1;
        }
}
```

Performance: Let n be the number of elements in the stack. The complexities for operations with this representation can be given as:

Space Complexity (for n push operations)	O(n)
Time Complexity of create Stack: DynArrayStack ()	O(1)
Time Complexity of push()	O(1) (Average)
Time Complexity of pop()	O(1)
Time Complexity of top()	O(1)
Time Complexity of isEmpty()	O(1)
Time Complexity of isStackFull ()	O(1)
Time Complexity of deleteStack()	O(1)

Note: Too many doublings may cause memory overflow exception.

Linked List Implementation

The other way of implementing stacks is by using Linked lists. Push operation is implemented by inserting element at the beginning of the list. Pop operation is implemented by deleting the node from the beginning (the header/top node).

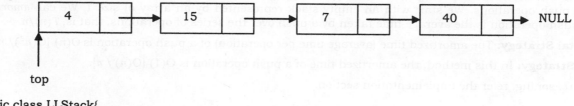

top

```java
public class LLStack{
        private LLNode headNode;
        public LLStack(){
                this.headNode = new LLNode(null);
        }
        public void Push(int data){
                if(headNode == null){
                        headNode = new LLNode(data);
                }else if(headNode.getData() == null){
                        headNode.setData(data);
                }else{
                        LLNode llNode = new LLNode(data);
                        llNode.setNext(headNode);
                        headNode = llNode;
                }
        }
        public int top(){
                if(headNode == null)
                        return null;
                else   return headNode.getData();
        }
        public int pop(){
                if(headNode == null){
                        throw new EmptyStackException("Stack empty");
                }else{
                        int data = headNode.getData();
                        headNode = headNode.getNext();
                        return data;
                }
        }
        public boolean isEmpty(){
                if(headNode == null)      return true;
                else     return false;
        }
        public void deleteStack(){
                headNode null;
        }
}
```

Performance

Let n be the number of elements in the stack. Let n be the number of elements in the stack. The complexities for operations with this representation can be given as:

Space Complexity (for n push operations)	$O(n)$
Time Complexity of create Stack: DynArrayStack()	$O(1)$
Time Complexity of push()	$O(1)$ (Average)
Time Complexity of pop()	$O(1)$
Time Complexity of top()	$O(1)$
Time Complexity of isEmpty()	$O(1)$
Time Complexity of deleteStack()	$O(n)$

4.7 Comparison of Implementations

Comparing Incremental Strategy and Doubling Strategy

We compare the incremental strategy and doubling strategy by analyzing the total time $T(n)$ needed to perform a series of n push operations. We start with an empty stack represented by an array of size 1. We call *amortized* time of a push operation is the average time taken by a push over the series of operations, that is, $T(n)/n$.

Incremental Strategy: The amortized time (average time per operation) of a push operation is O(n) [O(n^2)/ n].

Doubling Strategy: In this method, the amortized time of a push operation is O(1) [O(n) / n].

Note: For reasoning, refer the Implementation section.

Comparing Array Implementation & Linked List Implementation

Array Implementation

- Operations take constant time.
- Expensive doubling operation every once in a while.
- Any sequence of n operations (starting from empty stack) -- "amortized" bound takes time proportional to n.

Linked list Implementation

- Grows and shrinks gracefully.
- Every operation takes constant time O(1).
- Every operation uses extra space and time to deal with references.

4.8 Problems on Stacks

Problem-1   Discuss how stacks can be used for checking balancing of symbols?

Solution: Stacks can be used to check whether the given expression has balanced symbols. This algorithm is very useful in compilers. Each time parser reads one character at a time. If the character is an opening delimiter such as (, {, or [- then it is written to the stack. When a closing delimiter is encountered like), }, or]- is encountered the stack is popped. The opening and closing delimiters are then compared. If they match, the parsing of the string continues. If they do not match, the parser indicates that there is an error on the line. A linear-time O(n) algorithm based on stack can be given as:

Algorithm
a)   Create a stack.
b)   while (end of input is not reached)
     1)   If the character read is not a symbol to be balanced, ignore it.
     2)   If the character is an opening symbol like (, [, {, push it onto the stack
     3)   If it is a closing symbol like),],}, then if the stack is empty report an error. Otherwise pop the stack.
     4)   If the symbol popped is not the corresponding opening symbol, report an error.
c)   At end of input, if the stack is not empty report an error

Example	Valid?	Description
(A+B)+(C-D)	Yes	The expression is having balanced symbol
((A+B)+(C-D)	No	One closing brace is missing
((A+B)+[C-D])	Yes	Opening and immediate closing braces correspond
((A+B)+[C-D]}	No	The last closing brace does not correspond with the first opening parenthesis

For tracing the algorithm let us assume that the input is: () (() [()])

Input Symbol, A[i]	Operation	Stack	Output
(	Push (	(	
)	Pop (		

	Test if (and A[i] match? YES		
(	Push (	(	
(	Push (	((	
)	Pop (Test if(and A[i] match? YES	(	
[	Push [	([	
(	Push (	([(	
)	Pop (Test if(and A[i] match? YES	([	
]	Pop [Test if [and A[i] match? YES	(	
)	Pop (Test if(and A[i] match? YES		
	Test if stack is Empty? YES		TRUE

Time Complexity: O(n). Since, we are scanning the input only once. Space Complexity: O(n) [for stack].

Problem-2   Discuss infix to postfix conversion algorithm using stack.

Solution: Before discussing the algorithm, first let us see the definitions of infix, prefix and postfix expressions.

Infix: An infix expression is a single letter, or an operator, proceeded by one infix string and followed by another Infix string.

      A
      A+B
      (A+B)+ (C-D)

Prefix: A prefix expression is a single letter, or an operator, followed by two prefix strings. Every prefix string longer than a single variable contains an operator, first operand and second operand.

      A
      +AB
      ++AB-CD

Postfix: A postfix expression (also called Reverse Polish Notation) is a single letter or an operator, preceded by two postfix strings. Every postfix string longer than a single variable contains first and second operands followed by an operator.

      A
      AB+
      AB+CD-+

Prefix and postfix notions are methods of writing mathematical expressions without parenthesis. Time to evaluate a postfix and prefix expression is O(n), were n is the number of elements in the array.

Infix	Prefix	Postfix
A+B	+AB	AB+
A+B-C	-+ABC	AB+C-
(A+B)*C-D	-*+ABCD	AB+C*D-

Now, let us focus on the algorithm. In infix expressions, the operator precedence is implicit unless we use parentheses. Therefore, for the infix to postfix conversion algorithm we have to define the operator precedence (or priority) inside the algorithm. The table shows the precedence and their associatively (order of evaluation) among operators.

Token	Operator	Precedence	Associatively
( ) [ ] → .	function call array element struct or union member	17	left-to-right
-- ++	increment, decrement	16	left-to-right

-- ++ ! - - + & * sizeof	decrement, increment logical not one's complement unary minus or plus address or indirection size (in bytes)	15	right-to-left
(type)	type cast	14	right-to-left
* / %	multiplicative	13	Left-to-right
+ -	binary add or subtract	12	left-to-right
<< >>	shift	11	left-to-right
> >= < <=	relational	10	left-to-right
== !=	equality	9	left-to-right
&	bitwise and	8	left-to-right
^	bitwise exclusive or	7	left-to-right
|	bitwise or	6	left-to-right
&&	logical and	5	left-to-right
||	logical or	4	left-to-right
?:	conditional	3	right-to-left
= += -= /= *= %= <<= >>= &= ^=	assignment	2	right-to-left
,	Comma	1	left-to-right

Important Properties

- Let us consider the infix expression 2 + 3 * 4 and its postfix equivalent 2 3 4 * +. Notice that between infix and postfix the order of the numbers (or operands) is unchanged. It is 2 3 4 in both cases. But the order of the operators * and + is affected in the two expressions.
- Only one stack is enough to convert an infix expression to postfix expression. The stack that we use in the algorithm will be used to change the order of operators from infix to postfix. The stack we use will only contain operators and the open parentheses symbol '('. Postfix expressions do not contain parentheses. We shall not output the parentheses in the postfix output.

Algorithm

a) Create a stack
b) for each character t in the input stream{
   if(t is an operand) output t
   else if(t is a right parenthesis)
        Pop and output tokens until a left parenthesis is popped (but not output)
   else // t is an operator or left parenthesis{
        pop and output tokens until one of lower priority than t is encountered or a left parenthesis
        is encountered or the stack is empty
        Push t
   }
 }
c) pop and output tokens until the stack is empty

For better understanding let us trace out some example: A * B- (C + D) + E

Input Character	Operation on Stack	Stack	Postfix Expression
A		Empty	A
*	Push	*	A
B		*	AB
-	Check and Push	-	AB*
(	Push	-(	AB*
C		-(	AB*C
+	Check and Push	-(+	AB*C
D			AB*CD
)	Pop and append to postfix till '('	-	AB*CD+
+	Check and Push	+	AB*CD+-
E		+	AB*CD+-E

| End of input | Pop till empty | AB*CD+-E+ |

Problem-3   For a given array with *n* symbols how many stack permutations are possible?

Solution: The number of stack permutations with *n* symbols is represented by *Catalan number* and we will discuss this in *Dynamic Programming* chapter.

Problem-4   Discuss postfix evaluation using stacks?

Solution:

Algorithm:

1   Scan the Postfix string from left to right.
2   Initialize an empty stack.
3   Repeat steps 4 and 5 till all the characters are scanned.
4   If the scanned character is an operand, push it onto the stack.
5   If the scanned character is an operator, and if the operator is unary operator then pop an element from the stack. If the operator is binary operator then pop two elements from the stack. After popping the elements, apply the operator to those popped elements. Let the result of this operation be retVal onto the stack.
6   After all characters are scanned, we will have only one element in the stack.
7   Return top of the stack as result.

Example: Let us see how the above algorithm works using an example. Assume that the postfix string is 123*+5-. Initially the stack is empty. Now, the first three characters scanned are 1, 2 and 3, which are operands. They will be pushed into the stack in that order.

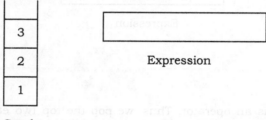

Next character scanned is "*", which is an operator. Thus, we pop the top two elements from the stack and perform the "*" operation with the two operands. The second operand will be the first element that is popped.

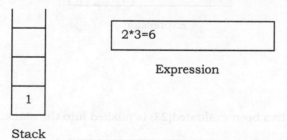

The value of the expression (2*3) that has been evaluated (6) is pushed into the stack.

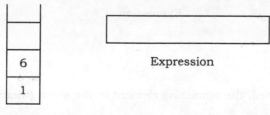

Next character scanned is "+", which is an operator. Thus, we pop the top two elements from the stack and perform the "+" operation with the two operands.

The second operand will be the first element that is popped.

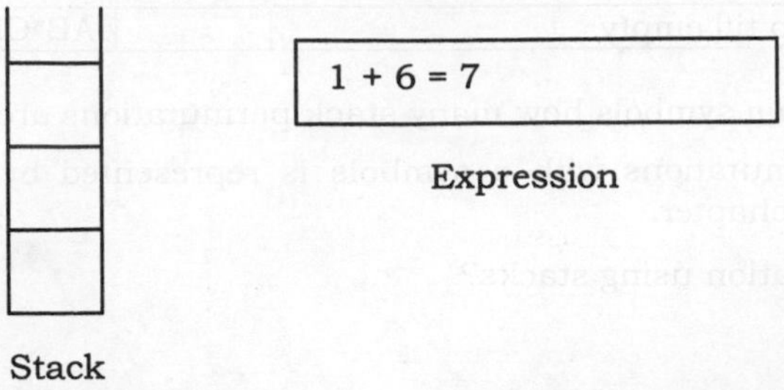

	1 + 6 = 7
	Expression

Stack

The value of the expression (1+6) that has been evaluated (7) is pushed into the stack.

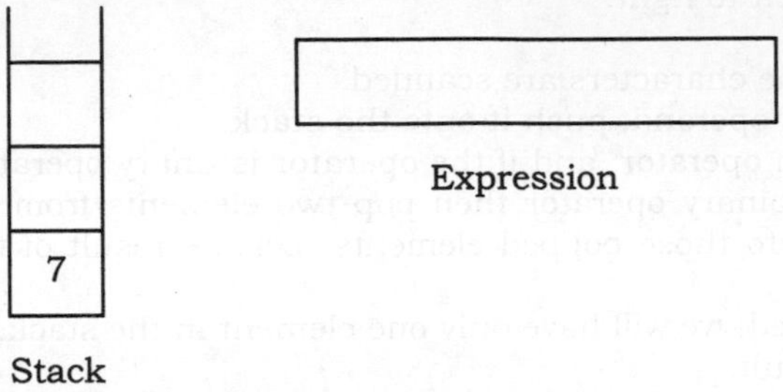

	Expression
7	

Stack

Next character scanned is "5", which is added to the stack.

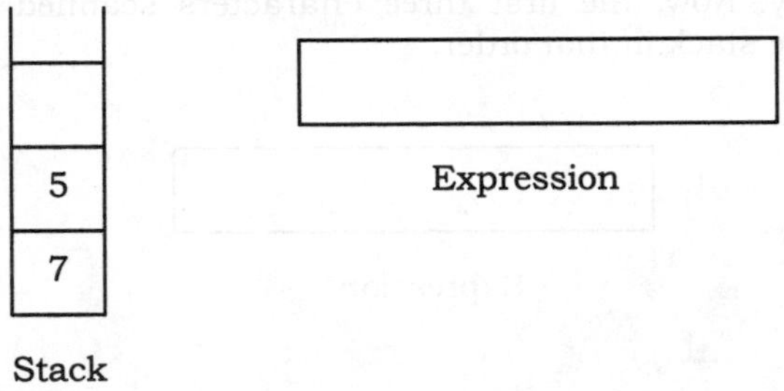

5	Expression
7	

Stack

Next character scanned is "-", which is an operator. Thus, we pop the top two elements from the stack and perform the "-" operation with the two operands. The second operand will be the first element that is popped.

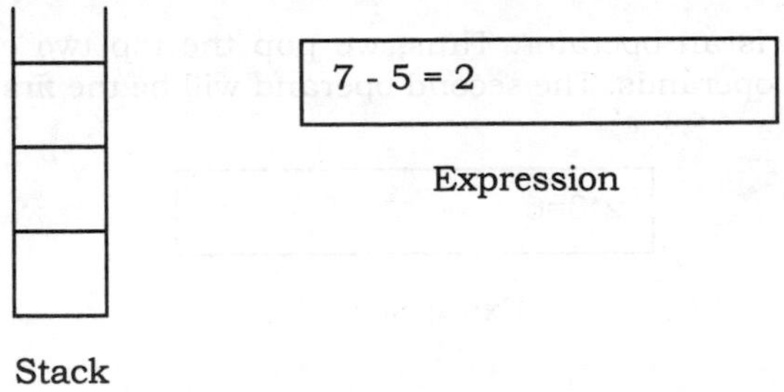

	7 - 5 = 2
	Expression

Stack

The value of the expression(7-5) that has been evaluated(23) is pushed into the stack.

	Expression
2	

Stack

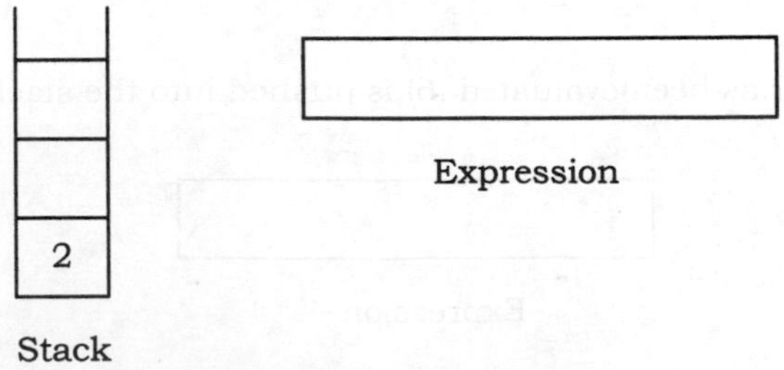

Now, since all the characters are scanned, the remaining element in the stack (there will be only one element in the stack) will be returned. End result:

- Postfix String : 123*+5-
- Result : 2

Problem-5   Can we evaluate the infix expression with stacks in one pass?

Solution: Using 2 stacks we can evaluate an infix expression in 1 pass without converting to postfix.

Algorithm
1) Create an empty operator stack
2) Create an empty operand stack
3) For each token in the input string
   a. Get the next token in the infix string
   b. If next token is an operand, place it on the operand stack
   c. If next token is an operator
      i. Evaluate the operator (next op)
4) While operator stack is not empty, pop operator and operands (left and right), evaluate left operator right and push result onto operand stack
5) Pop result from operator stack

Problem-6   How to design a stack such that getMinimum( ) should be O(1)?

Solution: Take an auxiliary stack that maintains the minimum of all values in the stack. Also, assume that, each element of the stack is less than its below elements. For simplicity let us call the auxiliary stack as *min stack*.

When we *pop* the main stack, *pop* the min stack too. When we push the main stack, push either the new element or the current minimum, whichever is lower. At any point, if we want to get the minimum then we just need to return the top element from the min stack. Let us take some example and trace out. Initially let us assume that we have pushed 2, 6, 4, 1 and 5. Based on above-mentioned algorithm the *min stack* will look like:

Main stack	Min stack
5 →top	1→top
1	1
4	2
6	2
2	2

After popping twice we get:

Main stack	Min stack
4 -→ top	2→top
6	2
2	2

Based on the discussion above, now let us code the push, pop and GetMinimum() operations.

```java
public class AdvancedStack implements Stack{
        private Stack elementStack = new LLStack();
        private Stack minStack = new LLStack();
        public void push(int data){
                elementStack.push(data);
                if(minStack.isEmpty() || (Integer)minStack.top() >= (Integer)data){
                        minStack.push(data);
                }else{
                        minStack.push(minStack.top());
                }
        }
        public int pop(){
                if(elementStack.isEmpty()) return null;
                minStack.pop();
                return elementStack.pop();
        }
        public int getMinimum(){
                return minStack.top();
        }
        public int top(){
                return elementStack.top();
        }
        public boolean isEmpty(){
                return elementStack.isEmpty();
        }
}
```

Time complexity: O(1).

Space complexity: O(n) [for Min stack]. This algorithm has much better space usage if we rarely get a "new minimum or equal".

Problem-7   For Problem-6 is it possible to improve the space complexity?

Solution: **Yes.** The main problem of the previous approach is, for each push operation we are pushing the element on to *min stack* also (either the new element or existing minimum element). That means, we are pushing the duplicate minimum elements on to the stack.

Now, let us change the algorithm to improve the space complexity. We still have the min stack, but we only pop from it when the value we pop from the main stack is equal to the one on the min stack. We only *push* to the min stack when the value being pushed onto the main stack is less than *or equal* to the current min value. In this modified algorithm also, if we want to get the minimum then we just need to return the top element from the min stack. For example, taking the original version and pushing 1 again, we'd get:

Main stack	Min stack
1→top	
5	
1	
4	1→top
6	1
2	2

Popping from the above pops from both stacks because 1 == 1, leaving:

Main stack	Min stack
5 →top	
1	
4	
6	1→top
2	2

Popping again *only* pops from the main stack, because 5 > 1:

Main stack	Min stack
1 →top	
4	
6	1→top
2	2

Popping again pops both stacks because 1 == 1:

Main stack	Min stack
4→top	
6	
2	2→top

Note: The difference is only in push & pop operations.

```java
public class AdvancedStack  implements Stack{
        private Stack elementStack = new LLStack();
        private Stack minStack = new LLStack();
        public void Push(int data){
                elementStack.push(data);
                if(minStack.isEmpty() || (Integer)minStack.top() >= (Integer)data){
                        minStack.push(data);
                }
        }
        public int Pop(){
                if(elementStack.isEmpty())
                        return null;
                Integer minTop = (Integer) minStack.top();
                Integer elementTop = (Integer) elementStack.top();
                if(minTop.intValue() == elementTop.intValue())
                        minStack.pop();
                return elementStack.pop();
        }
        public int GetMinimum(){
                return minStack.top();
```

```
        }
        public int Top(){
                return elementStack.top();
        }
        public boolean isEmpty(){
                return elementStack.isEmpty();
        }
}
```

Time complexity: O(1).
Space complexity: O(n) [for Min stack]. But this algorithm has much better space usage if we rarely get a "new minimum or equal".

Problem-8   Given an array of characters formed with a's and b's. The string is marked with special character X which represents the middle of the list (for example: ababa...ababXbabab.....baaa). Check whether the string is palindrome.

Solution: This is one of the simplest algorithms. What we do is, start two indexes one at the beginning of the string and other at the ending of the string. Each time compare whether the values at both the indexes are same or not. If the values are not same then we say that the given string is not a palindrome. If the values are same then increment the left index and decrement the right index. Continue this process until both the indexes meet at the middle (at X) or if the string is not palindrome.

```
int isPalindrome(String inputStr) {
        int i=0, j = inputStr.length;
        while(i < j && A[i] == A[j]) {
                i++;
                j--;
        }
        if(i < j ) {
                System.out.println("Not a Palindrome");
                return 0;
        }
        else {
                System.out.println("Palindrome");
                return 1;
        }
}
```

Time Complexity: O(n).
Space Complexity: O(1).

Problem-9   For Problem-8, if the input is in singly linked list then how do we check whether the list elements form a palindrome (That means, moving backward is not possible).

Solution: Refer *Linked Lists* chapter.

Problem-10   Can we solve Problem-8 using stacks?

Solution: Yes.

Algorithm
*   Traverse the list till we encounter X as input element.
*   During the traversal push all the elements (until X) on to the stack.
*   For the second half of the list, compare each elements content with top of the stack. If they are same then pop the stack and go to the next element in the input list.
*   If they are not same then the given string is not a palindrome.
*   Continue this process until the stack is empty or the string is not a palindrome.

```
boolean isPalindrome(String inputStr){
        char inputChar[] = inputStr.toCharArray();
        Stack s = new LLStack();
        int i=0;
        while(inputChar[i] != 'X'){
                s.push(inputChar[i]);
                i++;
        }
        i++;
        while(i<inputChar.length){
                if(s.isEmpty()) return false;
```

```
                if(inputChar[i] != ((Character)s.pop()).charValue()) return false;
                i++;
        }
        return true;
}
```

Time Complexity: O(*n*).
Space Complexity: O(*n*/2) ≈ O(*n*).

Problem-11   Given a stack, how to reverse the contents of stacks using only stack operations (push and pop)?

Solution:
Algorithm
- First pop all the elements of the stack till it becomes empty.
- For each upward step in recursion, insert the element at the bottom of stack.

```
public class StackReversal {
        public static void reverseStack(Stack stack){
                if(stack.isEmpty()) return;
                int temp = stack.pop();
                reverseStack(stack);
                insertAtBottom(stack, temp);
        }
        private static void insertAtBottom(Stack stack , int data){
                if(stack.isEmpty()){
                        stack.push(data);
                        return;
                }
                int temp = stack.pop();
                insertAtBottom(stack, data);
                stack.push(temp);
        }
}
```

Time Complexity: O(*n*²).
Space Complexity: O(*n*), for recursive stack.

Problem-12   Show how to implement one queue efficiently using two stacks. Analyze the running time of the queue operations.

Solution: Refer *Queues* chapter.

Problem-13   Show how to implement one stack efficiently using two queues. Analyze the running time of the stack operations.

Solution: Refer *Queues* chapter.

Problem-14   How do we implement 2 stacks using only one array? Our stack routines should not indicate an exception unless every slot in the array is used?

Solution:

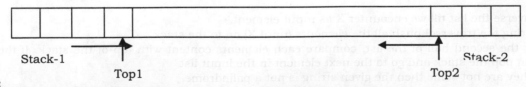

Stack-1   Top1   Top2   Stack-2

Algorithm:
- Start two indexes one at the left end and other at the right end.
- The left index simulates the first stack and the right index simulates the second stack.
- If we want to push an element into the first stack then put the element at left index.
- Similarly, if we want to push an element into the second stack then put the element at right index.
- First stack gets grows towards right, second stack grows towards left.

Time Complexity of push and pop for both stacks is O(1). Space Complexity is O(1).

```
public class ArrayWithTwoStacks{
        private int[] dataArray;
        private int size;
        private int topOne;
        private int topTwo;
```

```java
        public ArrayWithTwoStacks(int size){
                if(size<2) throw new IllegalStateException("size < 2 is no persmissible");
                dataArray = new int[size];
                this.size = size;
                topOne = -1;
                topTwo = size;
        }
        public void push(int stackId, int data){
                if(topTwo == topOne+1) throw new StackOverflowException("Array is full");
                if(stackId == 1){
                        dataArray[++topOne] = data;
                }else if(stackId == 2){
                        dataArray[--topTwo] = data;
                }else return;
        }
        public int pop(int stackId){
                if(stackId == 1){
                        if(topOne == -1) throw new EmptyStackException("First Stack is Empty");
                        int toPop = dataArray[topOne];
                        dataArray[topOne--] = null;
                        return toPop;
                }else if(stackId == 2){
                        if(topTwo == this.size) throw new EmptyStackException("Second Stack is Empty");
                        int toPop = dataArray[topTwo];
                        dataArray[topTwo++] = null;
                        return toPop;
                }else return null;
        }
        public int top(int stackId){
                if(stackId == 1){
                        if(topOne == -1) throw new EmptyStackException("First Stack is Empty");
                                return dataArray[topOne];
                        }else if(stackId == 2){
                                if(topTwo == this.size)
                                        throw new EmptyStackException("Second Stack is Empty");
                                return dataArray[topTwo];
                        }else return null;
        }
        public boolean isEmpty(int stackId){
                if(stackId == 1){
                                return topOne == -1;
                        }else if(stackId == 2){
                                return topTwo == this.size;
                        }else return true;
        }
}
```

Problem-15   3 stacks in one array: How to implement 3 stacks in one array?

Solution: For this problem, there could be other way of solving it. Given below is one such possibility and it works as long as there is an empty space in the array.

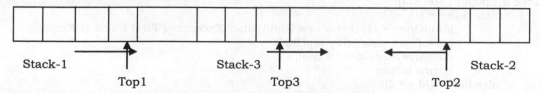

To implement 3 stacks we keep the following information.
- The index of the first stack (Top1): this indicates the size of the first stack.
- The index of the second stack (Top2): this indicates the size of the second stack.
- Starting index of the third stack (base address of third stack).
- Top index of the third stack.

Now, let us define the push and pop operations for this implementation.

Pushing:
- For pushing on to the first stack, we need to see if adding a new element causes it to bump into the third stack. If so, try to shift the third stack upwards. Insert the new element at (start1 + Top1).
- For pushing to the second stack, we need to see if adding a new element causes it to bump into the third stack. If so, try to shift the third stack downward. Insert the new element at (start2 – Top2).
- When pushing to the third stack, see if it bumps the second stack. If so, try to shift the third stack downward and try pushing again. Insert the new element at (start3 + Top3).

Time Complexity: O(n). Since, we may need to adjust the third stack. Space Complexity: O(1).

Popping: For popping, we don't need to shift, just decrement the size of the appropriate stack.
Time Complexity: O(1). Space Complexity: O(1).

One Possible Implementation

```java
public class ArrayWithThreeStacks {
        private int[] dataArray;
        private int size, topOne, topTwo, baseThree, topThree;
        public ArrayWithThreeStacks(int size){
                if(size<3) throw new IllegalStateException("Size < 3 is no persmissible");
                dataArray = new int[size];
                this.size = size;
                topOne = -1;
                topTwo = size;
                baseThree = size/2;
                topThree = baseThree;
        }
        public void push(int stackId, int data){
                if(stackId == 1){
                        if(topOne+1 == baseThree){
                                if(stack3IsRightShiftable()){
                                        shiftStack3ToRight();
                                        dataArray[++topOne] = data;
                                }else throw new StackOverflowException("Stack1 has reached max limit");
                        }else dataArray[++topOne] = data;
                }else if(stackId == 2){
                        if(topTwo-1 == topThree){
                                if(stack3IsLeftShiftable()){
                                        shiftStack3ToLeft();
                                        dataArray[--topTwo] = data;
                                }else throw new StackOverflowException("Stack2 has reached max limit");
                        }else dataArray[--topTwo] = data;
                }else if(stackId == 3){
                        if(topTwo-1 == topThree){
                                if(stack3IsLeftShiftable()){
                                        shiftStack3ToLeft();
                                        dataArray[++topThree] = data;
                                }else throw new StackOverflowException("Stack3 has reached max limit");
                        }else dataArray[++topThree] = data;
                }else return;
        }
        public int pop(int stackId){
                if(stackId == 1){
                        if(topOne == -1) throw new EmptyStackException("First Stack is Empty");
                        int toPop = dataArray[topOne];
                        dataArray[topOne--] = null;
                        return toPop;
                }else if(stackId == 2){
                        if(topTwo == this.size) throw new EmptyStackException("Second Stack is Empty");
                        int toPop = dataArray[topTwo];
                        dataArray[topTwo++] = null;
                        return toPop;
                }else if(stackId == 3){
                        if(topThree == this.size && dataArray[topThree] == null)
```

```
                            throw new EmptyStackException("Third Stack is Empty");
                        int toPop = dataArray[topThree];
                        if(topThree > baseThree) dataArray[topThree--] = null;
                        if(topThree == baseThree) dataArray[topThree] = null;
                        return toPop;
                    }else return null;
            }
        public int top(int stackId){
                if(stackId == 1){
                    if(topOne == -1) throw new EmptyStackException("First Stack is Empty");
                        return dataArray[topOne];
                    }else if(stackId == 2){
                        if(topTwo == this.size)
                                throw new EmptyStackException("Second Stack is Empty");
                        return dataArray[topTwo];
                    }else if(stackId == 3){
                            if(topThree == baseThree && dataArray[baseThree] == null)
                                throw new EmptyStackException("Third Stack is Empty");
                            return dataArray[topThree];
                    }else return null;
            }
        public boolean isEmpty(int stackId){
                if(stackId == 1){
                            return topOne == -1;
                    }else if(stackId == 2){
                        return topTwo == this.size;
                    }else if(stackId == 3){
                        return (topThree == baseThree) && (dataArray[baseThree] == null);
                    }else return true;
            }
        private void shiftStack3ToLeft() {
                for(int i=baseThree-1; i<=topThree-1;i++){
                    dataArray[i] = dataArray[i+1];
                }
                dataArray[topThree--] = null;
                baseThree--;
            }
        private boolean stack3IsLeftShiftable() {
                if(topOne+1 < baseThree){
                        return true;
                }
                return false;
            }
        private void shiftStack3ToRight() {
                for(int i=topThree+1; i>=baseThree+1;i--){
                    dataArray[i] = dataArray[i-1];
                }
                dataArray[baseThree++] = null;
                topThree++;
            }
        private boolean stack3IsRightShiftable() {
                if(topThree+1 < topTwo){
                        return true;
                }
                return false;
            }
    }
}
```

Problem-16   For Problem-15, is there any other way implementing middle stack?

Solution: Yes. When either the left stack (which grows to the right) or the right stack (which grows to the left) bumps into the middle stack, we need to shift the entire middle stack to make room. The same happens if a push on the middle stack causes it to bump into the right stack. To solve the above-mentioned problem (number of shifts) what we can do is, alternating pushes could be added at alternating sides of the middle list (For example, even elements are pushed to the left, odd elements are pushed to the right). This would keep the middle stack balanced in the center of the array but it would still need to be shifted when it bumps into the left or right stack, whether by growing on its own or by the growth of a neighboring stack.

We can optimize the initial locations of the three stacks if they grow/shrink at different rates and if they have different average sizes. For example, suppose one stack doesn't change much. If you put it at the left then the middle stack will eventually get pushed against it and leave a gap between the middle and right stacks, which grow toward each other. If they collide, then it's likely you've run out of space in the array. There is no change in the time complexity but the average number of shifts will get reduced.

Problem-17   Multiple (m) stacks in one array: Similar to Problem-15, what if we want to implement m stacks in one array?

Solution: Let us assume that array indexes are from 1 to n. Similar to the discussion of Problem-15, to implement m stacks in one array, we divide the array into m parts (as shown below). The size of each part is $\frac{n}{m}$.

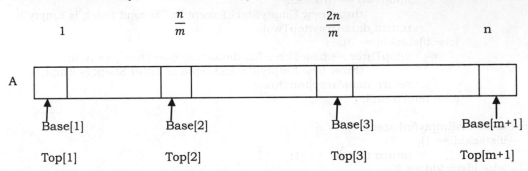

From the above representation we can see that, first stack is starting at index 1 (starting index is stored in Base[1]), second stack is starting at index $\frac{n}{m}$ (starting index is stored in Base[2]), third stack is starting at index $\frac{2n}{m}$ (starting index is stored in Base[3]) and so on.

Similar to *Base* array, let us assume that *Top* array stores the top indexes for each of the stack. Consider the following terminology for the discussion.

- Top[i], for $1 \leq i \leq m$ will point to the topmost element of the stack i.
- If Base[i] == Top[i], then we can say the stack i is empty.
- If Top[i] == Base[i+1], then we can say the stack i is full.
  Initially Base[i] = Top[i] = $\frac{n}{m}(i-1)$, for $1 \leq i \leq m$.
- The ith stack grows from Base[i]+1 to Base[i+1].

Pushing on to i^{th} stack:

1) For pushing on to the ith stack, we check whether top of ith stack is pointing to Base[i+1] (this case defines that i^{th} stack is full). That means, we need to see if adding a new element causes it to bump into the $i + 1^{th}$ stack. If so, try to shift the stacks from $i + 1^{th}$ stack to m^{th} stack towards right. Insert the new element at (Base[i] + Top[i]).
2) If right shifting is not possible then try shifting the stacks from 1 to $i - 1^{th}$ stack towards left.
3) If both of them are not possible then we can say that all stacks are full.

```
void Push(int StackID, int data){
        if(Top[i] == Base[i+1])
                Print i^{th} Stack is full and does the necessary action (shifting);
        Top[i] = Top[i]+1;
        A[Top[i]] = data;
}
```

Time Complexity: O(n). Since, we may need to adjust the stacks.
Space Complexity: O(1).

Popping from ith stack: For popping, we don't need to shift, just decrement the size of the appropriate stack. The only case we need to check is stack empty case.

```
int Pop(int StackID) {
        if(Top[i] == Base[i])
                Print i^{th} Stack is empty;
        return  A[Top[i]--];
}
```

Time Complexity: O(1).
Space Complexity: O(1).

Problem-18   Consider an empty stack of integers. Let the numbers $1, 2, 3, 4, 5, 6$ be pushed on to this stack only in the order they appeared from left to right. Let S indicates a push and X indicate a pop operation. Can they be permuted in to the order 325641(output) and order 154623? (If a permutation is possible give the order string of operations.

Solution: SSSXXSSXSXXX outputs 325641. 154623 cannot be output as 2 is pushed much before 3 so can appear only after 3 is output.

Problem-19   Suppose there are two singly linked lists, which intersect at some point and become a single linked list. The head or start pointers of both the lists are known, but the intersecting node is not known. Also, the number of nodes in each of the list before they intersect are unknown and both list may have it different. *List*1 may have n nodes before it reaches intersection point and *List*2 might have m nodes before it reaches intersection point where m and n may be $m = n, m < n$ or $m > n$. Can we solve this problem using stacks?

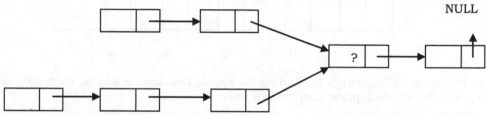

Solution: Yes. For algorithm refer *Linked Lists* chapter.

Problem-20   Earlier in this chapter, we discussed that for dynamic array implementation of stack, 'repeated doubling' approach is used. For the same problem what is the complexity if we create a new array whose size is $n + K$ instead of doubling?

Solution: Let us assume that the initial stack size is 0. For simplicity let us assume that $K = 10$. For inserting the element we create a new array whose size is $0 + 10 = 10$. Similarly, after 10 elements we again create a new array whose size is $10 + 10 = 20$ and this process continues at values: $30, 40 \ldots$ That means, for a given n value, we are creating the new arrays at: $\frac{n}{10}, \frac{n}{20}, \frac{n}{30}, \frac{n}{40} \ldots$

The total number of copy operations are: $= \frac{n}{10} + \frac{n}{20} + \frac{n}{30} + \cdots 1 = \frac{n}{10}\left(\frac{1}{1} + \frac{1}{2} + \frac{1}{3} + \cdots \frac{1}{n}\right) = \frac{n}{10} logn \approx O(nlogn)$. If we are performing n push operations, the cost of per operation is O($logn$).

Problem-21   Given a string containing n $S's$ and n $X's$ where S indicates a push operation and X indicates a pop operation, and with the stack initially empty, Formulate a rule to check whether a given string S of operations is admissible or not?

Solution: Given a string of length $2n$, we wish to check whether the given string of operations is permissible or not with respect to its functioning on a stack. The only restricted operation is pop whose prior requirement is that the stack should not be empty. So while traversing the string from left to right, prior to any pop the stack shouldn't be empty which means the no of S's is always greater than or equal to that of X's. Hence the condition is at any stage on processing of the string, number of push operations (S) should be greater than the number of pop operations (X).

Problem-22   Finding of Spans: Given an array A the span $S[i]$ of $A[i]$ is the maximum number of consecutive elements $A[j]$ immediately preceding $A[i]$ and such that $A[j] \leq A[j + 1]$?

Solution: This is a very common problem in stock markets to find the peaks. Spans are used in financial analysis (E.g., stock at 52-week high). The span of a stock price on a certain day, i, is the maximum number of consecutive days (up to the current day) the price of the stock has been less than or equal to its price on i. As an example, let us consider the following table and the corresponding spans diagram. In the figure the arrows indicates the length of the spans.

Day: Index i	Input Array A[i]	S[i]: Span of A[i]
0	6	1
1	3	1
2	4	2
3	5	3
4	2	1

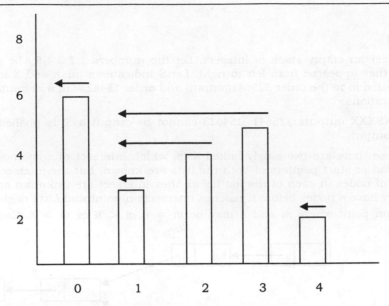

Now, let us concentrate on the algorithm for finding the spans. One simple way is, each day, check how many contiguous days are with less stock price than current price.

```java
int[] FindingSpans(int[] inputArray){
        int[] spans = new int[inputArray.length];
        for(int i=0;i<inputArray.length;i++){
                int span = 1;
                int j=i-1;
                while(j>=0 && inputArray[j]<=inputArray[j+1]){
                        span++;
                        j--;
                }
                spans[i] = span;
        }
        return spans;
}
```

Time Complexity: $O(n^2)$. Space Complexity: $O(1)$.

Problem-23   Can we improve the complexity of Problem-22?

Solution: From the example above, we can see that the span $S[i]$ on day i can be easily calculated if we know the closest day preceding i, such that the price is greater than on that day than the price on day i. Let us call such a day as P. If such a day exists then the span is now defined as $S[i] = i - P$.

```java
int[] FindingSpans(int[] inputArray){
        int[] spans = new int[inputArray.length];
        Stack stack = new LLStack();
        int p = 0;
        for(int i=0;i<inputArray.length;i++){
                while (!stack.isEmpty() && inputArray[i] > inputArray[(Integer) stack.top()])
                        stack.pop();
                if( stack.isEmpty())
                        p = -1;
                else     p = (Integer) stack.top();
                spans[i] = i - p;
                stack.push(i);
        }
        return spans;
}
```

Time Complexity: Each index of the array is pushed into the stack exactly one and also popped from the stack at most once. The statements in the while loop are executed at most n times. Even though the algorithm has nested loops, the complexity is $O(n)$ as the inner loop is executing only n times during the course of algorithm (trace out an example and see how many times the inner loop is becoming success). Space Complexity: $O(n)$ [for stack].

Problem-24   **Largest rectangle under histogram:** A histogram is a polygon composed of a sequence of rectangles aligned at a common base line. For simplicity, assume that the rectangles are having equal widths but may have different heights. For example, the figure on the left shows the histogram that consists of rectangles with the heights 3, 2, 5, 6, 1, 4, 4, measured in units where 1 is the width of the rectangles. Here our problem is: given an array with heights of rectangles (assuming width is 1), we need to find the largest rectabgle possible. For the given example the largest rectangle is the shared part.

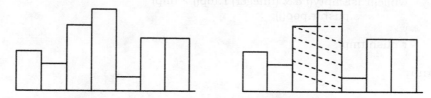

Solution: Linear search using a stack of incomplete subproblems: There are many ways of solving this problem. *Judge* has given a nice algorithm for this problem which is based on stack. We process the elements in left-to-right order and maintain a stack of information about started but yet unfinished sub histograms. If the stack is empty, open a new subproblem by pushing the element onto the stack. Otherwise compare it to the element on top of the stack. If the new one is greater we again push it. If the new one is equal we skip it. In all these cases, we continue with the next new element.

If the new one is less, we finish the topmost subproblem by updating the maximum area with respect to the element at the top of the stack. Then, we discard the element at the top, and repeat the procedure keeping the current new element. This way, all subproblems are finished until the stack becomes empty, or its top element is less than or equal to the new element, leading to the actions described above. If all elements have been processed, and the stack is not yet empty, we finish the remaining subproblems by updating the maximum area with respect to the elements at the top.

```java
public class StackItem {
        public int height;
        public int index;
}
int MaxRectangleArea(int A[], int n){
        long maxArea = 0;
        if (A == null || A.length == 0)
            return maxArea;
        Stack<StackItem> S = new Stack<StackItem>();
        S.push(new StackItem(Integer.MIN_VALUE, -1));
        for (int i = 0; i <= n; i++) {
            StackItem cur = new StackItem((i < n ? A[i] :  Integer.MIN_VALUE), i);
            if (cur.height > S.top().height) {
              S.push(cur);
              continue;
            }
            while (S.size() > 1) {
              StackItem prev = S.top();
              long area = (i - prev.index) * prev.height;
              if (area > maxArea) {
                    maxArea = area;
              }
              prev.height = cur.height;
              if (prev.height > S.get(S.size() - 2).height) {
                    break;
              }
              S.pop();
            }
        }
        return maxArea;
}
```

Every element is pushed and popped at most once and in every step of the function at least one element is pushed or popped. Since the amount of work for the decisions and the update is constant, the complexity of the algorithm is O(n) by amortized analysis. Space Complexity: O(n) [for stack].

Problem-25   Give an algorithm for sorting a stack in ascending order. We should not make any assumptions about how the stack is implemented.

Solution:

```java
public class StackSorter {
    public static Stack sort(Stack s) {
        LLStack r = new LLStack();
        while(!s.isEmpty()) {
            int tmp = (Integer) s.pop();
            while(!r.isEmpty() && (Integer) r.top() > tmp) {
                s.push(r.pop());
            }
            r.push(tmp);
        }
        return r;
    }
}
```

Time Complexity: $O(n^2)$. Space Complexity: $O(n)$, for stack.

Problem-26   Given a stack of integers, how do check whether each successive pair of numbers in the stack is consecutive or not. The pairs can be increasing or decreasing, and if the stack has an odd number of elements, the element at the top is left out of a pair. For example, if the stack of elements are [4, 5, -2, -3, 11, 10, 5, 6, 20], then the output should be true because each of the pairs (4, 5), (-2, -3), (11, 10), and (5, 6) consists of consecutive numbers.

Solution: Refer *Queues* chapter.

Problem-28   Recursively remove all adjacent duplicates: Given an array of numbers, recursively remove adjacent duplicate numbers. The output array should not have any adjacent duplicates.

Input: 1,5,6, 8,8,8,0,1,1,0,6,5	*Input*: 1,9,6, 8,8,8,0,1,1,0,6,5}
Output: 1	*Output*: 1, 9, 5

Solution: This solution runs with the concept of in-place stack. When element on stack doesn't match to the current number, we add it to stack. When it matches to stack top, we skip numbers until the element match the top of stack and remove the element from stack.

```java
public class RemoveAdjacentDuplicates {
    public      int removeAdjacentDuplicates(int []A){
        int stkptr=-1;
        int i=0;
        while (i<A.length){
            if (stkptr == -1 || A[stkptr]!=A[i]){
                stkptr++;
                A[stkptr]=A[i];
                i++;
            }else {
                while(i < A.length&& A[stkptr]==A[i])
                    i++;
                stkptr--;
            }
        }
        return stkptr;
    }
}

public class TestRemoveAdjacentDuplicates {
    public static void main(String[] args) {
        RemoveAdjacentDuplicates obj = new RemoveAdjacentDuplicates();
        int[] A = {1,5,6, 8,8,8,0,1,1,0,6,5};
        int index = obj.removeAdjacentDuplicates(A);
        for (int i = 0; i <= index; i++) {
            System.out.print(" " + A[i]);
        }
    }
}
```

Time Complexity: $O(n)$. Space Complexity: $O(n)$, for stack.

Chapter-5

QUEUES

5.1 What is a Queue?

A queue is a data structure used for storing data (similar to Linked Lists and Stacks). In queue, the order in which data arrives is important. In general, a queue is a line of people or things waiting to be served in sequential order starting at the beginning of the line or sequence.

Definition: A *queue* is an ordered list in which insertions are done at one end (*rear*) and deletions are done at other end (*front*). The first element to be inserted is the first one to be deleted. Hence, it is called First in First out (FIFO) or Last in Last out (LILO) list.

Similar to *Stacks*, special names are given to the two changes that can be made to a queue. When an element is inserted in a queue, the concept is called *EnQueue*, and when an element is removed from the queue, the concept is called *DeQueue*. *DeQueueing* an empty queue is called *underflow* and *EnQueuing* an element in a full queue is called *overflow*. Generally, we treat them as exceptions. As an example, consider the snapshot of the queue.

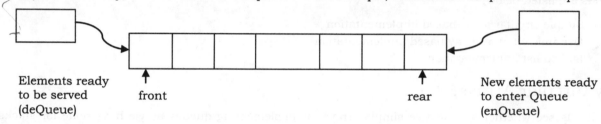

Elements ready to be served (deQueue)   front   rear   New elements ready to enter Queue (enQueue)

5.2 How are Queues Used?

The concept of a queue can be explained by observing a line at a reservation counter. When we enter the line we stand at the end of the line and the person who is at the front of the line is the one who will be served next. He will exit the queue and be served.

As this happens, the next person will come at head of the line, will exit the queue and will be served. As each person at the head of the line keeps exiting the queue we move towards the head of the line. Finally we will reach head of the line and we will exit the queue and be served. This behavior is very useful in cases where there is a need to maintain the order of arrival.

5.3 Queue ADT

The following operations make a queue an ADT. Insertions and deletions in queue must follow the FIFO scheme. For simplicity we assume the elements are integers.

Main Queue Operations

- enQueue(int data): Inserts an element at the end of the queue
- int deQueue(): Removes and returns the element at the front of the queue

Auxiliary Queue Operations

- int Front(): Returns the element at front without removing it
- int QueueSize(): Returns the number of elements stored in the queue
- int isEmpty(): Indicates whether no elements are stored in the queue or not

5.4 Exceptions

Similar to other ADTs, executing *DeQueue* on an empty queue throws an "*Empty Queue Exception*" and executing *EnQueue* on a full queue throws an "*Full Queue Exception*".

5.5 Applications

Following are the some of the applications that are using queues.

Direct Applications

- Operating systems schedule jobs (with equal priority) in the order of arrival (e.g., a print queue).
- Simulation of real-world queues such as lines at a ticket counter, or any other first-come first-served scenario requires a queue.
- Multiprogramming.
- Asynchronous data transfer (file IO, pipes, sockets).
- Waiting times of customers at call center.
- Determining number of cashiers to have at a supermarket.

Indirect Applications

- Auxiliary data structure for algorithms
- Component of other data structures

5.6 Implementation

There are many ways (similar to Stacks) of implementing queue operations and some of the commonly used methods are listed below.

- Simple circular array based implementation
- Dynamic circular array based implementation
- Linked list implementation

Why Circular Arrays?

First, let us see whether we can use simple arrays for implementing queues as we have done for stacks. We know that, in queues, the insertions are performed at one end and deletions are performed at other end. After performing some insertions and deletions the process becomes easy to understand.

In the example shown below, it can be seen clearly that the initial slots of the array are getting wasted. So, simple array implementation for queue is not efficient. To solve this problem we assume the arrays as circular arrays. That means, we treat last element and first array elements as contiguous. With this representation, if there are any free slots at the beginning, the rear pointer can easily go to its next free slot.

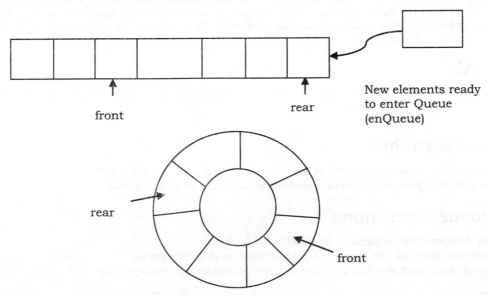

Note: The simple circular array and dynamic circular array implementations are very similar to stack array implementations. Refer *Stacks* chapter for analysis of these implementations.

Simple Circular Array Implementation

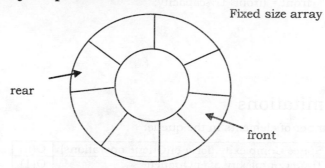

Fixed size array

rear

front

This simple implementation of Queue ADT uses an array. In the array, we add elements circularly and use two variables to keep track of start element and end element. Generally, *front* is used to indicate the start element and *rear* is used to indicate the end element in the queue.

The array storing the queue elements may become full. An *EnQueue* operation will then throw a *full queue exception*. Similarly, if we try deleting an element from empty queue then it will throw *empty queue exception*.

Note: Initially, both front and rear points to -1 which indicates that the queue is empty.

```java
public class ArrayQueue {
        private int front;
        private int rear;
        private int capacity;
        private int [] array;
        private ArrayQueue(int size){
                capacity = size;
                front = -1;
                rear = -1;
                array = new int [size];
        }
        public static ArrayQueue createQueue(int size){
                return new ArrayQueue(size);
        }
        public boolean isEmpty(){
                return (front == -1);
        }
        public boolean isFull(){
                return ((rear+1)%capacity == front);
        }
        public int getQueueSize(){
                return((capacity-front+rear+1)%capacity);
        }
        public void enQueue(int  data){
                if(isFull()){
                        throw new QueueOverflowException("Queue Overflow");
                }else{
                        rear = (rear+1)%capacity;
                        array[rear] = data;
                        if(front == -1){
                                front = rear;
                        }
                }
        }
        public int deQueue(){
                int  data = null;
                if(isEmpty()){
                        throw new EmptyQueueException("Queue Empty");
                }else{
                        data = array[front];
                        if(front == rear){
                                front = rear-1;
```

```
                    }else{
                            front = (front+1)%capacity;
                    }
            }
            return data;
        }
}
```

Performance and Limitations

Performance: Let n be the number of elements in the queue:

Space Complexity (for n enQueue operations)	O(n)
Time Complexity of enQueue()	O(1)
Time Complexity of deQueue()	O(1)
Time Complexity of isEmpty()	O(1)
Time Complexity of isFull ()	O(1)
Time Complexity of getQueueSize ()	O(1)

Limitations

The maximum size of the queue must be defined a prior and cannot be changed. Trying to *EnQueue* a new element into a full queue causes an implementation-specific exception.

Dynamic Circular Array Implementation

```
public class DynArrayQueue implements Queue{
        private int front;
        private int rear;
        private int capacity;
        private int[] array;
        private DynArrayQueue(){
                capacity = 1;
                front = -1;
                rear = -1;
                array = new int[1];
        }
        public static DynArrayQueue createDynArrayQueue(){
                return new DynArrayQueue();
        }
        public boolean isEmpty(){
                return (front == -1);
        }
        private boolean isFull(){
                return ((rear+1)%capacity == front);
        }
        public int getQueueSize(){
                if(front == -1) return 0;
                int size = (capacity-front+rear+1)%capacity;
                if(size == 0) {
                        return capacity;
                }else    return size;
        }
        private void resizeQueue(){
                int initCapacity = capacity;
                capacity*=2;
                int[] oldArray = array;
                array = new int[this.capacity];
                for(int i=0;i<oldArray.length;i++){
                        array[i] = oldArray[i];
                }
                if(rear<front){
                        for(int i=0;i<front;i++){
```

```
                                        array[i+initCapacity] = this.array[i];
                                        array[i] = null;
                                }
                                rear = rear + initCapacity;
                        }
                }
                public void enQueue(int data){
                        if(isFull())
                                resizeQueue();
                        rear = (rear+1)%capacity;
                        array[rear] = data;
                        if(front == -1)
                                front = rear;
                }
                public int deQueue(){
                        int data = null;
                        if(isEmpty())
                                throw new EmptyQueueException("Queue Empty");
                        else{
                                data = array[front];
                                if(front == rear) front = rear = -1;
                                else front = (front+1)%capacity;
                        }
                        return data;
                }
        }
}
```

Performance

Let *n* be the number of elements in the queue.

Space Complexity (for *n* enQueue operations)	O(*n*)
Time Complexity of enQueue()	O(1) (Average)
Time Complexity of deQueue()	O(1)
Time Complexity of getQueueSize()	O(1)
Time Complexity of isEmpty()	O(1)
Time Complexity of isFull()	O(1)

Linked List Implementation

Another way of implementing queues is by using Linked lists. *EnQueue* operation is implemented by inserting element at the ending of the list. *DeQueue* operation is implemented by deleting an element from the beginning of the list.

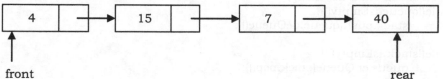

```
public class LLQueue{
        private LLNode frontNode; //represents headNode
        private LLNode rearNode; //represents lastNode
        private LLQueue(){
                this.frontNode = null;
                this.rearNode = null;
        }
        public static LLQueue createQueue(){
                return new LLQueue();
        }
        public boolean isEmpty(){
                return (frontNode == null);
        }
        public void enQueue(int data){
                LLNode newNode = new LLNode(data);
```

```
                    if(rearNode != null) {
                            rearNode.setNext(newNode);
                    }
                    rearNode = newNode;
                    if(frontNode == null) {
                            frontNode = rearNode;
                    }
            }
            public int deQueue(){
                    int data = null;
                    if(isEmpty()){
                            throw new EmptyQueueException("Queue Empty");
                    }else{
                            data = frontNode.getData();
                            frontNode = frontNode.getNext();
                    }
                    return data;
            }
    }
```

Performance

Let n be the number of elements in the queue, then

Space Complexity (for n enQueue operations)	O(n)
Time Complexity of enQueue()	O(1) (Average)
Time Complexity of deQueue()	O(1)
Time Complexity of isEmpty()	O(1)
Time Complexity of deleteQueue()	O(1)

Comparison of Implementations

Note: Comparison is very similar to stack implementations and *Stacks* chapter.

5.7 Problems on Queues

Problem-1   Give an algorithm for reversing a queue Q. To access the queue, you are only allowed to use the methods of queue ADT.

Solution:
```
public class QueueReversal {
        public static Queue reverseQueue(Queue queue){
                Stack stack = new LLStack();
                while(!queue.isEmpty()){
                        stack.push(queue.deQueue());
                }
                while(!stack.isEmpty()){
                        queue.enQueue(stack.pop());
                }
                return queue;
        }
}
```
Time Complexity: O(n).

Problem-2   How can you implement a queue using two stacks?

Solution: Let S1 and S2 be the two stacks to be used in the implementation of queue. All we have to do is to define the enQueue and deQueue operations for the queue.

enQueue Algorithm:
- Just push on to stack S1

Time Complexity: O(1).

deQueue Algorithm:
- If stack S2 is not empty then pop from S2 and return that element.

- If stack is empty, then transfer all elements from S1 to S2 and pop the top element from S2 and return that popped element [we can optimize the code little by transferring only $n - 1$ elements from S1 to S2 and pop the nth element from S1 and return that popped element].
- If stack S1 is also empty then throw error.

Time Complexity: From the algorithm, if the stack S2 is not empty then the complexity is O(1). If the stack S2 is empty then, we need to transfer the elements from S1 to S2. But if we carefully observe, the number of transferred elements and the number of popped elements from S2 are equal. Due to this the average complexity of pop operation in this case is O(1). Amortized complexity of pop operation is O(1).

```java
public class QueueWithTwoStacks {
        Stack stack1;
        Stack stack2;
        public QueueWithTwoStacks(){
                stack1 = new LLStack();
                stack2 = new LLStack();
        }
        //default implementation
        public boolean isEmpty(){
                if(stack2.isEmpty()){
                        while(!stack1.isEmpty()){
                                stack2.push(stack1.pop());
                        }
                }
                return stack2.isEmpty();
        }
        public void enQueue(Object data){
                stack1.push(data);
        }
        public Object deQueue(){
                if(!stack2.isEmpty()){
                        return stack2.pop();
                }else{  while(!stack1.isEmpty()){
                                stack2.push(stack1.pop());
                        }
                        return stack2.pop();
                }
        }
}
```

Problem-3   Show how can you efficiently implement one stack using two queues. Analyze the running time of the stack operations.

Solution: Let Q1 and Q2 be the two queues to be used in the implementation of stack. All we have to do is to define the push and pop operations for the stack.

In the algorithms below, we make sure that one queue is always empty.

Push Operation Algorithm: Insert the element in whichever queue is not empty.
- Check whether queue Q1 is empty or not. If Q1 is empty then Enqueue the element into Q2.
- Otherwise enQueue the element into Q1.

Time Complexity: O(1).

Pop Operation Algorithm: Transfer $n - 1$ elements to the other queue and delete last from queue for performing pop operation.
- If queue Q1 is not empty then transfer $n - 1$ elements from Q1 to Q2 and then, deQueue the last element of Q1 and return it.
- If queue Q2 is not empty then transfer $n - 1$ elements from Q2 to Q1 and then, deQueue the last element of Q2 and return it.

Time Complexity: Running time of pop operation is $O(n)$ as each time pop is called, we are transferring all the elements from one queue to the other.

```java
public class StackWithTwoQueues{
        LLQueue queue1;
        LLQueue queue2;
        public StackWithTwoQueues(){
```

```
                    queue1 = new LLQueue();
                    queue1 = new LLQueue();
            }
            public void push(int data){
                    if(queue1.isEmpty())
                            queue2.enQueue(data);
                    else    queue1.enQueue(data);
            }
            public int Pop() {
                    int i, size;
                    if(isEmpty(S?Q2)) {
                            size = queue1.getQueueSize();
                            i = 0;
                            while(i < size-1) {
                                    queue2.enQueue(queue1.deQueue());
                                    i++;
                            }
                            return queue.deQueue();
                    }
                    else {  size = queue2.getQueueSize();
                            while(i < size-1) {
                                    queue1.enQueue(queue2.deQueue());
                                    i++;
                            }
                            return queue2.deQueue();
                    }
            }

}
```

Problem-4   Maximum sum in sliding window: Given array A[] with sliding window of size w which is moving from the very left of the array to the very right. Assume that we can only see the w numbers in the window. Each time the sliding window moves rightwards by one position. For example: The array is [1 3 -1 -3 5 3 6 7], and w is 3.

Window position	Max
[1 3 -1] -3 5 3 6 7	3
1 [3 -1 -3] 5 3 6 7	3
1 3 [-1 -3 5] 3 6 7	5
1 3 -1 [-3 5 3] 6 7	5
1 3 -1 -3 [5 3 6] 7	6
1 3 -1 -3 5 [3 6 7]	7

Input: A long array A[], and a window width w. **Output**: An array B[], B[i] is the maximum value from A[i] to A[i+w-1]. **Requirement**: Find a good optimal way to get B[i]

Solution: This problem can be solved with doubly ended queue (which support insertion and deletions at both ends). Refer *Priority Queues* chapter for algorithms.

**Problem-5   ** Given a queue Q containing n elements, transfer these items on to a stack S (initially empty) so that front element of Q appears at the top of the stack and the order of all other items is preserved. Using enqueue and dequeue operations for the queue and push and pop operations for the stack, outline an efficient O(n) algorithm to accomplish the above task, using only a constant amount of additional storage.

Solution: Assume the elements of queue Q are $a_1, a_2 \ldots a_n$. Dequeuing all elements and pushing them onto the stack will result in a stack with a_n at the top and a_1 at the bottom. This is done in O(n) time as dequeue and each push require constant time per operation. The queue is now empty. By popping all elements and pushing them on the the queue we will get a_1 at the top of the stack. This is done again in O(n) time. As in big-oh arithmetic we can ignore constant factors, the process is carried out in O(n) time. The amount of additional storage needed here has to be big enough to temporarily hold one item.

**Problem-6   ** A queue is set up in a circular array A[0..n - 1] with front and rear defined as usual. Assume that $n - 1$ locations in the array are available for storing the elements (with the other element being used to detect full/empty condition). Give a formula for the number of elements in the queue in terms of *rear*, *front*, and n.

Solution: Consider the following figure to get clear idea about the queue.

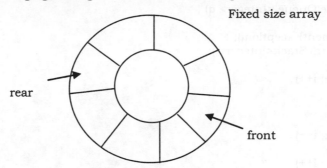

Fixed size array

- Rear of the queue is somewhere clockwise from the front
- To enqueue an element, we move *rear* one position clockwise and write the element in that position
- To dequeue, we simply move *front* one position clockwise
- Queue migrates in a clockwise direction as we enqueue and dequeue
- Emptiness and fullness to be checked carefully.
- Analyze the possible situations (make some drawings to see where *front* and *rear* are when the queue is empty, and partially and totally filled). We will get this:

$$Number\ Of\ Elements = \begin{cases} rear - front + 1 & \text{if } rear = front \\ rear - front + n & \text{otherwise} \end{cases}$$

Problem-7   What is the most appropriate data structure to print elements of queue in reverse order?

Solution: Stack.

Problem-8   Given a stack of integers, how do check whether each successive pair of numbers in the stack is consecutive or not. The pairs can be increasing or decreasing, and if the stack has an odd number of elements, the element at the top is left out of a pair. For example, if the stack of elements are [4, 5, -2, -3, 11, 10, 5, 6, 20], then the output should be true because each of the pairs (4, 5), (-2, -3), (11, 10), and (5, 6) consists of consecutive numbers.

Solution:
```java
public static boolean checkStackPairwiseOrder(Stack<Integer> s) {
    Queue<Integer> q = new LinkedList<Integer>();
    boolean pairwiseOrdered = true;
    while (!s.isEmpty())
        q.add(s.pop());
    while (!q.isEmpty())
        s.push(q.remove());
    while (!s.isEmpty()) {
        int n = s.pop();
        q.add(n);
        if (!s.isEmpty()) {
            int m = s.pop();
            q.add(m);
            if (Math.abs(n - m) != 1) {
                pairwiseOrdered = false;
            }
        }
    }
    while (!q.isEmpty())
        s.push(q.remove());
    return pairwiseOrdered;
}
```
Time Complexity: O(n). Space Complexity: O(n).

Problem-9   Given a queue of integers, rearrange the elements by interleaving the first half of the list with the second half of the list. For example, suppose a queue stores the following sequence of values: [11, 12, 13, 14, 15, 16, 17, 18, 19, 20]. Consider the two halves of this list: first half: [11, 12, 13, 14, 15] second half: [16, 17, 18, 19, 20]. These are combined in an alternating fashion to form a sequence of interleave pairs: the first values from each half (11 and 16), then the second values from each half (12 and 17), then the third values from each half (13 and 18), and so on. In each pair, the value from the first half appears before the value from the second half. Thus, after the call, the queue stores the following values: [11, 16, 12, 17, 13, 18, 14, 19, 15, 20].

Solution:

```
public void interLeavingQueue(Queue <Integer> q) {
    if (q.size() % 2 != 0)
        throw new IllegalArgumentException();
    Stack<Integer> s = new ArrayStack<Integer>();
    int halfSize = q.size() / 2;
    for (int i = 0; i < halfSize; i++)
        s.push(q.dequeue());
    while (!s.isEmpty())
        q.enqueue(s.pop());
    for (int i = 0; i < halfSize; i++)
        q.enqueue(q.dequeue());
    for (int i = 0; i < halfSize; i++)
        s.push(q.dequeue());
    while (!s.isEmpty()) {
        q.enqueue(s.pop());
        q.enqueue(q.dequeue());
    }
}
```

Time Complexity: $O(n)$. Space Complexity: $O(n)$.

Problem-10　　Given an integer k and a queue of integers, how do you reverse the order of the first k elements of the queue, leaving the other elements in the same relative order? For example, if $k=4$ and queue has the elements [10, 20, 30, 40, 50, 60, 70, 80, 90]; the output should be [40, 30, 20, 10, 50, 60, 70, 80, 90].

Solution:

```
public static void reverseQueueFirstKElements(int k, Queue<Integer> q) {
    if (q == null || k > q.size()) {
        throw new IllegalArgumentException();
    }
    else if (k > 0) {
        Stack<Integer> s = new Stack<Integer>();
        for (int i = 0; i < k; i++) {
            s.push(q.remove());
        }
        while (!s.isEmpty()) {
            q.add(s.pop());
        }
        for (int i = 0; i < q.size() - k; i++) { // wrap around rest of elements
            q.add(q.remove());
        }
    }
}
```

Time Complexity: $O(n)$. Space Complexity: $O(n)$.

TREES

6.1 What is a Tree?

A *tree* is a data structure similar to a linked list but instead of each node pointing simply to the next node in a linear fashion, each node points to a number of nodes. Tree is an example of non-linear data structures. A *tree* structure is a way of representing the hierarchical nature of a structure in a graphical form.

In trees ADT (Abstract Data Type), order of the elements is not important. If we need ordering information linear data structures like linked lists, stacks, queues, etc. can be used.

6.2 Glossary

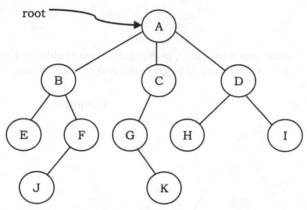

- The *root* of a tree is the node with no parents. There can be at most one root node in a tree (node *A* in the above example).
- An *edge* refers to the link from parent to child (all links in the figure).
- A node with no children is called *leaf* node (E, J, K, H and I).
- Children of same parent are called *siblings* (B, C, D are siblings of A and E, F are the siblings of B).
- A node p is an *ancestor* of node q if there exists a path from *root* to q and p appears on the path. The node q is called a *descendant* of p. For example, A, C and G are the ancestors of K.
- Size of a node is the number of descendants it has including itself (size of the subtree C is 3).
- Set of all nodes at a given depth is called *level* of the tree (B, C and D are same level). The root node is at level zero.

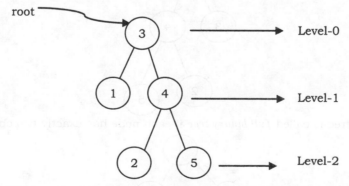

- The *depth* of a node is the length of the path from the root to the node (depth of G is 2, $A - C - G$).
- The *height* of a node is the length of the path from that node to the deepest node. The height of a tree is the length of the path from the root to the deepest node in the tree. A (rooted) tree with only one node (the root) has a height of zero. In the previous example, height of B is 2 ($B - F - J$).

Height of the tree is the maximum height among all the nodes in the tree and *depth of the tree* is the maximum depth among all the nodes in the tree. For a given tree depth and height returns the same value. But for individual nodes we may get different results.

- If every node in a tree has only one child (except leaf nodes) then we call such trees *skew trees*. If every node has only left child then we call them as *left skew trees*. Similarly, if every node has only right child then we call them *right skew trees*.

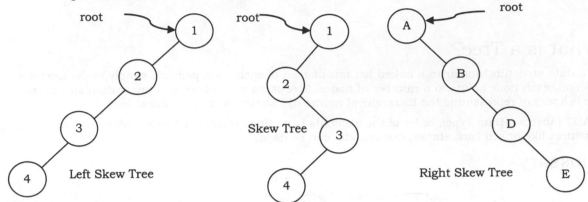

6.3 Binary Trees

A tree is called *binary tree* if each node has zero child, one child or two children. Empty tree is also a valid binary tree. We can visualize a binary tree as consisting of a root and two disjoint binary trees, called the left and right subtrees of the root.

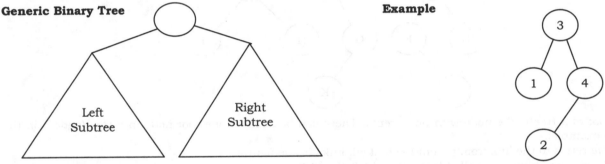

Types of Binary Trees

Strict Binary Tree: A binary tree is called *strict binary tree* if each node has exactly two children or no children.

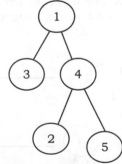

Full Binary Tree: A binary tree is called *full binary tree* if each node has exactly two children and all leaf nodes are at same level.

Complete Binary Tree: Before defining the *complete binary tree,* let us assume that the height of the binary tree is h. In complete binary trees, if we give numbering for the nodes by starting at root (let us say the root node has 1) then we get a complete sequence from 1 to number of nodes in the tree. While traversing we should give numbering for NULL pointers also. A binary tree is called complete binary tree if all leaf nodes are at height h or $h - 1$ and also without any missing number in the sequence.

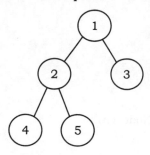

Properties of Binary Trees

For the following properties, let us assume that the height of the tree is h. Also, assume that root node is at height zero.

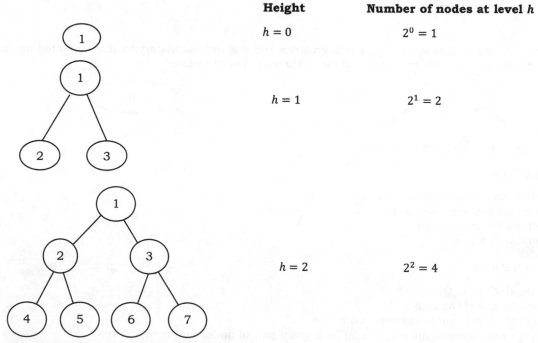

Height	Number of nodes at level h
$h = 0$	$2^0 = 1$
$h = 1$	$2^1 = 2$
$h = 2$	$2^2 = 4$

From the below diagram we can infer the following properties:

- The number of nodes n in a full binary tree is $2^{h+1} - 1$. Since, there are h levels we need to add all nodes at each level $[2^0 + 2^1 + 2^2 + \cdots + 2^h = 2^{h+1} - 1]$.
- The number of nodes n in a complete binary tree is between 2^h (minimum) and $2^{h+1} - 1$ (maximum). For more information on this, refer *Priority Queues* chapter.
- The number of leaf nodes in a full binary tree is 2^h.
- The number of NULL links (wasted pointers) in a complete binary tree of n nodes is $n + 1$.

Structure of Binary Trees

Now let us define structure of the binary tree. For simplicity, assume that the data of the nodes are integers. One way to represent a node (which contains data) is to have two links which points to left and right children along with data fields as shown below:

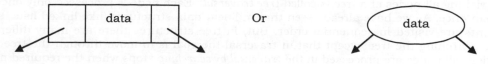

```java
public class BinaryTreeNode {
    private int data;
    private BinaryTreeNode left;
    private BinaryTreeNode right;
    public int getData() {
        return data;
    }
    public void setData(int data) {
        this.data = data;
    }
    public BinaryTreeNode getLeft() {
        return left;
    }
    public void setLeft(BinaryTreeNode left) {
        this.left = left;
    }
    public BinaryTreeNode getRight() {
        return right;
    }
    public void setRight(BinaryTreeNode right) {
        this.right = right;
    }
}
```

Note: In trees, the default flow is from parent to children and it is not mandatory to show directed branches. For our discussion, we assume both the representations shown below are same.

   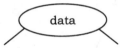

Operations on Binary Trees

Basic Operations

- Inserting an element into a tree
- Deleting an element from a tree
- Searching for an element
- Traversing the tree

Auxiliary Operations

- Finding size of the tree
- Finding height of the tree
- Finding the level which has maximum sum
- Finding least common ancestor (LCA) for a given pair of nodes and many more.

Applications of Binary Trees

Following are the some of the applications where *binary trees* play important role:
- Expression trees are used in compilers.
- Huffman coding trees that are used in data compression algorithms.
- Binary Search Tree (BST), which supports search, insertion and deletion on a collection of items in O(*logn*) (average).
- Priority Queues (PQ), which supports search and deletion of minimum(or maximum) on a collection of items in logarithmic time (in worst case).

6.4 Binary Tree Traversals

In order to process trees, we need a mechanism for traversing them and that forms the subject of this section. The process of visiting all nodes of a tree is called *tree traversal*. Each node is processed only once but it may be visited more than once. As we have already seen that in linear data structures (like linked lists, stacks, queues, etc.), the elements are visited in sequential order. But, in tree structures there are many different ways. Tree traversal is like searching the tree except that in traversal the goal is to move through the tree in a particular order. In addition, all nodes are processed in the *traversal by searching* stops when the required node is found.

Traversal Possibilities

Starting at the root of a binary tree, there are three main steps that can be performed and the order in which they are performed defines the traversal type. These steps are: performing an action on the current node (referred to as "visiting" the node and denoted with "*D*"), traversing to the left child node (denoted with "*L*"), and traversing to the right child node (denoted with "*R*"). This process can be easily described through recursion. Based on the above definition there are 6 possibilities:

1. *LDR*: Process left subtree, process the current node data and then process right subtree
2. *LRD*: Process left subtree, process right subtree and then process the current node data
3. *DLR*: Process the current node data, process left subtree and then process right subtree
4. *DRL*: Process the current node data, process right subtree and then process left subtree
5. *RDL*: Process right subtree, process the current node data and then process left subtree
6. *RLD*: Process right subtree, process left subtree and then process the current node data

Classifying the Traversals

The sequence in which these entities (nodes) processed defines a particular traversal method. The classification is based on the order in which current node is processed. That means, if we are classifying based on current node (*D*) and if *D* comes in the middle then it does not matter whether *L* is on left side of *D* or *R* is on left side of *D*. Similarly, it does not matter whether *L* is on right side of *D* or *R* is on right side of *D*. Due to this, the total 6 possibilities are reduced to 3 and these are:

*   Preorder (*DLR*) Traversal
*   Inorder (*LDR*) Traversal
*   Postorder (*LRD*) Traversal

There is another traversal method which does not depend on above orders and it is:
*   Level Order Traversal: This method is inspired from Breadth First Traversal (BFS of Graph algorithms).

Let us use the diagram below for remaining discussion.

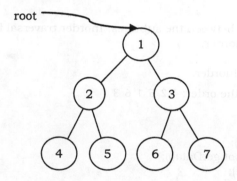

PreOrder Traversal

In pre-order traversal, each node is processed before (pre) either of its sub-trees. This is the simplest traversal to understand. However, even though each node is processed before the subtrees, it still requires that some information must be maintained while moving down the tree. In the example above, 1 is processed first, then the left sub-tree, and this is followed by the right subtree. Therefore, processing must return to the right sub-tree after finishing the processing of the left subtree. To move to right subtree after processing left subtree, we must maintain the root information. The obvious ADT for such information is a stack. Because of its LIFO structure, it is possible to get the information about the right subtrees back in the reverse order.

Preorder traversal is defined as follows:

*   Visit the root.
*   Traverse the left subtree in Preorder.
*   Traverse the right subtree in Preorder.

The nodes of tree would be visited in the order: 1 2 4 5 3 6 7

```
void PreOrder(BinaryTreeNode root){
        if(root != null) {
                System.out.println(root.getData());
                PreOrder(root.getLeft());
                PreOrder(root.getRight());
```

```
        }
}
```

Time Complexity: O(*n*). Space Complexity: O(*n*).

Non-Recursive Preorder Traversal

In recursive version a stack is required as we need to remember the current node so that after completing the left subtree we can go to right subtree. To simulate the same, first we process the current node and before going to left subtree, we store the current node on stack. After completing the left subtree processing, *pop* the element and go to its right subtree. Continue this process until stack is nonempty.

```
void PreOrderNonRecursive(BinaryTreeNode  root){
        if(root == null) return null;
        LLStack S = new LLStack();
        while(true){
                while(root  != null){
                        System.out.println(root.getData());
                        S.push(root);
                        root = root.getLeft();
                }
                if(S.isEmpty())
                        break;
                root = (BinaryTreeNode ) S.pop();
                root = root.getRight();
        }
        return;
}
```

Time Complexity: O(*n*). Space Complexity: O(*n*).

InOrder Traversal

In Inorder traversal the root is visited between the subtrees. Inorder traversal is defined as follows:
*   Traverse the left subtree in Inorder.
*   Visit the root.
*   Traverse the right subtree in Inorder.

The nodes of tree would be visited in the order: 4 2 5 1 6 3 7

```
void InOrder(BinaryTreeNode root){
        if(root != null) {
                InOrder(root.getLeft());
                System.out.println(root.getData());
                InOrder(root.getRight);
        }
}
```

Time Complexity: O(*n*). Space Complexity: O(*n*).

Non-Recursive Inorder Traversal

Non-recursive version of Inorder traversal is similar to Preorder. The only change is, instead of processing the node before going to left subtree, process it after popping (which indicates after completion of left subtree processing).

```
void InOrderNonRecursive(BinaryTreeNode  root ){
        if(root == null) return null;
        LLStack S = new LLStack();
        while(true){
                while(root != null){
                        S.push(root );
                        root = root.getLeft();
                }
                if(stack.isEmpty())
                        break;
                root = (BinaryTreeNode) S.pop();
                System.out.println(root.getData());
```

```
                        root = root.getRight();
                }
                return;
        }
```

Time Complexity: O(n). Space Complexity: O(n).

PostOrder Traversal

In postorder traversal, the root is visited after both subtrees. Postorder traversal is defined as follows:
- Traverse the left subtree in Postorder.
- Traverse the right subtree in Postorder.
- Visit the root.

The nodes of tree would be visited in the order: 4 5 2 6 7 3 1

```
void PostOrder(BinaryTreeNode root){
        if(root != null)    {
                PostOrder(root.getLeft());
                PostOrder(root.getRight());
                System.out.println(root.getData());
        }
}
```

Time Complexity: O(n). Space Complexity: O(n).

Non-Recursive Postorder Traversal

In preorder and inorder traversals, after popping the stack element we do not need to visit the same vertex again. But in postorder traversal, each node is visited twice. That means, after processing left subtree we will visit the current node and after processing the right subtree we will visit the same current node. But we should be processing the node during the second visit. Here the problem is how to differentiate whether we are returning from left subtree or right subtree?

Trick to solving this problem is that after popping an element from stack, check whether that element and right of top of the stack are same or not. If they are same then we have completed the process of left subtree and right subtree. In this case we just need to pop the stack one more time and print its data.

```
void PostOrderNonRecursive(BinaryTreeNode root){
        LLStack S = new LLStack();
        while (1) {
                if  (root != null) {
                        S.push(root);
                        root = root.getLeft();
                }
                else {
                        if(S.isEmpty()) {
                                System.out.println("Stack is Empty");
                                return;
                        }
                        else
                                if(S.top().getRight() == null) {
                                        root= S.pop();
                                        System.out.println(root.getData());
                                        if(root == S.top().getRight()) {
                                                System.out.println(S.top(S.getData()));
                                                S.pop();
                                        }
                                }
                        if(!S.isEmpty())
                                root=S.top().getRight();
                        else    root= null;
                }
        }
        S.deleteStack();
}
```

Time Complexity: O(n). Space Complexity: O(n).

Level Order Traversal

Level order traversal is defined as follows:
- Visit the root.
- While traversing level l, keep all the elements at level l+1 in queue.
- Go to the next level and visit all the nodes at that level.
- Repeat this until all levels are completed.

The nodes of tree would be visited in the order: 1 2 3 4 5 6 7

```java
void LevelOrder(BinaryTreeNode root){
        BinaryTreeNode temp;
        LLQueue Q = new LLQueue();
        if(root == null)
                return;
        Q.enQueue(root);
        while(!Q.isEmpty()) {
                temp = Q.deQueue();
                //Process current node
                System.out.println(temp.getData());
                if(temp.getLeft())
                        Q.enQueue(temp.getLeft());
                if(temp.getRight())
                        Q.enQueue(temp.getRight());

        }
        Q.deleteQueue();
}
```

Time Complexity: $O(n)$. Space Complexity: $O(n)$. Since, in the worst case, all the nodes on the entire last level could be in the queue simultaneously.

Problems on Binary Trees

Problem-1   Give an algorithm for finding maximum element in binary tree.

Solution: One simple way of solving this problem is: find the maximum element in left subtree, find maximum element in right sub tree, compare them with root data and select the one which is giving the maximum value. This approach can be easily implemented with recursion.

```java
int FindMax(BinaryTreeNode  root) {
        int root_val, left, right, max = INT_MIN;
        if(root != null) {
                root_val = root.getData();
                left = FindMax(root.getLeft());
                right = FindMax(root.getRight());
                // Find the largest of the three values.
                if(left > right)
                        max = left;
                else
                        max = right;
                if(root_val > max)
                        max = root_val;
        }
        return max;
}
```

Time Complexity: $O(n)$. Space Complexity: $O(n)$.

Problem-2   Give an algorithm for finding maximum element in binary tree without recursion.

Solution: Using level order traversal: just observe the elements data while deleting.

```java
int FindMaxUsingLevelOrder(BinaryTreeNode root){
        BinaryTreeNode temp;
        int max = INT_MIN;
        LLQueue Q = new LLQueue();
        Q.enQueue(root);
        while(!Q.isEmpty()) {
                temp = Q.deQueue();
```

```
                        //largest of the three values
                        if(max < temp.getData())
                                max = temp.getData();
                        if(temp.getLeft())
                                Q.enQueue(temp.getLeft());
                        if(temp.getRight())
                                Q.enQueue(temp.getRight());
                }
                Q.deleteQueue();
                return max;
        }
```

Time Complexity: O(n). Space Complexity: O(n).

Problem-3   Give an algorithm for searching an element in binary tree.

Solution: Given a binary tree, return true if a node with data is found in the tree. Recurse down the tree, choose the left or right branch by comparing data with each nodes data.

```
Boolean FindInBinaryTreeUsingRecursion(BinaryTreeNode root, int data) {
        Boolean temp;
        // Base case == empty tree, in that case, the data is not found so return false
        if(root == null)
                return false;
        else {    //see if found here
                if(data == root.getData())
                        return true;
                else {    // otherwise recur down the correct subtree
                        temp = FindInBinaryTreeUsingRecursion(root.getLeft(), data)
                        if(temp != true)
                                return temp;
                        else    return(FindInBinaryTreeUsingRecursion(root.getRight(), data));
                }
        }
        return 0;
}
```

Time Complexity: O(n). Space Complexity: O(n).

Problem-4   Give an algorithm for searching an element in binary tree without recursion.

Solution: We can use level order traversal for solving this problem. The only change required in level order traversal is, instead of printing the data we just need to check whether the root data is equal to the element we want to search.

```
Boolean SearchUsingLevelOrder(BinaryTreeNode root, int data){
        BinaryTreeNode temp;
        LLQueue Q = new LLQueue();
        if(root == null) return -1;
        Q.enQueue(root);
        while(!Q.isEmpty()) {
                temp = Q.deQueue();
                //see if found here
                if(data == root.getData())
                        return true;
                if(temp.getLeft())
                        Q.enQueue(temp.getLeft());
                if(temp.getRight())
                        Q.enQueue(temp.getRight());
        }
        Q.deleteQueue();
        return false;
}
```

Time Complexity: O(n). Space Complexity: O(n).

Problem-5   Give an algorithm for inserting an element into binary tree.

Solution: Since the given tree is a binary tree, we can insert the element wherever we want. To insert an element, we can use the level order traversal and insert the element wherever we found the node whose left or right child is NULL.

```java
void InsertInBinaryTree(BinaryTreeNode root, int data){
        LLQueue Q = new LLQueue();
        BinaryTreeNode temp;
        BinaryTreeNode newNode = new BinaryTreeNode();
        newNode.setLeft(null);
        newNode.setRight(null);
        if(newNode == null) {
                System.out.println("Memory Error");
                return;
        }
        if(root == null) {
                root = newNode;
                return;
        }
        Q.enQueue(root);
        while(!Q.isEmpty()) {
                temp = Q.deQueue();
                if(temp.getLeft())
                        Q.enQueue(temp.getLeft());
                else {
                        temp.setLeft(newNode);
                        Q.deleteQueue();
                        return;
                }
                if(temp.getRight())
                        Q.enQueue(temp.getRight());
                else {
                        temp.setRight(newNode);
                        Q.deleteQueue();
                        return;
                }
        }
        Q.deleteQueue();
}
```

Time Complexity: O(n). Space Complexity: O(n).

Problem-6 Give an algorithm for finding the size of binary tree.

Solution: Calculate the size of left and right subtrees recursively, add 1 (current node) and return to its parent.
// Compute the number of nodes in a tree.

```java
int SizeOfBinaryTree(BinaryTreeNode root) {
        if(root == null) return 0;
        else    return(SizeOfBinaryTree(root.getLeft()) + 1 +  SizeOfBinaryTree(root.getRight()));
}
```

Time Complexity: O(n). Space Complexity: O(n).

Problem-7 Can we solve Problem-6 without recursion?

Solution: Yes, using level order traversal.

```java
int SizeofBTUsingLevelOrder(BinaryTreeNode root) {
        BinaryTreeNode temp;
        LLQueue Q = new LLQueue();
        int count = 0;
        if(root == null) return 0;
        Q.enQueue(root);
        while(!Q.isEmpty()) {
                temp = Q.deQueue();
                count++;
                if(temp.getLeft())
                        Q.enQueue(temp.getLeft());
                if(temp.getRight())
```

```
                Q.enQueue(temp.getRight());
        }
        Q.deleteQueue();
        return count;
}
```
Time Complexity: O(n). Space Complexity: O(n).

Problem-8   Give an algorithm for deleting the tree.

Solution: To delete a tree we must traverse all the nodes of the tree and delete them one by one. So which traversal should we use Inorder, Preorder, Postorder or Level order Traversal?

Before deleting the parent node we should delete its children nodes first. We can use postorder traversal as it does the work without storing anything. We can delete tree with other traversals also with extra space complexity. For the following tree nodes are deleted in order – 4, 5, 2, 3, 1.

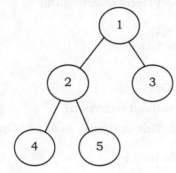

```
void DeleteBinaryTree(BinaryTreeNode root) {
        if(root == null)
                return;
        /* first delete both subtrees */
        DeleteBinaryTree(root.getLeft());
        DeleteBinaryTree(root.getRight());
        //Delete current node only after deleting subtrees
        root = null;                    //In Java, it will be taken care by garbage collector
}
```
Time Complexity: O(n). Space Complexity: O(n).

Problem-9   Give an algorithm for printing the level order data in reverse order. For example, the output for the below tree should be: 4 5 6 7 2 3 1

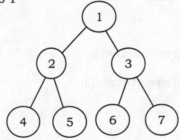

Solution:
```
void LevelOrderTraversalInReverse(BinaryTreeNode root) {
        LLQueue Q = new LLQueue();
        LLStack S = new LLStack();
        BinaryTreeNode temp;
        if(root == null)   return;
        Q.enQueue( root);
        while(!Q.isEmpty()) {
                temp = Q.deQueue();
                if(temp.getRight())
                        Q.enQueue(temp.getRight());
                if(temp.getLeft())
                        Q.enQueue(temp.getLeft());
                S.push(temp);
        }
        while(!S.isEmpty())
```

```
                    System.out.println(S.pop().getData());
}
```

Time Complexity: O(n). Space Complexity: O(n).

Problem-10   Give an algorithm for finding the height (or depth) of the binary tree.

Solution: Recursively calculate height of left and right subtrees of a node and assign height to the node as max of the heights of two children plus 1. This is similar to *PreOrder* tree traversal (and *DFS* of Graph algorithms).

```
int HeightOfBinaryTree(BinaryTreeNode  root) {
        int leftheight, rightheight;
        if(root == null) return 0;
        else {   /* compute the depth of each subtree */
                leftheight = HeightOfBinaryTree(root.getLeft());
                rightheight = HeightOfBinaryTree(root.getRight());
                if(leftheight > rightheight)
                        return (leftheight + 1);
                else     return (rightheight + 1);
        }
}
```

Time Complexity: O(n). Space Complexity: O(n).

Problem-11   Can we solve Problem-10 without recursion?

Solution: Yes. Using level order traversal. This is similar to *BFS* of Graph algorithms. End of level is identified with NULL.
```
int FindHeightofBinaryTree(BinaryTreeNode root) {
        int level=1;
        LLQueue Q = new LLQueue();
        if(root == null)  return 0;
        Q.enQueue(root);
        // End of first level
        Q.enQueue(null);
        while(!Q.isEmpty()) {
                root=Q.deQueue();
                // Completion of current level.
                if(root==null) {
                        //Put another marker for next level.
                        if(!Q.isEmpty())
                                Q.enQueue(null);
                        level++;
                }
                else {  if(root.getLeft())
                                Q.enQueue( root.getLeft());
                        if(root.getRight())
                                Q.enQueue( root.getRight());
                }
        }
        return level;
}
```

Time Complexity: O(n). Space Complexity: O(n).

Problem-12   Give an algorithm for finding the deepest node of the binary tree.

Solution:
```
BinaryTreeNode DeepestNodeinBinaryTree(BinaryTreeNode root) {
        BinaryTreeNode temp;
        LLQueue Q = new LLQueue();
        if(root == null) return null;
        Q.enQueue(root);
        while(!Q.isEmpty()) {
                temp = Q.deQueue();
                if(temp.getLeft())
                        Q.enQueue(temp.getLeft());
                if(temp.getRight())
                        Q.enQueue(temp.getRight());
        }
```

```
            Q.deleteQueue();
            return temp;
}
```

Time Complexity: O(n). Space Complexity: O(n).

Problem-13   Give an algorithm for deleting an element (assuming data is given) from binary tree.

Solution: The deletion of a node in binary tree can be implemented as
- Starting at root, find the node which we want to delete.
- Find the deepest node in the tree.
- Replace the deepest nodes data with node to be deleted.
- Then delete the deepest node.

Problem-14   Give an algorithm for finding the number of leaves in the binary tree without using recursion.

Solution: The set of nodes whose both left and right children are NULL are called leaf nodes.

```
int NumberOfLeavesInBTusingLevelOrder(BinaryTreeNode root) {
        BinaryTreeNode temp;
        LLQueue Q = new LLQueue();
        int count = 0;
        if(root == null)
                return 0;
        Q.enQueue(root);
        while(!Q.isEmpty()) {
                temp = Q.deQueue();
                if(!temp.getLeft() && !temp.getRight())
                        count++;
                else {  if(temp.getLeft())
                                Q.enQueue(temp.getLeft());
                        if(temp.getRight())
                                Q.enQueue(temp.getRight());
                }
        }
        Q.deleteQueue();
        return count;
}
```

Time Complexity: O(n). Space Complexity: O(n).

Problem-15   Give an algorithm for finding the number of full nodes in the binary tree without using recursion.

Solution: The set of all nodes with both left and right children are called full nodes.

```
int NumberOfFullNodesInBTusingLevelOrder(BinaryTreeNode root) {
        BinaryTreeNode temp;
        LLQueue Q = new LLQueue();
        int count = 0;
        if(root == null)
                return 0;
        Q.enQueue(root);
        while(!Q.isEmpty()) {
                temp = Q.deQueue();
                if(temp.getLeft() && temp.getRight())
                        count++;
                if(temp.getLeft())
                        Q.enQueue(temp.getLeft());
                if(temp.getRight())
                        Q.enQueue(temp.getRight());
        }
        Q.deleteQueue();
        return count;
}
```

Time Complexity: O(n). Space Complexity: O(n).

Problem-16   Give an algorithm for finding the number of half nodes (nodes with only one child) in the binary tree without using recursion.

Solution: The set of all nodes with either left or either right child (but not both) are called half nodes.

```java
int NumberOfHalfNodesInBTusingLevelOrder(BinaryTreeNode root) {
        BinaryTreeNode temp;
        LLQueue Q = new LLQueue();
        int count = 0;
        if(root == null) return 0;
        Q.enQueue(root);
        while(!Q.isEmpty()) {
                temp = Q.deQueue();
                //we can use this condition also instead of two temp.getLeft() ^ temp.getRight()
                if(!temp.getLeft() && temp.getRight() || temp.getLeft() && !temp.getRight())
                        count++;
                if(temp.getLeft())
                        Q.enQueue(temp.getLeft());
                if(temp.getRight())
                        Q.enQueue(temp.getRight());
        }
        Q.deleteQueue();
        return count;
}
```

Time Complexity: O(n). Space Complexity: O(n).

Problem-17   Given two binary trees, return true if they are structurally identical.

Solution:
Algorithm:
   - If both trees are NULL then return true.
   - If both trees are not NULL, then compare data and recursively check left and right subtree structures.

```java
//Return true if they are structurally identical.
Boolean AreStructurullySameTrees(BinaryTreeNode root1, BinaryTreeNode root2) {
        // both empty→1
        if(root1== null && root2== null)
                return true;
        if(root1== null || root2== null)
                return false;
        // both non-empty→compare them
        return(root1.getData() == root2.getData() &&
                AreStructurullySameTrees(root1.getLeft(), root2.getLeft()) &&
                AreStructurullySameTrees(root1.getRight(), root2.getRight()));
}
```

Time Complexity: O(n). Space Complexity: O(n), for recursive stack.

Problem-18   Give an algorithm for finding the diameter of the binary tree. The diameter of a tree (sometimes called the *width*) is the number of nodes on the longest path between two leaves in the tree.

Solution: To find the diameter of a tree, first calculate the diameter of left subtree and right sub trees recursively. Among these two values, we need to send maximum value along with current level (+1).

```java
// assume diameter is a static variable in class
int DiameterOfTree(BinaryTreeNode root, int diameter) {
        int left, right;
        if(root == null) return 0;
        left = DiameterOfTree(root.getLeft(), diameter);
        right = DiameterOfTree(root.getRight(), diameter);
        if(left + right > diameter)
                diameter = left + right;
        return Math.max(left, right)+1;
}
```

Time Complexity: O(n). Space Complexity: O(n).

Problem-19   Give an algorithm for finding the level that has the maximum sum in the binary tree.

Solution: The logic is very much similar to finding number of levels. The only change is, we need to keep track of sums as well.

```java
int FindLevelwithMaxSum(BinaryTreeNode root) {
        BinaryTreeNode temp;
        int level=0, maxLevel=0;
```

```
                LLQueue Q = new LLQueue();
                int currentSum = 0, maxSum = 0;
                if(root == null) return 0;
                Q.enQueue(root);
                Q.enQueue(null);                                //End of first level.
                while(!Q.isEmpty()) {
                        temp =Q.deQueue();
                        // If the current level is completed then compare sums
                        if(temp == null) {
                                if(currentSum> maxSum) {
                                        maxSum = currentSum;
                                        maxLevel = level;
                                }
                                currentSum = 0;
                                //place the indicator for end of next level at the end of queue
                                if(!Q.isEmpty())
                                        Q.enQueue(null);
                                level++;
                        }
                        else {  currentSum    += temp.getData();
                                if(temp.getLeft())
                                        temp.enQueue(temp.getLeft());
                                if(root.getRight())
                                        temp.enQueue(temp.getRight());
                        }
                }
        return maxLevel;
}
```

Time Complexity: O(n). Space Complexity: O(n).

Problem-20   Given a binary tree, print out all its root-to-leaf paths.

Solution: Refer comments in functions.

```
public void printPaths() {
        int[] path = new int[256];
        printPaths(node, path, 0);
}
private void printPaths(BinaryTreeNode  node, int[] path, int pathLen) {
        if (node == null) return;
        // append this node to the path array
        path[pathLen] = node.getData();
        pathLen++;
        // it's a leaf, so print the path that led to here
        if (node.getLeft() == null && node.getRight() == null) {
                printArray(path, pathLen);
        }
        else {  // otherwise try both subtrees
                printPaths(node.getLeft(), path, pathLen);
                printPaths(node.getRight(), path, pathLen);
        }
}
private void printArray(int[] ints, int len) {
        for (int i=0; i<len; i++) {
                System.out.print(ints[i] + " ");
        }
        System.out.println();
}
```

Time Complexity: O(n). Space Complexity: O(n), for recursive stack.

Problem-21   Give an algorithm for checking the existence of path with given sum. That means, given a sum check whether there exists a path from root to any of the nodes.

Solution: For this problem, the strategy is: subtract the node value from the sum before calling its children recursively, and check to see if the sum is 0 when we run out of tree.

```
public boolean hasPathSum(int sum) {
```

```
        return(hasPathSum(root, sum));
}
boolean hasPathSum(BinaryTreeNode node, int sum) {
        // return true if we run out of tree and sum==0
        if (node == null)
                return (sum == 0);
        else {    // otherwise check both subtrees
                int subSum = sum – node.getData();
                return(hasPathSum(node.getLeft(), subSum) || hasPathSum(node.getRight(), subSum));
        }
}
```

Time Complexity: O(n). Space Complexity: O(n).

Problem-22   Give an algorithm for finding the sum of all elements in binary tree.

Solution: Recursively, call left subtree sum, right subtree sum and add their values to current nodes data.

```
int Add(BinaryTreeNode  root) {
        if(root == null) return 0;
        else return(root.getData() + Add(root.getLeft()) +  Add(root.getRight()));
}
```

Time Complexity: O(n). Space Complexity: O(n).

Problem-23   Can we solve Problem-22 without recursion?

Solution: We can use level order traversal with simple change. Every time after deleting an element from queue, add the nodes data value to *sum* variable.

```
int SumofBTusingLevelOrder(BinaryTreeNode root){
        BinaryTreeNode temp;
        LLQueue Q = new LLQueue();
        int sum = 0;
        if(root == null)
                return 0;
        Q.enQueue(root);
        while(!Q.isEmpty()) {
                temp = Q.deQueue();
                sum += temp.getData();
                if(temp.getLeft())
                        Q.enQueue(temp.getLeft());
                if(temp.getRight())
                        Q.enQueue(temp.getRight());
        }
        Q.deleteQueue();
        return sum;
}
```

Time Complexity: O(n). Space Complexity: O(n).

Problem-24   Give an algorithm for converting a tree to its mirror. Mirror of a tree is another tree with left and right children of all non-leaf nodes interchanged. The trees below are mirrors to each other.

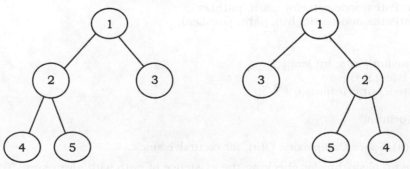

Solution:

```
BinaryTreeNode MirrorOfBinaryTree(BinaryTreeNode root) {
        BinaryTreeNode  temp;
        if(root) {
                MirrorOfBinaryTree(root.getLeft());
```

```
            MirrorOfBinaryTree(root.getRight());
            /* swap the pointers in this node */
            temp = root.getLeft();
            root.setLeft(root.getRight());
            root.setRight(temp);
    }
    return root;
}
```

Time Complexity: O(*n*). Space Complexity: O(*n*).

Problem-25   Given two trees, give an algorithm for checking whether they are mirrors of each other.

Solution:

```
int AreMirrors(BinaryTreeNode root1, BinaryTreeNode root2) {
        if(root1 == null && root2 == null)
                return 1;
        if(root1 == null || root2 == null)
                return 0;
        if(root1.getData() != root2.getData())
                return 0;
        else return (AreMirrors(root1.getLeft(), root2.getRight()) && AreMirrors(root1.getRight(), root2.getLeft()));
}
```

Time Complexity: O(*n*). Space Complexity: O(*n*).

Problem-26   Give an algorithm for constructing binary tree from given Inorder and Preorder traversals.

Solution: Let us consider the traversals below:

Inorder sequence: D B E A F C
Preorder sequence: A B D E C F

In a Preorder sequence, leftmost element denotes the root of the tree. So we know '*A*' is root for given sequences. By searching '*A*' in Inorder sequence we can find out all elements on left side of '*A*', which come under left subtree and elements right side of '*A*', which come under right subtree. So we get the structure as given below.

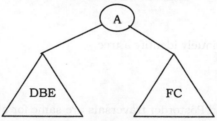

We recursively follow above steps and get the following tree.

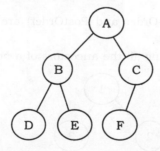

Algorithm: BuildTree()

1   Select an element from Preorder. Increment a Preorder index variable (preIndex in below code) to pick next element in next recursive call.
2   Create a new tree node (newNode) with the data as selected element.
3   Find the selected elements index in Inorder. Let the index be inIndex.
4   Call BuildBinaryTree for elements before inIndex and make the built tree as left subtree of newNode.
5   Call BuildBinaryTree for elements after inIndex and make the built tree as right subtree of newNode.
6   return newNode.

```
BinaryTreeNode BuildBinaryTree(int inOrder[], int preOrder[], int inStrt, int inEnd) {
        static int preIndex = 0;
        BinaryTreeNode newNode = new BinaryTreeNode();
```

```
        if(inStrt > inEnd) return null;
        if(newNode == null) {
                System.out.println("Memory Error");
                return null;
        }
        // Select current node from Preorder traversal using preIndex
        newNode.setData(preOrder[preIndex]);
        preIndex++;
        if(inStrt == inEnd)                        /* if this node has no children then return */
                return newNode;
        /* else find the index of this node in Inorder traversal */
        int inIndex = Search(inOrder, inStrt, inEnd, newNode.getData());
        /* Using index in Inorder traversal, construct left and right subtress */
        newNode.setLeft(BuildBinaryTree(inOrder, preOrder, inStrt, inIndex-1));
        newNode.setRight(BuildBinaryTree(inOrder, preOrder, inIndex+1, inEnd));
        return newNode;
}
```

Time Complexity: $O(n)$. Space Complexity: $O(n)$.

Problem-27   If we are given two traversal sequences, can we construct the binary tree uniquely?

Solution: It depends on what traversals are given. If one of the traversal methods is *Inorder* then the tree can be constructed uniquely, otherwise not.

Therefore, following combination can uniquely identify a tree:
- Inorder and Preorder
- Inorder and Postorder
- Inorder and Level-order

The following combinations do not uniquely identify a tree.
- Postorder and Preorder
- Preorder and Level-order
- Postorder and Level-order

For example, Preorder, Level-order and Postorder traversals are same for above trees:

```
        Preorder Traversal    = AB
        Postorder Traversal   = BA
        Level-order Traversal = AB
```

So, even if three of them (PreOrder, Level-Order and PostOrder) are given, the tree cannot be constructed uniquely.

Problem-28   Give an algorithm for printing all the ancestors of a node in a Binary tree. For the tree below, for 7 the ancestors are 1 3 7.

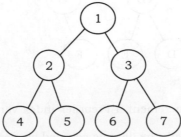

Solution: Apart from the Depth First Search of this tree, we can use the following recursive way to print the ancestors.

```
int PrintAllAncestors(BinaryTreeNode root, BinaryTreeNode node){
        if(root == null)
                return 0;
        if(root.getLeft() == node || root.getRight() == node ||
           PrintAllAncestors(root.getLeft(), node) || PrintAllAncestors(root.getRight(), node)) {
```

```
            System.out.println(root.getData());
            return 1;
        }
        return 0;
}
```

Time Complexity: O(*n*). Space Complexity: O(*n*) for recursion.

Problem-29   Give an algorithm for finding LCA (Least Common Ancestor) of two nodes in a Binary Tree.

Solution:
```
BinaryTreeNode LCA(BinaryTreeNode root, BinaryTreeNode α, BinaryTreeNode β) {
        BinaryTreeNode left, right;
        if(root == null)
                return root;
        if(root == α || root == β)
            return root;
        left = LCA(root.getLeft(), α, β );
        right = LCA(root.getRight(), α, β );

        if(left && right) return root;
        else      return(left? left: right)
}
```
Time Complexity: O(*n*). Space Complexity: O(*n*) for recursion.

Problem-30   **Zigzag Tree Traversal:** Give an algorithm to traverse a binary tree in Zigzag order. For example, the output for the tree below should be: 1 3 2 4 5 6 7

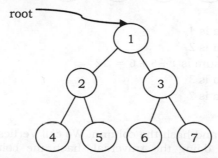

Solution: This problem can be solved easily using two stacks. Let us say the two stacks are: *currentLevel* and *nextLevel*. We would also need a variable to keep track of the current level order (whether it is left to right or right or left). We pop from *currentLevel* stack and print the nodes value. Whenever the current level order is from left to right, push the nodes left child, then its right child to stack *nextLevel*. Since a stack is a Last In First OUT (*LIFO*) structure, next time when nodes are popped off nextLevel, it will be in the reverse order.

On the other hand, when the current level order is from right to left, we would push the nodes right child first, then its left child. Finally, don't forget to swap those two stacks at the end of each level (i.e., when *currentLevel* is empty).

```
void ZigZagTraversal(BinaryTreeNode root) {
        BinaryTreeNode temp;
        int leftToRight = 1;
        if(root == null)
            return;
        Stack currentLevel currentLevel = new CreateStack(), nextLevel = new CreateStack();
        Push(currentLevel, root);
        while(!isEmpty(currentLevel)) {
                temp = Pop(currentLevel);
                if(temp) {
                        System.out.println(temp.getData());
                        if(leftToRight) {
                                if(temp.getLeft())
                                        Push(nextLevel, temp.getLeft());
                                if(temp.getRight())
                                        Push(nextLevel, temp.getRight());
                        }
                        else {  if(temp.getRight())
                                        Push(nextLevel, temp.getRight());
```

```
                              if(temp.getLeft())
                                  Push(nextLevel, temp.getLeft());
                  }
          }
          if(isEmpty(currentLevel)) {
                  leftToRight = 1-leftToRight;
                  swap(currentLevel, nextLevel);
          }
      }
}
```

Time Complexity: $O(n)$. Space Complexity: Space for two stacks = $O(n) + O(n) = O(n)$.

Problem-31   Give an algorithm for finding the vertical sum of a binary tree. For example,

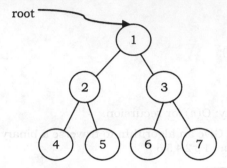

The tree has 5 vertical lines
       Vertical-1: nodes-4 => vertical sum is 4
       Vertical-2: nodes-2 => vertical sum is 2
       Vertical-3: nodes-1,5,6 => vertical sum is $1 + 5 + 6 = 12$
       Vertical-4: nodes-3 => vertical sum is 3
       Vertical-5: nodes-7 => vertical sum is 7
       We need to output: 4 2 12 3 7

Solution: We can do an inorder traversal and hash the column. We call VerticalSumInBinaryTree(root, 0) which means the root is at column 0. While doing the traversal, hash the column and increase its value by *root.getData()*.

```
void VerticalSumInBinaryTree(BinaryTreeNode root, int column) {
      if(root==null)
            return;
      VerticalSumInBinaryTree(root.getLeft(), column-1);
      //Refer Hashing chapter for implementation of hash table
      Hash[column] += root.getData();
      VerticalSumInBinaryTree(root.getRight(), column+1);
}
VerticalSumInBinaryTree(root, 0);
Print Hash;
```

Problem-32   How many different binary trees are possible with n nodes?

Solution: For example, consider a tree with 3 nodes ($n = 3$). It will have the maximum combination of 5 different (i.e., $2^3 - 3 = 5$) trees.

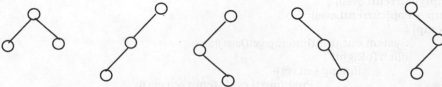

In general, if there are n nodes, there exist $2^n - n$ different trees.

Problem-33   Given a tree with a special property where leaves are represented with 'L' and internal node with 'I'. Also, assume that each node has either 0 or 2 children. Given preorder traversal of this tree, construct the tree.

    Example: Given preorder string => ILILL

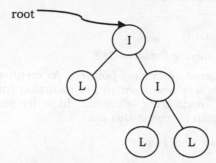

Solution: First, we should see how preorder traversal is arranged. Pre-order traversal means first put root node, then pre-order traversal of left subtree and then pre-order traversal of right subtree. In normal scenario, it's not possible to detect where left subtree ends and right subtree starts using only pre-order traversal. Since every node has either 2 children or no child, we can surely say that if a node exists then its sibling also exists. So every time when we are computing a subtree, we need to compute its sibling subtree as well.

Secondly, whenever we get 'L' in the input string, that is a leaf and we can stop for a particular subtree at that point. After this 'L' node (left child of its parent 'L'), its sibling starts. If 'L' node is right child of its parent, then we need to go up in the hierarchy to find next subtree to compute. Keeping above invariant in mind, we can easily determine when a subtree ends and the next one starts. It means that we can give any start node to our method and it can easily complete the subtree it generates going outside of its nodes. We just need to take care of passing correct start nodes to different sub-trees.

```java
BinaryTreeNode BuildTreeFromPreOrder(char[] A, int i) {
        if(A == null)                          //Boundary Condition
                return null;
        BinaryTreeNode newNode = new BinaryTreeNode();
        newNode.setData(A[i]);
        newNode.setLeft(null);
        newNode.setRight(null);
        if(A[i] == 'L')                        //On reaching leaf node, return
                return newNode;
        i = i + 1;                             //Populate left sub tree
        newNode.setLeft(BuildTreeFromPreOrder(A, i));
        i = i + 1;                             //Populate right sub tree
        newNode.setRight(BuildTreeFromPreOrder(A, i));
        return newNode;
}
```

Time Complexity: O(n).

Problem-34   Given a binary tree with three pointers (left, right and nextSibling), give an algorithm for filling the *nextSibling* pointers assuming they are NULL initially.

Solution: We can use simple queue.

```java
void FillNextSiblings(BinaryTreeNode root) {
        LLQueue Q = new LLQueue();
        BinaryTreeNode temp;
        if(root == null)  return 0;
        Q.enQueue(root);
        Q.enQueue(null);
        while(!Q.isEmpty()) {
                root=Q.deQueue();
                // Completion of current level.
                if(root == null) { //Put another marker for next level.
                        if(!Q.isEmpty())
                                Q.enQueue(null);
                }
                else {   temp.setNextSibling(Q.getFront());
                        if(root.getLeft())
                                Q.enQueue( root.getLeft());
                        if(root.getRight())
                                Q.enQueue( root.getRight());
                }
        }
}
```

}

Time Complexity: O(*n*). Space Complexity: O(*n*).

Problem-35   Is there any other way of solving Problem-34?

Solution: The trick is to re-use the populated *nextSibling* pointers. As mentioned earlier, we just need one more step for it to work. Before we passed the *left* and *right* to the recursion function itself, we connect the right childs *nextSibling* to the current nodes nextSibling left child. In order for this to work, the current node *nextSibling* pointer must be populated, which is true in this case.

```
void FillNextSiblings(BinaryTreeNode root) {
        if (root == null) return;
        if (root.getLeft())
                root.getLeft().setNextSibling(root.getRight());
        if (root.getRight())
                if(root.getNextSibling())
                        root.getRight().setNextSibling(root.getNextSibling().getLeft());
                else       root.getRight().setNextSibling(null);
        FillNextSiblings(root.getLeft());
        FillNextSiblings(root.getRight());
}
```

Time Complexity: O(*n*).

6.5 Generic Trees (N-ary Trees)

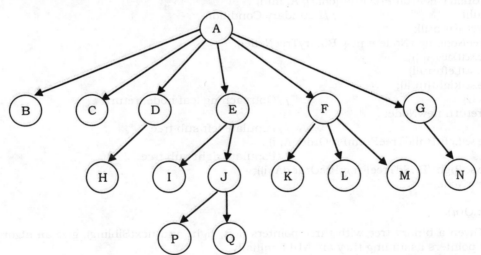

In the previous section we discussed binary trees where each node can have maximum of two children and these are represented easily with two pointers. But suppose if we have a tree with many children at every node and also if we do not know how many children a node can have, how do we represent them? For example, consider the tree shown above.

How do we represent the tree?

In the above tree, there are nodes with 6 children, with 3 children, 2 children, with 1 child, and with zero children (leaves). To present this tree we have to consider the worst case (6 children) and allocate those many child pointers for each node. Based on this, the node representation can be given as:

```
public class TreeNode {
        public int data;
        public TreeNode firstChild;
        public TreeNode secondChild;
        public TreeNode thirdChild;
        public TreeNode fourthChild;
        public TreeNode fifthChild;
        public TreeNode sixthChild;
        .....
}
```

Since we are not using all the pointers in all the cases there is a lot of memory wastage. Also, another problem is that, in advance we do not know the number of children for each node.

In order to solve this problem we need a representation that minimizes the wastage and also accept nodes with any number of children.

Representation of Generic Trees

Since our objective is to reach all nodes of the tree, a possible solution to this is as follows:

- At each node link children of same parent (siblings) from left to right.
- Remove the links from parent to all children except the first child.

What these above statements say is if we have a link between children then we do not need extra links from parent to all children. This is because we can traverse all the elements by starting at the first child of the parent. So if we have link between parent and first child and also links between all children of same parent then it solves our problem.

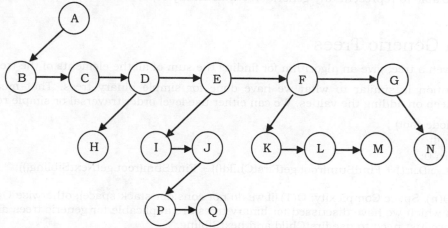

This representation is sometimes called first child/next sibling representation. First child/next sibling representation of the generic tree is shown above. The actual representation for this tree is:

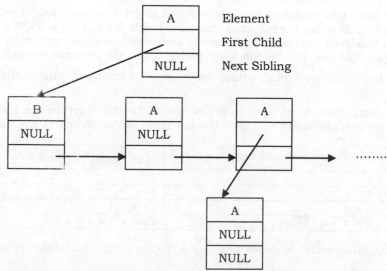

Based on this discussion, the tree node declaration for general tree can be given as:

```java
public class TreeNode {
        public int data;
        public TreeNode firstChild;
        public TreeNode nextSibling;
        public int getData() {
                return data;
        }
        public void setData(int data) {
                this.data = data;
        }
        public BinaryTreeNode getFirstChild() {
```

```
                    return firstChild;
        }
        public void setFirstChild(BinaryTreeNode firstChild) {
                this.firstChild = firstChild;
        }
        public BinaryTreeNode getNextSibling () {
                return nextSibling;
        }
        public void setNextSibling(BinaryTreeNode nextSibling) {
                this.nextSibling = nextSibling;
        }
}
```

Note: Since we are able to represent any generic tree with binary representation, in practice we use only binary tree.

Problems on Generic Trees

Problem-36   Given a tree, give an algorithm for finding the sum of all the elements of the tree.

Solution: The solution is similar to what we have done for simple binary trees. That means, traverse the complete list and keep on adding the values. We can either use level order traversal or simple recursion.

```
int FindSum(TreeNode root) {
        if(root == null)
                return 0;
        return root.getData() + FindSum(root.getFirstChild()) + FindSum(root.getNextSibling());
}
```

Time Complexity: $O(n)$. Space Complexity: $O(1)$ (if we do not consider stack space), otherwise $O(n)$.
Note: All problems which we have discussed for binary trees are applicable for generic trees also. Instead of left and right pointers we just need to use firstChild and nextSibling.

Problem-37   For a 4-ary tree (each node can contain maximum of 4 children), what is the maximum possible height with 100 nodes? Assume height of a single node is 0.

Solution: In 4-ary tree each node can contain 0 to 4 children and to get maximum height, we need to keep only one child for each parent. With 100 nodes the maximum possible height we can get is 99. If we have a restriction that at least one node has 4 children, then we keep one node with 4 children and remaining nodes with 1 child. In this case, the maximum possible height is 96. Similarly, with n nodes the maximum possible height is $n - 4$.

Problem-38   For a 4-ary tree (each node can contain maximum of 4 children), what is the minimum possible height with n nodes?

Solution: Similar to above discussion, if we want to get minimum height, then we need to fill all nodes with maximum children (in this case 4). Now let's see the following table, which indicates the maximum number of nodes for a given height.

Height, h	Maximum Nodes at height, $h = 4^h$	Total Nodes height $h = \frac{4^{h+1}-1}{3}$
0	1	1
1	4	1+4
2	4×4	$1 + 4 \times 4$
3	$4 \times 4 \times 4$	$1 + 4 \times 4 + 4 \times 4 \times 4$

For a given height h the maximum possible nodes are: $\frac{4^{h+1}-1}{3}$. To get minimum height, take logarithm on both sides:

$$n = \frac{4^{h+1}-1}{3} \implies 4^{h+1} = 3n + 1 \implies (h+1)log4 = log(3n + 1)$$
$$\implies h + 1 = log_4(3n + 1) \implies h = log_4(3n + 1) - 1$$

Problem-39   Given a parent array P, where $P[i]$ indicates the parent of ith node in the tree (assume parent of root node is indicated with -1). Give an algorithm for finding the height or depth of the tree.

Solution: From the problem definition, the given array represents the parent array. That means, we need to consider the tree for that array and find the depth of the tree.

For example: if the P is

-1	0	1	6	6	0	0	2	7
0	1	2	3	4	5	6	7	8

Its corresponding tree is:

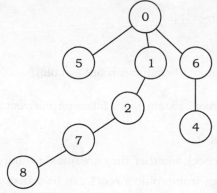

The depth of this given tree is 4. If we carefully observe, we just need to start at every node and keep going to its parent until we reach −1 and also keep track of the maximum depth among all nodes.

```
int FindDepthInGenericTree(int P[], int n) {
        int maxDepth =-1, currentDepth =-1, j;
        for(int i = 0; i < n; i++)   {
                currentDepth = 0; j = i;
                while(P[j] != -1) {
                        currentDepth++; j = P[j];
                }
                if(currentDepth > maxDepth)
                        maxDepth = currentDepth;
        }
        return maxDepth;
}
```

Time Complexity: $O(n^2)$. For skew trees we will be calculating the same values again and again. Space Complexity: $O(1)$.

Note: We can optimize the code by storing the previous calculated nodes depth in some hash table or other array. This reduces the time complexity but uses extra space.

Problem-40   Given a node in the generic tree. Give an algorithm for counting the number of siblings for that node.

Solution: For a given node in the tree, we just need to traverse all its nextsiblings.

```
int SiblingsCount(TreeNode current) {
        int count = 0;
        while(current)   {
                count++;
                current = current.getNextSibling();
        }
        reutrn count;
}
```

Time Complexity: $O(n)$. Space Complexity: $O(1)$.

Problem-41   Given two trees how do we check whether the trees are isomorphic to each other or not?

Solution: Two binary trees *root*1 and *root*2 are isomorphic if they have the same structure. The values of the nodes does not affect whether two trees are isomorphic or not. In the diagram below, the tree in the middle is not isomorphic to the other trees, but the tree on the right is isomorphic to the tree on the left.

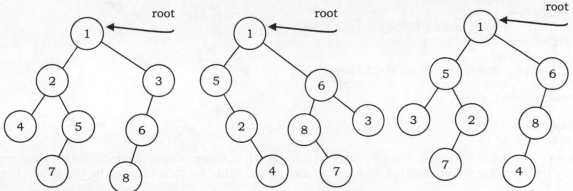

```java
int IsIsomorphic(TreeNode  root1, TreeNode root2) {
        if(root1 == null && root2 == null)
                return 1;
        if((root1 == null && root2 != null) || (root1 != null && root2 == null))
                return 0;
        return (IsIsomorphic(root1.getLeft(), root2.getLeft())  && IsIsomorphic(root1.getRight(), root2.getRight()));
}
```

Time Complexity: O(n). Space Complexity: O(n).

Problem-42   Given two trees how do we check whether they are quasi-isomorphic to each other or not?

Solution: Two trees *root*1 and *root*2 are quasi-isomorphic if *root*1 can be transformed into *root*2 by swapping left and right children of some of the nodes of *root*1. Data in the nodes are not important in determining quasi-isomorphism, only the shape is important. The trees below are quasi-isomorphic because if the children of the nodes on the left are swapped, the tree on the right is obtained.

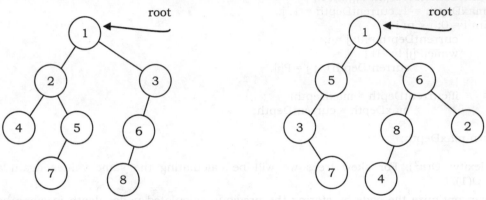

```java
int QuasiIsomorphic(TreeNode  root1, TreeNode  root2) {
        if(root1 == null && root2 == null)
                return true;
        if((root1 == null && root2 != null) || (root1 != null && root2 == null))
                return false;
        return (QuasiIsomorphic(root1.getLeft(), root2.getLeft()) &&
                QuasiIsomorphic(root1.getRight(), root2.getRight()) ||
                QuasiIsomorphic(root1.getRight(), root2.getLeft()) &&
                QuasiIsomorphic(root1.getLeft(), root2.getRight()));
}
```

Time Complexity: O(n). Space Complexity: O(n).

Problem-43   Given a node in the generic tree, give an algorithm for counting the number of children for that node.

Solution: For a given node in the tree, we just need to point to its first child and keep traversing all its nextsiblings.

```java
int ChildCount(TreeNode current) {
        int count = 0;
        current = current.getFirstChild();
        while(current != null)    {
                count++;
                current = current.getNextSibling();
        }
        reutrn count;
}
```

Time Complexity: O(n).
Space Complexity: O(1).

Problem-44   A full k −ary tree is a tree where each node has either 0 or k children. Given an array which contains the preorder traversal of full k −ary tree, give an algorithm for constructing the full k −ary tree.

Solution: In k −ary tree, for a node at i^{th} position its children will be at $k * i + 1$ to $k * i + k$. For example, the example below is for full 3-ary tree.

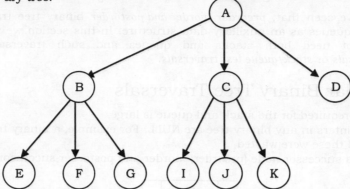

As we have seen, in preorder traversal first left subtree is processed then followed by root node and right subtree. Because of this, to construct a full k-ary, we just need to keep on creating the nodes without bothering about the previous constructed nodes. We can use this trick to build the tree recursively by using one global index. Declaration for k-ary tree can be given as:

```java
public class K-aryTreeNode {
        public int data;
        public K-aryTreeNode[] child;
        public K-aryTreeNode(int k){
                child = new K-aryTreeNode[k];
        }
        public void setData(int dataInput){
                data = dataInput;
        }
        public int getChild(){
                return data;
        }
        public void setChild(int i, K-aryTreeNode childNode){
                child[i]= childNode;
        }
        public K-aryTreeNode getChild(int i){
                return child[i];
        }
        ...
}
int Ind = 0;
K-aryTreeNode BuildK-aryTree(int A[], int n, int k) {
        if(n <= 0)
                return null;
        K-aryTreeNode newNode = new K-aryTreeNode(k);
        if(newNode == null) {
                System.out.println("Memory Error");
                return;
        }
        newNode.setData(A[Ind]);
        for(int i = 0; i<k; i++) {
                if(k * Ind + i <n) {
                        Ind++;
                        newNode.setChild(BuildK-aryTree(A, n, k,Ind ));
                }
                else  newNode.setChild(null);
        }
        return newNode;
}
```

Time Complexity: $O(n)$, where n is the size of the pre-order array. This is because we are moving sequentially and not visiting the already constructed nodes.

6.6 Threaded [Stack or Queue less] Binary Tree Traversals

In earlier sections we have seen that, *preorder, inorder and postorder* binary tree traversals used stacks and *level order* traversal used queues as an auxiliary data structure. In this section we will discuss new traversal algorithms which do not need both stacks and queues and such traversal algorithms are called *threaded binary tree traversals* or *stack/queue less traversals*.

Issues with Regular Binary Tree Traversals

- The storage space required for the stack and queue is large.
- The majority of pointers in any binary tree are NULL. For example, a binary tree with n nodes has $n + 1$ NULL pointers and these were wasted.
- It is difficult to find successor node (preorder, inorder and postorder successors) for a given node.

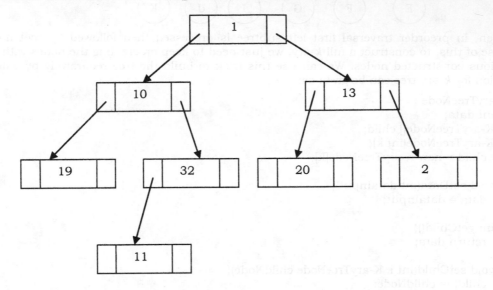

Motivation for Threaded Binary Trees

To solve these problems, one idea is to store some useful information in NULL pointers. If we observe previous traversals carefully, stack/queue is required because we have to record the current position in order to move to right subtree after processing the left subtree. If we store the useful information in NULL pointers, then we don't have to store such information in stack/queue. The binary trees which store such information in NULL pointers are called *threaded binary trees*. From the above discussion, let us assume that we want to store some useful information in NULL pointers. The next question is what to store?

The common convention is to put predecessor/successor information. That means, if we are dealing with preorder traversals then for a given node, NULL left pointer will contain preorder predecessor information and NULL right pointer will contain preorder successor information. These special pointers are called *threads*.

Classifying Threaded Binary Trees

The classification is based on whether we are storing useful information in both NULL pointers or only in one of them.

- If we store predecessor information in NULL left pointers only then we call such binary trees as *left threaded binary trees*.
- If we store successor information in NULL right pointers only then we call such binary trees as *right threaded binary trees*.
- If we store predecessor information in NULL left pointers only then we call such binary trees as *fully threaded binary trees* or simply *threaded binary trees*.

Note: For the remaining discussion we consider only (*fully*) *threaded binary trees*.

Types of Threaded Binary Trees

Based on above discussion we get three representations for threaded binary trees.

- *Preorder Threaded Binary Trees*: NULL left pointer will contain PreOrder predecessor information and NULL right pointer will contain PreOrder successor information

- *Inorder Threaded Binary Trees*: NULL left pointer will contain InOrder predecessor information and NULL right pointer will contain InOrder successor information
- *Postorder Threaded Binary Trees*: NULL left pointer will contain PostOrder predecessor information and NULL right pointer will contain PostOrder successor information

Note: As the representations are similar, for the remaining discussion we will use InOrder threaded binary trees.

Threaded Binary Tree structure

Any program examining the tree must be able to differentiate between a regular *left/right* pointer and a *thread*. To do this, we use two additional fields into each node giving us, for threaded trees, nodes of the following form:

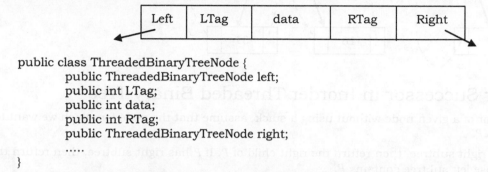

```
public class ThreadedBinaryTreeNode {
        public ThreadedBinaryTreeNode left;
        public int LTag;
        public int data;
        public int RTag;
        public ThreadedBinaryTreeNode right;
        .....
}
```

Difference between Binary Tree and Threaded Binary Tree Structures

	Regular Binary Trees	Threaded Binary Trees
if LTag == 0	NULL	left points to the in-order predecessor
if LTag == 1	left points to the left child	left points to left child
if RTag == 0	NULL	right points to the in-order successor
if RTag == 1	right points to the right child	right points to the right child

Note: Similarly, we can define for preorder/postorder differences as well.

As an example, let us try representing a tree in inorder threaded binary tree form. The tree below shows what an inorder threaded binary tree will look like. The dotted arrows indicate the threads. If we observe, the left pointer of left most node (2) and right pointer of right most node (31) are hanging.

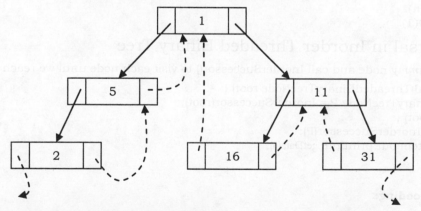

What should leftmost and rightmost pointers point to?

In the representation of a threaded binary tree, it is convenient to use a special node *Dummy* which is always present even for an empty tree. Note that right tag of dummy node is 1 and its right child points to itself.

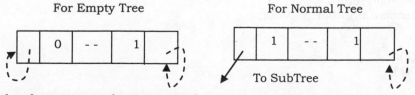

For Empty Tree   For Normal Tree

To SubTree

With this convention the above tree can be represented as:

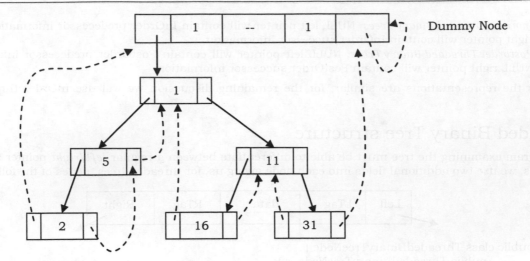

Finding Inorder Successor in Inorder Threaded Binary Tree

To find inorder successor of a given node without using a stack, assume that the node for which we want to find the inorder successor is P.

Strategy: If P has a no right subtree, then return the right child of P. If P has right subtree, then return the left of the nearest node whose left subtree contains P.

```
ThreadedBinaryTreeNode InorderSuccessor(ThreadedBinaryTreeNode P) {
        ThreadedBinaryTreeNode Position;
        if(P→RTag == 0)
                return P.getRight();
        else {
                Position = P.getRight();
                while(Position.getLTag() == 1)
                        Position = Position.getLeft();
                return Position;
        }
}
```

Time Complexity: O(n).
Space Complexity: O(1).

Inorder Traversal in Inorder Threaded Binary Tree

We can start with *dummy* node and call InorderSuccessor() to visit each node until we reach *dummy* node.

```
void InorderTraversal(ThreadedBinaryTreeNode root) {
        ThreadedBinaryTreeNode P = InorderSuccessor(root);
        while(P != root) {
                P = InorderSuccessor(P);
                System.out.println(P.getData());
        }
}
```

Alternative way of coding:

```
void InorderTraversal(ThreadedBinaryTreeNode root) {
        ThreadedBinaryTreeNode P = root;
        while(1) {
                P = InorderSuccessor(P);
                if(P == root) return;
                System.out.println(P.getData());
        }
}
```

Time Complexity: O(n).
Space Complexity: O(1).

Finding PreOrder Successor in InOrder Threaded Binary Tree

Strategy: If *P* has a left subtree, then return the left child of *P*. If *P* has no left subtree, then return the right child of the nearest node whose right subtree contains *P*.

```
ThreadedBinaryTreeNode* PreorderSuccessor(ThreadedBinaryTreeNode P) {
        ThreadedBinaryTreeNode Position;
        if(P.getLTag() == 1)  return P.getLeft();
        else {
                Position = P;
                while(Position.getRTag() == 0)
                        Position = Position.getRight();
                return Position.getRight();
        }
}
```

Time Complexity: O(*n*). Space Complexity: O(1).

PreOrder Traversal of InOrder Threaded Binary Tree

As in inorder traversal, start with *dummy* node and call PreorderSuccessor() to visit each node until we get *dummy* node again.

```
void PreorderTraversal(ThreadedBinaryTreeNode root) {
        ThreadedBinaryTreeNode P;
        P = PreorderSuccessor(root);
        while(P != root) {
                P = PreorderSuccessor(P);
                System.out.println(P.getData());
        }
}
```

Alternative way of coding:
```
void PreorderTraversal(ThreadedBinaryTreeNode root) {
        ThreadedBinaryTreeNode P = root;
        while(1) {
                P = PreorderSuccessor(P);
                if(P == root) return;
                System.out.println(P.getData());
        }
}
```

Time Complexity: O(*n*). Space Complexity: O(1).

Note: From the above discussion, it should be clear that inorder and preorder successor finding is easy with threaded binary trees. But finding postorder successor is very difficult if we do not use stack.

Insertion of Nodes in InOrder Threaded Binary Trees

For simplicity, let us assume that there are two nodes *P* and *Q* and we want to attach *Q* to right of *P*. For this we will have two cases.

- Node *P* does not have right child: In this case we just need to attach *Q* to *P* and change its left and right pointers.

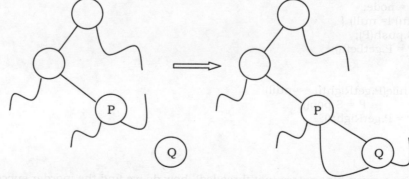

- Node *P* has right child (say, *R*): In this case we need to traverse *R's* left subtree and find the left most node and then update the left and right pointer of that node (as shown below).

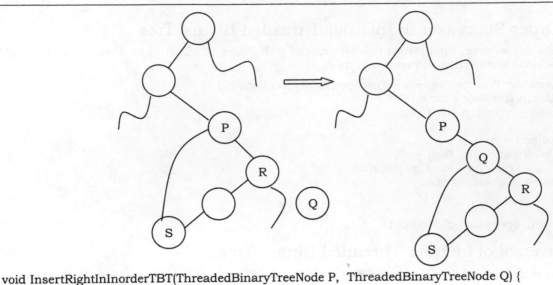

```
void InsertRightInInorderTBT(ThreadedBinaryTreeNode P,  ThreadedBinaryTreeNode Q) {
      ThreadedBinaryTreeNode Temp;
      Q.setRight(P.getRight());
      Q.setRTag(P.getRTag());
      Q.setLeft(P);
      Q.setLTag(0);
      P.setRight(Q);
      P.setRTag( 1);
      if(Q.getRTag() == 1) {                                        //Case-2
             Temp = Q.getRight();
             while(Temp.getLTag())
                     Temp = Temp.getLeft();
             Temp.setLeft(Q);
      }
}
```

Time Complexity: O(*n*). Space Complexity: O(1).

Problems on Threaded binary Trees

Problem-45   For a given binary tree (not threaded) how do we find the preorder successor?

Solution: For solving this problem, we need to use an auxiliary stack S. On the first call, the parameter node is a pointer to the head of the tree, thereafter its value is NULL. Since we are simply asking for the successor of the node we got last time we called the function. It is necessary that the contents of the stack S and the pointer P to the last node "visited" are preserved from one call of the function to the next; they are defined as static variables.

```
// pre-order successor for an unthreaded binary tree
BinaryTreeNode PreorderSuccssor(BinaryTreeNode node) {
      static BinaryTreeNode P;
      LLStack S = new LLStack();
      if(node != null)
             P = node;
      if(P.getLeft() != null) {
             S.push(P);
             P = P.getLeft();
      }
      else {
             while(P.getRight() == null)
                     P = S.pop();
             P = P.getRight();
      }
      return P;
}
```

Problem-46   For a given binary tree (not threaded) how do we find the inorder successor?

Solution: Similar to above discussion, we can find the inorder successor of a node as:
// In-order successor for an unthreaded binary tree

```
BinaryTreeNode InorderSuccssor(BinaryTreeNode node) {
        static BinaryTreeNode P;
        LLStack S = new LLStack();
        if(node != null)
                P = node;
        if(P.getRight() == null)
                P = S.pop();
        else {
                P = P.getRight();
                while(P.getLeft() != null)
                        S.push(P);
                P = P.getLeft();
        }
        return P;
}
```

6.7 Expression Trees

A tree representing an expression is called an *expression tree*. In expression trees leaf nodes are operands and non-leaf nodes are operators. That means, an expression tree is a binary tree where internal nodes are operators and leaves are operands. Expression tree consists of binary expression. But for a u-nary operator, one subtree will be empty. The figure below shows a simple expression tree for (A + B * C) / D.

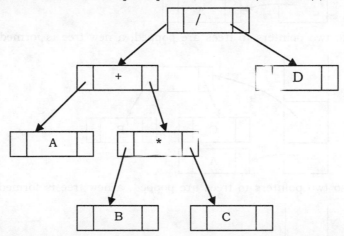

Algorithm for Building Expression Tree from Postfix Expression

```
BinaryTreeNode BuildExprTree(char postfixExpr[], int size) {
        LLStack S = new LLStack();
        for(int i = 0; i< size; i++) {
                if(postfixExpr[i] is an operand) {
                        BinaryTreeNode newNode = new BinaryTreeNode();
                        if(newNode == null) {
                                System.out.println("Memory Error");
                                return null;
                        }
                        newNode.setData(postfixExpr[i]);
                        newNode.setLeft(null);
                        newNode.setRight(null);
                        S.push(newNode);
                }
                else {  BinaryTreeNode T2 = S.pop(), T1 = S.pop();
                        BinaryTreeNode newNode = new BinaryTreeNode();
                        if(newNode == null) {
                                System.out.println("Memory Error");
                                return null;
                        }
                        newNode.setData(postfixExpr[i]);
                        //Make T2 as right child and T1 as left child for new node
```

```
                    newNode.setLeft(T1); newNode.setRight(T2);
                    S.push(newNode);
            }
    }
    return S;
}
```

Example

Assume that one symbol is read at a time. If the symbol is an operand, we create a tree node and push a pointer to it onto a stack. If the symbol is an operator, pop pointers to two trees T_1 and T_2 from the stack (T_1 is popped first) and forms a new tree whose root is the operator and whose left and right children point to T_2 and T_1 respectively. A pointer to this new tree is then pushed onto the stack. As an example, assume the input is A B C * + D /. The first three symbols are operands, so create tree nodes and push pointers to them onto a stack as shown below.

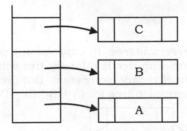

Next, an operator '*' is read, so two pointers to trees are popped, a new tree is formed and a pointer to it is pushed onto the stack.

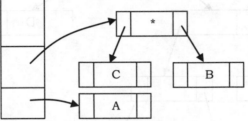

Next, an operator '+' is read, so two pointers to trees are popped, a new tree is formed and a pointer to it is pushed onto the stack.

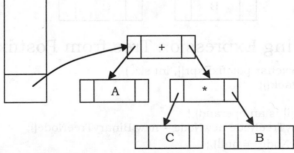

Next, an operand 'D' is read, a one-node tree is created and a pointer to the corresponding tree is pushed onto the stack.

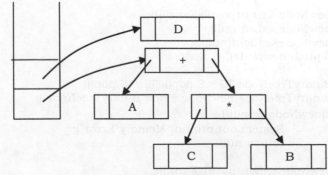

Finally, the last symbol ('/') is read, two trees are merged and a pointer to the final tree is left on the stack.

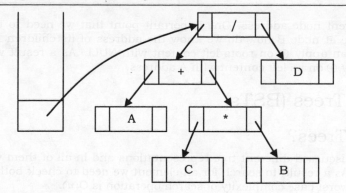

6.8 XOR Trees

This concept is similar to *memory efficient doubly linked lists* of *Linked Lists* chapter. Also, like threaded binary trees this representation does not need stacks or queues for traversing the trees. This representation is used for traversing back (to parent) and forth (to children) using $\oplus$ operation. To represent the same in XOR trees, for each node below are the rules used for representation:

- Each nodes left will have the $\oplus$ of its parent and its left children.
- Each nodes right will have the $\oplus$ of its parent and its right children.
- The root nodes parent is NULL and also leaf nodes children are NULL nodes.

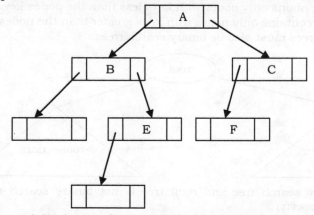

Based on the above rules and discussion the tree can be represented as:

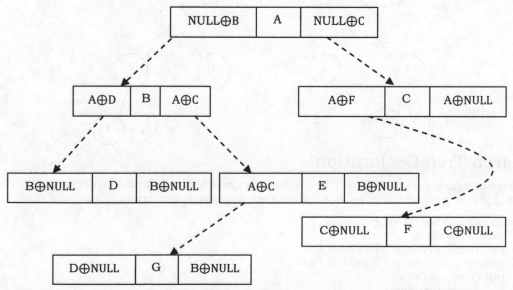

The major objective of this presentation is ability to move to parent as well to children. Now, let us see how to use this representation for traversing the tree. For example, if we are at node B and want to move to its parent node A, then we just need to perform $\oplus$ on its left content with its left child address (we can use right child also for going to parent node). Similarly, if we want to move to its child (say, left child D) then we have to perform $\oplus$

on its left content with its parent node address. One important point that we need to understand about this representation is: When we are at node B how do we know the address of its children D? Since the traversal starts at node root node, we can apply ⊕ on roots left content with NULL. As a result we get its left child, B. When we are at B, we can apply ⊕ on its left content with A address.

6.9 Binary Search Trees (BSTs)

Why Binary Search Trees?

In previous sections we have discussed different tree representations and in all of them we did not impose any restriction on the nodes data. As a result, to search for an element we need to check both in left subtree and in right subtree. Due to this, the worst case complexity of search operation is O(*n*).

In this section, we will discuss another variant of binary trees: Binary Search Trees (BSTs). As the name suggests, the main use of this representation is for *searching*. In this representation we impose restriction on the kind of data a node can contain. As a result, it reduces the worst case average search operation to O(*logn*).

Binary Search Tree Property

In binary search trees, all the left subtree elements should be less than root data and all the right subtree elements should be greater than root data. This is called binary search tree property. Note that, this property should be satisfied at every node in the tree.

- The left subtree of a node contains only nodes with keys less than the nodes key.
- The right subtree of a node contains only nodes with keys greater than the nodes key.
- Both the left and right subtrees must also be binary search trees.

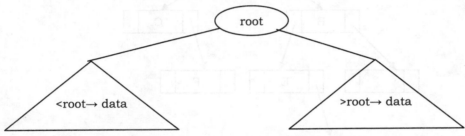

Example: The left tree is a binary search tree and right tree is not binary search tree (at node 6 it's not satisfying the binary search tree property).

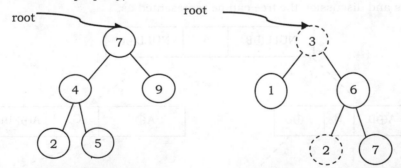

Binary Search Tree Declaration

There is no difference between regular binary tree declaration and binary search tree declaration. The difference is only in data but not in structure. But for our convenience we change the structure name as:

```java
public class BinarySearchTreeNode {
        private int data;
        private BinarySearchTreeNode left;
        private BinarySearchTreeNode right;
        public int getData() {
                return data;
        }
        public void setData(int data) {
                this.data = data;
        }
```

```
            public BinarySearchTreeNode getLeft() {
                  return left;
            }
            public void setLeft(BinarySearchTreeNode left) {
                  this.left = left;
            }
            public BinarySearchTreeNode getRight() {
                  return right;
            }
            public void setRight(BinarySearchTreeNode right) {
                  this.right = right;
            }
      }
```

Operations on Binary Search Trees

Main operations

Following are the main operations that are supported by binary search trees:
- Find/ Find Minimum / Find Maximum in binary search trees
- Inserting an element in binary search trees
- Deleting an element from binary search trees

Auxiliary operations

- Checking whether the given tree is a binary search tree or not
- Finding k^{th}-smallest element in tree
- Sorting the elements of binary search tree and many more

Notes on Binary Search Trees

- Since root data is always between left subtree data and right subtree data, performing inorder traversal on binary search tree produces a sorted list.
- While solving problems on binary search trees, first we process left subtree, then root data and finally we process right subtree. This means, depending on the problem only the intermediate step (processing root data) changes and we do not touch the first and third steps.
- If we are searching for an element and if the left subtree roots data is less than the element we want to search then skip it. Same is the case with right subtree.. Because of this binary search trees take less time for searching an element than regular binary trees. In other words, the binary search trees consider either left or right subtrees for searching an element but not both.

Finding an Element in Binary Search Trees

Find operation is straightforward in a BST. Start with the root and keep moving left or right using the BST property. If the data we are searching is same as nodes data then we return current node. If the data we are searching is less than nodes data then search left subtree of current node; otherwise search right subtree of current node. If the data is not present, we end up in a *null* link.

```
BinarySearchTreeNode Find(BinarySearchTreeNode root, int data) {
      if( root == null) return null;
      if( data < root.getData() )
            return Find(root.getLeft(), data);
      else if( data > root.getData() )
            return( Find(root.getRight(), data );
      return root;
}
```

Time Complexity: O(n), in worst case (when the given binary search tree is a skew tree). Space Complexity: O(n), for recursive stack.

Non recursive version of the above algorithm can be given as:

```
BinarySearchTreeNode Find(BinarySearchTreeNode root, int data ) {
      if( root == null)  return null;
      while(root != null) {
            if(data == root.getData())
                  return root;
            else if(data > root.getData())
```

```
                          root = root.getRight();
            else          root = root.getLeft();
      }
      return null;
}
```
Time Complexity: O(n). Space Complexity: O(1).

Finding Minimum Element in Binary Search Trees

In BSTs, the minimum element is the left-most node, which does not has left child. In the BST below, the minimum element is **4**.

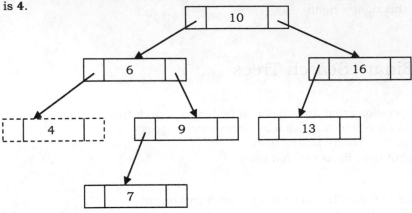

```
BinarySearchTreeNode FindMin(BinarySearchTreeNode root) {
      if(root == null)
            return null;
      else
            if( root.getLeft() == null ) return root;
            else return FindMin(root.getLeft() );
}
```
Time Complexity: O(n), in worst case (when BST is a *left skew* tree).
Space Complexity: O(n), for recursive stack.

Non recursive version of the above algorithm can be given as:

```
BinarySearchTreeNode FindMin(BinarySearchTreeNode  root ) {
      if( root == null)
            return null;
      while( root.getLeft() != null) root = root.getLeft();
      return root;
}
```
Time Complexity: O(n).
Space Complexity: O(1).

Finding Maximum Element in Binary Search Trees

In BSTs, the maximum element is the right-most node, which does not have right child. In the BST below, the maximum element is **16**.

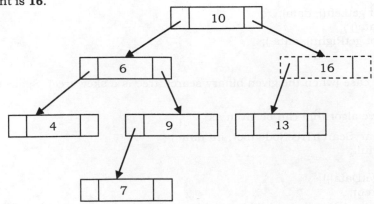

```
BinarySearchTreeNode FindMax(BinarySearchTreeNode root) {
        if(root == null)
                return null;
        else
                if( root.getRight() == null)
                        return root;
                else     return FindMax( root.getRight());
}
```
Time Complexity: O(n), in worst case (when BST is a *right skew* tree).
Space Complexity: O(n), for recursive stack.

Non recursive version of the above algorithm can be given as:

```
BinarySearchTreeNode FindMax(BinarySearchTreeNode  root ) {
        if( root == null)
                return null;
        while( root.getRight() != null)
            root = root.getRight();
        return root;
}
```
Time Complexity: O(n).
Space Complexity: O(1).

Where is Inorder Predecessor and Successor?

Where is the inorder predecessor and successor of node X in a binary search tree assuming all keys are distinct?

If X has two children then its inorder predecessor is the maximum value in its left subtree and its inorder successor the minimum value in its right subtree.

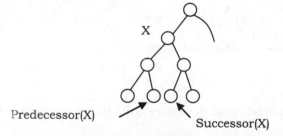

If it does not have a left child a nodes inorder predecessor is its first left ancestor.

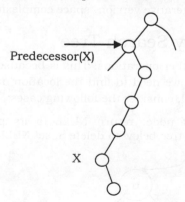

Inserting an Element from Binary Search Tree

To insert *data* into binary search tree, first we need to find the location for that element. We can find the location of insertion by following the same mechanism as that of *find* operation. While finding the location if the *data* is already there then we can simply neglect and come out. Otherwise, insert *data* at the last location on the path traversed. As an example let us consider the following tree. The dotted node indicates the element (5) to be inserted.

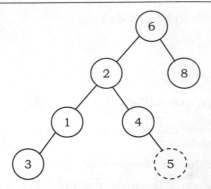

To insert 5, traverse the tree as using *find* function. At node with key 4, we need to go right, but there is no subtree, so 5 is not in the tree, and this is the correct location for insertion.

```
BinarySearchTreeNode Insert(BinarySearchTreeNode root, int data) {
        if( root == null) {
                root = new BinarySearchTreeNode();
                if( root == null) {
                        System.out.println("Memory Error");
                        return;
                }
                else {
                        root.setData(data);
                        root.setLeft(null); root.setRight(null);
                }
        }
        else {
                if( data < root.getData() )
                        root.setLeft(Insert(root.getLeft(), data));
                else if( data > root.getData() )
                        root.setRight(Insert(root.getRight(), data));
        }
        return root;
}
```

Note: In the above code, after inserting an element in subtrees, the tree is returned to its parent. As a result, the complete tree will get updated.

Time Complexity: O(n).
Space Complexity: O(n), for recursive stack. For iterative version, space complexity is O(1).

Deleting an Element from Binary Search Tree

The delete operation is more complicated than other operations. This is because the element to be deleted may not be the leaf node. In this operation also, first we need to find the location of the element which we want to delete. Once we have found the node to be deleted, consider the following cases:

- If the element to be deleted is a leaf node: return NULL to its parent. That means make the corresponding child pointer NULL. In the tree below to delete 5, set NULL to its parent node 2.

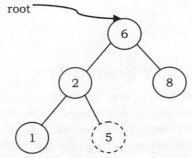

- If the element to be deleted has one child: In this case we just need to send the current nodes child to its parent. In the tree below, to delete 4, 4 left subtree is set to its parent node 2.

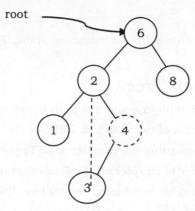

- If the element to be deleted has both children: The general strategy is to replace the key of this node with the largest element of the left subtree and recursively delete that node (which is now empty). The largest node in the left subtree cannot have a right child, the second *delete* is an easy one..

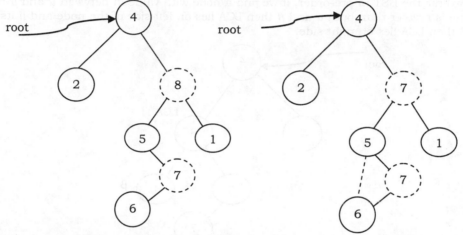

As an example, let us consider the following tree. In the tree below, to delete 8, it is the right child of root. The key value is 8. It is replaced with the largest key in its left subtree (7), and then that node is deleted as before (second case).

Note: We can replace with minimum element in right subtree also.

```
BinarySearchTreeNode Delete(BinarySearchTreeNode root, int data) {
        BinarySearchTreeNode temp;
        if( root == null)
                System.out.println("Element not there in tree");
        else if(data < root.data)
                root.left = Delete(root.getLeft(),data);
        else if(data > root→ data)
                root.right = Delete(root.getRight(), data);
        else {    //Found element
                if( root.getLeft() && root.getRight() ) {
                        /* Replace with largest in left subtree */
                        temp = FindMax( root.getLeft() );
                        root.getData() = temp.data;
                        root.left = Delete(root.getLeft(), root.getData());
                }
                else {               /* One child */
                        temp = root;
                        if( root.getLeft() == null )
                                root = root.getRight();
                        if( root.getRight() == null)
                                root = root.getLeft();
                        free( temp );
                }
        }
}
```

```
        return root;
}
```
Time Complexity: $O(n)$. Space Complexity: $O(n)$ for recursive stack. For iterative version, space complexity is $O(1)$.

Problems on Binary Search Trees

Problem-47   Give an algorithm for finding the shortest path between two nodes in a BST.

Solution: It's nothing but finding the LCA of two nodes in BST.

Problem-48   Give an algorithm for counting the number of BSTs possible with n nodes.

Solution: This is a DP problem and refer to chapter on *Dynamic Programming* for algorithm.

Problem-49   Given pointers to two nodes in a binary search tree, find lowest common ancestor (*LCA*). Assume that both values already exist in the tree.

Solution: The main idea of the solution is: while traversing BST from root to bottom, the first node we encounter with value between α and β, i.e., $\alpha < node \rightarrow data < \beta$ is the Least Common Ancestor(LCA) of α and β (where $\alpha < \beta$). So just traverse the BST in pre-order, if we find a node with value in between α and β then that node is the LCA. If its value is greater than both α and β then LCA lies on left side of the node and if its value is smaller than both α and β then LCA lies on right side.

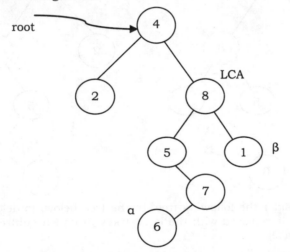

```
BinarySearchTreeNode FindLCA(BinarySearchTreeNode root, BinarySearchTreeNode α, BinarySearchTreeNode β) {
        while(1) {
                if((α.getData() < root.getData() && β.getData() > root.getData()) ||
                    (α.getData() > root.getData() && β.getData() < root.getData()))
                        return root;
                if(α.getData() < root.getData())
                        root = root.getLeft();
                else        root = root.getRight();
        }
}
```
Time complexity: $O(n)$. Space complexity: $O(n)$, for skew trees.

Problem-49   Give an algorithm to check whether the given binary tree is a BST or not.

Solution: Consider the following simple program. For each node, check if node on its left is smaller and check if the node on its right is greater.

```
int IsBST(BinaryTreeNode root) {
        if(root == null) return 1;
        /* false if left is > than root */
        if(root.getLeft() != null && root.getLeft().getData() > root.getData())
                return 0;
        /* false if right is < than root */
        if(root.getRight() != null && root.getRight().getData() < root.getData())
                return 0;
        /* false if, recursively, the left or right is not a BST */
        if(!IsBST(root.getLeft()) || !IsBST(root.getRight()))
```

```
            return 0;
      /* passing all that, it's a BST */
      return 1;
}
```

This approach is wrong as this will return true for binary tree below. Checking only at current node is not enough.

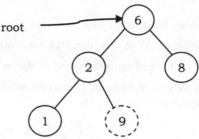

Problem-50   Can we think of getting the correct algorithm?

Solution: For each node, check if max value in left subtree is smaller than the current node data and min value in right subtree greater than the node data.

```
/* Returns true if a binary tree is a binary search tree */
int IsBST(BinaryTreeNode root) {
      if(root == null)
            return 1;
      /* false if the max of the left is > than us */
      if(root.getLeft() != null && FindMax(root.getLeft()) > root.getData())
            return 0;
      /* false if the min of the right is <= than us */
      if(root.getRight() != null && FindMin(root.getRight()) < root.getData())
            return 0;
      /* false if, recursively, the left or right is not a BST */
      if(!IsBST(root.getLeft()) || !IsBST(root.getRight()))
            return 0;
      /* passing all that, it's a BST */
      return 1;
}
```

It is assumed that we have helper functions *FindMin()* and *FindMax()* that return the min or max integer value from a non-empty tree.

Time complexity: $O(n^2)$. Space Complexity: $O(n)$.

Problem-51   Can we improve the complexity of Problem-50?

Solution: Yes. A better solution looks at each node only once. The trick is to write a utility helper function IsBSTUtil(BinaryTreeNode* root, int min, int max) that traverses down the tree keeping track of the narrowing min and max allowed values as it goes, looking at each node only once. The initial values for min and max should be INT_MIN and INT_MAX — they narrow from there.

```
Initial call: IsBST(root, INT_MIN, INT_MAX);
int IsBST(BinaryTreeNode root, int min, int max) {
      if(root == null)
            return 1;
      return (root.getData() >min && root.getData() < max &&
            IsBSTUtil(root.getLeft(), min, root.getData()) &&
            IsBSTUtil(root.getRight(),   root.getData(), max));
}
```

Time Complexity: $O(n)$. Space Complexity: $O(n)$, for stack space.

Problem-52   Can we further improve the complexity of Problem-50?

Solution: Yes, by using inorder traversal. The idea behind this solution is that, inorder traversal of BST produces sorted lists. While traversing the BST in inorder, at each node check the condition that its key value should be greater than the key value of its previous visited node. Also, we need to initialize the prev with possible minimum integer value (say, INT_MIN).

```
int prev = INT_MIN;
int IsBST(BinaryTreeNode root, int prev) {
```

```
        if(root == null) return 1;
        if(!IsBST(root.getLeft(), prev))
            return 0;
        if(root.getData() < prev)
            return 0;
        prev = root.getData();
        return IsBST(root.getRight(), prev);
}
```

Time Complexity: O(n). Space Complexity: O(n), for stack space.

Problem-53   Give an algorithm for converting BST to circular DLL with space complexity O(1).

Solution: Convert left and right subtrees to DLLs and maintain end of those lists. Then, adjust the pointers.

```
BinarySearchTreeNode BST2DLL(BinarySearchTreeNode root, BinarySearchTreeNode Ltail) {
        BinarySearchTreeNode left, ltail, right, rtail;
        if(root == null) {
                ltail = null;
                return null;
        }
        left = BST2DLL(root.getLeft(), ltail);
        right = BST2DLL(root.getRight(), rtail);
        root.setLeft(ltail);
        root.setRight(right);
        if(right == null)
                ltail = root;
        else {
                right.setLeft(root);
                ltail = rtail;
        }
        if(left == null)
                return root;
        else {  ltail.setRight(root);
                return left;
        }
}
```

Time Complexity: O(n).

Problem-54   Given a sorted doubly linked list, give an algorithm for converting it into balanced binary search tree.

Solution: Find the middle node and adjust the pointers.
```
DLLNode  DLLtoBalancedBST(DLLNode  head) {
        DLLNode  temp, p, q;
        if( head == null || head.getNext() == null)
                return head;
        temp = FindMiddleNode(head);
        p = head;
        while(p.getNext()!  = temp)
                p = p.getNext();
        p.setNext(null);
        q = temp.getNext();
        temp.setNext(null);
        temp.setPrev(DLLtoBalancedBST(head));
        temp.setNext(DLLtoBalancedBST(q));
        return temp;
}
```

Time Complexity: $2T(n/2) + $ O(n) [for finding the middle node]=O($nlogn$).

Note: For *FindMiddleNode* function refer *Linked Lists* chapter.

Problem-55   Given a sorted array, give an algorithm for converting the array to BST.

Solution: If we have to choose an array element to be the root of a balanced BST, which element should we pick? The root of a balanced BST should be the middle element from the sorted array. We would pick the middle element from the sorted array in each iteration. We then create a node in the tree initialized with this element. After the element is chosen, what is left? Could you identify the sub-problems within the problem? There are two arrays left — The one on its left and the one on its right. These two arrays are the sub-problems of the original problem, since both of them are sorted. Furthermore, they are subtrees of the current node's left and right child.

The code below creates a balanced BST from the sorted array in O(n) time (n is the number of elements in the array). Compare how similar the code is to a binary search algorithm. Both are using the divide and conquer methodology.

```java
BinaryTreeNode  BuildBST(int A[], int left, int right) {
        BinaryTreeNode  newNode;
        if(left > right)
                return null;
        newNode = new BinaryTreeNode();
        if(newNode == null) {
                System.out.println("Memory Error"); return;
        }
        if(left == right) {
                newNode.setData(A[left]);
                newNode.setLeft(null);
                newNode.setRight(null);
        }
        else {
                int mid = left + (right-left)/ 2;
                newNode.setData(A[mid]);
                newNode.setLeft(BuildBST(A, left, mid - 1));
                newNode.setRight(BuildBST(A, mid + 1, right));
        }
        return newNode;
}
```

Time Complexity: O(n). Space Complexity: O(n), for stack space.

Problem-56   Given a singly linked list where elements are sorted in ascending order, convert it to a height balanced BST.

Solution: A naive way is to apply the Problem-54 solution directly. In each recursive call, we would have to traverse half of the list's length to find the middle element. The run time complexity is clearly O($nlogn$), where n is the total number of elements in the list. This is because each level of recursive call requires a total of $n/2$ traversal steps in the list, and there are a total of $logn$ number of levels (ie, the height of the balanced tree).

Problem-57   For Problem-56, can we improve the complexity?

Solution: Hint: How about inserting nodes following the list order? If we can achieve this, we no longer need to find the middle element, as we are able to traverse the list while inserting nodes to the tree.

Best Solution: As usual, the best solution requires us to think from another perspective. In other words, we no longer create nodes in the tree using the top-down approach. Create nodes bottom-up, and assign them to their parents. The bottom-up approach enables us to access the list in its order while creating nodes [42].

Isn't the bottom-up approach precise? Each time we are stuck with the top-down approach, give bottom-up a try. Although bottom-up approach is not the most natural way we think, it is helpful in some cases. However, we should prefer top-down instead of bottom-up in general, since the latter is more difficult to verify.

Below is the code for converting a singly linked list to a balanced BST. Please note that the algorithm requires the list length to be passed in as the function's parameters. The list length could be found in O(n) time by traversing the entire list once. The recursive calls traverse the list and create tree nodes by the list order, which also takes O(n) time. Therefore, the overall run time complexity is still O(n).

```java
BinaryTreeNode SortedListToBST(ListNode list, int start, int end) {
        if(start > end)
                return null;
        // same as (start+end)/2, avoids overflow
        int mid = start + (end - start) / 2;
        BinaryTreeNode leftChild = SortedListToBST(list, start, mid-1);
        BinaryTreeNode  parent = new BinaryTreeNode();
        if(parent == null)
                System.out.println("Memory Error"); return;
        parent.setData(list.getData());
        parent.setLeft(leftChild);
        list = list.getNext();
```

```
        parent.setRight(SortedListToBST(list, mid+1, end));
        return parent;
}
BinaryTreeNode  SortedListToBST(ListNode head, int n) {
        return SortedListToBST(head, 0, n-1);
}
```

Problem-58   Give an algorithm for finding the kth smallest element in BST.

Solution: The idea behind this solution is that, inorder traversal of BST produces sorted lists. While traversing the BST in inorder, keep track of the number of elements visited.

```
BinarySearchTreeNode kthSmallestInBST(BinarySearchTreeNode root, int k, int count) {
        if(root == null)
            return null;
        BinarySearchTreeNode left = kthSmallestInBST(root.getLeft(), k, count);
        if( left != null)
            return left;
        if(++count == k)
            return root;
        return kthSmallestInBST(root.getRight(), k, count);
}
```

Time Complexity: $O(n)$. Space Complexity: $O(1)$.

Problem-59   **Floor and ceiling:** If a given key is less than the key at the root of a BST then floor of key (the largest key in the BST less than or equal to key) must be in the left subtree. If key is greater than the key at the root then floor of key could be in the right subtree, but only if there is a key smaller than or equal to key in the right subtree; if not (or if key is equal to the key at the root) then the key at the root is the floor of key. Finding the ceiling is similar with interchanging right and left. For example, if the sorted with input array is {1, 2, 8, 10, 10, 12, 19}, then

For $x = 0$:   floor doesn't exist in array, ceil = 1,   For $x = 1$:   floor = 1, ceil = 1
For $x = 5$:   floor = 2, ceil = 8,   For $x = 20$:   floor = 19, ceil doesn't exist in array

Solution: The idea behind this solution is that, inorder traversal of BST produces sorted lists. While traversing the BST in inorder, keep track of the values being visited. If the roots data is greater than the given value then return the previous value which we have maintained during traversal. If the roots data is equal to the given data then return root data.

```
BinaryTreeNode FloorInBST(BinaryTreeNode root, int data) {
        BinaryTreeNode prev=null;
        return FloorInBSTUtil(root, prev, data);
}
BinaryTreeNode FloorInBSTUtil(BinaryTreeNode root, BinaryTreeNode prev, int data)  {
            if(root == null) return null;
            if(!FloorInBSTUtil(root.getLeft(), prev, data))
                    return 0;
            if(root.getData() == data) return root;
            if(root.getData() > data) return prev;
            prev = root;
            return FloorInBSTUtil(root.getRight(), prev, data);
}
```

Time Complexity: $O(n)$. Space Complexity: $O(n)$, for stack space.

For ceiling, we just need to call the right subtree first and then followed by left subtree.

```
BinaryTreeNode CeilingInBST(BinaryTreeNode root, int data) {
        BinaryTreeNode prev=null;
        return CeilingInBSTUtil(root, prev, data);
}
BinaryTreeNode CeilingInBSTUtil(BinaryTreeNode root,          BinaryTreeNode prev, int data) {
            if(root == null) return null;
            if(!CeilingInBSTUtil(root.getRight(), prev, data))          return 0;
            if(root.getData() == data)
                    return root;
            if(root.getData() < data)
                    return prev;
```

```
            prev = root;
            return CeilingInBSTUtil(root.getLeft(), prev, data);
}
```
Time Complexity: O(n). Space Complexity: O(n), for stack space.

Problem-60   Give an algorithm for finding the union and intersection of BSTs. Assume parent pointers are available (say threaded binary trees). Also, assume the lengths of two BSTs are m and n respectively.

Solution: If parent pointers are available then the problem is same as merging of two sorted lists. This is because if we call inorder successor each time we get the next highest element. It's just a matter of which InorderSuccessor to call.

Time Complexity: O($m + n$). Space complexity: O(1).

Problem-61   For Problem-60, what if parent pointers are not available?

Solution: If parent pointers are not available then, the BSTs can be converted to linked lists and then merged.
1   Convert both the BSTs into sorted doubly linked lists in O($n + m$) time. This produces 2 sorted lists.
2   Merge the two double linked lists into one and also maintain the count of total elements in O($n + m$) time.
3   Convert the sorted doubly linked list into height balanced tree in O($n + m$) time.

Problem-62   For Problem-60, is there any alternative way of solving the problem?

Solution: Yes, by using inorder traversal.
• Perform inorder traversal on one of the BST.
• While performing the traversal store them in table (hash table).
• After completion of the traversal of first *BST*, start traversal of the second *BST* and compare them with hash table contents.

Time Complexity: O($m + n$). Space Complexity: O($Max(m, n)$).

Problem-63   Given a *BST* and two numbers $K1$ and $K2$, give an algorithm for printing all the elements of *BST* in the range $K1$ and $K2$.

Solution:
```
void RangePrinter(BinarySearchTreeNode root, int  K1, int K2) {
        if(root == null)
              return;
        if(root.getData() >= K1)
              RangePrinter(root.getLeft(), K1, K2);
        if(root.getData() >= K1 && root.getData() <= K2)
                   System.out.println( root.getData());
        if(root.getData() <= K2)
              RangePrinter(root.getRight(), K1, K2);
}
```
Time Complexity: O(n). Space Complexity: O(n), for stack space.

Problem-64   For Problem-63, is there any alternative way of solving the problem?

Solution: We can use level order traversal: while adding the elements to queue check for the range.
```
void  RangeSeachLevelOrder(BinarySearchTreeNode root, int  K1, int K2) {
        BinarySearchTreeNode temp;
        LLQueue Q = new LLQueue();
        if(root == null)   return null;
        Q.enQueue( root);
        while(!Q.isEmpty()) {
              temp=Q.deQueue();
              if(temp.getData() >= K1 && temp.getData() <= K2)
                    System.out.println(temp.getData());
              if(temp.getLeft() && temp.getData() >= K1)
                    Q.enQueue( temp.getLeft());
              if(temp.getRight() && temp.getData() <= K2)
                    Q.enQueue( temp.getRight());
        }
        Q.deleteQueue();
        return null;
}
```
Time Complexity: O(n). Space Complexity: O(n), for queue.

Problem-65   For Problem-63, can we still think of alternative way for solving the problem?

Solution: First locate $K1$ with normal binary search and after that use InOrder successor until we encounter $K2$. For algorithm, refer problems section of threaded binary trees.

Problem-66   Given root of a Binary Search tree, trim the tree, so that all elements in the new tree returned are between the inputs A and B.

Solution: It's just another way of asking the Problem-63.

Problem-67   Given two BSTs, check whether the elements of them are same or not. For example: two BSTs with data 10 5 20 15 30 and 10 20 15 30 5 should return true and the dataset with 10 5 20 15 30 and 10 15 30 20 5 should return false. **Note:** BSTs data can be in any order.

Solution: One simple way is performing an inorder traversal on first tree and storing its data in hash table. As a second step perform inorder traversal on second tree and check whether that data is already there in hash table or not (if it exists in hash table then mark it with -1 or some unique value). During the traversal of second tree if we find any mismatch return false. After traversal of second tree check whether it has all -1s in the hash table or not (this ensures extra data available in second tree).

Time Complexity: O($max(m, n)$), where m and n are the number of elements in first and second BST. Space Complexity: O($max(m, n)$). This depends on the size of the first tree.

Problem-68   For Problem-67, can we reduce the time complexity?

Solution: Instead of performing the traversals one after the other, we can perform $in - order$ traversal of both the trees in parallel. Since the $in - order$ traversal gives the sorted list, we can check whether both the trees are generating the same sequence or not.

Time Complexity: O($max(m, n)$). Space Complexity: O(1). This depends on the size of the first tree.

6.10 Balanced Binary Search Trees

In earlier sections we have seen different trees whose worst case complexity is O(n), where n is the number of nodes in the tree. This happens when the trees are skew trees. In this section we will try to reduce this worst case complexity to O($logn$) by imposing restrictions on the heights.

In general, the height balanced trees are represented with $HB(k)$, where k is the difference between left subtree height and right subtree height. Sometimes k is called balance factor.

Full Balanced Binary Search Trees

In $HB(k)$, if $k = 0$ (if balance factor is zero), then we call such binary search trees as *full* balanced binary search trees. That means, in $HB(0)$ binary search tree, the difference between left subtree height and right subtree height should be at most zero. This ensures that the tree is a full binary tree. For example,

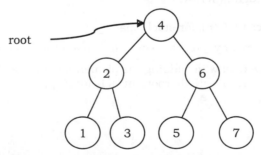

Note: For constructing $HB(0)$ tree refer problems section.

6.11 AVL (Adelson-Velskii and Landis) Trees

In $HB(k)$, if $k = 1$ (if balance factor is one), such binary search tree is called an AVL tree. That means an AVL tree is a binary search tree with a *balance* condition: the difference between left subtree height and right subtree height is at most 1.

Properties of AVL Trees

A binary tree is said to be an AVL tree, if:

- It is a binary search tree, and

- For any node X, the height of left subtree of X and height of right subtree of X differ by at most 1.

As an example among the below binary search trees, the left one is not an AVL tree, whereas the right binary search tree is an AVL tree.

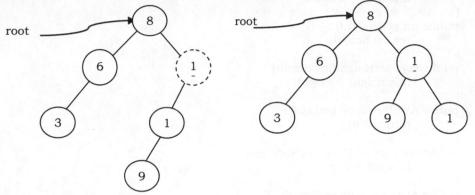

Minimum/Maximum Number of Nodes in AVL Tree

For simplicity let us assume that the height of an AVL tree is h and $N(h)$ indicates the number of nodes in AVL tree with height h.

To get minimum number of nodes with height h, we should fill the tree with as minimum nodes as possible. That means if we fill the left subtree with height $h - 1$ then we should fill the right subtree with height $h - 2$. As a result, the minimum number of nodes with height h is:

$$N(h) = N(h-1) + N(h-2) + 1$$

In the above equation:
- $N(h-1)$ indicates the minimum number of nodes with height $h-1$.
- $N(h-2)$ indicates the minimum number of nodes with height $h-2$.
- In the above expression, "1" indicates the current node.

We can give $N(h-1)$ either for left subtree or right subtree. Solving the above recurrence gives:

$$N(h) = O(1.618^h) \Rightarrow h = 1.44 log n \approx O(log n)$$

Where n is the number of nodes in AVL tree. Also, the above derivation says that the maximum height in AVL trees is $O(log n)$.

Similarly, to get maximum number of nodes, we need to fill both left and right subtrees with height $h - 1$. As a result, we get $N(h) = N(h-1) + N(h-1) + 1 = 2N(h-1) + 1$. The above expression defines the case of full binary tree. Solving the recurrence we get:

$$N(h) = O(2^h) \Rightarrow h = log n \approx O(log n)$$

∴ In both the cases, AVL tree property is ensuring that the height of an AVL tree with n nodes is $O(log n)$.

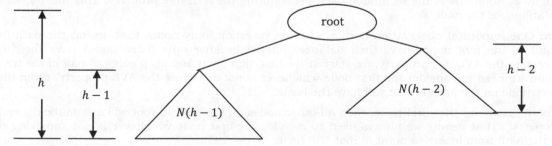

AVL Tree Declaration

Since AVL tree is a BST, the declaration of AVL is similar to that of BST. But just to simplify the operations, we include the height also as part of declaration.

```
public class AVLTreeNode {
    private int data;
    private int height;
    private AVLTreeNode left;
    private AVLTreeNode right;
    public int getData() {
```

```
                    return data;
            }
            public void setData(int data) {
                    this.data = data;
            }
            public int getHeight() {
                    return height;
            }
            public void setHeight(int height) {
                    this.height = height;
            }
            public AVLTreeNode getLeft() {
                    return left;
            }
            public void setLeft(AVLTreeNode left) {
                    this.left = left;
            }
            public AVLTreeNode getRight() {
                    return right;
            }
            public void setRight(AVLTreeNode right) {
                    this.right = right;
            }
    }
```

Finding Height of an AVL tree

```
int Height(AVLTreeNode root ) {
        if( root == null)
            return -1;
        else
            return root.getHeight();
}
```
Time Complexity: $O(1)$.

Rotations

When the tree structure changes (e.g., with insertion or deletion), we need to modify the tree to restore the AVL tree property. This can be done using single rotations or double rotations. Since an insertion/deletion involves adding/deleting a single node, this can only increase/decrease the height of some subtree by 1. So, if the AVL tree property is violated at a node X, it means that the heights of left(X) and right(X) differ by exactly 2. This is because, if we balance the AVL tree every time, then at any point, the difference in heights of left(X) and right(X) differ by exactly 2. Rotations is the technique used for restoring the AVL tree property. This means, we need to apply the rotations for the node X.

Observation: One important observation is that, after an insertion, only nodes that are on the path from the insertion point to the root might have their balances altered because only those nodes have their subtrees altered. To restore the AVL tree property, we start at the insertion point and keep going to root of the tree. While moving to root, we need to consider the first node whichever is not satisfying the AVL property. From that node onwards every node on the path to root will have the issue.

Also, if we fix the issue for that first node, then all other nodes on the path to root will automatically satisfy the AVL tree property. That means we always need to care for the first node whichever is not satisfying the AVL property on the path from insertion point to root and fix it.

Types of Violations

Let us assume the node that must be rebalanced is X. Since any node has at most two children, and a height imbalance requires that $X's$ two subtree heights differ by two, we can easily observe that a violation might occur in four cases:

1. An insertion into the left subtree of the left child of X.
2. An insertion into the right subtree of the left child of X.
3. An insertion into the left subtree of the right child of X.
4. An insertion into the right subtree of the right child of X.

Cases 1 and 4 are symmetric and easily solved with single rotations. Similarly, cases 2 and 3 are also symmetric and can be solved with double rotations (needs two single rotations).

Single Rotations

Left Left Rotation (LL Rotation) [Case-1]: In the case below, at node X, the AVL tree property is not satisfying.

As discussed earlier, rotation does not have to be done at the root of a tree. In general, we start at the node inserted and travel up the tree, updating the balance information at every node on the path. For example, in below figure, after the insertion of 7 in the original AVL tree on the left, node 9 becomes unbalanced. So, we do a single left-left rotation at 9. As a result we get the tree on the right.

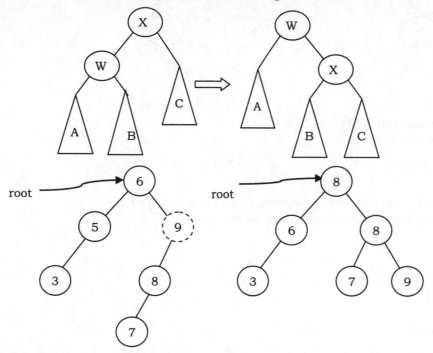

```
AVLTreeNode SingleRotateLeft(AVLTreeNode X ) {
        AVLTreeNode W = X.getLeft();

        X.setLeft(W.getRight());
        W.setRight(X);

        X.setHeight(Math.max( Height(X→left), Height(X.getRight()) ) + 1);
        W.setHeight(Math.max( Height(W→left), X→height ) + 1);

        return W;          /* New root */
}
```

Time Complexity: O(1). Space Complexity: O(1).

Right Right Rotation (RR Rotation) [Case-4]: In this case, the node X is not satisfying the AVL tree property.

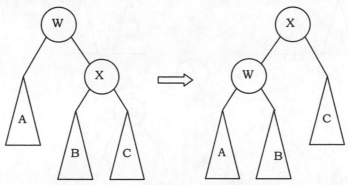

For example, in the figure above, after the insertion of 7 in the original AVL tree on the left, node 9 becomes unbalanced. So, we do a single left-left rotation at 9. As a result we get the tree on the right.

6.11 AVL (Adelson-Velskii and Landis) Trees

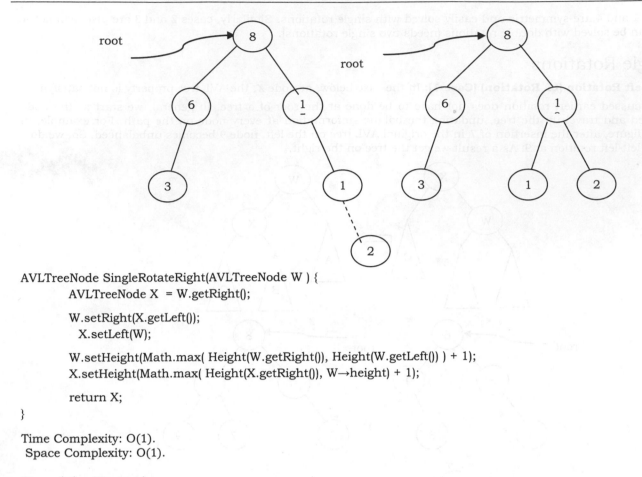

```
AVLTreeNode SingleRotateRight(AVLTreeNode W ) {
        AVLTreeNode X  = W.getRight();

        W.setRight(X.getLeft());
          X.setLeft(W);

        W.setHeight(Math.max( Height(W.getRight()), Height(W.getLeft()) ) + 1);
        X.setHeight(Math.max( Height(X.getRight()), W→height) + 1);

        return X;
}
```

Time Complexity: O(1).
 Space Complexity: O(1).

Double Rotations

Left Right Rotation (LR Rotation) [Case-2]: For case-2 and case-3 single rotation does not fix the problem. We need to perform two rotations.

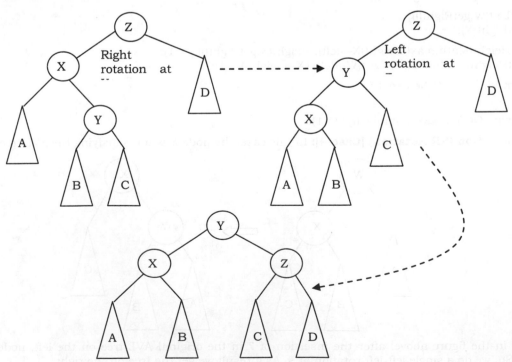

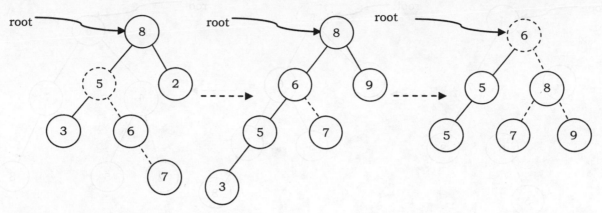

As an example, let us consider the following tree: Insertion of 7 is creating the case-2 scenario and right side tree is the one after double rotation.

```
AVLTreeNode DoubleRotatewithLeft( AVLTreeNode Z ) {
        Z.setLeft( SingleRotateRight(Z.getLeft()) );
        return SingleRotateLeft(Z);
}
```

Right Left Rotation (RL Rotation) [Case-3]: Similar to case-2, we need to perform two rotations for fixing this scenario.

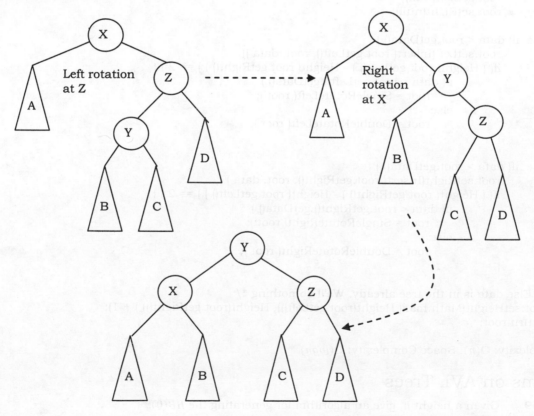

As an example, let us consider the following tree: Insertion of 6 is creating the case-3 scenario and right side tree is the one after double rotation.

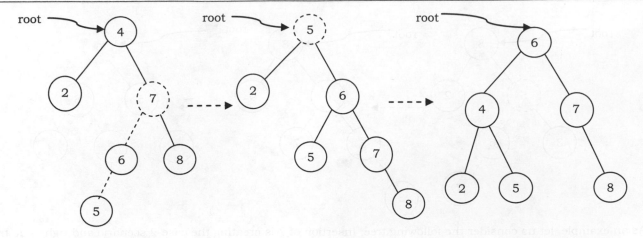

Insertion into an AVL tree

Insertion in AVL tree is similar to BST insertion. After inserting the element, we just need to check whether there is any height imbalance. If there is any imbalance, we just need to call the appropriate rotation functions.

```java
AVLTreeNode Insert( AVLTreeNode root, AVLTreeNode parent, int data) {
    if( root == null) {
        root = new AVLTreeNode();
        root.setData(data);
        root.setHeight(0);
        root.setLeft(null);
        root.setRight(null);
    }
    else  if( data < root.getData() ) {
        root.setLeft(Insert( root.getLeft(), root, data ));
        if( ( Height( root.getLeft() ) - Height( root.getRight() ) ) == 2 ) {
            if( data < root.getLeft().getData() )
                root = SingleRotateLeft( root );
            else
                root = DoubleRotateLeft( root );
        }
    }
    else  if( data > root.getData() ) {
        root.setRight(Insert( root.getRight(), root, data ) );
        if( ( Height( root.getRight() ) - Height( root.getLeft() ) ) == 2 ) {
            if( data < root.getRight().getData() )
                root = SingleRotateRight( root );
            else
                root = DoubleRotateRight( root );
        }
    }
    /* Else data is in the tree already. We'll do nothing */
    root.setHeight(Math.max( Height(root.getLeft()), Height(root.getRight()) ) + 1);
    return root;
}
```

Time Complexity: O(n). Space Complexity: O($logn$).

Problems on AVL Trees

Problem-69   Given a height h, give an algorithm for generating the $HB(0)$.

Solution: As we have discussed, $HB(0)$ is nothing but generating full binary tree. In full binary tree the number of nodes with height h are: $2^{h+1} - 1$ (let us assume that the height of a tree with one node is 0). As a result the nodes can be numbered as: 1 to $2^{h+1} - 1$.

```java
BinarySearchTreeNode BuildHB0(int h) {
    BinarySearchTreeNode temp;
    if(h == 0)
      return null;
```

```
        temp = newBinarySearchTreeNode();
        temp.setLeft(BuildHB0 (h-1));
        temp.getData(count++); //assume count is a global variable
        temp.setRight(BuildHB0 (h-1));
        return temp;
}
```

Time Complexity: O(n). Space Complexity: O($logn$), where $logn$ indicates the maximum stack size which is equal to height of the tree.

Problem-70   Is there any alternative way of solving Problem-69?

Solution: Yes, we can solve following Mergesort logic. That means, instead of working with height, we can take the range. With this approach we do not need any global counter to be maintained.

```
Struct BinarySearchTreeNode BuildHB0(int l, int r) {
        BinarySearchTreeNode temp;
        int mid = l + (r−l)/2;
        if( l > r)
            return null;
        temp = (BinarySearchTreeNode ) malloc (sizeof(BinarySearchTreeNode));
        temp.setData(mid);
        temp.setLeft(BuildHB0(l, mid-1));
        temp.setRight(BuildHB0(mid+1, r));
        return temp;
}
```

The initial call to *BuildHB*0 function could be: *BuildHB*0(1, 1 ≪ h). 1 ≪ h does the shift operation for calculating the $2^{h+1} - 1$.

Time Complexity: O(n). Space Complexity: O($logn$). Where $logn$ indicates maximum stack size which is equal to height of the tree.

Problem-71   Construct minimal AVL trees of height 0, 1, 2, 3, 4, and 5. What is the number of nodes in a minimal AVL tree of height 6?

Solution Let $N(h)$ be the number of nodes in a minimal AVL tree with height h.

$N(0) = 1$

$N(1) = 2$

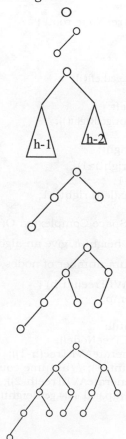

$N(h) = 1 + N(h - 1) + N(h - 2)$

$N(2) = 1 + N(1) + N(0)$
$\quad\quad = 1 + 2 + 1 = 4$

$N(3) = 1 + N(2) + N(1)$
$\quad\quad = 1 + 4 + 2 = 7$

$N(4) = 1 + N(3) + N(2)$
$\quad\quad = 1 + 7 + 4 = 12$

$$N(5) = 1 + N(4) + N(3)$$
$$= 1 + 12 + 7 = 20$$

Problem-72   For Problem-69, how many different shapes can there be of a minimal AVL tree of height?

Solution: Let $NS(h)$ be the number of different shapes of a minimal AVL tree of height h.

$$NS(0) = 1$$

$$NS(1) = 2$$

$$NS(2) = 2 * NS(1) * NS(0)$$
$$= 2 * 2 * 1 = 4$$

$$NS(3) = 2 * NS(2) * NS(1)$$
$$= 2 * 4 * 1 = 8$$

$$...$$

$$NS(h) = 2 * NS(h-1) * NS(h-2)$$

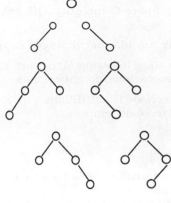

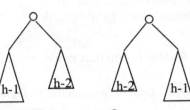

Problem-73   Given a binary search tree check whether it is an AVL tree or not?

Solution: Let us assume that *IsAVL* is the function which checks whether the given binary search tree is an AVL tree or not. *IsAVL* returns −1 if the tree is not an AVL tree. During the checks each node sends height of it to their parent.

```
int IsAVL(BinarySearchTreeNode root) {
        int left, right;
        if(root == null)
                return 0;
        left = IsAVL(root.getLeft());
        if(left == -1)
                return left;
        right = IsAVL(root.getRight());
        if(right == -1)
                return right;
        if(Math.abs(left-right)>1)
                return -1;
        return Math.max(left, right)+1;
}
```
Time Complexity: O(n). Space Complexity: O(n).

Problem-74   Given a height h, give an algorithm for generating an AVL tree with minimum number of nodes.

Solution: To get minimum number of nodes, fill one level with $h-1$ and other with $h-2$.

```
AVLTreeNode GenerateAVLTree(int h) {
        AVLTreeNode temp;
        if(h == 0)
                return null;
        temp = new AVLTreeNode();
        temp.setLeft(GenerateAVLTree(h-1));
        temp.getData(count++); //assume count is a global variable
        temp.setRight(GenerateAVLTree(h-2));
        temp.setHeight(temp.getLeft().getHeight()+1); // or temp→height = h;
        return temp;
}
```

Problem-75   Given an AVL tree with n integer items and two integers a and b, where a and b can be any integers with $a <= b$. Implement an algorithm to count the number of nodes in the range $[a, b]$.

Solution:

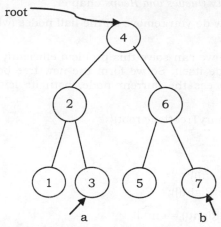

The idea is to make use of the recursive property of binary search trees. There are three cases to consider, whether the current node is in the range $[a, b]$, on the left side of the range $[a, b]$, or on the right side of the range $[a, b]$. Only subtrees that possibly contain the nodes will be processed under each of the three cases.

```
int RangeCount(AVLNode root, int a, int b) {
        if(root == null)
                return 0;
        else if(root.getData() > b)
                return RangeCount(curr.getLeft(), a, b);
        else if(root.getData() < a)
                return RangeCount(root.getRight(), a, b);
        else if(root.getData() >= a && root.getData() <= b)
                return RangeCount(root.getLeft(), a, b) + RangeCount(root.getRight(), a, b) + 1;
}
```

The complexity is similar to $in-order$ traversal of the tree but skipping left or right sub-trees when they do not contain any answers. So in the worst case, if the range covers all the nodes in the tree, we need to traverse all the n nodes to get the answer. The worst time complexity is therefore $O(n)$.

If the range is small, which only covers few elements in a small subtree at the bottom of the tree, the time complexity will be $O(h) = O(logn)$, where h is the height of the tree. This is because only a single path is traversed to reach the small subtree at the bottom and many higher level subtrees have been pruned along the way.

Note: Refer similar problem in BST.

Problem-76   Median in an infinite series of integers

Solution: Median is the middle number in a sorted list of numbers (if we have odd number of elements). If we have even number of elements, median is the average of two middle numbers in a sorted list of numbers.

For solving this problem we can use binary search tree with additional information at each node, number of children on the left and right subtrees. We also keep the number of total nodes in the tree. Using this additional information we can find the median in $O(logn)$ time, taking the appropriate branch in the tree based on number of children on the left and right of the current node. But, the insertion complexity is $O(n)$ because a standard binary search tree can degenerate into a linked list if we happen to receive the numbers in sorted order.

So, let's use a balanced binary search tree to avoid worst case behavior of standard binary search trees. For this problem, the balance factor is the number of nodes in the left subtree minus the number of nodes in the right subtree. And only the nodes with balance factor of +1 or 0 are considered to be balanced. So, the number of nodes on the left subtree is either equal to or 1 more than the number of nodes on the right subtree, but not less.

If we ensure this balance factor on every node in the tree, then the root of the tree is the median, if the number of elements is odd. In the even case, the median is the average of the root and its inorder successor, which is the leftmost descendent of its right subtree.

So, complexity of insertion maintaining balance condition is $O(logn)$ and find median operation is O(1) assuming we calculate the inorder successor of the root at every insertion if the number of nodes is even. Insertion and balancing is very similar to AVL trees. Instead of updating the heights, we update the number of nodes information. Balanced binary search trees seem to be the most optimal solution, insertion is O(*logn*) and find median is O(1).

Note: For efficient algorithm refer *Priority Queues and Heaps* chapter.

Problem-82   Given a binary tree, how do you remove all the half nodes (which has only one child)? Note that we should not touch leaves.

Solution: By using post-order traversal we can solve this problem efficiently. We first process the left children, then right children, and finally the node itself. So we form the new tree bottom up, starting from the leaves towards the root. By the time we process the current node, both its left and right subtrees were already processed.

```
BinaryTreeNode removeHalfNodes(BinaryTreeNode root){
    if (root == null)
        return null;

    root.left=removeHalfNodes(root.getLeft());
    root.right=removeHalfNodes(root.getRight());

    if (root.getLeft() == null && root.getRight() == null)
        return root;

    if (root.getLeft() == null)
        return root.getRight();

    if (root.getRight() == null)
        return root.getLeft();

    return root;
}
```

Time Complexity: O(*n*).

Problem-83   Given a binary tree, how do you remove leaves of it?

Solution: By using post-order traversal we can solve this problem (other traversals would also work).

```
BinaryTreeNode removeLeaves(BinaryTreeNode root) {
    if (root != null) {
        if (root.getLeft() == null && root.getRight() == null) {
            root = null;
        } else {
            root.left = removeLeaves(root.getLeft());
            root.right = removeLeaves(root.getRight());
        }
    }
    return root;
}
```

Time Complexity: O(*n*).

Problem-84   Given a BST and two integers (minimum and maximum integers) as parameters, how do you remove (prune) elements from the tree any elements that are not within that range, inclusive.

Sample Tree

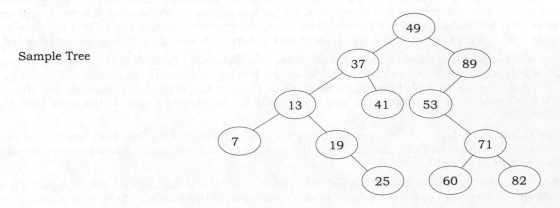

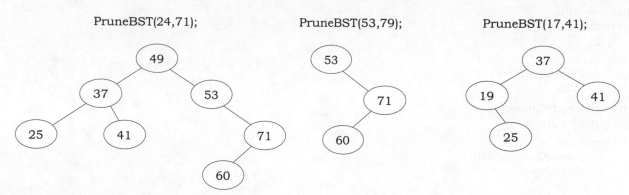

PruneBST(24,71);   PruneBST(53,79);   PruneBST(17,41);

Solution: Observation: Since we need to check each and every element in tree and the subtree changes should reflect in parent, we can think of using post order traversal. So we process the nodes starting from the leaves towards the root. As a result while processing the node itself; both its left and right subtrees are valid pruned BSTs.

At each node we will return a pointer based on its value, which will then be assigned to its parent's left or right child pointer, depending on whether the current node is left or right child of the parent. If current node's value is between A and B ($A <= node's\ data <= B$) then there's no action need to be taken, so we return the reference to the node itself.

If current node's value is less than A, then we return the reference to its right subtree, and discard the left subtree. Because if a node's value is less than A, then its left children are definitely less than A since this is a binary search tree. But its right children may or may not be less than A we can't be sure, so we return the reference to it. Since we're performing bottom-up post-order traversal, its right subtree is already a trimmed valid binary search tree (possibly NULL), and left subtree is definitely NULL because those nodes were surely less than A and they were eliminated during the post-order traversal.

Similar situation occurs when node's value is greater than B, we now return the reference to its left subtree. Because if a node's value is greater than B, then its right children are definitely greater than B. But its left children may or may not be greater than B. So we discard the right subtree and return the reference to the already valid left subtree.

```java
BinarySearchTreeNode PruneBST(BinarySearchTreeNode root, int A, int B){
    if(root == null)
        return null;
    root.left= PruneBST(root->getLeft(),A,B);
    root.right= PruneBST(root->getRight(),A,B);
    if(A<=root.getData() && root.getData()<=B)
        return root;
    if(root.getData()<A)
        return root.getRight();
    if(root.getData()>B)
        return root.getLeft();
}
```

Time Complexity: O(n) in worst case and in average case it is O($logn$).

Note: If the given BST is an AVL tree then O(n) is the average time complexity.

Problem-85   Given a binary tree, how do you connect all the adjacent nodes at the same level? Assume that given binary tree has next pointer along with left and right pointers.

Solution: One simple approach is to use level-order traversal and keep updating the next pointers. While traversing, we will link the nodes on next level. If the node has left and right node, we will link left to right. If node has next node, then link rightmost child of current node to leftmost child of next node.

```java
public void linkLevelNodes(BinaryTreeNode root){
    Queue Q = CreateQueue();
    BinaryTreeNode prev;      // Pointer to the revious node of the current level
    BinaryTreeNode temp;
    int currentLevelNodeCount;
    int nextLevelNodeCount;
```

```
   if(root == null)
      return;

EnQueue(Q, root);
currentLevelNodeCount = 1;
nextLevelNodeCount = 0;
prev = NULL;

while (!IsEmptyQueue(Q)) {
   temp = DeQueue(Q);

   if (temp.left != null){
      EnQueue(Q, temp.left);
      nextLevelNodeCount++;
   }
   if (temp.right != null){
      EnQueue(Q, temp.right);
      nextLevelNodeCount++;
   }

   // Link the previous node of the current level to this node
   if (prev)
      prev.next = temp;

   //Set the previous node to the current
   prev = temp;

   currentLevelNodeCount--;
   if (currentLevelNodeCount == 0) {   // if this is the last node of the current level
      currentLevelNodeCount = nextLevelNodeCount;
      nextLevelNodeCount = 0;
      prev = NULL;
   }
 }
}
```

Time Complexity: O(*n*).
Space Complexity: O(*n*).

Problem-86   Can we improve space complexity for the Problem-85?

Solution: We can process the tree level by level, but without a queue. The logical part is that when we process the nodes of next level, we make sure that the current level has already been linked.

```
   public void linkLevelNodes(BinaryTreeNode root) {
      if(root==null)
         return;
      BinaryTreeNode rightMostNode = null;
      BinaryTreeNode nextHead = null;
      BinaryTreeNode temp = root;
      //connect next level of current root node level
      while(temp!=null){
         if(temp.left!=null)
            if(rightMostNode==null){
               rightMostNode=temp.left;
               nextHead=temp.left;
            }
            else{
               rightMostNode.next = temp.left;
               rightMostNode = rightMostNode.next;
            }
         if(temp.right!=null)
            if(rightMostNode==null){
               rightMostNode=temp.right;
               nextHead=temp.right;
            }
            else{
               rightMostNode.next = temp.right;
               rightMostNode = rightMostNode.next;
```

```
        }
    temp=temp.next;
    }
    connect(nextHead);
}
```

Time Complexity: O(*n*).
Space Complexity: O(*depth of tree*) for stack space.

6.12 Other Variations in Trees

In this section, let us enumerate the other possible representations of trees. In the earlier sections, we have seen AVL trees which is a binary search tree (BST) with balancing property. Now, let us see few more balanced binary search trees: Red-Black Trees and Splay Trees.

6.12.1 Red-Black Trees

In red-black trees each node is associated with extra attribute: the color, which is either red or black. To get logarithmic complexity we impose the following restrictions.

Definition: A red-black tree is a binary search tree that satisfies the following properties:
- Root Property: the root is black
- External Property: every leaf is black
- Internal Property: the children of a red node are black
- Depth Property: all the leaves have the same black

Similar to AVL trees, if the Red-black tree becomes imbalanced then we perform rotations to reinforce the balancing property. With Red-black trees, we can perform the following operations in O(*logn*) in worst case, where *n* is the number of nodes in the trees.
- Insertion
- Deletion
- Find predecessor
- Find successor
- Find minimum
- Find maximum

6.12.2 Splay Trees

Splay-trees are BSTs with self-adjusting property. Another interesting property of splay-trees is: starting with empty tree, any sequence of *K* operations with maximum of *n* nodes takes O(*Klogn*) time complexity in worst case.

Splay trees are easier to program and also ensures faster access to recently accessed items. Similar to *AVL* and Red-Black trees, at any point if the splay tree becomes imbalanced then we perform rotations to reinforce the balancing property.

Splay-trees cannot guarantee the O(*logn*) complexity in worst case. But it gives amortized O(*logn*) complexity. Even though individual operations can be expensive, any sequence of operations gets the complexity of logarithmic behavior. One operation may take more time (a single operation may take O(*n*) time) but the subsequent operations may not take worst case complexity and on the average *per operation* complexity is O(*logn*).

6.12.3 Augmented Trees

In earlier sections, we have seen the problems like finding K^{th} −smallest element in the tree and many other similar problems. For all those problems the worst complexity is O(*n*), where *n* is the number of nodes in the tree. To perform such operations in O(*logn*) augmented trees are useful. In these trees, extra information is added to each node and that extra data depends on the problem we are trying to solve.

For example, to find K^{th} −smallest in binary search tree, let us see how augmented trees solve the problem. Let us assume that we are using Red-Black trees as balanced BST (or any balanced BST) and augment the size information in the nodes data.

For a given node X in Red-Black tree with a field $size(X)$ equal to the number of nodes in the subtree and can be calculated as:

$$size(X) = size(X \rightarrow left) + size(X \rightarrow right)) + 1$$

Example: With the extra size information, the augmented tree will look like:

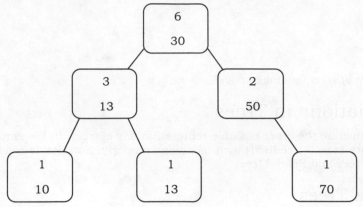

Kth-smallest operation can be defined as:

```
BinarySearcTreeNode KthSmallest (BinarySearcTreeNode X, int K) {
        int r = size(X.getLeft()) + 1;
        if(K == r)
                return X;
        if(K < r)
                return KthSmallest (X.getLeft(), K);
        if(K > r)
                return KthSmallest (X.getRight(), K-r);
}
```

Time Complexity: O($logn$). Space Complexity: O($logn$).

6.12.4 Scapegoat Trees

Scapegoat tree is a self-balancing binary search tree, discovered by Arne Andersson. It provides worst-case O($logn$) search time, and O($logn$) amortized (average) insertion and deletion time.

AVL tree rebalance whenever the heights of two sibling subtrees differ by more than one, scapegoat tree rebalance whenever the size of a child exceeds a certain ratio of its parent's, a ratio known as a. After inserting the element, we traverse back up the tree. If we find an imbalance where a child's size exceeds the parent's size times alpha, we must rebuild the subtree at the parent, the *scapegoat*.

There might be more than possible scapegoat, but we only have to pick one. The most optimal scapegoat is actually determined by height balance. When removing, we see if the total size of the tree is less than alpha of the largest size since the last rebuilding of the tree. If so, we rebuild the entire tree. The alpha for a scapegoat tree can be any number between 0.5 and 1.0. The value 0.5 will force perfect balance, while 1.0 will cause rebalancing to never occur, effectively turning it into a BST.

6.12.5 Interval Trees

Interval trees are also binary search trees and store interval information in the node structure. That means, we maintain a set of n intervals [i_1, i_2] such that one of the intervals containing a query point Q (if any) can be found efficiently. Interval trees are used for performing range queries efficiently.

Example: Given a set of intervals: S = {[2-5], [6-7], [6-10], [8-9], [12-15], [15-23], [25-30]}. A query with Q = 9 returns [6,10] or [8,9] (assume these are the intervals which contains 9 among all the intervals). A query with Q = 23 returns [15, 23].

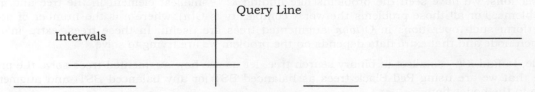

Construction of Interval Trees

Let us assume that we are given a set S of n intervals (also called segments). These n intervals will have 2n endpoints. Now, let us see how to construct the interval tree.

Algorithm

Recursively build tree on interval set S as follows:

- Sort the $2n$ endpoints
- Let X_{mid} be the median point

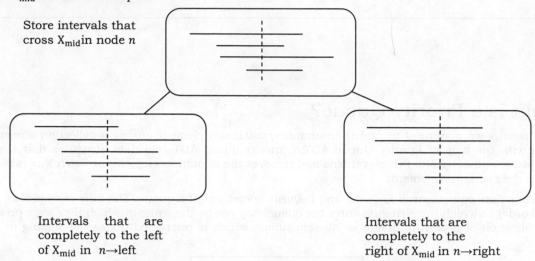

Store intervals that cross X_{mid} in node n

Intervals that are completely to the left of X_{mid} in $n \rightarrow$ left

Intervals that are completely to the right of X_{mid} in $n \rightarrow$ right

Time Complexity for building interval trees: O($nlogn$). Since we are choosing the median, Interval Trees will be approximately balanced. This ensures that, we split the set of end points up in half each time. The depth of the tree is O($logn$). To simplify the search process, generally X_{mid} is stored with each node.

Chapter-7

PRIORITY QUEUE AND HEAPS

7.1 What is a Priority Queue?

In some situations we may need to find the minimum/maximum element among a collection of elements. We can do this with the help of Priority Queue ADT.A priority queue ADT is a data structure that supports the operations *Insert* and *DeleteMin* (which returns and removes the minimum element) or *DeleteMax* (which returns and removes the maximum element).

These operations are equivalent to *EnQueue* and *DeQueue* operations of a queue. The difference is that, in priority queues, the order in which the elements enter the queue may not be the same in which they were processed. An example application of a priority queue is job scheduling, which is prioritized instead of serving in first come first serve.

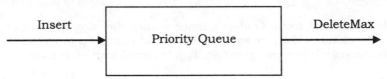

A priority queue is called an *ascending − priority* queue, if the item with smallest key has the highest priority (that means, delete smallest element always). Similarly, a priority queue is said to be a *descending − priority* queue if the item with largest key has the highest priority (delete maximum element always). Since these two types are symmetric we will be concentrating on one of them, say, ascending-priority queue.

7.2 Priority Queue ADT

The following operations make priority queues an ADT.

Main Priority Queues Operations

A priority queue is a container of elements, each having an associated key.
- Insert(key, data): Inserts data with *key* to the priority queue. Elements are ordered based on key.
- DeleteMin/DeleteMax: Remove and return the element with the smallest/largest key.
- GetMinimum/GetMaximum: Return the element with the smallest/largest key without deleting it.

Auxiliary Priority Queues Operations

- k^{th} −Smallest/k^{th} −Largest: Returns the kth −Smallest/k^{th} −Largest key in priority queue.
- Size: Returns number of elements in priority queue.
- Heap Sort: Sorts the elements in the priority queue based on priority (key).

7.3 Priority Queue Applications

Priority queues have many applications and few of them are listed below:
- Data compression: Huffman Coding algorithm
- Shortest path algorithms: Dijkstra's algorithm
- Minimum spanning tree algorithms: Prim's algorithm
- Event-driven simulation: customers in a line
- Selection problem: Finding k^{th}-smallest element

7.4 Priority Queue Implementations

Before discussing the actual implementation, let us enumerate the possible options.

Unordered Array Implementation

Elements are inserted into the array without bothering about the order. Deletions (DeleteMax) are performed by searching the key and then followed by deletion. Insertions complexity: O(1). DeleteMin complexity: O(n).

Unordered List Implementation

It is very much similar to array implementation, but instead of using arrays linked lists are used. Insertions complexity: O(1). DeleteMin complexity: O(n).

Ordered Array Implementation

Elements are inserted into the array in sorted order based on key field. Deletions are performed at only one end.

Insertions complexity: O(n). DeleteMin complexity: O(1).

Ordered List Implementation

Elements are inserted into the list in sorted order based on key field. Deletions are performed at only one end, hence preserving the status of the priority queue. All other functionalities associated with a linked list ADT are performed without modification. Insertions complexity: O(n). DeleteMin complexity: O(1).

Binary Search Trees Implementation

Both insertions and deletions take O($logn$) on average if insertions are random (refer *Trees* chapter).

Balanced Binary Search Trees Implementation

Both insertions and deletion take O($logn$) in the worst case (refer *Trees* chapter).

Binary Heap Implementation

In subsequent sections we will discuss this in full detail. For now assume that binary heap implementation gives O($logn$) complexity for search, insertions and deletions and O(1) for finding the maximum or minimum element.

Comparing Implementations

Implementation	Insertion	Deletion (DeleteMax)	Find Min
Unordered array	1	n	n
Unordered list	1	n	n
Ordered array	n	1	1
Ordered list	n	1	1
Binary Search Trees	$logn$ (average)	$logn$ (average)	$logn$ (average)
Balanced Binary Search Trees	$logn$	$logn$	$logn$
Binary Heaps	$logn$	$logn$	1

7.5 Heaps and Binary Heap

What is a Heap?

A heap is a tree with some special properties. The basic requirement of a heap is that the value of a node must be ≥ (or ≤) to the values of its children. This is called *heap property*. A heap also has the additional property that all leaves should be at h or $h - 1$ levels (where h is the height of the tree) for some $h > 0$ (*complete binary trees*). That means heap should form a *complete binary tree* (as shown below).

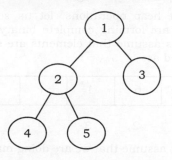

In the examples below, the left tree is a heap (each element is greater than its children) and right tree is not a heap (since, 11 is greater than 2).

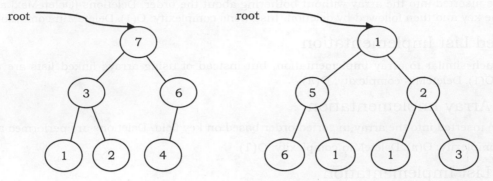

Types of Heaps?

Based on the property of a heap we can classify heaps into two types:
- **Min heap:** The value of a node must be less than or equal to the values of its children

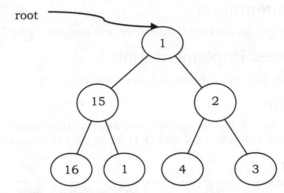

- **Max heap:** The value of a node must be greater than or equal to the values of its children

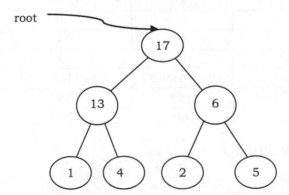

7.6 Binary Heaps

In binary heap each node may have up to two children. In practice, binary heaps are enough and we concentrate on binary min heaps and binary max heaps for remaining discussion.

Representing Heaps: Before looking at heap operations, let us see how heaps can be represented. One possibility is using arrays. Since heaps are forming complete binary trees, there will not be any wastage of locations. For the discussion below let us assume that elements are stored in arrays, which starts at index 0. The previous max heap can be represented as:

17	13	6	1	4	2	5
0	1	2	3	4	5	6

Note: For the remaining discussion let us assume that we are doing manipulations in max heap.

Declaration of Heap

```
public class  Heap {
        public int[] array;
        public int count;                              // Number of elements in Heap
        public int capacity;                           // Size of the heap
        public int heap_type;                          // Min Heap or Max Heap
        public Heap(int capacity, int heap_type)       { //Refer Below sections }
        public Parent(int capacity, int heap_type)         { //Refer Below sections }
        public int LeftChild(int i)                    {//Refer Below sections }
        public int RightChild(int i)                   {//Refer Below sections }
        public int GetMaximum(int i)                   {//Refer Below sections }
        .........
}
```

Note: Assume all the below functions are part of class.

Creating Heap

```
public Heap(int capacity, int heap_type) {
        this.heap_type = heap_type;
        this.count = 0;
        this.capacity = capacity;
        this.array = new int[capacity];
}
```

Time Complexity: O(1).

Parent of a Node

For a node at i^{th} location, its parent is at $\frac{i-1}{2}$ location. In the previous example, the element 6 is at second location and its parent is at 0th location.

```
public int Parent (int i) {
        if(i <= 0 || i >= this.count)
                return -1;
        return i-1/2;
}
```

Time Complexity: O(1).

Children of a Node

Similar to above discussion for a node at i^{th} location, its children are at $2*i+1$ and $2*i+2$ locations. For example, in the above tree the element 6 is at second location and its children 2 and 5 are at 5 ($2*i+1 = 2*2+1$) and 6 ($2*i+2 = 2*2+2$) locations.

```
public int LeftChild(int i) {                    public int RightChild(int i) {
        int left = 2 * i + 1;                            int right = 2 * i + 2;
        if(left >= this.count)                           if(right >= this.count)
                return -1;                                       return -1;
        return left;                                     return right;
}                                                }
Time Complexity: O(1).                           Time Complexity: O(1).
```

Getting the Maximum Element

Since the maximum element in max heap is always at root, it will be stored at this.array[0].

```
public int GetMaximum() {
        if(this.count == 0)
                return -1;
        return this.array[0];
}
```

Time Complexity: O(1).

Heapifying an Element

After inserting an element into heap, it may not satisfy the heap property. In that case we need to adjust the locations of the heap to make it heap again. This process is called *heapifying*. In max-heap, to heapify an element, we have to find the maximum of its children and swap it with the current element and continue this process until the heap property is satisfied at every node.

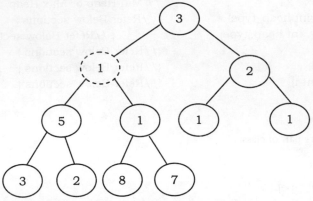

Observation: One important property of heap is that, if an element is not satisfying the heap property then all the elements from that element to root will also have the same problem. In the example below, element 1 is not satisfying the heap property and its parent 31 is also having the issue. Similarly, if we heapify an element then all the elements from that element to root will also satisfy the heap property automatically. Let us go through an example. In the above heap, the element 1 is not satisfying the heap property. Let us try heapifying this element.

To heapify 1, find maximum of its children and swap with that.

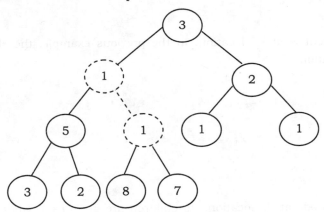

We need to continue this process until the element satisfies the heap properties. Now, swap 1 with 8.

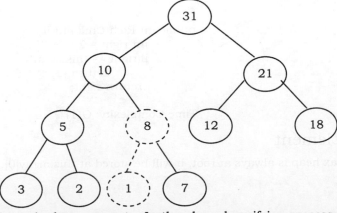

Now the tree is satisfying the heap property. In the above heapifying process, since we are moving from top to bottom, this process is sometimes called *percolate down*.

```
//Heapifying the element at location i.
public void PercolateDown(int i) {
```

```
        int l, r, max, temp;
        l = LeftChild(i);
        r = RightChild(i);
        if(l != -1 && this.array[l] > this.array[i])
                max = l;
        else
                max = i;
        if(r != -1&& this.array[r] > this.array[max])
                max = r;
        if(max != i) {  //Swap this.array[i] and  this.array[max];
                temp = this.array[i]; this.array[i] = this.array[max]; this.array[max] = temp;
        }
        PercolateDown(max);
}
```

Time Complexity: O(*logn*). Heap is a complete binary tree and in the worst case we start at root and come down till the leaf. This is equal to the height of the complete binary tree.
Space Complexity: O(1).

Deleting an Element

To delete an element from heap, we just need to delete the element from root. This is the only operation (maximum element) supported by standard heap. After deleting the root element, copy the last element of the heap (tree) and delete that last element. After replacing the last element the tree may not satisfy the heap property. To make it heap again, call *PercolateDown* function.

- Copy the first element into some variable
- Copy the last element into first element location
- *PercolateDown* the first element

```
int DeleteMax() {
        if(this.count == 0)
                return -1;
        int data = this.array[0];
        this.array[0] = this.array[this.count-1];
        this.count--; //reducing the heap size
        PercolateDown(0);
        return data;
}
```

Note: Deleting an element uses *percolate down*.
Time Complexity: same as Heapify function and it is O(*logn*).

Inserting an Element

Insertion of an element is similar to heapify and deletion process.

- Increase the heap size
- Keep the new element at the end of the heap (tree)
- Heapify the element from bottom to top (root)

Before going through code, let us look at an example. We have inserted the element 19 at end of the heap and this is not satisfying the heap property.

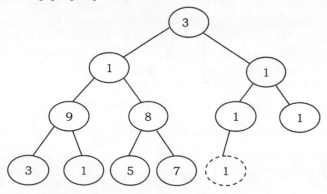

In-order to heapify this element (19), we need to compare it with its parent and adjust them. Swapping 19 and 14 gives:

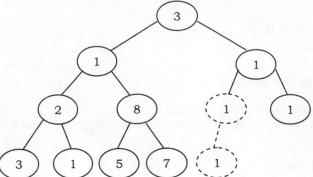

Again, swap 19 and16:

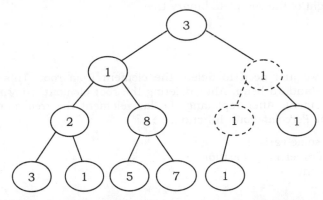

Now the tree is satisfying the heap property. Since we are following the bottom-up approach we sometimes call this process is *percolate up*.

```
int Insert(int data) {
        int i;
        if(this.count == this.capacity)
                ResizeHeap();
        this.count++;              //increasing the heap size to hold this new item
        i = this.count-1;
        while(i >=0 && data > this.array[(i-1)/2]) {
                this.array[i] = this.array[(i-1)/2];
                i = i-1/2;
        }
        this.array[i] = data;
}
void ResizeHeap() {
        int[] array_old = new int[this.capacity];
        System.arraycopy(this.array, 0, array_old, this.count-1);
        this.array = new int[this.capacity * 2];
        if(this.array == null) {
                System.out.println("Memory Error");
                return;
        }
        for (int i = 0; i < this.capacity; i ++)
                this.array[i] = array_old[i];
        this.capacity *= 2;
        array_old = null;
}
```

Time Complexity: O(*logn*). The explanation is same as that of Heapify function.

Destroying Heap

```
void DestroyHeap() {
        this.count = 0;
        this.array = null;
```

}

Heapifying the Array

One simple approach for building the heap is, take *n* input items and place them into an empty heap. This can be done with *n* successive inserts and takes O(*nlogn*) in the worst case. This is due to the fact that each insert operation takes O(*logn*).

Observation: Leaf nodes always satisfy the heap property and do not need to care for them. The leaf elements are always at the end and to heapify the given array it should be enough if we heapify the non-leaf nodes. Now let us concentrate on finding the first non leaf node. The last element of the heap is at location $h \to count - 1$, and to find the first non-leaf node it is enough to find the parent of last element.

```java
void BuildHeap(Heap h, int A[], int n) {
    if(h == null) return;
    while (n > this.capacity)
        h.ResizeHeap();
    for (int i = 0; i < n; i ++)
        h.array[i] = A[i];
    this.count = n;
    for (int i = (n-1)/2; i >=0; i --)
        h.PercolateDown(i);
}
```

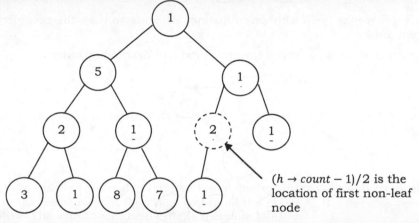

$(h \to count - 1)/2$ is the location of first non-leaf node

Time Complexity: The linear time bound of building heap, can be shown by computing the sum of the heights of all the nodes. For a complete binary tree of height *h* containing $n = 2^{h+1} - 1$ nodes, the sum of the heights of the nodes is $n - h - 1 = n - logn - 1$ (for proof refer *Problems Section*). That means, building heap operation can be done in linear time (O(*n*)) by applying a *PercolateDown* function to nodes in reverse level order.

Heapsort

One main application of heap ADT is sorting (heap sort). Heap sort algorithm inserts all elements (from an unsorted array) into a heap, then removes them from the root of a heap until the heap is empty. Note that heap sort can be done in place with the array to be sorted. Instead of deleting an element, exchange the first element (maximum) with the last element and reduce the heap size (array size). Then, we heapify the first element. Continue this process until the number of remaining elements is one.

```java
void Heapsort(int A[], in n) {
    Heap h = new Heap(n, 0);
    int old_size, i, temp;
    BuildHeap(h, A, n);
    old_size = h.count;
    for(i = n-1; i > 0; i--) { //h.array[0] is the largest element
        temp = h.array[0]; h.array[0] = h.array[h.count-1];
        h.count--;
        h.PercolateDown(i);
    }
    h.count = old_size;
}
```

Time complexity: As we remove the elements from the heap, the values become sorted (since maximum elements are always *root* only). Since the time complexity of both the insertion algorithm and deletion algorithms is O(*logn*) (where n is the number of items in the heap), the time complexity of the heap sort algorithm is O(*nlogn*).

7.7 Problems on Priority Queues [Heaps]

Problem-1   Is there a min-heap with seven distinct elements so that, the preorder traversal of it gives the elements in sorted order?

Solution: Yes. For the tree below, preorder traversal produces ascending order.

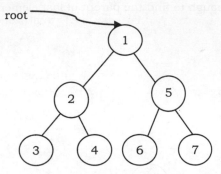

Problem-2   Is there a max-heap with seven distinct elements so that, the preorder traversal of it gives the elements in sorted order?

Solution: Yes. For the tree below, preorder traversal produces descending order.

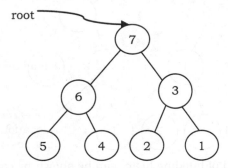

Problem-3   Is there a min-heap/max-heap with seven distinct elements so that, the inorder traversal of it gives the elements in sorted order?

Solution: No, since a heap must be either a min-heap or a max-heap, the root will hold the smallest element or the largest. An inorder traversal will visit the root of tree as its second step, which is not the appropriate place if trees root contains the smallest or largest element.

Problem-4   Is there a min-heap/max-heap with seven distinct elements so that, the postorder traversal of it gives the elements in sorted order?

Solution: Yes, if tree is a max-heap and we want descending order (below left), or if tree is a min-heap and we want ascending order (below right).

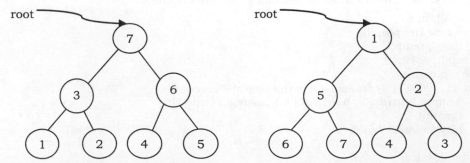

Problem-5   What are the minimum and maximum number of elements in a heap of height h?

Solution: Since heap is a complete binary tree (all levels contain full nodes except possibly the lowest level), it has at most $2^{h+1} - 1$ elements (if it is complete). This is because, to get maximum nodes, we need to fill all the h levels completely and the maximum number of nodes is nothing but sum of all nodes at all h levels.

To get minimum nodes, we should fill the $h - 1$ levels fully and last level with only one element. As a result, the minimum number of nodes is nothing but sum of all nodes from $h - 1$ levels plus 1 (for last level) and we get $2^h - 1 + 1 = 2^h$ elements (if the lowest level has just 1 element and all the other levels are complete).

Problem-6   Show that the height of a heap with n elements is $logn$?

Solution: A heap is a complete binary tree. All the levels, except the lowest, are completely full. So the heap has at least 2^h element and atmost elements. $2^h \le n \le 2^{h+1} - 1$. This implies, $h \le logn \le h + 1$. Since h is integer, $h = logn$.

Problem-7   Given a min-heap, give an algorithm for finding the maximum element.

Solution: For a given min heap the maximum element will always be at leaf only. Now, the next question is how to find the leaf nodes in tree. If we carefully observe, the next node of last elements parent is the first leaf node. Since the last element is always at $h \to count - 1^{th}$ location, the next node of its parent (parent at location $\frac{h \to count - 1}{2}$) can be calculated as:

$$\frac{h \to count - 1}{2} + 1 \approx \frac{h \to count + 1}{2}$$

Now, the only step remaining is scanning the leaf nodes and finding the maximum among them.

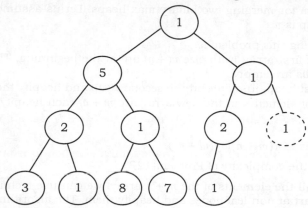

```
int FindMaxInMinHeap(Heap h) {
        int Max = -1;
        for(int i = (h.count+1)/2; i < h.count; i++)
                if(h→array[i] > Max)
                        Max = h.array[i];
}
```

Time Complexity: $O(\frac{n}{2}) \approx O(n)$.

Problem-8   Give an algorithm for deleting an arbitrary element from min heap.

Solution: To delete an element, first we need to search for an element. Let us assume that we are using level order traversal for finding the element. After finding the element we need to follow the DeleteMin process.

Time Complexity = Time for finding the element + Time for deleting an element
= $O(n)$ + $O(logn) \approx O(n)$. //Time for searching is dominated.

Problem-9   Give an algorithm for deleting the ith indexed element in a given min-heap.

Solution:
```
Int Delete(Heap h, int i) {
        int key;
        if(n < i) {
                System.out.println("Wrong position"); return;
        }
        key = h.array[i];
        h.array[i]= h.array[h.count-1];
        h.count--;
        h.PercolateDown(i);
        return key;
}
```

Time Complexity = O($logn$).

Problem-10   Prove that, for a complete binary tree of height h the sum of the heights of all nodes is O($n - h$).

Solution: A complete binary tree has 2^i nodes on level i. Also, a node on level i has depth i and height $h - i$. Let us assume that S denotes the sum of the heights of all these nodes and S can be calculated as:

$$S = \sum_{i=0}^{h} 2^i(h-i)$$
$$S = h + 2(h-1) + 4(h-2) + \cdots + 2^{h-1}(1)$$

Multiplying with 2 on both sides gives: $2S = 2h + 4(h-1) + 8(h-2) + \cdots + 2^h(1)$. Now, subtract S from $2S$: $2S - S = -h + 2 + 4 + \cdots + 2^h \Rightarrow S = (2^{h+1} - 1) - (h-1)$. But, we already know that the total number of nodes n in a complete binary tree with height h is $n = 2^{h+1} - 1$. This gives us: $h = log(n+1)$. Finally, replacing $2^{h+1} - 1$ with n, gives: $S = n - (h-1)$ =O($n - logn$) =O($n - h$).

Problem-11   Give an algorithm to find all elements less than some value k in a binary heap.

Solution: Start from the root of the heap. If the value of the root is smaller than k then print its value and call recursively once for its left child and once for its right child. If the value of a node is greater or equal than k then the function stops without printing that value. The complexity of this algorithm is O(n), where n is the total number of nodes in the heap. This bound takes place in the worst case, where the value of every node in the heap will be smaller than k, so the function has to call each node of the heap.

Problem-12   Give an algorithm for merging two binary max-heaps. Let us assume that the size of first heap is $m + n$ and size of second heap is n.

Solution: One simple way of solving this problem is:
- Assume that elements of first array (with size $m + n$) are at the beginning. That means, first m cells are filled and remaining n cells are empty.
- Without changing the first heap, just append the second heap and heapify the array.
- Since the total number of elements in the new array are $m + n$, each heapify operation takes O($log(m + n)$).

The complexity of this algorithm is : O($(m + n)log(m + n)$).

Problem-13   Can we improve the complexity of Problem-12?

Solution: Instead of heapifying all the elements of the $m + n$ array, we can use technique of "building heap with an array of elements". We can start at non leaf nodes and heapify them. The algorithm can be given as:
- Assume that elements of first array (with size $m + n$) are at the beginning. That means, first m cells are filled and remaining n cells are empty.
- Without changing the first heap, just append the second heap.
- Now, find the first non leaf node and start heapifying from that element.

In theory section, we have already seen that, building a heap with n elements takes O(n) complexity. The complexity of merging with this technique is: O($m + n$).

Problem-14   Is there an efficient algorithm for merging 2 max-heaps (stored as an array)? Assume both arrays have n elements.

Solution: The alternative solution for this problem depends on what type of heap it is. If it's a standard heap where every node has up to two children and which gets filled up that the leaves are on a maximum of two different rows, we cannot get better than O(n) for merge. There is an O($logm \times logn$) algorithm for merging two binary heaps with sizes m and n. For $m = n$, this algorithm takes O($log^2 n$) time complexity. We will be skipping it due to its difficulty and scope. For better merging performance, we can use another variant of binary heap like a *Fibonacci-Heap* which can merge in O(1) on average (amortized).

Problem-15   Give an algorithm for finding the kth smallest element in min-heap.

Solution: One simple solution to this problem is: perform deletion k times from min-heap.
```
int FindKthLargestEle(Heap h, int k) {
        //Just delete first k-1 elements and return the k-th element.
        for(int i=0;i<k-1;i++)
                h.DeleteMin();
        return h.DeleteMin();
}
```
Time Complexity: O($klogn$). Since we are performing deletion operation k times and each deletion takes O($logn$).

Problem-16   For the Problem-15, can we improve the time complexity?

Solution: Assume that the original min-heap is called *HOrig* and the auxiliary min-heap is named *HAux*. Initially, the element at the top of *HOrig*, the minimum one, is inserted into *HAux*. Here we don't do the operation of DeleteMin with *HOrig*.

```java
Heap HOrig, HAux;
int FindKthLargestEle( int k ) {
        int heapElement;//Assuming heap data is of integers
        int count=1;
        HAux.Insert(HOrig.DeleteMin());
        while( true ) {
                //return the minimum element and delete it from the HA heap
                heapElement = HAux.DeleteMin();
                if(++count == k ) {
                        return heapElement;
                }
                else {    //insert the left and right children in HO into the HA
                        HAux.Insert(heapElement.LeftChild());
                        HAux.Insert(heapElement.RightChild());
                }
        }
}
```

Every while-loop iteration gives the kth smallest element and we need k loops to get the kth smallest elements. Because the size of the auxiliary heap is always less than k, every while-loop iteration the size of the auxiliary heap increases by one, and the original heap *HOrig* has no operation during the finding, the running time is $O(klogk)$.

Problem-17   Find k max elements from max heap.

Solution: One simple solution to this problem is: build max-heap and perform deletion k times.
$$T(n) = \text{DeleteMin from heap } k \text{ times} = \Theta(klogn).$$

Problem-18   For Problem-17, is there any alternative solution?

Solution: We can use the Problem-16 solution. At the end the auxiliary heap contains the k-largest elements. Without deleting the elements we should keep on adding elements to *HAux*.

Problem-19   How do we implement stack using heap?

Solution: To implement a stack using a priority queue PQ (using min heap), let us assume that we are using one extra integer variable c. Also, assume that c is initialized equal to any known value (e.g. 0). The implementation of the stack ADT is given below. Here c is used as the priority while inserting/deleting the elements from PQ.

```java
void Push(int element) {
      PQ.Insert(c, element);
      c--;
}
int Pop() {
      return PQ.DeleteMin();
}
int Top() {
      return PQ.Min();
}
int Size() {
      return PQ.Size();
}
int isEmpty() {
      return PQ.isEmpty();
}
```

Note: We could also increment c back when popping.

Observation: We could use the negative of the current system time instead of c (to avoid overflow). The implementation based on this can be given as:

```java
void Push(int element) {
      PQ.insert(-gettime(),element);
}
```

Problem-20   How do we implement Queue using heap?

Solution: To implement a queue using a priority queue PQ (using min heap), as similar to stacks simulation, let us assume that we are using one extra integer variable, c. Also, assume that c is initialized equal to any known value (e.g. 0). The implementation of the queue ADT is given below. Here the c, is used as the priority while inserting/deleting the elements from PQ.

```java
void Push(int element) {
        PQ.Insert(c, element);
        c++;
}
int Pop() {
        return PQ.DeleteMin();
}
int Top() {
        return PQ.Min();
}
int Size() {
        return PQ.Size();
}
int isEmpty() {
        return PQ.isEmpty();
}
```

Note: We could also decrement c when popping.

Observation: We could use just the negative of the current system time instead of c (to avoid overflow). The implementation based on this can be given as:

```java
void Push(int element) {
        PQ.insert(gettime(),element);
}
```

Note: The only change is that we need to take positive c value instead of negative.

Problem-21   Given a big file containing billions of numbers. How can you find the the 10 maximum numbers from that file?

Solution: Always remember that when need to find max n elements, best data structure to use is priority queues.

One solution for this problem is to divide the data in sets of 1000 elements (let's say 1000), make a heap of them, and take 10 elements from each heap one by one. Finally heap sort all the sets of 10 elements and take top 10 among those. But the problem in this approach is where to store 10 elements from each heap. That may require a large amount of memory as we have billions of numbers.

Reusing top 10 elements from earlier heap in subsequent elements can solve this problem. That means to take first block of 1000 elements and subsequent blocks of 990 elements each. Initially Heapsort first set of 1000 numbers, take max 10 elements and mix them with 990 elements of 2nd set. Again Heapsort these 1000 numbers (10 from first set and 990 from 2nd set), take 10 max element and mix those with 990 elements of 3rd set. Repeat till last set of 990 (or less) elements and take max 10 elements from final heap. These 10 elements will be your answer.

Time Complexity: $O(n) = n/1000 \times$(complexity of Heapsort 1000 elements) Since complexity of heap sorting 1000 elements will be a constant so the $O(n) = n$ i.e. linear complexity.

Problem-22   **Merge k sorted lists with total of n elements:** We are given k sorted lists with total n inputs in all the lists. Give an algorithm to merge them into one single sorted list.

Solution: Since there are k equal size lists with a total of n elements, size of each list is $\frac{n}{k}$. One simple way of solving this problem is:

- Take the first list and merge it with second list. Since the size of each list is $\frac{n}{k}$, this step produces a sorted list with size $\frac{2n}{k}$. This is similar to merge sort logic. Time complexity of this step is: $\frac{2n}{k}$. This is because we need to scan all the elements of both the lists.
- Then, merge the second list output with third list. As a result this step produces the sorted list with size $\frac{3n}{k}$. Time complexity of this step is: $\frac{3n}{k}$. This is because we need to scan all the elements of both the lists (one with size $\frac{2n}{k}$ and other with size $\frac{n}{k}$).
- Continue this process until all the lists are merged to one list.

Total time complexity: $= \frac{2n}{k} + \frac{3n}{k} + \frac{4n}{k} + \cdots \cdot \frac{kn}{k} = \sum_{i=2}^{n} \frac{in}{k} = \frac{n}{k} \sum_{i=2}^{n} i \approx \frac{n(k^2)}{k} \approx O(nk)$. Space Complexity: O(1).

Problem-23   For the Problem-22, can we improve the time complexity?

Solution:
1   Divide the lists into pairs and merge them. That means, first take two lists at a time and merge them so that the total elements parsed for all lists is $O(n)$. This operation gives $k/2$ lists.
2   Repeat step-1 until the number of lists becomes one.

Time complexity: Step-1 executes $logk$ times and each operation parses all n elements in all the lists for making $k/2$ lists. For example, if we have 8 lists then first pass would make 4 lists by parsing all n elements. Second pass would make 2 lists by parsing again n elements and third pass would give 1 list again by parsing n elements. As a result the total time complexity is $O(nlogn)$. Space Complexity: $O(n)$.

Problem-24   For the Problem-23, can we improve the space complexity?

Solution: Let us use heaps for reducing the space complexity.
1.   Build the max-heap with all first elements from each list in $O(k)$.
2.   In each step extract the maximum element of the heap and add it at the end of the output.
3.   Add the next element from the list of the one extracted. That means, we need to select the next element of the list which contains the extracted element of the previous step.
4.   Repeat step−2 and step-3 until all the elements are completed from all the lists.

Time Complexity = $O(n\ logk\ )$. At a time we have k elements max heap and for all n elements we have to read just the heap in $logk$ time so total time = $O(nlogk)$. Space Complexity: $O(k)$ [for Max-heap].

Problem-25   Given 2 arrays A and B each with n elements. Give an algorithm for finding largest n pairs $(A[i], B[j])$.

Solution:
Algorithm:
•   Heapify A and B. This step takes $O(2n) \approx O(n)$.
•   Then keep on deleting the elements from both the heaps. Each step takes $O(2logn) \approx O(logn)$.
Total Time complexity: $O(nlogn)$.

Problem-26   **Min-Max heap:** Give an algorithm that supports min and max in $O(1)$ time, insert, delete min, and delete max in $O(logn)$ time. That means, design a data structure which supports the following operations:

Operation	Complexity
Init	$O(n)$
Insert	$O(logn)$
FindMin	$O(1)$
FindMax	$O(1)$
DeleteMin	$O(logn)$
DeleteMax	$O(logn)$

Solution: This problem can be solved using two heaps. Let us say two heaps are: Minimum-Heap H_{min} and Maximum-Heap H_{max}. Also, assume that elements in both the arrays have mutual pointers. That means, an element in H_{min} will have a pointer to the same element in H_{max} and an element in H_{max} will have a pointer to the same element in H_{min}.

Init	Build H_{min} in $O(n)$ and H_{max} in $O(n)$
Insert(x)	Insert x to H_{min} in $O(logn)$. Insert x to H_{max} in $O(logn)$. Update the pointers in $O(1)$
FindMin()	Return root(H_{min}) in $O(1)$
FindMax	Return root(H_{max}) in $O(1)$
DeleteMin	Delete the minimum from H_{min} in $O(logn)$. Delete the same element from H_{max} by using the mutual pointer in $O(logn)$
DeleteMax	Delete the maximum from H_{max} in $O(logn)$. Delete the same element from H_{min} by using the mutual pointer in $O(logn)$

Problem-27   Dynamic median finding. Design a heap data structure that supports finding the median.

Solution: In a set of n elements, median is the middle element, such that the number of elements lesser than the median is equal to the number of elements larger than the median. If n is odd, we can find the median by sorting the set and taking the middle element. If n is even, the median is usually defined as the average of the two middle elements. This algorithm work even when some of the elements in the list are equal. For example, the median of the multiset $\{1, 1, 2, 3, 5\}$ is 2, and the median of the multiset $\{1, 1, 2, 3, 5, 8\}$ is 2.5.

"*Median heaps*" are the variant of heaps that give access to the median element. A median heap can be implemented using two heaps, each containing half the elements. One is a max-heap, containing the smallest elements, the other is a min-heap, containing the largest elements. The size of the max-heap may be equal to the size of the min-heap, if the total number of elements is even. In this case, the median is the average of the maximum element of the max-heap and the minimum element of the min-heap. If there are an odd number of elements, the max-heap will contain one more element than the min-heap. The median in this case is simply the maximum element of the max-heap.

Problem-28 **Maximum sum in sliding window:** Given array A[] with sliding window of size w which is moving from the very left of the array to the very right. Assume that we can only see the w numbers in the window. Each time the sliding window moves rightwards by one position. For example: The array is [1 3 -1 -3 5 3 6 7], and w is 3.

Window position	Max
[1 3 -1] -3 5 3 6 7	3
1 [3 -1 -3] 5 3 6 7	3
1 3 [-1 -3 5] 3 6 7	5
1 3 -1 [-3 5 3] 6 7	5
1 3 -1 -3 [5 3 6] 7	6
1 3 -1 -3 5 [3 6 7]	7

Input: A long array A[], and a window width w. **Output**: An array B[], B[i] is the maximum value of from A[i] to A[i+w-1]. **Requirement**: Find a good optimal way to get B[i]

Solution: Brute force solution is, every time the window is moved, we can search for a total of w elements in the window.
Time complexity of O(nw).

Problem-29 For Problem-28, can we reduce the complexity?

Solution: Yes, we can use heap data structure. This reduces the time complexity to O($nlogw$). Insert operation takes O($logw$) time, where w is the size of the heap. However, getting the maximum value is cheap, it merely takes constant time as the maximum value is always kept in the root (head) of the heap. As the window slides to the right, some elements in the heap might not be valid anymore (range is outside of the current window). How should we remove them? We would need to be somewhat careful here. Since we only remove elements that are out of the window's range, we would need to keep track of the elements' indices too.

Problem-30 For Problem-28, can we further reduce the complexity?

Solution: Yes, The double-ended queue is the perfect data structure for this problem. It supports insertion/deletion from the front and back. The trick is to find a way such that the largest element in the window would always appear in the front of the queue. How would you maintain this requirement as you push and pop elements in and out of the queue?

Besides, you will notice that there are some redundant elements in the queue that we shouldn't even consider. For example, if the current queue has the elements: [10 5 3], and a new element in the window has the element 11. Now, we could have emptied the queue without considering elements 10, 5, and 3, and insert only element 11 into the queue.

Typically, most people try to maintain the queue size the same as the window's size. Try to break away from this thought and think out of the box. Removing redundant elements and storing only elements that need to be considered in the queue is the key to achieving the efficient O(n) solution below. This is because each element in the list is being inserted and removed at most once. Therefore, the total number of insert + delete operations is $2n$.

```java
void MaxSlidingWindow(int A[], int n, int w, int B[]) {
        DoubleEndQueue Q = new DoubleEndQueue();
        for (int i = 0; i < w; i++) {
                while (!Q.isEmpty() && A[i] >= A[Q.QBack()])
                        Q.PopBack();
                Q.PushBack(i);
        }
        for (int i = w; i < n; i++) {
                B[i-w] = A[Q.QFront()];
                while (!Q.isEmpty() && A[i] >= A[Q.QBack()])
                        Q.PopBack();
                while (!Q.isEmpty() && Q.QFront() <= i-w)
                        Q.PopFront();
                Q.PushBack(i);
        }
        B[n-w] = A[Q.QFront()];
}
```

Problem-31   A priority queue is a list of items in which each item has associated with it a priority. Items are withdrawn from a priority queue in order of their priorities starting with the highest priority item first. If the maximum priority item is required, then a heap is constructed such than priority of every node is greater than the priority of its children.

Design such a heap where the item with the middle priority is withdrawn first. If there are n items in the heap, then the number of items with the priority smaller than the middle priority is $\frac{n}{2}$ if n is odd, else $\frac{n}{2} \mp 1$.

Explain how the withdraw and insert operations work, calculate their complexity, and how the data structure is constructed.

Solution: We can use one min heap and one max heap such that root of the min heap is larger than the root of the max heap. The size of the min heap should be equal or one less than the size of the max heap. So the middle element is always the root of the max heap.

For the insert operation, if the new item is less than the root of max heap, then insert it into the max heap, else insert it into the min heap. After the withdraw or insert operation, if the size of heaps are not as specified above than transfer the root element of the max heap to min heap or vice-versa.

With this implementation, insert and withdraw operation will be in O(*logn*) time.

Problem-32   Given two heaps, how do you merge (union) them?

Solution: Binary heap supports various operations quickly: Find-min, insert, decrease-key. If we have two min-heaps, H1 and H2, there is no efficient way to combine them into a single min-heap.

For solving this problem efficiently, we can use mergeable heaps. Mergeable heaps support efficient union operation. It is a data structure that supports the following operations:

- Create-Heap(): creates an empty heap
- Insert(H,X,K) : insert an item x with key K into a heap H
- Find-Min(H) : return item with min key
- Delete-Min(H) : return and remove
- Union(H1, H2) : merge heaps H1 and H2

Examples of mergeable heaps are:

- Binomial Heaps
- Fibonacci Heaps

Both heaps also support:

- Decrease-Key(H,X,K): assign item Y with a smaller key K
- Delete(H,X) : remove item X

Binomial Heaps: Unlike binary heap which consists of a single tree, a *binomial* heap consists of a small set of component trees and no need to rebuild everything when union is performed. Each component tree is in a special format, called a *binomial tree*.

A binomial tree of order k, denoted by B_k is defined recursively as follows:

- B_0 is a tree with a single node
- For $k \geq 1$, B_k is formed by joining two B_{k-1}, such that the root of one tree becomes the leftmost child of the root of the other.

Example:

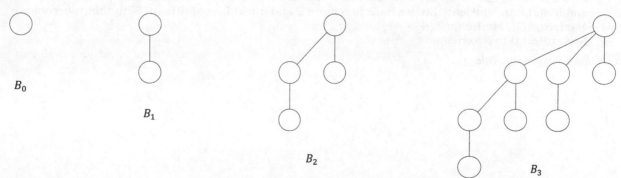

Fibonacci Heaps: Fibonacci heap is another example of mergeable heap. It has no good worst-case guarantee for any operation (except Insert/Create-Heap). Fibonacci Heaps have excellent amortized cost to perform each operation. Like *binomial* heap, *fibonacci* heap consists of a set of min-heap ordered component trees. However, unlike binomial heap, it has

- No limit on number of trees (up to O(n)), and
- No limit on height of a tree (up to O(n))

Also, *Find-Min, Delete-Min, Union, Decrease-Key, Delete* all have worst-case O(n) running time. However, in the amortized sense, each operation performs very quickly.

Operation	Binary Heap	Binomial Heap	Fibonacci Heap
Create-Heap	$\Theta(1)$	$\Theta(1)$	$\Theta(1)$
Find-Min	$\Theta(1)$	$\Theta(\log n)$	$\Theta(1)$
Delete-Min	$\Theta(\log n)$	$\Theta(\log n)$	$\Theta(\log n)$
Insert	$\Theta(\log n)$	$\Theta(\log n)$	$\Theta(1)$
Delete	$\Theta(\log n)$	$\Theta(\log n)$	$\Theta(\log n)$
Decrease-Key	$\Theta(\log n)$	$\Theta(\log n)$	$\Theta(1)$
Union	$\Theta(n)$	$\Theta(\log n)$	$\Theta(1)$

Problem-33   Median in an infinite series of integers

Solution: Median is the middle number in a sorted list of numbers (if we have odd number of elements). If we have even number of elements, median is the average of two middle numbers in a sorted list of numbers.

We can solve this problem efficiently by using 2 heaps: One MaxHeap and one MinHeap.

1. MaxHeap contains the smallest half of the received integers
2. MinHeap contains the largest half of the received integers

The integers in MaxHeap are always less than or equal to the integers in MinHeap. Also, the number of elements in MaxHeap is either equal to or 1 more than the number of elements in the MinHeap.

In the stream if we get $2n$ elements (at any point of time), MaxHeap and MinHeap will both contain equal number of elements (in this case, n elements in each heap). Otherwise, if we have received $2n + 1$ elements, MaxHeap will contain $n + 1$ and MinHeap n.

Let us find the Median: If we have $2n + 1$ elements (odd), the Median of received elements will be the largest element in the MaxHeap (nothing but the root of MaxHeap). Otherwise, the Median of received elements will be the average of largest element in the MaxHeap (nothing but the root of MaxHeap) and smallest element in the MinHeap (nothing but the root of MinHeap). This can be calculated in O(1).

Inserting an element into heap can be done in O($\log n$). Note that, any heap containing $n + 1$ elements might need one delete operation (and insertion to other heap) as well.

Example:
   Insert 1: Insert to MaxHeap.
   MaxHeap: {1}, MinHeap:{}

   Insert 9: Insert to MinHeap. Since 9 is greater than 1 and MinHeap maintains the maximum elements.
   MaxHeap: {1}, MinHeap:{9}

   Insert 2: Insert MinHeap. Since 2 is less than all elements of MinHeap.
   MaxHeap: {1,2}, MinHeap:{9}

   Insert 0: Since MaxHeap already has more than half; we have to drop the max element from MaxHeap and insert it to MinHeap. So, we have to remove 2 and insert into MinHeap. With that it becomes:
   MaxHeap: {1}, MinHeap:{2,9}
   Now, insert 0 to MaxHeap.

Total Time Complexity: O($\log n$).

Chapter-8

DISJOINT SETS ADT

8.1 Introduction

In this chapter, we will represent an important mathematics concept *sets*. This means how to represent a group of elements which do not need any order. The disjoint sets ADT is the one used for this purpose. It is used for solving the equivalence problem. It is very simple to implement and a simple array can be used for the implementation and each function takes only a few lines of code. Disjoint sets ADT acts as an auxiliary data structure for many other algorithms (for example, Kruskal's algorithm in graph theory). Before starting our discussion on disjoint sets ADT, let us see some basic properties of sets.

8.2 Equivalence Relations and Equivalence Classes

For the discussion below let us assume that S is a set containing the elements and a relation R is defined on it. That means for every pair of elements in $a, b \in S$, $a \, R \, b$ is either true or false. If $a \, R \, b$ is true, then we say a is related to b, otherwise a is not related to b. A relation R is called an *equivalence relation* if it satisfies the following properties:

- *Reflexive*: For every element $a \in S, a \, R \, a$ is true.
- *Symmetric*: For any two elements $a, b \in S$, if $a \, R \, b$ is true then $b \, R \, a$ is true.
- *Transitive*: For any three elements a, b, c ∈ S, if a R b and $b \, R \, c$ are true then $a \, R \, c$ is true.

As an example, relations ≤ (less than or equal to) and ≥ (greater than or equal to) on a set of integers are not equivalence relations. They are reflexive (since $a \leq a$) and transitive ($a \leq b$ and $b \leq c$ implies $a \leq c$) but it is not symmetric ($a \leq b$ does not imply $b \leq a$).

Similarly, *rail connectivity* is an equivalence relation. This relation is reflexive because any location is connected to itself. If there is a connectivity from city a to city b, then city b also has connectivity to city a, so the relation is symmetric. Finally, if city a is connected to city b and city b is connected to city c, then city a is also connected to city c.

The *equivalence class* of an element $a \in S$ is a subset of S that contains all the elements that are related to a. Equivalence classes creates a *partition* of S. Every member of S appears in exactly one equivalence class. To decide if $a \, R \, b$, we just need to check whether a and b are in the same equivalence class (group) or not.

In the above example, two cities will be in same equivalence class if they have rail connectivity. If they do not have connectivity then they will be part of different equivalence classes.

Since the intersection of any two equivalence classes is empty (ϕ), the equivalence classes are sometimes called *disjoint sets*. In the subsequent sections, we will try to see the operations that can be performed on equivalence classes. The possible operations are:

- Creating an equivalence class (making a set)
- Finding the equivalence class name (Find)
- Combining the equivalence classes (Union)

8.3 Disjoint Sets ADT

To manipulate the set elements we need basic operations defined on sets. In this chapter, we concentrate on following set operations:
- MAKESET(X): Creates a new set containing a single element X.
- UNION(X, Y): Creates a new set containing the elements X and Y with their union and deletes the sets containing the elements X and Y.
- FIND(X): Returns the name of the set containing the element X.

8.4 Applications

Disjoint sets ADT have many applications and few of them are:
- To represent network connectivity

- Image processing
- To find least common ancestor
- To define equivalence of finite state automata
- Kruskal's minimum spanning tree algorithm (graph theory)
- In game algorithms

8.5 Tradeoffs in Implementing Disjoint Sets ADT

Let us see the possibilities for implementing disjoint set operations. Initially, assume the input elements are collection of n sets, each with one element. That means, initial representation assumes all relations (except reflexive relations) are false. Each set has a different element, so that $S_i \cap S_j = \phi$. This makes the sets *disjoint*.

To add the relation $a\ R\ b$ (UNION), we first need to check whether a and b are already related or not. This can be verified by performing FINDs on both a and b and checking whether they are in the same equivalence class (set) or not. If they are not, then we apply UNION. This operation merges the two equivalence classes containing a and b into a new equivalence class by creating a new set $S_k = S_i \cup S_j$ and deletes S_i and S_j. Basically there are two ways to implement the above FIND/UNION operations:

- Fast FIND implementation (also called Quick FIND)
- Fast UNION operation implementation (also called Quick UNION)

Fast FIND Implementation (Quick FIND)

In this method, we use an array. As an example, in the representation below the array contains the set name for each element. For simplicity, let us assume that all the elements are numbered sequentially from 0 to $n - 1$.

In the example below, element 0 has the set name 3, element 1 has the set name 5 and so on. With this representation FIND takes only O(1) since for any element we can find the set name by accessing its array location in constant time.

In this representation, to perform UNION(a, b) [assuming that a is in set i and b is in set j] we need to scan the complete array and change all $i's$ to j. This takes O(n). A sequence of $n - 1$ unions take O(n^2) time in the worst case. If there are O(n^2) FIND operations, this performance is fine, as the average time complexity is O(1) for each UNION or FIND operation. If there are fewer FINDs, this complexity is not acceptable.

Fast UNION Implementation (Quick UNION)

In this and subsequent sections, we will discuss the faster *UNION* implementations and its variants. There are different ways of implementing this approach and following is a list of a few of them.

- Fast UNION implementations (Slow FIND)
- Fast UNION implementations (Quick FIND)
- Fast UNION implementations with path compression

8.6 Fast UNION implementation (Slow FIND)

As we have discussed, FIND operation returns same answer (set name) if and only if they are in the same set. In representing disjoint sets, our main objective is to give different set name for each group. In general we do not care for the name of the set. One possibility for implementing the set is *tree* as each element has only one *root* and we can use it as the set name.

How are these represented?

One possibility is using an array: for each element keep the *root* as its set name. But with this representation, we will have the same problem as that of FIND array implementation. To solve this problem, instead of storing the *root* we can keep parent of element. Therefore, using an array which stores the parent of each element solves our problem. To differentiate the root node, let us assume its parent is same as that of element in the array. Based on this representation, MAKESET, FIND, UNION operations can be defined as:

- MAKESET(X): Creates a new set containing a single element X and in the array update the parent of X as X. That means root (set name) of X is X.

- UNION(X, Y): Replaces the two sets containing X and Y by their union and in the array update the parent of X as Y.

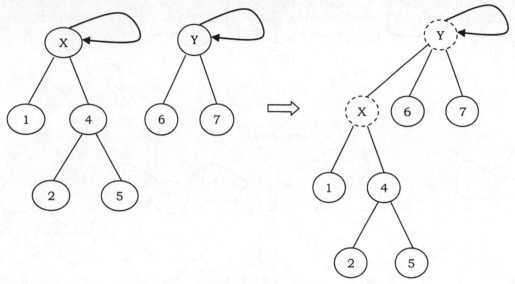

- FIND(X): Returns the name of the set containing the element X. We keep on searching for $X's$ set name until we come to root of the tree.

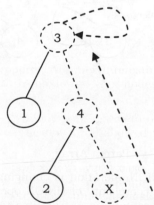

For the elements 0 to $n-1$ the initial representation is:

Parent Array

To perform a UNION on two sets, we merge the two trees by making the root of one tree point to the root of the other.

Initial Configuration for the elements 0 to 6

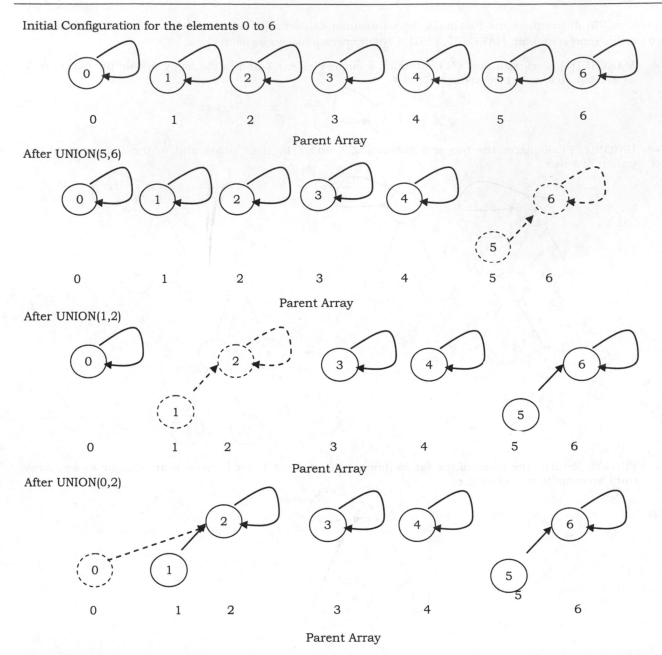

Parent Array

After UNION(5,6)

Parent Array

After UNION(1,2)

Parent Array

After UNION(0,2)

Parent Array

One important thing to observe here is, UNION operation is changing the roots parent only but not for all the elements in the sets. Due to this, the time complexity of UNION operation is O(1). A FIND(X) on element X is performed by returning the root of the tree containing X. The time to perform this operation is proportional to the depth of the node representing X. Using this method, it is possible to create a tree of depth $n - 1$ (Skew Trees) and the worst-case running time of a FIND is O(n) and m consecutive FIND operations take O(mn) time in the worst case.

```
public class  DisjointSet {
        public int[] S;
        public int size;                          // Number of elements in set
        public MAKESET(int size)                  { //Refer Below sections }
        public int FIND(int X)                     { //Refer Below sections }
        public int UNION(int root1, int root2)     {//Refer Below sections }
        .........

}
```

MAKESET

public void MAKESET(int size){

```
        S = new int[size];
        for(int i = size-1; i >=0; i-- )
                S[i] = i;
}
```

FIND

```
public int FIND(int X){
        if(! (X >= 0 && X < size)) )
                return;
        if( S[X] == X )
                return X;
        else
                return FIND(S, S[X]);
}
```

UNION

```
public void UNION(int root1, int root2){
        if(FIND(root1) == FIND(root2))
                return;
        if(! ((root1 >= 0 && root1 < size) && (root1 >= 0 && root1 < size) ) )
                return;
        S[root1] = root2;
}
```

8.7 Fast UNION implementations (Quick FIND)

The main problem with the previous approach is that, in the worst case we are getting the skew trees and as a result the FIND operation is taking O(n) time complexity. There are two ways to improve it:

- UNION by Size (also called UNION by Weight): Make the smaller tree as a subtree of the larger tree
- UNION by Height (also called UNION by Rank): Make the tree with smaller height as a subtree of the tree with larger height

UNION by Size

In the earlier representation, for each element i we have stored i (in the parent array) for the root element and for other elements we have stored the parent of i. But in this approach we store negative of size of the tree (that means, if the size of the tree is 3 then store −3 in the parent array for root element). For the previous example (after UNION(0,2)), the new representation will look like:

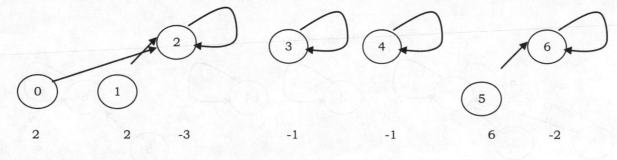

| 2 | 2 | -3 | -1 | -1 | 6 | -2 |

Parent Array

Assume that the size of one element set is 1 and store −1. Other than this there is no change.

MAKESET

```
public void MAKESET(int size) {
        for(int i = size-1; i >= 0; i-- )
                S[i] = -1;
}
```

FIND

```java
public int FIND(int X) {
        if(! (X >= 0 && X < size)) )
                return;
        if( S[X] == -1 )
                return X;
        else        return FIND(S, S[X]);
}
```

UNION by Size

```java
public void UNIONBySize(int root1, int root2) {
        if(FIND(root1) == FIND(root2))
                return;
        if( S[root2] < S[root1] )   {
                S[root1] = root2;
                S[root2] += S[root1];
        }
        else {
                S[root2] = root1;
                S[root1] += S[root2];
        }
}
```

Note: There is no change in FIND operation implementation.

UNION by Height (UNION by Rank)

As in UNION by size, in this method we store negative of height of the tree (that means, if the height of the tree is 3 then we store -3 in the parent array for root element). We assume the height of a tree with one element set is 1. For the previous example (after UNION(0,2)), the new representation will look like:

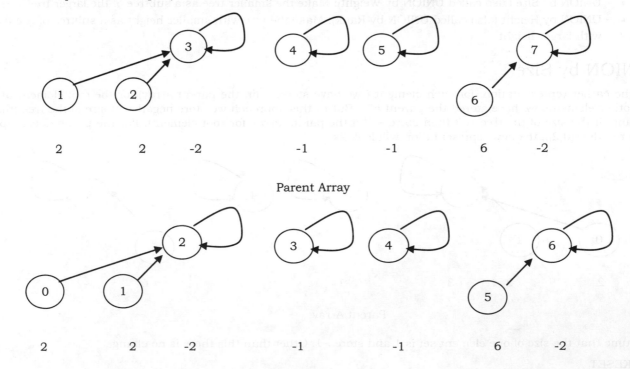

Parent Array

Parent Array

UNION by Height

```java
public void UNIONByHeight(int root1, int root2) {
        if(FIND(root1) == FIND(root2))
```

```
                return;
        if( S[root2] < S[root1] )
                S[root1] = root2;
        else {
                if( S[root2] == S[root1] )
                        S[root1]--;
                S[root2] = root1;
        }
}
```

Note: For FIND operation there is no change in the implementation.

Comparing UNION by Size and UNION by Height

With UNION by size, the depth of any node is never more than *logn*. This is because a node is initially at depth 0. When its depth increases as a result of a UNION, it is placed in a tree that is at least twice as large as before. That means its depth can be increased at most *logn* times. This means that the running time for a FIND operation is O(*logn*), and a sequence of *m* operations takes O(*m logn*).

Similarly with UNION by height, if we take the UNION of two trees of the same height, the height of the UNION is one larger than the common height, and otherwise equal to the max of the two heights. This will keep the height of tree of *n* nodes from growing past O(*logn*). A sequence of *m* UNIONs and FINDs can then still cost O(*m logn*).

8.8 Path Compression

FIND operation traverses list of nodes on the way to the root. We can make later FIND operations efficient by making each of these vertices point directly to the root. This process is called *path compression*. For example, in the FIND(*X*) operation, we travel from *X* till the root of the tree. The effect of path compression is that every node on the path from *X* to the root has its parent changed to the root.

With path compression the only change to the FIND function is that *S*[*X*] is made equal to the value returned by FIND. That means, after the root of the set is found recursively, *X* is made to point directly to it. This happen recursively to every node on the path to the root.

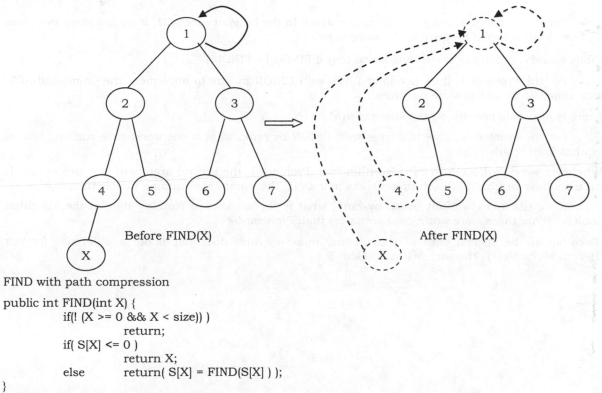

Before FIND(X)   After FIND(X)

FIND with path compression

```java
public int FIND(int X) {
        if(! (X >= 0 && X < size)) )
                return;
        if( S[X] <= 0 )
                return X;
        else        return( S[X] = FIND(S[X] ) );
}
```

Note: Path compression is compatible with UNION by size but not with UNION by height as there is no efficient way to change the height of the tree.

8.9 Summary

Performing m union-find operations on a set of n objects.

Algorithm	Worst-case time
Quick-find	mn
Quick-union	mn
Quick-Union by Size/Height	$n + m\,logn$
Path compression	$n + m\,logn$
Quick-Union by Size/Height + Path Compression	$(m + n)\,logn$

8.10 Problems on Disjoint Sets

Problem-1   Consider a list of cities c_1, c_2,...,c_n. Assume that we have a relation R such that, for any i, j, $R(c_i, c_j)$ is 1 if cities c_i and c_j are in the same state, and 0 otherwise. If R is stored as a table, how much space does it require?

Solution: R must have an entry for every pair of cities. There are $\Theta(n^2)$ of these.

Problem-2   For the Problem-1, using a Disjoint sets ADT, give an algorithm that puts each city in a set such that c_i and c_j are in the same set if and only if they are in the same state.

Solution:
```
for (int i = 1; i<= n; i++) {
        MAKESET(c_i);
        for (int j = 1; j <= i-1; j++) {
                if(R(c_j, c_i)) {
                        UNION(c_j, c_i);
                        break;
                }
        }
}
```

Problem-3   For the Problem-1, when the cities are stored in the Disjoint sets ADT, if we are given two cities c_i and c_j, how do we check if they are in the same state?

Solution: Cities c_i and c_j are in the same state if and only if FIND(c_i) = FIND(c_j).

Problem-4   For the Problem-1, if we use linked-lists with UNION by size to implement the union-find ADT, how much space do we use to store the cities?

Solution: There is one node per city, so the space is $\Theta(n)$.

Problem-5   For the Problem-1, if we use trees with UNION by rank, what is the worst-case running time of the algorithm from Problem-2?

Solution: Whenever we do a UNION in the algorithm from Problem-2, the second argument is a tree of size 1. Therefore, all trees have height 1, so each union takes time O(1). The worst-case running time is then $\Theta(n^2)$.

Problem-6   If we use trees without union-by-rank, what is the worst-case running time of the algorithm from Problem-2. Are there more worst-case scenarios than Problem-5?

Solution: Because of the special case of the unions, union-by-rank does not make a difference for our algorithm. Hence, everything is the same as in Problem-5.

Chapter-9

Graph Algorithms

9.1 Introduction

In real world, many problems are represented in terms of objects and connections between them. For example, in an airline route map, we might be interested in questions like: "What's the fastest way to go from Hyderabad to New York?" *or* "What is the cheapest way to go from Hyderabad to New York?" To answer these questions we need information about connections (airline routes) between objects (towns). Graphs are data structures used for solving these kinds of problems.

9.2 Glossary

Graph: A graph is a pair (*V*, *E*), where *V* is a set of nodes, called *vertices* and *E* is a collection of pairs of vertices, called *edges*.

- *Vertices* and *edges* are positions and store elements
- Definitions that we use:
    - *Directed edge*:
        - ordered pair of vertices (u, v)
        - first vertex u is the origin
        - second vertex v is the destination
        - Example: One-way road traffic

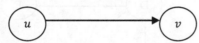

    - *Undirected edge*:
        - unordered pair of vertices (u, v)
        - Example: Railway lines

    - *Directed graph*:
        - all the edges are directed
        - Example: route network

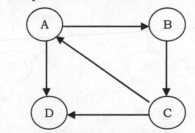

    - *Undirected graph*:
        - all the edges are undirected
        - Example: flight network

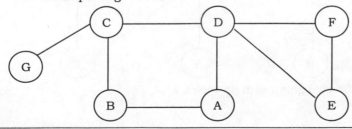

- When an edge connects two vertices, the vertices are said to be adjacent to each other and that the edge is incident on both vertices.
- A graph with no cycles is called a *tree*. A tree is an acyclic connected graph.

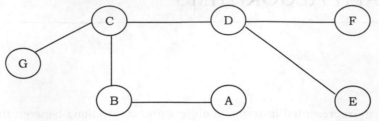

- A self loop is an edge that connects a vertex to itself.

- Two edges are parallel if they connect the same pair of vertices.

- Degree of a vertex is the number of edges incident on it.
- A subgraph is a subset of a graphs edges (with associated vertices) that forms a graph.
- A path in a graph is a sequence of adjacent vertices. *Simple* path is a path with no repeated vertices. In the graph below, dotted lines represent a path from *G* to *E*.

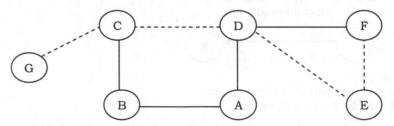

- A cycle is a path where first and last vertices are the same. A simple cycle is a cycle with no repeated vertices or edges (except the first and last vertices).

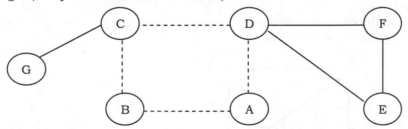

- We say that one vertex is connected to another if there is a path that contains both of them.
- A graph is connected if there is a path from *every* vertex to every other vertex.
- If a graph is not connected then it consists of a set of connected components.

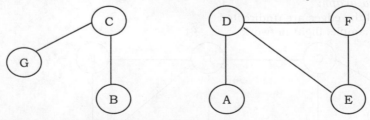

- A *directed* acyclic graph is a directed graph with no cycles.

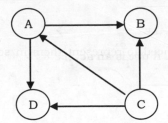

- A forest is a disjoint set of trees.
- A spanning tree of a connected graph is a subgraph that contains all of that graph's vertices and is a single tree. A spanning forest of a graph is the union of spanning trees of its connected components.
- A bipartite graph is a graph whose vertices can be divided into two sets such that all edges connect a vertex in one set with a vertex in the other set.

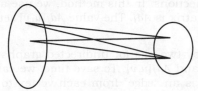

- In *weighted graphs* integers *(weights)* are assigned to each edge to represent (distances or costs).

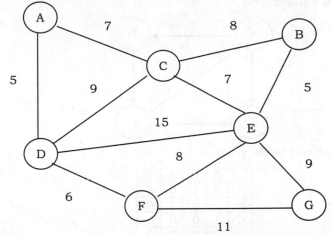

- We will denote the number of vertices in a given graph by |V|, the number of edges by |E|. Note that E can range anywhere from 0 to |V|(|V| − 1)/2 (in undirected graph). This is because each node can connect to every other node.
- Graphs with all edges present are called *complete* graphs.

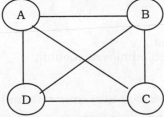

- Graphs with relatively few edges (generally if it edges < |V| log |V|) are called *sparse graphs*.
- Graphs with relatively few of the possible edges missing are called *dense*.
- Directed weighted graphs are sometimes called *networks*.

9.3 Applications of Graphs

- Representing relationships between components in electronic circuits
- Transportation networks: Highway network, Flight network
- Computer networks: Local area network, Internet, Web
- Databases: For representing ER (Entity Relationship) diagrams in databases, for representing dependency of tables in databases

9.4 Graph Representation

As in other ADTs, to manipulate graphs we need to represent them in some useful form. Basically, there are three ways of doing this:

- Adjacency Matrix
- Adjacency List

Adjacency Matrix

Graph Declaration for Adjacency Matrix

First, let us see the components of the graph data structure. To represent graphs, we need number of vertices, number of edges and also their interconnections. In this method, we use a matrix with size $V \times V$. The values of matrix are boolean. Let us assume the matrix is *Adj*. The value $Adj[u, v]$ set to 1 if there is an edge from vertex u to vertex v and 0 otherwise.

In the matrix, each edge is represented by two bits for undirected graphs. That means, an edge from u to v is represented by 1 values in both $Adj[u, v]$ and $Adj[u, v]$. To save time, we can process only half of this symmetric matrix. Also, we can assume that there is an "edge" from each vertex to itself. So, $Adj[u, u]$ is set to 1 for all vertices. If the graph is a directed graph then we need to mark only one entry in the adjacency matrix. As an example, consider the directed graph below.

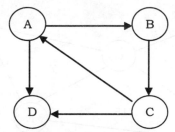

Adjacency matrix for this graph can be given as:

	A	B	C	D
A	0	1	0	1
B	0	0	1	0
C	1	0	0	1
D	0	0	0	0

Now, let us concentrate on the implementation. To read a graph, one way is to first read the vertex names and then read pairs of vertex names (edges). The code below reads an undirected graph.

```java
public class Graph {
        private boolean adjMatrix[][];
        private int vertexCount;
        public Graph(int vertexCount) {
                this.vertexCount = vertexCount;
                adjMatrix = new boolean[vertexCount][vertexCount];
        }
        public void addEdge(int i, int j) {
                if (i >= 0 && i < vertexCount && j > 0 && j < vertexCount) {
                        adjMatrix[i][j] = true;
                        adjMatrix[j][i] = true;
                }
        }
        public void removeEdge(int i, int j) {
                if (i >= 0 && i < vertexCount && j > 0 && j < vertexCount) {
                        adjMatrix[i][j] = false;
                        adjMatrix[j][i] = false;
                }
        }
        public boolean isEdge(int i, int j) {
                if (i >= 0 && i < vertexCount && j > 0 && j < vertexCount)
                        return adjMatrix[i][j];
                else      return false;
```

```
        }
}
```

The adjacency matrix representation is good if the graphs are dense. The matrix requires $O(V^2)$ bits of storage and $O(V^2)$ time for initialization. If the number of edges is proportional to V^2, then there is no problem because V^2 steps are required to read the edges. If the graph is sparse, since initializing the matrix takes V^2 and it dominates the running time of algorithm.

Adjacency List

Graph Declaration for Adjacency List

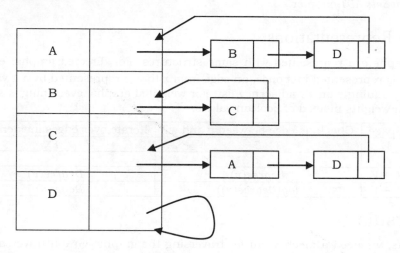

In this representation all the vertices connected to a vertex *v* are listed on an adjacency list for that vertex *v*. This can be easily implemented with linked lists. That means, for each vertex *v* we use a linked list and list nodes represents the connections between *v* and other vertices to which *v* has an edge. The total number of linked lists is equal to the number of vertices in the graph. Considering the same example as that of adjacency matrix, the adjacency list representation can be given as ashown above. Since vertex A has an edge for B and D, we have added them in the adjacency list for A. Same is the case with other vertices as well.

```
public class Graph {
        private ArrayList<Integer> vertices;
        private ListNode[] edges;
        private int vertexCount = 0;
        public Graph(int vertexCount) {
                this.vertexCount = vertexCount;
                vertices = new ArrayList<Integer>();
                edges = new ListNode[vertexCount];
                for (int i = 0; i < vertexCount; i++) {
                        vertices.add(i);
                        edges[i] = new ListNode ();
                }
        }
        public void addEdge(int source, int destination) {
                int i = vertices.indexOf(source);
                int j = vertices.indexOf(destination);
                if (i != -1 || j != -1) {
                        edges[i].insertAtBeginning(destination);
                        edges[j].insertAtBeginning(source);
                }
        }
}
```

For this representation, the order of edges in the input is *important*. This is because they determine the order of the vertices on the adjacency lists. Same graph can be represented in many different ways in an adjacency list. The order in which edges appear on the adjacency list affects the order in which edges are processed by algorithms.

Disadvantages of Adjacency Lists

Using adjacency list representation we cannot perform some operations efficiently. As an example, consider the case of deleting a node. In adjacency list representation, if we delete a node from the adjacency list then that is enough. For each node on the adjacency list of that node specifies another vertex. We need to search other nodes linked list also for deleting it. This problem can be solved by linking the two list nodes which correspond to a particular edge and make the adjacency lists doubly linked. But all these extra links are risky to process.

Adjacency Set

It is very much similar to adjacency list but instead of using Linked lists, Disjoint Sets [Union-Find] are used. For more details refer *Disjoint Sets ADT* chapter.

Comparison of Graph Representations

Directed and undirected graphs are represented with same structures. For directed graphs, everything is the same, except that each edge is represented just once, an edge from x to y is represented by a 1 value in $Adj[x][y]$ in the adjacency matrix or by adding y on x's adjacency list. For weighted graphs, everything is same except that fill the adjacency matrix with weights instead of boolean values.

Representation	Space	Checking edge between v and w?	Iterate over edges incident to v?
List of edges	E	E	E
Adj Matrix	V^2	1	V
Adj List	$E + V$	$Degree(v)$	$Degree(v)$
Adj Set	$E + V$	$log(Degree(v))$	$Degree(v)$

9.5 Graph Traversals

To solve problems on graphs, we need a mechanism for traversing the graphs. Graph traversal algorithms are also called as *graph search* algorithms. Like trees traversal algorithms (Inorder, Preorder, Postorder and Level-Order traversals), graph search algorithms can be thought of as starting at some source vertex in a graph, and "search" the graph by going through the edges and marking the vertices. Now, we will discuss two such algorithms for traversing the graphs.

- Depth First Search [DFS]
- Breadth First Search [BFS]

Depth First Search [DFS]

DFS algorithm works in a manner similar to preorder traversal of the trees. Like preorder traversal, internally this algorithm also uses stack.

Let us consider the following example. Suppose a person is trapped inside a maze. To come out from that maze, the person visits each path and each intersection (in the worst case). Let us say the person uses two colors of paint, to mark the intersections already passed. When discovering a new intersection, it is marked grey, and he continues to go deeper. After reaching a "dead end" the person knows that there is no more unexplored path from the grey intersection, which now is completed and he marks it with black. This "dead end" is either an intersection which has already been marked grey or black, or simply a path that does not lead to an intersection.

Intersections of the maze are the vertices and the paths between the intersections are the edges of the graph. The process of returning from the "dead end" is called *backtracking*. We are trying to go away from starting vertex into the graph as deep as possible, until we have to backtrack to the preceding grey vertex. In DFS algorithm, we encounter the following types of edges.

> *Tree edge*: encounter new vertex
> *Back edge*: from descendent to ancestor
> *Forward edge:* from ancestor to descendent
> *Cross edge*: between a tree or subtrees

For most algorithms boolean classification unvisited/visited is enough (for three color implementation refer to problems section). That means, for some problems we need to use three colors, but for our discussion two colors are enough.

false   ⟶   Vertex is unvisited

true   ⟶   Vertex is visited

Initially all vertices are marked unvisited (false). DFS algorithm starts at a vertex u in graph. By starting at vertex u it considers the edges from u to other vertices. If the edge leads to an already visited vertex, then backtrack to current vertex u. If an edge leads to an unvisited vertex, then go to that vertex and start processing from that vertex. That means the new vertex becomes the current vertex. Follow this process until we reach the dead-end. At this point start *backtracking*. The process terminates when backtracking leads back to the start vertex. The algorithm based on this mechanism is given below: assume Visited[] is a global array.

```java
class Vertex {
        public char label;
        public boolean visited;
        public Vertex(char lab)  {
                label = lab;
                visited = false;
        }
}
class Graph {
        private final int maxVertices = 20;
        private Vertex vertexList[];
        private int adjMatrix[][];
        private int vertexCount;
        private Stack theStack;
        public Graph() {
                vertexList = new Vertex[maxVertices];
                adjMatrix = new int[maxVertices][maxVertices];
                vertexCount = 0;
                for(int y=0; y<maxVertices; y++)
                        for(int x=0; x<maxVertices; x++)
                                adjMatrix[x][y] = 0;
                theStack = new Stack();
        }
        public void addVertex(char lab) {
                vertexList[vertexCount++] = new Vertex(lab);
        }
        public void addEdge(int start, int end) {
                adjMatrix[start][end] = 1;
                adjMatrix[end][start] = 1;
        }
        public void displayVertex(int v) {
                System.out.print(vertexList[v].label);
        }
        public void dfs() {
                vertexList[0].visited = true;
                displayVertex(0);
                theStack.push(0);
                while( !theStack.isEmpty() ) {
                        // get an unvisited vertex adjacent to stack top
                        int v = getAdjUnvisitedVertex( theStack.peek() );
                        if(v == -1)
                                theStack.pop();
                        else  {
                                vertexList[v].visited = true;
                                displayVertex(v);
                                theStack.push(v);
                        }
                }
                for(int j=0; j<vertexCount; j++)        // reset flags
                        vertexList[j].visited = false;
        }
        public int getAdjUnvisitedVertex(int v) {
                for(int j=0; j<vertexCount; j++)
```

```
            if(adjMatrix[v][j]==1 && vertexList[j].visited==false)
                return j;
        return -1;
    }
}
```

As an example consider the following graph. We can see that sometimes an edge leads to an already discovered vertex. These edges are called *back edges*, and the other edges are called *tree edges* because deleting the back edges from the graph generates a tree. The final generated tree is called *DFS tree* and the order in which the vertices processed are called *DFS numbers* of the vertices. In the below graph gray color indicates that the vertex is visited (there is no other significance). We need to see when *Visited* table is being updated.

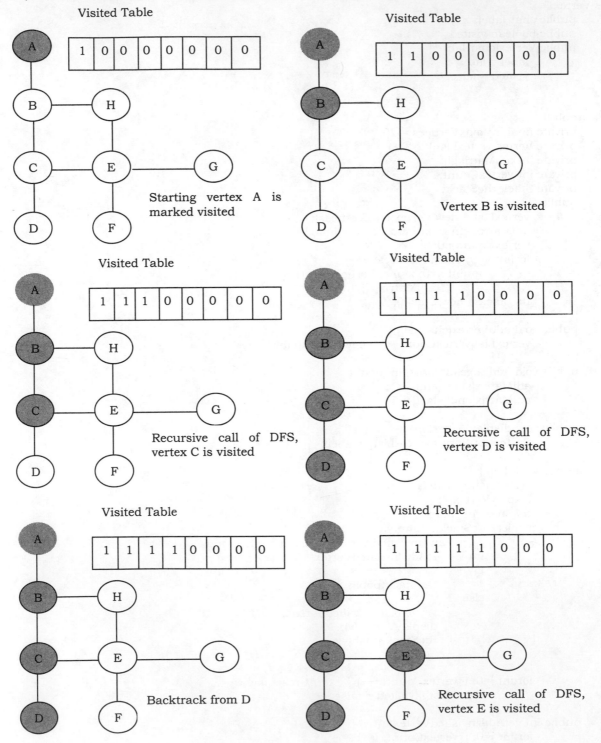

Visited Table

| 1 | 0 | 0 | 0 | 0 | 0 | 0 | 0 |

Starting vertex A is marked visited

Visited Table

| 1 | 1 | 0 | 0 | 0 | 0 | 0 | 0 |

Vertex B is visited

Visited Table

| 1 | 1 | 1 | 0 | 0 | 0 | 0 | 0 |

Recursive call of DFS, vertex C is visited

Visited Table

| 1 | 1 | 1 | 1 | 0 | 0 | 0 | 0 |

Recursive call of DFS, vertex D is visited

Visited Table

| 1 | 1 | 1 | 1 | 0 | 0 | 0 | 0 |

Backtrack from D

Visited Table

| 1 | 1 | 1 | 1 | 1 | 0 | 0 | 0 |

Recursive call of DFS, vertex E is visited

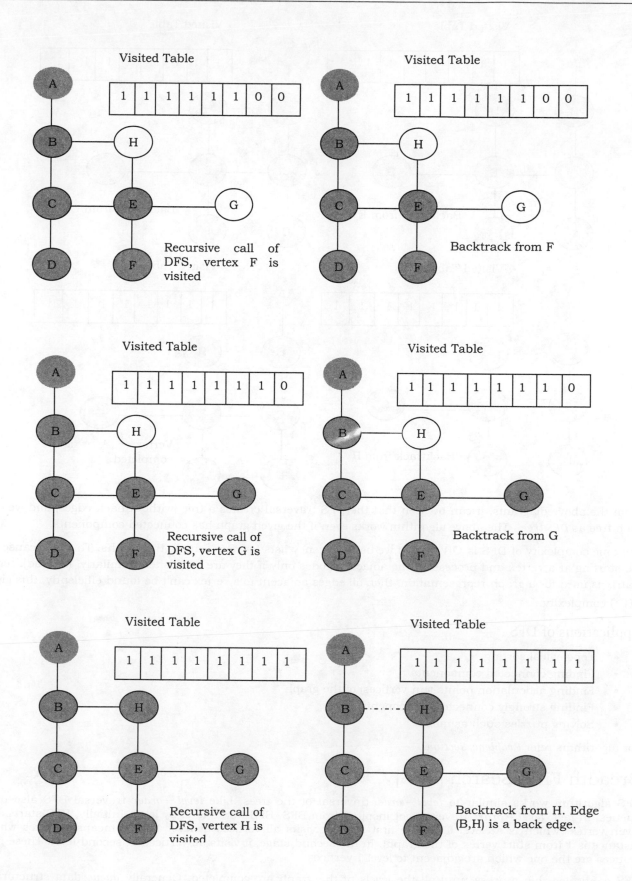

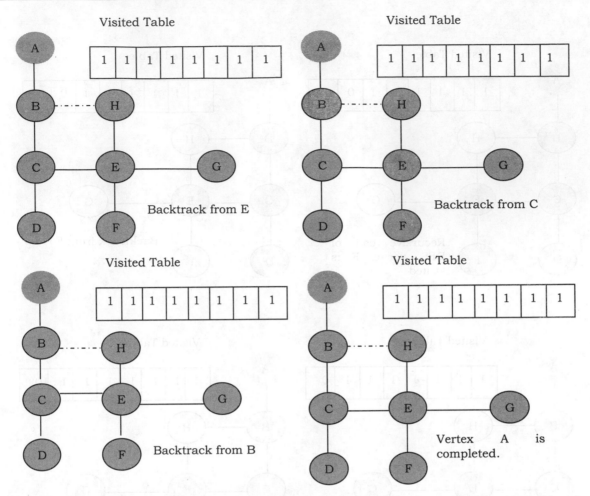

Visited Table

Backtrack from E

Visited Table

Backtrack from C

Visited Table

Backtrack from B

Visited Table

Vertex   A   is completed.

From the above diagrams, it can be seen that the DFS traversal creates a tree (without back edges) and we call such tree as *DFS tree*. The above algorithm works even if the given graph has connected components.

The time complexity of DFS is $O(V + E)$, if we use adjacency lists for representing the graphs. This is because we are starting at a vertex and processing the adjacent nodes only if they are not visited. Similarly, if an adjacency matrix is used for a graph representation, then all edges adjacent to a vertex can't be found efficiently, this gives $O(V^2)$ complexity.

Applications of DFS

- Topological sorting
- Finding connected components
- Finding articulation points (cut vertices) of the graph
- Finding strongly connected components
- Solving puzzles such as mazes

For algorithms refer *Problems Section*.

Breadth First Search [BFS]

BFS algorithm works similar to *level − order* traversal of the trees. Like *level − order* traversal BFS also uses queues. In fact, *level − order* traversal got inspired from BFS. BFS works level by level. Initially, BFS starts at a given vertex, which is at level 0. In the first stage it visits all vertices at level 1 (that means, vertices whose distance is 1 from start vertex of the graph). In the second stage, it visits all vertices at second level. These new vertices are the one which are adjacent to level 1 vertices.

BFS continues this process until all the levels of the graph are completed. Generally *queue* data structure is used for storing the vertices of a level. As similar to DFS, assume that initially all vertices are marked *unvisited* (*false*). Vertices that have been processed and removed from the queue are marked *visited* (*true*). We use a queue to represent the visited set as it will keep the vertices in order of when they were first visited. The implementation for the above discussion can be given as:

```java
class Vertex {
        public char label;
        public boolean visited;
        public Vertex(char lab)  {
                label = lab;
                visited = false;
        }
}
class Graph {
        private final int maxVertices = 20;
        private Vertex vertexList[];
        private int adjMatrix[][];
        private int vertexCount;
        private Queue theQueue;
        public Graph() {
                vertexList = new Vertex[maxVertices];
                adjMatrix = new int[maxVertices][maxVertices];
                vertexCount = 0;
                for(int y=0; y<maxVertices; y++)
                        for(int x=0; x<maxVertices; x++)
                                adjMatrix[x][y] = 0;
                theQueue = new Queue();
        }
        public void addVertex(char lab) {
                vertexList[vertexCount++] = new Vertex(lab);
        }
        public void addEdge(int start, int end) {
                adjMatrix[start][end] = 1;
                adjMatrix[end][start] = 1;
        }
        public void displayVertex(int v) {
                System.out.print(vertexList[v].label);
        }
        public void bfs() {
                vertexList[0].wasVisited = true;
                displayVertex(0);
                theQueue.insert(0);
                int v2;
                while( !theQueue.isEmpty() ) {
                        int v1 = theQueue.remove();
                        while( (v2=getAdjUnvisitedVertex(v1)) != -1 ) {
                                vertexList[v2].wasVisited = true;
                                displayVertex(v2);
                                theQueue.insert(v2);
                        }
                }
                for(int j=0; j<nVerts; j++)
                        vertexList[j].wasVisited = false;
        }
        public int getAdjUnvisitedVertex(int v) {
                for(int j=0; j<vertexCount; j++)
                        if(adjMatrix[v][j]==1 && vertexList[j].visited==false)
                                return j;
```

```
        return -1;
    }
}
```

As an example, let us consider the same graph as that of DFS example. The BFS traversal can be shown as:

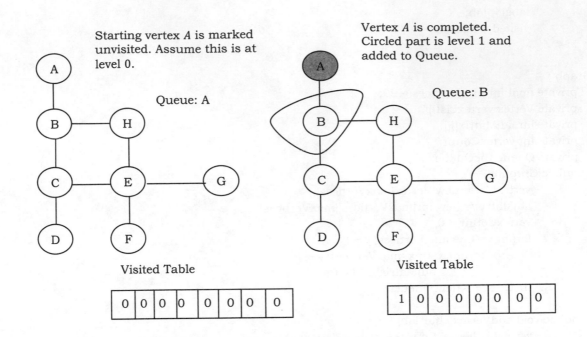

Starting vertex *A* is marked unvisited. Assume this is at level 0.

Queue: A

Visited Table

0	0	0	0	0	0	0	0

Vertex *A* is completed. Circled part is level 1 and added to Queue.

Queue: B

Visited Table

1	0	0	0	0	0	0	0

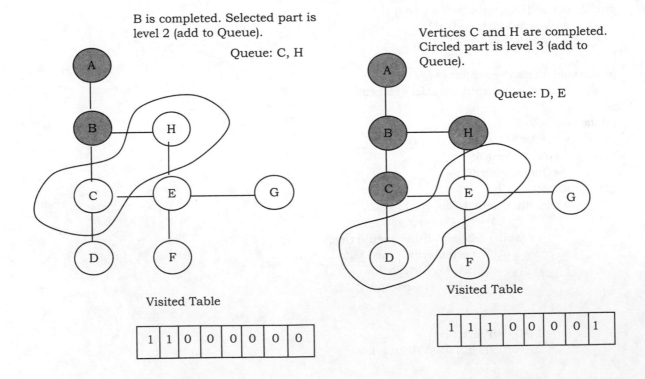

B is completed. Selected part is level 2 (add to Queue).

Queue: C, H

Visited Table

1	1	0	0	0	0	0	0

Vertices C and H are completed. Circled part is level 3 (add to Queue).

Queue: D, E

Visited Table

1	1	1	0	0	0	0	1

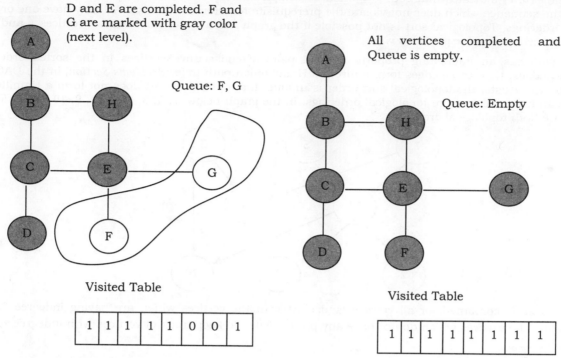

D and E are completed. F and G are marked with gray color (next level).

Queue: F, G

All vertices completed and Queue is empty.

Queue: Empty

Visited Table

1	1	1	1	1	0	0	1

Visited Table

1	1	1	1	1	1	1	1

Time complexity of BFS is $O(V + E)$, if we use adjacency lists for representing the graphs and $O(V^2)$ for adjacency matrix representation.

Applications of BFS

- Finding all connected components in a graph
- Finding all nodes within one connected component
- Finding the shortest path between two nodes
- Testing a graph for bipartiteness

Comparing DFS and BFS

Comparing BFS and DFS, the big advantage of DFS is that it has much lower memory requirements than BFS, because it's not required to store all of the child pointers at each level. Depending on the data and what we are looking for, either DFS or BFS could be advantageous. For example, in a family tree if we are looking for someone who's still alive and if we assume that person would be at bottom of the tree then DFS is a better choice. BFS would take a very long time to reach that last level.

DFS algorithm finds the goal faster. Now, if we were looking for a family member who died a very long time ago, then that person would be closer to the top of the tree. In this case, BFS finds faster than DFS. So, the advantages of either vary depending on the data and what we are looking for.

DFS is related to preorder traversal of a tree. Like *preorder* traversal simply DFS visits each node before its children. BFS algorithm works similar to *level − order* traversal of the trees.

If someone asks whether DFS is better or BFS is better? The answer depends on the type of the problem that we are trying to solve. BFS visits each level one at a time, and if we know the solution we are searching for is at a low depth then BFS is good. DFS is better choice if the solution is at maximum depth. Below table shows the differences between DFS and BFS in terms of their applications.

Applications	DFS	BFS
Spanning forest, connected components, paths, cycles	Yes	Yes
Shortest paths		Yes
Minimal use of memory space	Yes	

9.6 Topological Sort

Topological sort is an ordering of vertices in a directed acyclic graph [DAG] in which each node comes before all nodes to which it has outgoing edges. As an example, consider the course prerequisite structure at universities.

A directed *edge* (v, w) indicates that course v must be completed before course w. Topological ordering for this example is the sequence which does not violate the prerequisite requirement. Every DAG may have one or more topological orderings. Topological sort is not possible if the graph has a cycle, since for two vertices v and w on the cycle, v precedes w and w precedes v.

Topological sort has an interesting property that all pairs of consecutive vertices in the sorted order are connected by edges; then these edges form a directed Hamiltonian path [refer *Problems Section*] in the DAG. If a Hamiltonian path exists, the topological sort order is unique. If a topological sort does not form a Hamiltonian path, DAG can have two or more topological orderings. In the graph below: 7, 5, 3, 11, 8, 2, 9, 10 and 3, 5, 7, 8, 11, 2, 9, 10 are both topological orderings.

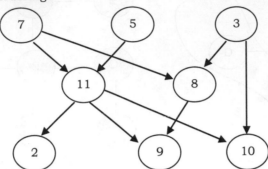

Initially, *indegree* is computed for all vertices and start with the vertices which are having indegree 0. That means consider the vertices which do not have any prerequisite. To keep track of vertices with indegree zero we can use a queue.

All vertices of indegree 0 are placed on queue. While the queue is not empty, a vertex v is removed, and all edges adjacent to v have their indegrees decremented. A vertex is put on the queue as soon as its indegree falls to 0. The topological ordering then is the order in which the vertices deQueue. The time complexity of this algorithm is $O(|E| + |V|)$ if adjacency lists are used.

```java
void TopologicalSort( Graph G ) {
        LLQueue Q = new LLQueue();
        int counter;
        int v, w;
        counter = 0;
        for (v = 0; v< G.vertexCount; v++)
                if( indegree[v] ==  0 )
                        Q.enQueue(v );
        while( !Q.isEmpty() ) {
                v = Q.deQueue();
                topologicalOrder[v] = ++counter;
                for each w adjacent to v
                        if( --indegree[w] ==  0 )
                                Q.enQueue(w);
        }
        if( counter != G.vertexCount)
                System.out.println("Graph has cycle");
        Q.deleteQueue();
}
```

Total running time of topological sort is $O(V + E)$.

Note: Topological sorting problem can be solved with DFS. Refer *Problems Section* for algorithm.

Applications of Topological Sorting

- Representing course prerequisites
- In detecting deadlocks
- Pipeline of computing jobs
- Checking for symbolic link loop

•   Evaluating formulae in spreadsheet

9.7 Shortest Path Algorithms

Let us consider the other important problem of graph. Given a graph $G = (V, E)$ and a distinguished vertex s, we need to find the shortest path from s to every other vertex in G. There are variations in the shortest path algorithms which depend on the type of the input graph and are given below.

Variations of Shortest Path Algorithms

Shortest path in unweighted graph
Shortest path in weighted graph
Shortest path in weighted graph with negative edges

Applications of Shortest Path Algorithms

•   Finding fastest way to go from one place to another
•   Finding cheapest way to fly/send data from one city to another

Shortest Path in Unweighted Graph

Let s be the input vertex from which we want to find shortest path to all other vertices. Unweighted graph is a special case of the weighted shortest-path problem, with all edges a weight of 1. The algorithm is similar to BFS and we need to use the following data structures:

•   A distance table with three columns (each row corresponds to a vertex):
    ○   Distance from source vertex.
    ○   Path - contains the name of the vertex through which we get the shortest distance.
•   A queue is used to implement breadth-first search. It contains vertices whose distance from the source node has been computed and their adjacent vertices are to be examined.

As an example, consider the following graph and its adjacency list representation.

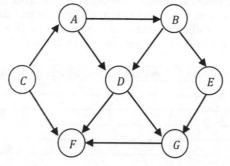

The adjacency list for this graph is:

$A: B \rightarrow D$
$B: D \rightarrow E$
$C: A \rightarrow F$
$D: F \rightarrow G$
$E: G$
$F: -$
$G: F$

Let $s = C$. The distance from C to C is 0. Initially, distances to all other nodes are not computed, and we initialize the second column in the distance table for all vertices (except C) with -1 as below.

Vertex	Distance[v]	Previous vertex which gave Distance[v]
A	-1	-
B	-1	-
C	0	-
D	-1	-
E	-1	-
F	-1	-
G	-1	-

Algorithm

```
void UnweightedShortestPath(Graph G, int s) {
```

```
LLQueue Q = new LLQueue();
int v, w;
Q.enQueue( s);
for (int i = 0; i< G.vertexCount;i++)
        Distance[i]=-1;
Distance[s]= 0;
while (!Q.isEmpty()) {
        v = Q.deQueue();

        for each w adjacent to v
                if(Distance[w] == -1)      {
                        Distance[w] = Distance[v] + 1;
                        Path[w] = v;
                        Q.enQueue(w);

                }

}
        Q.deleteQueue();
}
```

Each vertex examined at most once

Each vertex enQueue'd at most once

Running time: $O(|E| + |V|)$, if adjacency lists are used. In for loop, we are checking the outgoing edges for a given vertex and the sum of all examined edges in the while loop is equal to the number of edges which gives $O(|E|)$.

If we use matrix representation the complexity is $O(|V|^2)$, because we need to read an entire row in the matrix of length $|V|$ in order to find the adjacent vertices for a given vertex.

Shortest path in Weighted Graph [Dijkstra's]

A famous solution for shortest path problem was given by *Dijkstra*. *Dijkstra's* algorithm is a generalization of BFS algorithm. The regular BFS algorithm cannot solve the shortest path problem as it cannot guarantee that the vertex at the front of the queue is the vertex closest to source *s*.

Before going to code let us understand how the algorithm works. As in unweighted shortest path algorithm, here too we use the distance table. The algorithm works by keeping the shortest distance of vertex *v* from the source in *Distance* table. The value *Distance[v]* holds the distance from s to v. The shortest distance of the source to itself is zero. *Distance* table for all other vertices is set to −1 to indicate that those vertices are not already processed.

Vertex	Distance[v]	Previous vertex which gave Distance[v]
A	-1	-
B	-1	-
C	0	-
D	-1	-
E	-1	-
F	-1	-
G	-1	-

After the algorithm finishes *Distance* table will have the shortest distance from source *s* to each other vertex *v*. To simplify the understanding of *Dijkstra's* algorithm, let us assume that the given vertices are maintained in two sets. Initially the first set contains only the source element and the second set contains all the remaining elements. After the kth iteration, the first set contains *k* vertices which are closest to the source. These *k* vertices are the ones for which we have already computed shortest distances from source.

Notes on Dijkstra's Algorithm

- It uses greedy method: Always pick the next closest vertex to the source.
- Uses priority queue to store unvisited vertices by distance from *s*.
- Does not work with negative weights.

Difference Between Unweighted Shortest Path and Dijkstra's Algorithm

1) To represent weights in adjacency list, each vertex contains the weights of the edges (in addition to their identifier).
2) Instead of ordinary queue we use priority queue [distances are the priorities] and the vertex with the smallest distance is selected for processing.
3) The distance to a vertex is calculated by the sum of the weights of the edges on the path from the source to that vertex.
4) We update the distances in case the newly computed distance is smaller than old distance which we have already computed.

```
void Dijkstra(Graph G, int s) {
      Heap PQ = new Heap();
      int v, w;
      PQ.enQueue(s);
      for (int i = 0; i< G.vertexCount;i++)
             Distance[i]=-1;
      Distance[s] = 0;
      while ((!PQ .isEmpty()) {
             v = PQ.deleteMin();
             for all adjacent vertices w of v {
                    Compute new distance d= Distance[v] + weight[v][w];
                    if(Distance[w] == -1) {
                          Distance[w] = new distance d;
                          Insert w in the priority queue with priority d
                          Path[w] = v;
                    }
                    if(Distance[w]  > new distance d) {
                          Distance[w] = new distance d;
                          Update priority of vertex w to be d;
                          Path[w] = v;
                    }
             }
      }
}
```

The above algorithm can be better understood through an example, which will explain each step that is taken and how *Distance* is calculated. The weighted graph below has 5 vertices from $A - E$. The value between the two vertices is known as the edge cost between two vertices. For example, the edge cost between A and C is 1. Dijkstra's algorithm can be used to find shortest path from source A to the remaining vertices in the graph.

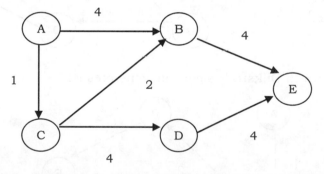

Initially the *Distance* table is:

Vertex	Distance[v]	Previous vertex which gave Distance[v]
A	0	-
B	-1	-
C	-1	-
D	-1	-
E	-1	-

After the first step, from vertex A, we can reach B and C. So, in the *Distance* table we update the reachability of B and C with their costs and same is shown below.

A	0	-
B	4	A
C	1	A
D	-1	-
E	-1	-

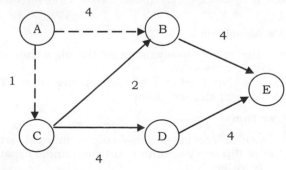

Now, let us select the minimum distance among all. The minimum distance vertex is *C*. That means, we have to reach other vertices from these two vertices (*A* and *C*). For example *B* can be reached from *A* and also from *C*. In this case we have to select the one which gives low cost. Since reaching *B* through *C* is giving minimum cost (1 + 2), we update the *Distance* table for vertex *B* with cost 3 and the vertex from which we got this cost as *C*.

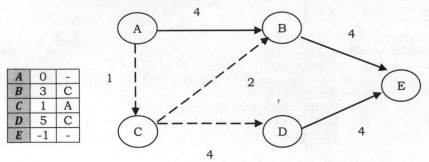

A	0	-
B	3	C
C	1	A
D	5	C
E	-1	-

Shortest path to B, D using C as intermediate vertex

The only vertex remaining is *E*. To reach *E*, we have to see all the paths through which we can reach *E* and select the one which gives minimum cost. We can see that if we use *B* as intermediate vertex through *C* then we get the minimum cost.

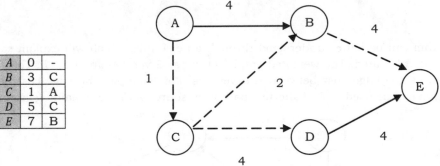

A	0	-
B	3	C
C	1	A
D	5	C
E	7	B

The final minimum cost tree which Dijkstra's algorithm generates is:

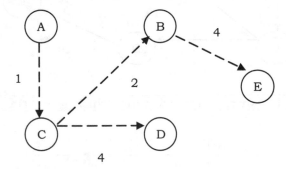

Performance

In Dijkstra's algorithm, the efficiency depends on the number of DeleteMins (*V* DeleteMins) and updates for priority queues (*E* updates) that were used. If a *standard binary heap* is used then the complexity is O(*E logV*). The term *E logV* comes from *E* updates (each update takes *logV*) for the standard heap. If the set used is an array then the complexity is O(*E* + *V²*).

Disadvantages of Dijkstra's Algorithm

- As discussed above, the major disadvantage of the algorithm is that it does a blind search thereby wasting time and necessary resources.
- Another disadvantage is that it cannot handle negative edges. This leads to acyclic graphs and most often cannot obtain the right shortest path.

Relatives of Dijkstra's Algorithm

- The *Bellman–Ford* algorithm computes single-source shortest paths in a weighted digraph. It uses the same concept as that of *Dijkstra's* algorithm but can handle negative edges as well. It has more running time than *Dijkstra's* algorithm.

- Prim's algorithm finds a minimum spanning tree for a connected weighted graph. It implies that a subset of edges that form a tree where the total weight of all the edges in the tree is minimized.

Bellman-Ford Algorithm

If the graph has negative edge costs, then *Dijkstra's* algorithm does not work. The problem is that once a vertex u is declared known, it is possible that from some other, unknown vertex v there is a path back to u that is very negative. In such a case, taking a path from s to v back to u is better than going from s to u without using v.

A combination of Dijkstra's algorithm and unweighted algorithms will solve the problem. Initialize the queue with s. Then, at each stage, we *DeQueue* a vertex v. We find all vertices w adjacent to v such that,

$$distance\ to\ v\ +\ weight(v,w) <\ old\ distance\ to\ w$$

We update w old distance and path, and place w on a queue if it is not already there. A bit can be set for each vertex to indicate presence in the queue. We repeat the process until the queue is empty.

```
void BellmanFordAlgorithm(Graph G, int s) {
        LLQueue Q = new LLQueue();
        int v, w;
        Q.enQueue( s);
        // assume the Distance table is filled with INT_MAX
        Distance[s] = 0;
        while ((!Q.isEmpty()) {
                v = Q.deQueue();
                for all adjacent vertices w of v {
                        Compute new distance d= Distance[v] + weight[v][w];

                        if(old distance to w > new distance d ) {
                                Distance[v] = (distance to v) + weight[v][w];
                                Path[w] = v;
                                if(w is there in queue)
                                        Q.enQueue( w);
                        }
                }
        }
}
```

This algorithm works if there are no negative-cost cycles. Each vertex can deQueue at most $|V|$ times, so the running time is $O(|E|.|V|)$ if adjacency lists are used.

Overview of Shortest Path Algorithms

Shortest path in unweighted graph [*Modified BFS*]	$O(|E| + |V|)$
Shortest path in weighted graph [*Dijkstra's*]	$O(|E| \log |V|)$
Shortest path in weighted graph with negative edges [*Bellman − Ford*]	$O(|E|.|V|)$
Shortest path in weighted acyclic graph	$O(|E| + |V|)$

9.8 Minimal Spanning Tree

Spanning tree of a graph is a subgraph that contains all the vertices and is also a tree. A graph may have many spanning trees. As an example, consider a graph with 4 vertices as shown below. Let us assume that the corners of the graph are vertices.

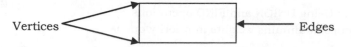

For this simple graph, we can have multiple spanning trees as shown below.

The algorithm we will discuss now is *minimum spanning tree* in an undirected graph. We assume that the given graphs are weighted graph. If the graphs are unweighted graphs then we can still the weighted graph algorithms by treating all weights are equal. A *minimum spanning tree* of an undirected graph G is a tree formed from graph edges that connects all the vertices of G with minimum total cost (weights). A minimum spanning tree exists only if the graph is connected.

There are two famous algorithms for this problem:

- *Prim's* Algorithm
- *Kruskal's* Algorithm

Prim's Algorithm

Prim's algorithm is almost same as Dijkstra's algorithm. Like in Dijkstra's algorithm, in Prim's algorithm also we keep values *distance* and *paths* in distance table. The only exception is that since the definition of *distance* is different and as a result the updating statement also changes little. The update statement is simpler than before.

```
void Prims(Graph G, int s) {
        Heap PQ = new Heap();
        int v, w;
        PQ.enQueue(s);

        // assume the Distance table is filled with -1
        Distance[s] = 0;
        while ((!PQ.isEmpty()) {
                v = PQ.DeleteMin();

                for all adjacent vertices w of v {
                        Compute new distance d= Distance[v] + weight[v][w];

                        if(Distance[w] == -1) {
                                Distance[w] = weight[v][w];
                                Insert w in the priority queue with priority d
                                Path[w] = v;
                        }

                        if(Distance[w]  > new distance d) {
                                Distance[w] = weight[v][w];
                                Update priority of vertex w to be d;
                                Path[w] = v;
                        }
                }
        }
}
```

The entire implementation of this algorithm is identical to that of Dijkstra's algorithm. The running time is $O(|V|^2)$ without heaps [good for dense graphs], and $O(ElogV)$ using binary heaps [good for sparse graphs].

Kruskal's Algorithm

The algorithm starts with V different trees (V is the vertices in graph). While constructing the minimum spanning tree, every time it selects the edge which has minimum weight and adds that edge if it doesn't creates a cycle. So, initially, there are $|V|$ single-node trees in the forest. Adding an edge merges two trees into one. When the algorithm is completed, there will be only one tree, and that is the minimum spanning tree. There are two ways of implementing Kruskal's algorithm:

- By using Disjoint Sets: Using UNION and FIND operations
- By using Priority Queues: Maintains weights in priority queue

The appropriate data structure is the UNION/FIND algorithm [for implementing forests]. Two vertices belong to the same set if and only if they are connected in the current spanning forest. Each vertex is initially in its own set. If u and v are in the same set, the edge is rejected, because it forms a cycle. Otherwise, the edge is accepted, and a UNION is performed on the two sets containing u and v. As an example, consider the following graph (edges shows the weights).

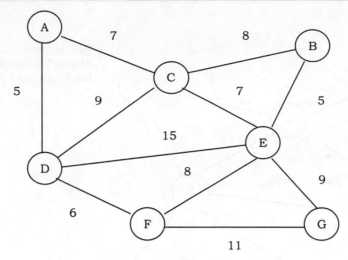

Now let us perform Kruskal's algorithm on this graph. We always select the edge which is having minimum weight (cost).

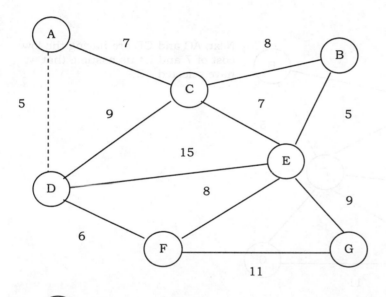

From the above graph, the edges which are having minimum weight (cost) are: AD and BE. Among these two we can select one of them and let us assume that we have selected AD (dotted line).

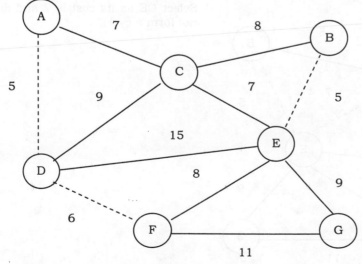

DF is the next edge which having the low cost (6).

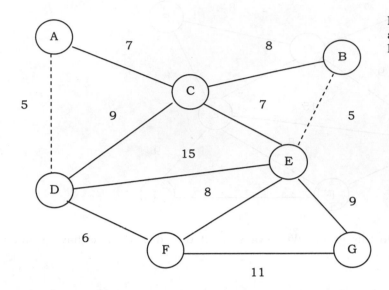

BE is now having the low cost among all and we select that (dotted lines indicates selected edges).

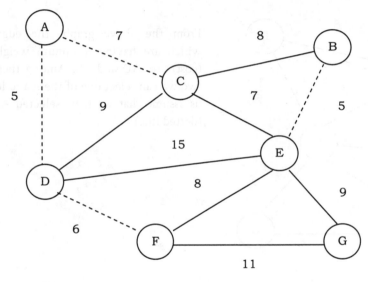

Next, AC and CE are having the low cost of 7 and let us assume that we have selected AC.

Select CE as its cost is 7 and does not form a cycle.

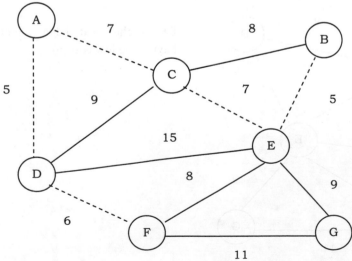

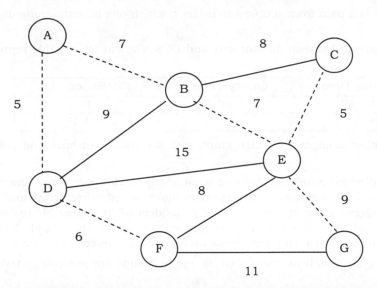

Next low cost edges are CB and EF. But if we select CB then it forms a cycle. So we discard that. Same is the case with EF also. So we should not select these 2. And the next low cost is 9 (BD and EG). Selecting BD forms a cycle and we discard that. Adding EG will not form a cycle and with this edge we complete all vertices of the graph.

```
void Kruskal(Graph G) {
    //Refer DisjointSets Chapter
    S = ф;  // At the end S will contains the edges of minimum spanning trees
    for (int v = 0; v< G→V; v++)
        MakeSet (v);
    Sort edges of E by increasing weights w;
    for each edge (u, v) in E { //from sorted list
        if(FIND (u) != FIND (v)) {
            S = S ∪ {(u, v)};
            UNION (u, v);
        }
    }
    return S;
}
```

Note: For implementation of UNION and FIND operations refer *Disjoint Sets ADT* chapter.

The worst-case running time of this algorithm is O(*ElogE*), which is dominated by the heap operations. That means, since we are constructing the heap with E edges we need O(*ElogE*) time for doing that.

9.9 Problems on Graph Algorithms

Problem-1   In an undirected simple graph with n vertices, what is the maximum number of edges? Self loops are not allowed.

Solution: Since every node can connect to all other nodes, first node can connect o $n - 1$ nodes. Second node can connect to $n - 2$ nodes [since one edge is already there from first node]. The total number of edges is: $1 + 2 + 3 + \cdots + n - 1 = \frac{n(n-1)}{2}$ edges.

Problem-2   How many different adjacency matrices does a graph with n vertices and E edges have?

Solution: It's equal to the number of permutations of n elements. i.e., $n!$.

Problem-3   How many different adjacency lists does a graph with n vertices have?

Solution: It's equal to the number of permutations of edges. i.e., $E!$.

Problem-4   Which undirected graph representation is most appropriate for determining whether or not a vertex is isolated (is not connected to any other vertex)?

Solution: Adjacency List. If we use adjacency matrix then we need to check the complete row for determining whether that vertex has any edges or not. By using adjacency list it is very easy to check and it can be done just by checking whether that vertex has NULL for next pointer or not [NULL indicates that vertex is not connected to any other vertex].

Problem-5   For checking whether there is a path from source *s* to target *t*, which one is best among disjoint sets and DFS?

Solution: The table below shows the comparison between disjoint sets and DFS. The entries in table represent the case for any pair of nodes (for *s* and *t*).

Method	Processing Time	Query Time	Space
Union-Find	$V + E\ logV$	$logV$	V
DFS	$E + V$	1	$E + V$

Problem-6   What is the maximum number of edges a directed graph with *n* vertices can have and still not contain a directed cycle?

Solution: The number is $V(V-1)/2$. Any directed graph can have at most n^2 edges. However, since the graph has no cycles it cannot contain a self loop and for any pair x,y of vertices at most one edge from (x,y) and (y,x) can be included. Therefore the number of edges can be at most $(V^2 - V)/2$ as desired. It is possible to achieve $V(V-1)/2$ edges. Label *n* nodes $1, 2...n$ and add an edge (x, y) if and only if $x < y$. This graph has the appropriate number of edges and cannot contain a cycle (any path visits an increasing sequence of nodes).

Problem-7   How many simple directed graphs with no parallel edges and self loops are possible in terms of *V*?

Solution: $(V) \times (V-1)$. Since, each vertex can connect to $V-1$ vertices without self loops.

Problem-8   Earlier in this chapter, we have discussed minimum spanning tree algorithms. Now, give an algorithm for finding the maximum-weight spanning tree in a graph?

Solution:

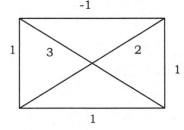

Given graph

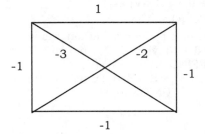

Transformed graph with negative edge weights

Using the given graph, construct a new graph with same nodes and edges. But instead of using same weights take the negative of their weights. That means, weight of an edge = negative of weight of the corresponding edge in the given graph. Now, we can use existing *minimum spanning tree* algorithms on this new graph. As a result, we will get the maximum weight spanning tree in the original one.

Problem-9   Differences between DFS and BFS?

Solution:

DFS	BFS
Backtracking is possible from a dead end	Backtracking is not possible
Vertices from which exploration is incomplete are processed in a LIFO order	The vertices to be explored are organized as a FIFO queue
Search is done in one particular direction	The vertices at the same level are maintained in parallel

Problem-10   Give an algorithm for checking whether a given graph *G* has simple path from source *s* to destination *d*. Assume the graph *G* is represented using adjacent matrix.

Solution: Let us assume that the structure for the graph is:

For each vertex call *DFS* and check whether the current vertex is same as destination vertex or not. If they are same, then return 1. Otherwise, call the *DFS* on its unvisited neighbors. One important thing to note here is that, we are calling the DFS algorithm on vertices which are not visited already.

```java
void HasSimplePath(Graph G, int s, int d) {
        Viisited[s] = 1;
        if(s == d) return 1;
        for(int t = 0; t < G.vertexCount; t++) {
                if(G.adjMatrix[s][t] && !Viisited[t])
                        if(DFS(G, t, d))  return 1;
```

```
        }
        return 0;
}
```

Time Complexity:O(E). In the above algorithm, for each node since we are not calling *DFS* on all of its neighbors (discarding through *if* condition), Space Complexity: O(V).

Problem-11   Count simple paths for a given graph G has simple path from source s to destination d? Assume the graph is represented using adjacent matrix.

Solution: As similar to the discussion of Problem-9, start at one node and call DFS on that node. As a result of this call, it visits all the nodes in the given graph which it can reach. That means it visits all the nodes of the connected component of that node. If there are any nodes left without visiting, then again start at one of those nodes and call DFS. Before the first call of DFS in each connected component, increment the connected components *count*. Continue this process until all of the graph nodes are visited. As a result, at the end we will get the total number of connected components. The implementation based on this logic is given below.

```
void CountSimplePaths(Graph G, int s, int d) {
        Viisited[s] = 1;
        if(s == d) {
                count++;
                Visited[s] = 0;
                return;
        }
        for(int t = 0; t < G.vertexCount; t++) {
                if(G.adjMatrix[s][t] && !Viisited[t]){
                        DFS(G, t, d);
                        Visited[t] = 0;
                }
        }
}
```

Problem-12   **All pairs shortest path problem:** Find the shortest graph distances between every pair of vertices in a given graph. Let us assume that given graph doesn't have negative edges.

Solution: The problem can be solved using n applications of *Dijkstra's* algorithm. That means we apply the *Dijkstra's* algorithm on each vertex of the given graph. This algorithm does not work if the graph has edges with negative weights.

Problem-13   In Problem-12, how do we solve the all pairs shortest path problem if the graph has edges with negative weights?

Solution: This can be solved by using *Floyd − Warshall algorithm*. This algorithm also works in the case of a weighted graph where the edges have negative weights. This algorithm is an example of Dynamic Programming and refer *Dynamic Programming* chapter.

Problem-14   **DFS Application:** *Cut Vertex* or *Articulation Points*

Solution: In an undirected graph, a *cut vertex* (or articulation point) is a vertex and if we remove it then the graph splits into two disconnected components. As an example, consider the following figure. Removal of "*D*" vertex divides the graph in to two connected components ({E, F} and {A, B, C, G}). Similarly, removal of C vertex divides the graph into ({G} and {A, B, D, E, F}). For this graph A and C are the cut vertices.

Note: A connected, undirected graph is called *bi − connected* if the graph is still connected after removing any vertex.

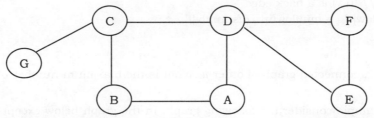

DFS provides a linear-time algorithm (O(n)) to find all cut vertices in a connected graph. Starting at any vertex, call a *DFS* and number the nodes as they are visited. For each vertex v, we call this DFS number $dfsnum(v)$. The tree generated with DFS traversal is called *DFS spanning tree*. Then, for every vertex v in the *DFS* spanning tree, we compute the lowest-numbered vertex, which we call $low(v)$, that is reachable from v by taking zero or more tree edges and then possibly one back edge (in that order).

Based on the above discussion we need the following information for this algorithm. The *dfsnum* of each vertex in the *DFS* tree (once it gets visited), and for each vertex *v*, the lowest depth of neighbors of all descendants of *v* in the *DFS* tree, called the *low*. The *dfsnum* can be computed during DFS. The low of *v* can be computed after visiting all descendants of *v* (i.e., just before *v* gets popped off the *DFS* stack) as the minimum of the *dfsnum* of all neighbors of *v* (other than the parent of *v* in the *DFS* tree) and the *low* of all children of *v* in the *DFS* tree.

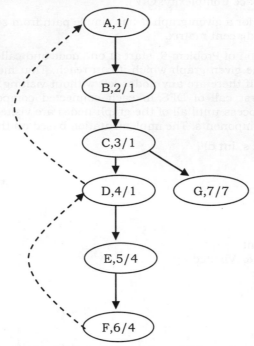

The root vertex is a cut vertex if and only if it has at least two children. A non-root vertex u is a cut vertex if and only if there is a son *v* of *u* such that $low(v) \geq dfsnum(u)$. This property can be tested once the *DFS* returned from every child of *u* (that means, just before u gets popped off the DFS stack), and if true, *u* separates the graph into different bi-connected components. This can be represented by computing one bi-connected component out of every such *v* (a component which contains *v* will contain the sub-tree of *v*, plus *u*), and then erasing the sub-tree of *v* from the tree For the given graph, the *DFS* tree with *dfsnum/low* can be given as shown in above figure. The implementation for the above discussion is:

```java
int adjMatrix [256] [256] ;
int dfsnum [256], num = 0, low [256];
void CutVertices( int u ) {
        low[u] = dfsnum[u] = num++;
        for (int v = 0 ; v < 256; ++v ) {
                if(adjMatrix[u][v] && dfsnum[v] == -1) {
                        CutVertices( v ) ;
                        if(low[v] > dfsnum[u])
                                System.out.println("Cut Vetex:" + u);
                        low[u] = min ( low[u] , low[v] ) ;
                }
                else    // (u,v) is a back edge
                        low[u ] = min(low[u] , dfsnum[v]) ;

        }
}
```

Problem-15   Let *G* be a connected graph of order *n*. What is the maximum number of cut-vertices that *G* can contain?

Solution: $n - 2$. As an example consider the following graph. In the graph below except the vertices 1 and *n* all the remaining vertices are cut vertices. This is because removing 1 and *n* vertices do not split the graph into two. This is a case where we can get maximum number of cut vertices.

Problem-16   **DFS Application:** *Cut Bridges* or *Cut Edges*

Solution:

Definition: Let *G* be a connected graph. An edge *uv* in *G* is called a *bridge* of *G* if *G – uv* is disconnected.

As an example, consider the following graph.

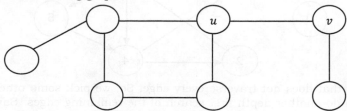

In the above graph, if we remove the edge *uv* then the graph splits into two components. For this graph, *uv* is a bridge. The discussion we had for cut vertices holds good for bridges also. The only change is instead of printing the vertex we give the edge. The main observation is that an edge (u, v) cannot be a bridge if it is part of a cycle. If (u, v) is not part of a cycle then it is a bridge.

We can detect cycles in *DFS* by the presence of back edges. (u, v) is a bridge if and only if none of v or *v's* children has a back edge to *u* or any of *u's* ancestors. To detect whether any of *v's* children has a back edge to *u's* parent, we can use a similar idea as above to see what is the smallest *dfsnum* reachable from the subtree rooted at *v*.

```
int dfsnum[256], num = 0, low [256];
void Bridges( Graph G, int u ) {
        low[u] = dfsnum[u] = num++;
        for (int v = 0 ; G.vertexCount; ++v ) {
                if(G.adjMatrix[u][v] && dfsnum[v] == -1) {
                        cutVertices( v ) ;
                        if(low[v] > dfsnum[u])
                                print (u,v)  as a bridge
                        low[u] = min ( low[u] , low[v] ) ;
                }
                else      // (u,v) is a back edge
                        low[u ] = min(low[u] , dfsnum[v]) ;
        }
}
```

Problem-17   **DFS Application:** Discuss *Euler* Circuits

Solution: Before discussing this problem let us see the terminology:
- *Eulerian tour* – a path that contains all edges without repetition.
- *Eulerian circuit* – a path that contains all edges without repetition starts and ends in the same vertex.
- *Eulerian graph* – a graph that contains an Eulerian circuit.
- *Even vertex*: a vertex that has an even number of incident edges.
- *Odd vertex*: a vertex that has an odd number of incident edges.

Euler circuit: For a given graph we have to reconstruct them using a pen, drawing each line exactly once. We should not lift the pen from the paper while drawing. That means, we must find a path in the graph that visits every edge exactly once and this problem is called an *Euler path* (also called *Euler tour*) or *Euler circuit problem*. This puzzle has a simple solution based on DFS.

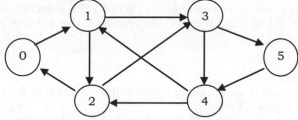

An *Euler* circuit exists if and only if the graph is connected and the number of neighbors of each vertex is even. Start with any node, select any untraversed outgoing edge, and follow it. Repeat until there are no more remaining unselected outgoing edges. For example, consider the following graph: A legal Euler Circuit of this graph is 0 1 3 4 1 2 3 5 4 2 0.

If we start at vertex 0, we can select the edge to vertex 1, then select the edge to vertex 2, then select the edge to vertex 0. There are now no remaining unchosen edges from vertex 0:

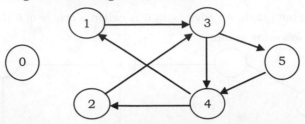

We now have a circuit 0,1,2,0 that does not traverse every edge. So, we pick some other vertex that is on that circuit, say vertex 1. We then do another depth first search of the remaining edges. Say we choose the edge to node 3, then 4, then 1. Again we are stuck. There are no more unchosen edges from node 1. We now splice this path 1,3,4,1 into the old path 0,1,2,0 to get: 0,1,3,4,1,2,0. The unchosen edges now look like this:

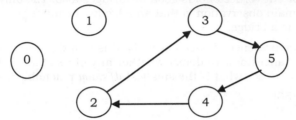

We can pick yet another vertex to start another DFS. If we pick vertex 2, and splice the path 2,3,5,4,2, then we get the final circuit 0,1,3,4,1,2,3,5,4,2,0. A similar problem is to find a simple cycle, in an undirected graph that visits every vertex. This is known as the *Hamiltonian cycle problem*. Although it seems almost identical to the *Euler* circuit problem, no efficient algorithm for it is known.

Notes:
- A connected undirected graph is *Eulerian* if and only if every graph vertex has an even degree, or exactly two vertices with odd degree.
- A directed graph is *Eulerian* if it is strongly connected and every vertex has equal *in* and *out* degree.

Application: A postman has to visit a set of streets in order to deliver mails and packages. He needs to find a path that starts and ends at the post-office, and that passes through each street (edge) exactly once. This way the postman will deliver mails and packages to all streets he has to, and in the same time will spend minimum efforts/time on the road.

Problem-18   **DFS Application:** Finding Strongly Connected Components.

Solution: This is another application of DFS. In a directed graph, two vertices u and v are strongly connected if and only if there exists a path from u to v and there exists a path from v to u. The strongly connectedness is an equivalence relation.
- A vertex is strongly connected with itself
- If a vertex u is strongly connected to a vertex v, then v is strongly connected to u
- If a vertex u is strongly connected to a vertex v and v is strongly connected to a vertex x, then u is strongly connected to x

What this says is, for a given directed graph we can divide it into strongly connected components. This problem can be solved by performing two depth-first searches. With two DFS searches we can test whether a given directed graph is strongly connected or not. We can also produce the subsets of vertices that are strongly connected.

Algorithm
- Perform DFS on given graph G
- Number vertices of given graph G according to a post-order traversal of depth-first spanning forest.
- Construct graph G_r by reversing all edges in G
- Perform DFS on G_r: Always start a new DFS (initial call to Visit) at the highest-numbered vertex
- Each tree in resulting depth-first spanning forest corresponds to a strongly-connected component.

Why this algorithm works?

Let us consider two vertices, v and w. If they are in same strongly connected component, then there are paths from v to w and from w to v in the original graph G, and hence also in G_r. If two vertices v and w are not in the same depth-first spanning tree of G_r, clearly they cannot be in the same strongly connected component. As an example, consider the graph shown below. Let us assume this graph is G.

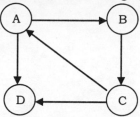

Now, as per the algorithm, performing *DFS* on this graph G the following diagram. The dotted line from C to A indicates a back edge.

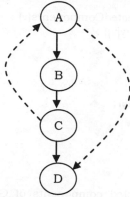

Now, performing post order traversal on this tree gives: D, C, B and A.

Vertex	Post Order Number
A	4
B	3
C	2
D	1

Now reverse the given graph, G and call it G_r and at the same time assign postorder numbers to the vertices. The reversed graph G_r will look like:

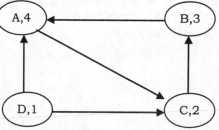

Last step is, performing DFS on this revered graph G_r. While doing *DFS* we need to consider the vertex which has largest DFS number. So, first we start at A and with *DFS* we go to C and then B. At B, we cannot move further. This says that $\{A, B, C\}$ is strongly connected component. Now the only remaining element is D and we end our second *DFS* at D itself. So the connected components are: $\{A, B, C\}$ and $\{D\}$.

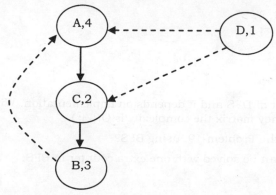

The implementation based on this discussion can be given as:

```
//Graph represented in adj matrix.
int adjMatrix [256][256], table[256];
vector <int> st ;
int counter = 0 ;
//This table contains the DFS Search number
int dfsnum [256], num = 0, low[256] ;
void StronglyConnectedComponents( int u ) {
        low[u] = dfsnum[ u ] = num++;
        Push(st, u) ;
        for( int v = 0 ; v < 256; ++v ) {
                if(graph[u][v] && table[v] == -1) {
                        if( dfsnum[v] == -1)
                                StronglyConnectedComponents(v) ;
                        low[u] = min(low[u] , low[v]) ;
                }
        }
        if(low[u] == dfsnum[u]) {
                while( table[u] != counter) {
                        table[st.back()] = counter;
                        Push(st) ;
                }
                ++ counter;
        }
}
```

Problem-19   Count the number of connected components of Graph *G* which is represented in adjacent matrix.

Solution: This problem can be solved with one extra counter in *DFS*.

```
//Visited[] is a global array.
int Visited[G→V];
void DFS(Graph G, int u) {
        Visited[u] = 1;
        for( int v = 0; v < G.vertexCount; v++ ) {
                /* For example, if the adjacency matrix is used for representing the
                   graph, then the condition to be used for finding unvisited adjacent
                   vertex of u  is: if( !Visited[v] && G→Adj[u][v] ) */
                for each unvisited adjacent node v of u {
                        DFS(v);
                }
        }
}
void DFSTraversal(Graph G) {
        int count = 0;
        for (int i = 0; i< G.vertexCount;i++)
                Visited[i]=0;
        //This loop is required if the graph has more than one component
        for (int i = 0; i< G.vertexCount;i++)
                if(!Visited[i]) {
                        DFS(G, i);
                        count++;
                }

        return count;
}
```

Time Complexity: Same as that of DFS and it depends on implementation. With adjacency matrix the complexity is $O(|E| + |V|)$ and with adjacency matrix the complexity is $O(|V|^2)$.

Problem-20   Can we solve the Problem-19, using BFS?

Solution: Yes. This problem can be solved with one extra counter in BFS.

```
void BFS(Graph G, int u) {
        int v,
```

```
                LLQueue Q = new LLQueue();
                Q.enQueue( u);
                while(!Q.isEmpty()) {
                        u = Q.deQueue();
                        Process u; //For example, print
                        Visited[s]=1;
                        /* For example, if the adjacency matrix is used for representing the
                        graph, then the condition be used for finding unvisited adjacent
                        vertex of u  is: if( !Visited[v] && G→Adj[u][v] ) */
                        for each unvisited adjacent node v of u {
                                Q.enQueue( v);
                        }
                }
        }
}
void BFSTraversal(Graph G) {
        for (int i = 0; i< G.vertexCount;i++)
                Visited[i]=0;
        //This loop is required if the graph has more than one component
        for (int i = 0; i< G.vertexCount; i++)
                if(!Visited[i])
                        BFS(G, i);
}
```

Time Complexity: Same as that of *BFS* and it depends on implementation. With adjacency matrix the complexity is $O(|E| + |V|)$ and with adjacency matrix the complexity is $O(|V|^2)$.

Problem-21   Let us assume that $G(V, E)$ is an undirected graph. Give an algorithm for finding a spanning tree which takes $O(|E|)$ time complexity (not necessarily a minimum spanning tree).

Solution: The test for a cycle can be done in constant time, by marking vertices that have been added to the set *S*. An edge will introduce a cycle, if both its vertices have already been marked.

Algorithm:
```
        S = {}; //Assume S is a set
        for each edge e ∈ E {
                if(adding e to S doesn't form a cycle) {
                        add e to S;
                        mark e;
                }
        }
```

Problem-22   Is there any other way of solving Problem-20?

Solution: Yes. We can run *BFS* and find the *BFS* tree for the graph (level order tree of the graph). Then start at the root element and keep moving to next levels and at the same time we have to consider the nodes in the next level only once. That means, if we have a node with multiple input edges then we should consider only of them, otherwise they will form a cycle.

Problem-23   Detecting a cycle in undirected graph

Solution: An undirected graph is acyclic if and only if a *DFS* yields no back edges, edges (u, v) where v has already been discovered and is ancestor of u.
*   Execute *DFS* on the graph.
*   If there is a back edge - the graph has a cycle.
If the graph does not contain a cycle then $|E| < |V|$ and *DFS* cost $O(|V|)$. If the graph contains a cycle, then a back edge is discovered after $2|V|$ steps at most.

Problem-24   Detecting a cycle in DAG

Solution:

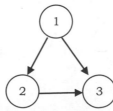

Cycle detection on a graph is different than on a tree. This is because in graph a node can have multiple parents. In a tree, the algorithm for detecting a cycle is to do a depth first search, marking nodes as they are encountered. If a previously marked node is seen again, then a cycle exists. This won't work on a graph. Let us consider the graph shown in the figure below. If we use tree cycle detection algorithm, then it will report wrong result. That means that this graph has cycle in it. But the given graph does not have any cycle in it. This is because node 3 will be seen twice in a *DFS* starting at node 1.

The cycle detection algorithm for trees can easily be modified to work for graphs. The key is that in a *DFS* of an acyclic graph, a node whose descendants have all been visited can be seen again without implying a cycle. But, if a node is seen for the second time before all its descendants have been visited, then there must be a cycle.

Can you see why this is? Suppose there is a cycle containing node A. This means that A must be reachable from one of its descendants. When the *DFS* is visiting that descendant, it will see *A* again, before it has finished visiting all of *A's* descendants. So there is a cycle. In order to detect cycles, we can modify the depth first search.

```
int DetectCycle(Graph G) {
        for (int i = 0; i< G.vertexCount; i++) {
                Visited[s]=0;
                Predecessor[i] = 0;
        }
        for (int i = 0; i < G.vertexCount;i++) {
                if(!Visited[i] && HasCycle(G, i))
                        return 1;
        }
        return false;;
}
int HasCycle(Graph G, int u) {
        Visited[u]=1;
        for (int i = 0; i< G.vertexCount; i++) {
                if(G→Adj[s][i]) {
                        if(Predecessor[i] != u && Visited[i])
                                return 1;
                        else {
                                Predecessor[i] = u;
                                return  HasCycle(G, i);
                        }
                }
        }
        return 0;
}
```

Time Complexity: $O(V + E)$.

Problem-25   Given a directed acyclic graph, give an algorithm for finding its depth.

Solution: We can solve this problem by following the similar approach which we used for finding the depth in trees. In trees, we have solved this problem using level order traversal (with one extra special symbol to indicate the end of the level).

```
//Assuming the given  graph is a DAG
int DepthInDAG( Graph G ) {
        LLQueue Q = new LLQueue();
        int counter;
        int v, w;
        counter =  0;
        for (v = 0; v< G.vertexCount; v++)
                if( indegree[v] ==  0 )
                        Q.enQueue(v);
        Q.enQueue( '$' );
        while( !Q.isEmpty()) {
                v = Q.deQueue();
                if(v == '$') {
                        counter++;
                        if(!Q.isEmpty())
                                Q.enQueue( '$' );
                }
                for each w adjacent to v
                        if( --indegree[w] ==  0 )
                                Q.enQueue(w );
        }
```

```
        Q.deleteQueue();
        return counter;
}
```

Total running time is $O(V + E)$.

Problem-26   How many topological sorts of the following dag are there?

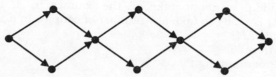

Solution: If we observer the above graph there are three stages with 2 vertices. In the early discussion of this chapter, we have seen that topological sort picks the elements with zero indegree at any point of time. At each of the two vertices stages, we can either first process the top vertex of bottom vertex. As a result at each of these stages we have two possibilities. So the total number of possibilities is the multiplication of possibilities at each stage and that is, $2 \times 2 \times 2 = 8$.

Problem-27   Unique topological ordering: Design an algorithm to determine whether a directed graph has a unique topological ordering.

Solution: A directed graph has a unique topological ordering if and only if there is a directed edge between each pair of consecutive vertices in the topological order. This can also be defined as: a directed graph has a unique topological ordering if and only if it has a Hamiltonian path. If the digraph has multiple topological orderings, then a second topological order can be obtained by swapping a pair of consecutive vertices.

Problem-28   Let us consider the prerequisites for courses at *IIT Bombay*. Suppose that all prerequisites are mandatory, every course is offered every semester, and there is no limit to the number of courses we can take in one semester. We would like to know the minimum number of semesters required to complete the major. Describe the data structure to represent this problem, and outline a linear time algorithm for solving it.

Solution: Use a directed acyclic graph (DAG). The vertices represent courses and the edges represent the prerequisite relation between courses at *IIT Bombay*. It is a DAG, because the prerequisite relation has no cycles.

The number of semesters required to complete the major is one more than the longest path in the dag. This can be calculated on the DFS tree recursively in linear time. The longest path out of a vertex x is 0 if x has outdegree 0, otherwise it is $1 + max \{longest\ path\ out\ of\ y \mid (x,y)\ is\ an\ edge\ of\ G\}$.

Problem-29   At one of the universities (say, *IIT Bombay*), there is a list of courses along with their prerequisites. That means, two lists are given:

A - Courses list

B – Prerequisites: B contains couples (x,y) where $x,y \in A$ indicating that course x can't be taken before course y.

Let us consider a student who wants to take only one course in a semester. Design a schedule for this student.

Example: A = {C-Lang, Data Structures, OS, CO, Algorithms, Design Patterns, Programming }. B = { (C-Lang, CO), (OS, CO), (Data Structures, Algorithms), (Design Patterns, Programming) }. *One possible schedule could be*:

> Semester 1: Data Structures
> Semester 2: Algorithms
> Semester 3: C-Lang
> Semester 4: OS
> Semester 5: CO
> Semester 6: Design Patterns
> Semester 7: Programming

Solution: The solution to this problem is exactly the same as that of topological sort. Assume that the courses names are integers in the range $[1..n]$, n is known (n is not constant). The relations between the courses will be represented by a directed graph $G = (V, E)$, where V are the set of courses and if course i is prerequisite of course j, E will contain the edge (i, j). Let us assume that the graph will be represented as an Adjacency list. First, let's observe another algorithm to topologically sort a DAG in $O(|V| + |E|)$.

- Find in-degree of all the vertices - $O(|V| + |E|)$
- Repeat:
  Find a vertex v with in-degree=0 - $O(|V|)$

Output v and remove it from G, along with its edges - O(|V|)

Reduce the in-degree of each node u such as (v, u) was an edge in G and keep a list of vertices with in-degree=0 - O($degree(v)$)

Repeat the process until all the vertices are removed

Time complexity of this algorithm is also same as that of topological sort and it is O(|V| + |E|).

Problem-30   In Problem-29, a student wants to take all the courses in A, in the minimal number of semesters. That means the student is ready to take any number of courses in a semester. Design a schedule for this scenario. *One possible schedule is:*

Semester 1: C-Lang, OS, Design Patterns
Semester 2: Data Structures, CO, Programming
Semester 3: Algorithms

Solution: A variation of the above topological sort algorithm with a slight change: In each semester, instead of taking one subject, take all the subjects with zero indegree. That means, execute the algorithm on all the nodes with degree 0 (instead of dealing with one source in each stage, all the sources will be dealt and printed).

Time Complexity: O(|V| + |E|).

Problem-31   LCA of a DAG: Given a DAG and two vertices v and w, find the *lowest common ancestor* of v and w. The LCA of v and w is an ancestor of v and w that has no descendants which are also ancestors of v and w.

Hint: Define the height of a vertex v in a DAG to be the length of the longest path from *root* to v. Among the vertices that are ancestors of both v and w, the one with the greatest height is an LCA of v and w.

Problem-32   Shortest ancestral path: Given a DAG and two vertices v and w, find the *shortest ancestral path* between v and w. An ancestral path between v and w is a common ancestor x along with a shortest path from v to x and a shortest path from w to x. The shortest ancestral path is the ancestral path whose total length is minimized.

Hint: Run BFS two times. First run from v and second time from w. Find a DAG where the shortest ancestral path goes to a common ancestor x that is not an LCA.

**Problem-33   Let us assume that we have two graphs G_1 and G_2. How do we check whether they are isomorphic or not?

Solution: There are many ways of representing the same graph. As an example, consider the following simple graph. It can be seen that all the representations below have the same number of vertices and same number of edges.

Definition: Graphs $G_1 = \{V_1, E_1\}$ and $G_2 = \{V_2, E_2\}$ are isomorphic if
1)   There is a one-to-one correspondence from V_1 to V_2 and
2)   There is a one-to-one correspondence from E_1 to E_2 that map each edge of G_1 to G_2.

Now, for the given graphs how do we check whether they are isomorphic or not?

In general, it is not a simple task to prove that two graphs are isomorphic. For that reason we consider some properties of isomorphic graphs. That means those properties must be satisfied if the graphs are isomorphic. If the given graph does not satisfy these properties then we say they are not isomorphic graphs.

Property: Two graphs are isomorphic if and only if for some ordering of their vertices their adjacency matrices are equal.

Based on the above property we decide whether the given graphs are isomorphic or not. For checking the property we need to do some matrix transformation operations.

Problem-34   How many simple undirected non-isomorphic graphs are there with n vertices?

Solution: We will try to answer this question in two steps. First, we count all labeled graphs. Assume all the representations below are labeled with $\{1, 2, 3\}$ as vertices. The set of all such graphs for $n = 3$ are:

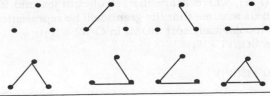

There are only two choices for each edge, it either exists or it does not. Therefore, since the maximum number of edges is $\binom{n}{2}$ (since, the maximum number of edges in an undirected graph with n vertices are $\frac{n(n-1)}{2} = n_{c_2} = \binom{n}{2}$), the total number of undirected labeled graphs is $2^{\binom{n}{2}}$.

Problem-35   For a given graph G with n vertices how many spanning trees can we construct?

Solution: There is a simple formula for this problem and it is named after Arthur Cayley. For a given graph with n labeled vertices the formula for finding number of trees on is n^{n-2}. Below, the number of trees with different n values is shown.

n value	Formula value: n^{n-2}	Number of Trees
2	1	1 ———— 2
3	3	(three tree diagrams)

Problem-36   For a given graph G with n vertices how many spanning trees can we construct?

Solution: The solution to this problem is same as that of Problem-35. It is just other way of asking the same problem. Because, the number of edges in both regular tree and spanning tree are same.

Problem-37   **Hamiltonian path in DAGs:** Given a DAG, design a linear time algorithm to determine whether there is a path that visits each vertex exactly once.

Solution: *Hamiltonian* path problem is a NP-Complete problem (for more details ref *Complexity Classes* chapter). To solve this problem, we will try to give the approximation algorithm (which solves the problem but it may not always produce the optimal solution).

Let us consider the topological sort algorithm for solving this problem. Topological sort has an interesting property that all pairs of consecutive vertices in the sorted order are connected by edges then these edges form a directed *Hamiltonian* path in the DAG. If a *Hamiltonian* path exists, the topological sort order is unique. Also, if a topological sort does not form a *Hamiltonian* path, the DAG will have two or more topological orderings.

Approximation Algorithm: Compute a topological sort and check if there is an edge between each consecutive pair of vertices in the topological order.

In an unweighted graph, finding a path from s to t that visits each vertex exactly once. The basic solution based on backtracking is, we start at *s* and try all of its neighbors recursively, making sure we never visit the same vertex twice. The algorithm based on this implementation can be given as:

```
bool seenTable[32];
void HamiltonianPath( Graph G, int u ) {
    if( u == t )
            /* Check that we have seen all vertices. */
    else {
        for( int v = 0; v < n; v++ )
            if( !seenTable[v] && G.adjMatrix [u][v] ) {
                seenTable[v] = true;
                HamiltonianPath( v );
                seenTable[v] = false;
            }
    }
}
```

Note that if we have a partial path from s to u using vertices $s = v_1, v_2, ..., v_k = u$, then we don't care about the order in which we visited these vertices in order to figure out which vertex to visit next. All that we need to know is the set of vertices we have seen (the seenTable[] array) and which vertex we are at right now (u). There are 2^n possible sets of vertices and n choices for u. In other words, there are 2^n possible *seenTable*[] arrays and n different parameters to HamiltonianPath(). What HamiltonianPath() does during any particular recursive call is completely determined by the *seenTable*[] array and the parameter u.

Problem-38   The *Hamiltonian cycle* problem: Is it possible to traverse each of the vertices of a graph exactly once, starting and ending at the same vertex?

Solution: Since *Hamiltonian* path problem is a NP-Complete problem *Hamiltonian* cycle problem is a NP-Complete problem. A *Hamiltonian* cycle is a cycle that traverses every vertex of a graph exactly once. There are no known conditions which are both necessary and sufficient. There are a few sufficient conditions.

- For a graph to have a *Hamiltonian* cycle the degree of each vertex must be two or more.
- The Petersen graph does not have a *Hamiltonian* cycle and the graph is given below.

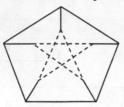

- In general, the more edges a graph has, the more likely it is to have a *Hamiltonian* cycle.
- Let G be a simple graph with n ≥ 3 vertices. If every vertex has degree at least $\frac{n}{2}$, then G has a *Hamiltonian* cycle.
- The best known algorithm for finding a *Hamiltonian* cycle has an exponential worst-case complexity.

As stated above, for approximation algorithm of *Hamiltonian* path, refer *Dynamic Programming* chapter.

Problem-39   What is the difference between *Dijkstra's* and *Prim's* algorithm?

Solution: *Dijkstra's* algorithm is almost identical to that of *Prim's*. The algorithm begins at a specific vertex and extends outward within the graph, until all vertices have been reached. The only distinction is that *Prim's* algorithm stores a minimum cost edge whereas *Dijkstra's* algorithm stores the total cost from a source vertex to the current vertex. More simply, *Dijkstra's* algorithm stores a summation of minimum cost edges whereas *Prim's* algorithm stores at most one minimum cost edge.

Problem-40   **Reversing Graph:** Give an algorithm that returns the reverse of the directed graph (each edge from *v* to *w* is replaced by an edge from *w* to *v*).

Solution: In graph theory, the reverse (also called as transpose) of a directed graph *G* is another directed graph on the same set of vertices with all the edges reversed. That means, if *G* contains an edge (*u*, *v*) then the reverse of *G* contains an edge (*v*, *u*) and vice versa.

Algorithm:
```
Graph ReverseTheDirectedGraph(Graph G) {
        Create new graph with name ReversedGraph and
                let us assume that this will contain the reversed graph.

        //The reversed graph also will contain same number of vertices and edges.
        for each vertex of given graph G {
                for each vertex w adjacent to v {
                        Add the w to v edge in ReversedGraph;
                        //That means we just need to reverse
                        //the bits in adjacency matrix.
                }
        }
        return ReversedGraph;
}
```

Problem-41   **Travelling Sales Person Problem:** Find the shortest path in a graph that visits each vertex at least once, starting and ending at the same vertex?

Solution: The Traveling Salesman Problem (*TSP*) is related to finding a Hamiltonian cycle. Given a weighted graph *G*, we want to find the shortest cycle (may be non-simple) that visits all the vertices.

Approximation algorithm: This algorithm does not solve the problem but gives a solution which is within a factor of 2 of optimal (in the worst-case).
1) Find a Minimal Spanning Tree (MST).
2) Do a DFS of the MST.
or details, refer to chapter on *Complexity Classes*.

Problem-42   Discuss Bipartite matchings?

Solution: In Bipartite graphs, we divide the graphs in to two disjoint sets and each edge connects a vertex from one set to a vertex in another subset (as shown in figure).

Definition: A simple graph $G = (V, E)$ is called bipartite graph if its vertices can be divided into two disjoint sets $V = V_1 \cup V_2$, such that every edge has the form $e = (a, b)$ where $a \in V_1$ and $b \in V_2$. One important condition is that no vertices both in V_1 or both in V_2 are connected.

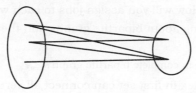

Properties of Bipartite Graphs

- A graph is called bipartite if and only if the given graph does not have an odd length cycle.
- A *complete bipartite graph* $K_{m,n}$ is a bipartite graph that has each vertex from one set adjacent to each vertex to another set.

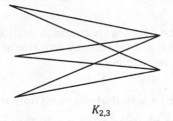   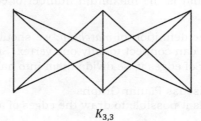

$K_{2,3}$ $K_{3,3}$

- A subset of edges $M \subset E$ is a *matching* if no two edges have a common vertex. As example, matching sets of edges are represented with dotted lines. A matching M is called *maximum* if it has a largest number of possible edges. In the graphs, the dotted edges represent the alternative matching for the given graph.

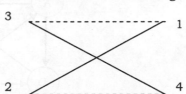

- A matching M is *perfect*, if it matches all vertices. We must have $V_1 = V_2$ in order to have perfect matching.
- An *alternating path* is a path whose edges alternate between matched and unmatched edges. If we find an alternating path then we can improve the matching. This is because an alternating path consists of matched and unmatched edges. The number of unmatched edges exceed the number of matched edges by one. Therefore, an alternating path always increases the matching by one.

Next question is, how do we find a perfect matching?

Based on the above theory and definition we can find the perfect matching with the following approximation algorithm.

Matching Algorithm (Hungarian algorithm)

1) Start at unmatched vertex.
2) Find an alternating path.
3) If it exists, change matching edges to no matching edges and conversely. If it does not exist, choose another unmatched vertex.
4) If the number of edges equals $V/2$ stop, otherwise proceed to step 1 and repeat as long all vertices have been examined without finding any alternating paths.

Time Complexity of the Matching Algorithm

The number of iterations is in $O(V)$.
The complexity of finding an alternating path using BFS is $O(E)$.
Therefore, the total time complexity is $O(V \times E)$.

Problem-43   Marriage and Personnel Problem?

Marriage Problem: There are X men and Y women who desire to get married. Participants indicate who among the opposite sex could be a potential spouse for them. Every woman can be married to at most one man, and every man to at most one woman. How can we marry everybody to someone they liked?

Personnel Problem: You are the boss of a company. The company has M workers and N jobs. Each worker is qualified to do some jobs, but not others. How will you assign jobs to each worker?

Solution: This is just another way of asking about bipartite graphs and the solution is same as that of Problem-42.

Problem-44   How many edges will be there in complete bipartite graph $K_{m,n}$?

Solution: $m \times n$. This is because each vertex in first set can connect all vertices in second set.

Problem-45   A graph is called regular graph if it has no loops and multiple edges where each vertex has the same number of neighbors; i.e. every vertex has the same degree. Now, if $K_{m,n}$ is a regular graph what is the relation between m and n?

Solution: Since each vertex should have the same degree the relation should be $m = n$.

Problem-46   What is the maximum number of edges in the maximum matching of a bipartite graph with n vertices?

Solution: From the definition of *matching*, we should not have the edges with common vertices. So in bipartite graph, each vertex can connect to only one vertex. Since we divide the total vertices into two sets, we can get the maximum number of edges if we divide them into half. Finally the answer is $\frac{n}{2}$.

Problem-47   Discuss Planar Graphs
   Planar graph: Is it possible to draw the edges of a graph in such a way that edges do not cross?

Solution: A graph G is said to be planar if it can be drawn in the plane in such a way that no two edges meet each other except at a vertex to which they are incident. Any such drawing is called a plane drawing of G. As an example consider the below graph:

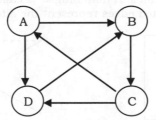

This graph we can easily convert to planar graph as below (without any cross edges).

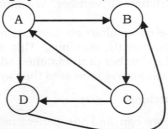

How do we decide whether a given graph is planar or not?

The solution to this problem is not simple. Instead some researchers found some interesting properties based on which we can decide whether the given graph is a planar graph or not.

Properties of Planar Graphs

• If a graph G is a connected planar simple graph with V vertices, where $V = 3$ and E edges then $E = 3V - 6$.

• K_5 is non-planar [K_5 stands for complete graph with 5 vertices].

• If a graph G is a connected planar simple graph with V vertices and E edges, and no triangles then $E = 2V - 4$.

• $K_{3,3}$ is non-planar [$K_{3,3}$ stands for bipartite graph with 3 vertices on one side and other 3 vertices on other side. $K_{3,3}$ contains 6 vertices].

• If a graph G is connected planar simple graph then G contains at least one vertex of degree 5 or less.

- A graph is planar if and only if it does not contain a subgraph which has K_5 and $K_{3,3}$ as a contraction.
- If a graph G contains a nonplanar graph as a subgraph, then G is non-planar.
- If a graph G is a planar graph, then every subgraph of G is planar;
- For any connected planar graph $G = (V, E)$, the following formula should holds $V + F - E = 2$, where F stands for the number of faces.
- For any planar graph $G = (V, E)$ with K components, the following formula holds $V + F - E = 1 + K$.

Inorder to test planarity of a given graph we use these properties and decide whether it is planar graph or not. Note that all the above properties are only the necessary conditions but not sufficient.

Problem-48   How many faces do $K_{2,3}$ have?

Solution: From the above discussion, we know that $V + F - E = 2$ and from earlier problem we know that $E = m \times n = 2 \times 3 = 6$ and $V = m + n = 5$.

$$\therefore 5 + F - 6 = 2 \Rightarrow F = 3.$$

Problem-49   Discuss Graph Coloring

Solution: A k −coloring of a graph G is an assignment of one color to each vertex of G such that no more than k colors are used and no two adjacent vertices receive the same color. A graph is called k −colorable if and only if it has a k −coloring.

Applications of Graph Coloring: The graph coloring problem has many applications such as scheduling, register allocation in compilers, frequency assignment in mobile radios, etc.

Clique: A *clique* in a graph G is the maximum complete subgraph is denoted by $\omega(G)$.

Chromatic number: The chromatic number of a graph G is the smallest number k such that G is k −colorable, and it is denoted by $X(G)$.

Lower bound for $X(G)$ is $\omega(G)$, that means $\omega(G) \leq X(G)$.

Properties of Chromatic number: Let G be a graph with n vertices and G' is its complement. Then,

- $X(G) \leq \Delta(G) + 1$, where $\Delta(G)$ is the maximum degree of G.
- $X(G)\,\omega(G') \geq n$
- $X(G) + \omega(G') \leq n + 1$
- $X(G) + (G') \leq n + 1$

K-colorability problem: Given a graph $G = (V, E)$ and a positive integer $k \leq V$. Check whether G is k −colorable?

This problem is NP-complete and will be discussed in detail in the chapter on *Complexity Classes*.

Graph coloring algorithm: As discussed earlier, this problem is *NP*-Complete. So we do not have a polynomial time algorithm to determine $X(G)$. Let us consider the following approximation (no efficient) algorithm.

- Consider a graph G with two non-adjacent vertices a and b. The connection G_1 is obtained by joining the two non-adjacent vertices a and b with an edge. The contraction G_2 is obtained by shrinking $\{a, b\}$ into a single vertex $c(a, b)$ and by joining it to each neighbor in G of vertex a and of vertex b (and eliminating multiple edges).
- A coloring of G in which a and b have the same color yields a coloring of G_1. A coloring of G in which a and b have different colors yields a coloring of G_2.
- Repeat the operations of connection and contraction in each graph generated, until the resulting graphs are all cliques. If the smallest resulting clique is a K −clique, then $(G) = K$.

Important notes on Graph Coloring

- Any simple planar graph G can be colored with 6 colors.
- Every simple planar graph can be colored with less than or equal to 5 colors.

Problem-50   What is the four coloring problem?

Solution: A graph can be constructed from any map. The regions of the map are represented by the vertices of the graph and two vertices are joined by an edge if the regions corresponding to the vertices are adjacent. The resulting graph is planar. That means it can be drawn in the plane without any edges crossing.

The *Four Color Problem* is whether if the vertices of a planar graph can be colored with at most 4 colors so that no two adjacent vertices use the same color.

History: The *Four − Color* problem was first given by *Francis Guthrie*. He was a student at *University College London* where he studied under *Augusts De Morgan*. After graduating from London he studied law but some years later his brother Frederick Guthrie had become a student of *De Morgan*. One day Francis asked his brother to discuss this problem with *De Morgan*.

Problem-51　　When an adjacency-matrix representation is used, most graph algorithms require time $O(V^2)$. Show that determining whether a directed graph, represented in an adjacency-matrix contains a sink can be done in time $O(V)$. A sink is a vertex with in-degree $|V| - 1$ and out-degree 0 (Only one can exist in a graph).

Solution: A vertex i is a sink if and only if $M[i,j] = 0$ for all j and $M[j,i] = 1$ for all $j \neq i$. For any pair of vertices i and j:

$$M[i,j] = 1 \rightarrow \text{vertex i can't be a sink}$$
$$M[i,j] = 0 \rightarrow \text{vertex j can't be a sink}$$

Algorithm:
- Start at $i = 1, j = 1$
- If $M[i,j] = 0 \rightarrow i$ wins, $j++$
- If $M[i,j] = 1 \rightarrow j$ wins, $i++$
- Proceed this process until $j = n$ or $i = n + 1$
- If $i == n + 1$, the graph does not contain a sink
- Otherwise, check row i - it should be all zeros, and column i - it should be all but $M[i,i]$ ones - if so, i is a sink.

Time Complexity: $O(V)$, because at most $2|V|$ cells in the matrix are examined.

Problem-52　　What is the worst – case memory usage of DFS?

Solution: It occurs when the$O(|V|)$, which happens if the graph is actually a list. So the algorithm is memory efficient on graphs with small diameter.

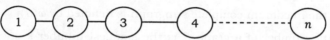

Problem-53　　Does DFS find the shortest path from start node to some node w ?

Solution: No. In DFS it is not compulsory to select smallest weight edge.

Chapter-10

SORTING

10.1 What is Sorting?

Sorting is an algorithm that arranges the elements of a list in certain order [either *ascending* or *descending*]. The output is a permutation or reordering of the input.

10.2 Why is Sorting Necessary?

Sorting is one of the important categories of algorithms in computer science. Sometimes sorting significantly reduces the complexity of the problem. We can use sorting as a technique to reduce the search complexity. Great research went into this category of algorithms because of its importance. These algorithms are used in many computer algorithms [for example, searching elements], database algorithms and many more.

10.3 Classification

Sorting algorithms are generally categorized based on the following parameters.

By Number of Comparisons

In this method, sorting algorithms are classified based on the number of comparisons. For comparison based sorting algorithms best case behavior is $O(nlogn)$ and worst case behavior is $O(n^2)$. Comparison-based sorting algorithms evaluate the elements of the list by key comparison operation and need at least $O(nlogn)$ comparisons for most inputs.

Later in this chapter we will discuss few *non – comparison* (*linear*) sorting algorithms like Counting sort, Bucket sort, and Radix sort, etc. Linear Sorting algorithms impose few restrictions on the inputs to improve the complexity.

By Number of Swaps

In this method, sorting algorithms are categorized by number of *swaps* (also called *inversions*).

By Memory Usage

Some sorting algorithms are "*in place*" and they need O(1) or O(*logn*) memory to create auxiliary locations for sorting the data temporarily.

By Recursion

Sorting algorithms are either recursive [quick sort] or non-recursive [selection sort, and insertion sort]. There are some algorithms which use both (merge sort).

By Stability

Sorting algorithm is stable if for all indices i and j such that the key A[i] equals key A[j], if record R[i] precedes record R[j] in the original file, record R[i] precedes record R[j] in the sorted list. Few sorting algorithms maintain the relative order of elements with equal keys (equivalent elements retain their relative positions even after sorting).

By Adaptability

Few sorting algorithms complexity changes based on presortedness [quick sort]: presortedness of the input affects the running time. Algorithms that take this into account are known to be adaptive.

10.4 Other Classifications

Another method of classifying sorting algorithms is:
- Internal Sort
- External Sort

Internal Sort

Sort algorithms that use main memory exclusively during the sort are called *internal* sorting algorithms. This kind of algorithm assumes high-speed random access to all memory.

External Sort

Sorting algorithms that use external memory, such as tape or disk, during the sort come under this category.

10.5 Bubble sort

Bubble sort is the simplest sorting algorithm. It works by iterating the input array from the first element to last, comparing each pair of elements and swapping them if needed. Bubble sort continues its iterations until no more swaps are needed. The algorithm gets its name from the way smaller elements "*bubble*" to the top of the list. Generally, insertion sort has better performance than bubble sort. Some researchers suggest that we should not teach bubble sort because of its simplicity and complexity.

The only significant advantage that bubble sort has over other implementations is that it can detect whether the input list is already sorted or not.

```
void BubbleSort(int A[], int n) {
        for (int pass = n - 1; pass >= 0; pass--)   {
                for (int i = 0; i < pass - 1 ; i++)   {
                        if(A[i] > A[i+1]) {
                                // swap elements
                                int temp = A[i];
                                A[i] = A[i+1];
                                A[i+1] = temp;
                        }
                }
        }
}
```

Algorithm takes O(n^2) (even in best case). We can improve it by using one extra flag. No more swaps indicate the completion of sorting. If the list is already sorted, we can use this flag to skip the remaining passes.

```
void BubbleSortImproved(int A[], int n) {
        int pass, i, temp, swapped = 1;
        for (pass = n - 1; pass >= 0 && swapped; pass--) {
                swapped = 0;
                for (i = 0; i < pass - 1 ; i++) {
                        if(A[i] > A[i+1]) {
                                // swap elements
                                temp = A[i];
                                A[i] = A[i+1];
                                A[i+1] =  temp;
                                swapped = 1;
                        }
                }
        }
}
```

This modified version improves the best case of bubble sort to O(n).

Performance

Worst case complexity : O(n^2)
Best case complexity (Improved version) : O(n)
Average case complexity (Basic version) : O(n^2)
Worst case space complexity : O(1) auxiliary

10.6 Selection Sort

Selection sort is an in-place sorting algorithm. Selection sort works well for small files. It is used for sorting the files with very large values and small keys. This is because selection is made based on keys and swaps are made only when required.

Advantages:

- Easy to implement
- In-place sort (requires no additional storage space)

Disadvantages:

- Doesn't scale well: $O(n^2)$

Algorithm

1. Find the minimum value in the list
2. Swap it with the value in the current position
3. Repeat this process for all the elements until the entire array is sorted

This algorithm is called *selection sort* since it repeatedly *selects* the smallest element.

```
void Selection(int A[], int n) {
        int i, j, min, temp;
        for (i = 0; i < n - 1; i++) {
                min = i;
                for (j = i+1; j < n; j++) {
                        if(A [j] < A [min])
                                min = j;
                }
                // swap elements
                temp = A[min];
                A[min] = A[i];
                A[i] = temp;
        }
}
```

Performance

Worst case complexity : $O(n^2)$	
Best case complexity : $O(n)$	
Average case complexity : $O(n^2)$	
Worst case space complexity: $O(1)$ auxiliary	

10.7 Insertion sort

Insertion sort is a simple and efficient comparison sort. In this algorithm each iteration removes an element from the input data and inserts it into the correct position in the list being sorted. The choice of the element being removed from the input is random and this process is repeated until all input elements have gone through.

Advantages

- Simple implementation
- Efficient for small data
- Adaptive: If the input list is presorted [may not be completely] then insertions sort takes O(n + d), where d is the number of inversions
- Practically more efficient than selection and bubble sorts even though all of them have $O(n^2)$ worst case complexity
- Stable: Maintains relative order of input data if the keys are same
- In-place: It requires only a constant amount O(1) of additional memory space
- Online: Insertion sort can sort the list as it receives it

Algorithm

Every repetition of insertion sort removes an element from the input data, inserts it into the correct position in the already-sorted list until no input elements remain. Sorting is typically done in-place. The resulting array after k iterations has the property where the first $k + 1$ entries are sorted.

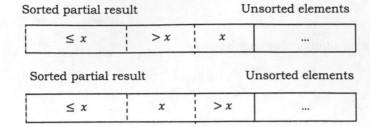

Each element greater than x copied to the right as it is compared against x.

```java
void InsertionSort(int A[], int n) {
        int i, j, v;
        for (i = 2; i <= n - 1; i++) {
                v = A[i];
                j = i;

                while (A[j-1] > v && j >= 1) {
                        A[j] = A[j-1];
                        j--;
                }
                A[j] = v;

        }

}
```

Example

Given an array: 6 8 1 4 5 3 7 2 and the goal is to put them in ascending order.

> **6** 8 1 4 5 3 7 2 (Consider index 0)
> **6 8** 1 4 5 3 7 2 (Consider indices 0 - 1)
> **1 6 8** 4 5 3 7 2 (Consider indices 0 - 2: insertion places 1 in front of 6 and 8)
> **1 4 6 8** 5 3 7 2 (Process same as above is repeated until array is sorted)
> **1 4 5 6 8** 3 7 2
> **1 3 4 5 6 7 8** 2
> **1 2 3 4 5 6 7 8** (The array is sorted!)

Analysis

Worst case analysis: Worst case occurs when for every i the inner loop has to move all elements $A[1], \ldots, A[i-1]$ (which happens when $A[i]$ = key is smaller than all of them), that takes $\Theta(i-1)$ time.

$$T(n) = \Theta(1) + \Theta(2) + \Theta(2) + \ldots \ldots + \Theta(n-1)$$
$$= \Theta(1 + 2 + 3 + \ldots + n - 1) = \Theta(\tfrac{n(n-1)}{2}) \approx \Theta(n^2)$$

Average case analysis: For the average case, the inner loop will insert $A[i]$ in the middle of $A[1], \ldots, A[i-1]$. This takes $\Theta(i/2)$ time.

$$T(n) = \sum_{i=1}^{n} \Theta(i/2) \approx \Theta(n^2)$$

Performance

Worst case complexity : $O(n^2)$
Best case complexity : $O(n^2)$
Average case complexity : $O(n^2)$
Worst case space complexity: $O(n^2)$ total, $O(1)$ auxiliary

Comparisons to Other Sorting Algorithms

Insertion sort is one of the elementary sorting algorithms with $O(n^2)$ worst-case time. Insertion sort is used when the data is nearly sorted (due to its adaptiveness) or when the input size is small (due to its low overhead). For these reasons and due to its stability, insertion sort is used as the recursive base case (when the problem size is small) for higher overhead divide-and-conquer sorting algorithms, such as merge sort or quick sort.

Note:

- Bubble sort takes $\frac{n^2}{2}$ comparisons and $\frac{n^2}{2}$ swaps (inversions) in both average case and in worst case.
- Selection sort takes $\frac{n^2}{2}$ comparisons and n swaps.
- Insertion sort takes $\frac{n^2}{4}$ comparisons and $\frac{n^2}{8}$ swaps in average case and in the worst case they are double.
- Insertion sort is almost linear for partially sorted input.
- Selection sort is best suits for elements with bigger values and small keys.

10.8 Shell sort

Shell sort (also called *diminishing increment sort*) was invented by *Donald Shell*. This sorting algorithm is a generalization of insertion sort. Insertion sort works efficiently on input that is already almost sorted. Shell sort is also known as n-gap insertion sort. Instead of comparing only adjacent pair, shell sort makes several passes and uses various gaps between adjacent elements (ending with the gap of 1 or classical insertion sort).

In insertion sort, comparisons are made between the adjacent elements. At most 1 inversion is eliminated for each comparison done with insertion sort. The variation used in shell sort is to avoid comparing adjacent elements until the last step of the algorithm. So, the last step of shell sort is effectively the insertion sort algorithm. It improves insertion sort by allowing the comparison and exchange of elements that are far away. This is the first algorithm which got less than quadratic complexity among comparison sort algorithms.

Shellsort is actually a simple extension for insertion sort. The primary difference is its capability of exchanging elements that are far apart, making it considerably faster for elements to get to where it should be. For example if the smallest element happens to be at the end of an array, with insertion sort it will require a full array steps to put this element at the beginning of the array. However with shellsort, this element can jump further instead of just one step a time and reach the proper destination in less exchanges.

The basic idea in shellsort is to exchange every hth element in the array. Now this can be confusing so we'll talk more on this. h determine how far apart element exchange can happen, say for example take h as 13, the first element (index-0) is exchanged with the 14th element (index-13) if necessary (of course). The second element with the 15th element, and so on. Now if we take h as 1, it is exactly the same as a regular insertion sort.

Shellsort works by starting with big enough (but not larger than the array size) h as to allow elligible element exchanges that are far apart. Once a sort is complete with a particular h, the array can be said as h-sorted. The next step is to reduce h by a certain sequence, and again performing another complete h-sort. Once h is 1 and h-sorted, the array is completely sorted. Notice that the last sequence for h is 1 so the last sort is always an insertion sort, except by this time the array is already well-formed and easier to sort.

Shell sort uses a sequence $h1, h2, ..., ht$ called the *increment sequence*. Any increment sequence is fine as long as $h1 = 1$ and some choices are better than others. Shell sort makes multiple passes through input list and sorts a number of equally sized sets using the insertion sort. Shell sort improves the efficiency of insertion sort by *quickly* shifting values to their destination.

```java
void ShellSort(int A[], int array_size) {
    int i, j, h, v;
    for (h = 1; h = array_size/9; h = 3*h+1);
    for ( ; h > 0; h = h/3) {
        for (i = h+1; i = array_size; i += 1) {
            v = A[i];
            j = i;
            while (j > h && A[j-h] > v) {
                A[j] = A[j-h];
                j -= h;
            }
            A[j] = v;
        }
    }
}
```

Note that when $h == 1$, the algorithm makes a pass over the entire list, comparing adjacent elements, but doing very few element exchanges. For $h == 1$, shell sort works just like insertion sort, except the number of inversions that have to be eliminated is greatly reduced by the previous steps of the algorithm with $h > 1$.

Analysis

Shell sort is efficient for medium size lists. For bigger lists, the algorithm is not the best choice. It is the fastest of all $O(n^2)$ sorting algorithms.

The disadvantage of shell sort is that it is a complex algorithm and not nearly as efficient as the merge, heap, and quick sorts. Shell sort is significantly slower than the merge, heap, and quick sorts, but is a relatively simple algorithm, which makes it a good choice for sorting lists of less than 5000 items unless speed is important. It is also a good choice for repetitive sorting of smaller lists.

The best case in Shell sort is when the array is already sorted in the right order. The number of comparisons is less. Running time of Shell sort depends on the choice of increment sequence.

Performance

Worst case complexity depends on gap sequence. Best known: $O(nlog^2n)$
Best case complexity: $O(n)$
Average case complexity depends on gap sequence
Worst case space complexity: $O(n)$

10.9 Merge sort

Merge sort is an example of the divide and conquer.

Important Notes

- *Merging* is the process of combining two sorted files to make one bigger sorted file.
- *Selection* is the process of dividing a file into two parts: k smallest elements and $n - k$ largest elements.
- Selection and merging are opposite operations
  - o   selection splits a list into two lists
  - o   merging joins two files to make one file
- Merge sort is Quick sorts complement
- Merge sort accesses the data in a sequential manner
- This algorithm is used for sorting a linked list
- Merge sort is insensitive to the initial order of its input
- In Quick sort most of the work is done before the recursive calls. Quick sort starts with the largest subfile and finishes with the small ones and as a result it needs stack. Moreover, this algorithm is not stable. Merge sort divides the list into two parts; then each part is conquered individually. Merge sort starts with the small subfiles and finishes with the largest one. As a result it doesn't need stack. This algorithm is stable.

```
void Mergesort(int A[], int temp[], int left, int right) {
        int mid;
        if(right > left) {
                mid = (right + left) / 2;
                Mergesort(A, temp, left, mid);
                Mergesort(A, temp, mid+1, right);
                Merge(A, temp, left, mid+1, right);
        }
}
void Merge(int A[], int temp[], int left, int mid, int right) {
        int i, left_end, size, temp_pos;
        left_end = mid - 1;
        temp_pos = left;
        size = right - left + 1;
        while ((left <= left_end) && (mid <= right)) {
                if(A[left] <= A[mid]) {
                        temp[temp_pos] = A[left];
                        temp_pos = temp_pos + 1;
                        left = left +1;
                }
```

```
            else {
                    temp[temp_pos] = A[mid];
                    temp_pos = temp_pos + 1;
                    mid = mid + 1;
            }
    }
    while (left <= left_end) {
            temp[temp_pos] = A[left];
            left = left + 1;
            temp_pos = temp_pos + 1;
    }
    while (mid <= right) {
            temp[temp_pos] = A[mid];
            mid = mid + 1;
            temp_pos = temp_pos + 1;
    }
    for (i = 0; i <= size; i++) {
            A[right] = temp[right];
            right = right - 1;
    }
}
```

Analysis

In Merge sort the input list is divided into two parts and these are solved recursively. After solving the sub problems they are merged by scanning the resultant sub problems. Let us assume $T(n)$ is the complexity of Merge sort with n elements. The recurrence for the Merge Sort can be defined as:

Recurrence for Mergesort is $T(n) = 2T(\frac{n}{2}) + \Theta(n)$. Using Master theorem, we get, $T(n) = \Theta(n \log n)$.

Note: For more details, refer *Divide and Conquer* chapter.

Performance

Worst case complexity : $\Theta(nlogn)$
Best case complexity : $\Theta(nlogn)$
Average case complexity : $\Theta(nlogn)$
Worst case space complexity: $\Theta(n)$ auxiliary

10.10 Heapsort

Heapsort is a comparison-based sorting algorithm and is part of the selection sort family. Although somewhat slower in practice on most machines than a good implementation of Quick sort, it has the advantage of a more favorable worst-case $\Theta(n \log n)$ runtime. Heapsort is an in-place algorithm but is not a stable sort.

Performance

Worst case performance: $\Theta(nlogn)$
Best case performance: $\Theta(nlogn)$
Average case performance: $\Theta(nlogn)$
Worst case space complexity: $\Theta(n)$ total, $\Theta(1)$ auxiliary

For other details on Heapsort refer to *Priority Queues* chapter.

10.11 Quicksort

Quick sort is an example of divide-and-conquer algorithmic technique. It is also called *partition exchange sort*. It uses recursive calls for sorting the elements. It is one of famous algorithms among comparison-based sorting algorithms.

Divide: The array $A[low \dots high]$ is partitioned into two non-empty sub arrays $A[low \dots q]$ and $A[q + 1 \dots high]$, such that each element of $A[low \dots high]$ is less than or equal to each element of $A[q + 1 \dots high]$. The index q is computed as part of this partitioning procedure.

Conquer: The two sub arrays $A[low \dots q]$ and $A[q + 1 \dots high]$ are sorted by recursive calls to Quick sort.

Algorithm

The recursive algorithm consists of four steps:
1) If there are one or no elements in the array to be sorted, return.
2) Pick an element in the array to serve as "*pivot*" point. (Usually the left-most element in the array is used.)
3) Split the array into two parts - one with elements larger than the pivot and the other with elements smaller than the pivot.
4) Recursively repeat the algorithm for both halves of the original array.

```
Quicksort( int A[], int low, int high ) {
        int pivot;
        /* Termination condition! */
        if( high > low ) {
                pivot = Partition( A, low, high );
                Quicksort( A, low, pivot-1 );
                Quicksort( A, pivot+1, high );
        }
}
int Partition( int A, int low, int high ) {
        int left, right, pivot_item = A[low];
        left = low;
        right = high;
        while ( left < right ) {
                /* Move left while item < pivot */
                while( A[left] <= pivot_item )
                        left++;
                /* Move right while item > pivot */
                while( A[right] > pivot_item )
                        right--;
                if( left < right )
                        swap(A,left,right);
        }
        /* right is final position for the pivot */
        A[low] = A[right];
        A[right] = pivot_item;
        return right;
}
```

Analysis

Let us assume that T(n) be the complexity of Quick sort and also assume that all elements are distinct. Recurrence for $T(n)$ depends on two subproblem sizes which depend on partition element. If pivot is i^{th} smallest element then exactly $(i - 1)$ items will be in left part and $(n - i)$ in right part. Let us call it as i −split. Since each element has equal probability of selecting it as pivot the probability of selecting i^{th} element is $\frac{1}{n}$.

Best Case: Each partition splits array in halves and gives

$$T(n) = 2T(\tfrac{n}{2}) + \Theta(n) = \Theta(nlogn), \text{ [using } Divide \text{ and } Conquer \text{ master theorem]}$$

Worst Case: Each partition gives unbalanced splits and we get

$$T(n) = T(n - 1) + \Theta(n) = \Theta(n^2) [using \ Subtraction \ and \ Conquer \ master \ theorem$$

The worst-case occurs when the list is already sorted and last element chosen as pivot.

Average Case: In the average case of Quick sort, we do not know where the split happens. For this reason, we take all possible values of split locations, add all their complexities and divide with n to get the average case complexity.

$$T(n) = \sum_{i=1}^{n} \frac{1}{n}(runtime \ with \ i - split) + n + 1$$

$$= \frac{1}{n}\sum_{i=1}^{N}(T(i-1) + T(n-i)) + n + 1$$

//since we are dealing with best case we can assume $T(n-i)$ and $T(i-1)$ are equal

$$= \frac{2}{n}\sum_{i=1}^{n} T(i-1) + n + 1$$

$$= \frac{2}{n}\sum_{i=0}^{n-1} T(i) + n + 1$$

Multiply both sides by n.

$$nT(n) = 2\sum_{i=0}^{n-1} T(i) + n^2 + n$$

Same formula for $n - 1$.

$$(n-1)T(n-1) = 2\sum_{i=0}^{n-2} T(i) + (n-1)^2 + (n-1)$$

Subtract the $n - 1$ formula from n.

$$nT(n) - (n-1)T(n-1) = 2\sum_{i=0}^{n-1} T(i) + n^2 + n - (2\sum_{i=0}^{n-2} T(i) + (n-1)^2 + (n-1))$$

$$nT(n) - (n-1)T(n-1) = 2T(n-1) + 2n$$

$$nT(n) = (n+1)T(n-1) + 2n$$

Divide with $n(n+1)$.

$$\frac{T(n)}{n+1} = \frac{T(n-1)}{n} + \frac{2}{n+1}$$

$$= \frac{T(n-2)}{n-1} + \frac{2}{n} + \frac{2}{n+1}$$

.
.
.

$$= O(1) + 2\sum_{i=3}^{n} \frac{1}{i}$$

$$= O(1) + O(2logn)$$

$$\frac{T(n)}{n+1} = O(logn)$$

$$T(n) = O((n+1)\,logn) = O(nlogn)$$

Time Complexity, $T(n) = O(nlogn)$.

Performance

Worst case Complexity: $O(n^2)$
Best case Complexity: O(*nlogn*)
Average case Complexity: O(*nlogn*)
Worst case space Complexity: O(1)

Randomized Quick sort

In average-case behavior of Quicksort, we assumed that all permutations of the input numbers are equally likely. However, we cannot always expect it to hold. We can add randomization to an algorithm in order to reduce the probability of getting worst case in Quick sort.

There are two ways of adding randomization in Quick sort: either by randomly placing the input data in the array or by randomly choosing an element in the input data for pivot. The second choice is easier to analyze and implement. The change will only be done at the Partition algorithm.

In normal Quicksort, *pivot* element was always the leftmost element in the list to be sorted. Instead of always using $A[low]$ as *pivot*, we will use a randomly chosen element from the subarray $A[low..high]$ in the randomized version of Quicksort. It is done by exchanging element $A[low]$ with an element chosen at random from $A[low..high]$. This ensures that the *pivot* element is equally likely to be any of the $high - low + 1$ elements in the subarray. Since the pivot element is randomly chosen, we can expect the split of the input array to be reasonably well balanced on average. This can help in preventing the worst-case behavior of quick sort which occurs in unbalanced partitioning.

Even though, randomized version improves the worst case complexity, its worst case complexity is still $O(n^2)$. One way to improve *Randomized − QuickSort* is to choose the pivot for partitioning more carefully than by picking a random element from the array. One common approach is to choose the pivot as the median of a set of 3 elements randomly selected from the array.

10.12 Tree Sort

Tree sort uses a binary search tree. It involves scanning each element of the input and placing it into its proper position in a binary search tree. This has two phases:

- First phase is creating a binary search tree using the given array elements.
- Second phase is traversing the given binary search tree in inorder, thus resulting in a sorted array.

Performance

The average number of comparisons for this method is O($nlogn$). But in worst case, number of comparisons is reduced by O(n^2), a case which arises when the sort tree is skew tree.

10.13 Comparison of Sorting Algorithms

Name	Average Case	Worst Case	Auxiliary Memory	Is Stable?	Other Notes
Bubble	O(n^2)	O(n^2)	1	yes	Small code
Selection	O(n^2)	O(n^2)	1	no	Stability depends on the implementation.
Insertion	O(n^2)	O(n^2)	1	yes	Average case is also O($n + d$), where d is the number of inversions
Shell	-	O($nlog^2 n$)	1	no	
Merge	O($nlogn$)	O($nlogn$)	depends	yes	
Heap	O($nlogn$)	$\underline{O(nlogn)}$	1	no	
Quick Sort	O($nlogn$)	O(n^2)	O($logn$)	depends	Can be implemented as a stable sort depending on how the pivot is handled.
Tree sort	O($nlogn$)	O(n^2)	O(n)	depends	Can be implemented as a stable sort.

Note: n denotes the number of elements in the input.

10.14 Linear Sorting Algorithms

In earlier sections, we have seen many examples on comparison-based sorting algorithms. Among them, the best comparison-based sorting can has the complexity O($nlogn$). In this section, we will discuss other types of algorithms: Linear Sorting Algorithms. To improve the time complexity of sorting these algorithms, make some assumptions about the input. Few examples of Linear Sorting Algorithms are:

- Counting Sort
- Bucket Sort
- Radix Sort

10.15 Counting Sort

Counting sort is not a comparison sort algorithm and gives O(n) complexity for sorting. To achieve O(n) complexity, Counting sort assumes that each of the elements is an integer in the range 1 to K, for some integer K. When $K = $ O(n), the Counting-sort runs in O(n) time. The basic idea of Counting sort is to determine, for each input element X, the number of elements less than X. This information can be used to place directly into its correct position. For example, if 10 elements are less than X, then X belongs to position 11 in output.

In the code below, $A[0..n-1]$ is the input array with length n. In counting sort we need two more arrays: let us assume array $B[0..n-1]$ contains the sorted output and the array $C[0..K-1]$ provides temporary storage.

```
void CountingSort (int A[], int n, int B[], int K) {
    int C[K], i, j;
    //Complexity: O(K)
    for (i =0 ; i<K; i++)
        C[i] = 0;
    //Complexity: O(n)
    for (j =0 ; j<n; j++)
        C[A[j]] = C[A[j]] + 1;
    //C[i] now contains the number of elements equal to i
```

```
        //Complexity: O(K)
        for (i =1 ; i<K; i++)
            C[i] = C[i] + C[i-1];
         // C[i] now contains the number of elements ≤ i
        //Complexity: O(n)
        for (j = n-1; j>=0; j--) {
            B[C[A[j]]] = A[j];
            C[A[j]] = C[A[j]] - 1;
        }
}
```

Total Complexity: $O(K) + O(n) + O(K) + O(n) = O(n)$ if $K = O(n)$. Space Complexity: $O(n)$ if $K = O(n)$.

Note: Counting works well if $K = O(n)$. Otherwise, the complexity will be more.

10.16 Bucket sort [or Bin Sort]

Like *Counting* sort, *Bucket* sort also imposes restrictions on the input to improve the performance. In other words, Bucket sort works well if the input is drawn from fixed set. *Bucket* sort is the generalization of *Counting* Sort. For example, suppose that all the input elements from {0, 1, . . . , $K - 1$}, i.e., the set of integers in the interval [0, $K - 1$]. That means, K is the number of distant elements in the input. *Bucket* sort uses K counters. The ith counter keeps track of the number of occurrences of the ith element. Bucket sort with two buckets is effectively a version of Quick sort with two buckets.

```
#define BUCKETS 10
void BucketSort(int A[], int array_size) {
    int i, j, k;
    int buckets[BUCKETS];
    for(j =0; j < BUCKETS; j++)
            buckets[j] = 0;
    for(i =0; i < array_size; i++)
            ++ buckets[A[i]];
    for(i =0, j=0; j < BUCKETS; j++)
            for(k = buckets[j];k > 0; --k)
                    A[i++] = j;
}
```

Time Complexity: $O(n)$. Space Complexity: $O(n)$.

10.17 Radix sort

Similar to *Counting* sort and *Bucket* sort, this sorting algorithm also assumes some kind of information about the input elements. Suppose that the input values to be sorted are from base d. That means all numbers are d-digit numbers.

In radix sort, first sort the elements based on last digit [least significant digit]. These results were again sorted by second digit [next to least significant digits]. Continue this process for all digits until we reach most significant digits. Use some stable sort to sort them by last digit. Then stable sort them by the second least significant digit, then by the third, etc. If we use counting sort as the stable sort, the total time is $O(nd) \approx O(n)$.

Algorithm:
1) Take the least significant digit of each element.
2) Sort the list of elements based on that digit, but keep the order of elements with the same digit (this is the definition of a stable sort).
3) Repeat the sort with each more significant digit.

The speed of Radix sort depends on the inner basic operations. If the operations are not efficient enough, Radix sort can be slower than other algorithms such as Quick sort and Merge sort. These operations include the insert and delete functions of the sub-lists and the process of isolating the digit we want. If the numbers were not of equal length then a test is needed to check for additional digits that need sorting. This can be one of the slowest parts of Radix sort and also one of the hardest to make efficient.

Since Radix sort depends on the digits or letters, it is less flexible than other sorts. For every different type of data, Radix sort needs to be rewritten and if the sorting order changes, the sort needs to be rewritten again. In short, Radix sort takes more time to write, and it is very difficult to write a general purpose Radix sort that can handle all kinds of data.

For many programs that need a fast sort, Radix sort is a good choice. Still, there are faster sorts, which is one reason why Radix sort is not used as much as some other sorts.

Time Complexity: $O(nd) \approx O(n)$, if d is small.

10.18 Topological Sort

Refer *Graph Algorithms* Chapter.

10.19 External Sorting

External sorting is a generic term for a class of sorting algorithms that can handle massive amounts of data. These External sorting algorithms are useful when the files are too big and cannot fit into main memory.

Like internal sorting algorithms, there are number for algorithms for external sorting also. One such algorithm is External Mergesort. In practice these external sorting algorithms are being supplemented by internal sorts.

Simple External Mergesort

A number of records from each tape would be read into main memory and sorted using an internal sort and then output to the tape. For the sake of clarity, let us assume that 900 megabytes of data needs to be sorted using only 100 megabytes of RAM.

1) Read 100MB of the data into main memory and sort by some conventional method (let us say Quick sort).

2) Write the sorted data to disk.

3) Repeat steps 1 and 2 until all of the data is sorted in chunks of 100MB. Now we need to merge them into one single sorted output file.

4) Read the first 10MB of each sorted chunk (call them input buffers) in main memory (90MB total) and allocate the remaining 10MB for output buffer.

5) Perform a 9-way Mergesort and store the result in the output buffer. If the output buffer is full, write it to the final sorted file. If any of the 9 input buffers gets empty, fill it with the next 10MB of its associated 100MB sorted chunk or otherwise mark it as exhausted if there is no more data in the sorted chunk and do not use it for merging.

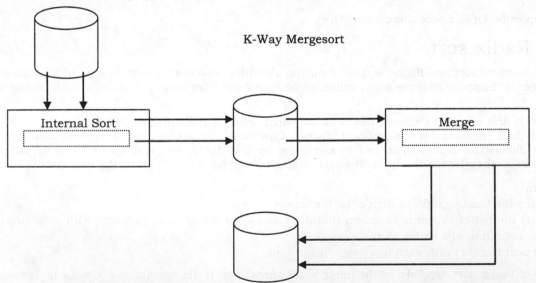

K-Way Mergesort

The above algorithm can be generalized by assuming that the amount of data to be sorted exceeds the available memory by a factor of K. Then, K chunks of data need to be sorted and a K-way merge has to be completed.

If X is the amount of main memory available, there will be K input buffers and 1 output buffer of size $X/(K+1)$ each. Depending on various factors (how fast is the hard drive?) better performance can be achieved if the output buffer is made larger (for example, twice as large as one input buffer).

Complexity of the 2-way External Merge sort: In each pass we read + write each page in file. Let us assume that there are n pages in file. That means we need $\lceil logn \rceil + 1$ number of passes. The total cost is $2n(\lceil logn \rceil + 1)$.

10.20 Problems on Sorting

Problem-1   Given an array $A[0 \dots n-1]$ of n numbers containing repetition of some number. Give an algorithm for checking whether there are repeated elements or not. Assume that we are not allowed to use additional space (i.e., we can use a few temporary variables, O(1) storage).

Solution: Since we are not allowed to use any extra space, one simple way is to scan the elements one by one and for each element check whether that elements appears in the remaining elements. If we find a match we return true.

```java
int CheckDuplicatesInArray(in A[], int n) {
        for (int i  =  0; i < n; i++)
                for (int j   = i + 1; j < n; j++)
                        if(A[i]==A[j])
                                reutrn true;
        return false;
}
```

Each iteration of the inner, *j*-indexed loop uses O(1) space, and for a fixed value of *i*, the *j* loop executes $n - i$ times. The outer loop executes $n - 1$ times, so the entire function uses time proportional to

$$\sum_{i=1}^{n-1} n - i = n(n-1) - \sum_{i=1}^{n-1} i = n(n-1) - \frac{n(n-1)}{2} = \frac{n(n-1)}{2} = O(n^2)$$

Time Complexity: $O(n^2)$. Space Complexity: O(1).

Problem-2   Can we improve the time complexity of Problem-1?

Solution: **Yes**, using sorting technique.
```java
int CheckDuplicatesInArray(in A[], int n) {
        //for heap sort algorithm refer Priority Queues chapter
        Heapsort( A, n );
        for (int i  =  0; i < n-1; i++)
                if(A[i]==A[i+1])
                        reutrn true;
        return false;
}
```

Heapsort function takes $O(n \, logn)$ time, and requires O(1) space. The scan clearly takes for $n - 1$ iterations, each iteration using O(1) time. The overall time is $O(n \, logn + n) = O(n \, logn)$.

Time Complexity: $O(n \, logn)$. Space Complexity: O(1).

Note: For variations of this problem, refer *Searching* chapter.

Problem-3   Given an array $A[0 \dots n-1]$, where each element of the array represents a vote in the election. Assume that each vote is given as an integer representing the ID of the chosen candidate. Give an algorithm for determining who wins the election.

Solution: This problem is nothing but finding the element which repeated maximum number of times. Solution is similar to Problem-1 solution: keep track of counter.

```java
int CheckWhoWinsTheElection(in A[], int n) {
        int i, j, counter = A[0], maxCounter = 0, candidate;
        for (i  =  0; i < n; i++) {
                candidate = A[i];
                counter = 0;
                for (j   = i + 1; j < n; j++) {
                        if(A[i]==A[j])
                                counter++;
                }
                if(counter > maxCounter) {
                        maxCounter = counter;
                        candidate = A[i];

                }
        }
        return candidate;
}
```
Time Complexity: $O(n^2)$. Space Complexity: O(1).

Note: For variations of this problem, refer *Searching* chapter.

Problem-4   Can we improve the time complexity of Problem-3? Assume we don't have any extra space.

Solution: Yes. The approach is to sort the votes based on candidate ID, then scan the sorted array and count up which candidate so far has the most votes. We only have to remember the winner, so we don't need a clever data structure. We can use heapsort as it is an in-place sorting algorithm.

```java
int CheckWhoWinsTheElection(in A[], int n) {
        int i, j, currentCounter = 1, maxCounter = 1;
        int currentCandidate, maxCandidate;
        currentCandidate = maxCandidate= A[0];
        //for heap sort algorithm refer Priority Queues Chapter
        Heapsort( A, n );
        for (int i  =  0; i < n; i++) {
                if( A[i] == currentCandidate)
                        currentCounter ++;
                else {   currentCandidate = A[i];
                        currentCounter = 1;
                }
                if(currentCounter > maxCounter)
                        maxCounter = currentCounter;
                else {   maxCandidate = currentCandidate;
                        maxCounter = currentCounter;
                }
        }
        return candidate;
}
```

Since Heapsort time complexity is $O(n\,logn)$ and in-place, so it only uses an additional $O(1)$ of storage in addition to the input array. The scan of the sorted array does a constant-time conditional $n - 1$ times, thus using $O(n)$ time. The overall time bound is $O(n\,logn)$.

Problem-5   Can we further improve the time complexity of Problem-3?

Solution: In the given problem, number of candidates is less but the number of votes is significantly large. For this problem we can use counting sort.

Time Complexity: $O(n)$, n is the number of votes (elements) in array. Space Complexity: $O(k)$, k is the number of candidates participated in election.

Problem-6   Given an array A of n elements, each of which is an integer in the range $[1, n^2]$. How do we sort the array in $O(n)$ time?

Solution: If we subtract each number by 1 then we get the range $[0, n^2 - 1]$. If we consider all number as 2 −digit base n. Each digit ranges from 0 to n^2 - 1. Sort this using radix sort. This uses only two calls to counting sort. Finally, add 1 to all the numbers. Since there are 2 calls, the complexity is $O(2n) \approx O(n)$.

Problem-7   For the Problem-6, what if the range is $[1...n^3]$?

Solution: If we subtract each number by 1 then we get the range $[0, n^3 - 1]$. Considering all number as 3-digit base n: each digit ranges from 0 to n^3 - 1. Sort this using radix sort. This uses only three calls to counting sort. Finally, add 1 to all the numbers. Since there are 3 calls, the complexity is $O(3n) \approx O(n)$.

Problem-8   Given an array with n integers each of value less than n^{100}, can it be sorted in linear time?

Solution: Yes. Reasoning is same as in of Problem-6 and Problem-7.

Problem-9   Let A and B be two arrays of n elements, each. Given a number K, give an $O(nlogn)$ time algorithm for determining whether there exists a $\in A$ and b $\in B$ such that $a + b = K$.

Solution: Since we need $O(n\,logn)$, it gives us a pointer that we need sorting. So, we will do that.

```java
int Find( int A[], int B[], int n, K ) {
        int i, c;
        Heapsort( A, n );                              //O(nlogn)
        for (i =0; i < n; i++) {                       //O(n)
                c = k-B[i];                            //O(1)
                if(BinarySearch(A, c))                 //O(logn)
                        return 1;
        }
}
```

```
    return 0;
}
```

Note: For variations of this problem, refer *Searching* chapter.

Problem-10   Let A, B and C are three arrays of n elements, each. Given a number K, give an O($n \log n$) time algorithm for determining whether there exists $a \in A$, $b \in B$ and $c \in C$ such that $a + b + c = K$.

Solution: Refer *Searching* chapter.

Problem-11   Given an array of n elements, can we output in sorted order the K elements following the median in sorted order in time O($n + K \log K$).

Solution: Yes. Find the median and partition about the median. With this we can find all the elements greater than it. Now find the Kth largest element in this set and partition about it; and get all the elements less than it. Output the sorted list of final set of elements. Clearly, this operation takes O($n + K \log K$) time.

Problem-12   Consider the sorting algorithms: Bubble Sort, Insertion Sort, Selection Sort, Merge Sort, Heap Sort, and Quick Sort. Which of these are stable?

Solution: Let us assume that A is the array to be sorted. Also, let us say R and S have the same key and R appears earlier in the array than S. That means, R is at $A[i]$ and S is at $A[j]$, with $i < j$. To show any stable algorithm, in the sorted output R must precede S.

Bubble sort: Yes. Elements change order only when a smaller record follows a larger. Since S is not smaller than R it cannot precede it.

Selection sort: No. It divides the array into sorted and unsorted portions and iteratively finds the minimum values in the unsorted portion. After finding a minimum x, if the algorithm moves x into the sorted portion of the array by means of a swap then the element swapped could be R which then could be moved behind S. This would invert the positions of R and S, so in general it is not stable. If swapping is avoided, it could be made stable but the cost in time would probably be very significant.

Insertion sort: Yes. As presented, when S is to be inserted into sorted subarray $A[1..j - 1]$, only records larger than S are shifted. Thus R would not be shifted during $S's$ insertion and hence would always precede it.

Merge sort: Yes, In the case of records with equal keys, the record in the left subarray gets preference. Those are the records that came first in the unsorted array. As a result, they will precede later records with the same key.

Heap sort: No. Suppose $i = 1$ and R and S happen to be the two records with the largest keys in the input. Then R will remain in location 1 after the array is heapified, and will be placed in location n in the first iteration of Heapsort. Thus S will precede R in the output.

Quick sort: No. The partitioning step can swap the location of records many times, and thus two records with equal keys could swap position in the final output.

Problem-13   Consider the same sorting algorithms as that of Problem-12. Which of them are in-place?

Solution:

Bubble sort: Yes, because only two integers are required.

Insertion sort: Yes, since we need to store two integers and a record.

Selection sort: Yes. This algorithm would likely need space for two integers and one record.

Merge sort: No. Arrays need to perform the merge. (If the data is in the form of a linked list, the sorting can be done in-place, but this is a nontrivial modification.)

Heap sort: Yes, since the heap and partially-sorted array occupy opposite ends of the input array.

Quicksort: No, since it is recursive and stores O(*$\log n$*) activation records on the stack. Modifying it to be non-recursive is feasible but nontrivial.

Problem-14   Among, Quick sort, Insertion sort, Selection sort, Heap sort algorithms, which one needs the minimum number of swaps?

Solution: Selected sort, it needs n swaps only (refer theory section).

Problem-15   What is the minimum number of comparisons required to determine if an integer appears more than $n/2$ times in a sorted array of n integers?

Solution: Refer *Searching* chapter.

Problem-16   **Sort an array of 0's, 1's and 2's:** Given an array A[] consisting 0's, 1's and 2's, give an algorithm for sorting A[]. The algorithm should put all 0's first, then all 1's and all 2's in last.
  Example: Input = {0,1,1,0,1,2,1,2,0,0,0,1}, Output = {0, 0, 0, 0, 0, 1, 1, 1, 1, 1, 2, 2}

Solution: Use Counting Sort. Since there are only three elements and the maximum value is 2, we need a temporary array with 3 elements.

Time Complexity: O(n). Space Complexity: O(1).

Note: For variations of this problem, refer *Searching* chapter.

Problem-17   Is there any other way of solving Problem-16?

Solution: Using Quick Sort. Since we know that there are only 3 elements 0, 1 and 2 in the array, we can select 1 as a pivot element for Quick Sort. Quick Sort finds the correct place for 1 by moving all 0's to the left of 1 and all 2's to the right of 1. For doing this it uses only one scan.

Time Complexity: O(n). Space Complexity: O(1).
Note: For efficient algorithm, refer *Searching* chapter.

Problem-18   How do we find the number which appeared the maximum number of times in an array?

Solution: One simple approach is to sort the given array and scan the sorted array. While scanning, keep track of the elements that occur the maximum number of times.

Algorithm:
```
        QuickSort(A, n);
        int i, j, count=1, Number=A[0], j=1;
        for(i=1;i < n;i++) {
                if(arr[j]==A) {
                        count++;
                        Number=A[j];
                }
                j=i;
        }
        System.out.println("Number:" + Number + " , count: " + count);
```

Time Complexity = Time for Sorting + Time for Scan = O($n log n$) +O(n) = O($n log n$). Space Complexity: O(1).

Note: For variations of this problem, refer *Searching* chapter.

Problem-19   Is there any other way of solving Problem-18?

Solution: Using Binary Tree. Create a binary tree with an extra field *count* which indicates the number of times an element appeared in the input. Let us say we have created a Binary Search Tree [BST]. Now, do the In-Order of the tree. In-Order traversal of BST produces sorted list. While doing In-Order traversal keep track of maximum element.

Time Complexity: O(n) +O(n) ≈O(n). First parameter is for constructing the BST and the second parameter is for Inorder Traversal. Space Complexity: O($2n$) ≈O(n), since every node in BST needs two extra pointers.

Problem-20   Is there yet other way of solving the Problem-18?

Solution: Using Hash Table: For each element of the given array we use a counter and for each occurrence of the element we increment the corresponding counter. At the end we can just return the element which has the the maximum counter.

Time Complexity: O(n). Space Complexity: O(n). For constructing hash table we need O(n).

Note: For efficient algorithm, refer *Searching* chapter.

Problem-21   Given a 2 GB file with one string per line, which sorting algorithm would we use to sort the file and why?

Solution: When we have a size limit of 2GB, it means that we cannot bring all the data into main memory.

Algorithm:
How much memory do we have available? Let's assume we have X MB of memory available. Divide the file into K chunks, where $X * K$ 2 GB.
  • Bring each chunk into memory and sort the lines as usual (any O($n log n$) algorithm).
  • Save the lines back to the file.
  • Now bring next chunk into memory and sort.
  • Once we're done, merge them one by one; in case of one set finish bring more data from concerned chunk.

The above algorithm is also known as external sort. Step $3 - 4$ is known as K-way merge. The idea behind going for external sort is the size of data. Since data is huge and we can't bring it to the memory, we need e to go for a disk based sorting algorithm.

Problem-22   Nearly sorted: Given an array of n elements, each which is at most K positions from its target position, devise an algorithm that sorts in O($n\ logK$) time.

Solution: Divide the elements into n/K groups of size K, and sort each piece in O($KlogK$) time, say using Mergesort. This preserves the property that no element is more than K elements out of position. Now, merge each block of K elements with the block to its left.

**Problem-23   **Is there any other way of solving Problem-22?

Solution: Insert the first K elements into a binary heap. Insert the next element from the array into the heap, and delete the minimum element from the heap. Repeat.

Problem-24   Merging K sorted lists: Given K sorted lists with a total of n elements, give an O($nlogK$) algorithm to produce a sorted list of all n elements.

Solution: Simple Algorithm for merging K sorted lists: Consider groups each having $\frac{n}{K}$ elements. Take the first list and merge it with the second list using a linear-time algorithm for merging two sorted lists, such as the merging algorithm used in merge sort. Then, merge the resulting list of $\frac{2n}{K}$ elements with the third list, merge the list of $\frac{3n}{K}$ elements that results with the fourth list. Repeat this until we end up with a single sorted list of all n elements.

Time Complexity: In each iteration we are merging K elements.

$$T(n) = \frac{2n}{K} + \frac{3n}{K} + \frac{4n}{K} + \cdots \frac{Kn}{K}(n) = \frac{n}{K}\sum_{i=2}^{K} i$$

$$T(n) = \frac{n}{K}\left[\frac{K(K+1)}{2}\right] \approx O(nK)$$

**Problem-25   **Can we improve the time complexity of Problem-24?

Solution: One method is to repeatedly pair up the lists, and merge each pair. This method can also be seen as a tail component of the execution merge sort, where the analysis is clear. This is called Tournament Method. Maximum depth of Tournament Method is logK and in each iteration we are scanning all the n elements.

Time Complexity: O($nlogK$).

**Problem-26   **Is there any other way of solving Problem-24?

Solution: Other method is to use a *min* priority queue for the minimum elements of each of the K lists. At each step, we output the extracted minimum of the priority queue, and determine from which of the K lists it came, and insert the next element from that list into the priority queue. Since we are using priority queue, that maximum depth of priority queue is *logK*.

Time Complexity: O($nlogK$).

**Problem-27   **Which sorting method is better for Linked Lists?

Solution: Merge Sort is a better choice. At a first appearance, merge sort may not be a good selection since the middle node is required to subdivide the given list into two sub-lists of equal length. We can easily solve this problem by moving the nodes alternatively to two lists would also solve this problem (refer *Linked Lists* chapter). Then, sorting these two lists recursively and merging the results into a single list will sort the given one [27].

```
ListNode LinkedListMergeSort(ListNode first) {
        ListNode list1HEAD = null;
        ListNode list1TAIL = null;
        ListNode list2HEAD = null;
        ListNode list2TAIL = null;
        if(first==null || first.next==null)
                return first;
        while (first != null) {
                Append(first, list1HEAD, list1TAIL);
                if(first != null)
                        Append(first, list2HEAD, list2TAIL);
        }
        list1HEAD = LinkedListMergeSort(list1HEAD);
```

```
        list2HEAD = LinkedListMergeSort(list2HEAD);
        return Merge(list1HEAD, list2HEAD);
}
```

Note: Append() appends the first argument to the tail of a singly linked list whose head and tail are defined by the second and third arguments.

All external sorting algorithms can be used for sorting linked lists since each involved file can be considered as a linked list that can only be accessed sequentially. We can sort a doubly linked list using its next fields as if it is a singly linked one and reconstruct the prev fields after sorting with an additional scan.

Problem-28   Can we implement Linked Lists Sorting with Quick Sort?

Solution: Original Quick Sort cannot be used for sorting the Singly Linked Lists. This is because we cannot move backward in Singly Linked Lists. We can modify the original Quick Sort and make it work for Singly Linked Lists.

Let us consider the following modified Quick Sort implementation. The first node of the input list is considered as a *pivot* and is moved to *equal*. The value of each node is compared with the *pivot* and moved *to less* (*respectively, equal or larger*) if the nodes value is smaller than (respectively, *equal* to or *larger* than) the *pivot*. Then, *less* and *larger* are sorted recursively. Finally, joining *less*, *equal* and *larger* into a single list yields a sorted one.

Append() appends the first argument to the tail of a singly linked list whose head and tail are defined by the second and third arguments. On return, the first argument will be modified so that it *equal* points to the next node of the list. *Join*() appends the list whose head and tail are defined by the third and fourth arguments to the list whose head and tail are defined by the first and second arguments. For simplicity, the first and fourth arguments become the head and tail of the resulting list [27].

```
void Qsort(ListNode first, ListNode last){
        ListNode lesHEAD=null, lesTAIL=null;
        ListNode equHEAD=null, equTAIL=null;
        ListNode larHEAD=null, larTAIL=null;
        ListNode current = first;
        int pivot, info;
        if(current == null)
                return;
        pivot = current.getData();
        Append(current, equHEAD, equTAIL);
        while (current != null) {
                info = current.getData();
                if(info < pivot)
                        Append(current, lesHEAD, lesTAIL)
                else if(info > pivot)
                        Append(current, larHEAD, larTAIL)
                else    Append(current, equHEAD, equTAIL);
        }
        Quicksort(lesHEAD, lesTAIL);
        Quicksort(larHEAD, larTAIL);
        Join(lesHEAD, lesTAIL,equHEAD, equTAIL);
        Join(lesHEAD, equTAIL,larHEAD, larTAIL);
        first = lesHEAD;
        last = larTAIL;
}
```

Problem-29   Given an array of $1,00,000$ pixel color values, each of which is an integer in the range $[0,255]$. Which sorting algorithm is preferable for sorting them?

Solution: Counting Sort. There are only 256 key values, so the auxiliary array would only be of size 256, and there would be only two passes through the data which would be very efficient in both time and space.

Problem-30   Similar to Problem-29, if we have a telephone directory with $1,00,000$ entries, which sorting algorithm is best?

Solution: Bucket sort. In Bucket sort the buckets are defined by the last 7 digits. This requires an auxiliary array of size 10 million, and has the advantage of requiring only one pass through the data on disk. Each bucket contains all telephone numbers with the same last 7 digits but different area codes. The buckets can then be sorted on area code by selection or insertion sort; there are only a handful of area codes.

Problem-31   Give an algorithm for merging K-sorted lists.

Solution: Refer *Priority Queues* chapter.

Problem-32   Given a big file containing billions of numbers. Find maximum 10 numbers from those file.

Solution: Refer *Priority Queues* chapter.

Problem-33   There are two sorted arrays A and B. First one is of size $m + n$ containing only m elements. Another one is of size n and contains n elements. Merge these two arrays into the first array of size $m + n$ such that the output is sorted.

Solution: The trick for this problem is to start filling the destination array from the back with the largest elements. We will end up with a merged and sorted destination array.

```
void Merge(int[] A[], int m, int B[], int n) {
        int count = m;
        int i = n – 1, j = count – 1, k = m - 1;
        for(;k>=0;k--) {
                if(B[i] > A[j] || j < 0) {
                        A[k] =B[i];
                        i--;
                        if(i<0)
                                break;
                }
                else {    A[k] = A[j];
                        j--;
                }
        }
}
```

Time Complexity: O($m + n$). Space Complexity: O(1).

Problem-34   **Nuts and Bolts Problem:** Given a set of n nuts of different sizes and n bolts such that there is a one-to-one correspondence between the nuts and the bolts, find for each nut its corresponding bolt. Assume that we can only compare nuts to bolts: we cannot compare nuts to nuts and bolts to bolts.
Otherway of asking: We are given a box which contains bolts and nuts. Assume there are n nuts and n bolts and that each nut matches exactly one bolt (and vice versa). By trying to match a bolt and a nut we can see which one is bigger, but we cannot compare two bolts or two nuts directly. Design an efficient algorithm for matching the nuts and bolts.

Solution: Brute Force Approach: Start with the first bolt and compare it with each nut until we find a match. In the worst case, we require n comparisons. Repeat this for successive bolts on all remaining gives O(n^2) complexity.

Problem-35   For Problem-34, can we improve the complexity?

Solution: In Problem-34, we got O(n^2) complexity in the worst case (if bolts are in ascending order and nuts are in descending order). Its analysis is same as that of quick sort. The improvement is also on same line.

To reduce the worst case complexity, instead of selecting the first bolt every time, we can select a random bolt and match it with nuts. This randomized selection reduces the probability of getting the worst case but still the worst case is O(n^2) only.

Problem-36   For Problem-34, can we further improve the complexity?

Solution: We can use a divide-and-conquer technique for solving this problem and the solution is very similar to randomized Quicksort. For simplicity let us assume that bolts and nuts are represented in two arrays B and N.

The algorithm first performs a partition operation as follows: pick a random bolt $B[i]$. Using this bolt, rearrange the array of nuts into three groups of elements:
- First the nuts smaller than $B[i]$
- Nut that matches $B[i]$, and
- Finally, the nuts larger than $B[i]$.

Next, using the nut that matches $B[i]$ perform a similar partition of the array of bolts. This pair of partitioning operations can easily implemented in O(n) time, and it leaves the bolts and nuts nicely partitioned so that the "*pivot*" bolt and nut are aligned with each-other and all other bolts and nuts are on the correct side of these pivots -- smaller nuts and bolts precede the pivots, and larger nuts and bolts follow the pivots. Our algorithm then completes by recursively applying itself to the subarray to the left and right of the pivot position to match these remaining bolts and nuts. We can assume by induction on n that these recursive calls will properly match the remaining bolts.

To analyze the running time of our algorithm, we can use the same analysis as that of randomized Quicksort. Therefore, applying the analysis from Quicksort, the time complexity of our algorithm is O(*nlogn*).

Another way of Analysis: We can solve this problem by making little change to quick sort. Let us assume that we pick the last element as pivot, say it is a nut. Compare the nut with only bolts as we walk down the array. This will partition the array for the bolts. Every bolt less than the partition nut will be on the left. And every bolt greater than the partition nut will be on the right.

While traversing down the list, the matching bolt for the partition nut will have been found. Now we do the partition again using the matching bolt. As a result, all the nuts less than the matching bolt will be on the left side and all the nuts greater than the matching bolt will be on the right side. Recursively call on the left and right arrays.

The time complexity is O(2*nlogn*) ≈O(*nlogn*).

Problem-37   Given a binary tree, can we print its elements in sorted order in O(*n*) time by performing an In-order tree traversal?

Solution: Yes, if the tree is a Binary Search Tree [BST]. For more details refer *Trees* chapter.

Chapter-11

SEARCHING

11.1 What is Searching?

In computer science, *searching* is the process of finding an item with specified properties from a collection of items. The items may be stored as records in a database, simple data elements in arrays, text in files, nodes in trees, vertices and edges in graphs, or may be elements of other search space.

11.2 Why do we need Searching?

Searching is one of core computer science algorithms. We know that today's computers store a lot of information. To retrieve this information proficiently we need very efficient searching algorithms.

There are certain ways of organizing the data which improves the searching process. That means, if we keep the data in a proper order, it is easy to search the required element. Sorting is one of the techniques for making the elements ordered. In this chapter we will see different searching algorithms.

11.3 Types of Searching

Following are the types of searches which we will be discussing in this book.

- Unordered Linear Search
- Sorted/Ordered Linear Search
- Binary Search
- Symbol Tables and Hashing
- String Searching Algorithms: Tries, Ternary Search and Suffix Trees

Unordered Linear Search

Let us assume that given an array whose elements order is not known. That means the elements of the array are not sorted. In this case if we want to search for an element then we have to scan the complete array and see if the element is there in the given list or not.

```java
int UnsorteddLinearSearch (int A[], int n, int data) {
    for (int i  = 0; i < n; i++) {
        if(A[i] == data)
            return i;
    }
    return -1;
}
```

Time complexity: O(n), in the worst case we need to scan the complete array. Space complexity: O(1).

Sorted/Ordered Linear Search

If the elements of the array are already sorted then in many cases we don't have to scan the complete array to see if the element is there in the given array or not. In the algorithm below, it can be seen that, at any point if the value at $A[i]$ is greater than *data* to be searched then we just return −1 without searching the remaining array.

```java
int SortedLinearSearch(int A[], int n, int data) {
    for (int i  = 0; i < n; i++) {
        if(A[i] == data)    return i;
        else if(A[i] > data)
            return -1;
    }
    return -1;
}
```

Time complexity of this algorithm is O(*n*). This is because in the worst case we need to scan the complete array. But in the average case it reduces the complexity even though the growth rate is same. Space complexity: O(1).

Note: For the above algorithm we can make further improvement by incrementing the index at faster rate (say, 2). This will reduce the number of comparisons for searching in the sorted list.

Binary Search

Let us consider the problem of searching a word in a dictionary. Typically, we directly go to some approximate page [say, middle page] start searching from that point. If the *name* that we are searching is same then the search is complete. If the page is before the selected pages then apply the same process for the first half otherwise apply the same process to the second half. Binary search also works in the same way. The algorithm applying such a strategy is referred to as *binary search* algorithm.

```
//Iterative Binary Search Algorithm
int BinarySearchIterative[int A[], int n, int data) {
        int low =  0, high = n-1;
        while (low <= high) {
        mid  = low + (high-low)/2; //To avoid overflow
                if(A[mid] == data)
                        return mid;
                else if(A[mid] < data)
                        low =  mid + 1;
                else     high =  mid - 1;
        }
        return -1;
}
//Recursive Binary Search Algorithm
int BinarySearchRecursive[int A[], int low, int high, int data) {
        int mid  = low + (high-low)/2; //To avoid overflow
        if(A[mid] == data)          return mid;
        else if(A[mid] < data)
                return BinarySearchRecursive (A, mid + 1, high, data);
        else     return BinarySearchRecursive (A, low, mid - 1 , data);
        return -1;
}
```

Recurrence for binary search is $T(n) = T(\frac{n}{2}) + \Theta(1)$. This is because we are always considering only half of the input list and throwing out the other half. Using *Divide and Conquer* master theorem, we get, $T(n = O(log n)$.

Time Complexity: O(*log n*). Space Complexity: O(1) [for iterative algorithm].

Comparing Basic Searching Algorithms

Implementation	Search-Worst Case	Search-Avg. Case
Unordered Array	n	$\frac{n}{2}$
Ordered Array (Binary Search)	*log n*	*log n*
Unordered List	n	$\frac{n}{2}$
Ordered List	n	$\frac{n}{2}$
Binary Search Trees (for skew trees)	n	*log n*

Note: For discussion on binary search trees refer *Trees* chapter.

11.4 Symbol Tables and Hashing

Refer *Symbol Tables* and *Hashing* chapters.

11.5 String Searching Algorithms

Refer *String Algorithms* chapter.

11.6 Problems on Searching

Problem-1   Given an array of n numbers, give an algorithm for checking whether there are any duplicate elements in the array or not?

Solution: This is one of the simplest problems. One obvious answer to this is, exhaustively searching for duplicates in the array. That means, for each input element check whether there is any element with same value. This we can solve just by using two simple *for* loops. The code for this solution can be given as:

```java
void CheckDuplicatesBruteForce(int A[], int n) {
    for(int i = 0; i < n; i++) {
        for(int j = i+1; j < n; j++) {
            if(A[i] == A[j])    {
                System.out.println("Duplicates exist:" + A[i]);
                return;
            }
        }
    }
    System.out.println("No duplicates in given array.");
}
```

Time Complexity: $O(n^2)$, for two nested *for* loops.
Space Complexity: $O(1)$.

Problem-2   Can we improve the complexity of Problem-1's solution?

Solution: Yes. Sort the given array. After sorting all the elements with equal values come adjacent. Now, just do another scan on this sorted array and see if there are elements with same value and adjacent.

```java
void CheckDuplicatesSorting(int A[], int n) {
    Sort(A, n);                          //sort the array
    for(int i = 0; i < n-1; i++) {
        if(A[i] == A[i+1]) {
            System.out.println("Duplicates exist: " + A[i]);
            return;
        }
    }
    System.out.println("No duplicates in given array.");
}
```

Time Complexity: $O(nlogn)$, for sorting.
Space Complexity: $O(1)$.

Problem-3   Is there any other way of solving Problem-1?

Solution: Yes, using hash table. Hash tables are a simple and effective method used to implement dictionaries. *Average* time to search for an element is $O(1)$, while worst-case time is $O(n)$. Refer *Hashing* chapter for more details on hashing algorithms. As an example, consider the array, $A = \{3, 2, 1, 2, 2, 3\}$.

Scan the input array and insert the elements into the hash. For each inserted element, keep the *counter* as 1 (assume initially all entires are filled with zeros). This indicates that the corresponding element has occurred already. For the given array, the hash table will look like (after inserting first three elements 3, 2 and 1):

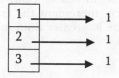

Now if we try inserting 2, since counter value of 2 is already 1, we can say the element has appeared twice.
Time Complexity: $O(n)$. Space Complexity: $O(n)$.

Problem-4   Can we further improve the complexity of Problem-1 solution?

Solution: Let us assume that the array elements are positive numbers and also all the elements are in the range 0 to $n - 1$. For each element $A[i]$, go to the array element whose index is $A[i]$. That means select $A[A[i]]$ and mark - $A[A[i]]$ (negate the value at $A[A[i]]$). Continue this process until we encounter the element whose value is already negated. If one such element exists then we say duplicate elements exist in the given array. As an example, consider the array, $A = \{3, 2, 1, 2, 2, 3\}$.

Initially,

3	2	1	2	2	3
0	1	2	3	4	5

At step-1, negate A[abs(A[0])],

3	2	1	-2	2	3
0	1	2	3	4	5

At step-2, negate A[abs(A[1])],

3	2	-1	-2	2	3
0	1	2	3	4	5

At step-3, negate A[abs(A[2])],

3	-2	- 1	-2	2	3
0	1	2	3	4	5

At step-4, negate A[abs(A[3])],

3	-2	- 1	-2	2	3
0	1	2	3	4	5

At step-4, we can observe that $A[abs(A[3])]$ is already negative. That means we have encountered the same value twice.

```java
void CheckDuplicates(int A[], int n) {
    for(int i = 0; i < n; i++) {
        if(A[Math.abs(A[i])] < 0) {
            System.out.println("Duplicates exist: " + A[i]);
            return;
        }
        else    A[A[i]] = - A[A[i]];
    }
    System.out.println("No duplicates in given array.");
}
```

Time Complexity: O(n). Since, only one scan is required. Space Complexity: O(1).

Notes:
- This solution does not work if the given array is read only.
- This solution will work only if all the array elements are positive.
- If the elements range is not in 0 to $n - 1$ then it may give exceptions.

Problem-5   Given an array of n numbers. Give an algorithm for finding the element which appears maximum number of times in the array?

Brute Force Solution: One simple solution to this is, for each input element check whether there is any element with same value and for each such occurrence, increment the counter. Each time, check the current counter with the max counter and update it if this value is greater than max counter. This we can solve just by using two simple *for* loops.

```java
int CheckDuplicatesBruteForce(int A[], int n) {
    int counter =0, max=0;
    for(int i = 0; i < n; i++) {
        counter=0;
        for(int j = 0; j < n; j++) {
            if(A[i] == A[j])
                counter++;
        }
        if(counter > max) max = counter;
    }
    return max;
}
```

Time Complexity: O(n^2), for two nested *for* loops. Space Complexity: O(1).

Problem-6   Can we improve the complexity of Problem-5 solution?

Solution: Yes. Sort the given array. After sorting all the elements with equal values come adjacent. Now, just do another scan on this sorted array and see which element is appearing maximum number of times.

Time Complexity: O($nlogn$). (for sorting). Space Complexity: O(1).

Problem-7   Is there any other way of solving Problem-5?

Solution: Yes, using hash table. For each element of the input keep track of how many times that element appeared in the input. That means the counter value represents the number of occurrences for that element.

Time Complexity: O(n). Space Complexity: O(n).

Problem-8   For Problem-5, can we improve the time complexity? Assume that the elements range is 0 to $n-1$. That means all the elements are within this range only.

Solution: Yes. We can solve this problem in two scans. We *cannot* use the negation technique of Problem-3 for this problem because of number of repetitions. In the first scan, instead of negating add the value n. That means for each of occurrence of an element add the array size to that element. In the second scan, check the element value by dividing it with n and return the element whichever gives the maximum value. The code based on this method is given below.

```java
void MaxRepititions(int A[], int n){
        int i =  0, max = 0, maxIndex;
        for(i = 0; i < n; i++)
                A[A[i]%n] +=n;
        for(i = 0; i < n; i++) {
                if(A[i]/n > max) {
                        max = A[i]/n;
                        maxIndex =i;
                }
        }
        return maxIndex;
}
```

Notes:

- This solution does not work if the given array is read only.
- This solution will work only if the array elements are positive.
- If the elements range is not in 0 to $n-1$ then it may give exceptions.

Time Complexity: O(n). Since no nested *for* loops are required. Space Complexity: O(1).

Problem-9   Given an array of n numbers, give an algorithm for finding the first element in the array which is repeated. For example, in the array, $A = \{3, 2, 1, 2, 2, 3\}$ the first repeated number is 3 (not 2). That means, we need to return the first element among the repeated elements.

Solution: We can use the brute force solution that we used for Problem-1. For each element since it checks whether there is a duplicate for that element or not, whichever element duplicates first will be returned.

Problem-10   For Problem-9, can we use sorting technique?

Solution: No. For proving the failed case, let us consider the following array. For example, $A = \{3, 2, 1, 2, 2, 3\}$. After sorting we get $A = \{1, 2, 2, 2, 3, 3\}$. In this sorted array the first repeated element is 2 but the actual answer is 3.

Problem-11   For Problem-9, can we use hashing technique?

Solution: Yes. But the simple hashing technique which we used for Problem-3 will not work. For example, if we consider the input array as $A = \{3, 2, 1, 2, 3\}$, then first repeated element is 3 but using our simple hashing technique we get the answer as 2. This is because 2 is coming twice before 3. Now let us change the hashing table behavior so that we get the first repeated element. Let us say, instead of storing 1 value, initially we store the position of the element in the array. As a result the hash table will look like (after inserting 3, 2 and 1):

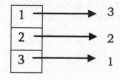

Now, if we see 2 again, we just negate the current value of 2 in the hash table. That means, we make its counter value as −2. The negative value in the hash table indicates that we have seen the same element two times. Similarly, for 3 (next element in input) also, we negate the current value of hash table and finally the hash table will look like:

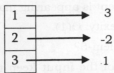

After processing the complete input array, scan the hash table and return the highest negative indexed value from it (i.e., −1 in our case). The highest negative value indicates that we have seen that element first (among repeated elements) and also repeating.

What if the element is repeated more than twice? In this case, just skip the element if the corresponding value i already negative.

Problem-12 For Problem-9, can we use the technique that we used for Problem-3 (negation technique)?

Solution: No. As a contradiction example, for the array $A = \{3, 2, 1, 2, 2, 3\}$ the first repeated element is 3. But with negation technique the result is 2.

Problem-13 **Finding the Missing Number:** We are given a list of $n - 1$ integers and these integers are in the range of 1 to n. There are no duplicates in list. One of the integers is missing in the list. Given an algorithm to find the missing integer. **Example**: I/P: [1, 2, 4, 6, 3, 7, 8] O/P: 5

Brute Force Solution: One simple solution to this is, for each number in 1 to n check whether that number is in the given array or not.

```
int FindMissingNumber(int A[], int n){
        int i, j, found=0;
        for (i = 1; i < =n; i ++) {
                found = 0;
                for (j = 0; j < n; j ++) {
                        if(A[j]==i)
                                found = 1;
                }
                if(!found) return i;
        }
        return -1;
}
```

Time Complexity: $O(n^2)$. Space Complexity: $O(1)$.

Problem-14 For Problem-13, can we use sorting technique?

Solution: Yes. Sorting the list will give the elements in increasing order and with another scan we can find the missing number.

Time Complexity: $O(n\log n)$, for sorting. Space Complexity: $O(1)$.

Problem-15 For Problem-13, can we use hashing technique?

Solution: Yes. Scan the input array and insert elements into the hash. For inserted element keep *counter* as 1 (assume initially all entires are filled with zeros). This indicates that the corresponding element has occurred already. Now, scan the hash table and return the element which has counter value zero.

Time Complexity: $O(n)$. Space Complexity: $O(n)$.

Problem-16 For Problem-13, can we improve the complexity?

Solution: Using summation formula
1) Get the sum of numbers, $sum = n * (n + 1)/2$.
2) Subtract all the numbers from sum and you will get the missing number.

Time Complexity: $O(n)$, for scanning the complete array.

Problem-17 In Problem-13, if the sum of the numbers goes beyond maximum allowed integer, then there can be integer overflow and we may not get correct answer. Can we solve this problem?

Solution:
1) *XOR* all the array elements, let the result of *XOR* be *X*.
2) *XOR* all numbers from 1 to n, let *XOR* be Y.

3) *XOR* of *X* and *Y* gives the missing number.

```
int FindMissingNumber(int A[], int n){
    int i, X, Y;
    for (i = 0; i < n; i ++)
        X ^= A[i];
    for (i = 1; i <= n; i ++)
        Y ^= i;
    //In fact, one variable is enough.
    return X ^ Y;
}
```

Time Complexity: $O(n)$, for scanning the complete array. Space Complexity: $O(1)$.

Problem-18 **Find the Number Occurring Odd Number of Times:** Given an array of positive integers, all numbers occurs even number of times except one number which occurs odd number of times. Find the number in $O(n)$ time & constant space. **Example**: I/P = [1,2,3,2,3,1,3] O/P = 3

Solution: Do a bitwise *XOR* of all the elements. We get the number which has odd occurrences. This is because, *A XOR A* = 0.

Time Complexity: $O(n)$. Space Complexity: $O(1)$.

Problem-19 **Find the two repeating elements in a given array:** Given an array with $n + 2$ elements, all elements of the array are in range 1 to n and also all elements occur only once except two numbers which occur twice. Find those two repeating numbers. For example: if the array is 4,2,4,5,2,3,1 with $n = 5$. This input has $n + 2 = 7$ elements with all elements occurring once except 2 and 4 which occur twice. So the output should be 4 2.

Solution: One simple way is to scan the complete array for each element of the input elements. That means use two loops. In the outer loop, select elements one by one and count the number of occurrences of the selected element in the inner loop. For the code below assume that *PrintRepeatedElements* is called with $n + 2$ to indicate the size.

```
void PrintRepeatedElements(int A[], int n){
    for(int i = 0; i < n; i++)
        for(int j = i+1; j <n; j++)
            if(A[i] == A[j])
                System.out.println( A[i]);
}
```

Time Complexity: $O(n^2)$. Space Complexity: $O(1)$.

Problem-20 For Problem-19, can we improve the time complexity?

Solution: Sort the array using any comparison sorting algorithm and see if there are any elements which contiguous with same value.

Time Complexity: $O(nlogn)$. Space Complexity: $O(1)$.

Problem-21 For Problem-19, can we improve the time complexity?

Solution: Use Count Array. This solution is like using a hash table. For simplicity we can use array for storing the counts. Traverse the array once and keep track of count of all elements in the array using a temp array *count*[] of size n. When we see an element whose count is already set, print it as duplicate. For the code below assume that *PrintRepeatedElements* is called with $n + 2$ to indicate the size.

```
void PrintRepeatedElements(int A[], int n){
    int *count = (int *)calloc(sizeof(int), (n - 2));
    for(int i = 0; i < size; i++) {
        count[A[i]]++;
        if(count[A[i]] == 2)
            System.out.println( A[i]);
    }
}
```

Time Complexity: $O(n)$. Space Complexity: $O(n)$.

Problem-22 Consider Problem-19. Let us assume that the numbers are in the range 1 to n. Is there any other way of solving the problem?

Solution: Yes by using XOR Operation. Let the repeating numbers be *X* and *Y*, if we *XOR* all the elements in the array and also all integers from 1 to n, then the result will be *X XOR Y*. The 1's in binary representation of

$X\,XOR\,Y$ correspond to the different bits between X and Y. If the kth bit of $X\,XOR\,Y$ is 1, we can XOR all the elements in the array and also all integers from 1 to n, whose k^{th} bits are 1. The result will be one of X and Y.

```java
void PrintRepeatedElements (int A[], int size){
        int XOR = A[0];
        int i, right_most_set_bit_no, X= 0, Y = 0;
        for(i = 1; i < size; i++)            /* Compute XOR of all elements in A[]*/
                XOR ^= A[i];
        for(i = 1; i <= n; i++)              /* Compute XOR of all elements {1, 2 ..n} */
                XOR ^= i;
        right_most_set_bit_no = XOR & ~( XOR -1);    // Get the rightmost set bit in right_most_set_bit_no

        /* Now divide elements in two sets by comparing rightmost set */
        for(i = 0; i < size; i++) {
                if(A[i] & right_most_set_bit_no)
                        X = X^ A[i];        /*XOR of first set in A[] */
                else    Y = Y ^ A[i];       /*XOR of second set inA[] */
        }
        for(i = 1; i <= n; i++) {
                if(i & right_most_set_bit_no)
                        X = X ^ i;          /*XOR of first set in A[] and {1, 2, ...n }*/
                else    Y = Y ^ i;          /*XOR of second set in A[] and {1, 2, ...n } */
        }
        System.out.println("Values X: "+ X " and Y:" + Y);
}
```

Time Complexity: O(n). Space Complexity: O(1).

Problem-23   Consider the Problem-19. Let us assume that the numbers are in the range 1 to n. Is there yet other way of solving the problem?

Solution: We can solve this by creating two simple mathematical equations. Let us assume that two numbers which we are going to find are X and Y. We know the sum of n numbers is $n(n+1)/2$ and product is $n!$. Make two equations using these sum and product formulae, and get values of two unknowns using the two equations. Let the summation of all numbers in array be S and product be P and the numbers which are being repeated are X and Y.

$$X + Y = \frac{n(n+1)}{2} - S$$
$$XY = n!/P$$

Using above two equations, we can find out X and Y. There can be addition and multiplication overflow problem with this approach.

Time Complexity: O(n). Space Complexity: O(1).

Problem-24   Similar to Problem-19, let us assume that the numbers are in the range 1 to n. Also, $n-1$ elements are repeating thrice and remaining element repeated twice. Find the element which is repeating twice.

Solution: If we XOR all the elements in the array and all integers from 1 to n, then all the elements which are thrice will become zero. This is because, since the element is repeating thrice and XOR with another time from range makes that element appearing four times. As a result, output of $a\,XOR\,a\,XOR\,a\,XOR\,a = 0$. Same is case with all elements which repeated three times.

With the same logic, for the element which repeated twice, if we XOR the input elements and also the range, then the total number of appearances for that element are 3. As a result, output of $a\,XOR\,a\,XOR\,a = a$. Finally, we get the element which repeated twice.

Time Complexity: O(n). Space Complexity: O(1).

Problem-25   Given an array of n elements. Find two elements in the array such that their sum is equal to given element K?

Brute Force Solution: One simple solution to this is, for each input element check whether there is any element whose sum is K. This we can solve just by using two simple for loops. The code for this solution can be given as:

```java
void BruteForceSearch[int A[], int n, int K){
        for (int i = 0; i < n; i++) {
                for(int j = i; j < n; j++) {
                        if(A[i]+A[j] == K) {
```

```
                        System.out.println("Items Found, i: " + i + " j:" + j);
                        return;
                    }
                }
            }
        System.out.println("Items not found: No such elements");
}
```

Time Complexity: $O(n^2)$. This is because of two nested for loops. Space Complexity: O(1).

Problem-26   For Problem-25, can we improve the time complexity?

Solution: Yes. Let us assume that we have sorted the given array. This operation takes O(*n logn*). On the sorted array, maintain indices *loIndex* = 0 and hiIndex = $n - 1$ and compute A[*loIndex*] + A[*hiIndex*]. If the sum equals K, then we are done with the solution. If the sum is less than K, decrement *hiIndex*, if the sum is greater than K, increment *loIndex*.

```
void Search[int A[], int n, int K]{
        int i, j, temp;
        Sort(A, n);
        for(i =  0, j = n-1; i < j) {
                temp  = A[i] + A[j];
                if(temp  == K) {
                        System.out.println("Items Found, i: " + i + " j:" + j);
                        return;
                }
                else if(temp  < K)
                        i = i + 1;
                else      j = j - 1;
        }
        return;
}
```

Time Complexity: O(*nlogn*). If the given array is already sorted then the complexity is O(*n*). Space Complexity: O(1).

Problem-27   Does the solution of Problem-25 work even if the array is not sorted?

Solution: Yes. Since we are checking all possibilities, the algorithm ensures that we get the pair of numbers if they exist.

Problem-28   Is there any other way of solving Problem-25?

Solution: Yes, using hash table. Since our objective is to find two indexes of the array whose sum is K. Let us say those indexes are X and Y. That means, A[X] + A[Y] = K. What we need is, for each element of the input array A[X], check whether K − A[X] also exists in input array. Now, let us simplify that searching with hash table.

Algorithm:
- For each element of the input array, insert into the hash table. Let us say the current element is A[X].
- Before proceeding to the next element we check whether K − A[X] also exists in hash table or not.
- Existence of such number indicates that we are able to find the indexes.
- Otherwise proceed to the next input element.

Time Complexity: O(*n*). Space Complexity: O(*n*).

Problem-29   Given an array A of *n* elements. Find three elements, *i, j* and *k* in the array such that $A[i]^2 + A[j]^2 = A[k]^2$?

Solution:
Algorithm:
- Sort the given array in-place.
- For each array index *i* compute $A[i]^2$ and store in array.
- Search for 2 numbers in array from 0 to $i − 1$ which adds to $A[i]$ similar to Problem-25. This will give us the result in O(*n*) time. If we find such sum return true otherwise continue.

```
Sort(A); // Sort the input array
for (int i=0; i < n; i++)
    A[i] = A[i]*A[i];
for (i=n; i > 0; i--) {
    res = false;
```

```
if(res) {
        //Problem-11/12 Solution
    }
}
```

Time Complexity: Time for sorting + n × (Time for finding the sum) = O($nlogn$) + n ×O(n)= n^2. Space Complexity: O(1).

Problem-30   Find two elements whose sum is closest to zero: Given an array with both positive and negative numbers, find the two elements such that their sum is closest to zero. For the below array, algorithm should give −80 and 85. Example: 1 60 − 10 70 − 80 85

Brute Force Solution: For each element, find the sum with every other element in the array and compare sums. Finally, return the minimum sum.

```
void TwoElementsWithMinSum(int A[], int n){
        int i, j, min_sum, sum, min_i, min_j, inv_count = 0;
        if(n < 2) {
                System.out.println("Invalid Input");
                return;

        }
        /* Initialization of values */
        min_i = 0;
        min_j = 1;
        min_sum = A[0] + A[1];
        for(i= 0; i < n - 1; i ++)    {
                for(j = i + 1; j < n; j++)    {
                        sum = A[i] + A[j];
                        if(Math.abs(min_sum) > Math.abs(sum)) {
                                min_sum = sum;
                                min_i = i;
                                min_j = j;
                        }
                }
        }
        System.out.println(" The two elements are " + arr[min_i] + " and " + arr[min_j]);
}
```

Time complexity: O(n^2). Space Complexity: O(1).

Problem-31   Can we improve the time complexity of Problem-30?

Solution Use Sorting.
Algorithm:
1. Sort all the elements of the given input array.
2. Maintain two indexes one at the beginning ($i = 0$) and other at the ending ($j = n - 1$). Also, maintina two variables to keep track of smallest positive sum closest to zero and smallest negative sum closest to zero.
3. While $i < j$:
    a. If the current pair sum is > zero and < postiveClosest then update the postiveClosest. Decrement j.
    b. If the current pair sum is < zero and > negativeClosest then update the negativeClosest. Increment i.
    c. Else, print the pair

```
void TwoElementsWithMinSum(int A[], int n) {
        int i = 0, j = n-1, temp, postiveClosest = INT_MAX, negativeClosest = INT_MIN;
        Sort(A, n);
        while(i < j) {
                temp  = A[i] + A[j];
                if(temp  > 0) {
                        if (temp < postiveClosest)
                                postiveClosest = temp;

                        j--;
                }
                else if (temp  < 0) {
                        if (temp > negativeClosest)
                                negativeClosest = temp;
```

```
                i++;
            }
            else printf("Closest Sum: %d ", A[i] + A[j]);
        }
        return (Math.abs(negativeClosest)> postiveClosest: postiveClosest: negativeCiosest);
    }
```

Time Complexity: O($nlogn$), for sorting. Space Complexity: O(1).

Problem-32 Given an array of n elements. Find three elements in the array such that their sum is equal to given element K?

Brute Force Solution: The default solution to this is, for each pair of input elements check whether there is any element whose sum is K. This we can solve just by using three simple for loops. The code for this solution can be given as:

```
void BruteForceSearch[int A[], int n, int data){
    for (int i = 0; i < n; i++) {
        for(int j = i+1; j < n; j++) {
            for(int k = j+1; k < n; k++)          {
                if(A[i] + A[j] + A[k]== data) {
                    System.out.println("Items Found, i:" + i + " j:" + j + " k:" + k);
                    return;
                }
            }
        }
    }
    System.out.println("Items not found: No such elements");
}
```

Time Complexity: O(n^3), for three nested *for* loops.Space Complexity: O(1).

Problem-33 Does the solution of Problem-32 work even if the array is not sorted?

Solution: Yes. Since we are checking all possibilities, the algorithm ensures that we can find three numbers whose sum is K if they exist.

Problem-34 Can we use sorting technique for solving Problem-32?

Solution: Yes.

```
void Search[int A[], int n, int data){
    Sort(A, n);
    for(int k = 0; k < n; k++) {
        for(int i =  k + 1, j = n-1; i < j;  ) {
            if(A[k] + A[i] + A[j]  == data) {
                System.out.println("Items Found, i:" + i + " j:" + j + " k:" + k);
                return;
            }
            else if(A[k] + A[i] + A[j]  < data)
                i = i + 1;
            else     j = j - 1;
        }
    }
    return;
}
```

Time Complexity: Time for sorting + Time for searching in sorted list = O($nlogn$) + O(n^2) $\approx$ O(n^2). This is because of two nested *for* loops. Space Complexity: O(1).

Problem-35 Can we use hashing technique for solving Problem-32?

Solution: Yes. Since our objective is to find three indexes of the array whose sum is K. Let us say those indexes are X, Y and Z. That means, $A[X] + A[Y] + A[Z] = K$.

Let us assume that we have kept all possible sums along with their pairs in hash table. That means the key to hash table is $K - A[X]$ and values for $K - A[X]$ are all possible pairs of input whose sum is $K - A[X]$.

Algorithm:
- Before starting the searching, insert all possible sums with pairs of elements into the hash table.
- For each element of the input array, insert into the hash table. Let us say the current element is $A[X]$.
- Check whether there exists a hash entry in the table with key: $K - A[X]$.

- If such element exists then scan the element pairs of $K - A[X]$ and return all possible pairs by including $A[X]$ also.
- If no such element exists (with $K - A[X]$ as key) then go to next element.

Time Complexity: Time for storing all possible pairs in Hash table + searching = $O(n^2) + O(n^2) \approx O(n^2)$. Space Complexity: $O(n)$.

Problem-36 Given an array of n integers, the $3 - sum\ problem$ is to find three integers whose sum is closest to $zero$.

Solution: This is same as that of Problem-32 with K value is zero.

Problem-37 Let A be an array of n distinct integers. Suppose A has the following property: there exists an index $1 \le k \le n$ such that $A[1],...,A[k]$ is an increasing sequence and $A[k+1],...,A[n]$ is a decreasing sequence. Design and analyze an efficient algorithm for finding k.

Similar question: Let us assume that the given array is sorted but starts with negative numbers and ends with positive numbers [such functions are called monotonically increasing function]. In this array find the starting index of the positive numbers. Assume that we know the length of the input array. Design a $O(logn)$ algorithm.

Solution: Let us use a variant of the binary search.

```
int Search (int A[], int n, int first, int last){
        int mid, first = 0, last = n-1;
        while(first <= last) {
                // if the current array has size 1
                if(first == last)
                        return A[first];
                // if the current array has size 2
                else if(first == last-1)
                        return max(A[first], A[last]);
                // if the current array has size 3 or more
                else {
                        mid = first + (last-first)/2;
                        if(A[mid-1] < A[mid] && A[mid] > A[mid+1])
                                return A[mid];
                        else if(A[mid-1] < A[mid] && A[mid] < A[mid+1])
                                first = mid+1;
                        else if(A[mid-1] > A[mid] && A[mid] > A[mid+1])
                                last = mid-1;
                        else    return INT_MIN ;
                } // end of else
        } // end of while
}
```

The recursion equation is $T(n) = 2T(n/2) + c$. Using master theorem, we get $O(logn)$.

Problem-38 If we don't know n, how do we solve the Problem-37?

Solution: Repeatedly compute $A[1], A[2], A[4], A[8], A[16]$, and so on until we find a value of n such that $A[n] > 0$.

Time Complexity: $O(logn)$, since we are moving at the rate of 2.
Refer *Introduction to Analysis of Algorithms* chapter for details on this.

Problem-39 Given an input array of size unknown with all 1's in the beginning and 0's in the end. Find the index in the array from where 0's start. Consider there are millions of 1's and 0's in the array. E.g. array contents 1111111.......1100000.........0000000.

Solution: This problem is almost similar to Problem-38. Check the bits at the rate of 2^K where $k = 0, 1, 2 ....$ Since we are moving at the rate of 2, the complexity is $O(logn)$.

Problem-40 Given a sorted array of n integers that has been rotated an unknown number of times, give a $O(logn)$ algorithm that finds an element in the array.
Example: Find 5 in array (15 16 19 20 25 1 3 4 5 7 10 14)
Output: 8 (the index of 5 in the array)

Solution: Let us assume that the given array is $A[]$ and use the solution of Problem-37 with extension. The function below *FindPivot* returns the k value (let us assume that this function return the index instead of value). Find the pivot point, divide the array into two sub-arrays and call binary search. The main idea for finding pivot is – for a sorted (in increasing order) and pivoted array, pivot element is the only element for which next element to it is smaller than it. Using above criteria and binary search methodology we can get pivot element in O(*logn*) time.

Algorithm:

1) Find out pivot point and divide the array in two sub-arrays.
2) Now call binary search for one of the two sub-arrays.
    a. if element is greater than first element then search in left subarray
    b. else search in right subarray
3) If element is found in selected sub-array then return index *else* return −1.

```
int FindPivot(int A[], int start, int finish) {
        if(finish - start == 0)
                return start;
        else if(start == finish - 1) {
                if(A[start] >= A[finish])
                        return start;
                else    return finish;
        }
        else {  mid = start + (finish-start)/2;
                if(A[start] >= A[mid])
                        return FindPivot(A, start, mid);
                else    return FindPivot(A, mid, finish);
        }
}

int Search(int A[], int n, int x) {
        int pivot = FindPivot(A, 0, n-1);
        if(A[pivot] == x) return pivot;
        if(A[pivot] <= x)
                return BinarySearch(A, 0, pivot-1, x);
        else    return BinarySearch(A, pivot+1, n-1, x);
}

int BinarySearch(int A[], int low, int high, int x) {
        if(high >= low)   {
                int mid = low + (high - low)/2;
                if(x == A[mid])
                        return mid;
                if(x > A[mid])
                        return BinarySearch(A, (mid + 1), high, x);
                else    return BinarySearch(A, low, (mid -1), x);
        }
        /*Return -1 if element is not found*/
        return -1;
}
```

Time complexity:O(*logn*).

Problem-41 For Problem-40, can we solve in one scan?

Solution: Yes.

```
int BinarySearchRotated(int A[], int start, int finish, int data) {
        if(start > finish) return -1;
        int mid = start + (finish - start) / 2;
        if(data == A[mid]) return mid;
        else if(A[start] <= A[mid]) {        // start half is in sorted order.
                if(data >= A[start] && data < A[mid])
                        return BinarySearchRotated(A, start, mid - 1, data);
                else    return BinarySearchRotated(A, mid + 1, finish, data);
        }
        else {  // A[mid] <= A[finish], finish half is in sorted order.
                if(data > A[mid] && data <= A[finish])
                        return BinarySearchRotated(A, mid + 1, finish, data);
                else    return BinarySearchRotated(A, start, mid - 1, data);
        }
}
```

Time complexity:O(*logn*).

Problem-42 **Bitonic search:** An array is *bitonic* if it is comprised of an increasing sequence of integers followed immediately by a decreasing sequence of integers. Given a bitonic array A of n distinct integers, describe how to determine whether a given integer is in the array in O(*logn*) steps.

Solution: The solution is the same as that for Problem-37.

Problem-43 Yet, other way of framing Problem-37.
Let A[] be an array that starts out increasing, reaches a maximum, and then decreases. Design an O(*logn*) algorithm to find the index of the maximum value.

Problem-44 Give an O(*nlogn*) algorithm for computing the median of a sequence of n integers.

Solution: Sort and return element at $\frac{n}{2}$.

Problem-45 Given two sorted lists of size m and n, find median of all elements in O(*log (m + n)*) time.

Solution: Refer *Divide and Conquer* chapter.

Problem-46 Given a sorted array A of n elements, possibly with duplicates, find the index of the first occurrence of a number in O(*logn*) time.

Solution: To find the first occurrence of a number we need to check for the following condition. Return the position if any one of the following is true:

mid == low && A[mid] == data || A[mid] == data && A[mid-1] < data

```
int BinarySearchFirstOccurrence(int A[], int low, int high, int data) {
    if(high >= low) {
        int mid = low + (high-low) / 2;
        if((mid == low && A[mid] == data) || (A[mid] == data && A[mid - 1] < data))
            return mid;
        // Give preference to left half of the array
        else if(A[mid] >= data)
            return BinarySearchFirstOccurrence (A, low, mid - 1, data);
        else    return BinarySearchFirstOccurrence (A, mid + 1, high, data);
    }
    return -1;
}
```
Time Complexity: O(*logn*).

Problem-47 Given a sorted array A of n elements, possibly with duplicates. Find the index of the last occurrence of a number in O(*logn*) time.

Solution: To find the last occurrence of a number we need to check for the following condition. Return the position if any one of the following is true:

mid == high && A[mid] == data || A[mid] == data && A[mid+1] > data

```
int BinarySearchLastOccurrence(int A[], int low, int high, int data) {
    if(high >= low) {
        int mid = low + (high-low) / 2;
        if((mid == high && A[mid] == data) || (A[mid] == data && A[mid + 1] > data))
            return mid;
        // Give preference to right half of the array
        else if(A[mid] <= data)
            return BinarySearchLastOccurrence (A, mid + 1, high, data);
        else    return BinarySearchLastOccurrence (A, low, mod - 1, data);
    }
    return -1;
}
```
Time Complexity: O(*logn*).

Problem-48 Given a sorted array of n elements, possibly with duplicates. Find the number of occurrences of a number.

Brute Force Solution: Do a linear search over the array and increment count as and when we find the element data in the array.

```
int LinearSearchCount(int A[], int n, int data) {
    int count = 0;
    for (int i = 0; i < n; i++)  {
        if(A[i] == k)
            count++;
```

```
    }
    return count;
}
```

Time Complexity: O(n).

Problem-49 Can we improve the time complexity of Problem-48?

Solution: Yes. We can solve this by using one binary search call followed by another small scan.
Algorithm:

- Do a binary search for the *data* in the array. Let us assume its position is K.
- Now traverse towards left from K and count the number of occurrences of *data*. Let this count be *leftCount*.
- Similarly, traverse towards right and count the number of occurrences of *data*. Let this count be *rightCount*.
- Total number of occurrences = *leftCount* + 1 + *rightCount*

Time Complexity – O($logn + S$) where S is the number of occurrences of *data*.

Problem-50 Is there any alternative way of solving Problem-48?

Solution:
Algorithm:

- Find first occurrence of *data* and call its index as *firstOccurrence* (for algorithm refer Problem-46)
- Find last occurrence of *data* and call its index as *lastOccurrence* (for algorithm refer Problem-47)
- Return *lastOccurrence – firstOccurrence* + 1

Time Complexity = O($logn + logn$) =O($logn$).

Problem-51 What is the next number in the sequence $1, 11, 21$ and why?

Solution: Read the given number loudly. This is just a fun problem.

> One One
> Two Ones
> One two, one one→ 1211

So answer is, the next number is the representation of previous number by reading it loudly.

Problem-52 Finding second smallest number efficiently.

Solution: We can construct a heap of the given elements using up just less than n comparisons (Refer *Priority Queues* chapter for algorithm). Then we find the second smallest using $logn$ comparisons for the GetMax() operation. Overall, we get $n + logn + constant$.

Problem-53 Is there any other solution for Problem-52?

Solution: Alternatively, split the n numbers into groups of 2, perform $n/2$ comparisons successively to find the largest using a tournament-like method. The first round will yield the maximum in $n - 1$ comparisons. The second round will be performed on the winners of the first round and the ones the maximum popped. This will yield $logn - 1$ comparisons for a total of $n + logn - 2$. The above solution is called *tournament problem*.

Problem-54 An element is a majority if it appears more than $n/2$ times. Give an algorithm takes an array of n element as argument and identifies a majority (if it exists).

Solution: The basic solution is to have two loops and keep track of maximum count for all different elements. If maximum count becomes greater than $n/2$ then break the loops and return the element having maximum count. If maximum count doesn't become more than $n/2$ then majority element doesn't exist.

Time Complexity: O(n^2). Space Complexity: O(1).

Problem-55 Can we improve Problem-54 time complexity to O($nlogn$)?

Solution: Using binary search we can achieve this. Node of the Binary Search Tree (used in this approach) will be as follows.

```
public class TreeNode {
        public int element;
        public int count;
        public TreeNode left;
        public TreeNode right;
        ......
}
```

Insert elements in BST one by one and if an element is already present then increment the count of the node. At any stage, if count of a node becomes more than $n/2$ then return. The method works well for the cases where

$n/2 + 1$ occurrences of the majority element is present in the starting of the array, for example $\{1, 1, 1, 1, 1, 2, 3,$ and $4\}$.

Time Complexity: If a binary search tree is used then worst time complexity will be $O(n^2)$. If a balanced-binary-search tree is used then $O(nlogn)$. Space Complexity: $O(n)$.

Problem-56 Is there any other of achieving $O(nlogn)$ complexity for Problem-54?

Solution: Sort the input array and scan the sorted array to find the majority element.

Time Complexity: $O(nlogn)$. Space Complexity: $O(1)$.

Problem-57 Can we improve the complexity for Problem-54?

Solution: If an element occurs more than $n/2$ times in A then it must be the median of A. But, the reverse is not true, so once the median is found, we must check to see how many times it occurs in A. We can use linear selection which takes $O(n)$ time (for algorithm refer *Selection Algorithms* chapter).

```
int CheckMajority(int A[], in n) {
    1) Use linear selection to find the median m of A.
    2) Do one more pass through A and count the number of occurrences of m.
        a. If m occurs more than n/2 times then return true;
        b. Otherwise return false.
}
```

Problem-58 Is there any other way of solving Problem-54?

Solution: Since only one element is repeating, we can use simple scan of the input array by keeping track of count for the elements. If the count is 0 then we can assume that the element is coming first time otherwise that the resultant element.

```
int MajorityNum(int[] A, int n) {
    int majNum, count = 0, element = -1;
    for(int i = 0; i < n; i++) {
        // If the counter is 0 then set the current candidate to majority num and set the counter to 1.
        if(count == 0) {
            element = A[i];
            count = 1;
        }
        else if(element == A[i]) {
            // Increment counter If the counter is not 0 and
            // element is same as current candidate.
            count++;
        }
        else {  // Decrement counter If the counter is not 0 and
            // element is different from current candidate.
            count--;
        }
    }
    return element;
}
```

Time Complexity: $O(n)$. Space Complexity: $O(1)$.

Problem-59 Given an array of $2n$ elements of which n elements are same and the remaining n elements are all different. Find the majority element.

Solution: The repeated elements will occupy half the array. No matter what arrangement it is, only one of the below will be true,

- All duplicate elements will be at a relative distance of 2 from each other. Ex: n, 1, n, 100, n, 54, n ...
- At least two duplicate elements will be next to each other
  Ex: $n, n, 1, 100, n, 54, n, \ldots.$
       $n, 1, n, n, n, 54, 100 \ldots$
       $1, 100, 54, n, n, n, n \ldots.$

In worst case, we will need two passes over the array,
- First Pass: compare $A[i]$ and $A[i + 1]$
- Second Pass: compare $A[i]$ and $A[i + 2]$

Something will match and that's your element. This will cost $O(n)$ in time and $O(1)$ in space.

Problem-60 Given an array with $2n + 1$ integer elements, n elements appear twice in arbitrary places in the array and a single integer appears only once somewhere inside. Find the lonely integer with O(n) operations and O(1) extra memory.

Solution: Except one element all other elements are repeated. We know that $A\ XOR\ A = 0$. Based on this if we *XOR* all the input elements then we get the remaining element.

```
int Solution(int A[], int n) {
        int i, res;
        for (i = res = 0; i < 2n+1; i++)
                res = res ^ A[i];
        return res;
}
```

Time Complexity: O(n). Space Complexity: O(1).

Problem-61 **Throwing eggs from an n-story building:** Suppose we have an n story building and a number of eggs. Also assume that an egg breaks if it is thrown off floor F or higher, and will not break otherwise. Devise a strategy to determine the floor F, while breaking O($logn$) eggs.

Solution: Refer *Divide and Conquer* chapter.

Problem-62 **Local minimum of an array:** Given an array A of n distinct integers, design an O($logn$) algorithm to find a *local minimum*: an index i such that $A[i-1] < A[i] < A[i+1]$.

Solution: Check the middle value $A[n/2]$, and two neighbors $A[n/2 - 1]$ and $A[n/2 + 1]$. If $A[n/2]$ is local minimum, stop; otherwise search in half with smaller neighbor.

Problem-63 Give an $n \times n$ array of elements such that each row is in ascending order and each column is in ascending order, devise an O(n) algorithm to determine if a given element x in the array. You may assume all elements in the $n \times n$ array are distinct.

Solution: Let us assume that the given matrix is $A[n][n]$. Start with the last row, first column [or first row - last column]. If the element we are searching for is greater than the element at $A[1][n]$, then the column 1 can be eliminated. If the search element is less than the element at $A[1][n]$, then the last row can be completely eliminated. Once the first column or the last row is eliminated, start over the process again with left-bottom end of the remaining array. In this algorithm, there would be maximum n elements that the search element would be compared with.

Time Complexity: O(n). This is because we will traverse at most $2n$ points. Space Complexity: O(1).

Problem-64 Given an $n \times n$ array a of n^2 numbers, give an O(n) algorithm to find a pair of indices i and j such that $A[i][j] < A[i+1][j], A[i][j] < A[i][j+1], A[i][j] < A[i-1][j]$, and $A[i][j] < A[i][j-1]$.

Solution: This problem is same as Problem-63.

Problem-65 Given $n \times n$ matrix, and in each row all 1's are followed 0's. Find row with maximum number of 0's.

Solution: Start with first row, last column. If the element is 0 then move to the previous column in the same row and at the same time increase the counter to indicate the maximum number of 0's. If the element is 1 then move to next row in the same column. Repeat this process until we reach last row, first column.

Time Complexity: O($2n$) ≈O(n) (similar to Problem-63).

Problem-66 Given an input array of size unknown with all numbers in the beginning and special symbols in the end. Find the index in the array from where special symbols start.

Solution: Refer *Divide and Conquer* chapter.

Problem-67 **Separate Even and Odd numbers:** Given an array $A[\ ]$, write a function that segregates even and odd numbers. The functions should put all even numbers first, and then odd numbers. **Example**: Input = $\{12, 34, 45, 9, 8, 90, 3\}$ Output = $\{12, 34, 90, 8, 9, 45, 3\}$

Note: In the output, order of numbers can be changed, i.e., in the above example 34 can come before 12 and 3 can come before 9.

Solution: The problem is very similar to *Separate 0's and 1's* (Problem-68) in an array, and both problems are variations of the famous *Dutch national flag problem*.

Algorithm: Logic is similar to Quick sort.
1) Initialize two index variables left and right: *left* = 0, *right* = $n - 1$
2) Keep incrementing left index until we see an odd number.
3) Keep decrementing right index until we see an even number.
4) If *left* < *right* then swap $A[left]$ and $A[right]$

```
void DutchNationalFlag(int A[], int n) {
        int left = 0, right = n-1;                          /* Initialize left and right indexes */
        while(left < right) {
                /* Increment left index while we see 0 at left */
                while(A[left]%2 == 0 && left < right)
                        left++;
                /* Decrement right index while we see 1 at right */
                while(A[right]%2 == 1 && left < right)
                        right--;
                if(left < right) {
                        /* Swap A[left] and A[right]*/
                        swap(&A[left], &A[right]);
                        left++;
                        right--;
                }
        }
}
```

Time Complexity: O(n).

Problem-68   The following is another way of structuring Problem-67, but with little difference.

   Separate 0's and 1's in an array: We are given an array of 0's and 1's in random order. Separate 0's on left side and 1's on right side of the array. Traverse array only once.

> Input array   = [0, 1, 0, 1, 0, 0, 1, 1, 1, 0]
> Output array = [0, 0, 0, 0, 0, 1, 1, 1, 1, 1]

Solution: Counting 0's or 1's

1.   Count the number of 0's. Let count be C.
2.   Once we have count, put C 0's at the beginning and 1's at the remaining $n - C$ positions in array.

Time Complexity: O(n). This solution scans the array two times.

Problem-69   Can we solve Problem-68 in one scan?

Solution: Yes. Use two indexes to traverse: Maintain two indexes. Initialize first index left as 0 and second index right as $n - 1$. Do following while *left* < *right*:

1)   Keep incrementing index left while there are 0s at it
2)   Keep decrementing index right while there are 1s at it
3)   If left < right then exchange $A[left]$ and $A[right]$

```
/*Function to put all 0s on left and all 1s on right*/
void Separate0and1(int A[], int n) {
        /* Initialize left and right indexes */
        int left = 0, right = n-1;
        while(left < right) {
                /* Increment left index while we see 0 at left */
                while(A[left] == 0 && left < right)
                        left++;
                /* Decrement right index while we see 1 at right */
                while(A[right] == 1 && left < right)
                        right-;
                /* If left is smaller than right then there is a 1 at left
                and a 0 at right.  Swap A[left] and A[right]*/
                if(left < right) {
                        A[left] = 0;
                        A[right] = 1;
                        left++;
                        right-;
                }
        }
}
```

Time Complexity: O(n). Space Complexity: O(1).

Problem-70   **Sort an array of 0's, 1's and 2's [or R's, G's and B's]:** Given an array A[] consisting 0's, 1's and 2's, give an algorithm for sorting A[].The algorithm should put all 0's first, then all 1's and finally all the 2's at the end. **Example** Input = {0,1,1,0,1,2,1,2,0,0,0,1}, Output = {0, 0, 0, 0, 0, 1, 1, 1, 1, 1, 2, 2}

Solution:

```
void Sorting012sDutchFlagProblem(int A[],int n){
        int low=0,mid=0,high=n-1;
        while(mid <=high){
                switch(A[mid]){
                        case 0:
                                swap(A[low],A[mid]);
                                low++;mid++;
                                break;
                        case 1:
                                mid++;
                                break;
                        case 2:
                                swap(A[mid],A[high]);
                                high--;
                                break;
                }
        }
}
```

Time Complexity: O(n). Space Complexity: O(1).

Problem-71   **Maximum difference between two elements:** Given an array $A[]$ of integers, find out the difference between any two elements such that larger element appears after the smaller number in $A[]$.
Examples: If array is [2, 3, 10, 6, 4, 8, 1] then returned value should be 8 (Diff between 10 and 2). If array is [7, 9, 5, 6, 3, 2] then returned value should be 2 (Difference between 7 and 9)

Solution: Refer *Divide and Conquer* chapter.

Problem-72   Given an array of 101 elements. Out of them 25 elements are repeated twice, 12 elements are repeated 4 times and one element is repeated 3 times. Find the element which repeated 3 times in O(1).

Solution: Before solving this problem let us consider the following *XOR* operation property: $a\ XOR\ a = 0$. That means, if we apply the *XOR* on same elements then the result is 0.

Algorithm:
*   *XOR* all the elements of the given array and assume the result is A.
*   After this operation, 2 occurrences of number which appeared 3 times becomes 0 and one occurrence remains the same.
*   The 12 elements that are appearing 4 times become 0.
*   The 25 elements that are appearing 2 times become 0.
*   So just *XOR'ing* all the elements give the result.

Time Complexity: O(n), because we are doing only one scan. Space Complexity: O(1).

Problem-73   Given a number n, give an algorithm for finding the number of trailing zeros in $n!$.

Solution:
```
int NumberOfTrailingZerosInNumber(int n) {
        int i, count = 0;
        if(n < 0)
                return -1;
        for (i = 5; n / i > 0; i *= 5)
                count += n / i;
        return count;
}
```
Time Complexity: O($logn$).

Problem-74   Given an array of $2n$ integers in the following format $a1\ a2\ a3\ldots an\ b1\ b2\ b3\ldots bn$. Shuffle the array to $a1\ b1\ a2\ b2\ a3\ b3\ldots an\ bn$ without any extra memory.

Solution: A brute force solution involves two nested loops to rotate the elements in the second half of the array to the left. The first loop runs n times to cover all elements in the second half of the array. The second loop rotates the elements to the left. Note that the start index in the second loop depends on which element we are rotating and the end index depends on how many positions we need to move to the left.
```
void ShuffleArray() {
        int n = 4, A[] = {1,3,5,7,2,4,6,8};
        for (int i = 0, q =1, k = n; i < n; i++, k++, q++) {
                for (int j = k; j > i + q; j--) {
                        int tmp = A[j-1];
```

```
                    A[j-1] = A[j];
                    A[j] = tmp;
            }
    }
    for (int i = 0; i  < 2*n; i++)
            System.out.println(A[i]);
}
```

Time Complexity: O(n^2).

Problem-75   Can we improve Problem-74 solution?

Solution: Refer Divide and Concur chapter. A better solution of time complexity O($nlogn$) can be achieved using *Divide and Concur* technique. Let us take an example
1. Start with the array: $a1$ $a2$ $a3$ $a4$ $b1$ $b2$ $b3$ $b4$
2. Split the array into two halves: $a1$ $a2$ $a3$ $a4$: $b1$ $b2$ $b3$ $b4$
3. Exchange elements around the center: exchange $a3$ $a4$ with $b1$ $b2$ you get: $a1$ $a2$ $b1$ $b2$ $a3$ $a4$ $b3$ $b4$
4. Split $a1$ $a2$ $b1$ $b2$ into $a1$ $a2$: $b1$ $b2$ then split $a3$ $a4$ $b3$ $b4$ into $a3$ $a4$: $b3$ $b4$
5. Exchange elements around the center for each subarray you get: $a1$ $b1$ $a2$ $b2$ and $a3$ $b3$ $a4$ $b4$

Please note that this solution only handles the case when $n = 2^i$ where $i = 0, 1, 2, 3$ etc. In our example $n = 2^2 = 4$ which makes it easy to recursively split the array into two halves. The basic idea behind swapping elements around the center before calling the recursive function is to produce smaller size problems. A solution with linear time complexity may be achieved if the elements are of specific nature. For example, if you can calculate the new position of the element using the value of the element itself. This is nothing but a hashing technique.

Problem-76   Given an Aay A[], find the maximum j – i such that A[j] > A[i]. For example, Input: {34, 8, 10, 3, 2, 80, 30, 33, 1} and Output: 6 (j = 7, i = 1).

Solution: Brute Force Approach: Run two loops. In the outer loop, pick elements one by one from left. In the inner loop, compare the picked element with the elements starting from right side. Stop the inner loop when you see an element greater than the picked element and keep updating the maximum j-i so far.

```
    int maxIndexDiff(int A[], int n){
        int maxDiff = -1;
        int i, j;

        for (i = 0; i < n; ++i){
            for (j = n-1; j > i; --j){
                if(A[j] > A[i] && maxDiff < (j - i))
                    maxDiff = j - i;
            }
        }
        return maxDiff;
    }
```

Time Complexity: O(n^2). Space Complexity: O(1).

Problem-77   Can we improve the complexity of Problem-76?

Solution: To solve this problem, we need to get two optimum indexes of A[]: left index i and right index j. For an element A[i], we do not need to consider A[i] for left index if there is an element smaller than A[i] on left side of A[i]. Similarly, if there is a greater element on right side of A[j] then we do not need to consider this j for right index.

So we construct two auxiliary Aays LeftMins[] and RightMaxs[] such that LeftMins[i] holds the smallest element on left side of A[i] including A[i], and RightMaxs[j] holds the greatest element on right side of A[j] including A[j]. After constructing these two auxiliary arrays, we traverse both these arrays from left to right.

While traversing LeftMins[] and RightMaxs[] if we see that LeftMins[i] is greater than RightMaxs[j], then we must move ahead in LeftMins[] (or do i++) because all elements on left of LeftMins[i] are greater than or equal to LeftMins[i]. Otherwise we must move ahead in RightMaxs[j] to look for a greater $j - i$ value.

```
    int maxIndexDiff(int A[], int n){
        int maxDiff;
        int i, j;
        int *LeftMins = (int *)malloc(sizeof(int)*n);
        int *RightMaxs = (int *)malloc(sizeof(int)*n);
        LeftMins[0] = A[0];
        for (i = 1; i < n; ++i)
            LeftMins[i] = min(A[i], LeftMins[i-1]);

        RightMaxs[n-1] = A[n-1];
```

```
        for (j = n-2; j >= 0; --j)
           RightMaxs[j] = max(A[j], RightMaxs[j+1]);

       i = 0, j = 0, maxDiff = -1;
       while (j < n && i < n){
          if (LeftMins[i] < RightMaxs[j]){
             maxDiff = max(maxDiff, j-i);
             j = j + 1;
          }
          else
             i = i+1;
       }
        return maxDiff;
   }
```

Time Complexity: O(*n*). Space Complexity: O(*n*).

Problem-78   Given an array of elements, how do you check whether the list is pairwise sorted or not? A list is considered pairwise sorted if each successive pair of numbers is in sorted (non-decreasing) order.

Solution:

```
     public boolean isPairwiseSorted(int A[], int n) {
         if (n == 0 || n == 1)
            return true;
         for (int i = 0; i < n - 1; i += 2){
            if (A[i] > A[i+1])
               return false;
         }
     }
```

Time Complexity: O(*n*). Space Complexity: O(1).

SELECTION ALGORITHMS [MEDIANS]    Chapter-12

12.1 What are Selection Algorithms?

Selection algorithm is an algorithm for finding the kth smallest/largest number in a list (also called as k^{th} order statistic). This includes, finding the minimum, maximum, and median elements. For finding k^{th} order statistic, there are multiple solutions which provide different complexities and in this chapter we will enumerate those possibilities.

12.2 Selection by Sorting

Selection problem can be converted to sorting problem. In this method, we first sort the input elements and then get the desired element. It is efficient if we want to perform many selections. For example, let us say we want to get the minimum element. After sorting the input elements we can simply return the first element (assuming the array is sorted in ascending order). Now, if we want to find the second smallest element, we can simply return the second element from the sorted list. That means, for the second smallest element we are not performing the sorting again. Same is the case with subsequent queries too. Even if we want to get k^{th} smallest element, just one scan of sorted list is enough for finding the element (or we can return the kth-indexed value if the elements are in the array).

From the above discussion what we can say is, with the initial sorting we can answer any query in one scan, $O(n)$. In general, this method requires $O(nlogn)$ time (for *sorting*), where n is the length of the input list. If we are performing n queries then the average cost per operation is just $\frac{n\,logn}{n} \approx O(logn)$. This kind of analysis is called *amortized* analysis.

12.3 Partition-based Selection Algorithm

For algorithm check Problem-6. This algorithm is similar to Quick sort.

12.4 Linear Selection algorithm - Median of Medians algorithm

Worst-case performance	$O(n)$
Best case performance	$O(n)$
Worst case space complexity	$O(1)$ auxiliary

Refer to Problem-11.

12.5 Finding the K Smallest Elements in Sorted Order

For algorithm check Problem-16.

12.6 Problems on Selection Algorithms

Problem-1   Find the largest element in an array *A* of size *n*.

Solution: Scan the complete array and return the largest element.

```java
void FindLargestInArray(int n, int[] A) {
        int large = A[0];
        for (int i = 1; i <= n-1; i++)
            if(A[i] > large)
                large = A[i];
        System.out.println("Largest: " + large);
}
```

Time Complexity - $O(n)$.
Space Complexity - $O(1)$.

Note: Any deterministic algorithm that can find the largest of n keys by comparisons of keys takes at least $n-1$ comparisons.

Problem-2   Find the smallest and largest elements in an array A of size n.

Solution:

```java
void FindSmallestAndLargestInArray (int[] A, int n) {
        int small = A[0];
        int large = A[0];
        for(int i = 1; i <= n-1; i++)
                if(A[i] < small)
                        small = A[i];
                else if(A[i] > large)
                        large = A[i];
        System.out.println("Smallest: " + small + " Largest: " + large);
}
```

Time Complexity - O(n).

Space Complexity - O(1). The worst-case number of comparisons is $2(n-1)$.

Problem-3   Can we improve the previous algorithms?

Solution: Yes. We can do this by comparing in pairs.

```java
void FindWithPairComparison (int A[], int n) {// n is assumed to be even. Compare in pairs.
        int large = small = -1;
        for (int i = 0; i <= n - 1; i = i + 2) {          // Increment i by 2.
                if(A[i] < A[i + 1]) {
                        if(A[i] < small)
                                small = A[i];
                        if(A[i + 1] > large)
                                large = A[i + 1];
                }
                else {
                        if(A[i + 1] < small)
                                small = A[i + 1];
                        if(A[i] > large)
                                large = A[i];
                }
        }
        System.out.println("Smallest: " + small + " Largest: " + large);
}
```

Time Complexity - O(n).

Space Complexity - O(1).

Number of comparisons: $\begin{cases} \frac{3n}{2} - 2, & \text{if } n \text{ is even} \\ \frac{3n}{2} - \frac{3}{2} & \text{if } n \text{ is odd} \end{cases}$

Summary:

Straightforward comparison – $2(n-1)$ comparisons
Compare for min only if comparison for max fails
Best case: increasing order – $n-1$ comparisons
Worst case: decreasing order – $2(n-1)$ comparisons
Average case: $3n/2 - 1$ comparisons

Note: For divide and conquer techniques refer to *Divide and Conquer* chapter.

Problem-4   Give an algorithm for finding the second largest element in the given input list of elements.

Solution: Brute Force Method

Algorithm:

- Find largest element: needs $n-1$ comparisons
- Delete (discard) the largest element
- Again find largest element: needs $n-2$ comparisons

Total number of comparisons: $n-1+n-2 = 2n-3$

Problem-5   Can we reduce the number of comparisons in Problem-4 solution?

Solution: The Tournament method: For simplicity, assume that the numbers are distinct and that n is a power of 2. We pair the keys and compare the pairs in rounds until only one round remains.

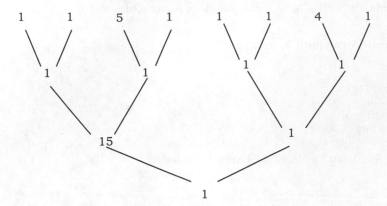

If the input has eight keys, there are four comparisons in the first round, two in the second, and one in the last. The winner of the last round is the largest key. The figure below shows the method. The tournament method directly applies only when n is a power of 2. When this is not the case, we can add enough items to the end of the array to make the array size a power of 2. If the tree is complete then the maximum height of the tree is $logn$. If we construct the complete binary tree, we need $n - 1$ comparisons to find the largest.

The second largest key has to be among the ones that were lost in a comparison with the largest one. That means, the second largest element should be one of the opponents of largest element. The number of keys that are lost to the largest key is the height of the tree, i.e. $logn$ [if the tree is a complete binary tree]. Then using the selection algorithm to find the largest among them take $logn - 1$ comparisons. Thus the total number of comparisons to find the largest and second largest keys is $n + logn - 2$.

Problem-6   Find the k-smallest elements in an array S of n elements using partitioning method.

   Input: positive integers n and k, where $k = n$, array of elements S indexed from 1 to n.

   Output: the k-smallest elements in S. It is returned as the value of function selection.

Solution: Brute Force Approach: Scan through the numbers k times to have the desired element. This method is the one used in bubble sort (and selection sort), every time we find out the smallest element in the whole sequence by comparing every element. In this method, the sequence has to be traversed k times. So the complexity is $O(n \times k)$.

Problem-7   Can we use sorting technique for solving Problem-6?

Solution: Yes. Sort and take first k elements.

1. Sort the numbers.
2. Pick the first k elements.

The complexity is very trivial. Sorting of n numbers is of $O(nlogn)$ and picking k^{th} element is of $O(k)$. Total complexity is $O(nlogn + k) = O(nlogn)$.

Problem-8   Can we use *tree sorting* technique for solving Problem-6?

Solution: Yes.
1. Insert all the elements to a binary search tree.
2. Do an InOrder traversal until and print k elements which will be the smallest ones. So, we have the k smallest elements.

The cost of creating a binary search tree with n elements is $O(nlogn)$ and the traversal upto k elements is $O(k)$. Hence the complexity is $O(nlogn + k) = O(nlogn)$.

Disadvantage: If the numbers are sorted in descending order, we will be getting a tree which will be skewed towards left. In that case, construction of the tree will be $0 + 1 + 2 + ... + (n - 1) = \frac{n(n-1)}{2}$ which is $O(n^2)$. To escape from this, we can keep the tree balanced, so that the cost of constructing the tree will be only $nlogn$.

Problem-9   Can we improve *tree sorting* technique for solving Problem-6?

Solution: Yes. Use a smaller tree to give the same result.

1. Take the first k elements of the sequence to create a balanced tree of k nodes (this will cost $klogk$).

2. Take the remaining numbers one by one, and
   a. If the number is larger than the largest element of the tree, return
   b. If the number is smaller than the largest element of the tree, remove the largest element of the tree and add the new element. This step is to make sure that a smaller element replaces a larger element from the tree. The cost of this operation is $logk$ since the tree is a balanced tree of k elements.

Once Step 2 is over, the balanced tree with k elements will have the smallest k elements. The only remaining task is to print out the largest element of the tree.

Time Complexity:
1. For the first k elements, we make the tree. Hence the cost is $klogk$.
2. For the rest $n - k$ elements, the complexity is $O(logk)$.

Step 2 has a complexity of $(n - k)\, logk$. The total cost is $klogk + (n - k)logk = nlogk$ which is $O(nlogk)$. This bound is actually better than the ones provided earlier.

Problem-10   Can we use partitioning technique for solving Problem-6?

Solution: Yes.
Algorithm
1. Choose a pivot from the array.
2. Partition the array so that: $A[low...pivotpoint - 1] <= pivotpoint <= A[pivotpoint + 1..high]$.
3. if $k < pivotpoint$ then it must be on the left of pivot, so do the same method recursively on the left part
4. if $k = pivotpoint$ then it must be the pivot and print all the elements from *low* to *pivotpoint*.
5. if $k > pivotpoint$ then it must be on the right of pivot, so do the same method recursively on the right part.

The top-level call would be kthSmallest = Selection(1, n, k).

```
int Selection (int low, int high, int k) {
        int pivotpoint;
        if(low == high)
                return S[low];
        else {
                pivotpoint = Partition (low, high);
                if(k == pivotpoint)
                        return S[pivotpoint];
                else if(k < pivotpoint)
                        return Selection (low, pivotpoint - 1, k);
                else    return Selection (pivotpoint + 1, high, k);
        }
}
void Partition (int low, int high) {
        int i, j = low, pivotitem= S[low];
        for (i = low + 1; i <= high; i++)
                if(S[i] < pivotitem) {
                        j++;
                        Swap S[i] and S[j];
                }
        pivotpoint = j;
        Swap S[low] and S[pivotpoint];
        return pivotpoint;
}
```

Time Complexity: $O(n^2)$ in worst case as similar to Quicksort. Although the worst case is the same as that of Quicksort, this performs much better on the average [$O(nlogk)$ – Average case].

Problem-11   Find the kth-smallest element in an array S of n elements in best possible way.

Solution: This problem is similar to Problem-6 and all the solutions discussed for Problem-6 are valid for this problem. The only difference is that instead of printing all the k elements we print only the k^{th}element. We can improve the solution by using *median of medians* algorithm. Median is a special case of the selection algorithm. The algorithm Selection(A, k) to find the kth smallest element from set A of n elements is as follows:

Algorithm: *Selection(A, k)*

1. Partition A into $ceil\left(\frac{length(A)}{5}\right)$ groups, with each group having five items (last group may have fewer items).
2. Sort each group separately (e.g., insertion sort).
3. Find the median of each of the $\frac{n}{5}$ groups and store them in some array (let us say A').
4. Use *Selection* recursively to find the median of A' (median of medians). Let us asay the median of medians is m.

$$m = Selection(A', \frac{\frac{length(A)}{5}}{2});$$

5. Let q = # elements of A smaller than m;
6. If($k == q + 1$)
    return m;
    /* Partition with pivot */
7. Else partition A into X and Y
    - X = {items smaller than m}
    - Y = {items larger than m}

    /* Next, form a subproblem */
8. If($k < q + 1$)
    return Selection(X, k);
9. Else
    return Selection(Y, k – (q+1));

Before developing recurrence, let us consider the representation below of the input. In the figure each circle is an element and each column is grouped with 5 elements. The black circles indicate the median in each group of 5 elements. As discussed, sort each column using constant time insertion sort.

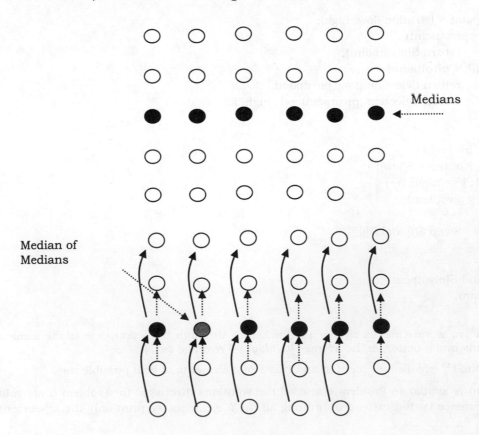

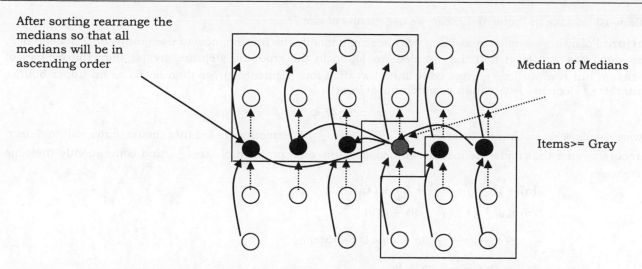

After sorting rearrange the medians so that all medians will be in ascending order

Median of Medians

Items>= Gray

In the figure above the gray circled item is the median of medians (let us call this m). It can be seen that at least 1/2 of 5 element group medians $\leq m$. Also, these 1/2 of 5 element groups contribute 3 elements that are $\leq m$ except 2 groups [last group which may contain fewer than 5 elements and other group which contains m]. Similarly, at least 1/2 of 5 element groups contribute 3 elements that are $\geq m$ as shown above. 1/2 of 5 element groups contribute 3 elements except 2 groups gives: $3(\frac{1}{2}\lceil\frac{n}{5}\rceil\text{-}2) \approx \frac{3n}{10} - 6$. The remaining are $n - \frac{3n}{10} - 6 \approx \frac{7n}{10} + 6$. Since $\frac{7n}{10} + 6$ is greater than $\frac{3n}{10} - 6$ we need to consider $\frac{7n}{10} + 6$ for worstcase analysis.

Components in recurrence:

*   In our selection algorithm, we choose m, which is the median of medians, to be a pivot and partition A into two sets X and Y. We need to select the set which gives maximum size.
*   The time in function *Selection* when called from procedure *partition*. The number of keys in the input to this call to *Selection* is $\frac{n}{5}$.
*   The number of comparisons required to partition the array. This number is $length(S)$, let us say n.

We have established the following recurrence: $T(n) = T\left(\frac{n}{5}\right) + \Theta(n) + Max\{T(X), T(Y)\}$

From the above discussion we have seen that, if we select median of medians m as pivot, the partition sizes are: $\frac{3n}{10} - 6$ and $\frac{7n}{10} + 6$. If we select the maximum of these, then we get:

$$\begin{aligned} T(n) &= T\left(\frac{n}{5}\right) + \Theta(n) + T\left(\frac{7n}{10} + 6\right) \\ &\approx T\left(\frac{n}{5}\right) + \Theta(n) + T\left(\frac{7n}{10}\right) + O(1) \\ &\leq c\frac{7n}{10} + c\frac{n}{5} + \Theta(n) + O(1) \end{aligned}$$

Finally, $T(n) = \Theta(n)$.

Problem-12   In Problem-11, we divided the input array into groups of 5 elements. The constant 5 play an important part in the analysis. Can we divide in groups of 3 which work in linear time?

Solution: In this case the modification causes the routine to take more than linear time. In the worst case, at least half the $\lceil\frac{n}{3}\rceil$ medians found in the grouping step are greater than the median of medians m, but two of those groups contribute less than two elements larger than m. So as an upper bound, the number of elements larger than pivotpoint is at least:

$$2(\frac{1}{2}\lceil\frac{n}{3}\rceil - 2) \geq \frac{n}{3} - 4$$

Likewise this is a lower bound. Thus up to $n - (\frac{n}{3} - 4) = \frac{2n}{3} + 4$ elements are fed into the recursive call to *Select*. The recursive step that finds the median of medians runs on a problem of size $\lceil\frac{n}{3}\rceil$, and consequently the time recurrence is:

$$T(n) = T(\lceil n/3 \rceil) + T(2n/3 + 4) + \Theta(n).$$

Assuming that $T(n)$ is monotonically increasing, we may conclude that $T(\frac{2n}{3} + 4) \geq T(\frac{2n}{3}) \geq 2T(\frac{n}{3})$, and we can say upper bound for this as $T(n) \geq 3T(\frac{n}{3}) + \Theta(n)$, which is O($nlogn$). Therefore, we cannot select 3 as the group size.

Problem-13   Like in Problem-12, can we use groups of size 7?

Solution: Following a similar reasoning, we once more modify the routine, now to use groups of 7 instead of 5. In the worst case, at least half the $\lceil \frac{n}{7} \rceil$ medians found in the grouping step are greater than the median of medians m, but two of those groups contribute less than four elements larger than m. So as an upper bound, the number of elements larger than pivotpoint is at least:

$$4(\lceil \frac{1}{2} \lceil \frac{n}{7} \rceil \rceil - 2) \geq \frac{2n}{7} - 8.$$

Likewise this is a lower bound. Thus up to $n - (\frac{2n}{7} - 8) = \frac{5n}{7} + 8$ elements are fed into the recursive call to Select. The recursive step that finds the median of medians runs on a problem of size $\lceil \frac{n}{7} \rceil$, and consequently the time recurrence is

$$T(n) = T(\lceil \frac{n}{7} \rceil) + T(\frac{5n}{7} + 8) + O(n)$$

$$T(n) \leq c\lceil \frac{n}{7} \rceil + c(\frac{5n}{7} + 8) + O(n)$$

$$\leq c\frac{n}{7} + c\frac{5n}{7} + 8c + an, a \text{ is a constant}$$

$$= cn - c\frac{n}{7} + an + 9c$$

$$= (a + c)n - (c\frac{n}{7} - 9c).$$

This is bounded above by $(a + c)n$ provided that $c\frac{n}{7} - 9c \geq 0$.

∴ We can select 7 as the group size.

Problem-14   Given two arrays each containing n sorted elements, give an O($logn$)-time algorithm to find the median of all $2n$ elements.

Solution: The simple solution to this problem is to merge the two lists and then take the average of the middle two elements (note the union always contains an even number of values). But, the merge would be $\Theta(n)$, so that doesn't satisfy the problem statement. To get $logn$ complexity, the general idea which we get is using binary search. Let $medianA$ and $medianB$ be the medians of the respective lists (which are easily found since both lists are sorted). If $medianA == medianB$, then that's the overall median of the union and we are done. Otherwise, the median of the union must be between $medianA$ and $medianB$. Suppose that $medianA < medianB$ (opposite case is entirely similar). Then we need to find the median of the union of the following two sets:

$$\{x \text{ in } A \mid x >= medianA\} \, \{x \text{ in } B \mid x <= medianB\}$$

So, we can do this recursively by resetting the "boundaries" of the two arrays. The algorithm tracks both arrays (which are sorted) using two indices. These indices are used to access and compare the median of both arrays to find where the overall median lies.

```
FindMedian(int A[], int alo , int ahi, int B[], int blo int bhi) {
        amid = alo + (ahi-alo)/2;
        amed = a[amid];
        bmid = blo + (bhi-blo)/2;
        bmed = b[bmid];
        if( ahi - alo + bhi - blo < 4) {
                Handle the boundary cases and solve it smaller problem in O(1) time.
                return;
        }
        else if(amed < bmed)
                FindMedian(A, amid, ahi, B, blo, bmid+1);
        else    FindMedian(A, alo, amid+1,B, bmid+1, bhi);
}
```

Time Complexity: O($logn$), since we are reducing the problem size by half every time.

Problem-15   Let A and B be two sorted arrays of n elements each. We can easily find the kth smallest element in A in O(1) time by just outputting $A[k]$. Similarly, we can easily find the kth smallest element in B. Give an O($logk$) time algorithm to find the kth smallest element overall { *i.e.*, the kth smallest in the union of A and B.

Solution: It's just another way of asking Problem-14.

Problem-16   **Find the k smallest elements in sorted order:** Given a set of n elements from a totally-ordered domain, find the k smallest elements, and list them in sorted order. Analyze the worst-case running time of the best implementation of the approach.

Solution: Sort the numbers, and list the k smallest.

$T(n)$ = Time complexity of sort + listing k smallest elements = $\Theta(n\, log n) + \Theta(n) = \Theta_{(n\, log n)}$

Problem-17   For Problem-16, if we follow the approach below then what is the complexity?

Solution: Using the priority queue data structure from heap sort, construct a min-heap over the set, and perform extract-min k times. Refer *Priority Queues (Heaps)* chapter for more details.

Problem-18   For Problem-16, if we follow the approach below then what is the complexity?
Find the kth-smallest element of the set, partition around this pivot element, and sort the k smallest elements.

Solution:
$T(n)$ = *Time complexity of kth − smallest + Finding pivot + Sorting prefix*
     = $\Theta(n) + \Theta(n) + \Theta(k\, log k)$
     = $\Theta(n + k\, log k)$

Since, $k \leq n$, this approach is bettern than Problem-16 and Problem-17.

Problem-19   Find k nearest neighbors to the median of n distinct numbers in $O(n)$ time.

Solution: Let us assume that the array elements are sorted. Now find the median of n numbers and call its index as X (since array is sorted, median will be at $\frac{n}{2}$ location). All we need to do is to select k elements with the smallest absolute differences from the median moving from $X - 1$ to 0 and $X + 1$ to $n - 1$ when the median is at index m.

Time Complexity: Each step takes $\Theta(n)$. So the total time complexity of the algorithm is $\Theta(n)$.

Problem-20   Is there any other way of solving the Problem-19?

Solution: Assume for simplicity that n is odd and k is even. If set A is in sorted order, the median is in position $n/2$ and the k numbers in A that are closest to the median are in positions $(n - k)/2$ through $(n + k)/2$.

We first use linear time selection to find the $(n - k)/2, n/2$, and $(n + k)/2$ elements and then pass through the set A to find the numbers less than $(n + k)/2$ element, greater than the $(n - k)/2$ element, and not equal to the $n/2$ element. The algorithm takes $O(n)$ time as we use linear time selection exactly three times and traverse the n numbers in A once.

Problem-21   Given (x, y) coordinates of n houses, where should you build a road parallel to x-axis to minimize construction cost of building driveways?

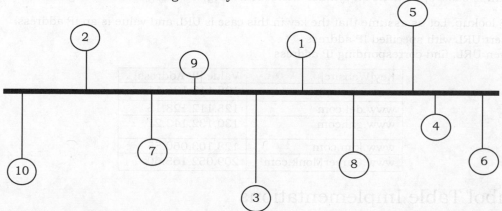

Solution: The road costs nothing to build. It is the driveways that cost money. Driveway cost is proportional to its distance to road. Obviously, they will be perpendicular. Solution is to put street at median of y coordinates.

Problem-22   Given a big file containing billions of numbers. Find maximum 10 numbers from that file.

Solution: Refer *Priority Queues* chapter.

Problem-23   Suppose there is a milk company. The company collects milk everyday from all its agents. The agents are located at different places. To collect the milk, what is the best place to start so that the least amount of total distance is travelled?

Solution: Starting at median reduces total distance travelled because it is the place which is at the center to all remaining places.

Chapter-13

SYMBOL TABLES

13.1 Introduction

Since childhood, we all have used a dictionary, and many of us have a word processor (say, Microsoft Word), which comes with spell checker. The spell checker is also a dictionary but limited in scope. There are many real time examples for dictionaries and few of them are:

- Spelling checker
- The data dictionary found in database management applications
- Symbol tables generated by loaders, assemblers, and compilers
- Routing tables in networking components (DNS lookup)

In computer science, we generally use the term symbol table rather than dictionary, when referring to the ADT.

13.2 What are Symbol Tables?

We can define the *symbol table* as a data structure that associates a *value* with a *key*. It supports the following operations:

- Search whether a particular name is in the table
- Get the attributes of that name
- Modify the attributes of that name
- Insert a new name and its attributes
- Delete a name and its attributes

There are only three basic operations on symbol tables: searching, inserting, and deleting.

Example: DNS lookup. Let us assume that the key in this case is URL and value is an IP address.

- Insert URL with specified IP address
- Given URL, find corresponding IP address

Key[Website]	Value [IP Address]
www.abc.com	128.112.136.11
www.def.com	128.112.128.15
www.ghi.com	130.132.143.21
www.klm.com	128.103.060.55
www.CareerMonk.com	209.052.165.60

13.3 Symbol Table Implementations

Before implementing symbol tables, let us enumerate the possible implementations. Symbol tables can be implemented in many ways and some of them are listed below.

Unordered Array Implementation

With this method, just maintaining an array is enough. It needs O(n) time for searching, insertion and deletion in the worst case.

Ordered [Sorted] Array Implementation

In this we maintain a sorted array of keys and values.

- Store in sorted order by key
- keys[i] = i^{th} largest key
- values[i] = value associated with i^{th} largest key

Since the elements are sorted and stored in arrays, we can use simple binary search for finding an element. It takes O($logn$) time for searching and O(n) time for insertion and deletion in the worst case.

Unordered Linked List Implementation

Just maintaining a linked list with two data values is enough for this method. It needs O(n) time for searching, insertion and deletion in the worst case.

Ordered Linked List Implementation

In this method, while inserting the keys, maintain the order of keys in the linked list. Even if the list is sorted, in the worst case it needs O(n) time for searching, insertion and deletion.

Binary Search Trees Implementation

Refer *Trees* chapter. Advantages of this method are it does not need much code and fast search [O($logn$) on average].

Balanced Binary Search Trees Implementation

Refer *Trees* chapter. It is an extension of binary search trees implementation and takes O($logn$) in worst case for search, insert and delete operations.

Ternary Search Implementation

Refer *String Algorithms* chapter. This is one of the important methods used for implementing dictionaries.

Hashing Implementation

This method is important. For complete discussion refer to *Hashing* chapter.

13.4 Comparison of Symbol Table Implementations

Let us consider the following comparison table for all the implementations.

Implementation	Search	Insert	Delete
Unordered Array	n	n	n
Ordered Array (can be implemented with array binary search)	$logn$	n	n
Unordered List	n	n	n
Ordered List	n	n	n
Binary Search Trees (O($logn$) on average)	$logn$	$logn$	$logn$
Balanced Binary Search Trees (O($logn$) in worst case)	$logn$	$logn$	$logn$
Ternary Search (only change is in logarithms base)	$logn$	$logn$	$logn$
Hashing (O(1) on average)	1	1	1

Notes:

- In the above table, n is the input size.
- Table indicates the possible implementations discussed in this book. But, there could be other implementations.

Chapter-14

HASHING

14.1 What is Hashing?

Hashing is a technique used for storing and retrieving information as fast as possible. It is used to perform optimal search and is useful in implementing symbol tables.

14.2 Why Hashing?

In *Trees* chapter we have seen that balanced binary search trees support operations such as *insert*, *delete* and *search* in O(*logn*) time. In applications if we need these operations in O(1), then hashing provides a way. Remember that worst case complexity of hashing is still O(*n*), but it gives O(1) on the average.

14.3 HashTable ADT

The common operations on hash table are:

- CreatHashTable: Creates a new hash table
- HashSearch: Searches the key in hash table
- HashInsert: Inserts a new key into hash table
- HashDelete: Deletes a key from hash table
- DeleteHashTable: Deletes the hash table

14.4 Understanding Hashing

In simple terms we can treat *array* as a hash table. For understanding the use of hash tables, let us consider the following example: Give an algorithm for printing the first repeated character if there are duplicated elements in it.

Let us think about the possible solutions. The simple and brute force way of solving is: given a string, for each character check whether that character is repeated or not. Time complexity of this approach is O(n^2) with O(1) space complexity.

Now, let us find the better solution for this problem. Since our objective is to find the first repeated character, what if we remember the previous characters in some array?

We know that the number of possible characters is 256 (for simplicity assume *ASCII* characters only). Create an array of size 256 and initialize it with all zeros. For each of the input characters go to the corresponding position and increment its count. Since we are using arrays, it takes constant time for reaching any location. While scanning the input, if we get a character whose counter is already 1 then we can say that the character is the one which is repeating first time.

```
char FirstRepeatedChar ( char [] str ) {
        int count[256]; //additional array
        for(int i=0; i<256; ++i)
               count[i] = 0;
        for(int i=0; i< str.length; ++i) {
               if(count[str[i]]==1) {
                       System.out.println(str[i]);
                       break;
               }
               else
                       count[str[i]]++;
        }
        if(i==len)
               System.out.println("No Repeated Characters");
        return 0;
}
```

Why not Arrays?

In the previous problem, we have used an array of size 256 because we know the number of different possible characters [256] in advance. Now, let us consider a slight variant of the same problem. Suppose the given array has numbers instead of characters then how do we solve the problem?

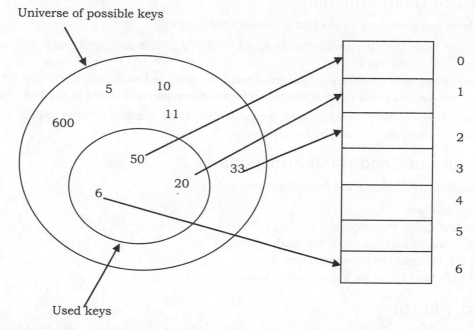

In this case the set of possible values is infinity (or at least very big). Creating a huge array and storing the counters is not possible. That means there are a set of universal keys and limited locations in the memory. If we want to solve this problem we need to somehow map all these possible keys to the possible memory locations.

From the above discussion and diagram it can be seen that we need a mapping of possible keys to one of the available locations. As a result using simple arrays is not the correct choice for solving the problems whose possible keys are very big. The process of mapping the keys to locations is called *hashing*.

Note: For now, do not worry about how the keys are mapped to locations. That depends on the function used for conversions. One such simple function is *key % table size*.

14.5 Components of Hashing

Hashing has four key components:
1) Hash Table
2) Hash Functions
3) Collisions
4) Collision Resolution Techniques

14.6 Hash Table

Hash table is a generalization of array. With an array, we store the element whose key is k at a position k of the array. That means, given a key k, we find the element whose key is k by just looking in the kth position of the array. This is called *direct addressing*.

Direct addressing is applicable when we can afford to allocate an array with one position for every possible key. Suppose we do not have enough space to allocate a location for each possible key then we need a mechanism to handle this case. Other way of defining the scenario is, if we have less locations and more possible keys then simple array implementation is not enough.

In these cases one option is to use hash tables. Hash table or hash map is a data structure that stores the keys and their associated values. Hash table uses a hash function to map keys to their associated values. General convention is that we use a hash table when the number of keys actually stored is small relative to the number of possible keys.

14.7 Hash Function

The hash function is used to transform the key into the index. Ideally, the hash function should map each possible key to a unique slot index, but it is difficult to achieve in practice.

How to Choose Hash Function?

The basic problems associated with the creation of hash tables are:

- An efficient hash function should be designed so that it distributes the index values of inserted objects uniformly across the table.
- An efficient collision resolution algorithm should be designed so that it computes an alternative index for a key whose hash index corresponds to a location previously inserted in the hash table.
- We must choose a hash function which can be calculated quickly, returns values within the range of locations in our table, and minimizes collisions.

Characteristics of Good Hash Functions

A good hash function should have the following characteristics:

- Minimize collision
- Be easy and quick to compute
- Distribute key values evenly in the hash table
- Use all the information provided in the key
- Have a high load factor for a given set of keys

14.8 Load Factor

The load factor of a non empty hash table is the number of items stored in the table divided by the size of the table. This is the decision parameter used when we want to rehash *or* expand the existing hash table entries. This also helps us in determining the efficiency of the hashing function. That means, it tells whether the hash function is distributing the keys uniformly or not.

$$Load\ factor = \frac{Number\ of\ elements\ in\ hash\ table}{Hash\ Table\ size}$$

14.9 Collisions

Hash functions are used to map each key to different address space but practically it is not possible to create such a hash function and the problem is called *collision*. Collision is the condition where two records are stored in the same location.

14.10 Collision Resolution Techniques

The process of finding an alternate location is called *collision resolution*. Even though hash tables are having collision problem, they are more efficient in many cases comparative to all other data structures like search trees. There are a number of collision resolution techniques, and the most popular are open addressing and chaining.

- **Direct Chaining:** An array of linked list application
  - Separate chaining
- **Open Addressing:** Array based implementation
  - Linear probing (linear search)
  - Quadratic probing (non linear search)
  - Double hashing (use two hash functions)

14.11 Separate Chaining

Collision resolution by chaining combines linked representation with hash table. When two or more records hash to the same location, these records are constituted into a singly-linked list called a *chain*.

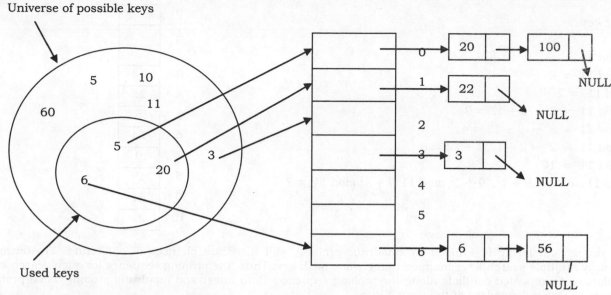

14.12 Open Addressing

In open addressing all keys are stored in the hash table itself. This approach is also known as *closed hashing*. This procedure is based on probing. A collision is resolved by probing.

Linear Probing

Interval between probes is fixed at 1. In linear probing, we search the hash table sequentially starting from the original hash location. If a location is occupied, we check the next location. We wrap around from the last table location to the first table location if necessary. The function for rehashing is the following:

$$rehash(key) = (n+1)\% \, tablesize$$

One of the problems with linear probing is that table items tend to cluster together in the hash table. This means that table contains groups of consecutively occupied locations that are called *clustering*.

Clusters can get close to one another, and merge into a larger cluster. Thus, the one part of the table might be quite dense, even though another part has relatively few items. Clustering causes long probe searches and therefore decreases the overall efficiency.

The next location to be probed is determined by the step-size, where other step-sizes (than one) are possible. The step-size should be relatively prime to the table size, i.e. their greatest common divisor should be equal to 1. If we choose the table size to be a prime number, then any step-size is relatively prime to the table size. Clustering cannot be avoided by larger step-sizes.

Quadratic Probing

Interval between probes increases proportional to the hash value (the interval thus increasing linearly and the indices are described by a quadratic function). Clustering problem can be eliminated if we use quadratic probing method. In quadratic probing, we start from the original hash location i. If a location is occupied, we check the locations $i + 1^2$, $i + 2^2$, $i + 3^2$, $i + 4^2$...We wrap around from the last table location to the first table location if necessary. The function for the rehashing is the following:

$$rehash(key) = (n + k^2)\% \, tablesize$$

Example: Let us assume that the table size is 11 (0..10)
Hash Function: h(key) = key mod 11

Insert keys:

$31 \bmod 11 = 9$

$19 \bmod 11 = 8$

$2 \bmod 11 = 2$

$13 \bmod 11 = 2 \rightarrow 2 + 12 = 3$

$25 \bmod 11 = 3 \rightarrow 3 + 12 = 4$

$24 \bmod 11 = 2 \rightarrow 2 + 12, 2 + 22 = 6$

$21 \bmod 11 = 10$

$9 \bmod 11 = 9 \rightarrow 9 + 1^2, 9 + 2^2 \bmod 11, 9 + 3^2 \bmod 11 = 7$

0	
1	
2	2
3	13
4	25
5	5
6	24
7	9
8	19
9	31
10	21

Even though clustering is avoided by quadratic probing, still there are chances of clustering. Clustering is caused by multiple search keys mapped to the same hash key. Thus, the probing sequence for such search keys is prolonged by repeated conflicts along the probing sequence. Both linear and quadratic probing use a probing sequence that is independent of the search key.

Double Hashing

Interval between probes is computed by another hash function. Double hashing reduces clustering in a better way. The increments for the probing sequence are computed by using a second hash function. The second hash function $h2$ should be:

$$h2(key) \neq 0 \text{ and } h2 \neq h1$$

We first probe the location $h1(key)$. If the location is occupied, we probe the location $h1(key) + h2(key)$, $h1(key) + 2 * h2(key)$, ...

Example:

Table size is 11 (0..10)
Hash Function: assume $h1(key) = key \bmod 11$ and
$$h2(key) = 7 - (key \bmod 7)$$

Insert keys:

$58 \bmod 11 = 3$

$14 \bmod 11 = 3 \rightarrow 3 + 7 = 10$

$91 \bmod 11 = 3 \rightarrow 3 + 7, 3 + 2 * 7 \bmod 11 = 6$

$25 \bmod 11 = 3 \rightarrow 3 + 3, 3 + 2 * 3 = 9$

0	
1	
2	
3	58
4	25
5	
6	91
7	
8	
9	25
10	14

14.13 Comparison of Collision Resolution Techniques

Comparisons: Linear Probing vs. Double Hashing

The choice between linear probing and double hashing depends on the cost of computing the hash function and on the load factor [number of elements per slot] of the table. Both use few probes but double hashing take more time because it hashes to compare two hash functions for long keys.

Comparisons: Open Addressing vs. Separate Chaining

It is somewhat complicated because we have to account for the memory usage. Separate chaining uses extra memory for links. Open addressing needs extra memory implicitly within the table to terminate probe sequence. Open-addressed hash tables cannot be used if the data does not have unique keys. An alternative is to use separate chained hash tables.

Comparisons: Open Addressing methods

Linear Probing	Quadratic Probing	Double hashing
Fastest among three	Easiest to implement and deploy	Makes more efficient use of memory
Uses few probes	Uses extra memory for links and it does not probe all locations in the table	Use few probes but take more time
A problem occurs known as primary clustering	A problem occurs known as secondary clustering	More complicated to implement
Interval between probes is fixed - often at 1.	Interval between probes increases proportional to the hash value	Interval between probes is computed by another hash function

14.14 How Hashing Gets O(1) Complexity?

From the previous discussion, one doubts how hashing gets O(1) if multiple elements map to the same location? The answer to this problem is simple. By using load factor we make sure that each block (for example linked list in separate chaining approach) on the average stores maximum number of elements less than *load factor*. Also, in practice this load factor is a constant (generally, 10 or 20). As a result, searching in 20 elements or 10 elements becomes constant.

If the average number of elements in a block is greater than load factor then we rehash the elements with bigger hash table size. One thing we should remember is that we consider average occupancy (total number of elements in the hash table divided by table size) while deciding the rehash.

The access time of table depends on the load factor which in turn depends on the hash function. This is because hash function distributes the elements to hash table. For this reason, we say hash table gives O(1) complexity on the average. Also, we generally use hash tables in cases where searches are more than insertion and deletion operations.

14.15 Hashing Techniques

There are two types of hashing techniques: static hashing and dynamic hashing

Static Hashing

If data is not fixed static hashing can give bad performance and dynamic hashing is the alternative for such types of data. The set of keys can change dynamically in this.

Dynamic Hashing

If data not fixed static hashing can give bad performance and dynamic hashing is the next alternative for such type of data. The set of keys can change dynamically in this.

14.16 Problems for which Hash Tables are not Suitable

- Problems for which data ordering is required.
- Problems having multidimensional data.
- Prefix searching especially if the keys are long and of variable-lengths.
- Problems that have dynamic data
- Problems in which the data does not have unique keys.

14.17 Bloom Filters

A Bloom filter is a probabilistic data structure which was designed to check whether an element is present in a set with memory and time efficiency. It tells us that the element either definitely is *not* in the set or may be in the set. The base data structure of a Bloom filter is a *Bit Vector*.

The algorithm was invented in 1970 by Burton Bloom and it relies on the use of a number of different hash functions.

How it works?

A Bloom filter starts off with a bit array initialized to zero. To store a data value we simply apply k different hash functions and treat the resulting k values as indices into the array and set each of the k array elements to 1. We repeat this for every element that we encounter.

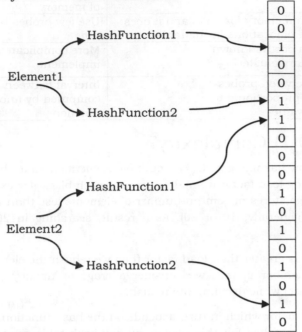

Now that the bits in the bit vector have been set for *Element*1 and *Element*2; we can query the bloom filter to tell us if something has been seen before.

The element is hashed but instead of setting the bits, this time a check is done and if the bits that would have been set are already set the bloom filter will return true that the element has been seen before.

Now suppose an element turns up and we want to know if we have seen it before. What we do is apply the k hash functions and look up the indicated array elements. If any of them are 0 we can be 100% sure that we have never encountered the element before - if we had the bit would have been set to 1. However even if all of them are one then we can't conclude that we have seen the element before because all of the bits could have been set by the k hash functions applied to multiple other elements. All we can conclude is that it is likely that we have encountered the element before.

Note that it is not possible to remove an element from a Bloom filter. The reason is simply that we can't unset a bit that appears to belong to an element because it might also be set by another element.

If the bit array is mostly empty i.e. set to zero and the k hash functions are independent of one another then the probability of a false positive (i.e. concluding that we have seen a data item when we actually haven't) is low. For example, if there are only k bits set we can conclude that the probability of a false positive is very close to zero as the only possibility of error is that we entered a data item that produced the same k hash values - which is unlikely as long as the has functions are independent.

As the bit array fills up the probability of a false positive slowly increases. Of course when the bit array is full every element queried is identified as having been seen before. So clearly we can trade space for accuracy as well as for time.

One-time removal of an element from a Bloom filter can be simulated by having a second Bloom filter that contains elements that have been removed. However, false positives in the second filter become false negatives in the composite filter, which may be undesirable. In this approach re-adding a previously removed item is not possible, as one would have to remove it from the *removed* filter.

Selecting hash functions

The requirement of designing k different independent hash functions can be prohibitive for large k. For a good hash function with a wide output, there should be little if any correlation between different bit-fields of such a hash, so this type of hash can be used to generate multiple *different* hash functions by slicing its output into multiple bit fields. Alternatively, one can pass k different initial values (such as 0, 1, ..., k - 1) to a hash function that takes an initial value; or add (or append) these values to the key. For larger m and/or k, independence among the hash functions can be relaxed with negligible increase in false positive rate.

Selecting size of bit vector

A Bloom filter with 1% error and an optimal value of k, in contrast, requires only about 9.6 bits per element — regardless of the size of the elements. This advantage comes partly from its compactness, inherited from arrays, and partly from its probabilistic nature. The 1% false-positive rate can be reduced by a factor of ten by adding only about 4.8 bits per element.

Space Advantages

While risking false positives, Bloom filters have a strong space advantage over other data structures for representing sets, such as self-balancing binary search trees, tries, hash tables, or simple arrays or linked lists of the entries. Most of these require storing at least the data items themselves, which can require anywhere from a small number of bits, for small integers, to an arbitrary number of bits, such as for strings (tries are an exception, since they can share storage between elements with equal prefixes). Linked structures incur an additional linear space overhead for pointers.

However, if the number of potential values is small and many of them can be in the set, the Bloom filter is easily surpassed by the deterministic bit array, which requires only one bit for each potential element.

Time Advantages

Bloom filters also have the unusual property that the time needed either to add items or to check whether an item is in the set is a fixed constant, $O(k)$, completely independent of the number of items already in the set. No other constant-space set data structure has this property, but the average access time of sparse hash tables can make them faster in practice than some Bloom filters. In a hardware implementation, however, the Bloom filter shines because its k lookups are independent and can be parallelized.

14.18 Problems on Hashing

Problem-1   Implement separate chaining collision resolution technique. Also, discuss time complexities of each function.

Solution: To create a hashtable of given size, say n, we allocate an array of n/L (whose value is usually between 5 and 20) pointers to list, initialized to NULL. To perform *Search/Insert/Delete* operations, we first compute the index of the table from the given key by using *hashfunction* and then do the corresponding operation in the linear list maintained at that location. To get uniform distribution of keys over a hashtable, maintain table size as prime number.

```java
public class ListNode {
        private int key;
        private int data;
        private ListNode next;
        public int getKey() {
                return key;
        }
        public void setKey(int key) {
                this.key = key;
        }
        public int getData() {
                return data;
        }
        public void setData(int data) {
                this.data = data;
        }
        public ListNode getNext() {
                return next;
        }
        public void setNext(ListNode next) {
                this.next = next;
        }
}
public class HashTableNode {
        private int blockCount;
        private ListNode startNode;
        public int getBlockCount() {
                return blockCount;
        }
        public void setBlockCount(int blockCount) {
                this.blockCount = blockCount;
        }
```

```java
        public ListNode getStartNode() {
                return startNode;
        }
        public void setStartNode(ListNode startNode) {
                this.startNode = startNode;
        }
}
public class HashTable {
        private int tSize;
        private int count;
        private HashTableNode[] table;
        public int getTSize() {
                return tSize;
        }
        public void setTSize(int size) {
                tSize = size;
                table = new HashTableNode[size];
        }
        public int getCount() {
                return count;
        }
        public void setCount(int count) {
                this.count = count;
        }
        public HashTableNode[] getTable() {
                return table;
        }
        public void setTable(HashTableNode[] table) {
                this.table = table;
        }
}
public class HashTableOperations {
        public final static int LOADFACTOR = 20;
        public static HashTable createHashTable(int size){
                HashTable h = new HashTable();
                //count is set to zero by default;
                h.setTSize(size/LOADFACTOR);
                for(int i=0;i<h.getTSize();i++){
                        h.getTable()[i].setStartNode(null);
                }
                return h;
        }
        public static int hashSearch(HashTable h, int data){
                ListNode temp;
                temp = h.getTable()[Hash(data, h.getTSize())].getStartNode();
                while(temp) {
                        if(temp.getData() == data)
                                return 1;
                        temp = temp.getNext();
                }
                return 0;

        }
        public static void hashInsert(HashTable h, int data){
                int index;
                ListNode temp, newNode;
                if(hashSearch(h, data))
                        return 0;
                index = Hash(data, h.getTSize()); //Assume Hash is a built-in function
                temp = h.getTable()[index].getNext();
                newNode = new ListNode();
                if(newNode == null) {
                        System.out.println("Memory Error");
                        return;
```

```
                }
                newNode.setKey(index);
                newNode.setData(data);
                newNode.setNext(h.getTable()[index].getNext());
                h.getTable()[index].setNext(newNode);
                h.getTable()[index].setBlockCount(h.getTable()[index].getBlockCount() + 1);
                h.setCount(h.getCount() + 1);
                if(h.getCount() / h.getTSize() > LOAD_FACTOR)
                        Rehash(h);
                return;
        }
        public static boolean hashDelete(HashTable h, int data){
                ListNode temp, prev;
                int index = Hash(data, h.getTSize());
                for(temp = h.getTable()[index].getNext(), prev = null; temp;
                                        prev = temp, temp = temp.getNext()) {
                        if(temp.getData() == data) {
                                if(prev != null)
                                        prev.setNext(temp.getNext());
                                temp = null;
                                h.getTable()[index].setBlockCount(h.getTable()[index].getBlockCount() - 1);
                                h.setCount(h.getCount() - 1);
                                return 1;
                        }
                }
                return 0;
        }
        public static void rehash(HashTable h){
                int oldsize, i, index;
                ListNode p, temp, temp2;
                HashTableNode oldTable;
                oldsize = h.getTSize();
                oldTable = h.getTable();
                h.setTSize(h.getTSize() * 2);
                h = new HashTable();
                if(!h.getTable()) {
                        System.out.println( "Memory Error");
                        return;
                }
                for(i = 0; i < oldsize; i++) {
                        for(temp = oldTable[i].getNext(); temp; temp = temp.getNext()) {
                                index = Hash(temp.getData(), h.getTSize());
                                temp2 = temp;
                                temp = temp.getNext();
                                temp2.setNext(h.getTable()[i].getNext());
                                h.getTable()[index].setNext(temp2);
                        }
                }
        }
}
```

CreatHashTable – O(n). HashSearch – O(1) average. HashInsert – O(1) average. HashDelete – O(1) average.

Problem-2   Given an array of characters, give an algorithm for removing the duplicates.

Solution: Start with the first character and check whether it appears in the remaining part of the string using simple linear search. If it repeats then bring the last character to that position and decrement the size of the string by one. Continue this process for each distinct character of the given string.

```
void RemoveDuplicates(char[] s, int n) {
        for(int i = 0; i < n; i++) {
                for(int j = i+1; j < n; ) {
                        if(s[i] == s[j])
                                s[j] = s[--n];
                        else    j++;
```

```
        }
    }
    s[i] = '\0';
}
```

Time Complexity: O(n^2). Space Complexity: O(1).

Problem-3   Can we find any other idea to solve this problem in better time than O(n^2)? Observe that order of characters in solutions do not matter.

Solution: Use sorting to bring the repeated characters together. Finally scan through the array to remove duplicates in consecutive positions.

```
//With Char[] as input
public static void removeDuplicates(char[] str, int len) {
        if (str == null)    return;
        if (len < 2)     return;
        int tail = 1;
        for (int i = 1; i < len; ++i) {
                for (int j = 0; j < tail; ++j) {
                        if (str[i] == str[j]) break;
                }
                if (j == tail) {
                        str[tail] = str[i];
                        ++tail;
                }
        }
        str[tail] = 0;
}
//With String as input
public static String removeDuplicates(String s) {
        StringBuilder noDupes = new StringBuilder();
        for (int i = 0; i < s.length(); i++) {
                String si = s.substring(i, i + 1);
                if (noDupes.indexOf(si) == -1) {
                        noDupes.append(si);
                }
        }
        return noDupes.toString();
}
//Sporting Approach
public static String removeDuplicates(String s) {
        char[] chars = s.toCharArray();
        Arrays.sort(chars);
        String sorted = new String(chars);
        System.out.println(sorted);
}
```

Time Complexity: $\Theta(nlogn)$. Space Complexity: O(1).

Problem-4   Can we solve this problem in single pass over given array?

Solution: We can use hash table to check whether a character is repeating in the given string or not. If the current character is not available in hash table then insert it into hash table and keep that character in the given string also. If the current character exists in the hash table then skip that character.

```
void RemoveDuplicates(char[] s) {
        int src, dst;
        HastTable h = new HashTable();
        current = last = 0;
        for(; s[current]; current++) {
                if( !HashSearch(h, s[current]))    {
                        s[last++] = s[current];
                        HashInsert(h, s[current]);
                }
        }
        s[last] = '\0';
}
```

Time Complexity: $\Theta(n)$ on average. Space Complexity: O(n).

Problem-5   Given two arrays of unordered numbers, check whether both arrays have the same set of numbers?

Solution: Let us assume that two given arrays are A and B. A simple solution to the given problem is: for each element of A check whether that element is in B or not. A problem arises with this approach if there are duplicates. For example consider the following inputs:

$$A = \{2,5,6,8,10,2,2\}$$
$$B = \{2,5,5,8,10,5,6\}$$

The above algorithm gives the wrong result because for each element of A there is an element in B also. But if we look at the number of occurrences then they are not the same. This problem we can solve by moving the elements which are already compared to the end of list. That means, if we find an element in B, then we move that element to the end of B and in the next searching we will not find those elements. But the disadvantage of this is it needs extra swaps. Time Complexity of this approach is $O(n^2)$. Since for each element of A we have to scan B.

Problem-6   Can we improve the time complexity of Problem-5?

Solution: Yes. To improve the time complexity, let us assume that we have sorted both the lists. Since the sizes of both arrays are n, we need $O(n \log n)$ time for sorting them. After sorting, we just need to scan both the arrays with two pointers and see whether they point to the same element every time and keep moving the pointers until we reach the end of arrays.

Time Complexity of this approach is $O(n \log n)$. This is because we need $O(n \log n)$ for sorting the arrays. After sorting, we need $O(n)$ time for scanning but it is less compared to $O(n \log n)$.

Problem-7   Can we further improve the time complexity of Problem-5?

Solution: Yes, by using hash table. For this, consider the following algorithm.

Algorithm:
- Construct the hash table with array *A* elements as keys.
- While inserting the elements keep track of number frequency for each number. That means, if there are duplicates, then increment the counter of that corresponding key.
- After constructing the hash table for *A's* elements, now scan the array *B*.
- For each occurrence of *B's* elements reduce the corresponding counter values.
- At the end, check whether all counters are zero or not
- If all counters are zero then both arrays are same otherwise the arrays are different.

Time Complexity: $O(n)$ for scanning the arrays Space Complexity: $O(n)$ for hash table.

Problem-8   Given a list of number pairs. If $pair(i,j)$ exist, and $pair(j,i)$ exist report all such pairs. For example, $\{\{1,3\},\{2,6\},\{3,5\},\{7,4\},\{3,5\},\{8,7\}\}$ here, $\{3,5\}$ and $\{5,3\}$ are present. To report this pair, when you encounter $\{5,3\}$. We call such pairs as symmetric pairs. So, given an efficient algorithm for finding all such pairs.

Solution: By using hashing, we can solve this problem just in one scan and consider the following algorithm.

Algorithm:
- Read pairs of elements one by one and insert them into the hash table. For each pair, consider the first element as key and second element as value.
- While inserting the elements, check if the hashing of second element of the current pair is same as of first number of the current pair.
- If they are same then that indicates symmetric pair exits and output that pair.
- Otherwise, insert that element in to that. That means, use first number of current pair as key and second number as value and insert into the hash table.
- By the time we complete the scanning of all pairs, we output all the symmetric pairs.

Time Complexity: $O(n)$ for scanning the arrays. Note that we are doing only scan of the input. Space Complexity: $O(n)$ for hash table.

Problem-9   Given a singly linked list, check whether it has any loop in it or not.

Solution: Using Hash Tables
Algorithm:
- Traverse the linked list nodes one by one.
- Check if the nodes address is there in the hash table or not.
- If it is already there in the hash table then that indicates that we are visiting the node which was already visited. This is possible only if the given linked list has a loop in it.

- If the address of the node is not there in the hash table then insert that nodes address into the hash table.
- Continue this process until we reach end of the linked list *or* we find loop.

Time Complexity: O(n) for scanning the linked list. Note that we are doing only scan of the input. Space Complexity: O(n) for hash table.

Note: for efficient solution refer *Linked Lists* chapter.

Problem-10   Given an array of 101 elements. Out of them 50 elements are distinct, 24 elements are repeated 2 times and one element is repeated 3 times. Find the element which repeated 3 times in O(1).

Solution: Using Hash Tables
Algorithm:
- Scan the input array one by one.
- Check if the element is already there in the hash table or not.
- If it is already there in the hash table then increment its counter value [this indicates the number of occurrence of the element].
- If the element is not there in the hash table then insert that node into the hash table with counter value 1.
- Continue this process until we reach end of the array.

Time Complexity: O(n), because we are doing two scans. Space Complexity: O(n), for hash table.

Note: For efficient solution refer *Searching* chapter.

Problem-11   Given m sets of integers that have n elements in them. Give an algorithm to find an element which appeared in maximum number of sets?

Solution: Using Hash Tables
Algorithm:
- Scan the input sets one by one.
- For each element keep track of the counter. Counter indicates the frequency of the occurrences in all the sets.
- After completing scanning of all the sets, select the one which has the maximum counter value.

Time Complexity: O(mn), because we need to scan all the sets. Space Complexity: O(mn), for hash table. Because, in the worst case all the elements may be different.

Problem-12   Given two sets A and B, and a number K, Give an algorithm for finding whether there exists a pair of elements, one from A and one from B, that add up to K.

Solution: For simplicity, let us assume that the size of A is m and size of B is n.

Algorithm:
- Select the set which has minimum elements.
- For the selected set create a hash table. We can use both key and value as the same.
- Now scan the second array and check whether (K-selected element) exits in the hash table or not.
- If it exits then return the pair of elements.
- Otherwise continue until we reach end of the set.

Time Complexity: O($Max(m,m)$), because we are doing two scans. Space Complexity: O($Min(m,m)$), for hash table. We can select the small set for creating the hash table.

Problem-13   Give an algorithm to remove the specified characters from a given string which are given in another string?

Solution: For simplicity, let us assume that the maximum number of different characters is 256. First we create an auxiliary array initialized to 0. Scan the characters to be removed and for each of those characters we set the value to 1, which indicates that we need to remove that character. After initialization, scan the input string and for each of the characters, we check whether that character needs to be deleted or not. If the flag is set then we simply skip to the next character otherwise we keep the character in the input string. Continue this process until we reach the end of the input string. All these operations we can do in-place as given below.

```java
void RemoveChars(char[] str, char[] removeTheseChars) {
        int srcInd, destInd;
        int auxi[256]; //additional array
        for(srcInd =0; srcInd<256; srcIndex++)
                auxi[srcInd]=0;
        //set true for all characters to be removed
        srcIndex=0;
```

```
        while(remove[srcInd]) {
                auxi[removeTheseChars[srcInd]]=1;
                srcInd++;
        }
        //copy chars unless it must be removed
        srcInd=destInd=0;
        while(str[srcInd++]) {
                if(!auxi[str[srcInd]])
                        str[destInd++]=str[srcInd];
        }
}
```

Time Complexity: Time for scanning the characters to be removed + Time for scanning the input array=$O(n) + O(m) \approx O(n)$. Where m is the length of the characters to be removed and n is the length of the input string.

Space Complexity: $O(m)$, length of the characters to be removed. But since we are assuming the maximum number of different characters is 256, we can treat this as a constant. But we should keep in mind that when we are dealing with multi-byte characters the total number of different characters is much more than 256.

Problem-13   Give an algorithm for finding the first non-repeated character in a string. For example, the first non-repeated character in the string "*abzddab*" is '*z*'.

Solution: The solution to this problem is trivial. For each character in the given string, we can scan the remaining string if that character appears in it. If does not appears then we are done with the solution and return that character. If the character appears in the remaining string then go to the next character.

```
char FirstNonRepeatedChar( char[] str , int len) {
        int i, j, repeated = 0;
        for(i = 0; i < len; i++ )    {
                repeated = 0;
                for( j = 0; j < len; j++ )    {
                        if( i != j && str[i] == str[j] ) {
                                repeated = 1;
                                break;
                        }
                }
                if( repeated == 0 ) {
                // Found the first non-repeated character
                        return str[i];
                }
        }
        return ";
}
```

Time Complexity: $O(n^2)$, for two for loops. Space Complexity: $O(1)$.

Problem-14   Can we improve the time complexity of Problem-13?

Solution: Yes. By using hash tables we can reduce the time complexity. Create a hash table by reading all the characters in the input string and keeping count of the number of times each character appears. After creating the hash table, we can read the hash table entries to see which element has a count equal to 1. This approach takes $O(n)$ space but reduces the time complexity also to $O(n)$.

```
char FirstNonRepeatedCharUsinghash( char[] str, int len ) {
        int i, count[256]; //additional array
        for(i=0;i<len;++i)
                count[i] = 0;
        for(i=0;i<len;++i)
                count[str[i]]++;
        for(i=0; i<len; ++i) {
                if(count[str[i]]==1) {
                        System.out.println(str[i]);
                        break;
                }
        }
        if(i==len) System.out.println("No Non-repeated Characters");
        return 0;
}
```

Time Complexity: We have $O(n)$ to create the hash table and another $O(n)$ to read the entries of hash table. So the total time is $O(n) + O(n) = O(2n) \approx O(n)$. Space Complexity: $O(n)$ for keeping the count values.

Problem-15   Given a string, give an algorithm for finding the first repeating letter in a string?

Solution: The solution to this problem is almost similar to Problem-13 and Problem-14. The only difference is, instead of scanning the hash table twice we can give the answer in one scan itself. This is because while inserting into the hash table we can see whether that element already exists or not. If it already exits then we just need to return that character.

```java
char FirstRepeatedCharUsinghash(char[] str, int len) {
        int i, count[256]; //additional array
        for(i=0;i<len;++i)
                count[i] = 0;
        for(i=0; i<len; ++i) {
                if(count[str[i]]==1) {
                        System.out.println("%s",str[i]);
                        break;
                }
                else    count[str[i]]++;
        }
        if(i==len) System.out.println("No Repeated Characters");
        return 0;
}
```

Time Complexity: We have $O(n)$ for scanning and create the hash table. Note that we need only one scan for this problem. So the total time is $O(n)$. Space Complexity: $O(n)$ for keeping the count values.

Problem-16   Given an array of n numbers. Give an algorithm which displays all pairs whose sum is S.

Solution: This problem is similar to Problem-12. But instead of using two sets we use only one set.

Algorithm:
- Scan the elements of the input array one by one and create a hash table. We can use both key and value are same.
- After creating the hash table, again scan the input array and check whether $(S - selected\ element)$ exits in the hash table *or* not.
- If it exits then return the pair of elements.
- Otherwise continue until we read all the elements of the array.

Time Complexity: We have $O(n)$ to create the hash table and another $O(n)$ to read the entries of hash table. So the total time is $O(n) + O(n) = O(2n) \approx O(n)$. Space Complexity: $O(n)$ for keeping the count values.

Problem-17   Is there any other way of solving Problem-16?

Solution: Yes. The alternative solution to this problem involves sorting. First sort the input array. After sorting, use two pointers one at the starting and another at the ending. Each time add the values of both the indexes and see if their sum is equal to S. If they are equal then print that pair. Otherwise increase left pointer if the sum is less than S and decrease the right pointer if the sum is greater than S.

Time Complexity: Time for sorting + Time for scanning = $O(n \log n) + O(n) \approx O(n \log n)$. Space Complexity: $O(1)$.

Problem-18   We have a file with millions of lines of data. Only two lines are identical; the rest are all unique. Each line is so long that it may not even fit in memory. What is the most efficient solution for finding the identical lines?

Solution: Since complete line may not fit into the main memory, read the line partially and compute the hash from that partial line. Next, again read the next part of line and compute the hash. This time use the previous has also while computing the new hash value. Continue this process until we find the hash for complete line.

Do this for each line and store all the hash values in some file [or maintain some hash table of these hashes]. At any point if we get same hash value, then read the corresponding lines part by part and compare.

Note: Refer *Searching* chapter for related problems.

Problem-19   If h is the hashing function and is used to hash n keys in to a table of size s, where $n <= s$, the expected number of collisions involving a particular key X is :
    (A) less than 1.   (B) less than n.   (C) less than s.   (D) less than $\frac{n}{2}$.

Solution: A.

Chapter-15

STRING ALGORITHMS

☀ ☀ ☀

15.1 Introduction

To understand the importance of string algorithms let us consider the case of entering the URL (Uniform Resource Locator) in any browser (say, Internet Explorer, Firefox, or Google Chrome). You will observe that after typing the prefix of the URL, a list of all possible URLs is displayed. That means, the browsers are doing some internal processing and giving us the list of matching URLs. This technique is sometimes called *auto − completion*.

Similarly, consider the case of entering the directory name in command line interface (in both *Windows* and *UNIX*). After typing the prefix of the directory name if we press *tab* button, then we get a list of all matched directory names available. This is another example of auto completion.

In order to support these kind of operations, we need a data structure, which stores the sting data efficiently. In this chapter, we will look at the data structures that are useful for implementing string algorithms.

We start our discussion with the basic problem of strings: given a string, how do we search a substring (pattern)? This is called *string matching* problem. After discussing various string matching algorithms, we will see different data structures for storing strings.

15.2 String Matching Algorithms

In this section, we concentrate on checking whether a pattern P is a substring of another string T (T stands for text) or not. Since we are trying to check a fixed string P, sometimes these algorithms are called *exact string matching* algorithms. To simplify our discussion let us assume that the length of given text T is n and the length of the pattern P which we are trying to match has the length m. That means, T has the characters from 0 to $n − 1$ ($T[0 ... n − 1]$) and P has the characters from 0 to $m − 1$ ($P[0 ... m − 1]$).

In the subsequent sections, we start with brute force method and gradually move towards better algorithms.

- Brute Force Method
- Robin-Karp String Matching Algorithm
- String Matching with Finite Automata
- KMP Algorithm
- Boyce-Moore Algorithm
- Suffix Trees

15.3 Brute Force Method

In this method, for each possible position in the text T we check whether the pattern P matches or not. Since the length of T is n, we have $n − m + 1$ possible choices for comparisons. This is because we do not need to check last $m − 1$ locations of T as the pattern length is m. The following algorithm searches for the first occurrence of a pattern string P in a text string T.

Algorithm:

```
int BruteForceStringMatch (int T[], int n,  int P[], int m) {
        for (int i  = 0; i <=n - m; i++) {
                int j  = 0;
                while (j < m && P[j] == T[i + j])
                        j  = j + 1;
                if(j == m ) return i;
        }
        return -1;
}
```

Time Complexity: $O((n − m + 1) \times m) \approx O(n \times m)$.
Space Complexity: $O(1)$.

15.4 Robin-Karp String Matching Algorithm

In this method, we will use the hashing technique and instead of checking for each possible position in T, we check only if the hashing of P and hashing of m characters of T gives the same result. Initially, apply hash function to first m characters of T and check whether this result and P's hashing result is same or not. If they are not same then go to the next character of T and again apply hash function to m characters (by starting at second character). If they are same then we compare those m characters of T with P.

Selecting Hash Function

At each step, since we are finding the hash of m characters of T, we need an efficient hash function. If the hash function takes $O(m)$ complexity in every step then the total complexity is $O(n \times m)$. This is worse than brute force method because first we are applying the hash function and also comparing.

Our objective is to select a hash function which takes $O(1)$ complexity for finding the hash of m characters of T every time. Then only we can reduce the total complexity of the algorithm. If the hash function is not good (worst case), then the complexity of Robin-Karp algorithm complexity is $O(n - m + 1) \times m) \approx O(n \times m)$. If we select a good hash function then the complexity of Robin-Karp algorithm complexity is $O(m + n)$. Now let us see how to select a hash function which can compute the hash of m characters of T at each step in $O(1)$.

For simplicity, let's assume that the characters used in string T are only integers. That means, all characters in $T, \in \{0,1,2,\ldots,9\}$. Since all of them are integers, we can view a string of m consecutive characters as decimal numbers. For example, string "61815" corresponds to the number 61815.

With the above assumption, the pattern P is also a decimal value and let us assume that decimal value of P is p. For the given text $T[0..n-1]$, let $t(i)$ denote the decimal value of length$-m$ substring $T[i..i+m-1]$ for $i = 0,1,\ldots,n-m-1$. So, $t(i) == p$ if and only if $T[i..i+m-1] == P[0..m-1]$. We can compute p in $O(m)$ time using Horner's Rule as:

$$p = P[m-1] + 10(P[m-2] + 10(P[m-3] + \ldots + 10 \, (P[1] + 10 \, P[0])\ldots))$$

```
value = 0;
for (int i = 0; i <= m-1; i++) {
        value = value * 10;
        value = value + P[i];
}
```

We can compute all $t(i)$, for $i = 0,1,\ldots,n-m-1$ values in a total of $O(n)$ time. The value of $t(0)$ can be similarly computed from $T[0..m-1]$ in $O(m)$ time. To compute the remaining values $t(0), t(1), \ldots, t(n-m-1)$, understand that $t(i+1)$ can be computed can be computed from $t(i)$ in constant time.

$$t(i+1) = 10 * (t(i) - 10^{m-1} * T[i+1]) + T[i+m+1]$$

For example, if T = "123456" and $m = 3$, $t(0) = 123, t(1) = 10 * (123 - 100 * 1) + 4 = 234$

Step by Step explanation

> First : remove the first digit : $123 - 100 * 1 = 23$
> Second: Multiply by 10 to shift it : $23 * 10 = 230$
> Third : Add last digit : $230 + 4 = 234$

The algorithm runs by comparing, $t(i)$ with p. When $t(i) == p$, then we have found the substring P in T, starting from position i.

15.5 String Matching with Finite Automata

In this method we use the finite automata which is the concept of Theory of Computation (ToC). Before looking at the algorithm, first let us see the definition of finite automata.

Finite Automata

A finite automaton F is a 5-tuple $(Q, q_0, A, \Sigma, \delta)$, where

- Q is a finite set of states
- $q_0 \in Q$ is the start state
- $A \subseteq Q$ is a set of accepting states
- Σ is a finite input alphabet
- δ is the transition function that gives the next state for a given current state and input

---

How does Finite Automata Work?

- The finite automaton F begins in state q_0
- Reads characters from Σ one at a time
- If F is in state q and reads input character a, F moves to state $\delta(q, a)$
- At the end if its state is in A, then we say, F accepted the input string read so far
- If the input string is not accepted is called rejected string

Example: Let us assume that $Q = \{0,1\}, q_0 = 0, A = \{1\}, \Sigma = \{a, b\}$. $\delta(q, a)$ as shown in the transition table/diagram. This accepts strings that end in an odd number of a's; e.g., *abbaaa* is accepted, *aa* is rejected.

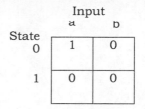

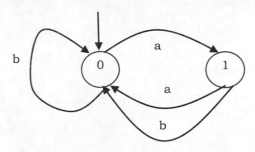

Transition Function/Table

Important Notes for Constructing the Finite Automata

For building the automata, first we start with initial state. The FA will be in state k if k characters of the pattern have been matched. If the next text character is equal to pattern character c, we have matched $k + 1$ characters, and the FA enters state $k + 1$. If the next text character is not equal to pattern character, then the FA go to a state $0, 1, 2, \ldots, or\ k$, depending on how many initial pattern characters match text characters ending with c.

Matching Algorithm

Now, let us concentrate on the matching algorithm.
- For a given pattern $P[0..m-1]$, first we need to build a finite automaton F
  - The state set is $Q = \{0, 1, 2, \ldots, m\}$
  - The start state is 0
  - The only accepting state is m
  - Time to build F can be large if Σ is large
- Scan the text string $T[0..n-1]$ to find all occurrences of the pattern $P[0..m-1]$
- String matching is efficient: $\Theta(n)$
  - Each character is examined exactly once
  - Constant time for each character
  - But the time to compute δ (transition function) is $O(m|\Sigma|)$. This is because δ has $O(m|\Sigma|)$ entries. If we assume $|\Sigma|$ is constant then the complexity becomes $O(m)$.

Algorithm

```
//Input: Pattern string P[0..m-1], δ and F,   Goal: All valid shifts displayed
FiniteAutomataStringMatcher(int P[], int m, F, δ) {
        q = 0;
        for (i = 0; i < m; i++)
                q = δ(q,T[i]);
                if(q == m)
                        System.out.println("Pattern occurs with shift:" + (i-m));
}
```

Time Complexity: $O(m)$.

15.6 KMP Algorithm

As before, let us assume that T is the string to be searched and P is the pattern to be matched. This algorithm was given by Knuth, Morris and Pratt. It takes $O(n)$ time complexity for searching a pattern. To get $O(n)$ time complexity, it avoids the comparisons with elements of T that were previously involved in comparison with some element of the pattern P.

The algorithm uses a table and in general we call it as *prefix function* or *prefix table* or *fail function* F. First we will see how to fill this table and later how to search for a pattern using this table.

The prefix function, F for a pattern stores the knowledge about how the pattern matches against shifts of itself. This information can be used to avoid useless shifts of the pattern P. It means that, this table can be used for avoiding backtracking on the string T.

Prefix Table

```
int F[]; //assume F is a global array
void Prefix-Table(int P[], int m) {
        int i=1, j=0, F[0]=0;
        while(i<m) {
                if(P[i]==P[j]) {
                        F[i]=j+1;
                        i++;
                        j++;
                }
                else if(j>0)
                        j=F[j-1];
                else {  F[i]=0;
                        i++;
                }
        }
}
```

As an example, assume that $P = a\,b\,a\,b\,a\,c\,a$. For this pattern, les us follow the step-by-step instructions for filling the prefix table F. Initially: $m = length[P] = 7, F[0] = 0$ and $F[1] = 0$.

Step 1: $i = 1, j = 0, F[1] = 0$

	0	1	2	3	4	5	6
P	a	b	a	b	a	c	a
F	0	0					

Step 2: $i = 2, j = 0, F[2] = 1$

	0	1	2	3	4	5	6
P	a	b	a	b	a	c	a
F	0	0	1				

Step 3: $i = 3, j = 1, F[3] = 2$

	0	1	2	3	4	5	6
P	a	b	a	b	a	c	a
F	0	0	1	2			

Step 4: $i = 4, j = 2, F[4] = 3$

	0	1	2	3	4	5	6
P	a	b	a	b	a	c	a
F	0	0	1	2	3		

Step 5: $i = 5, j = 3, F[5] = 1$

	0	1	2	3	4	5	6
P	a	b	a	b	a	c	a
F	0	0	1	2	3	0	

Step 6: $i = 6, j = 1, F[6] = 1$

	0	1	2	3	4	5	6
P	a	b	a	b	a	c	a
F	0	0	1	2	3	0	1

At this step filling of prefix table is complete.

Matching Algorithm

The KMP algorithm takes pattern P, string T and prefix function F as input, finds a match of P in T.

```
int KMP(char T[], int n, int P[], int m) {
        int i=0,j=0;
        Prefix-Table(P,m);
        while(i<n) {
                if(T[i]==P[j]) {
                        if(j==m-1)
                                return i-j;
                        else {  i++;
                                j++;
                        }
                }
```

```
            else if(j>0)
                    j=F[j-1];
            else    i++;
    }
    return -1;
}
```

Time Complexity: $O(m + n)$, where m is the length of the pattern and n is the length of the text to be searched.
Space Complexity: $O(m)$.

Now, to understand the process let us go through an example. For our example, assume that $T = b\,a\,c\,b\,a\,b\,a\,b\,a\,b\,a\,c\,a\,c\,a$ & $P = a\,b\,a\,b\,a\,c\,a$. Since we have already filled the prefix table, let us use it and go to the matching algorithm. Initially: $n = size\ of\ T = 15$; $m = size\ of\ P = 7$.

Step 1: $i = 0$, $j = 0$, comparing $P[0]$ with $T[0]$. $P[0]$ does not match with $T[0]$. P will be shifted one position to the right.

T	b	a	c	b	a	b	a	b	a	b	a	c	a	c	a
P	a	b	a	b	a	c	a								

Step 2: $i = 1$, $j = 0$, comparing $P[0]$ with $T[1]$. $P[0]$ matches with $T[1]$. Since there is a match, P is not shifted.

T	b	a	c	b	a	b	a	b	a	b	a	c	a	c	a
P		a	b	a	b	a	c	a							

Step 3: $i = 2$, $j = 1$, comparing $P[1]$ with $T[2]$. $P[1]$ does not match with $T[2]$. Backtracking on P, comparing $P[0]$ and $T[2]$.

T	b	a	c	b	a	b	a	b	a	b	a	c	a	c	a
P		a	b	a	b	a	c	a							

Step 4: $i = 3$, $j = 0$, comparing $P[0]$ with $T[3]$. $P[0]$ does not match with $T[3]$.

T	b	a	c	b	a	b	a	b	a	b	a	c	a	c	a
P			a	b	a	b	a	c	a						

Step 5: $i = 4$, $j = 0$, comparing $P[0]$ with $T[4]$. $P[0]$ matches with $T[4]$.

T	b	a	c	b	a	b	a	b	a	b	a	c	a	c	a
P				a	b	a	b	a	c	a					

Step 6: $i = 5$, $j = 1$, comparing $P[1]$ with $T[5]$. $P[1]$ matches with $T[5]$.

T	b	a	c	b	a	b	a	b	a	b	a	c	a	c	a
P				a	b	a	b	a	c	a					

Step 7: $i = 6$, $j = 2$, comparing $P[2]$ with $T[6]$. $P[2]$ matches with $T[6]$.

T	b	a	c	b	a	b	a	b	a	b	a	c	a	c	a
P				a	b	a	b	a	c	a					

Step 8: $i = 7$, $j = 3$, comparing $P[3]$ with $T[7]$. $P[3]$ matches with $T[7]$.

T	b	a	c	b	a	b	a	b	a	b	a	c	a	c	a
P				a	b	a	b	a	c	a					

Step 9: $i = 8$, $j = 4$, comparing $P[4]$ with $T[8]$. $P[4]$ matches with $T[8]$.

T	b	a	c	b	a	b	a	b	a	b	a	c	a	c	a
P				a	b	a	b	a	c	a					

Step 10: $i = 9$, $j = 5$, comparing $P[5]$ with $T[9]$. $P[5]$ does not matches with $T[9]$. Backtracking on P, comparing $P[4]$ with $T[9]$ because after mismatch $j = F[4] = 3$.

T	b	a	c	b	a	b	a	b	a	b	a	c	a	c	a
P				a	b	a	b	a	c	a					

Comparing $P[3]$ with $T[9]$.

T	b	a	c	b	a	b	a	b	a	b	a	c	a	c	a
P						a	b	a	b	a	c	a			

Step 11: $i = 10$, $j = 4$, comparing $P[4]$ with $T[10]$. $P[4]$ matches with $T[10]$.

T	b	a	c	b	a	b	a	b	a	b	a	c	a	c	a
P							a	b	a	b	a	c	a		

Step 12: $i = 11$, $j = 5$, comparing $P[5]$ with $T[11]$. $P[5]$ matches with $T[11]$.

T	b	a	c	b	a	b	a	b	a	b	a	c	a	c	a
P							a	b	a	b	a	c	a		

Step 13: $i = 12$, $j = 6$, comparing $P[6]$ with $T[12]$. $P[6]$ matches with $T[12]$.

T	b	a	c	b	a	b	a	b	a	b	a	c	a	c	a
P							a	b	a	b	a	c	a		

Pattern P has been found to completely occur in string T. The total number of shifts that took place for the match to be found are: $i - m = 13 - 7 = 6$ shifts.

Notes:
- KMP performs the comparisons from left to right
- KMP algorithm needs a preprocessing (prefix function) which takes O(m) space and time complexity
- Searching takes in O($n + m$) time complexity (does not depend on alphabet size)

15.7 Boyce-Moore Algorithm

Like KMP algorithm, this also does some pre-processing and we call it *last function*. The algorithm scans the characters of the pattern from right to left beginning with the rightmost character. During the testing of a possible placement of pattern P in T, a mismatch is handled as follows: Let us assume that the current character being matched is $T[i] = c$ and the corresponding pattern character is $P[j]$. If c is not contained anywhere in P, then shift the pattern P completely past $T[i]$. Otherwise, shift P until an occurrence of character c in P gets aligned with $T[i]$. This technique avoids needless comparisons by shifting pattern relative to text.

The *last* function takes O($m + |\Sigma|$) time and actual search takes O(nm) time. Therefore the worst case running time of Boyer-Moore algorithm is O($nm + |\Sigma|$). This indicates that the worst-case running time is quadratic, in case of $n == m$, the same as the brute force algorithm.

- Boyer-Moore algorithm is very fast on large alphabet (relative to the length of the pattern).
- For small alphabet, Boyce-Moore is not preferable.
- For binary strings KMP algorithm is recommended.
- For the very shortest patterns, the brute force algorithm is better.

15.8 Data Structures for Storing Strings

If we have a set of strings (for example, all words in dictionary) and a word which we want to search in that set. Inorder to perform the search operation faster, we need an efficient way of storing the strings. To store sets of strings we can use any of the following data structures.

- Hashing Tables
- Binary Search Trees
- Tries
- Ternary Search Trees

15.9 Hash Tables for Strings

As seen in *Hashing* chapter, we can use hash tables for storing the integers or strings. In this case, the keys are nothing but the strings. The problem with hash table implementation is that, we lose the ordering information. This is because, after applying the hash function, we do not know where it will map to. As a result some queries take more time. For example, to find all words starting with letter "*K*", then using hash table representation we need to scan the complete hash table. This is because the hash function takes the complete key, performs hash on it and we do not know the location of each word.

15.10 Binary Search Trees for Strings

In this representation, every node is used for sorting the strings alphabetically. This is possible because strings have a natural ordering: A comes before B, which comes before C, and so on. This is because words can be ordered and we can use a Binary Search Tree (BST) to store and retrieve them. For example, let us assume that we want to store the following strings using BSTs:

this is a career monk string

For the given string there are many ways of representing them in BST and one such possibility is shown in the tree below.

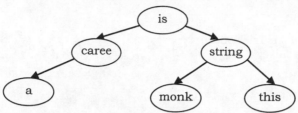

Issues with Binary Search Tree Representation

This method is good in terms of storage efficiency. But the disadvantage of this representation is that, at every node, the search operation performs the complete match of the given key with the node data and as a result the time complexity of search operation increases. So, from this we can say that BST representation of strings is good in terms of storage but not in terms of time.

15.11 Tries

Now, let us see the alternative representation which reduces the time complexity of search operation. The name *trie* is taken from the word re"trie".

What is a Trie?

A trie is a tree and each node in it contains the number of pointers equal to the number of characters of the alphabet. For example, if we assume that all the strings are formed with English alphabet characters "*a*" to "*z*" then each node of the trie contains 26 pointers. Suppose we want to store the strings "*a*", "*all*", "*als*" and "*as*", *trie* for these strings will look like:

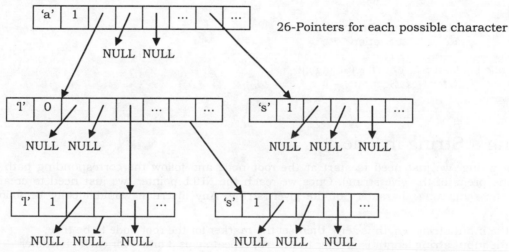

Why Tries?

Tries can insert and find strings in $O(L)$ time (where L represent the length of a single word). This is much faster than hash table and binary search tree representations.

Trie Node Declaration

The basic element - TrieNode of a TRIE data structure looks like this,

```
public class TrieNode {
    char data;
    boolean is_End_Of_String;
    Collection<TrieNode> child;
}
```

Node structure of the TRIE ADT had data (char), is_End_Of_String (boolean) and a collection of child nodes (Collection of TrieNode). It has one more method called as subNode(char). This method takes a character as argument and would return the child node of that character type if that is present.

```
public class TrieNode {
```

```
        char data;
        boolean is_End_Of_String;
        Collection<TrieNode> child;
        public TrieNode(char c){
                child = new LinkedList<TrieNode>();
                is_End_Of_String = false;
                data = c;
        }
        public TrieNode subNode(char c){
                if(child!=null){
                        for(TrieNode eachChild:child){
                                if(eachChild.data == c)
                                        return eachChild;
                        }
                }
                return null;
        }
}
```

Trie Declaration

Now that we have defined our Node, lets go ahead and look at the code for the TRIE class. Fortunately, the TRIE datastructure is insanely simple to implement since it has two major methods insert() and search(). Lets look at the elementary implementation of both these methods.

```
public class Trie{
        private TrieNode  root;
        public Trie(){
                root = new TrieNode(' ');
        }
        public void InsertInTrie(String s){
                //Refer Next Section
        }
        public boolean SearchInTrie(String s){
                //Refer Next Section
        }
}
```

Inserting a String in Trie

To insert a string, we just need to start at the root node and follow the corresponding path (path from root indicates the prefix of the give string). Once we reach the NULL pointer, we just need to create a skew of tail nodes for the remaining characters of the given string. Any insertion would ideally be following the below algorithm.

1) If the input string length is zero, then set the marker for the root node to be true.
2) If the input string length is greater than zero, repeat steps 3 and 4 for each character
3) If the character is present in the child node of the current node, set the current node point to the child node.
4) If the character is not present in the child node, then insert a new node and set the current node to that newly inserted node.
5) Set the marker flag to true when the end character is reached.

Time Complexity: $O(L)$, where L is the length of the string to be inserted.

Note: For real dictionary implementation we may need few more checks such as checking whether the given string is already there in dictionary or not.

Searching a String in Trie

Same is the case with search operation: we just need to start at root and follow the pointers. The time complexity of search operation is equal to the length of the given string which we want to search. The search alogirthm involves the following steps:

1) For each character in the string, see if there is a child node with that character as the content.
2) If that character does not exist, return false
3) If that character exist, repeat step 1.

4) Do the above steps until the end of string is reached.
5) When end of string is reached and if the marker of the current Node is set to true, return true, else return false.

Time Complexity: $O(L)$, where L is the length of the string to be searched.

Issues with Tries Representation

The main disadvantage of tries is that they need lot of memory for storing the strings. As we have seen above, for each node we have too many node pointers. In many cases, the occupancy of each node is less. The final conclusion regarding tries data structure is that they are faster but require huge memory for storing the strings.

Note: There are some improved tries representations called *trie compression techniques*. But, even with those techniques we can only reduce the memory at leaves but not at the internal nodes.

15.12 Ternary Search Trees

This representation was initially given by Jon Bentley and Sedgewick. A ternary search tree takes the advantages of binary search trees and tries. That means it combines the memory efficiency of BSTs and time efficiency of tries.

Ternary Search Trees Declaration

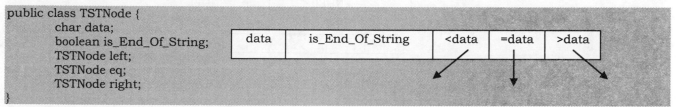

```
public class TSTNode {
        char data;
        boolean is_End_Of_String;
        TSTNode left;
        TSTNode eq;
        TSTNode right;
}
```

data	is_End_Of_String	<data	=data	>data

Ternary Search Tree (TST) uses three pointers:

- The *left* pointer points to the TST containing all the strings which are alphabetically less than *data*.
- The *right* pointer points to the TST containing all the strings which are alphabetically greater than *data*.
- The *eq* pointer points to the TST containing all the strings which are alphabetically equal to *data*. That means, if we want to search for a string, and if the current character of input string and *data* of current node in TST are same then we need to proceed to the next character in the input string and search it in the subtree which is pointed by *eq*.

Inserting strings in Ternary Search Tree

For simplicity let us assume that we want to store the following words in TST (also assume the same order): *boats, boat, bat* and *bats*. Initially, let us start with *boats* string.

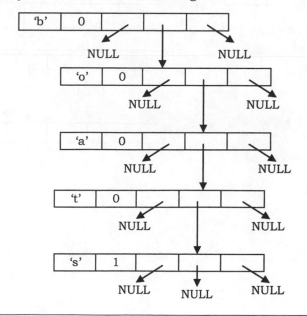

Now if we want to insert the string *boat*, then the TST becomes [the only change is setting the *is_End_Of_String* flag of "t" node to 1]:

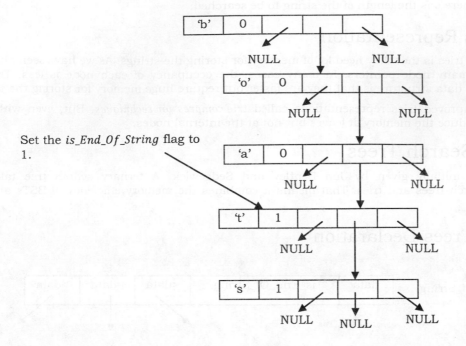

Set the *is_End_Of_String* flag to 1.

Now, let us insert the next string: *bat*

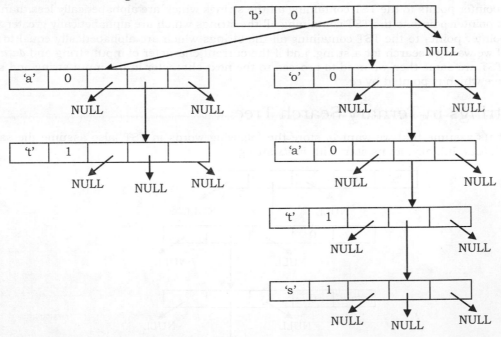

Now, let us insert the final word: *bat*.

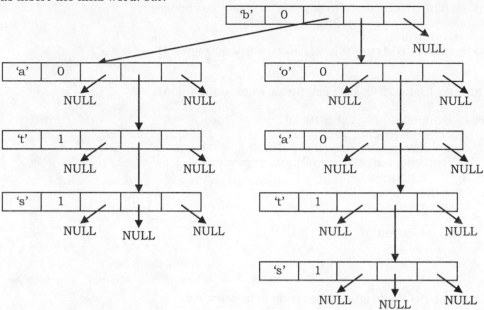

Based on these examples, we can write insertion algorithm as below. We will combine the insertion operation of BST and tries.

```
//initial value of position is zero
public TSTNode  InsertInTST(TSTNode  root, String word, int position) {
        if(root == null) {
                if(word.length() <= position) return root;
                root = new TSTNode();
                root.setData(word.charAt(position));
                root.setLeft(null);
                root.setEq(null);
                root.setRight(null);
                if(position == word.length()-1){
                        root.setMarker(true);
                    return root;
                }else return root.setEq(root, word, position+1);
        }
        if(word.charAt(position) < root.getData())
                root.setLeft( InsertInTST(root.getLeft(), word, position));
        else if(word.charAt(position) == root.getData()) {
                if(word.length <= position)
                        root.setEq(InsertInTST (root.getEq(), word, position + 1));
                else    root.setMarker(true);
        }
        else    root.setRight( InsertInTST(root.getRight(), word, position));
        return root;
}
```

Time Complexity: O(*L*), where *L* is the length of the string to be inserted.

Searching in Ternary Search Tree

If after inserting the words we want to search for them, then we have to follow the same rules as that of binary search. The only difference is, in case of match we should check for the remaining characters (in *eq* subtree) instead of return. Also, like BSTs we will see both recursive and non recursive versions of search method.

```
boolean SearchInTSTRecursive(TSTNode  root, String word, int position) {
        if(root == null)
                return false;
        if(word.charAt(position) < root.getData())
                return SearchInTSTRecursive(root.getLeft(), word, position);
```

```
        else if(word.charAt(position) > root.getData())
                return SearchInTSTRecursive(root.getRight(), word, position);
        else {    if(root.getMarker() && word.length == position)
                        return true;
                return SearchInTSTRecursive(root.getEq(), word, position + 1);
        }
}
boolean SearchInTSTNon-Recursive(TSTNode  root, String word, int position) {
        while (root) {
                if(word.charAt(position) < root.getData())
                        root = root.getLeft();
                else if(word.charAt(position)  == root.getData()) {
                        if(root.getMarker() && word.length == position)
                                return true;
                        position ++;
                        root = root.getEq();
                }
                else    root = root.getRight();
        }
        return false;
}
```

Time Complexity: O(L), where L is the length of the string to be searched.

Displaying All Words of Ternary Search Tree

Suppose we want to print all the strings of TST then we can use the following algorithm. If we want to print them in sorted order, we need to follow inorder traversal of TST.

```
String word;
int i = 0;
void DisplayAllWords(TSTNode  root) {
        if(root == null)    return;
        DisplayAllWords(root.getLeft());
        word.setCharAt(i, root.getData());
        if(root.getMarker()) {
                System.out.println(word);
        }
        i++;
        DisplayAllWords(root.getEq());
        i--;
        DisplayAllWords(root.getRight());
}
```

Finding Length of Largest Word in TST

This is similar to finding height of the BST and can be found as:

```
int MaxLengthOfLargestWordInTST(TSTNode  root) {
        if(root == null)    return 0;
        return Math.max(MaxLengthWordInTST(root.getLeft()),MaxLengthWordInTST(root.getEq())+1,
                MaxLengthWordInTST(root.getRight())));
}
```

15.13 Comparing BSTs, Tries and TSTs

- Hash table and BST implementation stores complete string at each node. As a result they take more time for searching. But they are memory efficient.
- TSTs can grow and shrink dynamically but hash tables resize only based on load factor.
- TSTs allow partial search where as BSTs and hash tables do not support them.
- TSTs can display the words in sorted order but in hash tables we cannot get the sorted order.
- Tries perform search operations very fast but they take huge memory for storing the string.
- TST combines the advantages of BSTs and Tries. That means it combines the memory efficiency of BSTs and time efficiency of tries.

15.14 Suffix Trees

Suffix trees are an important data structure for strings. With suffix trees we can answer the queries very fast. But it needs some preprocessing and construction of suffix tree. Even though construction of suffix tree is complicated, it solves many other string-related problems in linear time.

Note: Suffix trees use a tree (suffix tree) for one string whereas, Hash tables, BSTs, Tires and TSTs store a set of strings. That means, suffix tree answers the queries related to one string.

Let us see the terminology we use for this representation.

Prefix and Suffix

For given a string $T = T_1T_2 \ldots T_n$, *prefix* of T is a string $T_1 \ldots T_i$ where i can take values from 1 to n. For example, if $T = banana$, then the prefixes of T are: *b, ba, ban, bana, banan, banana*. Similarly, for given a string $T = T_1T_2 \ldots T_n$, *suffix* of T is a string $T_i \ldots T_n$ where i can take values from n to 1. For example, if $T = banana$, then the suffixes of T are: *a, na, ana, nana, anana, banana*.

Observation

From the above example, we can easily see that for a given text T and a pattern P, the exact string matching problem can also be defined as:
- Find a suffix of T such that P is a prefix of this suffix   *or*
- Find a prefix of T such that P is a suffix of this prefix.

Example: Let the text to be searched be $T = accbkkbac$ and the pattern be $P = kkb$. For this example, P is a prefix of the suffix *kkbac* and also a suffix of the prefix *accbkkb*.

What is a Suffix Tree?

In simple terms, suffix tree for a text T is a Trie-like data structure that represents the suffixes of T. The definition of suffix trees can be given as: A suffix tree for a n character string $T[1 \ldots n]$ is a rooted tree with the following properties.
- Suffix tree will contain n leaves which are numbered from 1 to n
- Each internal node (except root) should have at least 2 children
- Each edge in tree is labeled by a nonempty substring of T
- No two edges out of a node (children edges) begins with the same character
- The paths from the root to the leaves represent all the suffixes of T

Construction of Suffix Trees

Algorithm
1. Let S be the set of all suffixes of T. Append $ to each of the suffix.
2. Sort the suffixes in S based on their first character.
3. For each group S_c ($c \in \Sigma$):
   (i)   If S_c group has only one element, then create a leaf node.
   (ii)   Otherwise, find the longest common prefix of the suffixes in S_c group, create an internal node, and recursively continue with Step 2, S being the set of remaining suffixes from S_c after splitting off the longest common prefix.

For better understanding, let us go through an example. Let the given text be $T = tatat$. For this string, give a numbering to each of the suffixes.

Index	Suffix
1	$
2	t$
3	at$
4	tat$
5	atat$
6	tatat$

Now, sort the suffixes based on their initial characters.

Index	Suffix	
1	$	Group S_1 based on a
3	at$	Group S_2 based on a
5	atat$	
2	t$	
4	tat$	Group S_3 based on t
6	tatat$	

In the three groups the first group has only one element. So, as per the algorithm create a leaf node for it and the same is shown below.

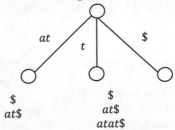

Now, for S_2 and S_3 (as they are having more than one element), let us find the longest prefix in the group and the result is shown below.

Group	Indices for this group	Longest Prefix of Group Suffices
S_2	3, 5	at
S_3	2, 4, 6	t

For S_2 and S_3, create internal nodes and the edge contains the longest common prefix of those groups.

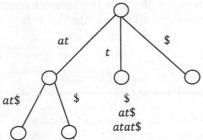

Now we have to remove the longest common prefix from S_2 and S_3 group elements.

Group	Indices for this group	Longest Prefix of Group Suffices	Resultant Suffixes
S_2	3, 5	at	$\$, at\$$
S_3	2, 4, 6	t	$\$, at\$, atat\$$

Our next step is, solving S_2 and S_3 recursively. First let us take S_2. In this group, if we sort them based on their first character, it is easy to see that the first group contains only one element $ and the second group also contains only one element, at$. Since both groups have only one element, we can directly create leaf nodes for them.

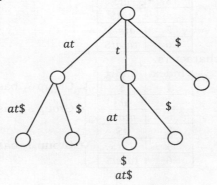

At this step, both S_1 and S_2 elements are done and the only remaining group is S_3. As similar to earlier steps, in S_3 group, if we sort them based on their first character, it is easy to see that there is only one element in first group and it is $. For S_3 remaining elements remove the longest common prefix.

Group	Indices for this group	Longest Prefix of Group Suffices	Resultant Suffixes
S_3	4, 6	at	$\$, at\$$

In the S_3 second group, there are two elements and among them one is $ and other is at$. We can directly add the leaf nodes for the first group element $. Let us add S_3 subtree as shown below.

Now, S_3 contains two elements. If we sort them based on their first character, it is easy to see that there are only two elements and among them one is $ and other is *at$*. We can directly add the leaf nodes for them. Let us add S_3 subtree as shown below.

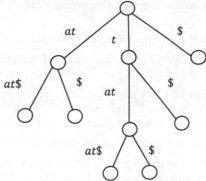

Since there are no more elements, this is the completion of construction of suffix tree for string $T = tatat$.

The time-complexity of the construction of a suffix tree using the above algorithm is $O(n^2)$ where n is the length of the input string because there are n distinct suffixes. The longest has length n, the second longest has length $n - 1$ and so on.

Note:

- There are $O(n)$ algorithms for constructing suffix trees.
- To improve the complexity, we can use indices instead of string for branches.

Applications of Suffix Trees

All the problems below (not limited to these) on strings can be solved with suffix trees very efficiently (for algorithms refer *Problems* section).

- **Exact String Matching Algorithm:** Given a text T and a pattern P, how do we check whether P appears in T or not?
- **Longest Repeated Substring:** Given a text T how do we find the substring of T which is the maximum repeated substring?
- **Longest Palindrome:** Given a text T how do we find the substring of T which is the longest palindrome of T?
- **Longest Common Substring:** Given two strings, how do we find the longest common substring?
- **Longest Common Prefix:** Given two strings $X[i \ldots n]$ and $Y[j \ldots m]$, how do we find the longest common prefix?
- How do we search for a regular expression in given text T?
- Given a text T and a pattern P, how do we find the first occurrence of P in T?

15.15 Problems on Strings

Problem-1   Given a paragraph of words, give an algorithm for finding the word which appears maximum number of times. If the paragraph is scrolled down(some words disappear from first frame, some words still appear and some are new words), give the maximum occurring word. Thus, it should be dynamic.

Solution: For this problem we can use combination of priority queues and tries. We start by creating a trie in which we insert a word as it appears and at every leaf of trie. Its node contains that word along with a pointer that points to the node in the heap [priority queue] which we also create. This heap contains nodes whose structure contains a *counter*. This is its frequency and also a pointer to that leaf of trie, which contain that word so that there is no need to store this word twice. Whenever a new word comes we find it in trie, if it is already there then we increase the frequency of node in heap corresponding to that word and call it heapify. This is done so that at any point of time we can get the word of maximum frequency. While scrolling, when a word goes out of scope, we decrement the counter in Heap. If the new frequency is still greater than zero, heapify the heap to incorporate the modification. If new frequency is zero, delete the node from heap and delete it from trie.

Problem-2   Given two strings how can we find the longest common substring?

Solution: Let us assume that the given two strings are T_1 and T_2. The longest common substring of two strings, T_1 and T_2, can be found by building a generalized suffix tree for T_1 and T_2. That means, we need to build a single suffix tree for both the strings. Each node is marked to indicate if it represents a suffix of T_1 or T_2 or both. This indicates that, we need to use different marker symbols for both the strings (for example, we can use $ for the first string and # for the second symbol). After constructing the common suffix tree, the deepest node marked for both T_1 and T_2 represents the longest common substring.

Other way of doing this is: We can build a suffix tree for the string $T_1\$T_2\#$. This is equivalent to building a common suffix tree for both the strings.

Time Complexity: $O(m + n)$, where m and n are the lengths of input strings T_1 and T_2.

Problem-3   **Longest Palindrome:** Given a text T how do we find substring of T which is the longest palindrome of T?

Solution: The longest palindrome of $T[1..n]$ can be found in $O(n)$ time. The algorithm is, first build a suffix tree for $T\$reverse(T)\#$ or build a generalized suffix tree for T and $reverse(T)$. After building the suffix tree, find the deepest node marked with both \$ and #. Basically it means to find the longest common substring.

Problem-4   Given a string (word), give an algorithm for finding the next word in dictionary.

Solution: Let us assume that we are using Trie for storing the dictionary words. To find the next word in Tries we can follow a simple approach as shown below. Starting from the rightmost character, increment the characters one by one. Once we reach Z, move to next character on left side. Whenever we increment, check if the word with the incremented character exists in dictionary or not. If it exists, then return the word, otherwise increment again. If we use *TST*, then we can find the inorder successor for the current word.

Problem-5   Give an algorithm for reversing a string.
Solution:
```
//If the str is editable
class ReverseString {
        public String ReversingString(String str) {
                char temp, start = 0, end = str.length();
                for (start = 0; start < end; start++, end--) {
                        temp = str.charAt(start);
                        str.setCharAt(start, str.charAt(end));
                        str.setCharAt(end, temp);
                }
                return str;
        }
}
```
Time Complexity: $O(n)$, where n is the length of the given string.Space Complexity: $O(n)$.

Problem-6   If the string is not editable, how do we create a string that is the reverse of given string?

Solution: If the string is not editable, then we need to create an array and return the pointer of that.
```
//If str is a const string (not editable)
class ReverseString {
        public static String reverseIt(String str) {
                int i, len = str.length();
                StringBuffer dest = new StringBuffer(len);
                for (i = (len - 1); i >= 0; i--)
                        dest.append(str.charAt(i));
                return dest.toString();
        }
}
```
Time Complexity: $O\left(\frac{n}{2}\right) \approx O(n)$, where n is the length of the given string.Space Complexity: $O(n)$.

Problem-7   Can we reverse the string without using any temporary variable?

Solution: Yes, we can use XOR logic for swapping the variables.
```
String ReversingString(String str) {
        int end= str.length()-1;
        int start = 0;
        while( start<end ) {
                str.setCharAt(start,  str.charAt(start)^ str.charAt(end));
                str.setCharAt(end,   str.charAt(end) ^  str.charAt(start));
                str.setCharAt(start,  str.charAt(start) ^ str.charAt(end));
                ++start;
                --end;
        }
        return str;
}
```

Time Complexity: $O\left(\frac{n}{2}\right) \approx O(n)$, where n is the length of the given string. Space Complexity: $O(n)$.

Problem-8   Give an algorithm for reversing words in a sentence.

Example: Input: "This is a Career Monk String", Output: "String Monk Career a is This"

Solution: Start from the beginning and keep on reversing the words. The below implementation assumes that ' ' (space) is the delimiter for words in given sentence.

```java
public class ReverseSentence {
        public static void ReversingSentence(String Line) {
                //specify delimiter as " " space
                StringTokenizer st = new StringTokenizer(strLine, " ");
                String strReversedLine = "";
                while(st.hasMoreTokens()) {
                        strReversedLine = st.nextToken() + " " + strReversedLine;
                }
                System.out.println("Reversed string by word is : " + strReversedLine);
        }
}
```

Time Complexity: $O(2n) \approx O(n)$, where n is the length of the string. Space Complexity: $O(1)$.

Problem-9   **Permutations of a string [anagrams]:** Give an algorithm for printing all possible permutations of the characters in a string. Unlike combinations, two permutations are considered distinct if they contain the same characters, but in a different order. For simplicity assume that each occurrence of a repeated character is a distinct character. That is, if the input is "aaa", the output should be six repetitions of "aaa". The permutations may be output in any order.

Solution: The solution is got by generating n! strings each of length n, where n is the length of the input string.

```java
public class Permutations {
        public  static void permutationsInOrder(String s) {
                permutationsInOrder("", s);
        }
        private static void permutationsInOrder(String prefix, String s) {
                int len = s.length();
                if (len == 0)
                        System.out.println(prefix);
                else {    for (int i = 0; i < len; i++)
                                permutationsInOrder(prefix + s.charAt(i), s.substring(0, i) + s.substring(i+1, len));
                }
        }
        public static void permutationsNotInOrder(String s) {
                int len = s.length();
                char[] a = new char[len];
                for (int i = 0; i < len; i++)
                        a[i] = s.charAt(i);
                permutationsNotInOrder(a, len);
        }
        private static void permutationsNotInOrder(char[] a, int n) {
                if (n == 1) {
                        System.out.println(a);
                        return;
                }
                for (int i = 0; i < n; i++) {
                        swap(a, i, n-1);
                        permutationsNotInOrder(a, n-1);
                        swap(a, i, n-1);
                }
        }
        // swap the characters at indices i and j
        private static void swap(char[] a, int i, int j) {
                char c;
                c = a[i]; a[i] = a[j]; a[j] = c;
        }
}
```

Problem-10 **Combinations of a String:** Unlike permutations, two combinations are considered to be the same if they contain the same characters, but may be in a different order. Give an algorithm that prints all possible combinations of the characters in a string. For example, "*ac*" and "*ab*" are different combinations from the input string "*abc*", but "*ab*" is the same as "*ba*".

Solution: The solution is got by generating $n!/r!(n-r)!$ strings each of length between 1 and n where n is the length of the given input string.

Algorithm:

For each of the input characters
- a. Put the current character in output string and print it.
- b. If there are any remaining characters, generate combinations with those remaining characters.

```java
public class Combinations {
    // print all subsets of the characters in str
    public static void CombinationsOne(String str) {
        CombinationsOne("", str);
    }
    // print all subsets of the remaining elements, with given prefix
    private static void CombinationsOne(String prefix, String str) {
        if (str.length() > 0) {
            System.out.println(prefix + str.charAt(0));
            CombinationsOne(prefix + str.charAt(0), str.substring(1));
            CombinationsOne(prefix,  str.substring(1));
        }
    }
    // alternate implementation
    public static void CombinationsTwo(String str) {
        comb2("", s);
    }
    private static void CombinationsTwo(String prefix, String str) {
        System.out.println(prefix);
        for (int i = 0; i < str.length(); i++)
            CombinationsTwo(prefix + str.charAt(i), str.substring(i + 1));
    }
}
```

Problem-11 Given a string "ABCCBCBA". Give an algorithm for recursively removing the adjacent characters if they are same. For example,   ABCCBCBA --> ABBCBA-->ACBA

Solution: First we need to check if we have character pair; if yes, then cancel it. Now check for next character and previous element. Keep canceling the characters until we either reach start of the array, end of the array or not find a pair [1].

```java
void RremoveAdjacentPairs(char[] str, int len)  {
    int j = 0;
    for (int i=1; i <= len; i++) {
        while ((str[i] == str[j]) && (j >= 0)){         //Cancel pairs
            i++;
            j--;
        }
        str[++j] = str[i];
    }
    return;
}
```

Problem-12 Given a set of characters *CHARS* and a input string *INPUT*, find the minimum window in *str* which will contain all the characters in *CHARS* in complexity O(n). For example, *INPUT* = *ABBACBAA* and *CHARS* = *AAB* has the minimum window *BAA*.

Solution: This algorithm is based on sliding window approach. In this approach, we start from the beginning of the array and move to right. As soon as we have a window, which have all the required elements, try sliding the window to as much right as possible with all the required elements. If current window length is less than min length found till now, update min length [1]. For example, if the input array is *ABBACBAA* and minimum window should cover characters *AAB* then sliding window will move like this:

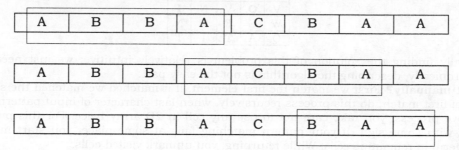

Algorithm
Input is the given array and chars is the array of character need to be found.

1. Make an integer array shouldfind[] of len 256. i^{th} element of this array will have a the count how many times we need to find element of ASCII value i.
2. Make another array hasfound of 256 elements, which will have the count of required element found till now.
3. Count <= 0
4. While input[i]
   a. If input[i] element is not to be found→continue
   b. If input[i] element is required => increase count by 1.
   c. If count is length of chars[] array, slide the window as much right as possible.
   d. If current window length is less than min length found till now. Update min length.

```
#define MAX 256
void MinLengthWindow(char[] input, int iplen, char[] chars, int charlen) {
        int shouldfind[MAX] = {0,}, hasfound[MAX] = {0,};
        int j=0, cnt = 0, start, finish, minwindow = INT_MAX;
        for (int i=0; i< charlen; i++)
                shouldfind[chars[i]] += 1;

        start = 0;
        finish = iplen;
        for (int i=0; i< iplen; i++) {
                if(!shouldfind[input[i]])
                        continue;
                hasfound[input[i]] += 1;

                if(shouldfind[input[i]] >= hasfound[input[i]])
                        cnt++;
                if(cnt == charlen) {
                        while (shouldfind[input[j]] == 0 || hasfound[input[j]] > shouldfind[input[j]])         {
                                if(hasfound[input[j]] > shouldfind[input[j]])
                                        hasfound[input[j]]--;
                                j++;
                        }
                        if(minwindow > (i - j +1)) {
                                minwindow = i - j +1;
                                finish = i;
                                start = j;
                        }
                }
        }
        System.out.println("Start: " + start +  " and Finish: " + finish);
}
```

Complexity: If we walk through the code, i and j can traverse at most n steps (where n is input size size) in the worst case, adding to a total of $2n$ times. Therefore, time complexity is $O(n)$.

Problem-13   We are given a 2D array of characters and a character pattern. Give an algorithm to find if pattern is present in 2D array. Pattern can be in any way (all 8 neighbors to be considered) but we can't use same character twice while matching. Return 1 if match is found, 0 if not. For example: Find "MICROSOFT" in below matrix.

A	C	P	**R**	C
X	**S**	**O**	P	**C**
V	**O**	V	N	**I**
W	G	**F**	**M**	N
Q	A	**T**	I	T

Solution: Manually finding the solution of this problem is relatively intuitive; we just need to describe an algorithm for it. Ironically, describing the algorithm is not the easy part.

How do we do it manually? First we match the first element, if it matched we matched the second element in the 8 neighbors of first match, do this process recursively, when last character of input pattern matches, return true. During above process, you take care not to use any cell in 2D array twice. For this purpose, you mark every visited cell with some sign. If your pattern matching fails at some place, you start matching from the beginning (of pattern) in remaining cells. While returning, you unmark visited cells.

Let's convert above intuitive method in algorithm. Since we are doing similar checks every time for pattern matching, a recursive solution is what we need here. In recursive solution, we need to check if the substring passed is matched in the given matrix or not. The condition is not to use the already used cell. For finding already used cell, we need to have another 2D array to the function (or we can use an unused bit in input array itself.) Also, we need the current position of input matrix, from where we need to start. Since we need to pass a lot more information than actually given, we should be having a wrapper function to initialize that extra information to be passed.

Algorithm:

        If we are past the last character in pattern
           Return true
        If we got an used cell again
           Return false if we got past the 2D matrix
           Return false
        If searching for first element and cell doesn't match
           FindMatch with next cell in row-first order (or column first order)
        otherwise if character matches
           mark this cell as used
           res = FindMatch with next position of pattern in 8 neighbors
           mark this cell as unused
           Return res
        Otherwise
           Return false

```
#define MAX 100
bool FindMatch_wrapper(char[][] mat, char[] pat, int patLen, int nrow, int ncol) {
        if(strlen(pat) > nrow*ncol)
                return false;
        int used[MAX][MAX] = {{0,},};
        return FindMatch(mat, pat, patLen, used, 0, 0, nrow, ncol, 0);
}
//level: index till which pattern is matched. x, y: current position in 2D array
boolean FindMatch(char[][] mat, char[] pat, int patLen, int used[MAX][MAX], int x, int y, int nrow, int ncol, int level) {
        if(level == patLen) //pattern matched
            return true;
        if(nrow == x || ncol == y)
            return false;
        if(used[x][y])
            return false;
        if(mat[x][y] != pat[level] && level == 0) {
            if(x < (nrow - 1))
                return FindMatch(mat, pat, patLen,used, x+1, y, nrow, ncol, level); //next element in same row
            else if(y < (ncol - 1))
                return FindMatch(mat, pat, patLen,used, 0, y+1, nrow, ncol, level); //first element from same
column
            else return false;
        }
        else if(mat[x][y] == pat[level]) {
            boolean res;
            used[x][y] = 1;        //marking this cell as used
```

```
                //finding subpattern in 8 neighbours
        res = (x > 0  ? FindMatch(mat, pat, used, x-1, y, nrow, ncol, level+1) :   false) ||
            (res = x < (nrow - 1)  ? FindMatch(mat, pat, used, x+1, y, nrow, ncol, level+1) :   false) ||
            (res = y > 0 ? FindMatch(mat, pat, used, x, y-1, nrow, ncol, level+1) :   false) ||
            (res = y < (ncol - 1)  ? FindMatch(mat, pat, used, x, y+1, nrow, ncol, level+1) :   false) ||
                    (res = x < (nrow - 1) && (y < ncol -1) ? FindMatch(mat, pat, used, x+1, y+1, nrow,
        ncol, level+1) :                                       false) ||
            (res = x < (nrow - 1) && y > 0  ? FindMatch(mat, pat, used, x+1, y-1, nrow, ncol, level+1) : false)
    ||
            (res = x > 0 && y < (ncol - 1) ? FindMatch(mat, pat, used, x-1, y+1, nrow, ncol, level+1) : false)
    ||
            (res = x > 0 && y > 0 ? FindMatch(mat, pat, used, x-1, y-1, nrow, ncol, level+1) : false);

        used[x][y] = 0;            //marking this cell as unused
        return res;
    }
        else return false;
}
```

Problem-14   Given a matrix with size $n \times n$ containing random integers. Give an algorithm which checks whether rows match with a column(s) or not. For example, If, i^{th} row matches with j^{th} column, and i^{th} row contains the elements - [2,6,5,8,9]. Then j^{th} column would also contain the elements - [2,6,5,8,9].

Solution: We can build a trie for the data in the columns (rows would also work). Then we can compare the rows with the trie. This would allow us to exit as soon as the beginning of a row does not match any column (backtracking). Also this would let us check a row against all columns in one pass.

If we do not want to waste memory for empty pointers then we can further improve the solution by constructing a suffix tree.

Chapter-16

ALGORITHMS DESIGN TECHNIQUES

16.1 Introduction

In the previous chapters, we have seen many algorithms for solving different kinds of problems. Before solving a new problem, the general tendency is to look for the similarity of current problem with other problems for which we have solutions. This helps us in getting the solution easily.

In this chapter, we will see different ways of classifying the algorithms and in subsequent chapters we will focus on a few of them (say, Greedy, Divide and Conquer and Dynamic Programming).

16.2 Classification

There are many ways of classifying algorithms and few of them are shown below:
- Implementation Method
- Design Method
- Other Classifications

16.3 Classification by Implementation Method

Recursion or Iteration

A *recursive* algorithm is one that calls itself repeatedly until a base condition is satisfied. It is a common method used in functional programming languages like $C, C++$, etc.. Iterative algorithms use constructs like loops and sometimes other data structures like stacks and queues to solve the problems.

Some problems are suited for recursive and other suited for iterative. For example, *Towers of Hanoi* problem can be easily understood in recursive implementation. Every recursive version has an iterative version, and vice versa.

Procedural or Declarative (Non-Procedural)

In *Declarative* programming languages, we say what we want without having to say how to do it. With *procedural* programming, we have to specify exact steps to get the result. For example, SQL is more declarative than procedural, because the queries don't specify steps to produce the result. Examples for procedural languages include: C, PHP, PERL, etc..

Serial or Parallel or Distributed

In general, while discussing the algorithms we assume that computers execute one instruction at a time. These are called *serial* algorithms. *Parallel* algorithms take advantage of computer architectures to process several instructions at a time. They divide the problem into subproblems and serve them to several processors or threads. Iterative algorithms are generally parallelizable. If the parallel algorithms are distributed on to different machines then we call such algorithms as *distributed* algorithms.

Deterministic or Non-Deterministic

Deterministic algorithms solve the problem with a predefined process whereas $non-deterministic$ algorithms guess the best solution at each step through the use of heuristics.

Exact or Approximate

As we have seen, for many problems we are not able to find the optimal solutions. That means, the algorithms for which we are able to find the optimal solutions are called *exact* algorithms. In computer science, if we do not have optimal solution, then we give approximation algorithms. Approximation algorithms are generally associated with NP-hard problems (refer *Complexity Classes* chapter for more details).

16.4 Classification by Design Method

Another way of classifying algorithms is by their design method.

Greedy Method

Greedy algorithms work in stages. In each stage, a decision is made that is good at that point, without bothering about the future consequences. Generally, this means that some *local best* is chosen. It assumes that local good selection makes the *global* optimal solution.

Divide and Conquer

The D&C strategy solves a problem by:
1) Divide: Breaking the problem into sub problems that are themselves smaller instances of the same type of problem.
2) Recursion: Recursively solving these sub problems.
3) Conquer: Appropriately combining their answers.

Examples: merge sort and binary search algorithms.

Dynamic Programming

Dynamic programming (DP) and memoization work together. The difference between DP and divide and conquer is that incase of the latter there is no dependency among the sub problems, whereas in DP there will be overlap of sub problems. By using memoization [maintaining a table for already solved sub problems], DP reduces the exponential complexity to polynomial complexity ($O(n^2)$, $O(n^3)$, etc.) for many problems.

The difference between dynamic programming and recursion is in memoization of recursive calls. When sub problems are independent and if there is no repetition, memoization does not help, hence dynamic programming is not a solution for all problems. By using memoization [maintaining a table of sub problems already solved], dynamic programming reduces the complexity from exponential to polynomial.

Linear Programming

In linear programming, there are inequalities in terms of inputs and *maximize* (or *minimize*) some linear function of the inputs. Many problems (example: maximum flow for directed graphs) can be discussed using linear programming.

Reduction [Transform and Conquer]

In this method we solve the difficult problem by transforming it into a known problem for which we have asymptotically optimal algorithms. In this method, the goal is to find a reducing algorithm whose complexity is not dominated by the resulting reduced algorithms. For example, selection algorithm for finding the median in a list involves first sorting the list and then finding out the middle element in the sorted list. These techniques are also called *transform and conquer*.

16.5 Other Classifications

Classification by Research Area

In computer science each field has its own problems and needs efficient algorithms. Examples: search algorithms, sorting algorithms, merge algorithms, numerical algorithms, graph algorithms, string algorithms, geometric algorithms, combinatorial algorithms, machine learning, cryptography, parallel algorithms, data compression algorithms and parsing techniques and more.

Classification by Complexity

In this classification, algorithms are classified by the time they take to find a solution based on their input size. Some algorithms take linear time complexity ($O(n)$) and others may take exponential time, and some never halt. Note that some problems may have multiple algorithms with different complexities.

Randomized Algorithms

Few algorithms make choices randomly. For some problems the fastest solutions must involve randomness. Example: Quick sort.

Branch and Bound Enumeration and Backtracking

These were used in Artificial Intelligence and we do not need to explore these fully. For backtracking method refer *Recusion and Backtracking* chapter.

Note: In the next few chapters we discuss these [greedy, divide and conquer and dynamic programming] design techniques. Importance is given to these techniques as the number of problems solved with these techniques is more as compared to others.

Chapter-17

GREEDY ALGORITHMS

17.1 Introduction

Let us start our discussion with simple theory which will give us an idea about the greedy technique. In the game of *Chess*, every time we make a decision about a move, we have to think about the future consequences as well. Whereas, in the game of *Tennis* (or *Volley Ball*), our action is based on current situation, which looks right at that moment, without bothering about the future consequences. This means that in some cases making a decision which looks right at that moment gives the best solution (*Greedy*) and for others it's not. Greedy technique is best suited for the second class of problems.

17.2 Greedy strategy

Greedy algorithms work in stages. In each stage, a decision is made that is good at that point, without bothering about the future. This means, some *local best* is chosen. It assumes that local good selection makes the global optimal.

17.3 Elements of Greedy Algorithms

The two basic properties of optimal greedy algorithms are:

1) Greedy choice property
2) Optimal substructure

Greedy choice property: This property says that globally optimal solution can be obtained by making a locally optimal solution (greedy). The choice made by a greedy algorithm may depend on earlier choices but not on future. It iteratively makes one greedy choice after another and reduces the given problem into a smaller one.

Optimal substructure: A problem exhibits optimal substructure if an optimal solution to the problem contains optimal solutions to the subproblems. That means we can solve subproblems and build up the solutions to solve larger problems.

17.4 Does Greedy Always Work?

Making locally optimal choices does not always work. Hence, greedy algorithms will not always give best solutions. We will see such examples in *Problems* section and in *Dynamic Programming* chapter.

17.5 Advantages and Disadvantages of Greedy Method

The main advantage of greedy method is that it is straightforward, easy to understand and easy to code. In greedy algorithms, once we make a decision, we do not have to spend time in re-examining already computed values.

Its main disadvantage is that for many problems there is no greedy algorithm. That means, in many cases there is no guarantee that making locally optimal improvements in a locally optimal solution gives the optimal global solution.

17.6 Greedy Applications

- Sorting: Selection sort, Topological sort
- Priority Queues: Heap sort
- Huffman coding compression algorithm
- Prim's & Kruskal's algorithms

- Shortest path in Weighted Graph [Dijkstra's]
- Coin change problem
- Fractional Knapsack problem
- Disjoint sets-UNION by size and UNION by height (or rank)
- Job scheduling algorithm
- Greedy techniques can be used as approximation algorithm for complex problems

17.7 Understanding Greedy Technique

For better understanding let us go through an example. For more details, refer the topics of *Greedy* applications.

Huffman coding algorithm

Definition: Given a set of n characters from the alphabet A [each character c ∈ A] and their associated frequency freq(c), find a binary code for each character c ∈ A, such that $\sum_{c \in A}$ freq(c)|binarycode(c)| is minimum, where | binarycode(c)| represents the length of binary code of character c. That means sum of lengths of all character codes should be minimum [sum of each characters frequency multiplied by number of bits in the representation].

The basic idea behind Huffman coding algorithm is to use fewer bits for more frequently occurring characters. Huffman coding algorithm compresses the storage of data using variable length codes. We know that each character takes 8 bits for representation. But in general, we do not use all of them. Also, we use some characters more frequently than others. When reading a file, generally system reads 8 bits at a time to read a single character. But this coding scheme is inefficient. The reason for this is that some characters are more frequently used than other characters. Let's say that the character 'e' is used 10 times more frequently than the character 'q'.

It would then be advantageous for us to use a 7 bit code for e and a 9 bit code for q instead because that could reduce our overall message length. On average, using Huffman coding on standard files can reduce them anywhere from 10% to 30% depending to the character frequencies. The idea behind the character coding is to give longer binary codes for less frequent characters and groups of characters. Also, the character coding is constructed in such a way that no two character codes are prefixes of each other.

Example: Let's assume that after scanning a file we found the following character frequencies:

Character	Frequency
a	12
b	2
c	7
d	13
e	14
f	85

In this, create a binary tree for each character that also stores the frequency with which it occurs (as shown below).

| b-2 | | c-7 | | a-12 | | d-13 | | e-14 | | f-85 |

The algorithm works as follows: Find the two binary trees in the list that store minimum frequencies at their nodes. Connect these two nodes at a newly created common node that will store no character but will store the sum of the frequencies of all the nodes connected below it. So our picture looks like follows:

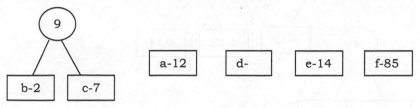

Repeat this process until only one tree is left:

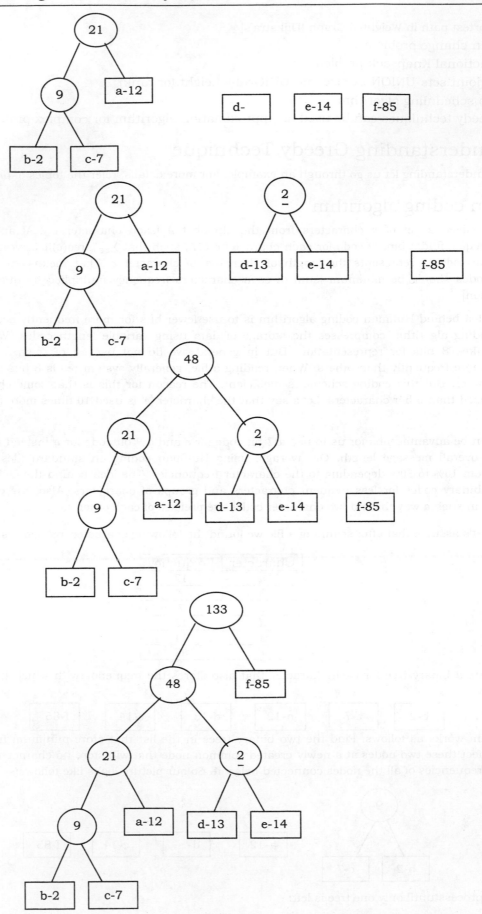

Once the tree is built, each leaf node corresponds to a letter with a code. To determine the code for a particular node, traverse from the root to the leaf node. For each move to the left, append a 0 to the code and for each move right append a 1. As a result for the above generated tree, we get the following codes:

Letter	Code
a	001
b	0000
c	0001
d	010
e	011
f	1

Calculating Bits Saved: Now, let us see how many bits that Huffman coding algorithm is saving. All we need to do for this calculation is see how many bits are originally used to store the data and subtract from that how many bits are used to store the data using the Huffman code.

In the above example, since we have six characters, let's assume each character is stored with a three bit code. Since there are 133 such characters (multiply total frequencies with 3), the total number of bits used is 3 * 133 = 399. Using the Huffman coding frequencies we can calculate the new total number of bits used:

Letter	Code	Frequency	Total Bits
a	001	12	36
b	0000	2	8
c	0001	7	28
d	010	13	39
e	011	14	42
f	1	85	85
Total			238

Thus, we saved 399 − 238 = 161 bits, or nearly 40% storage space.

```
HuffmanCodingAlgorithm(int A[], int n) {
        //Initialize a priority queue, PQ, to contain the n elements in A;
        Heap PQ = new Heap();
        BinaryTreeNode temp;
        for (i =  1; i<n; i++) {
                temp   = new BinaryTreeNode();
                temp.setLeft(PQ .deleteMin());
                temp.setRight(PQ.DeleteMin());
                temp.setData(temp.getLeft().getData() + temp.getRight().getData());
                PQ.insert(temp);
        }
        return PQ;
}
```

Time Complexity: O($nlogn$), since there will be *one* build_heap, $2n - 2$ delete_mins, and $n - 2$ inserts, on a priority queue that never has more than n elements. Refer *Priority Queues* chapter for details.

17.8 Problems on Greedy Algorithms

Problem-1   Given an array F with size n. Assume the array content $F[i]$ indicates the length of the ith file and we want to merge all these files into one single file. Check whether the following algorithm gives the best solution for this problem or not?

Algorithm: Merge the files contiguously. That means select the first two files and merge them. Then select the output of previous merge and merge with third file and keep going.

Note: Given two files A and B with sizes m and n, the complexity of merging is O($m + n$).

Solution: This algorithm will not produce the optimal solution. For counter example, let us consider the following file sizes array.

$$F = \{10,5,100,50,20,15\}$$

As per the above algorithm, we need to merge the first two files (10 and 5 size files) and as a result we get the following list of files. In the list below, 15 indicates the cost of merging two files with sizes 10 and 5.

$$\{15,100,50,20,15\}$$

Similarly, merging 15 with next file 100 produces: {115,50,20,15}. For the subsequent steps the list becomes,

{165,20,15}

{185,15}

Finally,   {200}

The total cost of merging = Cost of all merging operations = 15 + 115 + 165 + 185 + 200 = 680. To see whether the above result is optimal or not, consider the order: {5, 10, 15, 20, 50, 100}. For this example, following the same approach, the total cost of merging = 15 + 30 + 50 + 100 + 200 = 395. So, the given algorithm is not giving the best (optimal) solution.

Problem-2   Similar to Problem-1, does the following algorithm gives optimal solution?

Algorithm: Merge the files in pairs. That means after the first step, the algorithm produces the $n/2$ intermediate files. For the next step, we need to consider these intermediate files and merge them in pairs and keep going.

Note: Sometimes this algorithm is called 2-way merging. Instead of two files at a time, if we merge K files at a time then we call it as K-way merging.

Solution: This algorithm will not produce the optimal solution and consider the previous example for counter example. As per the above algorithm, we need to merge the first pair of files (10 and 5 size files), second pair of files (100 and 50) and third pair of files (20 and 15). As a result we get the following list of files.

{15, 150, 35}

Similarly, merge the output in pairs and this step produces [in the below, the third element does not have pair element, so keep it same]:

{165,35}

Finally,   {185}

The total cost of merging = Cost of all merging operations = 15 + 150 + 35 + 165 + 185 = 550. This is much more than 395 (of the previous problem). So, the given algorithm is not giving the best (optimal) solution.

Problem-3   In Problem-1, what is the best way to merge *all the files* into a single file?

Solution: Using greedy algorithm we can reduce the total time for merging the given files.

Algorithm

1.   Store file sizes in a priority queue. The key of elements are file lengths.
2.   Repeat the following until there is only one file:
     a.   Extract two smallest elements X and Y.
     b.   Merge X and Y and insert this new file in the priority queue.

Variant of same algorithm:

1.   Sort the file sizes in ascending order.
2.   Repeat the following until there is only one file:
     a.   Take first two elements (smallest) X and Y.
     b.   Merge X and Y and insert this new file in the sorted list.

To check the above algorithm, let us trace it with previous example. The given array is:

$$F = \{10,5,100,50,20,15\}$$

As per the above algorithm, sorting the list it becomes: {5, 10, 15, 20, 50, 100}. We need to merge the two smallest files (5 and 10 size files) and as a result we get the following list of files. In the list below, 15 indicates the cost of merging two files with sizes 10 and 5.

{15,15,20,50,100}

Similarly, merging two smallest elements (15 and 15) produces: {20,30,50,100}. For the subsequent steps the list becomes,   {50,50,100} //merging 20 and 30

{100,100}   //merging 20 and 30

Finally,   {200}

The total cost of merging = Cost of all merging operations = 15 + 30 + 50 + 100 + 200 = 395. So, this algorithm is producing the optimal solution for this merging problem.

Time Complexity: O($n\log n$) time using heaps to find best merging pattern plus the optimal cost of merging the files.

Problem-4   **Interval Scheduling Algorithm:** Given a set of n intervals $S = \{(start_i, end_i)|1 \le i \le n\}$. Let us assume that we want to find a maximum subset S' of S such that no pair of intervals in S' overlaps. Check whether the following algorithm works or not.

Algorithm: while (S is not empty) {

Select the interval I that overlaps the least number of other intervals.

Add I to final solution set S'.

Remove all intervals from S that overlap with I.
```
}
```
Solution: This algorithm does not solve the problem of finding a maximum subset of non-overlapping intervals. Consider the following intervals. The optimal solution is $\{M, O, N, K\}$. However, the interval that overlaps with the fewest others is C, and the given algorithm will select C first.

```
      _____              _____

      _____        C     _____

_____       _____       _____

  M          O         N          K
```

Problem-5 In Problem-4, if we select the interval that starts earliest (also not overlapping with already chosen intervals), does it gives optimal solution?

Solution: No. It will not give optimal solution. Let us consider the example below. It can be seen that optimal solution is 4 whereas the given algorithm gives 1.

Optimal Solution

```
_____   _____   _____   ←

_____   ←
```

Given Algorithm gives

Problem-6 In Problem-4, if we select the shortest interval (but is not overlapping the already chosen intervals), does it gives optimal solution?

Solution: This also will not give optimal solution. Let us consider the example below. It can be seen that optimal solution is 2 whereas the algorithm gives 1.

Optimal Solution

```
_____   _____   ←

           _____

                     _____   ←
```

Current Alg. gives

Problem-7 For Problem-4, what is the optimal solution?

Solution: Now, let us concentrate on the optimal greedy solution.

Algorithm:

Sort intervals according to the right-most ends [end times];
for every consecutive interval {
- If the left-most end is after the right-most end of the last selected interval then we select this interval
- Otherwise we skip it and go to the next interval
}

Time complexity = Time for sorting + Time for scanning = $O(n\log n + n) = O(n\log n)$.

Problem-8 Consider the following problem.

Input: $S = \{(start_i, end_i)|1 \le i \le n\}$ of intervals. The interval $(start_i, end_i)$, we can treat as a request for a room for a class with time $start_i$ to time end_i.

Output: Find an assignment of classes to rooms that uses the fewest number of rooms.

Algorithm: Assign as many classes as possible to the first room, then assign as many classes as possible to the second room, then assign as many classes as possible to the third room, etc. Does this algorithm give the best solution?

Note: In fact, this problem is similar to interval scheduling algorithm. The only difference is the application.

Solution: This algorithm does not solve the interval-coloring problem. Consider the following intervals:

```
              A
   _____
   B       C        D
  _____  _____  _____
       E          F   G
  _____     ___ __
```

Maximizing the number of classes in the first room results in having $\{B, C, F, G\}$ in one room, and classes $A, D,$ and G each in their own rooms, for a total of 4. The optimal solution is to put A in one room, $\{B, C, D\}$ in another, and $\{E, F, G\}$ in another, for a total of 3 rooms.

Problem-9   For Problem-8, consider the following algorithm. Process the classes in increasing order of start times. Assume that we are processing class C. If there is a room R such that R has been assigned to an earlier class, and C can be assigned to R without overlapping previously assigned classes, then assign C to R. Otherwise, put C in a new room. Does this algorithm solve the problem?

Solution: This algorithm solves the interval-coloring problem. Note that if the greedy algorithm creates a new room for the current class c_i, then because it examines classes in order of start times, c_i start point must intersect with the last class in all of the current rooms. Thus when greedy creates the last room, n, it is because the start time of the current class intersects with $n - 1$ other classes. But we know that for any single point in any class it can only intersect with at most s other class, it must then be that $n \le S$. As s is a lower bound on the total number needed and greedy is feasible it is thus also optimal.

Note: For optimal solution refer Problem-7 and for code refer Problem-10.

Problem-10   Suppose we are given two arrays $Start[1..n]$ and $Finish[1..n]$ listing the start and finish times of each class. Our task is to choose the largest possible subset $X \in \{1, 2, ..., n\}$ so that for any pair $i, j \in X$, either $Start[i] > Finish[j]$ or $Start[j] > Finish[i]$

Solution: Our aim is to finish the first class as early as possible, because that leaves us with the most remaining classes. We scan through the classes in order of finish time, whenever we encounter a class that doesn't conflict with latest class so far then take that class.

```java
int LargestTasks(int Start[], int n,  int Finish []) {
        sort Finish[];
        rearrange Start[] to match;
        count = 1;
        X[count]  = 1;
        for (int i  = 2; i<n; i++) {
                if(Start[i] > Finish[X[count]])       {
                        count  = count + 1;
                        X[count] = I;
                }
        }
        return X[1 .. count];
}
```

This algorithm clearly runs in O($nlogn$) time due to sorting.

Problem-11   Consider the making change problem in country India. The input to this problem is an integer M. The output should be the minimum number of coins to make M rupees of change. In India, assume the available coins are $1, 5, 10, 20, 25, 50$ rupees. Assume that we have an unlimited number of coins of each type.

For this problem, does the following algorithm produce optimal solution or not?
Take as many coins as possible from the highest denominations. For example, to make change for 234 rupees the greedy algorithms would take four 50 rupee coins, one 25 rupee coin, one 5 rupee coin, and four 1 rupee coins.

Solution: The greedy algorithm is not optimal for the problem of making change with the minimum number of coins when the denominations are $1, 5, 10, 20, 25,$ and 50. In order to make 40 rupees, the greedy algorithm would use three coins of $25, 10,$ and 5 rupees. The optimal solution is to use two 20-shilling coins.

Note: For optimal solution, refer *Dynamic Programming* chapter.

Problem-12   Let us assume that we are going for long drive between cities A and B. In preparation for our trip, we have downloaded a map that contains the distances in miles between all the petrol stations on our route. Assume that our cars tanks can hold petrol for n miles. Assume that the value n is given. Suppose we stop at every point, does it give the best solution?

Solution: Here the algorithm does not produce optimal solution. Obvious Reason: filling at each petrol station does not produce optimal solution.

Problem-13   For the Problem-12, stop if and only if you don't have enough petrol to make it to the next gas station, and if you stop, fill the tank up all the way. Prove/disprove that this algorithm solves the problem.

Solution: The greedy approach works: We start our trip from A with a full tank. We check our map to determine the farthest petrol station on our route within n miles. Stop at that petrol station, fill up our tank and we check our map again to determine the farthest petrol station on our route within n miles from this stop. Repeat the process until we get to B.

Note: For code, refer *Dynamic Programming* chapter.

Problem-14   **Fractional Knapsack problem:** Given items $t_1, t_2, ..., t_n$ (items we might want to carry in our backpack) with associated weights $s_1, s_2, ... , s_n$ and benefit values $v_1, v_2, ..., v_n$, how can we maximize the total benefit considering that we are subject to an absolute weight limit C?

Solution:
Algorithm:
   1)   Compute value per size density for each item $d_i = \frac{v_i}{s_i}$.
   2)   Sort each item by their value density.
   3)   Take as much as possible of the density item not already in the bag

Time Complexity: $O(n\ log n)$ for sorting and $O(n)$ for greedy selections.

Note: The items can be entered into a priority queue and retrieved one by one until either the bag is full or all items have been selected. This actually has a better runtime of $O(n + c log n)$ where c is the number of items that actually get selected in the solution. There is a savings in runtime if $c = O(n)$, but otherwise there is no change in the complexity.

Problem-15   **Number of railway-platforms:** At a rail-station, we have time-table of trains arrival and departure. We need to find the minimum number of platforms so that all the trains can be accommodated as per their schedule. **Example:** Time table is as given as below, the answer is 3. Otherwise, the railway station will not be able to accommodate all the trains.

Rail	Arrival	Departure
Rail A	0900 hrs	0930 hrs
Rail B	0915 hrs	1300 hrs
Rail C	1030 hrs	1100 hrs
Rail D	1045 hrs	1145 hrs

Solution: Let's take the same example as described above. Calculating the number of platforms is done by determining the maximum number of trains at the railway station at any time.

First, sort all the arrival(A) and departure(D) time in an array. Then, save the corresponding arrival or departure in the array also. After sorting our array will look like this:

0900	0915	0930	1030	1045	1100	1145	1300
A	A	D	A	A	D	D	D

Now modify the array by placing 1 for A and -1 for D. The new array will look like:

1	1	-1	1	1	-1	-1	-1

Finally make a cumulative array out of this:

1	2	1	2	3	2	1	0

Our solution will be the maximum value in this array. Here it is 3.

Note: If we have a train arriving and another departing at same time then put departure time first in sorted array.

Problem-16   Consider a country with very long roads and houses along the road. Assume that the residents of all houses use cell phones. We want to place cell phone towers along the road. Each cell phone tower covers a range of 7 kilometers. Give an efficient algorithm that gives the need for few cell phone towers.

Solution: The algorithm to locate the least number of cell phone towers:
1) Start from the beginning of the road
2) Find the first uncovered house on the road
3) If there is no such house, terminate this algorithm, otherwise, go to next step
4) Locate a cell phone tower 7 miles away after we find this house along the road
5) Go to step 2

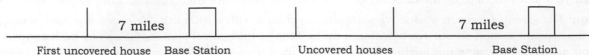

First uncovered house   Base Station   Uncovered houses   Base Station

Problem-17 **Preparing Songs Cassette:** Suppose we have a set of n songs and want to store these on a tape. In the future, users will want to read those songs from the tape. Reading a song from tape is not like reading from disk, first we have to fast-forward past all the other songs, and that takes a significant amount of time. Let $A[1..n]$ be an array listing the lengths of each song, specifically, song i has length $A[i]$. If the songs are stored in order from 1 to n, then the cost of accessing the kth song is:

$$C(k) = \sum_{i=1}^{k} A[i]$$

The cost reflects the fact that before we read song k we must first scan past all the earlier songs on the tape. If we change the order of the songs on the tape, we change the cost of accessing the songs, some songs become more expensive to read, but others become cheaper. Different song orders are likely to result in different expected costs. If we assume that each song is equally likely to be accessed, which order should we use if we want the expected cost to be as small as possible?

Solution: The answer is simple. We should store the songs in the order from shortest to longest. Storing the short songs at the beginning reduces the forwarding times for remaining jobs.

Problem-18 Let us consider a set of events at *HITEX (Hyderabad Convention Center)*. Assume that there are n events where each takes one unit of time. Event i will provide a profit of P[i] rupees (P[i] > 0) if started at or before time $T[i]$, where $T[i]$ is an arbitrary number. If an event is not started by $T[i]$ then there is no benefit in scheduling it at all. All events can start as early as time 0. Give the efficient algorithm to find a schedule that maximizes the profit.

Solution: Algorithm
- Sort the jobs according to floor($T[i]$) (sorted from largest to smallest).
- Let time t be the current time being considered (where initially t = floor($T[i]$)).
- All jobs i where floor($T[i]$) = t are inserted into a priority queue with the profit g_i used as the key.
- A *DeleteMax* is performed to select the job to run at time t.
- Then t is decremented and the process is continued.

Clearly the time complexity is O($nlogn$). The sort takes O($nlogn$) and there are at most n insert and DeleteMax operations performed on the priority queue, each of which takes O($logn$) time.

Problem-19 Let us consider a customer-care server (say, mobile customer-care) with n customers to be severed in the queue. For simplicity assume that the service time required by each customer is known in advance and it is w_i minutes for customer i. So if, for example, the customers are served in order of increasing i, then the ith customer has to wait: $\sum_{j=1}^{n-1} w_j$ *minutes*. The total waiting time of all customers can be given as = $\sum_{i=1}^{n} \sum_{j=1}^{i-1} w_j$

What is the best way to serve the customers so that the total waiting time can be reduced?

Solution: This problem can be easily solved using greedy technique. Since our objective is to reduce the total waiting time, what we can do is, select the customer whose service time is less. That means, if we process the customers in the increasing order of service time then we can reduce the total waiting time.

Time Complexity: O($nlogn$).

DIVIDE AND CONQUER ALGORITHMS

Chapter-18

18.1 Introduction

In *Greedy* chapter, we have seen that for many problems Greedy strategy failed to provide optimal solutions. Among those problems, there are some that can be easily solved by using *Divide and Conquer* (D & C) technique. Divide and Conquer is an important algorithm design technique based on recursion. The D & C algorithm works by recursively breaking down a problem into two or more sub problems of the same type, until they become simple enough to be solved directly. The solutions to the sub problems are then combined to give a solution to the original problem.

18.2 What is Divide and Conquer Strategy?

The D&C strategy solves a problem by:

1) Divide: Breaking the problem into sub problems that are themselves smaller instances of the same type of problem.
2) Recursion: Recursively solving these sub problems.
3) Conquer: Appropriately combining their answers.

18.3 Does Divide and Conquer Always Work?

It's not possible to solve all the problems with Divide and Conquer technique. As per the definition of D&C the recursion solves the subproblems which are of same type. For all problems it is not possible to find the subproblems which are same size and D&C is not a choice for all problems.

18.4 Divide and Conquer Visualization

For better understanding, consider the following visualization. Assume that n is the size of original problem. As described above, we can see that the problem is divided into sub problems with each of size n/b (for some constant b). We solve the sub problems recursively and combine their solutions to get the solution for the original problem.

```
DivideAndConquer ( P ) {
        if( small ( P ) )
        // P is very small so that a solution is obvious
                return solution ( n );
        divide the problem P into k sub problems P1, P2, ..., Pk;
        return (
                Combine (
                        DivideAndConquer ( P1 ),
                        DivideAndConquer ( P2 ),
                        ...
                        DivideAndConquer ( Pk )
                        )
                );
}
```

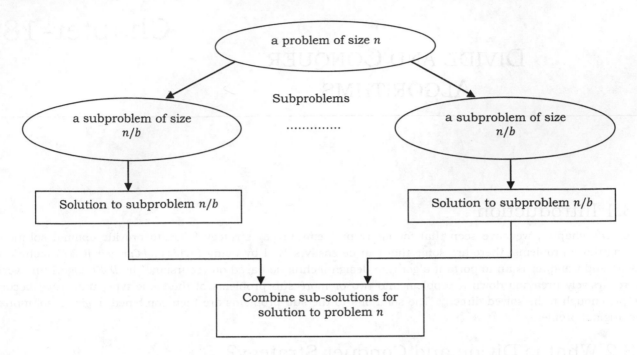

18.5 Understanding Divide and Conquer

For clear understanding of D & C, let us consider a story. There was an old man who was a rich farmer and had seven sons. He was afraid that when he died, his land and his possessions would be divided among his seven sons, and that they would quarrel with one another. He gathered them together and showed them seven sticks that he had tied together and told them that anyone who could break the bundle would inherit everything. They all tried, but no one could break the bundle. Then the old man untied the bundle and broke the sticks one by one. The brothers decided that they should stay together and work together and succeed together. The moral for problem solvers is different. If we can't solve the problem, divide it into parts, and solve one part at a time.

In earlier chapters we have already solved many problems based on D&C strategy: like Binary Search, Merge Sort, Quick Sort, etc.... Refer those topics to get an idea of how D&C works. Below are few other real-time problems which can easily be solved with D&C strategy. For all these problems we can find the subproblems which are similar to original problem.

1. Looking for a name in a phone book: We have a phone book with names in alphabetical order. Given a name, how do we find whether that name is there in the phone book or not?
2. Breaking a stone into dust: We want to convert a stone into dust (very small stones).
3. Finding the exit in a hotel: We are at the end of a very long hotel lobby with a long series of doors, with one door next to you. We are looking for the door that leads to the exit.
4. Finding our car in a parking lot.

Advantages of Divide and Conquer

Solving difficult problems: D & C is a powerful method for solving difficult problems. As an example, consider Tower of Hanoi problem. This requires breaking the problem into subproblems, solving the trivial cases and combining subproblems to solve the original problem. Dividing the problem into subproblems so that subproblems can be combined again is a major difficulty in designing a new algorithm. For many such problems D & C provides simple solution..

Parallelism: Since D&C allows us to solve the subproblems independently, they allow execution in multi-processor machines, especially shared-memory systems where the communication of data between processors does not need to be planned in advance, because different subproblems can be executed on different processors.

Memory access: D&C algorithms naturally tend to make efficient use of memory caches. This is because once a subproblem is small, all its subproblems can be solved within the cache, without accessing the slower main memory.

Disadvantages of Divide and Conquer

One disadvantage of $D \& C$ approach is that recursion is slow. This is because of the overhead of the repeated subproblem calls. Also, $D \& C$ approach needs stack for storing the calls (the state at each point in the recursion). Actually this depends upon the implementation style. With large enough recursive base cases, the overhead of recursion can become negligible for many problems.

Another problem with D&C is that, for some problems, it may be more complicated than an iterative approach. For example, to add n numbers, a simple loop to add them up in sequence is much easier than a divide-and-conquer approach that breaks the set of numbers into two halves, adds them recursively, and then adds the sums.

18.6 Master Theorem

As stated above, in $D \& C$ method, we solve the sub problems recursively. All problems are generally defined in terms of recursive definitions. These recursive problems can easily be solved using Master theorem. For details on Master theorem refer *Introduction to Analysis of Algorithms* chapter. Just for the continuity, let us reconsider the Master theorem.

If the recurrence is of the form $T(n) = aT(\frac{n}{b}) + \Theta(n^k log^p n)$, where $a \geq 1, b > 1, k \geq 0$ and p is a real number, then the complexity can be directly given as:

1) If $a > b^k$, then $T(n) = \Theta(n^{log_b^a})$
2) If $a = b^k$
    a. If $p > -1$, then $T(n) = \Theta(n^{log_b^a} log^{p+1} n)$
    b. If $p = -1$, then $T(n) = \Theta(n^{log_b^a} log log n)$
    c. If $p < -1$, then $T(n) = \Theta(n^{log_b^a})$
3) If $a < b^k$
    a. If $p \geq 0$, then $T(n) = \Theta(n^k log^p n)$
    b. If $p < 0$, then $T(n) = O(n^k)$

18.7 Divide and Conquer Applications

- Binary Search
- Merge Sort
- Quick Sort
- Median Finding
- Min and Max Finding
- Matrix Multiplication
- Closest Pair problem

18.8 Problems on Divide and Conquer

Problem-1   Let us consider an algorithm A which solves problems by dividing them into five subproblems of half the size, recursively solving each subproblem, and then combining the solutions in linear time. What is the complexity of this algorithm?

Solution: Let us assume that the input size is n and $T(n)$ defines the solution to the given problem. As per the description, algorithm divides the problem into 5 sub problems with each of size $\frac{n}{2}$. So we need to solve $5T(\frac{n}{2})$ subproblems. After solving these sub problems the given array (linear time) is scanned to combine these solutions. The total recurrence algorithm for this problem can be given as:

$$T(n) = 5T\left(\frac{n}{2}\right) + O(n)$$

Using Master theorem (of D&C), we get the complexity as $O(n^{log_2^5}) \approx O(n^{2+}) \approx O(n^3)$

Problem-2   Similar to Problem-1, an algorithm B solves problems of size n by recursively solving two subproblems of size $n - 1$ and then combining the solutions in constant time. What is the complexity of this algorithm?

Solution: Let us assume that input size is n and $T(n)$ defines the solution to the given problem. As per the description of algorithm we divide the problem into 2 sub problems with each of size $n - 1$. So we have to solve

$2T(n-1)$ sub problems. After solving these sub problems, the algorithm takes only a constant time to combine these solutions. The total recurrence algorithm for this problem can be given as:

$$T(n) = 2T(n-1) + O(1)$$

Using Master theorem (of *Subtract and Conquer*), we get the complexity as $O\left(n^0 2^{\frac{n}{1}}\right) = O(2^n)$. (Refer *Introduction to Analysis of Algorithms* chapter for more details).

Problem-3   Again similar to Problem-1, another algorithm C solves problems of size n by dividing them into nine subproblems of size $\frac{n}{3}$, recursively solving each subproblem, and then combining the solutions in $O(n^2)$ time. What is the complexity of this algorithm?

Solution: Let us assume that input size is n and $T(n)$ defines the solution to the given problem. As per the description of algorithm we divide the problem into 9 sub problems with each of size $\frac{n}{3}$. So we need to solve $9T(\frac{n}{3})$ sub problems. After solving the sub problems, the algorithm takes quadratic time to combine these solutions. The total recurrence algorithm for this problem can be given as:

$$T(n) = 9T\left(\frac{n}{3}\right) + O(n^2)$$

Using $D\ \&\ C$ Master theorem, we get the complexity as $O(n^2 logn)$.

Problem-4   Write a recurrence and solve it.

```
void function(int n) {
    if(n > 1) {
        System.out.println(("*");
        function(n/2);
        function(n/2);
    }
}
```

Solution: Let us assume that the input size is n and $T(n)$ defines the solution to the given problem. As per the given code after printing the character, and dividing the problem in to 2 subproblems with each of size $\frac{n}{2}$ and solving them. So we need to solve $2T(\frac{n}{2})$ subproblems.

After solving these subproblems, the algorithm is not doing anything for combining the solutions. The total recurrence algorithm for this problem can be given as:

$$T(n) = 2T\left(\frac{n}{2}\right) + O(1)$$

Using Master theorem (of D&C), we get the complexity as $O(n^{log_2^2}) \approx O(n^1) = O(n)$.

Problem-5   Given an array, give an algorithm for finding the maximum and minimum.

Solution: Refer *Selection Algorithms* chapter.

Problem-6   Discuss Binary Search and its complexity.

Solution: Refer *Searching* chapter for discussion on Binary Search.

Analysis: Let us assume that input size is n and $T(n)$ defines the solution to the given problem. The elements are in sorted order. In binary search we take the middle element and check whether the element to be searched is equal to that element or not. If it is equal then we return that element.

If the element to be searched is greater than the middle element then we consider the left sub-array for finding the element and discard the right sub-array. Similarly, if the element to be searched is less than the middle element then we consider the right sub-array for finding the element and discard the left sub-array.

What this means is, in both the cases we are discarding half of the sub-array and considering the remaining half only. Also, at every iteration we are dividing the elements into two equal halves.

As per the above discussion every time we divide the problem into 2 sub problems with each of size $\frac{n}{2}$ and solve one $T(\frac{n}{2})$ sub problem. The total recurrence algorithm for this problem can be given as:

$$T(n) = T\left(\frac{n}{2}\right) + O(1)$$

Using Master theorem (of D&C), we get the complexity as $O(logn)$.

Problem-7   Consider the modified version of binary search. Let us assume that the array is divided into 3 equal parts (ternary search) instead of two equal parts. Write the recurrence for this ternary search and find its complexity.

Solution: From the discussion on Problem-5, binary search has the recurrence relation: $T(n) = T\left(\frac{n}{2}\right) + O(1)$. Similar to Problem-5 discussion, instead of 2 in the recurrence relation we use "3". That indicates that we are dividing the array into 3 sub-arrays with equal size and considering only one of them. So, the recurrence for the ternary search can be given as:

$$T(n) = T\left(\frac{n}{3}\right) + O(1)$$

Using Master theorem (of D & C), we get the complexity as $O(log_3^n) \approx O(logn)$ (we don't have to worry about the base of log as they are constants).

Problem-8   In Problem-5, what if we divide the array into two sets of sizes approximately one-third and two-thirds.

Solution: We now consider a slightly modified version of ternary search in which only one comparison is made which creates two partitions, one of roughly $\frac{n}{3}$ elements and the other of $\frac{2n}{3}$. Here the worst case comes when the recursive call is on the larger $\frac{2n}{3}$ element part. So the recurrence corresponding to this worst case is:

$$T(n) = T\left(\frac{2n}{3}\right) + O(1)$$

Using Master theorem (of D&C), we get the complexity as $O(logn)$. It is interesting to note that we will get the same results for general k-ary search (as long as k is a fixed constant which does not depend on n) as n approaches infinity.

Problem-9   Discuss Merge Sort and its complexity.

Solution: Refer *Sorting* chapter for discussion on Merge Sort. In Merge Sort, if the number of elements are greater than 1 then divide them into two equal subsets, the algorithm is recursively invoked on the subsets, and the returned sorted subsets are merged to provide a sorted list of the original set. The recurrence equation of the Merge Sort algorithm is:

$$T(n) = \begin{cases} 2T\left(\frac{n}{2}\right) + O(n), if\ n > 1 \\ 0 \qquad\qquad\ , if\ n = 1 \end{cases}$$

If we solve this recurrence using D&C Master theorem gives O(nlogn) complexity.

Problem-10   Discuss Quick Sort and its complexity.

Solution: Refer *Sorting* chapter for discussion on Quick Sort. For Quick Sort we have different complexities for best case and worst case.

Best Case: In *Quick Sort,* if the number of elements is greater than 1 then they are divided into two equal subsets, and the algorithm is recursively invoked on the subsets. After solving the sub problems we don't need to combine them. This is because in *Quick Sort* they are already in sorted order. But, we need to scan the complete elements to partition the elements. The recurrence equation of *Quick Sort* best case is

$$T(n) = \begin{cases} 2T\left(\frac{n}{2}\right) + O(n), if\ n > 1 \\ 0 \qquad\qquad\ , if\ n = 1 \end{cases}$$

If we solve this recurrence using Master theorem of D&C gives O(*nlogn*) complexity.

Worst Case: In the worst case, Quick Sort divides the input elements into two sets and one of them contains only one element. That means other set has $n - 1$ elements to be sorted. Let us assume that the input size is n and $T(n)$ defines the solution to the given problem. So we need to solve $T(n-1)$, $T(1)$ subproblems. But to divide the input into two sets Quick Sort needs one scan of the input elements (this takes O(n)).

After solving these sub problems the algorithm takes only a constant time to combine these solutions. The total recurrence algorithm for this problem can be given as: $T(n) = T(n-1) + O(1) + O(n)$.

This is clearly a summation recurrence equation. So, $T(n) = \frac{n(n+1)}{2} = O(n^2)$.

Note: For the average case analysis, refer *Sorting* chapter.

Problem-11   Given an infinite array in which the first n cells contain integers in sorted order and the rest of the cells are filled with some special symbol (say, $). Assume we do not know the n value. Give an algorithm that takes an integer K as input and finds a position in the array containing K, if such a position exists, in O($logn$) time.

Solution: Since we need an O($logn$) algorithm, we should not search for all the elements of the given list (which gives O(n) complexity). To get O($logn$) complexity one possibility is to use binary search. But in the given scenario we cannot use binary search as we do not know the end of list. Our first problem is to find the end of the list. To do that, we can start at first element and keep searching with doubled index. That means we first search at index 1 then, $2, 4, 8 \dots$

```java
int FindInInfiniteSeries(int A[]) {
        int mid, l = r = 1;
        while( A[r] != '$') {
                l = r;
                r = r × 2;
        }
        while( (r – l > 1 ) {
```

```
        mid = (r – 1)/2 + 1;
        if( A[mid] == '$')
                r = mid;
        else    1 = mid;
    }
}
```

It is clear that, once we identified a possible interval $A[i,...,2i]$ in which K might be, its length is at most n (since we have only n numbers in the array A), so searching for K using binary search takes $O(logn)$ time.

Problem-12 Given a sorted array of non-repeated integers $A[1..n]$, check whether there is an index i for which $A[i] = i$. Give a divide-and-conquer algorithm that runs in time $O(logn)$.

Solution: We can use binary search to get the $O(logn)$ complexity.
```
int IndexSearcher(int A[] , int l, int r) {
        int mid = (r – 1)/2 + 1;
        if(r-1 <= 1) {
                if(A[l] == 1 || A[r] == r)
                        return 1;
                else    return 0;
        }
        if(A[mid] < mid )
                return IndexSearcher( A, mid + 1,r);
        if(A[mid] > mid)
                return IndexSearcher( A, 1, mid - 1);
        return mid;
}
```
Recurrence for the above function $T(n) = T(n/2) + O(1)$.
Using master theorem we get, $T(n) = O(logn)$.

Problem-13 We are given two sorted lists of size n. Give an algorithm for finding the median element in the union of the two lists.

Solution: We use the Merge Sort process. Use *merge* procedure of merge sort (refer *Sorting* chapter). Keep track of count while comparing elements of two arrays. If count becomes n (since there are $2n$ elements), we have reached the median. Take the average of the elements at indexes $n - 1$ and n in the merged array.

Time Complexity: $O(n)$.

Problem-14 Can we give algorithm if the sizes of two lists are not same?

Solution: The solution is similar to previous problem. Let us assume that the lengths of two lists are m and n. In this case we need to stop when counter reaches $(m + n)/2$.

Time Complexity: $O((m + n)/2)$.

Problem-15 Can we improve the time complexity of Problem-13 to $O(logn)$?

Solution: Yes, using D&C approach. Let us assume that the given two lists are $L1$ and $L2$.
Algorithm:
1) Find the medians of the given sorted input arrays $L1[]$ and $L2[]$. Also, assume that those medians are $m1$ and $m2$.
2) If $m1$ and $m2$ are equal then return $m1$ (or $m2$)
3) If $m1$ is greater than $m2$, then the final median will be below two sub arrays.
   a) From first element of $L1$ to $m1$
   b) From $m2$ to last element of $L2$
4) If $m2$ is greater than $m1$, then median is present in one of the two sub arrays below.
   a) From $m1$ to last element of $L1$
   b) From first element of $L2$ to $m2$
5) Repeat the above process until size of both the sub arrays becomes 2.
6) If size of the two arrays is 2 then use the formula below to get the median.
7) Median = $(\frac{max(L1[0],L2[0])+min(L1[1],L2[1])}{2})$

Time Complexity: $O(logn)$, as we are considering only half of the input and throwing the remaining half.

Problem-16 Given an input array A. Let us assume that there can be duplicates in the list. Now search for an element in the list in such a way that we get the highest index if there are duplicates.

Solution: Refer *Searching* chapter.

Problem-14   Discuss Strassen's Matrix Multiplication Algorithm using Divide and Conquer. That means, given two $n \times n$ matrices, A and B, compute the $n \times n$ matrix $C = A \times B$, where the elements of C are given by

$$C_{i,j} = \sum_{k=0}^{n-1} A_{i,k} B_{k,j}$$

Solution: Before Strassen's algorithm, first let us see the basic divide and conquer algorithm. The general approach we follow for solving this problem is given below. To determine, $C[i, j]$ we need to multiply the ith row of A with j^{th} column of B.

```
// Initialize C.
for i = 1 to n
  for j = 1 to n
    for k = 1 to n
      C[i, j] += A[i, k] * B[k, j];
```

The matrix multiplication problem can be solved with D&C technique. To implement a D&C algorithm we need to break the given problem into several subproblems that are similar to the original one. In this instance we view each of the $n \times n$ matrices as a 2×2 matrix, the elements of which are $\frac{n}{2} \times \frac{n}{2}$ submatrices. So, the original matrix multiplication, $C = A \times B$ can be written as:

$$\begin{bmatrix} C_{1,1} & C_{1,2} \\ C_{2,1} & C_{2,2} \end{bmatrix} = \begin{bmatrix} A_{1,1} & A_{1,2} \\ A_{2,1} & A_{2,2} \end{bmatrix} \times \begin{bmatrix} B_{1,1} & B_{1,2} \\ B_{2,1} & B_{2,2} \end{bmatrix}$$

where each $A_{i,j}$, $B_{i,j}$, and $C_{i,j}$ is a $\frac{n}{2} \times \frac{n}{2}$ matrix.

From the given definition o f $C_{i,j}$, we get that the result sub matrices can be computed as follows:

$$C_{1,1} = A_{1,1} \times B_{1,1} + A_{1,2} \times B_{2,1}$$
$$C_{1,2} = A_{1,1} \times B_{1,2} + A_{1,2} \times B_{2,2}$$
$$C_{2,1} = A_{2,1} \times B_{1,1} + A_{2,2} \times B_{2,1}$$
$$C_{2,2} = A_{2,1} \times B_{1,2} + A_{2,2} \times B_{2,2}$$

Here the symbols + and $\times$ are taken to mean addition and multiplication (respectively) of $\frac{n}{2} \times \frac{n}{2}$ matrices.

In order to compute the original $n \times n$ matrix multiplication we must compute eight $\frac{n}{2} \times \frac{n}{2}$ matrix products (*divide*) followed by four $\frac{n}{2} \times \frac{n}{2}$ matrix sums (*conquer*). Since matrix addition is an $O(n^2)$ operation, the total running time for the multiplication operation is given by the recurrence:

$$T(n) = \begin{cases} O(1) & ,for\ n = 1 \\ 8T\left(\frac{n}{2}\right) + O(n^2) & ,for\ n > 1 \end{cases}$$

Using master theorem, we get, $T(n) = O(n^3)$.

Fortunately, it turns out that one of the eight matrix multiplications is redundant (found by Strassen). Consider the following series of seven $\frac{n}{2} \times \frac{n}{2}$ matrices:

$$M_0 = \left(A_{1,1} + A_{2,2}\right) \times \left(B_{1,1} + B_{2,2}\right)$$
$$M_1 = \left(A_{1,2} - A_{2,2}\right) \times \left(B_{2,1} + B_{2,2}\right)$$
$$M_2 = \left(A_{1,1} - A_{2,1}\right) \times \left(B_{1,1} + B_{1,2}\right)$$
$$M_3 = \left(A_{1,1} + A_{1,2}\right) \times B_{2,2}$$
$$M_4 = A_{1,1} \times \left(B_{1,2} - B_{2,2}\right)$$
$$M_5 = A_{2,2} \times \left(B_{2,1} - B_{1,1}\right)$$
$$M_6 = \left(A_{21} + A_{2,2}\right) \times B_{1,1}$$

Each equation above has only one multiplication. Ten additions and seven multiplications are required to compute M_0 through M_6. Given M_0 through M_6, we can compute the elements of the product matrix C as follows:

$$C_{1,1} = M_0 + M_1 - M_3 + M_5$$
$$C_{1,2} = M_3 + M_4$$
$$C_{2,1} = M_5 + M_6$$
$$C_{2,2} = M_0 - M_2 + M_4 - M_6$$

This approach requires seven $\frac{n}{2} \times \frac{n}{2}$ matrix multiplications and 18 $\frac{n}{2} \times \frac{n}{2}$ additions. Therefore, the worst-case running time is given by the following recurrence:

$$T(n) = \begin{cases} O(1) & ,for\ n = 1 \\ 7T\left(\frac{n}{2}\right) + O(n^2) & ,for\ n = 1 \end{cases}$$

Using master theorem, we get, $T(n) = O\left(n^{\log_2^7}\right) = O(n^{2.81})$.

Problem-15   **Stock Pricing Problem:** Consider the stock price of *CareerMonk.com* in n consecutive days. That means the input consists of an array with stock prices of the company. We know that stock price will not be same on all the days. In the input stock prices there may be dates where the stock is high when we can sell the current holdings and there may be days when we can buy the stock. Now our problem is to find the day on which we can buy the stock and the day on which we can sell the stock so that we can make maximum profit.

Solution: As given in problem let us assume that the input is an array with stock prices [integers]. Let us say the given array is $A[1], ..., A[n]$. From this array we have to find two days [one for buy and one for sell] in such a way that we can make maximum profit. Also, another point to make is that buy date should be before sell date. One simple approach is to look at all possible buy and sell dates.

```java
void StockStrategy(int A[], int n, int *buyDateIndex, int *sellDateIndex) {
        int profit=0;
        *buyDateIndex =0; *sellDateIndex =0;;
        for (int i   = 1; i < n; i++)              //indicates buy date
                //indicates sell date
                for(int j  = i; j < n;  j++)
                        if(A[j] - A[i] > profit)        {
                                profit = A[j] - A[i];
                                *buyDateIndex = i;
                                *sellDateIndex = j;
                        }
}
```

The two nested loops takes $n(n + 1)/2$ computations, so this takes time $\Theta(n^2)$.

Problem-16   For Problem-15, can we improve the time complexity?

Solution: Yes, by opting for the Divide-and-Conquer $\Theta(nlogn)$ solution. Divide the input list into two parts and recursively find the solution in both the parts. Here, we get three cases:

- *buyDateIndex* and *sellDateIndex* both are in the earlier time period.
- *buyDateIndex* and *sellDateIndex* both are in the later time period.
- *buyDateIndex* is in the earlier part and *sellDateIndex* is in the later part of the time period.

The first two cases can be solved with recursion. The third case needs care. This is because *buyDateIndex* is one side and *sellDateIndex* is on other side. In this case we need to find the minimum and maximum prices in the two sub-parts and this we can solve in linear-time.

```java
void StockStrategy(int A[], int left, int right) {
        //Declare the necessary variables;
        if(left + 1 = right)
                return (0, left, left);
        mid   = left + (right - left) / 2;
        (profitLeft, buyDateIndexLeft, sellDateIndexLeft) =  StockStrategy(A, left, mid);
        (profitRight, buyDateIndexRight, sellDateIndexRight)  = StockStrategy(A, mid, right);
        minLeft  = Min(A, left, mid);
        maxRight  = Max(A, mid, right);
        profit  = A[maxRight] - A[minLeft];
        if(profitLeft > max{profitRight, profit})
                return (profitLeft, buyDateIndexLeft, sellDateIndexLeft);
        else if(profitRight > max{profitLeft, profit})
                return (profitRight, buyDateIndexRight, sellDateIndexRight);
        else
                return (profit, minLeft, maxRight);
}
```

Algorithm *StockStrategy* is used recursively on two problems of half the size of the input, and in addition $\Theta(n)$ time is spent searching for the maximum and minimum prices. So the time complexity is characterized by the recurrence $T(n) = 2T(n/2) + \Theta(n)$ and by the Master theorem we get O(nlogn).

Problem-17   We are testing "unbreakable" laptops and our goal is to find out how unbreakable they really are. In particular, we work in an n-story building and want to find out the lowest floor from which we can drop the laptop without breaking it (call this "the ceiling"). Suppose we are given two laptops and you want to find the highest ceiling possible. Give an algorithm that minimizes the number of tries we need to make $f(n)$ (hopefully, $f(n)$ is sub-linear, as a linear $f(n)$ yields a trivial solution).

Solution: For the given problem, we cannot use binary search as we cannot divide the problem and solve it recursively. Let us take some example for understanding the scenario. Let us say 14 is the answer. That means

---

we need 14 drops for finding the answer. First we drop from height 14, if it breaks we try all floors from 1 to 13. If it doesn't break then we are left 13 drops, so we will drop it from $14 + 13 + 1 = 28^{th}$ floor. The reason being if it breaks at 28th floor we can try all the floors from 15 to 27 in 12 drops (total of 14 drops). Now if it did not break then we are left with 11 drops and we can try to figure out the floor in 14 drops.

From the above example, it can be seen that we first tried with a gap of 14 floors, and then followed by 13 floors, then 12 and so on. So if the answer is k then we are trying the intervals at $k, k - 1, k - 2 ....1$. Given number of floors is n, we have to relate these two. Since the maximum floor from which we can try is n, the total skips should be less than n. This gives:

$$k + (k - 1) + (k - 2) + \cdots + 1 \le n$$
$$\frac{k(k + 1)}{2} \le n$$
$$k \le \sqrt{n}$$

Complexity of this process is $O(\sqrt{n})$.

Problem-18   Given n numbers, check if any two are equal.

Solution: Refer *Searching* chapter.

Problem-19   Give an algorithm to find out if an integer is a square? E.g. 16 is, 15 isn't.

Solution: Initially let us say $i = 2$. Compute the value $i \times i$ and see if it is equal to the given number. If it is equal then we are done otherwise increment the i vlaue. Continue this process until we reach $i \times i$ greater than or equal to the given number.

Time Complexity: $O(\sqrt{n})$. Space Complexity: $O(1)$.

Problem-20   **Nuts and Bolts Problem:** Given a set of n nuts of different sizes and n bolts such that there is a one-to-one correspondence between the nuts and the bolts, find for each nut its corresponding bolt. Assume that we can only compare nuts to bolts (cannot compare nuts to nuts and bolts to bolts).

Solution: Refer *Sorting* chapter.

Problem-21   **Closest-Pair of Points Problem:** Given a set of n points $S = \{p_1, p_2, p_3, \dots, p_n\}$, where $p_i = (x_i, y_i)$. Find the pair of points having smallest distance among all pairs. For simplicity, let us assume that all points are in one dimension.

Solution: Let us assume that we have sorted the points. Since the points are in one dimension, all the points are in a line after we sort them (either on X-axis or Y-axis). The complexity of sorting is $O(nlogn)$. After sorting we can go through them to find the consecutive points with least difference. So the problem in one dimension is solved in $O(nlogn)$ time which is mainly dominated by sorting time.

Time Complexity: $O(nlogn)$.

Problem-22   For the Problem-21, how do we solve if the points are in two dimensional space?

Solution: Before going to algorithm, let us consider the following mathematical equation:

$$distance(p_1, p_2) = \sqrt{(x_1 - x_2)^2 - (y_1 - y_2)^2}$$

The above equation calculates the distance between two points $p_1 = (x_1, y_1)$ and $p_2 = (x_2, y_2)$.

Brute Force Solution:

- Calculate the distances between all the pairs of points. From n points there are n_{c_2} ways of selecting 2 points. $(n_{c_2} = O(n^2))$.
- After finding distances for all n^2 possibilities, we select the one which is giving the minimum distance and this takes $O(n^2)$.

The overall time complexity is $O(n^2)$.

Problem-23   Give $O(nlogn)$ solution for *closest pair* problem (Problem-22)?

Solution: To find $O(nlogn)$ solution, we can use the $D \& C$ technique. Before starting the divide-and-conquer process let us assume that the points are sorted by increasing x-coordinate. Divide the points into two equal halves based on median of x- coordinates. That means problem is divided into that of finding the closest pair in each of the two halves. For simplicity let us consider the following algorithm to understand the process.

Algorithm:

1) Sort the given points in S (given set of points) based on their x −coordinates. Partition S into two subsets, S_1 and S_2, about the line l through median of S. This step is the *Divide* part of the D&C technique.
2) Find the closest-pairs in S_1 and S_2 and call them L and R recursively.

3) Now, steps-4 to 8 form the Combining component of the *D & C* technique.
4) Let us assume that $\delta = min(L, R)$.
5) Eliminate points that are farther than δ apart from l.
6) Consider the remaining points and sort based on their y-coordinates.
7) Scan the remaining points in the y order and compute the distances of each point to all its neighbors that are distanced no more than $2 \times \delta$ (that's the reason for sorting according to y).
8) If any of these distances is less than δ then update δ.

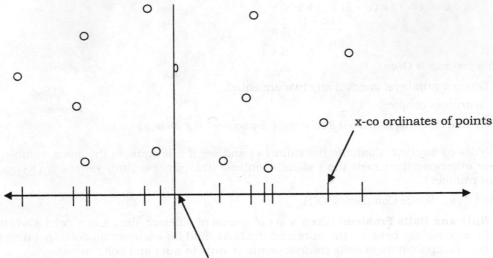

Line l passing through the median point and divides the set into 2 equal parts

Combining the results in linear time

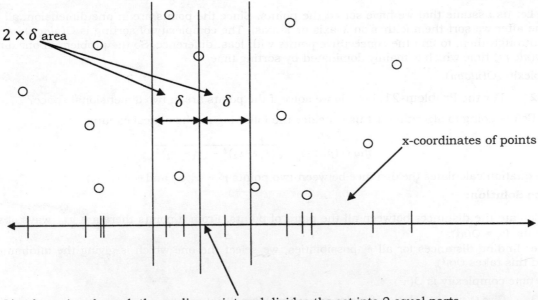

Line l passing through the median point and divides the set into 2 equal parts

Let $\delta = min(L, R)$, where L is the solution to first sub problem and R is the solution to second sub problem. The possible candidates for closest-pair, which are across the dividing line, are those which are less than δ distance from the line. So we need only the points which are inside the $2 \times \delta$ area across the dividing line as shown in the figure. Now, to check all points within distance δ from the line consider the following figure.

From the above diagram we can see that maximum of 12 points can be placed inside the square with a distance not less than δ. That means, we need to check only the distances which are within 11 positions in sorted list. This is similar to above one, but with the difference that in the above combining of subproblems, there are no vertical bounds. So we can apply the 12-point box tactic over all the possible boxes in the $2 \times \delta$ area with dividing line as middle line. As there can be a maximum of n such boxes in the area, the total time for finding the closest pair in the corridor is $O(n)$.

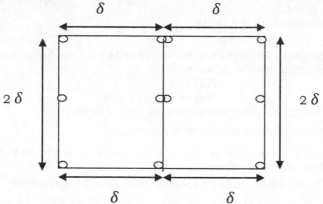

Analysis:

1) Step-1 and Step-2 take $O(nlogn)$ for sorting and recursively finding the minimum.
2) Step-4 takes $O(1)$.
3) Step-5 takes $O(n)$ for scanning and eliminating.
4) Step-6 takes $O(n \, logn)$ for sorting.
5) Step-7 takes $O(n)$ for scanning.

The total complexity, $T(n) = O(nlogn) + O(1) + O(n) + O(n) + O(n) \approx O(nlogn)$

Problem-24   Maximum Value Contiguous Subsequence: Given a sequence of n numbers $A(1)\dots A(n)$, give an algorithm for finding a contiguous subsequence $A(i)\dots A(j)$ for which the sum of elements in the subsequence is maximum. **Example**: {-2, **11, -4, 13**, -5, 2} →20 and {1, -3, **4, -2, -1, 6**}→7.

Solution: Divide this input into two halves. The maximum contiguous subsequence sum can occur in one of 3 ways:

- Case 1: It can be completely in the first half
- Case 2: It can be completely in the second half
- Case 3: It begins in the first half and ends in the second half

We begin by looking at case 3. To avoid the nested loop that results from considering all $n/2$ starting points and $n/2$ ending points independently. Replace two nested loops by two consecutive loops. The consecutive loops, each of size $n/2$ combine to require only linear work. Any contiguous subsequence that begins in the first half and ends in the second half must include both the last element of the first half and first element of the second half.

What we can do in cases 1 and 2 is apply the same strategy of dividing into more halves. In summary, we do the following:

1. Recursively compute the maximum contiguous subsequence that resides entirely in the first half.
2. Recursively compute the maximum contiguous subsequence that resides entirely in the second half.
3. Compute, via two consecutive loops, the maximum contiguous subsequence sum that begins in the first half but ends in the second half.
4. Choose the largest of the three sums.

```
int MaxSumRec(int A[], int left, int right) {
        int MaxLeftBorderSum = 0, MaxRightBorderSum = 0, LeftBorderSum = 0, RightBorderSum = 0;
        int mid = left + (right - left) / 2;
        if(left == right) // Base Case
                return A[left] > 0 ? A[left] : 0;
        int MaxLeftSum = MaxSumRec(A, left, mid);
        int MaxRightSum = MaxSumRec(A, mid + 1, right);
        for int i = mid; i >= left; i--) {
                LeftBorderSum += A[i];
                if(LeftBorderSum > MaxLeftBorderSum)
                        MaxLeftBorderSum = LeftBorderSum;
        }
        for (int j = mid + 1; j <= right; j++) {
                RightBorderSum += A[j];
                if(RightBorderSum > MaxRightBorderSum)
                        MaxRightBorderSum = RightBorderSum;
```

```
        }
        return Max(MaxLeftSum, MaxRightSum,MaxLeftBorderSum + MaxRightBorderSum);
}
int MaxSubsequenceSum(int A, int n) {
        return n > 0 ? MaxSumRec(A, 0, n – 1) : 0;
}
```

The base case cost is 1. The program performs two recursive calls plus the linear work involved in computing the maximum sum for case 3. The recurrence relation is:

$$T(1) = 1$$
$$T(n) = 2T(n/2) + n$$

Using *D & C* Master theorem, we get the time complexity as $T(n) = O(nlogn)$.

Note: For efficient solution refer *Dynamic Programming* chapter.

Problem-25   Given an array of $2n$ integers in the following format $a1\ a2\ a3\ ...\ an\ b1\ b2\ b3\ ...\ bn$. Shuffle the array to $a1\ b1\ a2\ b2\ a3\ b3\ ...\ an\ bn$ without any extra memory [MA].

Solution: Let us take an example (for brute force solution refer *Searching* chapter)

1. Start with the array: $a1\ a2\ a3\ a4\ b1\ b2\ b3\ b4$
2. Split the array into two halves: $a1\ a2\ a3\ a4 : b1\ b2\ b3\ b4$
3. Exchange elements around the center: exchange $a3\ a4$ with $b1\ b2$ you get: $a1\ a2\ b1\ b2\ a3\ a4\ b3\ b4$
4. Split $a1\ a2\ b1\ b2$ into $a1\ a2 : b1\ b2$ then split $a3\ a4\ b3\ b4$ into $a3\ a4 : b3\ b4$
5. Exchange elements around the center for each subarray you get: $a1\ b1\ a2\ b2$ and $a3\ b3\ a4\ b4$

Please note that this solution only handles the case when $n = 2^i$ where $i = 0, 1, 2, 3$ etc. In our example $n = 2^2 = 4$ which makes it easy to recursively split the array into two halves. The basic idea behind swapping elements around the center before calling the recursive function is to produce smaller size problems. A solution with linear time complexity may be achieved if the elements are of specific nature for example if you can calculate the new position of the element using the value of the element itself. This is nothing but a hashing technique.

```
void ShuffleArray(int A[], int l, int r) {
                //Array center
                int c = (l + r)/2, q = 1 + (l + c)/2;
                if(l == r) //Base case when the array has only one element
                        return;
                for (int k = 1, i = q; i <= c; i++, k++) {
                        //Swap elements around the center
                        int tmp = A[i];    A[i] = A[c + k];    A[c + k] = tmp;
                }
                ShuffleArray(A, l, c);         //Recursively call the function on the left and right
                ShuffleArray(A, c + 1, r); );   //Recursively call the function on the right
}
```

Time Complexity: O($nlogn$).

Problem-26   To calculate k^n, give algorithm and discuss its complexity.

Solution: The naive algorithm to compute k^n is: start with 1 and multiply by k until reaching k^n. For this approach; there are $n - 1$ multiplications and each takes constant time giving a $\Theta(n)$ algorithm.

But there is a faster way to compute k^n. For example,

$$9^{24} = (9^{12})^2 = ((9^6)^2)^2 = (((9^3)^2)^2)^2 = (((9^2.9)^2)^2)^2$$

Note that taking square of a number needs only one multiplication; this way, to compute 9^{24} we need only 5 multiplications instead of 23.

```
int Exponential(int k, int n) {
    if (k == 0)
        return 1;
    else{
        if (n%2 == 1){
            a = Exponential(k, n-1);
            return a*k;
        }
        else{
            a= Exponential(k, n/2);
            return a*a;
        }
    }
```

```
    }
}
```

Let T(n) be the number of multiplications required to compute k^n. For simplicity, assume $k = 2^i$ for some $i \geq 1$.

$$T(n) = T\left(\frac{n}{2}\right) + 1$$

Using master theorem we get T(n) = O(*logn*).

Chapter-19

DYNAMIC PROGRAMMING

19.1 Introduction

In this chapter we will try to solve the problems for which we failed to get the optimal solutions using other techniques (say, *Divide & Conquer* and *Greedy* methods). Dynamic Programming (DP) is a simple technique but it can be difficult to master. One easy way to identify and solve DP problems is by solving as many problems as possible. The term *Programming* is not related to coding but it is from literature, and means filling tables (similar to *Linear Programming*).

19.2 What is Dynamic Programming Strategy?

Dynamic programming and memoization work together. The main difference between dynamic programming and divide and conquer is that in-case of the latter, sub problems are independent, whereas in DP there can be an overlap of sub problems. By using memoization [maintaining a table of sub problems already solved], dynamic programming reduces the exponential complexity to polynomial complexity ($O(n^2)$, $O(n^3)$, etc.) for many problems. The major components of DP are:

- Recursion: Solves sub problems recursively.
- Memoization: Stores already computed values in table.

$$Dynamic\ Programming\ =\ Recursion\ +\ Memorization$$

19.3 Properties of Dynamic Programming Strategy

The two dynamic programming properties which can tell whether it can solve the given problem or not are:
- *Optimal substructure*: an optimal solution to a problem contains optimal solutions to sub problems.
- *Overlapping subproblems*: a recursive solution contains a small number of distinct sub problems repeated many times.

19.4 Can Dynamic Programming Solve All Problems?

Like Greedy and Divide and Conquer techniques, DP cannot solve every problem. There are problems which cannot be solved by any algorithmic technique [Greedy, Divide and Conquer and Dynamic Programming].

The difference between Dynamic Programming and straightforward recursion is in memoization of recursive calls. If the sub problems are independent and there is no repetition then memoization does not help, so dynamic programming is not a solution for all problems.

19.5 Dynamic Programming Approaches

Basically there are two approaches for solving DP problems:
- Bottom-up dynamic programming
- Top-down dynamic programming

Bottom-up Dynamic Programming

In this method, we evaluate the function starting with smallest possible input argument value and then we step through possible values, slowly increasing input argument value. While computing the values we store all computed values in a table (memory). As larger arguments are evaluated, pre-computed values for smaller arguments can be used.

Top-down Dynamic Programming

In this method, the problem is broken into sub problems; each of these sub problems solved; and the solutions remembered, in case they need to be solved. Also, we save each computed value as final action of recursive function and as the first action we check if pre-computed value exists.

Bottom-up versus Top-down Programming

In bottom-up programming, programmer has to select values to calculate and decide order of calculation. In this case, all sub problems that might be needed are solved in advance and then used to build up solutions to larger problems. In top-down programming, recursive structure of original code is preserved, but unnecessary recalculation is avoided. The problem is broken into sub problems, these sub problems are solved and the solutions remembered, in case they need to be solved again.

Note: Some problems can be solved with both the techniques and we will see such examples in next section.

19.6 Examples of Dynamic Programming Algorithms

- Many string algorithms including longest common subsequence, longest increasing subsequence, longest common substring, edit distance.
- Algorithms on graphs can be solved efficiently: Bellman-Ford algorithm for finding the shortest distance in a graph, Floyd's All-Pairs shortest path algorithm etc...
- Chain matrix multiplication
- Subset Sum
- 0/1 Knapsack
- Travelling salesman problem and many more

19.7 Understanding Dynamic Programming

Before going to problems, let us understand how DP works through examples.

Fibonacci Series

In Fibonacci series, the current number is the sum of previous two numbers. The Fibonacci series is defined as follows:

$$
\begin{aligned}
Fib(n) &= 0, & for\ n = 0 \\
&= 1, & for\ n = 1 \\
&= Fib(n-1) + Fib(n-2), & for\ n > 1
\end{aligned}
$$

The recursive implementation can be given as:

```
int RecursiveFibonacci(int n) {
        if(n == 0) return 0;
        if(n == 1) return 1;
        return RecursiveFibonacci(n -1) + RecursiveFibonacci(n -2);
}
```

Solving the above recurrence gives,

$$T(n) = T(n-1) + T(n-2) + 1 \approx \left(\tfrac{1+\sqrt{5}}{2}\right)^n \approx 2^n = O(2^n)$$

Note: For proof, refer *Introduction* chapter.

How does Memoization help? Calling $fib(5)$ produces a call tree that calls the function on the same value many times:

```
fib(5)
fib(4) + fib(3)
(fib(3) + fib(2)) + (fib(2) + fib(1))
((fib(2) + fib(1)) + (fib(1) + fib(0))) + ((fib(1) + fib(0)) + fib(1))
(((fib(1) + fib(0)) + fib(1)) + (fib(1) + fib(0))) + ((fib(1) + fib(0)) + fib(1))
```

In the above example, $fib(2)$ was calculated three times (overlapping of subproblems). If n is big then many more values of fib (sub problems) are recalculated, which leads to an exponential time algorithm. Instead of solving the same sub problems again and again we can store the previous calculated values and reduce the complexity.

Memoization works like this: Start with a recursive function and add a table that maps the functions parameter values to the results computed by the function. Then if this function is called twice with the same parameters, we simply look up the answer in the table.

Improving: Now, we see how DP reduces this problem complexity from exponential to polynomial. As discussed earlier, there are two ways of doing this. One approach is bottom-up: these methods starts with lower values of input and keep building the solutions for higher values.

```
int fib[n];
```

```
int fib(int n) {
        if(n == 0 || n == 1) return 1;
        fib[0] = 1;
        fib[1] = 1;
        for (int i = 2; i < n; i++)
                fib[i] = fib[i - 1] + fib[i - 2];
        return fib[n - 1];
}
```

Other approach is top-down. In this method, we preserve the recursive calls and use the values if they are already computed. The implementation for this is given as:

```
int fib[n];
int fibonacci( int n ) {
        if(n == 1) return 1;
        if(n == 2) return 1;
        if( fib[n] != 0)
                return fib[n] ;
        return fib[n] = fibonacci(n-1) + fibonacci(n -2) ;
}
```

Note: For all problems, it may not be possible to find both top-down and bottom-up programming solutions.

Both the versions of Fibonacci series implementations clearly reduce the problem complexity to $O(n)$. This is because if a value is already computed then we are not calling the subproblems again. Instead, we are directly taking its value from table.

Time Complexity: $O(n)$. Space Complexity: $O(n)$, for table.

Further Improving: One more observation from the Fibonacci series is: The current value is the sum of previous two calculations only. This indicates that we don't have to store all the previous values. Instead if we store just the last two values, we can calculate the current value. Implementation for this is given below:

```
int fibonacci(int n) {
        int a = 0, b = 1, sum, i;
        for (i=0;i < n;i++) {
                sum = a + b;
                a = b;
                b = sum;
        }
        return sum;
}
```

Time Complexity: $O(n)$. Space Complexity: $O(1)$.

Note: This method may not be applicable (available) for all problems.

Observations: While solving the problems using DP, try to figure out the following:
- See how problems are defined in terms of subproblems recursively.
- See if we can use some table [memoization] to avoid the repeated calculations.

Factorial of a Number

As another example consider the factorial problem: $n!$ is the product of all integers between n and 1. Definition of recursive factorial can be given as:

$$n! = n * (n-1)!$$
$$1! = 1$$
$$0! = 1$$

This definition can easily be converted to implementation. Here the problem is finding the value of $n!$, and sub problem is finding the value of $(n - l)!$. In the recursive case, when n is greater than 1, function calls itself to find the value of $(n - l)!$ and multiplies that with n. In the base case, when n is 0 or 1, the function simply returns 1.

```
int fact(int n) {
        if(n == 1)                              // base cases: fact of 0 or 1 is 1
            return 1;
        else if(n == 0)
            return 1;
        // recursive case: multiply n by (n -1) factorial
        else return n *fact(n -1);
```

}

The recurrence for the above implementation can be given as: $T(n) = n \times T(n-1) \approx O(n)$

Time Complexity: $O(n)$. Space Complexity: $O(n)$, recursive calls need a stack of size n.

In the above recurrence relation and implementation, for any n value, there are no repetitive calculations (*no overlapping of sub problems*) and the factorial function is not getting any benefits with dynamic programming. Now, let us say we want to compute a series of $m!$ for some arbitrary value m. Using the above algorithm, for each such call we can compute it in $O(m)$. For example, to find both $n!$ and $m!$ we can use the above approach, wherein the total complexity for finding $n!$ and $m!$ is $O(m + n)$.

Time Complexity: $O(n + m)$. Space Complexity: $O(max(m,n))$, recursive calls need a stack of size equal to the maximum of m and n.

Improving: Now let us see how DP reduces the complexity. From the above recursive definition it can be seen that $fact(n)$ is calculated from $fact(n-1)$ and n and nothing else. Instead of calling $fact(n)$ every time, we can store the previous calculated values in a table and use these values to calculate a new value. This implementation can be given as:

```java
int facto[n];
int fact(int n) {
        // base cases: fact of 0 or 1 is 1
        if(n == 1)
                return 1;
        else if(n == 0)
                return 1;
        //Already calculated case
        else if(facto[n]!=0) return facto[n];
        // recursive case: multiply n by (n -1) factorial
        else return facto[n]= n *fact(n -1);
}
```

For simplicity, let us assume that we have already calculated $n!$ and want to find $m!$. For finding $m!$, we just need to see the table and use the existing entries if they are already computed. If $m < n$ then we do not have to recalculate $m!$. If $m > n$ then we can use $n!$ and call the factorial on remaining numbers only.

The above implementation clearly reduces the complexity to $O(max(m,n))$. This is because if the $fact(n)$ is already there then we are not recalculating the value again. If we fill these newly computed values then the subsequent calls further reduces the complexity.

Time Complexity: $O(max(m,n))$. Space Complexity: $O(max(m,n))$ for table.

Longest Common Subsequence

Given two strings: string X of length m $[X(1..m)]$, and string Y of length n $[Y(1..n)]$, find longest common subsequence: the longest sequence of characters that appear left-to-right (but not necessarily in a contiguous block) in both strings. For example, if X = "ABCBDAB" and Y = "BDCABA", the $LCS(X, Y)$ = {"BCBA", "BDAB", "BCAB"}. As we can see there are several optimal solutions.

Brute Force Approach: One simple idea is to check every subsequence of $X[1..m]$ (m is the length of sequence X) to see if it is also a subsequence of $Y[1..n]$ (n is the length of sequence Y). Checking takes $O(n)$ time, and there are 2^m subsequences of X. The running time thus is exponential $O(n. 2^m)$ and is not good for large sequences.

Recursive Solution: Before going to DP solution, let us form the recursive solution for this and later we can add memoization to reduce the complexity. Let's start with some simple observations about the LCS problem. If we have two strings, say "ABCBDAB" and "BDCABA", if we draw lines from the letters in the first string to the corresponding letters in the second, no two lines cross:

From the above observation, we can see that current characters of X and Y may or may not match. That means, suppose that the two first characters differ. Then it is not possible for both of them to be part of a common subsequence - one or the other (or maybe both) will have to be removed. Finally, observe that once we have decided what to do with the first characters of the strings, the remaining sub problem is again a LCS problem, on two shorter strings. Therefore we can solve it recursively.

Solution to *LCS* should find two sequences in X and Y and let us say the starting index of sequence in X is i and starting index of sequence in T is j. Also, assume that $X[i \ldots m]$ is a substring of X starting at character i and going until the end of X and $Y[j \ldots n]$ is a substring of Y starting at character j and going until the end of Y.

Based on the above discussion, here we get the possibilities as described below:
1) If $X[i] == Y[j] : 1 + LCS(i+1, j+1)$
2) If $X[i] \neq Y[j]$: $LCS(i, j+1)$ // skipping j^{th} character of Y
3) If $X[i] \neq Y[j]$: $LCS(i+1, j)$ // skipping i^{th} character of X

In the first case, if $X[i]$ is equal to $Y[j]$, we get a matching pair and can count it towards the total length of the *LCS*. Otherwise, we need to skip either i^{th} character of X or j^{th} character of Y and find the longest common subsequence. Now, $LCS(i, j)$ can be defined as:

$$LCS(i, j) = \begin{cases} 0, & if\ i = m\ or\ j = n \\ Max\{LCS(i, j+1), LCS(i+1, j)\}, & if\ X[i] \neq Y[j] \\ 1 + LCS[i+1, j+1], & if\ X[i] == Y[j] \end{cases}$$

LCS has many applications. In web searching, if we find the smallest number of changes that are needed to change one word into another. A *change* here is an insertion, deletion or replacement of a single character.

```
//Initial Call: LCSLength(X, 0, m-1, Y, 0, n-1);
int LCSLength( int X[], int i, int m, int T[], int j, int n ) {
        if (i == m || j == n)
                return 0;
        else if (X[i] == Y[j]) return 1 + LCSLength(X, i+1, m, Y, j+1, n);
        else return max( LCSLength(X, i+1, m, Y, j, n),  LCSLength(X, i, m, Y, j+1, n));
}
```

This is a correct solution but it is very time consuming. For example, if the two strings have no matching characters, so the last line always gets executed which give (if $m == n$) are close to $O(2^n)$.

DP Solution: Adding Memoization: The problem with the recursive solution is that the same subproblems get called many different times. A subproblem consists of a call to LCSLength, with the arguments being two suffixes of X and Y, so there are exactly $(i + 1)(j + 1)$ possible subproblems (a relatively small number). If there are nearly 2^n recursive calls, some of these subproblems must be being solved over and over.

The DP solution is to check whenever we want to solve a sub problem, whether we've already done it before. So we look up the solution instead of solving it again. Implemented in the most direct way, we just add some code to our recursive solution. To do this, look up the code. This can be given as:

```
int LCS[1024][1024];
int LCSLength( int X[], int m, int Y[], int n ) {
        // base cases
        for( int i = 0; i <= m; i++ )
                LCS[i][n] = 0;
        for( int j = 0; j <= n; j++ )
                LCS[m][j] = 0;
        for( int i = m − 1; i >= 0; i) {
                for( int j = n − 1; j >= 0; j) {
                        LCS[i][j] = LCS[i + 1][j + 1]; // matching X[i] to Y[j]

                        if( X[i] == Y[j] )
                                LCS[i][j]++; // we get a matching pair

                        // the other two cases – inserting a gap
                        if(LCS[i][j + 1] > LCS[i][j] )
                                LCS[i][j] = LCS[i][j + 1];
                        if(LCS[i + 1][j] > LCS[i][j] )
                                LCS[i][j] = LCS[i + 1][j];

                }
        }
        return LCS[0][0];
}
```

First, take care of the base cases. We have created *LCS* table with one row and one column larger than the lengths of the two strings. Then run the iterative DP loops to fill each cell in the table. This is like doing recursion backwards, or bottom up.

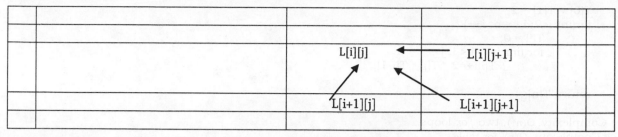

The value of $LCS[i][j]$ depends on 3 other values ($LCS[i+1][j+1]$, $LCS[i][j+1]$ and $LCS[i+1][j]$), all of which have larger values of i or j. They go through the table in the order of decreasing i and j values. This will guarantee that when we need to fill in the value of $LCS[i][j]$, we already know the values of all of the cells on which it depends.

Time Complexity: O(mn), since i takes values from 1 to m and and j takes values from 1 to n. Space Complexity: O(mn).

Note: In the above discussion, we have assumed $LCS(i, j)$ is the length of the LCS with $X[i ... m]$ and $Y[j ... n]$. We can solve the problem by changing the definition as $LCS(i, j)$ is the length of the LCS with $X[1 ... i]$ and $Y[1 ... j]$.

Printing the subsequence: Above algorithm can find the length of the longest common subsequence but cannot give the actual longest subsequence. To get the sequence, we trace it through the table. Start at cell $(0, 0)$. We know that the value of $LCS[0][0]$ was the maximum of 3 values of the neighboring cells. So we simply recompute $LCS[0][0]$ and note which cell gave the maximum value. Then we move to that cell (it will be one of $(1, 1)$, $(0, 1)$ or $(1, 0)$) and repeat this until we hit the boundary of the table. Every time we pass through a cell (i, j) where $X[i] == Y[j]$, we have a matching pair and print $X[i]$. At the end, we will have printed the longest common subsequence in O(mn) time.

An alternative way of getting path is to keep a separate table, for each cell. This will tell us which direction we came from when computing the value of that cell. At the end, we again start at cell $(0, 0)$ and follow these directions until the opposite corner of the table.

From the above examples, I hope you understood the idea behind DP. Now let us see more problems which can be easily solved using DP technique.

Note: As we have seen above, in DP the main component is recursion. If we know the recurrence then converting that to code is a minimal task. For the problems below, we concentrate on getting recurrence.

19.8 Problems on Dynamic Programming

Problem-1   Convert the following recurrence to code.

$$T(0) = T(1) = 2$$

$$T(n) = \sum_{i=1}^{n-1} 2 \times T(i) \times T(i-1), \text{for } n > 1$$

Solution: The code for the given recursive formula can be given as:

```java
int f(int n) {
        int sum = 0;
        if(n==0 || n==1)
                return 2;                //Base Case
        for(int i=1; i < n;i++)          //Recursive case
                sum += 2 * f(i) * f(i-1);
        return sum;
}
```

Problem-2   Can we improve the solution to Problem-1 using memoization of DP?

Solution: Yes. Before finding a solution, let us see how the values are calculated.

$$T(0) = T(1) = 2$$
$$T(2) = 2 * T(1) * T(0)$$
$$T(3) = 2 * T(1) * T(0) + 2 * T(2) * T(1)$$
$$T(4) = 2 * T(1) * T(0) + 2 * T(2) * T(1) + 2 * T(3) * T(2)$$

From the above calculations it is clear that, there are lots of repeated calculations with the same input values. Let us use table for avoiding these repeated calculations and the implementation can be given as:

```java
int f(int n) {
```

```
        T[0] = T[1] = 2;
        for(int i=2; i <= n; i++) {
                T[i] = 0;
                for (int j=1; j < i; j++)
                        T[i] +=2 * T[j] * T[j-1];
        }
        return T[n];
}
```

Time Complexity: $O(n^2)$, two *for* loops.
Space Complexity: $O(n)$, for table.

Problem-3   Can we further improve the complexity of Problem-2?

Solution: Yes, since all sub problem calculations are dependent only on previous calculations, code can be modified as:

```
int f(int n) {
        T[0] = T[1] = 2;
        T[2] = 2 * T[0] * T[1];
        for(int i=3; i <= n; i++)
                T[i]=T[i-1] + 2 * T[i-1] * T[i-2];
        return T[n];
}
```

Time Complexity: $O(n)$, since only one *for* loop.
Space Complexity: $O(n)$.

Problem-4   Maximum Value Contiguous Subsequence: Given an array of n numbers, give an algorithm for finding a contiguous subsequence $A(i) \ldots A(j)$ for which the sum of elements is maximum.
Example: {-2, **11, -4, 13**, -5, 2}→20 and {1, -3, **4, -2, -1, 6**} → 7

Solution:
Input: Array $A(1) \ldots A(n)$ of n numbers.
Goal: If there are no negative numbers then the solution is just the sum of all elements in the given array. If negative numbers are there, then our aim is to maximize the sum [there can be negative number in the contiguous sum].

One simple and brute force approach is to see all possible sums and select the one which has maximum value.

```
int MaxContigousSum(int A[], in n) {
        int maxSum = 0;
        for(int i = 0; i < n; i++)                    // for each possible start point
                for(int j = i; j < n; j++)    {       // for each possible end point
                        int currentSum = 0;
                        for(int k = i; k <= j; k++)
                                currentSum += A[k];
                        if(currentSum > maxSum)
                                maxSum = currentSum;

                }
        }
        return maxSum;
}
```

Time Complexity: $O(n^3)$.
Space Complexity: $O(1)$.

Problem-5   Can we improve the complexity of Problem-4?

Solution: Yes. One important observation is that, if we have already calculated the sum for the subsequence $i, \ldots, j - 1$, then we need only one more addition to get the sum for the subsequence $i, \ldots, j$. But, the Problem-4 algorithm ignores this information. If we use this fact, we can get an improved algorithm with the running time $O(n^2)$.

```
int MaxContigousSum(int A[], int n) {
        int maxSum = 0;
        for( int i = 0; i < n;  i++) {
                int currentSum = 0;
```

```
        for( int j = i; j < n; j++)   {
                currentSum += a[j];
                if(currentSum > maxSum)
                        maxSum = currentSum;

        }

    }
    return maxSum;
}
```

Time Complexity: $O(n^2)$.

Space Complexity: $O(1)$.

Problem-6   Can we solve Problem-4 using Dynamic Programming?

Solution: Yes. For simplicity, let us say, $M(i)$ indicates maximum sum over all windows ending at i.

Given Array, A: recursive formula considers the case of selecting i^{th} element

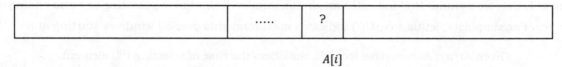

$$A[i]$$

To find maximum sum we have to do one of the following and select maximum among them.

- Either extend the old sum by adding $A[i]$
- or start new window starting with one element $A[i]$

$$M(i) = Max \begin{cases} M(i-1) + A[i] \\ 0 \end{cases}$$

Where, $M(i-1) + A[i]$ indicates the case of extending the previous sum by adding $A[i]$ and 0 indicates the new window starting at $A[i]$.

```
int MaxContigousSum(int A[], int n) {
        int M[n] = 0, maxSum = 0;
        if(A[0] > 0)
                M[0] = A[0];
        else M[0] = 0;
        for( int i = 1; i < n;   i++) {
                if( M[i-1] + A[i] > 0)
                        M[i] = M[i-1] + A[i];
                else
                        M[i] = 0;
        }
        maxSum = 0;
        for( int i = 0; i < n;   i++) {
                if(M[i] > maxSum) maxSum = M[i];
        }
        return maxSum;
}
```

Time Complexity: $O(n)$.

Space Complexity: $O(n)$, for table.

Problem-7   Is there any other way of solving Problem-4?

Solution: Yes. We can solve this problem without DP too (without memory). The algorithm is little tricky. One simple way is to look for all positive contiguous segments of the array (*sumEndingHere*) and keep track of maximum sum contiguous segment among all positive segments (*sumSoFar*). Each time we get a positive sum compare it with *sumSoFar* and update *sumSoFar* if it is greater than *sumSoFar*. Let us consider the following code for the above observation.

```
int MaxContigousSum(int A[], int n) {
        int sumSoFar = 0, sumEndingHere = 0;
        for(int i = 0; i < n; i++)   {
```

```
        sumEndingHere = sumEndingHere + A[i];
        if(sumEndingHere < 0) {
                sumEndingHere = 0;
                continue;
        }
        if(sumSoFar < sumEndingHere)
                sumSoFar = sumEndingHere;
    }
    return sumSoFar;
}
```

Note: Algorithm doesn't work if the input contains all negative numbers. It returns 0 if all numbers are negative. To overcoming this we can add an extra check before actual implementation. The phase will look if all numbers are negative, if they are it will return maximum of them (or smallest in terms of absolute value).

Time Complexity: $O(n)$, because we are doing only one scan. Space Complexity: $O(1)$, for table.

Problem-8   In Problem-7 solution, we have assumed that $M(i)$ indicates maximum sum over all windows ending at i. Can we assume $M(i)$ indicates maximum sum over all windows starting at i and ending at n?

Solution: Yes. For simplicity, let us say, $M(i)$ indicates maximum sum over all windows starting at i.

Given Array, A: recursive formula considers the case of selecting i^{th} element

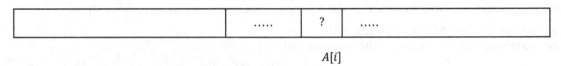

$$A[i]$$

To find maximum window we have to do one of the following and select maximum among them.

- Either extend the old sum by adding $A[i]$
- or start new window starting with one element A[i]

$$M(i) = Max \begin{cases} M(i+1) + A[i], & if\ M(i+1) + A[i] > 0 \\ 0 & , \quad if\ M(i+1) + A[i] <= 0 \end{cases}$$

Where, $M(i+1) + A[i]$ indicates the case of extending the previous sum by adding $A[i]$ and 0 indicates the new window starting at $A[i]$.

Time Complexity: $O(n)$.
Space Complexity: $O(n)$, for table.

Note: For $O(nlogn)$ solution refer *Divide and Conquer* chapter.

Problem-9   Given a sequence of n numbers $A(1)...A(n)$, give an algorithm for finding a contiguous subsequence $A(i)...A(j)$ for which the sum of elements in the subsequence is maximum. Here the condition is we should not select *two* contiguous numbers.

Solution: Let us see how DP solves this problem. Assume that $M(i)$ represents the maximum sum from 1 to i numbers without selecting two contiguous numbers. While computing $M(i)$, the decision we have to make is, whether to select i^{th} element or not. This gives us two possibilities and based on this we can write the recursive formula as:

$$M(i) = \begin{cases} Max\{A[i] + M(i-2), M(i-1)\}, & if\ i > 2 \\ A[1], & if\ i = 1 \end{cases}$$

Given Array, A: recursive formula considers the case of selecting i^{th} element

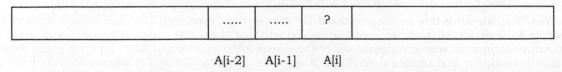

$$A[i-2] \quad A[i-1] \quad \quad A[i]$$

- The first case indicates whether we are selecting the ith element or not. If we don't select the ith element then we have to maximize the sum using the elements 1 to $i-1$. If i^{th} element is selected then we should not select $i-1^{th}$ element and need to maximize the sum using 1 to $i-2$ elements.
- In the above representation, the last two cases indicate the base cases.

```
int maxSumWithNoTwoContinuousNumbers(int A[], int n) {
    int M[n+1];
    M[0]=A[0];
    M[1]=(A[0]>A[1]?A[0]:A[i]);
    for(i=2, i<n; i++)
            M[i]= (M[i-1]>M[i-2]+A[i]? M[i-1]: M[i-2]+A[i]);
    return M[n-1];
}
```

Time Complexity: O(n).

Space Complexity: O(n).

Problem-10   In Problem-9, we assumed that $M(i)$ represents the maximum sum from 1 to i numbers without selecting two contiguous numbers. Can we solve the same problem by changing the definition as: $M(i)$ represents the maximum sum from i to n numbers without selecting two contiguous numbers?

Solution: Yes. Let us assume that $M(i)$ represents the maximum sum from i to n numbers without selecting two contiguous numbers.

Given Array, A: recursive formula considers the case of selecting i^{th} element

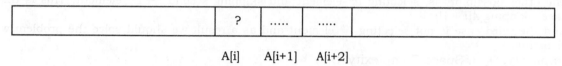

$$A[i] \qquad A[i+1] \qquad A[i+2]$$

As similar to Problem-9 solution, we can write the recursive formula as:

$$M(i) = \begin{cases} Max\{A[i] + M(i + 2), M(i + 1)\}, & if\ i > 2 \\ A[1], & if\ i = 1 \\ Max\{A[1], A[2]\}, & if\ i = 2 \end{cases}$$

- The first case indicates whether we are selecting the ith element or not. If we don't select the ith element then we have to maximize the sum using the elements $i + 1$ to n. If i^{th} element is selected then we should not select $i + 1^{th}$ element need to maximize the sum using $i + 2$ to n elements.
- In the above representation, the last two cases indicate the base cases.

Time Complexity: O(n). Space Complexity: O(n).

Problem-11   Given a sequence of n numbers $A(1) \ldots A(n)$, give an algorithm for finding a contiguous subsequence $A(i) \ldots A(j)$ for which the sum of elements in the subsequence is maximum. Here the condition is we should not select *three* continuous numbers.

Solution: Assume that $M(i)$ represents the maximum sum from 1 to i numbers without selecting three contiguous numbers. While computing $M(i)$, the decision we have to make is, whether to select i^{th} element or not. This gives us the following possibilities:

$$M(i) = Max \begin{cases} A[i] + A[i - 1] + M(i - 3) \\ A[i] + M(i - 2) \\ M(i - 1) \end{cases}$$

Given Array, A: recursive formula considers the case of selecting i^{th} element

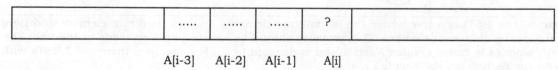

$$A[i-3] \qquad A[i-2] \qquad A[i-1] \qquad A[i]$$

- In the given problem the restriction is not to select three continuous numbers, but we can select two elements continuously and skip the third one. That is what the first case says in the above recursive formula. That means, skipping $A[i - 2]$.
- The other possibility is, selecting i^{th} element and skipping second $i - 1^{th}$ element. This is the second case (skipping $A[i - 1]$).
- The third term defines the case of not selecting i^{th} element and as a result we should solve the problem with $i - 1$ elements.

Time Complexity: O(n). Space Complexity: O(n).

Problem-12   In Problem-11, we assumed that $M(i)$ represents the maximum sum from 1 to i numbers without selecting three contiguous numbers. Can we solve the same problem by changing the definition as: $M(i)$ represents the maximum sum from i to n numbers without selecting three contiguous numbers?

Solution: Yes. Assume that $M(i)$ represents the maximum sum from i to n numbers without selecting three contiguous numbers. While computing $M(i)$, the decision we have to make is, whether to select i^{th} element or not. This gives us the following possibilities:

$$M(i) = Max \begin{cases} A[i] + A[i+1] + M(i+3) \\ A[i] + M(i+2) \\ M(i+1) \end{cases}$$

Given Array, A: recursive formula considers the case of selecting i^{th} element

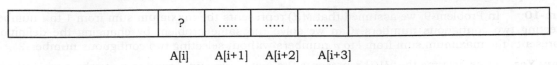

A[i]   A[i+1]   A[i+2]   A[i+3]

- In the given problem the restriction is not to select three continuous numbers, but we can select two elements continuously and skip the third one. That is what the first case says in the above recursive formula. That means we are skipping $A[i+2]$.
- The other possibility is, selecting i^{th} element and skipping second $i-1^{th}$ element. This is the second case (skipping $A[i+1]$).
- And the third case is not selecting i^{th} element and as a result we should solve the problem with $i+1$ elements.

Time Complexity: O(n). Space Complexity: O(n).

Problem-13   **Catalan Numbers:** How many binary search trees are there with n vertices?

Solution:

Number of nodes, n	Number of Trees
1	①
2	② ①
3	③ ① ③ ① ②

Binary Search Tree (BST) is a tree where the left subtree elements are less than root element and right subtree elements are greater than root element. This property should be satisfied at every node in the tree. The number of BSTs with n nodes is called *Catalan Number* and is denoted by C_n. For example, there are 2 BSTs with 2 nodes (2 choices for the root) and 5 BSTs with 3 nodes.

Let us assume that the nodes of the tree are number from 1 to n. Among the nodes, we have to select some node as root and divide the nodes which are less than root node into left sub tree and elements greater than root node into right sub tree. Since we have already numbered the vertices, let us assume that the root element we selected is i^{th} element. If we select i^{th} element as root then we get $i-1$ elements on left sub-tree and $n-i$ elements on right sub tree. Since C_n is the Catalan number for n elements, C_{i-1} represents the Catalan number for left sub tree elements ($i-1$ elements) and C_{n-i} represents the Catalan number for right sub tree elements. The two sub trees are independent of each other, so we simply multiply the two numbers. That means, the Catalan number for a fixed i value is $C_{i-1} \times C_{n-i}$. Since there are n nodes, for i we will get n choices. The total Catalan number with n nodes can be given as:

$$C_n = \sum_{i=1}^{n} C_{i-1} \times C_{n-i}$$

For this simple recursive definition, we can write the function as:

```java
int CatalanNumber( int n ) {
        if( n == 0 ) return 1;
        int count = 0;
        for( int i = 1; i <= n; i++ )
                count += CatalanNumber (i -1) * CatalanNumber (n -i);
        return count;
}
```

Time Complexity: $O(4^n)$. For proof, refer *Introduction* chapter.

Problem-14   Can we improve the time complexity of Problem-13 using DP?

Solution: The recursive call, C_n depends only on the numbers C_0 to C_{n-1} and for any value of i, there are lot of recalculations. We will keep a table of previously computed values of C_i. If the function *CatalanNumber*() is called with parameter i, and if it is already computed before then we can simply avoid recalculating the same subproblem.

```java
int Table[1024];
int CatalanNumber( int n ) {
        if( Table[n] ) != 1 )
                return Table[n];
        Table[n] = 0;
        for( int i = 1; i <= n; i++ )
                Table[n] += CatalanNumber( i -1) * CatalanNumber(n -i);
        return Table[n];
}
```

The time complexity of this implementation $O(n^2)$, because to compute *CatalanNumber*(n), we need to compute all of the *CatalanNumber*(i) values between 0 and $n-1$, and each one will be computed exactly once, in linear time.

In mathematics, Catalan Number can be represented by direct equation as: $\frac{(2n)!}{n!(n+1)!}$.

Problem-15   **Matrix Product Parenthesizations:** Given a series of matrices: $A_1 \times A_2 \times A_3 \times \ldots \times A_n$ with their dimensions, what is the best way to parenthesize them so that it produces the minimum number of total multiplications. Assume that we are using standard matrix and not Strassen's matrix multiplication algorithm.

Solution: For matrix multiplication problem, there are many possibilities. This is because matrix multiplication is associative. It does not matter how we parenthesize the product, the result will be the same. As an example, for four matrices A, B, C, and D, the possibilities could be:

$$(ABC)D = (AB)(CD) = A(BCD) = A(BC)D = ..$$

Multiplying $(p \times q)$ matrix with $(q \times r)$ matrix requires pqr multiplications. Each of the above possibility produces different number of products during multiplication. To select the best one, we can go through each possible parenthesizations (brute force), but this requires $O(2^n)$ time and is very slow.

Now let us use DP to improve this time complexity. Assume that, $M[i,j]$ represents the least number of multiplications needed to multiply $A_i \cdots A_j$.

$$M[i,j] = \begin{cases} 0 & ,if\ i = j \\ Min\{M[i,k] + M[k+1,j] + P_{i-1}P_kP_j\}, if\ i < j \end{cases}$$

The above recursive formula says that we have to find point k such that it produces the minimum number of multiplications. After computing all possible values for k, we have to select the k value which gives minimum value. We can use one more table (say, $S[i,j]$) to reconstruct the optimal parenthesizations. Compute the $M[i,j]$ and $S[i,j]$ in a bottom-up fashion.

```java
/* P is the sizes of the matrices, Matrix i has the dimension P[i-1] x P[i].
M[i,j] is the best cost of multiplying matrices i through j
S[i,j] saves the multiplication point and we use this for back tracing */
void MatrixChainOrder(int P[], int length) {
        int n = length - 1;
        int M[n][n], S[n][n];
        for (int i = 1; i <= n; i++)
                M[i][i] = 0;                 // Fills in matrix by diagonals
```

```java
for (int l=2; l<= n; l++)    {          // l is chain length
    for (int i=1; i<= n -l+1; i++) {
        int j = i+l-1;
        M[i][j] = MAX_VALUE;
        // Try all possible division points i..k and k..j
        for (int k=i; k<=j-1; k++) {
            int thisCost = M[i][k] + M[k+1][j] + P[i-1]*P[k]*P[j];
            if(thisCost < M[i][j]) {
                M[i][j] = thisCost;
                S[i][j] = k;
            }
        }
    }
}
}
```

How many sub problems are there? In the above formula, i can range from 1 to n and j can range from 1 to n. So there are a total of n^2 subproblems and also, we are doing $n - 1$ such operations [since the total number of operations we need for $A_1 \times A_2 \times A_3 \times \ldots \times A_n$ are $n - 1$]. So the time complexity is $O(n^3)$. Space Complexity: $O(n^2)$.

Problem-16   For the Problem-15, can we use greedy method?

Solution: *Greedy* method is not an optimal way of solving this problem. Let us go through some counter example for this. As we have seen already, *greedy* method makes the decision which is good locally and it does not consider the future optimal solutions. In this case, if we use *greedy* then we always do the cheapest multiplication first. Sometimes, it returns a parenthesization that is not optimal.

Example: Consider $A_1 \times A_2 \times A_3$ with dimentions 3×100, 100×2 and 2×2. Based on *greedy* we parenthesize them as: $A_1 \times (A_2 \times A_3)$ with $100 \cdot 2 \cdot 2 + 3 \cdot 100 \cdot 2 = 1000$ multiplications. But the optimal solution to this problem is: $(A_1 \times A_2) \times A_3$ with $3 \cdot 100 \cdot 2 + 3 \cdot 2 \cdot 2 = 612$ multiplications. $\therefore$ we cannot use *greedy* for solving this problem.

Problem-17   **Integer Knapsack Problem [Duplicate Items Permitted]:** Given n types of items, where the ith item type has an integer size s_i and a value v_i. We need to fill a knapsack of total capacity C with items of maximum value. We can add multiple items of the same type to the knapsack.
   Note: For Fractional Knapsack problem refer *Greedy Algorithms* chapter.

Solution:
Input: n types of items where i^{th} type item has the size s_i and value v_i. Also, assume infinite number of items for each item type.
Goal: Fill the knapsack with capacity C by using n types of items and with maximum value.

One important note is that it's not compulsory to fill the knapsack completely. That means, filling the knapsack completely [of size C] if we get a value V and without filling the knapsack completely [let us say $C - 1$] with value U and if V < U then we consider the second one. In this case, we are basically filling the knapsack of size $C - 1$. If we get the same situation for $C - 1$ also then we try to fill the knapsack with $C - 2$ size and get the maximum value.

Let us say $M(j)$ denote the maximum value we can pack into a j size knapsack. We can express $M(j)$ recursively in terms of solutions to sub problems as follows:

$$M(j) = \begin{cases} max\{M(j-1), max_{i=1\ to\ n}(M(j - s_i)) + v_i\}, & if\ j \geq 1 \\ 0, & if\ j \leq 0 \end{cases}$$

For this problem the decision depends on whether we select a particular i^{th} item or not for a knapsack of size j.
   • If we select i^{th} item then we add its value v_i to optimal solution and decrease the size of the knapsack to be solved to $j - s_i$.
   • If we do not select the item then check whether we can get better solution for the knapsack of size $j - 1$.

The value of $M(C)$ will contain the value of the optimal solution. We can find the list of items in the optimal solution by maintaining and following "back pointers".

Time Complexity: Finding each $M(j)$ value will require $\Theta(n)$ time, and we need to sequentially compute C such values. Therefore, total running time is $\Theta(nC)$. Space Complexity: $\Theta(C)$.

Problem-18   **0-1 Knapsack Problem:** For Problem-17, how do we solve if the items are not duplicated (not having infinite number of items for each type and each item is allowed to use for 0 or 1 time)?

Real-time example: Suppose we are going by flight, we know that there is a limitation on the luggage weight. Also, the items which we are carrying can be of different types (like laptops, etc.). In this case, our objective is to select the items with maximum value. That means, we need to tell the customs officer to select the items which have more weight and less value (profit).

Solution: Input: Set of n items with sizes s_i and values v_i and a Knapsack of size C which we need to fill with subset of items from the given set.

Let us try to find the recursive formula for this problem using DP. Let $M(i,j)$ represent the optimal value we can get for filling up a knapsack of size j with items $1 \ldots i$. The recursive formula can be given as:

$$M(i,j) = Max\{M(i-1,j), M(i-1,j-s_i) + v_i\}$$

i^{th} item is not used i^{th} item is used

Since i take values from $1 \ldots n$ and j takes values from $1 \ldots C$, there are a total of nC subproblems. Now let us see what the above formula says:

- $M(i-1,j)$: Indicates the case of not selecting i^{th} item. In this case, since we are not adding any size to knapsack we have to use the same knapsack size for subproblems but excluding i^{th} item. The remaining items are $i-1$.
- $M(i-1,j-s_i) + v_i$: Indicates the case where we have selected the ith item. If we add the ith item then we have to reduce the subproblem knapsack size to $j - s_i$ and at the same time we need to add the value v_i to optimal solution. The remaining items are $i-1$.

Now, after finding all $M(i,j)$ values the optimal objective value can be obtained as: $Max_j\{M(n,j)\}$
This is because we do not know what amount of capacity gives the best solution.

Time Complexity: $O(nC)$, since there are nC subproblems to be solved and each of them takes $O(1)$ to compute. Space Complexity: $O(nC)$, where as Integer Knapsack takes only $O(C)$.

Now let us consider the following diagram which helps us in reconstructing the optimal solution and also gives further understanding. Size of below matrix is M.

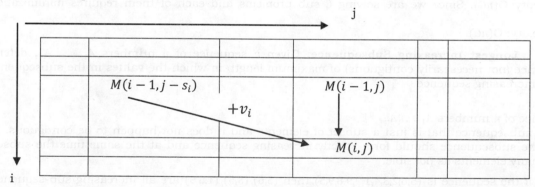

Inorder to compute some value M(i,j), we take the maximum of $M(i-1,j)$ and $M(i-1,j-s_i) + v_i$. These two values ($M(i,j)$ and $M(i-1,j-s_i)$) appears in previous row and also in some previous column. So, $M(i,j)$ can be computed just by looking at two values in the previous row in the table.

Problem-19   Making Change: Given n types of coin denominations of values $v_1 < v_2 < \ldots < v_n$ (integers). Assume $v_1 = 1$, so that we can always make change for any amount of money C. Give an algorithm which makes change for an amount of money C with as few coins as possible.

Solution: This problem is identical to the Integer Knapsack problem. In our problem, we have coin denominations, each of value v_i. We can construct an instance of a Knapsack problem for each item has a size s_i, which is equal to the value of v_i coin denomination. In the Knapsack we can give value of every item as -1.

Now it is easy to understand an optimal way to make money C with fewest coins is completely equivalent to the optimal way to fill the Knapsack of size C. This is because since every value has a value of -1, and the Knapsack algorithm uses as few items as possible which correspond to as few coins as possible.

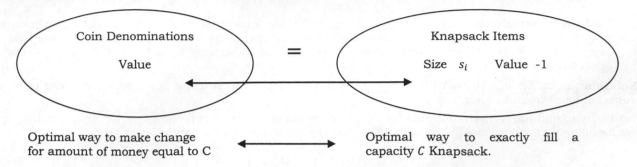

Let us try formulating the recurrence. Let $M(j)$ indicates the minimum number of coins required to make a change for the amount of money equal to j.

$$M(j) = Min_i\{M(j - v_i)\} + 1$$

What this says is, if coin denomination i was the last denomination coin added to solution, then the optimal way to finish the solution with that one is to optimally make change for the amount of money $j - v_i$ and then add one extra coin of value v_i.

```java
int Table[128];              //Initialization
int MakingChange(int n) {
        if(n < 0)
             return -1;
        if(n == 0)
             return 0;
        if(Table[n] != -1)
                return Table[n];
        int ans = -1;
        for ( int i = 0 ; i < num_denomination ; ++i )
                ans = Min( ans , MakingChange(n - denominations [ i ] ) ) ;
        return Table[ n ] = ans + 1 ;
}
```

Time Complexity: $O(nC)$. Since we are solving C sub problems and each of them requires minimization of n terms.

Space Complexity: $O(nC)$.

Problem-20   **Longest Increasing Subsequence:** Given a sequence of n numbers $A_1 \ldots A_n$, determine a subsequence (not necessarily contiguous) of maximum length in which the values in the subsequence form a strictly increasing sequence.

Solution:
Input: Sequence of n numbers $A_1 \ldots A_n$.
Goal: To find subsequence that is just a subset of elements and it does not happen to be contiguous. But the elements in the subsequence should form strictly increasing sequence and at the same time the subsequence contains as many elements as possible.

For example, if the sequence is $(5,6,2,3,4,1,9,9,8,9,5)$, then $(5,6)$, $(3,5)$, $(1,8,9)$ are all increasing sub-sequences. The longest one of them is $(2,3,4,8,9)$, and we want an algorithm for finding it.

First, let us concentrate on the algorithm for finding the longest subsequence. Later, we can try printing the sequence itself by tracing the table. Our first step is finding the recursive formula. First, let us create the base conditions. If there is only one element in the input sequence then we don't have to solve the problem and just need to return that element. For any sequence we can start with the first element ($A[1]$). Since we know the first number in the LIS, let's find the second number ($A[2]$). If $A[2]$ is larger than $A[1]$ then include $A[2]$ also. Otherwise, we are done – the LIS is the one element sequence ($A[1]$).

Now, let us generalize the discussion and decide about i^{th} element. Let $L(i)$ represent the optimal subsequence which is starting at position $A[1]$ and ending at $A[i]$. The optimal way to obtain a strictly increasing subsequence ending at position i is to extend some subsequence starting at some earlier position j. For this the recursive formula can written as:

$$L(i) = Max_{j<i \text{ and } A[j]<A[i]}\{L(j)\} + 1$$

The above recurrence says that we have to select some earlier position j which gives the maximum sequence. The 1 in the recursive formula indicates the addition of ith element.

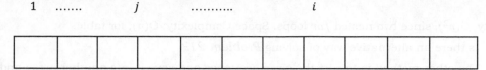

Now after finding maximum sequence for all positions we have to select the one among all positions which gives the maximum sequence and it is defined as:

$$Max_i\{L(i)\}$$

```java
int LISTable [1024];
int LongestIncreasingSequence( int A[], int n ) {
        int i, j, max = 0;
        for ( i = 0; i < n; i++ )
                LISTable[i] = 1;
        for ( i = 0; i< n; i++ ) {
                for ( j = 0; j < i; j++ ) {
                        if( A[i] > A[j] && LISTable[i] < LISTable[j] + 1 )
                                LISTable[i] = LISTable[j] + 1;
                }
        }
        for ( i = 0; i < n; i++)
                if( max < LISTable[i] )
                        max = LISTable[i];
        return max;
}
```

Time Complexity: $O(n^2)$, since two *for* loops. Space Complexity: $O(n)$, for table.

Problem-21   Longest Increasing Subsequence: In Problem-20, we assumed that $L(i)$ represents the optimal subsequence which is starting at position $A[1]$ and ending at $A[i]$. Now, let us change the definition of $L(i)$ as: $L(i)$ represents the optimal subsequence which is starting at position $A[i]$ and ending at $A[n]$. With this approach can we solve the problem?

Solution: Yes. The logic and reasoning is completely same.

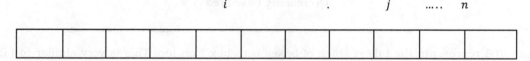

Let $L(i)$ represent the optimal subsequence which is starting at position $A[i]$ and ending at $A[n]$. The optimal way to obtain a strictly increasing subsequence starting at position i is going to be to extend some subsequence starting at some later position j. For this the recursive formula can be written as:

$$L(i) = Max_{i<j \text{ and } A[i]<A[j]}\{L(j)\} + 1$$

We have to select some later position j which gives the maximum sequence. The 1 in the recursive formula is the addition of ith element. After finding maximum sequence for all positions select the one among all positions which gives the maximum sequence and it is defined as:

$$Max_i\{L(i)\}$$

```java
int LISTable [1024];
int LongestIncreasingSequence( int A[], int n ) {
        int i, j, max = 0;
        for ( i = 0; i < n; i++ )
                LISTable[i] = 1;
        for(i = n – 1; i >= 0; i++) {
                // try picking a larger second element
                for( j = i + 1; j < n; j++ )  {
                        if( A[i] < A[j] && LISTable [i] < LISTable [j] + 1)
                                LISTable[i] = LISTable[j] + 1;
                }
        }
        for ( i = 0; i < n; i++ ) {
                if( max < LISTable[i] )
                        max = LISTable[i];
        }
        return max;
```

}
Time Complexity: $O(n^2)$, since two nested *for* loops. Space Complexity: $O(n)$, for table.

Problem-22   Is there an alternative way of solving *Problem-21?*

Solution: Yes. The other method is to sort the given sequence and save it into another array and then take out the "Longest Common Subsequence" (LCS) of the two arrays. This method has a complexity of $O(n^2)$. For LCS problem refer *theory section* of this chapter.

Problem-23   Box Stacking: Assume that we are given a set of n rectangular $3-D$ boxes. The dimensions of ith box are height h_i, width w_i and depth d_i. Now we want to create a stack of boxes which is as tall as possible, but we can only stack a box on top of another box if the dimensions of the $2-D$ base of the lower box are each strictly larger than those of the $2-D$ base of the higher box. We can rotate a box so that any side functions as its base. It is possible to use multiple instances of the same type of box.

Solution: Box stacking problem can be reduced to LIS [*Problem-21*].

Input: n boxes where i^{th} with height h_i, width w_i and depth d_i. For all n boxes we have to consider all the orientations with respect to rotation. That is, if we have, in the original set a box with dimensions $1 \times 2 \times 3$. Then we consider 3 boxes,

$$1 \times 2 \times 3 \Longrightarrow \begin{cases} 1 \times (2 \times 3), with\ height\ 1, base\ 2\ and\ width\ 3 \\ 2 \times (1 \times 3), with\ height\ 2, base\ 1\ and\ width\ 3 \\ 3 \times (1 \times 2), with\ height\ 3, base\ 1\ and\ width\ 2 \end{cases}$$

This simplification allows us to forget about the rotations of the boxes and we just focus on stacking of n boxes with each height as h_i and a base area of $(w_i \times d_i)$. Also assume that $w_i \le d_i$. Now what we do is, make a stack of boxes that is as tall as possible and has maximum height. We allow a box i on top of box j only if box i is smaller than box j in both the dimensions. That means, if $w_i < w_j$ && $d_i < d_j$. Now let us solve this using DP. First select the boxes in the order of decreasing base area.

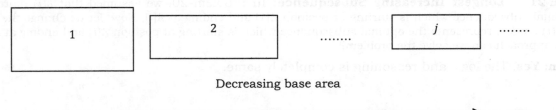

Decreasing base area

Now, let us say $H(j)$ represents the tallest stack of boxes with box j on top. This is very similar to LIS problem because stack of n boxes with ending box j is equal to finding a subsequence with first j boxes due to the sorting by decreasing base area. The order of the boxes on the stack is going to be equal to order of the sequence.

Now we can write $H(j)$ recursively. In order to form a stack which ends on box j, we need to extend some previous stack which is ending at i. That means, we need to put j box on top of stack [i box is the current top of stack]. To put j box on top of stack we should satisfy the condition $w_i > w_j$ and $d_i > d_j$ [these ensures the low level box has more base than boxes above it]. Based on this logic, we can write the recursive formula as:

$$H(j) = Max_{i<j\ and\ w_i>w_j and\ d_i>d_j}\ \{H(i)\} + h_i$$

As similar to LIS problem, at the end we have to select the best j over all potential values. This is because we are not sure which box might end up on top.

$$Max_j\{H(j)\}$$

Time Complexity: $O(n^2)$.

Problem-24   Building Bridges in India: Consider a very long, straight river which moves from north to south. Assume there are n cities on both sides of the river: n cities on left of the river and n cities on the right of the river. Also, assume that these cities are numbered from 1 to n but the order is not known. Now we want to connect as many left-right pairs of cities as possible with bridges such that no two bridges cross. When connecting cities, we can only connect city i on the left side to city i on the right side.

Solution:

Input: Two pairs of sets with each numbered from 1 to n.
Goal: Construct as many bridges as possible without any crosses between left side cities to right side cities of the river.

To understand better let us consider the diagram below. In the diagram it can be seen that there are n cities on left side of river and n cities on right side of river. Also, note that we are connecting the cities which have the same number [requirement in problem]. Our goal is to map maximum cities on left side of river to the cities on the right side of the river without any cross edges. Just to make it simple, let us sort the cities on one side of the river.

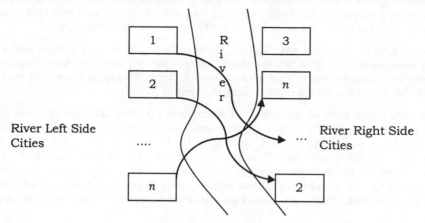

If we observe carefully, since the cities on left side are already sorted, the problem can be simplified to finding the maximum increasing sequence. That means we have to use LIS solution for finding the maximum in increasing sequence on the right side cities of the river.

Time Complexity: $O(n^2)$, (same as LIS).

Problem-25   **Subset Sum:** Given a sequence of n positive numbers $A_1 \ldots A_n$, give an algorithm which checks whether there exists a subset of A whose sum of all numbers is T?

Solution: This is a variation of the Knapsack problem. As an example, consider the following array:
$$A = [3, 2, 4, 19, 3, 7, 13, 10, 6, 11]$$

Suppose we want to check whether there is any subset whose sum is 17. The answer is yes, because the sum of $4 + 13 = 17$ and therefore $\{4, 13\}$ is such a subset.

Let us try solving this problem using DP. We will define $n \times T$ matrix, where n is the number of elements in our input array and T is the sum we want to check. Let, $M[i, j] = 1$ if it is possible to find a subset of the numbers 1 through i that produce sum j and $M[i, j] = 0$ otherwise.
$$M[i, j] = Max(M[i - 1, j], M[i - 1, j - A_i])$$

According to the above recursive formula similar to Knapsack problem, we check if we can get the sum j by not including the element i in our subset, and we check if we can get the sum j by including i by checking if the sum $j - A_i$ exists without the ith element. This is identical to Knapsack, except that we are storing a 0/1's instead of values. In the below implementation we can use binary OR operation to get the maximum among $M[i - 1, j]$ and $M[i - 1, j - A_i]$.

```java
int SubsetSum( int A[], int n, int T ) {
    int i, j, M[n+1][T +1];
    M[0][0]=0;
    for (i=1; i<= T; i++)
        M[0][i]= 0;
    for (i=1; i<=n; i++) {
        for (j = 0; j<= T; j++) {
            M[i][j] = M[i-1][j] || M[i-1][j] - A[i]];
        }
    }
    return M[n][T];
}
```

How many subproblems are there? In the above formula, i can range from $1\ to\ n$ and j can range from $1\ to\ T$. There are a total of nT subproblems and each one takes $O(1)$. So the time complexity is $O(nT)$ and this is not polynomial as the running time depends on two variables [n and T], and we can see that they are exponential function of the other. Space Complexity: $O(nT)$.

Problem-26   Given a set of n integers and sum of all numbers is at most K. Find the subset of these n elements whose sum is exactly half of the total sum of n numbers.

Solution:

Input: Given n numbers and sum of all numbers is at most K. Let us assume that the numbers are $A_1 \ldots A_n$.
Goal: Subset of these n elements whose sum is exactly half of the total sum of n numbers.

Let us use DP to solve this problem. We will create a boolean array T with size equal to $K + 1$. Assume that $T[x]$ is 1 if there exists a subset of given n elements whose sum is x. That means, after the algorithm finishes, $T[K]$ will be 1 if and only if there is a subset of the numbers that has sum K. Once we have that value then we just need to return $T[K/2]$. If it is 1, then there is a subset that adds up to half the total sum.

Initially we set all values of T to 0. Then we set $T[0]$ to 1. This is because we can always build 0 by taking an empty set. If we have no numbers in A, then we are done! Otherwise, we pick the first number, $A[0]$. We can either throw it away or take it into our subset. This means that the new $T[]$ should have $T[0]$ and $T[A[0]]$ set to 1. This creates the base case. We continue by taking the next element of A.

Suppose that we have already taken care of the first $i - 1$ elements of A. Now we take A[i] and look at our table T[]. After processing $i - 1$ elements, the array T has a 1 in every location that corresponds to a sum that we can make from the numbers we have already processed. Now we add the new number, A[i]. What should the table look like? First of all, we can simply ignore A[i]. That means, no one should disappear from T[] – we can still make all those sums. Now consider some location of T[j] that has a 1 in it. It corresponds to some subset of the previous numbers that add up to j. If we add A[i] to that subset, we will get a new subset with total sum j + A[i]. So we should set T[j + A[i]] to 1 as well. That's all. Based on above discussion, we can write the algorithm as:

```java
int T[10240];
int SubsetHalfSum( int  A[], int n ) {
        int K = 0;
        for( int i = 0; i < n; i++ )
                K += A[i];
        T[0] = 1;
        for( int i = 1; i <= K; i++ )          // initialize the table
                T[i] = 0;
        for( int i = 0; i < n; i++ ) {       // process the numbers one by one
                for( int j = K - A[i]; j >= 0; j--)    {
                        if( T[j] )
                                T[j + A[i]] = 1;
                }
        }
        return T[K / 2];
}
```

In the above code, j loop moves from right to left. This reduces the double counting problem. That means, if we move from left to right, then we may do the repeated calculations.

Time Complexity: $O(nK)$, for the two *for* loops. Space Complexity: $O(K)$, for the boolean table T.

Problem-27　　Can we improve the performance of Problem-26?

Solution: Yes. In the above code what we are doing is, the inner j loop is starting from K and moving left. That means, it is unnecessarily scanning the whole table every time.

What we actually want is to find all the 1 entries. At the beginning, only the 0th entry is 1. If we keep the location of the rightmost 1 entry in a variable, we can always start at that spot and go left instead of starting at the right end of the table.

To take full advantage of this, we can sort $A[]$ first. That way, the rightmost 1 entry will move to the right as slowly as possible. Finally, we don't really care about what happens in the right half of the table (after $T[K/2]$) because if $T[x]$ is 1, then $T[Kx]$ must also be 1 eventually – it corresponds to the complement of the subset that gave us x. The code based on above discussion is given below.

```java
int T[10240];
int SubsetHalfSumEfficient( int  A[], int n ) {
        int K = 0;
        for( int i = 0; i < n; i++ )
                K += A[i];
        Sort(A,n));
        T[0] = 1;          // initialize the table
        for( int i = 1; i <= sum; i++ )
                T[i] = 0;
```

```
            int R = 0;        // rightmost 1 entry
            for( int i = 0; i < n; i++)  {       // process the numbers one by one
                  for( int j = R; j >= 0; j--) {
                        if( T[j] )
                              T[j + A[i]] = 1;
                        R = min(K / 2, R + C[i] );
                  }
            }
            return T[K / 2];
}
```

After the improvements, the time complexity is still O(nK), but we have removed some useless steps.

Problem-28   Counting Boolean Parenthesizations: Let us assume that we are given a boolean expression consisting of symbols 'true', 'false', 'and', 'or', and 'xor'. Find the number of ways to parenthesize the expressions such that it will evaluate to *true*. For example, there is only 1 way to parenthesize 'true and false xor true' such that it evaluates to *true*.

Solution:
Input: A boolean expression consists of symbols T, F. Let the number of symbols are n and between symbols there are boolean operators like *and, or, xor* etc.. For example, if with $n = 4$, T or F and T xor F.
Goal: Count the numbers of ways to parenthesize the expression with boolean operators so that it evaluates to *true*. For example in the above case, if we use like T or ((F and T) xor F) then it evaluates to true.

$$T \; or(\; (F \; and \; T) xor \; F) = True$$

Now let us see how DP solves this problem. Let, $T(i,j)$ represent the number of ways to parenthesize the sub expression with symbols $i \dots j$ [symbols means only T and F and not the operators] with boolean operators so that it evaluates to *true*. Also, i and j takes the values from 1 to n. For example, in the above case, $T(2,4) = 0$ because there is no way to parenthesize the expression F and T xor F to make it *true*.

Just for simplicity and similarity, let $F(i,j)$ represent the number of ways to parenthesize the sub expression with symbols $i \dots j$ with boolean operators so that it evaluates to *false*. The base cases are $T(i,i)$ and $F(i,i)$.

Now we are going to compute T(i, i + 1) and F(i, i + 1) for all values of i. Similarly, $T(i, i + 2)$ and $F(i, i + 2)$ for all values of i and so on. Now let's generalize the solution.

$$T(i,j) = \sum_{k=i}^{j-1} \begin{cases} T(i,k)T(k+1,j), & \text{for "and"} \\ Total(i,k)Total(k+1,j) - F(i,k)F(k+1,j), & \text{for "or"} \\ T(i,k)F(k+1,j) + F(i,k)T(k+1,j), & \text{for "xor"} \end{cases}$$

Where, $Total(i,k) = T(i,k) + F(i,k)$.

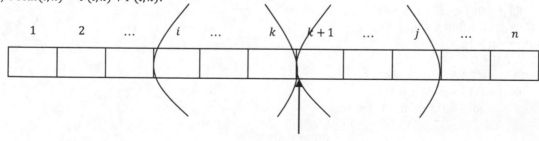

$$and, or, xor$$

What this above recursive formula says is, $T(i,j)$ indicates the number of ways to parenthesize the expression. Let us assume that we have some sub problems which are ending at k. Then the total number of ways to parenthesize from $i \; to \; j$ is the sum of counts of parenthesizing from $i \; to \; k$ and from $k + 1 \; to \; j$. To parenthesize between k and $k + 1$ there are three ways: *"and"*, *"or"* and *"xor"*.

- If we use *"and"* between k and $k + 1$ then the final expression becomes *true* only when both are *true*. If both are *true* then we can include them to get the final count.
- If we use *"or"*, then if at least one of them is *true* then the result becomes *true*. Instead of including all the three possibilities for *"or"*, we are giving one alternative where we are subtracting the "false" cases from total possibilities.
- Same is the case with *"xor"*. Conversation is as in above two cases.

After finding all the values we have to select the value of k which produces the maximum count and for k there are i *to* $j - 1$ possibilities.

How many subproblems are there? In the above formula, i can range from 1 *to* n and j can range from 1 *to* n. So there are a total of n^2 subproblems and also, we are doing summation for all such values. So the time complexity is $O(n^3)$.

Problem-29   **All Pairs Shortest Path Problem: Floyd's Algorithm:** Given a weighted directed graph $G = (V, E)$, where $V = \{1, 2, ..., n\}$. Find the shortest path between any pair of nodes in the graph. Assume the weights are represented in the matrix $C[V][V]$, where $C[i][j]$ indicates the weight (or cost) between the nodes i and j. Also, $C[i][j] = \infty$ or -1 if there is no path from node i to node j.

Solution: Let us try to find the DP solution (Floyd's algorithm) for this problem. The Floyd's algorithm for all pairs shortest path problem uses matrix $A[1..n][1..n]$ to compute the lengths of the shortest paths. Initially,

$$A[i, j] = C[i, j] \ if \ i \neq j$$
$$= 0 \quad if \ i = j$$

From the definition, $C[i, j] = \infty$ if there is no path from i to j. The algorithm makes n passes over A. Let $A_0, A_1, ..., A_n$ be the values of A on the n passes, with A_0 being the initial value.

Just after the $k - 1^{th}$ iteration, $A_{k-1}[i, j]$ = smallest length of any path from vertex i to vertex j that does not pass through the vertices $\{k + 1, k + 2, ... n\}$. That means, it passes through the vertices possibly through $\{1, 2, 3, ..., k - 1\}$.

In each iteration, the value $A[i][j]$ is updated with minimum of $A_{k-1}[i, j]$ and $A_{k-1}[i, k] + A_{k-1}[k, j]$.

$$A[i, j] = \min \begin{cases} A_{k-1}[i, j] \\ A_{k-1}[i, k] + A_{k-1}[k, j] \end{cases}$$

The kth pass explores whether the vertex k lies on an optimal path from i to j, for all i, j. The same is shown in the diagram below.

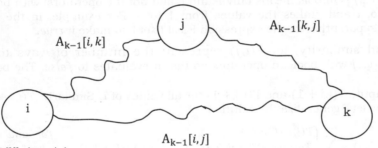

```
void Floyd(int C[][], int A[][], int n) {
    int i, j, k;
    for(i = 0, i <= n - 1;i + +)
            for(j = 0; j <= n - 1, j + +)
                A[i][j] = C[i][j];
    for(i = 0;i <= n - 1;i + +)
            A[i][i] = 0;
    for(k = 0;k <= n - 1;k + +) {
            for(i = 0;i <= n - 1;i + +) {
                for(j = 0;j <= n - 1, j + +)
                    if(A[i][k] + A[k][j] < A[i][j])
                        A[i][j] = A[i][k] + A[k][j];
            }
    }
}
```

Time Complexity: $O(n^3)$.

Problem-30   **Optimal Binary Search Trees:** Given a set of n (sorted) keys $A[1..n]$, build the best binary search tree for the elements of A. Also assume that, each element is associated with *frequency* which indicates the number of times that particular item is searched in the binary search trees. That means, we need to construct a binary search tree so that the total search time will be reduced.

Solution: Before solving the problem let us understand the problem with an example. Let us assume that the given array is $A = [3, 12, 21, 32, 35]$. There are many ways to represent these elements two of which are listed below.

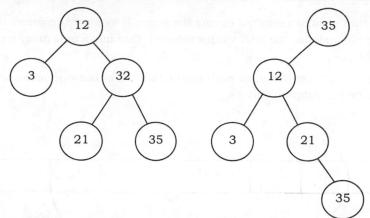

Of the two, which representation is better? The search time for an element depends on the depth of the node. The average number of comparisons for the first tree is: $\frac{1+2+2+3+3}{5} = \frac{11}{5}$ and for the second tree, the average number of comparisons is: $\frac{1+2+3+3+4}{5} = \frac{13}{5}$. Of the two, the first tree gives better results.

If frequencies are not given and if we want to search all elements then the above simple calculation is enough for deciding the best tree. If the frequencies are given then the selection depends on the frequencies of the elements and also the depth of the elements. For simplicity let us assume that, the given array is A and the corresponding frequencies are in array F. $F[i]$ indicates the frequency of ith element $A[i]$. With this, the total search time S(root) of the tree with *root* can be defined as:

$$S(root) = \sum_{i=1}^{n} (depth(root, i) + 1) \times F[i]$$

In the above expression, $depth(root, i) + 1$ indicates the number of comparisons for searching the ith element. Since we are trying to create binary search tree, the left subtree elements are less than root element and right subtree elements are greater than root element. If we separate the left subtree time and right subtree time then the above expression can be written as:

$$S(root) = \sum_{i=1}^{r-1} (depth(root, i) + 1) \times F[i] + \sum_{i=1}^{n} F[i] + \sum_{i=r+1}^{n} (depth(root, i) + 1) \times F[i]$$

Where r indicates the position of the root element in the array.

If we replace the left subtree and right subtree times with their corresponding recursive calls then the expression becomes:

$$S(root) = S(root \to left) + S(root \to right) + + \sum_{i=1}^{n} F[i]$$

Binary Search Tree node declaration

Refer *Trees* chapter.

```
BinarySearchTreeNode OptimalBST(int A[], int F[], int low, int high) {
        int r, minTime = 0;
        BinarySearchTreeNode newNode = new BinarySearchTreeNode();
        if(newNode == null) {
                System.out.println("Memory Error");
                return;
        }
        for (r =0, r <= n-1; r++)  {
                root.setLeft(OptimalBST(A, F, low, r-1));
                root.setRight(OptimalBST(A, F, r+1, high));
                root.setData(A[r]);
                if(minTime > S(root))
                        minTime = S(root);
        }
        return minTime;
}
```

Problem-31   Optimal Strategy for a Game: Consider a row of n coins of values $v_1 \ldots v_n$, where n is even [since it's a two player game]. We play this game with the opponent. In each turn, a player selects either the first or last coin from the row, removes it from the row permanently, and receives the value of the coin. Determine the maximum possible amount of money we can definitely win if we move first.

Solution: Goal: Maximize the sum of values selected during the game. If we start the game, then we should win the game. That means, we have to maximize the total values selected. One important note, we should not bother about the opponents moves.

Let us solve the problem using our DP technique. In each turn either we *or* our opponent selects the coin only from ends of the row. Let us define the subproblems as:

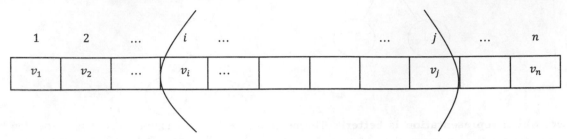

$V(i,j)$: denotes the maximum possible value we can definitely win if it is our turn and the only coins remaining are $v_i \ldots v_j$.

Base Cases: $V(i,i), V(i,i+1)$ for all values of i.

From these value, we can compute $V(i,i+2), V(i,i+3)$ and so on. Now let us define $V(i,j)$ for each sub problem as:

$$V(i,j) = Max\left\{Min\begin{cases}V(i+1,j-1)\\V(i+2,j)\end{cases} + v_i, Min\begin{cases}V(i,j-2)\\V(i+1,j-1)\end{cases} + v_j\right\}$$

In the recursive call we have to focus on i^{th} coin to j^{th} coin ($v_i \ldots v_j$). Since it is our turn to pick the coin, we have two possibilities: either we can pick v_i or v_j. The first term indicates the case if we select i^{th} coin (v_i) and second term indicates the case of selecting j^{th} coin (v_j). The outer Max indicates that we have to select the coin which gives maximum value. Now let us focus on the terms:

- Selecting i^{th} coin: If we select the ith coin then remaining range is from $i+1$ to j. Since we selected i^{th} coin we get the value v_i for that. From the remaining range $i+1$ to j, the opponents can select either $i+1^{th}$ coin or j^{th} coin. But the opoonents selection should be minimized as much as possible [the Min term]. Same is described in below figure.

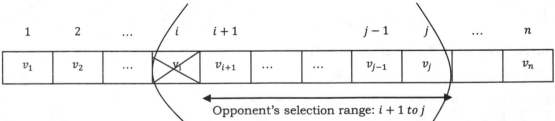

- Selecting j^{th} coin: Here also the a⸺⸺⸺⸺⸺⸺⸺⸺⸺⸺⸺⸺, ' coin then remaining range is from i to $j-1$. Since we selected j^{th} coin we get the value v_j for that. From the remaining range i to $j-1$, the opponent can select either i^{th} coin or $j-1^{th}$ coin. But the opoonents selection should be minimized as much as possible [the Min term].

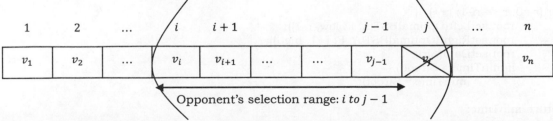

How many subproblems are there? In the above formula, i can range from 1 to n and j can range from 1 to n. There are a total of n^2 subproblems and each takes O(1) and the total time complexity is O(n^2).

Problem-32   **Tiling:** Assume that we use dominoes measuring 2×1 to tile an infinite strip of height 2. How many ways can one tile a $2 \times n$ strip of square cells with 1×2 dominoes?

Solution:

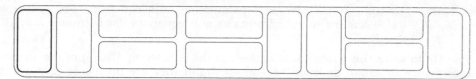

Notice that we can put tiles either vertically or horizontally. For putting vertical tiles, we need a gap of at least 2×2. For putting horizontal tiles, we need a gap of 2×1. In this manner, this problem reduces to find the number of ways to partition n using the numbers 1 and 2 with order considered relevant [1]. For example: $11 = 1 + 2 + 2 + 1 + 2 + 2 + 1$.

If we have to find such arrangements for 12, we can either place a 1 in the end or can add 2 in the arrangements possible with 10. Similarly, let us say we have F_n possible arrangements for n. Then for $(n + 1)$, we can either place just 1 at the end *or* we can find possible arrangements for $(n - 1)$ and put a 2 in the end. Going by above theory:

$$F_{n+1} = F_n + F_{n-1}$$

Let's verify above theory for our original problem:

- In how many ways, can we fill a 2×1, strip: 1→Only one vertical tile.
- In how many ways, can we fill a 2×2, strip: 2→Either 2 horizontal or 2 vertical tiles.
- In how many ways, can we fill a 2×3, strip: 3→Either put a vertical tile in 2 solutions possible for 2×2 strip or put 2 horizontal tiles in only solution possible for 2×1 strip. $(2 + 1 = 3)$.
- Similarly in how many ways, can we fill a $2 \times n$, strip: Either put a vertical tile in solutions possible for $2 \times (n - 1)$ strip or put 2 horizontal tiles in solution possible for $2 \times (n - 2)$ strip. $(F_{n-1} + F_{n-2})$.

- That's how, we verified that our final solution: $F_n = F_{n-1} + F_{n-2}$ with $F_1 = 1$ and $F_2 = 2$.

Problem-33   **Edit Distance:** Given two strings A of length m and B of length n, transform A into B with a minimum number of operations of the following types: delete a character from A, insert a character into A, or change some character in A into a new character. The minimal number of such operations required to transform A into B is called the *edit distance* between A and B.

Solution: Before going to solution, let us consider the possible operations for converting string A into B.
- If $m > n$, we need to remove some characters of A
- If $m == n$, we may need to convert some characters of A
- If $m < n$, we need to remove some characters from A

So the operations we need are insertion of a character, replacement of a character and deletion of character and their corresponding cost codes are defined below.

Costs of operations:

Insertion of a character	c_i
Replacement of a character	c_r
Deletion of character	c_d

Now let us concentrate on recursive formulation of the problem. Let, $T(i,j)$ represents the minimum cost required to transform first i characters of A to first j characters of B. That means, $A[1 \dots i]$ to $B[1 \dots j]$.

$$T(i,j) = min \begin{cases} c_d + T(i-1,j) \\ T(i,j-1) + c_i \\ T(i-1,j-1), & if\ A[i] == B[j] \\ T(i-1,j-1) + c_r & if\ A[i] \neq B[j] \end{cases}$$

Based on above discussion we have the following cases.
- If we delete i^{th} character from A, then we have to convert remaining $i - 1$ characters of A to j characters of B
- If we insert i^{th} character in A, then convert these i characters of A to $j - 1$ characters of B
- If $A[i] == B[j]$, then we have to convert remaining $i - 1$ characters of A to $j - 1$ characters of B
- If $A[i] \neq B[j]$, then we have to replace i^{th} character of A to j^{th} character of B and convert remaining $i - 1$ characters of A to $j - 1$ characters of B

After calculating all the possibilities we have to select the one which gives the lowest cost.

How many subproblems are there? In the above formula, i can range from 1 *to* m and j can range from 1 *to* n. This gives mn subproblems and each one take $O(1)$ and the time complexity is $O(mn)$. Space Complexity: $O(mn)$ where m is number of rows and n is number of columns in the given matrix.

Problem-34   **Longest Palindrome Subsequence:** A sequence is a palindrome if it reads the same whether we read it left to right or right to left. For example A, C, G, G, G, G, C, A. Given a sequence of length n devise an algorithm to output length of the longest palindrome subsequence. For example, the string, $A,G,C,T,C,B,M,A,A,C,T,G,G,A,M$ has many palindromes as subsequences, for instance: A,G,T,C,M,C,T,G,A has length 9.

Solution: Let us use DP to solve this problem. If we look at the sub-string $A[i,..,j]$ of the string A, then we can find a palindrome sequence of length at least 2 if $A[i] == A[j]$. If they are not same then we have to find the maximum length palindrome in subsequences $A[i+1,...,j]$ and $A[i,...,j-1]$.

Also every character $A[i]$ is a palindrome of length 1. Therefore base cases are given by $A[i,i] = 1$. Let us define the maximum length palindrome for the substring $A[i,...,j]$ as L(i,j).

$$L(i,j) = \begin{cases} L(i+1,j-1)+2, & if\ A[i] == A[j] \\ Max\{L(i+1,j), L(i,j-1)\}, & otherwise \end{cases}$$
$$L(i,i) = 1\ for\ all\ i = 1\ to\ n$$

```java
int LongestPalindromeSubsequence(int A[], int n) {
        int max = 1;
        int i,k, L[n][ n];
        for (i = 1; i<= n -1; i++) {
                L[i][i] =1;
                if(A[i]==A[i+1]) {
                        L[i][i + 1] = 1;
                        max = 2;
                }
                else     L[i][i + 1] = 0;
        }
        for (k=3;k<= n;k++) {
                for (i = 1;i <= n-k +1; i++) {
                        j = i + k - 1;
                        if(A[i] == A[j])    {
                                L[i, j] =  2 + L[i + 1][j - 1];
                                max = k;
                        }
                        else L[i, j]  = max(L[i + 1][j - 1], L[i][j - 1]);
                }
        }
        return max;
}
```

Time Complexity: First for loop takes O(n) time while the second for loop takes O($n - k$) which is also O(n). Therefore, the total running time of the algorithm is given by O(n^2).

Problem-35   **Longest Palindrome Substring:** Given a string A, we need to find the longest sub-string of A such that the reverse of it is exactly the same.

Solution: The basic difference between longest palindrome substring and longest palindrome subsequence is that, in case of longest palindrome substring the output string should be the contiguous characters which gives the maximum palindrome and in case of longest palindrome subsequence the output is the sequence of characters where the characters might not be in contiguous but they should be in increasing sequence with respect to their positions in the given string.

Brute-force solution exhaustively checks all $n(n+1)/2$ possible substrings of the given n-length string, tests each one if it's a palindrome, and keeps track of the longest one seen so far. This has worst-case complexity O(n^3), but we can easily do better by realizing that a palindrome is centered on either a letter (for odd-length palindromes) or a space between letters (for even-length palindromes). Therefore we can examine all $n + 1$ possible centers and find the longest palindrome for that center, keeping track of the overall longest palindrome. This has worst-case complexity O(n^2).

Let us use DP to solve this problem. It is worth noting that there are no more than O(n^2) substrings in a string of length n (while there are exactly 2^n subsequences). Therefore, we could scan each substring, check for palindrome and update the length of the longest palindrome substring discovered so far. Since the palindrome test takes time linear in the length of the substring, this idea takes O(n^3) algorithm. We can use DP to improve this. For $1 \leq i \leq j \leq n$,

$$L(i,j) = \begin{cases} 1, & if\ A[i]\ ....\ A[j]\ \text{is a palindrome substring,} \\ 0, & otherwise \end{cases}$$
$$L[i,i] = 1,$$
$$L[i,j] = L[i, i+1], if\ A[i] == A[i+1], for\ 1 \leq i \leq j \leq n-1.$$

Also, for string of length at least 3, $L[i,j] = (L[i + 1, j - 1]$ *and* $A[i] = A[j])$.

Note that in order to obtain a well-defined recurrence, we need to explicitly initialize two distinct diagonals of the boolean array $L[i,j]$, since the recurrence for entry $[i,j]$ uses the value $[i - 1, j - 1]$, which is two diagonals away from $[i,j]$ (that means, for a substring of length k, we need to know the status of a substring of length $k - 2$).

```java
int LongestPalindromeSubstring(int A[], int n) {
    int max  = 1;
    int i,k, L[n][n];
    for (i  = 1; i<=n-1; i++) {
        L[i][i] =1;
        if(A[i]==A[i+1]) {
            L[i][i + 1]  = 1;
            max = 2;
        }
        else L[i][i + 1]  = 0;
    }
    for (k=3;k<=n;k++) {
        for (i  = 1;i <= n-k +1; i++) {
            j =  i + k - 1;
            if(A[i] == A[j] && L[i + 1][j - 1]) {
                L[i][j] =  1;
                max = k;
            }
            else L[i][j]  = 0;
        }
    }
    return max;
}
```

Time Complexity: First for loop takes $O(n)$ time while the second for loop takes $O(n - k)$ which is also $O(n)$. Therefore the total running time of the algorithm is given by $O(n^2)$.

Problem-36   Given two strings S and T, give an algorithm to find the number of times S appears in T. It's not compulsory that all characters of S should appear contiguous to T. For example, if $S = ab$ and $T = abadcb$ then the solution is 4, because ab is appearing 4 times in $abadcb$.

Solution: Assume, $L(i,j)$ represents the count of how many times i characters of S appears in j characters of T.

$$L(i,j) = Max \begin{cases} 0, & if \ j = 0 \\ 1, & if \ i = 0 \\ L(i-1,j-1) + L(i,j-1), & if \ S[i] == T[j] \\ L(i-1,j), & if \ S[i] \neq T[j] \end{cases}$$

If we concentrate on the components of the above recursive formula,

- If $j = 0$, then since T is empty the count becomes 0.
- If $i = 0$, then we can treat empty string S also appearing in T and we can give the count as 1.
- If $S[i] == T[j]$, means i^{th} character of S and j^{th} character of T are same. In this case we have to check the subproblems with $i - 1$ characters of S and $j - 1$ characters of T and also we have to count the result of i characters of S with $j - 1$ characters of T. This is because even all i characters of S might be appearing in $j - 1$ characters of T.
- If $S[i] \neq T[j]$, then we have to get the result of subproblem with $i - 1$ characters of S and j characters of T.

After computing all the values, we have to select the one which gives maximum count.

How many subproblems are there? In the above formula, i can range from 1 *to* m and j can range from 1 *to* n. There are a total of mn subproblems and and each one takes $O(1)$. Time Complexity is $O(mn)$. Space Complexity: $O(mn)$ where m is number of rows and n is number of columns in the given matrix.

Problem-37   Given a matrix with n rows and m columns ($n \times m$). In each cell there are a number of apples. We start from the upper-left corner of the matrix. We can go down or right one cell. Finally, we need to arrive to the bottom-right corner. Find the maximum number of apples that we can collect. When we pass through a cell - we collect all the apples left there.

Solution: Let us assume that the given matrix is $A[n][m]$. The first thing that must be observed is that there are at most 2 ways we can come to a cell - from the left (if it's not situated on the first column) and from the top (if it's not situated on the most upper row).

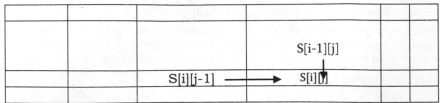

To find the best solution for that cell, we have to have already found the best solutions for all of the cells from which we can arrive to the current cell. From above, a recurrent relation can be easily obtained as:

$$S(i,j) = \left\{ A[i][j] + Max \begin{cases} S(i,j-1), & if\ j > 0 \\ S(i-1,j), & if\ i > 0 \end{cases} \right\}$$

$S(i,j)$ must be calculated by going first from left to right in each row and process the rows from top to bottom, or by going first from top to bottom in each column and process the columns from left to right.

```
int FindApplesCount(int A[][], int n, int m) {
        int S[n][m];
        for(int i = 0;i<n;i++) {
                for(int j = 0;i<m;j++) {
                        S[i][j] = A[i][j];
                        if(j>0 && S[i][j] < S[i][j] + S[i][j-1])
                                S[i][j] += S[i][j-1];
                        if(i>0 && S[i][j] < S[i][j] + S[i-1][j])
                                S[i][j] +=S[i-1][j];
                }
        }
        return S[n][m];
}
```

How many such subproblems are there? In the above formula, i can range from $1\ to\ n$ and j can range from $1\ to\ m$. There are a total of nm subproblems and each one takes $O(1)$. Time Complexity is $O(nm)$. Space Complexity: $O(nm)$, where m is number of rows and n is number of columns in the given matrix.

Problem-38   Similar to Problem-37, assume that, we can go down, right one cell or even in diagonal direction. We need to arrive at the bottom-right corner. Give DP solution to find the maximum number of apples we can collect.

Solution: Yes. The discussion is very similar to Problem-37. Let us assume that the given matrix is $A[n][m]$. The first thing that must be observed is that there are at most 3 ways we can come to a cell - from the left, from the top (if it's not situated on the uppermost row) or from top diagonal. To find the best solution for that cell, we have to have already found the best solutions for all of the cells from which we can arrive to the current cell. From above, a recurrent relation can be easily obtained:

$$S(i,j) = \left\{ A[i][j] + Max \begin{cases} S(i,j-1), & if\ j > 0 \\ S(i-1,j), & if\ i > 0 \\ S(i-1,j-1), if\ i > 0\ and\ j > 0 \end{cases} \right\}$$

$S(i,j)$ must be calculated by going first from left to right in each row and process the rows from top to bottom, or by going first from top to bottom in each column and process the columns from left to right.

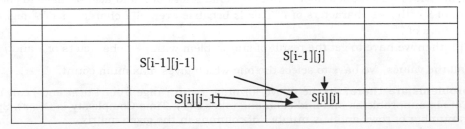

How many such subproblems are there? In the above formula, i can range from $1\ to\ n$ and j can range from $1\ to\ m$. There are a total of nm subproblems and each one takes $O(1)$. Time complexity is $O(nm)$.
Space Complexity: $O(nm)$ where m is number of rows and n is number of columns in the given matrix.

Problem-39   **Maximum size square sub-matrix with all 1's:** Given a matrix with 0's and 1's, give an algorithm for finding the maximum size square sub-matrix with all 1s. For example, consider the binary matrix below.

0 1 1 0 1

$$
\begin{array}{ccccc}
1 & 1 & 0 & 1 & 0 \\
0 & 1 & 1 & 1 & 0 \\
1 & 1 & 1 & 1 & 0 \\
1 & 1 & 1 & 1 & 1 \\
0 & 0 & 0 & 0 & 0
\end{array}
$$

The maximum square sub-matrix with all set bits is

$$
\begin{array}{ccc}
1 & 1 & 1 \\
1 & 1 & 1 \\
1 & 1 & 1
\end{array}
$$

Solution: Let us try solving this problem using DP. Let the given binary matrix be $B[m][m]$. The idea of the algorithm is to construct a temporary matrix $L[\ ][\ ]$ in which each entry $L[i][j]$ represents size of the square sub-matrix with all 1's including $B[i][j]$ and $B[i][j]$ is the rightmost and bottom-most entry in sub-matrix.

Algorithm:
1) Construct a sum matrix $L[m][n]$ for the given matrix $B[m][n]$.
   a. Copy first row and first columns as it is from $B[\ ][\ ]$ to $L[\ ][\ ]$.
   b. For other entries, use following expressions to construct $L[\ ][\ ]$
      if($B[i][j]$)
      $$L[i][j] = min(L[i][j-1], L[i-1][j], L[i-1][j-1]) + 1;$$
      else $L[i][j] = 0;$
2) Find the maximum entry in $L[m][n]$.
3) Using the value and coordinates of maximum entry in $L[i]$, print sub-matrix of $B[\ ][\ ]$.

```
void MatrixSubSquareWithAllOnes(int B[][], int m, int n) {
    int i, j, L[m][n], max_of_s, max_i, max_j;
    for(i = 0; i < m; i++)              // Setting first column of L[][]
        L[i][0] = B[i][0];
    // Setting first row of L[][]
    for(j = 0; j < n; j++)
        L[0][j] = B[0][j];
    // Construct other entries of L[][]
    for(i = 1; i < m; i++) {
        for(j = 1; j < n; j++) {
            if(B[i][j] == 1)
                L[i][j] = min(L[i][j-1], L[i-1][j], L[i-1][j-1]) + 1;
            else    L[i][j] = 0;
        }
    }
    max_of_s = L[0][0]; max_i = 0; max_j = 0;
    for(i = 0; i < m i++) {
        for(j = 0; j < n; j++) {
            if(L[i][j] > max_of_s) {
                max_of_s = L[i][j];
                max_i = i;
                max_j = j;
            }
        }
    }
    System.out.println("Maximum sub-matrix");
    for(i = max_i; i > max_i - max_of_s; i--) {
        for(j = max_j; j > max_j - max_of_s; j--)
            System.out.println(B[i][j]);
    }
}
```

How many subproblems are there? In the above formula, i can range from 1 to n and j can range from 1 to m. There are a total of nm subproblems and each one takes O(1). Time complexity is O(nm). Space Complexity: O(nm) where n is number of rows and m is number of columns in the given matrix.

Problem-40   Maximum sum sub-matrix: Given an $n \times n$ matrix M of positive and negative integers, give an algorithm to find the sub-matrix with the largest possible sum.

Solution: Let $Aux[r,c]$ represents the sum of rectangular subarray of M with one corner at entry $[1,1]$ and the other at $[r,c]$. Since there are n^2, such possibilities, we can them in O(n^2) time. After computing all possible sums, the sum of any rectangular subarray of M can be computed in constant time. This gives an O(n^4)

algorithm, we simply guess the lower-left and the upper-right corner of the rectangular subarray and use the *Aux* table to compute its sum.

Problem-41   Can we improve the complexity of Problem-40?

Solution: We can use Problem-4 solution with little variation. As we have seen that the maximum sum array of a $1 - D$ array algorithm scans the array one entry at a time and keeps a running total of the entries. At any point, if this total becomes negative then set it to 0. This algorithm is sometimes called *Kadane's* algorithm. We use this as an auxiliary function to solve the two dimensional problem in the following way [1].

```java
void FindMaximumSubMatrix(int A[][], int n){
    //computing the vertical prefix sum for columns
    int M[n][n];
    for (int i = 0; i < n; i++) {
        for (int j = 0; j < n; j++) {
            if (j == 0)
                M[j][i] = A[j][i];
            else
                M[j][i] = A[j][i] + M[j - 1][i];
        }
    }
    int maxSoFar = 0;
    int min , subMatrix;
    //iterate over the possible combinations applying Kadane's Alg.
    for (int i = 0; i < n; i++) {
        for (int j = i; j < n; j++) {
            min = 0;
            subMatrix = 0;
            for (int k = 0; k < n; k++) {
                if (i == 0) {
                    subMatrix += M[j][k];
                } else {
                    subMatrix += M[j][k] - M[i - 1 ][k];
                }
                if(subMatrix < min){
                    min = subMatrix;
                }
                if((subMatrix - min) > maxSoFar){
                    maxSoFar = subMatrix - min;
                }
            }
        }
    }
}
```

Time Complexity: $O(n^3)$.

Problem-42   Given a number n, find the minimum number of squares required to sum to a number n. *Examples*: $min[1] = 1 = 1^2$, $min[2] = 2 = 1^2 + 1^2$, $min[4] = 1 = 2^2$, $min[13] = 2 = 3^2 + 2^2$.

Solution: This problem can be reduced to coin change problem. The denominations are 1 to $\sqrt{n}$. Now, we just need to make change for n with minimum number of denominations.

Problem-43   **Finding Optimal Number Of Jumps To Reach Last Element:** Given an array, start from the first element and reach the last by jumping. The jump length can be at most the value at the current position in the array. Optimum result is when you reach the goal in minimum number of jumps.
Example: Given array A = {2,3,1,1,4}. Possible ways to reach the end (index list) are:
- 0,2,3,4 (jump 2 to index 2, and then jump 1 to index 3 and then jump 1 to index 4)
- 0,1,4 (jump 1 to index 1, and then jump 3 to index 4)

Since second solution has only 2 jumps it is the optimum result.

Solution: This problem is a classic example of Dynamic Programming. Though we can solve this by brute-force it will be complex. We can use LIS problem approach for solving this. As soon as we traverse the array, we should find the minimum number of jumps for reaching that position (index) and update our result array. Once we reach the end, we have the optimum solution at last index in result array.

How can we find optimum number of jump for every position (index)? For first index, optimum number of jumps will be zero. Please note that if value at first index is zero, we can't jump to any element and return infinite. For $n + 1^{th}$ element, initialize result[$n + 1$] as infinite. Then we should go through a loop from $0 \ldots n$, and at every index i, we should see if we are able to jump to $n + 1$ from i or not. If possible then see if total number of jump (result[i] + 1) is less than result[$n + 1$], then update result[$n + 1$] else just continue to next index.

```
//Define MAX 1 less so that adding 1 doesn't make it 0
#define MAX 0xFFFFFFFE;
unsigned int jump(int *array, int n) {
        unsigned answer, int *result = new unsigned int[n];
        int i, j;
        if(n==0 || array[0] == 0)
                return MAX;
        result[0] = 0;  //no need to jump at first element
        for (i = 1; i < n; i++) {
                result[i] = MAX; //Initialization of result[i]
                for (j = 0; j < i; j++) {
                        //check if jump is possible from j to is
                        if(array[j] >= (i-j)) {
                                //check if better solution available
                                if((result[j] + 1) < result[i])
                                        result[i] = result[j] + 1;  //updating result[i]
                        }
                }
        }
        answer = result[n-1];                           //return result[n-1]
        delete[] result;
        return answer;
}
```

Above code will return optimum number of jumps. To find the jump indexes as well, we can very easily modify the code as per requirement.

Time Complexity: Since we are running 2 loops here and iterating from 0 to i in every loop then total time takes will be $1 + 2 + 3 + 4 + \ldots + n - 1$. So time efficiency $O(n) = O(n * (n - 1)/2) = O(n^2)$. Space Complexity: $O(n)$ space for result array.

Problem-44   Explain what would happen if a dynamic programming algorithm is designed to solve a problem that does not have overlapping sub-problems.

Solution: It will be just a waste of memory, because the answers of sub-problems will never be used again. And the running time will be the same as using Divide & Conquer algorithm.

Chapter-20

COMPLEXITY CLASSES ☀ ☀ ☀

20.1 Introduction

In the previous chapters we have solved problems of different complexities. Some algorithms have lower rates of growth while others have higher rates of growth. The problems with lower rates of growth are called *easy* problems (or *easy solved problems*) and the problems with higher rates of growth are called *hard* problems (or *hard solved problems*). This classification is done based on the running time (or memory) that an algorithm takes for solving the problem.

Time Complexity	Name	Example	Problems
$O(1)$	Constant	Adding an element to the front of a linked list	Easy solved problems
$O(logn)$	Logarithmic	Finding an element in a binary search tree	Easy solved problems
$O(n)$	Linear	Finding an element in an unsorted array	Easy solved problems
$O(nlogn)$	Linear Logarithmic	Merge sort	Easy solved problems
$O(n^2)$	Quadratic	Shortest path between two nodes in a graph	Easy solved problems
$O(n^3)$	Cubic	Matrix Multiplication	Easy solved problems
$O(2^n)$	Exponential	The Towers of Hanoi problem	Hard solved problems
$O(n!)$	Factorial	Permutations of a string	Hard solved problems

There are lots of problems for which we do not know the solutions. All the problems we have seen so far are the ones, which can be solved by computer in deterministic time. Before starting our discussion let us see the basic terminology we use in this chapter.

20.2 Polynomial/Exponential time

Exponential time means, in essence, trying every possibility (for example, backtracking algorithms) and they are very slow in nature. Polynomial time means having some clever algorithm to solve a problem, and we don't try every possibility. Mathematically, we can represent these as:

- Polynomial time is $O(n^k)$, for some k.
- Exponential time is $O(k^n)$, for some k.

20.3 What is Decision Problem?

A decision problem is a question with a *yes/no* answer and the answer depends on the values of input. For example, the problem "Given an array of n numbers check whether there are any duplicates or not?" is a decision problem. The answer for this problem can be either *yes* or *no* depending on values of input array.

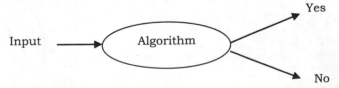

20.4 Decision Procedure

For a given decision problem let us assume we have given some algorithm for solving it. The process of solving a given decision problem in the form of an algorithm is called a *decision procedure* for that problem.

20.5 What is a Complexity Class?

In computer science, in order to understand the problems for which solutions are not there, the problems are divided into classes and we call them as complexity classes. In complexity theory, a *complexity class* is a set of problems with related complexity. It is the branch of theory of computation that studies the resources required during computation to solve a given problem. The most common resources are time (how much time the algorithm takes to solve a problem) and space (how much memory it takes).

20.6 Types of Complexity Classes

P Class

The complexity class *P* is the set of decision problems that can be solved by a deterministic machine in polynomial time (*P* stands for polynomial time). *P* problems are a set of problems whose solutions are easy to find.

NP Class

The complexity class *NP* (*NP* stands for non-deterministic polynomial time) is the set of decision problems that can be solved by a non-deterministic machine in polynomial time. *NP* class problems refer to a set of problems whose solutions are hard to find, but easy to verify.

For better understanding let us consider a college which has 500 students on its roll. Also, assume that there are 100 rooms available for students. Selection of 100 students must be paired together in rooms, but the dean of students has a list of pairings of certain students who cannot room together for some reason. The total possible number of pairings is too large. But the solutions (the list of pairings) provided to the dean, are easy to check for errors.

If one of the prohibited pairs is on the list, that's an error. In this problem, we can see that checking every possibility is very difficult but the result is easy to validate. That means, if someone gives us a solution to the problem, we can tell them whether it is right or not in polynomial time. Based on the above discussion, for *NP* class problems if the answer is *yes*, then there is a proof of this fact, which can be verified in polynomial time.

Co-NP Class

$Co - NP$ is the opposite of *NP* (complement of *NP*). If the answer to a problem in $Co - NP$ is *no*, then there is a proof of this fact that can be checked in polynomial time.

P	Solvable in polynomial time
NP	*Yes* answers can be checked in polynomial time
$Co - NP$	*No* answers can be checked in polynomial time

Relationship between P, NP and Co-NP

Every decision problem in *P* is also in *NP*. If a problem is in *P*, we can verify YES answers in polynomial time. Similarly, any problem in P is also in $Co - NP$. One of the important open questions in theoretical computer science is whether or not $P = NP$. Nobody knows. Intuitively, it should be obvious that $P \neq NP$, but nobody knows how to prove it.

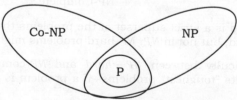

Another open question is whether *NP* and $Co - NP$ are different. Even if we can verify every YES answer quickly, there's no reason to think that we can also verify NO answers quickly. It is generally believed that $NP \neq Co - NP$, but again nobody knows how to prove it.

NP-hard Class

It is a class of problems such that every problem in *NP* reduces to it. All *NP*-hard problems are not in *NP*, so it takes a long time to even check them. That means, if someone gives us a solution for *NP*-hard problem, it takes a long time for us to check whether it is right or not.

A problem *K* is *NP*-hard indicates that if a polynomial-time algorithm (solution) exists for *K* then a polynomial-time algorithm for every problem is *NP*. Thus:

K is *NP*-hard implies that if *K* can be solved in polynomial time, then $P = NP$

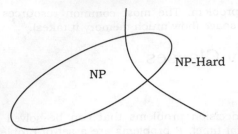

NP-complete Class

Finally, a problem is *NP*-complete if it is part of both *NP*-hard and *NP*. *NP*-complete problems are the hardest problems in *NP*. If anyone finds a polynomial-time algorithm for one *NP*-complete problem, then we can find polynomial-time algorithm for every *NP*-complete problem. This means that we can check an answer fast and every problem in *NP* reduces to it.

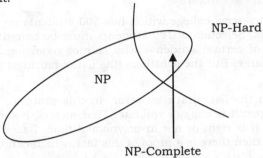

Relationship between P, NP Co-NP, NP-Hard and NP-Complete

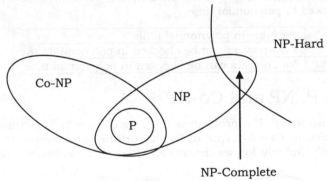

The set of problems that are *NP*-hard is a strict superset of the problems that are *NP*-complete. Some problems (like the halting problem) are *NP*-hard, but not in *NP*. *NP*-hard problems might be impossible to solve in general.

We can tell the difference in difficulty between $NP - hard$ and *NP*-complete problems because the class *NP* includes everything easier than its "toughest" problems--if a problem is not in *NP*, it is harder than all the problems in *NP*.

From the above discussion, we can write the relationships between different components as shown below (remember, this is just an assumption).

Does P==NP?

If $P = NP$, it means that every problem that can be checked quickly can be solved quickly (remember the difference between checking if an answer is right and actually solving a problem).

This is a big question (and nobody knows the answer), because right now there are lots of *NP*-Complete problems that can't be solved quickly. If $P = NP$, that means there is a way to solve them fast. Remember that "quickly" means not trial-and-error. It could take a billion years, but as long as we didn't use trial and error, it was quick. In future, a computer will be able to change that billion years into a few minutes.

20.7 Reductions

Before discussing reductions, let us consider the following scenario. Assume that we want to solve problem X but feel it's very complicated. In this case what do we do?

The first thing that comes to mind is, if we have similar problem as that of X (let us say Y), then we try to map X to Y and use Y's solution to solve X also. This process is called reduction.

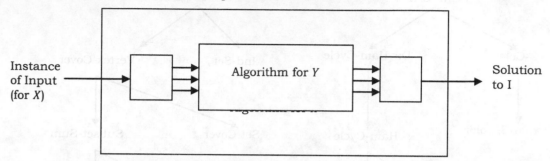

In order to map problem X to problem Y, we need some algorithm and that may take linear time or more. Based on this discussion the cost of solving problem X can be given as:

$$Cost\ of\ solving\ X = Cost\ of\ solving\ Y\ +\ Reduction\ time$$

Now, let us consider the other scenario. For solving problem X, sometimes we may need to use Y's algorithm (solution) multiple times. In that case,

$$Cost\ of\ solving\ X = Number\ of\ Times\ *\ Cost\ of\ solving\ X\ +\ Reduction\ time$$

The main thing in *NP*-Complete is reducibility. That means, we reduce (or transform) given *NP*-Complete problems to other known *NP*-Complete problem. Since the *NP*-Complete problems are hard to solve and in order to prove that given *NP*-Complete problem is hard, we take one existing hard problem (which we can prove is hard) and try to map given problem to that and finally we prove that the given problem is hard.

Note: It's not compulsory to reduce the given problem to known hard problem to prove its hardness. Sometimes, we reduce the known hard problem to given problem.

Important NP-Complete Problems (Reductions)

Satisfiability Problem: A boolean formula is in *conjunctive normal form* (CNF) if it is a conjunction (AND) of several clauses, each of which is the disjunction (OR) of several literals, each of which is either a variable or its negation. For example: $(a \lor b \lor c \lor d \lor e) \land (b \lor \sim c \lor \sim d) \land (\sim a \lor c \lor d) \land (a \lor \sim b)$

A 3-CNF formula is a CNF formula with exactly three literals per clause. The previous example is not a 3-CNF formula, since its first clause has five literals and its last clause has only two.

2-SAT Problem: 3-SAT is just SAT restricted to 3-CNF formulas: Given a 3-CNF formula, is there an assignment to the variables so that the formula evaluates to TRUE?

2-SAT Problem: 2-SAT is just SAT restricted to 2-CNF formulas: Given a 2-CNF formula, is there an assignment to the variables so that the formula evaluates to TRUE?

Circuit-Satisfiability Problem: Given a boolean combinational circuit composed of AND, OR and NOT gates, is it satisfiable?. That means, given a boolean circuit consisting of AND, OR and NOT gates properly connected by wires, the Circuit-SAT problem is to decide whether there exists an input assignment for which the output is TRUE.

Hamiltonian Path Problem (Ham-Path): Given an undirected graph, is there a path that visits every vertex exactly once?

Hamiltonian Cycle Problem (Ham-Cycle): Given an undirected graph, is there a cycle (where start and end vertices are same) that visits every vertex exactly once?

Directed Hamiltonian Cycle Problem (Dir-Ham-Cycle): Given a directed graph, is there a cycle (where start and end vertices are same) that visits every vertex exactly once?

Travelling Salesman Problem (TSP): Given a list of cities and their pair-wise distances, the problem is to find the shortest possible tour that visits each city exactly once.

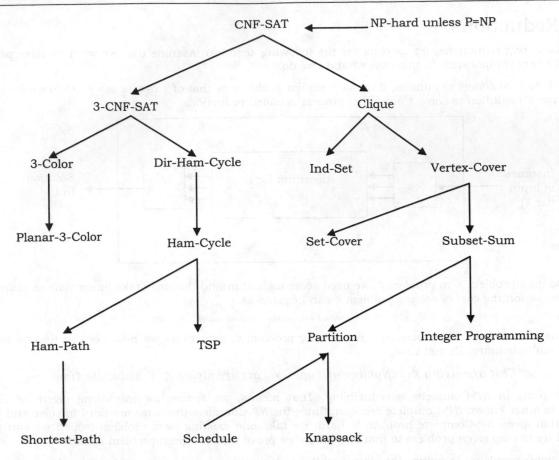

Shortest Path Problem (Shortest-Path): Given a directed graph and two vertices s and t, check whether there is a shortest simple path from *s* to *t*.

Graph Coloring: A *k*-coloring of a graph is to map one of *k* 'colors' to each vertex, so that every edge has two different colors at its endpoints. The graph coloring problem is to find the smallest possible number of colors in a legal coloring.

3-Color problem: Given a graph, is it possible to color the graph with 3 colors in such a way that every edge has two different colors?

Clique (also called complete graph): Given a graph, the *CLIQUE* problem is to compute the number of nodes in its largest complete subgraph. That means, we need to find the maximum subgraph which is also a complete graph.

Independent Set Problem (Ind_Set): Let *G* be an arbitrary graph. An independent set in *G* is a subset of the vertices of *G* with no edges between them. The maximum independent set problem is the size of the largest independent set in a given graph.

Vertex Cover Problem (Vertex-Cover): A vertex cover of a graph is a set of vertices that touches every edge in the graph. The vertex cover problem is to find the smallest vertex cover in a given graph.

Subset Sum Problem (Subset-Sum): Given a set *S* of integers and an integer *T*, determine whether *S* has a subset whose elements sum to *T*.

Integer Programming: Given integers b_i, a_{ij} find 0/1 variables x_i that satisfy a linear system of equations.

$$\sum_{j=1}^{N} a_{ij}x_j = b_i \quad 1 \leq i \leq M$$

$$x_j \in \{0,1\} \, 1 \leq j \leq N$$

In the figure, arrows indicate the reductions. For example, Ham-Cycle (Hamiltonian Cycle Problem) can be reduced to CNF-SAT. Same is the case with any pair of problems. For our discussion, we can ignore the reduction process for each of the problems. There is a theorem called *Cook's Theorem* which proves that Circuit satisfiability problem is NP-hard. That means, Circuit satisfiability is a known *NP*-hard problem.

Note: Since the problems below are *NP*-Complete, they are *NP* and *NP*-hard too. For simplicity we can ignore the proofs for these reductions.

20.8 Problems on Complexity Classes

Problem-1   What is a quick algorithm?

Solution: A quick algorithm (solution) means not trial-and-error solution. It could take a billion years, but as long as we do not use trial and error, it is efficient. Future computers will change those billion years to a few minutes.

Problem-2   What is an efficient algorithm?

Solution: An algorithm is said to be efficient if it satisfies the following properties:
- Scale with input size.
- Don't care about constants.
- Asymptotic running time: polynomial time.

Problem-3   Can we solve all problems in polynomial time?

Solution: No. The answer is trivial because we have seen lot of problems which take more than polynomial time.

Problem-4   Are there any problems which are *NP*-hard?

Solution: By definition, *NP*-hard implies that it is very hard. That means it is very hard to prove and verify that they are hard. Cook's Theorem proves that Circuit satisfiability problem is *NP*-hard.

Problem-5   For 2-SAT problem, which of the following are applicable?
(a) *P*   (b) *NP*   (c) *CoNP* (d) *NP*-Hard
(e) *CoNP*-Hard   (f) *NP*-Complete   (g) *CoNP*-Complete

Solution: 2-SAT is solvable in poly-time. So it is *P*, *NP*, and *CoNP*.

Problem-6   For 3-SAT problem, which of the following are applicable?
(a) *P*   (b) *NP*   (c) *CoNP* (d) *NP*-Hard
(e) *CoNP*-Hard   (f) *NP*-Complete   (g) *CoNP*-Complete

Solution: 3-SAT is NP-complete. So it is NP, NP-Hard, and NP-complete.

Problem-7   For 2-Clique problem, which of the following are applicable?
(a) *P*   (b) *NP*   (c) *CoNP*   (d) *NP*-Hard
(e) *CoNP*-Hard   (f) *NP*-Complete   (g) *CoNP*-Complete

Solution: 2-Clique is solvable in poly-time (check for an edge between all vertex-pairs in O(n²) time). So it is *P,NP*, and *CoNP*.

Problem-8   For 3-Clique problem, which of the following are applicable?
(a) *P*   (b) *NP*   (c) *CoNP*   (d) *NP*-Hard
(e) *CoNP*-Hard   (f) *NP*-Complete   (g) *CoNP*-Complete

Solution: 3-Clique is solvable in poly-time (check for a triangle between all vertex-triplets in O(n^3) time). So it is *P, NP*, and *CoNP*.

Problem-9   Consider the problem of determining. For a given boolean formula, check whether every assignment to the variables satisfies it. Which of the following is applicable?
(a) *P*   (b) *NP*   (c) *CoNP*   (d) *NP*-Hard
(e) CoNP-Hard   (f) *NP*-Complete   (g) *CoNP*-Complete

Solution: Tautology is the complimentary problem to Satisfiability, which is NP-complete, so Tautology is *CoNP*-complete. So it is *CoNP*, *CoNP*-hard, and *CoNP*-complete.

Problem-10   Let *S* be an *NP*-complete problem and *Q* and *R* be two other problems not known to be in *NP*. *Q* is polynomial time reducible to *S* and *S* is polynomial-time reducible to *R*. Which one of the following statements is true?
(a) *R* is *NP*-complete   (b) *R* is *NP*-hard   (c) *Q* is *NP*-complete   (d) *Q* is *NP*-hard.

Solution: *R* is *NP*-hard (b).

Problem-11   Let *A* be the problem of finding a Hamiltonian cycle in a graph *G* = (*V*,*E*), with |*V*| divisible by 3 and *B* the problem of determining if Hamiltonian cycle exists in such graphs. Which one of the following is true?
(a) Both *A* and *B* are *NP*-hard   (b) *A* is *NP*-hard, but *B* is not

(c) *A* is *NP*-hard, but *B* is not   (d) Neither *A* nor *B* is *NP*-hard

Solution: Both *A* and *B* are *NP*-hard (a).

Problem-12   Let *A* be a problem that belongs to the class *NP*. State which of the following is true?
(a) There is no polynomial time algorithm for *A*. (b) If *A* can be solved deterministically in polynomial time, then $P = NP$.
(c) If *A* is *NP*-hard, then it is *NP*-complete. (d) *A* may be undecidable.

Solution: If *A* is *NP*-hard, then it is *NP*-complete (c).

Problem-13   Suppose we assume *Vertex — Cover* is known to be *NP*-complete. Based on our reduction, can we say *Independent — Set* is *NP*-complete?

Solution: Yes. This follows from the two conditions necessary to be *NP*-complete:
  - Independent Set is in *NP*, as stated in the problem.
  - A reduction from a known *NP*-complete problem.

Problem-14   Suppose *Independent Set* is known to be *NP*-complete. Based on our reduction, is *Vertex Cover NP*-complete?

Solution: No. By reduction from Vertex-Cover to Independent-Set, we do not know the difficulty of solving Independent-Set. This is because Independent-Set could still be a much harder problem than Vertex-Cover. We have not proved that.

Problem-15   The class of NP is the class of languages that cannot be accepted in polynomial time. Is it true? Explain.

Solution:

  - The class of NP is the class of languages that can be *verified* in *polynomial time*.
  - The class of P is the class of languages that can be *decided* in *polynomial time*.
  - The class of P is the class of languages that can be *accepted* in *polynomial time*.

$P \subseteq NP$ and "languages in P can be accepted in polynomial time", the description "languages in NP cannot be accepted in polynomial time" is wrong.

The term NP comes from nondeterministic polynomial time and is derived from an alternative characterization by using nondeterministic polynomial time Turing machines. It has nothing to do with "cannot be accepted in polynomial time".

Problem-16   Different encodings would cause different time complexity for the same algorithm. Is it true?

Solution: True. The time complexity of the same algorithm are different between unary encoding and binary encoding. But if the two encodings are polynomially related (e.g. base 2 & base 3 encodings), then changing between them will not cause the time complexity to change.

Problem-17   If P = NP, then NPC (NP Complete) $\subseteq$ P. Is it true?

Solution: True. If P = NP, then for any language L ∈ NP C (1) L ∈ NPC (2) L is NP-hard. By the first condition, L ∈ NPC $\subseteq$ NP = P $\Rightarrow$ NPC $\subseteq$ P.

Problem-18   If NPC $\subseteq$ P, then P = NP. Is it true?

Solution: True. All the NP problem can be reduced to arbitrary NPC problem in polynomial time, and NPC problems can be solved in polynomial time because NPC $\subseteq$ P. $\Rightarrow$ NP problem solvable in polynomial time $\Rightarrow$ NP $\subseteq$ P and trivially P $\subseteq$ NP implies NP = P.

MISCELLANEOUS CONCEPTS

Chapter-21

21.1 Introduction

In this chapter we will cover the topics which are useful for interviews and exams.

21.2 Hacks on Bitwise Programming

In C and $C++$ we can work with bits effectively. First let us see the definitions of each bit operation and then move onto different techniques for solving the problems. Basically, there are six operators that C and $C++$ support for bit manipulation:

Symbol	Operation
&	Bitwise AND
|	Bitwise OR
^	Bitwise Exclusive-OR
«	Bitwise left shift
»	Bitwise right shift
~	Bitwise complement

21.2.1 Bitwise AND

The bitwise AND tests two binary numbers and returns bit values of 1 for positions where both numbers had a one, and bit values of 0 where both numbers did not have one:

```
      01001011
&     00010101
      ----------
      00000001
```

21.2.2 Bitwise OR

The bitwise OR tests two binary numbers and returns bit values of 1 for positions where either bit or both bits are one, the result of 0 only happens when both bits are 0:

```
      01001011
|     00010101
      ----------
      01011111
```

21.2.3 Bitwise Exclusive-OR

The bitwise Exclusive-OR tests two binary numbers and returns bit values of 1 for positions where both bits are different, if they are the same then the result is 0:

```
      01001011
^     00010101
      ----------
      01011110
```

21.2.4 Bitwise Left Shift

The bitwise left shift moves all bits in the number to the left and fills vacated bit positions with 0.

```
      01001011
« 2
      --------
      00101100
```

21.2.5 Bitwise Right Shift

The bitwise right shift moves all bits in the number to the right.

```
        01001011
 ≫ 2
        --------
        ??010010
```

Note the use of ? for the fill bits. Where the left shift filled the vacated positions with 0, a right shift will do the same only when the value is unsigned. If the value is signed then a right shift will fill the vacated bit positions with the sign bit or 0, which one is implementation-defined. So the best option is to never right shift signed values.

21.2.6 Bitwise Complement

The bitwise complement inverts the bits in a single binary number.

```
        01001011
 ~
        --------
        10110100
```

21.2.7 Checking whether K-th bit is Set or Not

Let us assume that the given number is n. Then for checking the Kth bit we can use the expression: $n \& (1 \ll K - 1)$. If the expression is true then we can say the Kth bit is set (that means, set to 1).

Example:
$$n = 01001011 \text{ and } K = 4$$
$$1 \ll K - 1 \quad 00001000$$
$$n \& (1 \ll K - 1) \quad 00001000$$

21.2.8 Setting K-th bit

For a given number n, to set the Kth bit we can use the expression: $n \mid 1 \ll (K - 1)$

Example:
$$n = 01001011 \text{ and } K = 3$$
$$1 \ll K - 1 \quad 00000100$$
$$n \mid (1 \ll K - 1) \quad 01001111$$

21.2.9 Clearing K-th bit

To clear K^{th} bit of a given number n, we can use the expression: $n \& \sim(1 \ll K - 1)$

Example:
$$n = 01001011 \text{ and } K = 4$$
$$1 \ll K - 1 \quad 00001000$$
$$\sim(1 \ll K - 1) \quad 11110111$$
$$n \& \sim(1 \ll K - 1) \quad 01000011$$

21.2.10 Toggling K-th bit

For a given number n, for toggling the Kth bit we can use the expression: $n \wedge (1 \ll K - 1)$

Example:
$$n = 01001011 \text{ and } K = 3$$
$$1 \ll K - 1 \quad 00000100$$
$$n \wedge (1 \ll K - 1) \quad 01001111$$

21.2.11 Toggling Rightmost One bit

For a given number n, for toggling rightmost one bit we can use the expression: $n \& n - 1$

Example:
$$n = 01001011$$
$$n - 1 \quad 01001010$$
$$n \& n - 1 \quad 01001010$$

21.2.12 Isolating Rightmost One bit

For a given number n, for isolating rightmost one bit we can use the expression: $n \& - n$

Example:
$$n = 01001011$$
$$-n \quad 10110101$$
$$n \& - n \quad 00000001$$

Note: For computing $-n$, use two's complement representation. That means, toggle all bits and add 1.

21.2.13 Isolating Rightmost Zero bit

For a given number n, for isolating rightmost zero bit we can use the expression: $\sim n \,\&\, n + 1$

Example:

$$n = 01001011$$

$\sim n$	10110100
$n + 1$	01001100
$\sim n \,\&\, n + 1$	00000100

21.2.14 Checking Whether Number is Power of 2 or Not

Given a number n, to check whether the number is in 2^n form for not, we can use the expression: $if (n \,\&\, n - 1 == 0)$

Example:

$$n = 01001011$$

$n - 1$	01001010
$n \,\&\, n - 1$	01001010
$if (n \,\&\, n - 1 == 0)$	0

21.2.15 Multiplying Number by Power of 2

For a given number n, to multiply the number with 2^K we can use the expression: $n \ll K$

Example:

$$n = 00001011 \text{ and } K = 2$$

$n \ll K$	00101100

21.2.16 Dividing Number by Power of 2

For a given number n, to divide the number with 2^K we can use the expression: $n \gg K$

Example:

$$n = 00001011 \text{ and } K = 2$$

$n \gg K$	00010010

21.2.17 Finding Modulo of a Given Number

For a given number n, to find the %8 we can use the expression: $n \,\&\, 0x7$. Similarly, to find %32, use the expression: $n \,\&\, 0x1F$

Note: Similarly, we can find modulo value of any number.

21.2.18 Reversing the Binary Number

For a given number n, to reverse the bits (reverse (mirror) of binary number)we can use the following code snippet:

```
unsigned int n, nReverse = n;
int s = sizeof(n);
for (; n; n >>= 1) {
        nReverse <<= 1;
        nReverse |= n & 1;
        s--;
}
nReverse <<= s;
```

Time Complexity: This requires one iteration per bit and the number of iterations depends on the size of the number.

21.2.19 Counting Number of One's in Number

For a given number n, to count the number of $1's$ in its binary representation we can use any of the following methods.

Method1: Process bit by bit

```
unsigned int n, count=0;
while(n) {
        count += n & 1;
        n >>= 1;
}
```

Time Complexity: This approach requires one iteration per bit and the number of iterations depends on system.

Method2: Using modulo approach

```
unsigned int n, count=0;
while(n) {
        if(n%2 ==1)
                count++;
```

```
        n = n/2;
}
```
Time Complexity: This requires one iteration per bit and the number of iterations depends on system.

Method3: Using toggling approach: $n \& n - 1$

```
unsigned int n, count=0;
while(n) {
        count++;
        n &= n - 1;
}
```
Time Complexity: The number of iterations depends on the number of 1 bits in the number.

Method4: Using preprocessing idea. In this method, we process the bits in groups. For example if we process them in groups of 4 bits at a time, we create a table which indicates the number of one's for of each those possibilities.

0000→0	0100→1	1000→1	1100→2
0001→1	0101→2	1001→2	1101→3
0010→1	0110→2	1010→2	1110→3
0011→2	0111→3	1011→3	1111→4

The following code to count the number of 1s in the number with this approach:

```
int Table = {0,1,1,2,1,2,2,3,1,2,2,3,2,3,3,4};
int count = 0;
for(; n; n >>= 4)
        count = count + Table[n & 0xF];
return count;
```
Time Complexity: This approach requires one iteration per 4 bits and the number of iterations depends on system.

21.2.20 Creating Mask for Trailing Zero's

For a given number n, to create a mask for trailing zeros, we can use the expression: $(n \& - n) - 1$

Example:
$$n = 01001011$$
$$-n \quad\quad 10110101$$
$$n \& - n \quad\quad 00000001$$
$$(n \& - n) - 1 \quad\quad 00000000$$

Note: In the above case we are getting the mask as all zeros because there are no trailing zeros.

27.2.21 Swap all odd and even bits

Example: $n =$ 01001011

Find even bits of given number (evenN) = n & 0xAA   00001010
Find odd bits of given number (oddN) = n & 0x55   01000001
evenN >>= 1   00000101
oddN <<= 1   10000010
Final Expresion: evenN | oddN   10000111

21.2.22 Performing Average without Division

Is there an algorithm to replace $mid = (low + high) / 2$ (used in Binary Search and Merge Sort) with something much faster? We can use $mid = (low + high) >> 1$. Note that using $(low + high) / 2$" for midpoint calculations won't work correctly when integer overflow becomes an issue. We can use bit shifting and also overcome a possible overflow issue: $low + ((high - low)/ 2)$ and the bit shifting operation for this is $low + ((high - low) >> 1)$.

21.3 Other Programming Questions

Problem-1   Give an algorithm for printing the matrix elements in spiral order.

Solution: Non-recursive solution involves directions right, left, up, down, and dealing their corresponding indices. Once the first row is printed, direction changes (from right) to down, the row is discarded by incrementing the upper limit. Once the last column is printed, direction changes to left, the column is discarded by decrementing the right hand limit.

```
void Spiral(int[][]values, int m, int n) {
        int rowStart=0, columnStart=0;
```

```
                int rowEnd=m-1, columnEnd=n-1;
                while(rowStart<=rowEnd && columnStart<=columnEnd) {
                    int i=rowStart, j=columnStart;
                    for(j=columnStart; j<=columnEnd; j++) printf("%d ",values[i][j]);
                    for(i=rowStart+1, j--; i<=rowEnd; i++) printf("%d ",values[i][j]);
                    for(j=columnEnd-1, i--; j>=columnStart; j--) printf("%d ",values[i][j]);
                    for(i=rowEnd-1, j++; i>=rowStart+1; i--) printf("%d ",values[i][j]);
                    rowStart++; columnStart++; rowEnd--; columnEnd--;
                }
        }
}
```

Time Complexity: $O(n^2)$. Space Complexity: $O(1)$.

Problem-2   Give an algorithm for shuffling the desk of cards.

Solution: Assume that we want to shuffle an array of 52 cards, from 0 to 51 with no repeats, such as we might want for a deck of cards. First fill the array with the values in order, then go through the array and exchange each element with a randomly chosen element in the range from itself to the end. It's possible that an element will swap with itself, but there is no problem with that.

```
void Shuffle(int[] cards, int n){ //assume  n = 52
    for (int i=0; i<n; i++)
        cards[i] = i;                              // filling the array with card number
    for (int i=0; i < n; i++) {
        // The random() method returns a random number between 0.0 and 1.0.
        int r = i + ( Math.random() * (n - i) );  // Random remaining position.
        int temp = cards[i]; cards[i] = cards[r]; cards[r] = temp;
    }
    System.out.println("Shuffled Cards:");
    for (int i=0; i<n; i++)
        System.out.println(cards[i]);
}
```

Time Complexity: $O(n)$. Space Complexity: $O(1)$.

Problem-3   Reversal algorithm for array rotation: Write a function rotate(A[], d, n) that rotates A[] of size n by d elements. For example, the array $1,2,3,4,5,6,7$ becomes $3,4,5,6,7,1,2$ after 2 rotations.

Solution: Consider the following algorithm.
Algorithm:

```
        rotate(Array[], d, n)
        reverse(Array[], 1, d) ;
        reverse(Array[], d + 1, n);
        reverse(Array[], 1, n);
```

Let AB be the two parts of the input Array where A = Array[0..d-1] and B = Array[d..n-1]. The idea of the algorithm is: Reverse A to get ArB. /* Ar is reverse of A */
Reverse B to get ArBr. /* Br is reverse of B */
Reverse all to get (ArBr) r = BA.
For example, if Array[] = [1, 2, 3, 4, 5, 6, 7], d =2 and n = 7 then, A = [1, 2] and B = [3, 4, 5, 6, 7]
Reverse A, we get ArB = [2, 1, 3, 4, 5, 6, 7], Reverse B, we get ArBr = [2, 1, 7, 6, 5, 4, 3]
Reverse all, we get (ArBr)r = [3, 4, 5, 6, 7, 1, 2]

Implementation:

```
        /* Function to left rotate Array[] of size n by d */
        void leftRotate(int[] Array, int d, int n) {
                rvereseArray(Array, 0, d-1);
                rvereseArray(Array, d, n-1);
                rvereseArray(Array, 0, n-1);
        }
        /*UTILITY FUNCTIONS: function to print an Array */
        void printArray(int[] Array, int size){
                for(int i = 0; i < size; i++)
                        printf("%d ", Array[i]);
                printf("%\n ");
        }
        /*Function to reverse Array[] from index start to end*/
        void rvereseArray(int[] Array, int start, int end) {
                int i;
```

```
            int temp;
            while(start < end){
              temp = Array[start];
              Array[start] = Array[end];
              Array[end] = temp;
              start++;
              end--;
            }
          }
```

Problem-4   Suppose you are given an array s[1...*n*] and a procedure reverse (s,i,j) which reverses the order of elements in between positions i and j (both inclusive). What does the following sequence do, where 1 < k <= n:

```
          reverse (s, 1, k);
          reverse (s, k + 1, n);
          reverse (s, 1, n);
```

   (a) Rotates s left by k positions (b) Leaves s unchanged (c) Reverses all elements of s (d) None of the above

Solution: (b). Effect of the above 3 reversals for any *k* is equivalent to left rotation of the array of size *n* by *k* [refer Problem-3].

Problem-5   Given a string that has set of words and spaces, write a program to move the spaces to *front* of string, you need to traverse the array only once and need to adjust the string in place.
   Input = "move these spaces to beginning" *Output* ="   movethesepacestobeginning"

Solution: Maintain two indices *i* and *j*; traverse from end to beginning. If the current index contains char, swap chars in index *i* with index *j*. This will move all the spaces to beginning of the array.

```
void mySwap(char[] A,int i,int j){
    char temp=A[i];
    A[i]=A[j];
    A[j]=temp;
}
void moveSpacesToBegin(char[] A){
    int i= A.length-1;
    int j=i;
    for(; j>=0; j--){
        if(!isspace(A[j]))
            mySwap(A,i--,j);
    }
}
```

Time Complexity: O(*n*) where *n* is the number of characters in input array. Space Complexity: O(1).

Problem-6   For the Problem-5, can we improve the complexity?

Solution: We can avoid swap operation with a simple counter. But, it does not reduce the overall complexity.

```
void moveSpacesToBegin(char[] A){
    int n=A.length-1,count=n;
    int i=n;
    for(;i>=0;i--){
        if(A[i]!=' ')
            A[count--]=A[i];
    }
    while(count>=0)
        A[count--]=' ';
}
```

Time Complexity: O(*n*) where *n* is the number of characters in input array. Space Complexity: O(1).

Problem-7   Given a string that has set of words and spaces, write a program to move the spaces to *end* of string, you need to traverse the array only once and need to adjust the string in place.
   Input = "move these spaces to end" *Output* ="movethesepacestoend   "

Solution: Traverse the array from left to right. While traversing, maintain a counter for non-space elements in array. For every non-space character A[*i*], put the element at A[*count*] and increment *count*. After complete traversal, all non-space elements have already been shifted to front end and *count* is set as index of first 0. Now, all we need to do is that run a loop which fills all elements with spaces from *count* till end of the array.

21.3 Other Programming Questions   390

```
void moveSpacesToEnd(char[] A){
    int count = 0;  // Count of non-space elements
    int n = A.length-1;
    int i =0;
    for (; i <= n; i++)
        if (!isspace(A[i]))
            A[count++] = A[i];

    while (count <= n)
        A[++count] = ' ';
}
```

Time Complexity: $O(n)$ where n is number of characters in input array. Space Complexity: $O(1)$.

Problem-8   Moving Zeros to end: Given an array of n integers, move all the zeros of a given array to the end of the array. For example, if the given arrays is {1, 9, 8, 4, 0, 0, 2, 7, 0, 6, 0}, it should be changed to {1, 9, 8, 4, 2, 7, 6, 0, 0, 0, 0}. The order of all other elements should be same.

Solution: Maintain two variables i and j; and initialize with 0. For each of the array element $A[i]$, if $A[i]$ non-zero element, then replace the element $A[j]$ with element $A[i]$. Variable i will always be incremented till $n - 1$ but we will increment j only when the element pointed by i is non-zero.

```
void moveZerosToEnd(int[] A){
    int i=0,j=0;
    while (i <= A.length - 1){
        if (A[i] != 0){
            A[j++] = A[i];
        }
        i++;
    }
    while (j <= size - 1)
        A[j++] = 0;
}
```

Time Complexity: $O(n)$. Space Complexity: $O(1)$.

Problem-9   For the Problem-8, can we improve the complexity?

Solution: Using simple swap technique we can avoid the unnecessary second *while* loop from the above code.

```
void mySwap(int[] A,int i,int j){
    int temp=A[i];
    A[i]=A[j];
    A[j]=temp;
}
void moveZerosToEnd(int[] A, int len){
    int i, j;
    for(i=0,j=0; i<len; i++)    {
        if (A[i] !=0)
            mySwap(A,j++,i);
    }
}
```

Time Complexity: $O(n)$. Space Complexity: $O(1)$.

Problem-10   Variant of Problem-9 and Problem-10: Given an array containing negative and positive numbers; give an algorithm for separating positive and negative numbers in it. Also, maintain the relative order of positive and negative numbers. Input: -5, 3, 2, -1, 4, -8 Output: -5 -1 -8 3 4 2

Solution: In the moveZerosToEnd function, just replace the condition $A[i]$!=0 with $A[i] < 0$.

References

[1] Akash. Programming Interviews. http://tech-queries.blogspot.com.

[2] Alfred V.Aho,J. E. (1983). Data Structures and Algorithms. Addison-Wesley.

[3] Algorithms.Retrieved from http://www.cs.princeton.edu/algs4/home

[4] Anderson., S. E. Bit Twiddling Hacks. Retrieved 2010, from Bit Twiddling Hacks: http://www-graphics.stanford.edu /~seander/ bithacks.html

[5] Bentley, J. AT&T Bell Laboratories. Retrieved from AT&T Bell Laboratories.

[6] Chen. Algorithms http://www2.hawaii.edu/~chenx.

[7] Database, P.Problem Database. Retrieved 2010, from Problem Database: datastructures.net

[8] Drozdek, A. (1996). Data Structures and Algorithms in C++.

[9] Ellis Horowitz, S. S. Fundamentals of Data Structures.

[10] Gilles Brassard, P. B. (1996). Fundamentals of Algorithmics.

[11] Hunter., J. Introduction to Data Structures and Algorithms. Retrieved 2010, from Introduction to Data Structures and Algorithms.:

[12] James F. Korsh, L. J. Data Structures, Algorithms and Program Style Using C.

[13] John Mongan, N. S. (2002). Programming Interviews Exposed. . Wiley-India. .

[14] Judges. Comments on Problems and solutions. http://www.informatik.uni-ulm.de.

[15] Kalid. P, NP, and NP-Complete. Retrieved from P, NP, and NP-Complete.: http://www.cs.princeton.edu

[16] Knuth., D. E. (1973). Fundamental Algorithms, volume 1 of The Art of Computer Programming. Addison-Wesley.

[17] Leon., J. S. Computer Algorithms. . Retrieved 2010, from Computer Algorithms. : math.uic.edu

[18] Leon., J. S. Computer Algorithms. http://www.math.uic.edu/~leon/cs-mcs401-s08.

[19] OCF. Algorithms. Retrieved 2010, from Algorithms: http://www.ocf.berkeley.edu

[20] Parlante., N. Binary Trees. Retrieved 2010, from cslibrary.stanford.edu: cslibrary.stanford.edu

[21] Patil., V. Fundamentals of data structures. Nirali Prakashan.

[22] Poundstone., W. HOW WOULD YOU MOVE MOUNT FUJI? New York Boston.: Little, Brown and Company. .

[23] Pryor, M. Tech Interview. Retrieved 2010, from Tech Interview: http://techinterview.org

[24] Questions, A. C. A Collection of Technical Interview Questions. Retrieved 2010, from A Collection of Technical Interview Questions: www.spellscroll.com

[25] Sedgewick., R. (1988). Algorithms. Addison-Wesley.

[26] Sells, C. (2010). Interviewing at Microsoft. Retrieved 2010, from Interviewing at Microsoft: http://www.sellsbrothers.com/fun/msiview

[27] Shene, C.-K. Linked Lists Merge Sort implementation. Retrieved 2010, from Linked Lists Merge Sort implementation: http://www.cs.mtu.edu/~shene

[28] Sinha, P. Linux Journal. Retrieved 2010, from http://www.linuxjournal.com/article/6828.

[29] Structures., d. D. www.math-cs.gordon.edu. Retrieved 2010, from www.math-cs.gordon.edu

[30] T. H. Cormen, C. E. (1997). Introduction to Algorithms. Cambridge: The MIT press.

[31] Tsiombikas, J. Pointers Explained. http://nuclear.sdf-eu.org.

[32] Warren., H. S. (2003). Hackers Delight. Addison-Wesley.

[33] Weiss., M. A. (1992). Data Structures and Algorithm Analysis in C.

[34] wikipedia, T. F. The Free wikipedia. Retrieved from The Free wikipedia: en.wikipedia.org

[35] Zhang., C. programheaven. Retrieved 2010, programheaven.blogspot.com

[36] Mohammed Abualrob, Interview Code Snippets, 2010, interviewcodesnippets.com

[37] Technical Questions. www.ihas1337code.com